Quantitative Research Methods for Professionals

W. Paul Vogt

Illinois State University

Boston • *New York* • *San Francisco*
Mexico City • *Montreal* • *Toronto* • *London* • *Madrid* • *Munich* • *Paris*
Hong Kong • *Singapore* • *Tokyo* • *Cape Town* • *Sydney*

Senior Editor: *Arnis E. Burvikovs*
Editorial Assistant: *Erin Reilly*
Marketing Manager: *Tara Kelly*
Editorial Production Service: *Omegatype Typography, Inc.*
Composition Buyer: *Linda Cox*
Manufacturing Manager: *Megan Cochran*
Electronic Composition: *Omegatype Typography, Inc.*
Cover Administrator: *Kristina Mose-Libon*

For related titles and support materials, visit our online catalog at www.ablongman.com.

Between the time Web site information is gathered and then published, it is not unusual for some sites to have closed. Also, the transcription of URLs can result in typographical errors. The publisher would appreciate notification where these errors occur so that they may be corrected in subsequent editions.

Library of Congress Cataloging-in-Publication Data

Vogt, W. Paul
    Quantitative research methods for professionals / W. Paul Vogt.
        p. cm.
    Includes bibliographical references and index.
    ISBN 0-205-35913-2
        1. Social sciences—Statistical methods. 2. Social sciences—Research—Methodology.   I. Title.
    HA29. V58 2007
    300.72'7—dc22

                                                                                2005049517

Printed in the United States of America
10   9   8   7   6   5   4   3   2   1   11   10   09   08   07   06

Contents

6   *Experiments and Random Assignment*   **95**

7   *Reliability and Validity*   **113**

Preface

About 20 years ago I started teaching my courses in research methods in a new way. This book reflects the changes and the new approaches I've developed over those years. The changes in my orientation to teaching were prompted by (1) what I learned about my students' needs and (2) innovations in quantitative analysis brought about by the computer revolution.

I teach graduate courses in research methods, mostly to doctoral-level students in education and other professional fields. The courses focus on quantitative research methods, and many have the word *statistics* in the title. However, it has long been clear to me that none of my students was ever going to become a statistician. And only a few would become professional researchers. Regardless of their areas of specialization—educational administration, social work, special education, business, nursing, curriculum, technology, and so on—virtually all envisioned becoming practitioners, not researchers. On the other hand, these students needed to know how to conduct research as part of their graduate programs, whether for a seminar paper, a master's thesis, or a doctoral dissertation. And they all realized that, as professional practitioners and students preparing for professional practice, they ought to base their work on up-to-date knowledge gained from the research in their fields.

The second reason I restructured the way I taught courses in quantitative research methods was the dramatic increase in the power and availability of computers. Equally dramatic, and delightful, is the astonishing reduction in the amount of time it takes to learn how to use statistical software such as SPSS (Statistical Package for the Social Sciences).[1] Today, as long as students know what they want the software to do, they typically need at most a few minutes of instruction to make it happen. By contrast, learning what the software is capable of and understanding how to interpret the output take much longer.

So, my students don't need the mathematical foundations of the statistics they use, because none of them is going to become a statistician. They don't need to know how to compute the statistics, because machines do that work. The machines and software are typically so user-friendly that students don't need intensive training in how to operate them. So what *do* students need? Two types of knowledge: First, an understanding of the elements of good research design. This understanding enables one to judge the research of others and to design one's own high-quality investigations, which can lead to improved professional practice. Second, the ability to read, interpret, and critically evaluate quantitative results. This is crucial for one to solve problems and to make knowledge-based decisions.

These are not easy things to learn. Most people find understanding research design and critically evaluating research results to be conceptually demanding. But this knowledge is not primarily technical. It requires no mathematics beyond grade-school arithmetic and no computer prerequisites other than elementary familiarity with a mouse and keyboard. Students with one introductory course in research methods or statistics or tests and measurement have the background to understand everything they will encounter in this book. Indeed, because the early chapters quickly review most of the basics of quantitative methods, students with no background could start with this volume, although many complete novices would find the review of elementary concepts too quick and condensed for them.

Because the technical parts of quantitative research methods are unnecessary for practitioners, and because they have been automated, this text can focus on the concepts. Concepts are compact. By focusing on them huge amounts of material can be covered in a relatively short span. This leads us to an unusual result, a seeming contradiction in terms: a short book that is quite comprehensive. It can be comprehensive but brief because it assumes some prior knowledge (so the basics are covered quickly) and because the discussions of advanced and specialized methods and concepts are thoroughly nontechnical.

Research methods and statistics is a field blessed with many excellent texts. What makes this text special, I believe, is that it exploits, more thoroughly than others, the opportunities provided by computer-assisted research. That is why this book can cover most topics in quantitative research methods in comparatively few pages. Indeed, it covers more parts of the field in less space than any other book with which I am familiar.

Whom Is This Book For?

First of all, this book is *not* "for dummies." It is for intelligent people who do not possess—and do not have the time or the inclination to acquire—knowledge of the mathematical foundations of quantitative research methods and statistics. It is possible for such individuals to gain a practical understanding of even the *most* advanced techniques and to do so without the mathematical foundations. Advanced quantitative techniques are technically complex, but the basic ideas behind them are comparatively simple. It is possible to discuss methods of analysis such as multilevel modeling and structural equation modeling in nontechnical, (almost) ordinary English. As Jerome Bruner (1977) put it in *The Process of Edu-*

cation, "any subject can be taught effectively in some intellectually honest form to any child," and surely, I would add, to any adult.

This book is for busy professionals working in fields based on the social and behavioral sciences—or for students preparing to become professionals in such fields as education, social work, and business. The book aims to help people whose approach to knowledge is verbal rather than mathematical. Ultimately the concepts involved are numerical, but a good approximation can be gained verbally or graphically. Also, even students planning to become researchers in the social and behavioral sciences, and the applied fields based on them, sometimes appreciate the kind of overview provided in this book. Although the book is not designed specifically for future full-time researchers, some will enjoy it anyway.

Main Features of the Book

Thinking about the intended audience for this volume has led me to design it with several distinct features. It approaches learning quantitative methods as one might learn a language; it makes extensive use of analogies and examples; it stresses understanding statistics rather than calculating them; it emphasizes all aspects of quantitative research, not only statistical analyses; it covers an unusually broad range of topics; it omits topics that are not absolutely essential; it prepares the reader for further work in the field; and, finally, it is based on many years of experience teaching thousands of students.

Quantitative Research Methods as Language

The grammar and vocabulary of research are often difficult, but no more difficult than those of other languages. As with learning a natural language, we will encounter strange labels for concepts that are not very unusual. With exposure, the foreignness of the language of research will gradually dissipate. However, you probably won't become "bilingual" by quickly reading this book. Despite the fact that it is written in as conversational tone as I can muster, most people will have to read it slowly, and more than once, to understand the concepts fully.

Analogies and Examples

Abstract concepts often become clear through analogies and examples. An analogy from everyday experience, such as using a vending machine, can throw much light on a jargon-filled topic such as hypothesis testing. The examples may be even more important than the analogies. Examples in this book are drawn primarily from the social sciences, especially as they are applied to educational research, and secondarily from medical research, especially public health and epidemiology. I have emphasized educational applications of the social sciences and the public health aspects of medical research because I know these areas best and because they are probably familiar and relevant to all readers. Everyone is likely to be vitally affected by the state of medical knowledge and its growth through research. Medical research is usually the kind of natural science most accessible to most people. Nearly all readers have also experienced the education system (and many are still experiencing it). Examples from educational research are especially helpful for considering a wide range of topics in research methods because educational research uses numerous methods and draws from many fields including psychology, sociology, anthropology, economics, and political science.

Stress on Understanding Rather Than Calculating

With a very few exceptions (mainly in Chapter 2), I devote no space in the following pages to how to calculate statistics. The exceptions in Chapter 2 mostly involve the standard deviation (including the variance) and the correlation coefficient. Because these two are so fundamental to most of the rest of the book, it is worth seeing how they are calculated. This is not because anyone ever would, unless compelled, calculate them by hand; rather, learning how they are calculated helps the reader get a better grasp of what they actually are. With the exception of the materials in Chapter

2, practicing professionals can *get by* with little or no knowledge of how statistics are calculated.

Emphasis beyond Statistical Analysis

This book will spend as much time on research design as on analysis. The methods of gathering evidence are, in most cases, probably more important than the techniques for analyzing evidence. Generally, it is more valuable to know how to plan good research, and thereby how to judge the research designs of others, than it is to know how to analyze the data. It is almost always true that a mistake in analyzing evidence is much easier to fix than an error in gathering it. In other words, there is much more to good research, even good quantitative research, than calculating and interpreting quantitative output. Analyzing data correctly is very important, but not so important that it should be allowed to overshadow the design components of good research practice.

Broad Coverage of Essentials

We must travel light because we are going far. This book will touch on almost every major research method in about half the number of pages of a typical introductory text that covers perhaps one-quarter of the subjects discussed here. Of course, all authors at some point sacrifice depth in order to gain breadth. What makes this book unusual is how far I have pushed that trade-off. Some of my colleagues, who *already know* a great deal about quantitative research methods, think I have gone too far and that my coverage of many topics is too light. Most people who are *still learning* about quantitative methods disagree. They like what some of them have called the "executive summary" approach. The idea is not to "dumb down" the material, but rather to focus on its most essential aspects.

Omission of Nonessentials

There are many things that it would be nice to know, but which you can (just barely) do without. For example, the statistical methods discussed are based on probability theory, calculus, and matrix algebra.

Yet the book will cover *none* of these. Doing so adequately would be impossible and, more important, it would divert attention from the basic concepts that professional practitioners require.

My question in writing this book has always been: What can readers without the "essential" math background learn about quantitative methods? The answer is almost everything—at some level. But there is a price to be paid for learning without the math background. You lose precision. Sentences using words are vaguer than formulas using abstract symbols. But for most readers of this book the choice is between learning at a somewhat lower level of precision and not learning anything at all. In the past, too many professionals, wrongly believing that they had to know math to grasp the essentials, settled for no understanding at all. But, rightly taught, the essential ideas are available to almost anyone willing to put in some time to acquire them. And once one has grasped the key ideas, one is ready to think about the process of research at a *high* level and thus to use research intelligently to enhance professional practice.

Preparation for Further Work

When you do your own research you will often need to read more advanced works and/or to consult with a specialist in research methods. This book gets you ready to do that. When you have finished this volume, you will have a good overview of the "forest." Your own research projects are likely to involve working with just a few "trees." In the pages that follow, I point out where it is most important to make sure to read more deeply or to get expert advice before tackling a research investigation on your own.

Students' Input

Every author accumulates many debts in writing a book. Many of mine in this book are to my students. I owe them a lot for helping me learn how to convey doctoral-level knowledge in ways that are broadly accessible. My students helped me to see that by making research methods more broadly accessible we can raise the level of discourse dramatically. We can move to more conceptually advanced discussions about the means and meaning of research, discussions that are consonant with the serious work done by professionals in education and other fields.

I have also used feedback from my students to design the pedagogical materials with which each chapter concludes. In keeping with the spirit of the book, these study aids focus on understanding rather than computations (your instructors may give you additional exercises that I have provided separately). Chapters end with (1) terms and concepts to review, (2) discussion questions that ask you to think about applying the concepts, and (3) a brief self-test that readers can use to assess their level of understanding.

Instructor's Resources

A complete *Instructor's Manual* is available to adopters of this book. For each chapter, the manual contains teaching suggestions, additional discussion questions, student exercises, explanations of the answers for the self-test questions, and a bank of test items instructors can use to construct their examinations. PowerPoint slides for illustrating and augmenting chapter content may also be obtained. These materials are available online at www.ablongman.com after finding this title under Educational Psychology. If you adopt this book, you can access the *Instructor's Manual* by contacting your local representative for an access code.

Acknowledgments

All authors know how important comments and, especially, criticisms can be to improving the quality of their work. Many people, mentioned briefly here, commented extensively on drafts of this work and deserve credit for several of its good points.

I continue to be awestruck by how seriously colleagues take the assignment to review another's work. I would like to thank the following reviewers, who worked diligently through the text and made numerous important suggestions: Kenneth Berk, Illinois State University; John Creswell, University of Nebraska–Lincoln; Jeanne Hilton, University of Nevada; Marie Kraska, Auburn University; Jeffrey Oescher, University of New Orleans;

Steven A. Schmitz, Central Washington University; and Alexander W. Wiseman, The University of Tulsa.

Many friends and colleagues at Illinois State University also read drafts of chapters, and I benefited greatly from their counsel. Members of my department used drafts of some of the chapters as a basis for our discussions of how to structure our curriculum. Those discussions were very helpful for thinking about how to improve the book.

I've also presented parts of this volume at various conferences and meetings, some small and regional, such as the Central Illinois branch of the American Statistical Association, and others large and national, such as the American Educational Research Association. I remain surprised, after many years of it, to see how a fleeting comment made at a paper session can start a train of thought that ultimately leads to important features of a book.

Finally, I am delighted to thank my students. I have long distributed my "lecture notes" to classes. The chapters that follow all grew out of such notes, especially for the doctoral-level courses I have taught on research design, applied educational research, and research methodology and statistics. Students in my classes have helped with the development of this book in more ways than I can remember and in more than they are probably aware. Particularly in the writing of a book focused on providing what practicing professionals need in their work, the great privilege of teaching classes of such professionals has been fundamental in the final decisions about the shape of the book.

In brief, I have gotten more help with this book than with any other I have written. I have even importuned, once again, my long-suffering wife, Elaine Vogt, to leave the piano and to help "just one more time" by performing her special magic with prose clarity. I have had the good fortune of having the above mentioned people willing to assist me in making this book better. My thanks to them all.

Of course, I can still use more help. I welcome your suggestions. Please send them to wpvogt@ ilstu.edu.

Endnote

1. Several good statistical packages exist. I do computations in this book with the PC version of SPSS, because it is widely available and easy to learn.

List of Abbreviations

AD	Average Deviation (a.k.a. Mean Average Deviation or MAD)
ANCOVA	Analysis of Covariance
ANOVA	Analysis of Variance
CI	Confidence Interval
d	Difference, usually standardized mean difference
DV	Dependent Variable
e	error
E	Expected value
ES	Effect Size
HLM	Hierarchical Linear Modeling
ICC	Intraclass Correlation
IV	Independent Variable
M	Mean
MAD	Mean Average Deviation
Md	Median
MLM	Multi-Level Modeling
Mo	Mode
MS	Mean Square (a.k.a. Variance)
MSE	Mean Squared Error
N	Number of cases (in a population)
n	Number of cases (in a sample)
OV	Outcome Variable
P	Probability
p	Probability (of Type I error)
PV	Predictor Variable
r	Correlation (bivariate, i.e., between 2 variables)
R	Correlation (multivariate, i.e., among 3 or more variables)
r^2	Squared bivariate correlation
R^2	Squared multivariate correlation
SD	Standard Deviation (in a population)
sd	Standard Deviation (in a sample)
SE	Standard Error
SEM	Structural Equation Modeling or Standard Error of the Mean
Sig.	Significance (statistical)
X	Usual symbol for an independent variable (IV)
Y	Usual symbol for a dependent variable (DV)
<	Less than
>	Greater than

Part I

The Basics

This book is designed to give professionals enough knowledge about how to consume and produce research that they can use research to improve their professional practice. "Enough" knowledge is a formidable standard. What is typically taught in the first course or two on research methods is rarely sufficient to give practitioners access to research in the main journals in their fields, and it is almost never adequate to provide the skills needed to do research.

After completing a beginning course on research methods and statistics, most students are prepared to read and interpret some descriptive statistics and the results of a standard experiment. But the vast majority of research articles published in most research journals are not experiments analyzed, following the oft-taught pattern, by comparing means and testing their significance with *t*-tests or ANOVAs. Much more specialized quantitative methods are routinely encountered in most key journals, including factor analysis, multiple and logistic regression, multilevel models, and structural equation modeling. Students who have completed a course or two in research methods are rarely prepared to read research employing these techniques. Professional practitioners, relying on what they have learned in their research courses, are also usually ill equipped

to apply the most commonly used advanced methods. But they could be.

It is possible in a relatively short time to prepare students and professionals to read and even to produce research employing quite advanced techniques. People with some minimal background in quantitative methods can accomplish this preparatory work fairly quickly. Students who have taken a good elementary course or two in tests and measurement, statistics, or research methods should be able to use this book (1) to learn how to read research with critical understanding and (2) to apply state-of-the-art quantitative techniques to problems that interest them. Of course, it would be ridiculous to claim that one book could provide readers with all they would ever need to know. My claim is more modest: This book should give readers enough to get started; it should enable them to understand advanced research and even to conduct a respectable investigation of a problem.

Important journals in the social sciences and applied fields such as education and social work also increasingly publish works using *qualitative* research methods, and that is a very healthy trend, but the growing array of qualitative techniques is not addressed here. This book focuses on *quantitative* techniques for two reasons: (1) The volume is more likely to be useful to its intended audience (practicing professionals) if it is comparatively short, and (2) it is better to address topics people seem to have most difficulty learning on their own, such as quantitative methods. However, the dichotomy between the "Quants" and the "Quals" is false. It is impossible to think about any moderately complex research problem without using both quantitative *and* qualitative reasoning. So this book will unavoidably contain qualitative elements. Nonetheless, its main target is quantitative methodologies.

My goal in this book is to discuss advanced quantitative concepts in simple language. For the most part, that means using natural language rather than equations. For experts, equations are much clearer and more concise than attempting to explain statistical methods in ordinary language. But this book is not for experts—future experts perhaps, but not current research experts. In many years of teaching professionals, I have found that equations are a source of confusion and anxiety for all but a very few students. Most cannot decipher equations and have little interest in learning how to do so. Fortunately, this reluctance is much less of a problem than it was a generation ago.

Today, of course, most quantitative analyses are done using computers. Professional *researchers* still need to know the formulas computer programs use to solve quantitative problems. Different programs sometimes use different algorithms and make different assumptions, occasionally with important consequences for their output. By contrast, professionals applying research to practice need to find a way to get along without this knowledge. Most professionals are consumers rather than producers of research. And even those who conduct research—whether the research produced is for an evaluation of a program or for a doctoral dissertation—cannot realistically be expected to have the kind of technical expertise that full-time researchers possess. Unfortunately, courses and textbooks are too often designed as though all students were aiming to become—in many, *many* small steps—technical experts rather than practitioners who want enough research expertise to get by in their professional practice.

This book is written for both consumers and producers of research. The gap between the two need not be as great as is often claimed. What was once an unbridgeable chasm can be jumped by the nimble. The distance between consuming and producing research is small and narrowing for three reasons. First, all producers must begin by finding and analyzing (that is, consuming) previous research on their subjects. They must "review the literature." So producers *are* consumers, almost by definition. Although most consumers of research do not produce it, many more could. This leads to the second reason the gap between producers and consumers has become relatively easier to bridge: The skills that competent consumers need are largely identical to those required by qualified producers of research. This was not always the case. The distinction between the needs of consumers and producers of research was increasingly emphasized in textbooks in the 1980s and 1990s. Several texts designed for consumers became available and went through multiple editions (e.g., Huck, 4th ed., 2004; Vogt, 3rd ed., 2005), and they filled an important need. Ironically, just as authors and publishers of textbooks came to recognize the special needs of consumers and how they differed from those of producers of research, the distinction began to evaporate. Today, to be competent, neither consumers nor producers of research absolutely require mathematical knowledge expressed in formulas. This brings us to the final reason that the producer/consumer distinction is increasingly outmoded. Because of technological advances, more people can produce research today than ever before.

Because we live in an age in which the "heavy lifting" in quantitative analyses is done by computer statistical packages, our descriptions of quantitative methods as carried out by computer programs need not be very technical. Many techniques of quantitative analysis that were once rare skills are now ordinary software routines. Because so much of the difficult work has been automated, researchers can be readied, with comparatively minimal instruction, to engage in research that only highly specialized professionals could have undertaken a couple of decades ago. Statistical software is increasingly easy to use and requires less and less direct instruction, which means that with the right approach, an author of a textbook can cover much of the field of quantitative methods in a relatively small volume. Of course, although many once rarefied skills of the producer of quantitative analyses have been automated, the critical intelligence of the consumer and the disciplined imagination of the designer of research are another matter altogether. These have yet to be reduced to ones and zeros.

Put simply, to use a quantitative method you first need to know which menu item to point at and click. This book aims to provide that knowledge, and the choice of the most effective technique is no simple matter. Then you need to know how to read the output with critical understanding—an equally formidable task, which is also addressed in this book. Ideally, perhaps, it would be nice if all folks who used computers also knew what went on in between the "click" and the output. But if busy professionals are to accomplish things at work, they cannot wait for optimal knowledge before deciding or acting. If specialists in decision science are right, we all have to learn to get by with *enough* knowledge to make *satisfactory* decisions. In the famous jargon, we "satisfice" because it is impossible to optimize.

The two routes to improving professional practice through research—consumption and production—require an overlapping set of skills, which is why they can be addressed in one book. Producers need to know how to understand their own output; consumers have to interpret the output of others. The knowledge needed to interpret the output of a quantitative analysis is the same whether you or someone else produces it.

People who think of themselves only as consumers of research often find that simply reviewing the research published by others does not yield what they need to know in order to answer their questions. To learn what they want to know, they have to conduct their own investigations. Because research production is no longer as remote a possibility as it once was, these consumers should be encouraged to undertake—or to sponsor—research projects of their own. If they do, both communities, researchers and the practitioners, will benefit. I hope this book fosters the ability of practicing professionals not only to use

the research of others but also to promote and even conduct it on their own.

A common query about texts such as this one is: Is this a work on design or measurement or statistics? The answer is all of the above. The book is a general study of quantitative research methods for professional practitioners, and, as such, it must deal with design *and* measurement *and* analysis. Although the three are clearly distinct, they are so closely dependent on one another that I personally do not know how to think about one without also thinking about the other two. Doing so is like trying to imagine how a human arm works without considering the complimentary interactions of bones, muscles, and nerves. All three are necessary. Leave out one and the other two are useless. The same is true of design, measurement, and analysis. Each chapter in this book integrates to one degree or another elements of design, measurement, and analysis. It is possible to take this balanced approach and include all three elements of good research because the highly specialized skills of analysis have been partly automated. Analysis no longer needs to overwhelm measurement and design in the education of those who would use quantitative research methods. The quality of research benefits when its main components are thus harmonized—and so does the quality of professional practice.

*   *   *

The book is divided into three main parts. Part 1 deals with basic concepts and techniques. It reviews in a selective way the fundamental concepts and methods covered in most elementary courses. Part 2 moves beyond these basics to specialized and advanced techniques, many of which were invented quite recently. The methods discussed in Part 2 are the ones readers are most likely to encounter in recent published research. Part 3 examines more specialized applications of the methods discussed in the first two parts. In Part 1 we survey the topics usually taught in an introductory course in quantitative research methods. This review is condensed and covers material that is typically presented in textbooks three or four times as long. Part 1 is necessary because students in the second or even the third course in a sequence on quantitative methods usually have to start from scratch, to begin at the beginning each time. But with each course in the sequence, students can cover the basics more easily and rapidly. And the basics are, well, basic. Knowledge of quantitative research methods is highly cumulative. It is difficult to understand advanced topics without knowing about the concepts on which they are built. So Part 1 provides the fundamentals needed to understand the more advanced material in Part 2 and the applications in Part 3.

Nine chapters comprise Part 1. They are divided about equally between design and analysis. By reviewing the three key components of research—design, measurement, and analysis—Chapter 1 provides an overview of the rest of the book. Then Chapter 2 looks at what might first seem an odd couple of statistics: standard deviation and correlation. The standard deviation (SD) is the building block with which most other statistics, including the correlation coefficient (r), are built. No statistic is more fundamental than the standard deviation (and its squared sibling, the variance) to understanding of the rest of statistics. From the standard deviation, we move to the correlation coefficient, r, which is a way to measure the degree of association between two variables. Considering the proper and improper uses of correlations helps us understand the kinds of relations there can be among variables. Relationships among variables are then discussed in greater depth in Chapter 3, "Variables and the Relations among Them." Here we examine different types of variables and the kinds of links between and among them. Variables can be causally linked, directly or indirectly, and they can interact to produce joint effects. Reviewing examples of these relationships enables us to understand the difficult topic of causation better and to design research projects that will help researchers to answer questions that interest them.

We return to more strictly statistical and analytic questions in Chapter 4 in which the methods of describing data are discussed. Particular emphasis is put on why this preliminary descriptive work is important to subsequent, more advanced analyses and how it can lead to wise interpretations of data. The next two chapters examine the most widely used general research designs and the statistical techniques usually associated with them. Surveys and random sampling are studied in Chapter 5. Experiments and random assignment are discussed in Chapter 6. Each of these chapters reviews approaches that lead to good-quality research by discussing the strengths and weaknesses of these designs for particular research questions. Then Chapter 7 focuses more intently on the issue of how to judge research by discussing the reliability and validity of measurements and designs. Ultimately, the question addressed in Chapter 7 is: What characteristics of research make it trustworthy?

From the design-focused issues discussed in Chapters 5, 6, and 7, the text moves to the two final chapters in Part 1. These are more statistically oriented and deal with the two main classes of quantitative analysis: statistical inference and regression. Chapter 8 gives special attention to a set of topics already encountered frequently, although briefly, in earlier chapters: How do we take information gleaned from a sample and generalize it to the population from which the sample was drawn? How do we know whether our findings are statistically significant? Chapter 9 then looks at the main methods of analysis used to explain and predict relationships among variables, which, by historical accident, have the peculiar name *regression analysis*. With a good grounding in statistical inference from Chapter 8 and in statistical associations among variables in Chapter 9, the reader is then ready to move on to the more advanced techniques discussed in Part 2 and the specialized applications of Part 3.

1

Research Design, Measurement, and Analysis

What is research and what is it for? Research is the systematic collection and/or study of evidence in order to answer a question, solve a problem, or create knowledge. Research methods are means of accomplishing the ends of using knowledge to answer questions, solve problems, and create knowledge. Studying research methods is meant to help indicate "how to" do what you want to accomplish. Research *methodology* focuses more on the prior question of *which* methods to use and compares the advantages and disadvantages of each. Methodology comes first. First you need to decide on your general strategy, or *which,* and then you need to figure out *how.* In other words, once you've made your methodological choice, then you are ready for methods.

The main way to judge methods is by their results. Results are the way to tell whether one method is better than another for a particular problem. There is no one best method for all problems, notwithstanding frequent claims about the superiority of experiments. What do I mean by results? Results in this context means getting a good answer to your question or finding a solution to your problem. Doing research, say for a dissertation, is not just a school exercise in which you show that you know the correct steps to solve a problem. In and of themselves, methods are uninteresting; they are not their own end; they matter only in terms

of the knowledge they help you generate. I remember sometimes getting credit in high school math classes for using the right method to solve a problem on a test, even when I got the answer wrong. This makes sense as a teaching technique, but not as a way to judge research. Because there is no one "right method" in research, the purpose of research cannot be to use it. Rather, the point is to learn something new, and not just new to you, but new to the community of researchers and professionals interested in your question. Imagine how we would react to a research report in the *New England Journal of Medicine* in which the editors explained that although the findings were inaccurate, they were publishing the article anyway. After all, the authors showed that they could follow the steps of the right method.

The approach in this book is to treat research as real, as a central element of a professional's practice. It is not treated merely as something one has to learn for school to obtain a credential. One trait that distinguishes a professional from a mere employee is that a professional is able and willing to make decisions about practice based on the best, most up-to-date research knowledge. As knowledge changes, a professional keeps up with it. Keeping up requires not only information about findings but also an understanding of research design, measurement, and analysis. One needs these three in order to be able to judge the quality of the research findings. To base professional practice on the best research knowledge, one needs to be able to assess the quality of knowledge claims.

This chapter begins by reviewing the relationships among research design, measurement, and analysis. Reviewing these three provides an overview of the book. Then follows the first extended look at analysis and an introduction to the basic categories of statistical analysis—descriptive, associational, and inferential statistics. More specifically, this chapter addresses the following questions.

1. What is the role of research questions in the process of planning research?
2. How are design, measurement, and analysis defined and related?
3. What are the main types of research design?
4. What is measurement, and what are its main types?
5. What different kinds of statistical analysis are there?
6. What is statistical significance?
7. How have recent controversies changed statistical practice?
8. What is the difference between Type I and Type II errors, and why does it matter?

What Is the Role of Research Questions in the Process of Planning Research?

The inextricable links among design, measurement, and analysis are illustrated in Figure 1.1. Design, measure-

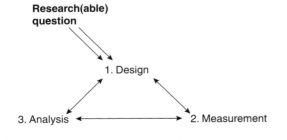

FIGURE 1.1 *Design, measurement, and analysis*

ment, and analysis are the three indispensable components of good research.[1] The figure also shows that *prior* to design, measurement, and analysis, one needs a research question. John Tukey is reported to have said that "if a thing is not worth doing, it is not worth doing well." The nature of the research question determines whether the thing is or is not worth doing. Even if you do it well, have good design, use excellent means of measurement, and use the most sophisticated analyses, all is naught if your question isn't worth looking into. A worthless project cannot be saved by technical sophistication in research methods. Having a good research question is essential to doing good research, but it is not itself a research method; there are no rules to follow to generate a good research question. A good research question addresses significant problems. It leads the researcher to focus on increasing important knowledge and addresses serious problems in a field of investigation and practice. Important knowledge and serious problems are determined by a substantive understanding of a field of research and practice. The methodologist must leave criteria for importance and seriousness to the experts in each field. There is no statistical test for these.

The question must also be research*able*. A researchable question is one about which you can gather evidence that would help you answer the question. *Researchability* is partly a matter of research methods, especially design. Topics or problems do not come with instructions. As a researcher you have to figure out not only what is the most important problem to focus on but also how to go about collecting evidence to solve it. And some problems may not be researchable. Creativity in design, measurement, and analysis has to do with figuring out innovative or newly effective ways to address problems.

How Are Design, Measurement, and Analysis Defined and Related?

Once one has a research question, design, measurement, and analysis are the pillars on which a research investigation is built. Each supports different aspects of the research enterprise. They answer separate but related questions about methods of gathering, recording, and interpreting evidence.

1. Design is focused on methods of *collecting* evidence. It addresses the question, How shall we conduct the study?
2. Measurement involves procedures for *recording* and handling evidence. It answers the question, How shall we sort, count, and assign numbers to the variables?
3. Analysis includes methods for *interpreting* evidence. It answers the question, How shall we produce, evaluate, and make sense of the results?

Note that the order I have used here—first design, then measurement, then analysis—is not invariant. Most arrows in Figure 1.1 point in both directions. Although I think it usually makes more sense to put design first, the really important point is that ultimately there is no "first." The design–measurement–analysis cycle describes an iterative process. Each step influences the others. In a research agenda, sometimes even in one research study, the researcher typically goes through the cycle more than once.

To repeat an earlier analogy, if a complete research project is like a human arm, design, measurement, and analysis are like the arm's bones, muscles, and nerves. The arm will not function well unless all three are in good working order. Though they are distinct, they must work together if they are to work at all. Like an arm, a well-functioning research project is a system; each part is tied to the other parts. How do researchers know where to start, where to enter the system?

Sometimes we can proceed in the order suggested in Figure 1.1. We (1) design the study so that it will yield the sort of (2) measurement data that will allow us to use (3) powerful analytic techniques. If researchers controlled the world they studied, this would almost always be the preferred order. Absent such control, it is sometimes difficult or impossible to follow that useful path. For example, the data may not be of our making. That means that the measurement question is settled; we have to build a research design and select analysis strategies that will work with the available data.

For example, in an evaluation of a big teacher education grant (Vogt, 2002a), the granting agency required that some of the measured outcomes be objective student achievement data. The evaluators did not have the resources to design and administer standardized tests to the students. And even if they had, the schools would not have allowed them to further clutter their crowded schedules with more standardized testing. In short, the outcome data used in the study had to be the standardized tests already given by the districts and/or the state. That fact simplified the design work, because designs were limited to those that could accommodate the available data. The range of analytic choices was restricted to techniques that worked well with the data generated by state and district tests. So, in this case, the researchers started with the measurements that had already been taken. They adopted design and analysis techniques that were perhaps not the ones they would have selected had they had unlimited resources to shape an ideal study. But, like all researchers, they had to compromise with reality.

Compromises are common in planning research, doubly so in field research in which investigators are studying real social life "on the fly" in functioning institutions. In laboratory research, on the other hand, investigators have the advantage of a "pure" setting in which to carry out their investigations. The purity of the laboratory is artificial, intentionally so. The idea is to simplify, or isolate aspects of, reality so as to be more certain about causal relations among the variables being studied. Is purity worth artificiality? The answer is clear: yes and no. It depends on the research question being investigated. Uncertainties about the answers to such questions as the one about trade-offs between purity and artificiality are the rule, not the exception, in research decisions. Do we investigate something that is real but hard to study or something that is artificial but easy to study? Despite what some simplistic textbooks suggest, there really is no typical or best approach to putting together a research design, a measurement model, or an analysis plan. Uncertainty leads to opportunities to be creative. Planning high-quality research requires flexibility. If it were a matter of following a recipe, anyone could do it. Planning a research project always involves weighing advantages and disadvantages in an elaborate series of interrelated choices.

Although design, measurement, and analysis mutually interact, it is also important to note that they are distinct. There is much sloppy use of these terms, which in turn can lead to sloppy thinking. Sometimes people talk about "quantitative designs." This is to confuse design with measurement. There are around seven (see later) main types of design. Each of them can be used to generate *both* quantitative and qualitative data.

Another common contrast is between experimental research and "correlational research." This contrast confuses design with analysis. Experiments are designs; correlations are analysis tools. Evidence from experimental designs can be analyzed with several statistical techniques, one cluster of which is correlational. Most researchers do not use correlation and regression to analyze experimental evidence, but that is because of tradition or convention, not necessity. Indeed, Keppel and Zedeck (1989) show how a wide range of techniques can be used to analyze the same data, a much wider range than is typically used. Traditions and restrictive labeling can lead researchers to follow well-worn paths and to neglect potentially better options (Johnson, 2001).

The word *qualitative* is also used in several ways; people often talk about "qualitative designs." Again, this is to confuse design with measurement. What is usually meant by qualitative design is a design in which it is not common practice to gather and analyze quantitative evidence. The expressions *qualitative data* and *qualitative variables* usually refer to the difference between evidence collected and analyzed in the form of words rather than in the form of numbers. However, it is quite common to use quantitative methods to analyze qualitative variables. For instance, pass/fail is a qualitative variable. But we can code pass/fail numerically—for example, pass = 1, fail = 0—and handle it like any other quantitative variable. Conversely, no matter how numerically loaded the measurement and analysis of a research project, a researcher cannot really avoid qualitative judgments when thinking about it. Any discussion of cause, for example, is inherently qualitative. Also, decisions about the design one has chosen and the reasons why it was selected will be qualitative. Design choice cannot be reduced to a formula.

What Are the Main Types of Research Design?

A research design is a plan for collecting evidence that can be used to answer a research question. There are at least seven basic types of research design. I have listed them in the order of how much the researcher using them has to interfere in people's lives—from the least to the most potential for intrusion. Experiments and participant observation have the greatest tendency to interfere. Those designs necessarily involve manipulation and/or interaction with other people. Document analysis and secondary analysis intrude the least. If the documents or data can be obtained via the Internet, researchers need not have any interactions whatsoever with another person to go about their work. The main types of research design are (1) document analysis; (2) secondary analysis of data, such as census data; (3) naturalistic observation; (4) surveys; (5) interviews; (6) experiments and quasi-experiments; and (7) participant observation.

Any one of these designs can produce evidence that can be handled in either quantitative or qualitative ways. For example, if you conduct a survey you can ask your respondents open-ended questions about public policies that require them to write paragraphs and that require you to use qualitative techniques to analyze the paragraphs; or you could ask respondents to rate public policies on a scale from 1 to 10 and then use quantitative techniques to tally and analyze the results. To take another example, you could conduct naturalistic observations of social interactions in a public place, such as a park. You could record your observations by carefully noting and describing what you observe and later using your notes to analyze your results qualitatively; or you could count and time the length of interactions of particular sorts and later use statistical techniques to organize and summarize your results.

The fact that any design can be used to collect either quantitative or qualitative data means that in battles between the Quants and the Quals what is at stake is more a matter of measurement and analysis than of design. Quantitative measurement and analysis will be the main focus in this book. That is no judgment on the relative merits of the Quants versus the Quals. Indeed, I think them equally meritorious. We focus on quantitative methods in this book because the complexity of studying quantitative approaches to research designs, measurements, and analyses is more than enough to occupy us. Attempts to bring the quantitative and qualitative research traditions together are not well advanced (Tashakkori & Teddlie, 1998). The rudimentary state of efforts to integrate them makes it very difficult to cover both approaches well in the same book, especially a short book.

What Is Measurement, and What Are Its Main Types?

A common definition of measurement is assigning numbers (or labels) to variables. A measurement is an observation expressed as a number. Such observations make it possible to link concepts and the empirical world. Most *operational definitions* involve rules for measurement. For example, one could define (or operationalize) students' "academic achievement" as their scores on the state's annual achievement tests or as their grade point averages. Thus the concept, achievement, could be defined and measured by test scores or grade point averages. Neither of these is a perfect measure of achievement, of course. Indeed, there is no such thing as a perfect or an errorless measurement. Good measurement techniques reduce error, and they are set up in such a way that one can estimate how much error there is likely to be, but there is no way to eliminate error.

Types or Levels of Measurement

Statistics texts often contain extensive discussions of types or levels of measurement. The most commonly used typology was created in the 1950s. It ranks levels of measurement (low to high) as nominal, ordinal, interval, and ratio (NOIR). The higher the rank, the more information the measurement scale contains. One can always convert a higher level of measurement into a lower, but the opposite is not true. These levels are listed with examples in Table 1.1.

Nominal measures are just names or categories or identifiers, such as social security numbers. The numbers assigned to categories convey no quantitative information. If my social security number is higher than yours, this does not mean that I'll receive more benefits. Or, to take another example, in research on religious affiliation Catholics might be labeled 1, Protestants 2, Jews 3, and Others 4. These numbers are just labels. It is silly to think, for example, that if you added two Catholics together you would get a Protestant. The main requirements of nominal or categorical measurement or categorization are that the categories must be *exhaustive* (not leave anything out) and *mutually exclusive* (each person or thing can be categorized in only one way). If these criteria are not met, then there is *no measurement whatsoever,* just sloppy labeling of the sort common in prejudice, stereotyping, and other forms of poor thinking.

Ordinal measures are ranks. The ranks can be few in number, such as low, middle, and high. Or, the number of ranks may be quite large, for instance, a graduating class of 500 students ranked from first to five hundredth by grade point average. Perhaps the most familiar ordinal scale is the common grading

TABLE 1.1 *Examples of Levels of Measurement*

Nominal	Religion	Social security number	Sex/gender
Ordinal	Class rank	Strongly (etc.) agree	Measurement levels
Interval*	GRE score	Grade point average	Years in a calendar
Ratio	Age	Class size	Years of experience

Note: Many measurements that are casually thought of and treated as interval level, such as GRE score and GPA, are really ordinal or rank-order measurements. The reason for the confusion is that they have many ranks, but the scales are ordinal because the intervals between the ranks are not necessarily equal.

system with its ranks of A, B, C, D, and F. The distances between the ranks in an ordinal scale are not necessarily equal. If they were, the scale would be an equal-*interval* scale. Also note that the measurement levels nominal, ordinal, interval, and ratio are arranged in an ordinal scale from lowest to highest.

Interval scales have equal distances between any two adjoining numbers, but they have no meaningful zero point. Common examples include the Fahrenheit and Celsius temperature scales and the way years are counted in various calendars. For instance, as I write this sentence it is the year 2005 in the Christian calendar, 5765 in the Jewish calendar, and 1363 in the Islamic calendar. From a measurement standpoint, though clearly not from a religious standpoint, the year at which one starts counting is arbitrary. It is hardly the case that time did not exist in the era before these calendars started marking it. Or, to consider the other common example, warmth exists at zero degrees Fahrenheit. Think of how much warmer it is at zero than at 30 below. Educational examples abound. If a student gets a zero on a vocabulary test, it probably is not the case that he has no vocabulary at all.

Ratio scales have equal intervals *and* a true zero point. In a ratio scale, zero means that the variable has none of the property. A class with no students in it has zero students. You can treat the numbers in a ratio scale as ratios, meaning you can divide them into one another. A class with 15 students is half the size of a class with 30. By contrast, a student who is ranked fifteenth in her graduating class does not have a GPA double that of the student who is ranked thirtieth. Most statistical techniques are built around the assumption that the measurement scales being used are ratio-level scales. Violating this assumption can be more or less serious, but few firm guidelines exist. Treating interval-level data as ratio is generally less serious than treating ordinal-level data as ratio, but the latter practice is very widespread. Whenever we compute a grade point average, we treat rankings (ordinal-level measures), which can vary widely from instructor to instructor, as though they were ratio-level measures that all instructors used to measure achievement in the same way.

A related distinction in measurement is between variables that can be measured on scales that are *continuous* versus those that are *discrete*. Examples of discrete scales include number of children in a family and number of heads in a coin toss experiment. You cannot have 3.7 children in a family. Examples of continuous scales include age, years of experience, and weight. A person can weigh 124.6 or 124.63 or 124.635 pounds and so on. Of course, measuring the weight of a person to the third decimal place is ridiculous, but it could be done.

Although all of these distinctions—continuous versus discrete and the nominal, ordinal, interval, and ratio levels of measurement—can sometimes be technically important, for most purposes three categories suffice. We can reduce levels of measurement or kinds of variables to a trio of distinctions: quantitative (including interval and ratio), rank (ordinal), and qualitative (nominal or categorical). Finer distinctions are rarely necessary, but these three are very important. They determine the choice of correct statistics to use. Different levels of measurement require different statistical techniques. Different types of correlation (measures of association) and different statistical tests (of significance) are used for different kinds of data.

Matching statistics to levels of measurement is a common source of mistakes by inexperienced researchers as well as a source of controversy among seasoned investigators. In practice, in research reports, data on interval and ratio scales are often treated the same way; that is, the same measures of association and the same statistical tests are used. In fact, ordinal measurements, as long as they contain many ranks, are also often treated as though they were measured at the ratio level, but this practice is open to dispute. Deciding which statistical techniques to use is sometimes quite difficult. This is one of those areas about which it is wise for beginning researchers to seek expert advice, always remembering that on many topics experts can disagree.

A main distinction among statistical techniques as determined by level of measurement is that between *parametric* and *nonparametric* measures. Parametric techniques can be used when the data being analyzed are quantitative (ratio or interval). Nonparametric techniques should be used in most other cases. Ranked data fall into a sometimes unclear middle area. There are specific rank-order measures of association and statistical tests, but ranked data are also sometimes analyzed with techniques developed either for quantitative or for qualitative data. Although various decision trees and algorithms exist for making these decisions, knowledgeable people can and do disagree about the best statistic to use in a particular case. Like most other decisions and choices discussed in this book, even these, which are among the most technical, have more to do with good thinking than good calculating.

What Different Kinds of Statistical Analysis Are There?

When people think of *statistics,* analysis is what they usually have in mind. Statistics involves examining and reasoning about quantitative data. One analyzes the data so as to be able to interpret them, to make sense of them, to figure out what they tell us—if anything. Generally, the idea in statistical analysis is to solve problems using quantitative information. The three main categories of statistics are descriptive, associational, and inferential. Descriptive statistics, as the name suggests, are focused on helping us describe and summarize data. Associational statistics are means by which we can assess how much variables go together or are associated. Inferential statistics are designed to help draw conclusions (make inferences) about populations on the basis of information about samples drawn from those populations.

These three types are described further in Table 1.2. This table can be thought of as a concept map. Students have found it to be a handy reference they could use to reorient themselves when they get lost in the thicket of terms and ideas. It can be reassuring to know that no matter what the statistical technique, it fits into one of three categories and can be described in general terms as having one of three purposes.

Descriptive statistics, such as means and standard deviations, are ways to investigate and explore quantitative evidence, usually one variable at a time; that is, they are usually univariate. *Associational* statistics, such as correlations, allow the researcher to investigate the relations between two variables (bi-

variate) or three or more variables (multivariate) in order to see how they "go together" statistically, how they are associated. The distinction between descriptive and associational statistics is not sharp, because associational statistics, such as correlations, describe relations between variables. *Inferential* statistics involve (1) making estimates, including margins of error, about populations on the basis of knowledge about samples and (2) significance or hypothesis testing. In both cases, *inference* means weighing evidence about the extent to which researchers can infer things about a population on the basis of sample data drawn from the population. The inferential question is: Can the statistics (descriptive and associational) that I have calculated on a sample be generalized to the population from which the sample was drawn? In the roughest terms we can say that associational statistics look at the relation between two or more variables and answer the question: *How big* is it? Inferential statistics answer the question: *How likely* is it to be true of the population? Is it just a coincidence?

Note that these two questions—How big? and How likely?—are quite distinct. A statistic can be big—but likely to be only a coincidence. Or a statistic can be very unlikely to be a coincidence—but still be small and unimportant. In other terms, a result can be *statistically* significant without being *practically* significant. Researchers have not always clearly distinguished in their writing between the two meanings of *significant:* (1) important and (2) unlikely to be only a coincidence. Readers should take care to guard against being misled by sloppy writing. The most common way careless writers mislead readers is by implying that statistical significance *necessarily* indicates importance. For example, suppose researchers gathered two large random samples of police officers in two states: one thousand in New York and one thousand in California. Then they carefully measured the officers' waist sizes and found that the average waist size of California cops was 36.3 inches, whereas for New York cops it was 37.4 inches. Because the samples were large and representative (because they were drawn randomly), the difference of 1.1 inches would be *statistically* significant; it was not just a coincidence that the California sample's waste sizes were smaller. Probably they are

TABLE 1.2   *Concept Map for Thinking about Statistics*

	Descriptive Statistics	*Measures of Association*	*Inferential Statistics*[*]
Also known as	Univariate statistics; measures of central tendency and frequency.	Correlations; strength of association indexes; effect sizes.	Significance tests; test statistics; hypothesis testing.
Common examples	Mean, mode, median, range, variance, standard deviation, proportion.	r, R, rho, eta, Cramer's V, phi coefficient, lambda, gamma, odds ratio, various regression coefficients.	t-test; F test (ANOVA); chi-squared test.
General purpose	To summarize information about a range of data, usually one variable at a time.	To tell you in one number the degree of relationship (statistical association) between two or more variables.	To tell you how likely a particular outcome (descriptive statistic or measure of association) is to be due to chance or sampling error. More specifically, they answer the question, "How likely is a result (a measurement or a statistic) of this size in a sample of this size, if the result in the population were zero?"
Differences among them	Different statistics focus on different features of distributions.	Different measures of association are used for different kinds of problems or variables or data.	Different statistical tests are used for different kinds of problems or variables or data.
What they have in common	The efficiency of the summaries always comes at the cost of losing/discarding data.	Often, but not always, they will range between 0 and 1.0 or between −1.0 and 0 and +1.0. Zero means there is no statistical association (no co-relation or covariance), and +1.0 or −1.0 means that the association is total, perfect, and complete.	Each leads to a p-value, such as $p < .05$ and $p = .0037$.

[*]Inferential statistics also include estimation with margins of error (confidence intervals)
   The most familiar example is political polling. Pollsters might say that a candidate was supported by 60% of those sampled and that they are 95% sure (confidence level) with a margin of error of 3% that the true value in the population is between (confidence interval) 57% and 63%.

smaller in the population of California police officers too. But few of us would think that this result was a large or important (practically significant) difference between law officers in the two states.

Traditionally, statistics courses and textbooks have focused on inferential statistics, especially methods of assessing statistical significance. This book puts more emphasis on associational techniques and, within inferential statistics, on estimation. The right balance between associational and inferential and, within inferential, between estimation and hypothesis testing has been a subject of long and complicated discussions—and surprisingly bitter debates. The current trend is to focus more on interpreting the size of associations and less on how to compute their statistical significance. This book advances that trend. Despite our *comparative* lack of emphasis on statistical significance in this book, it remains a *very* important topic. The rest of this chapter and all of Chapter 8 will be devoted to the subject, and it will come up in almost every other chapter as well. But for professionals wanting to interpret research or to conduct research in order to improve their practice, much more emphasis has to be put on associational statistics. Statistical significance can be adequately (not fully) covered in much less space than is usually devoted to it. Most practitioners will find it more valuable to be introduced to widely used advanced associational techniques than to learn several dozen additional ways to compute a *p*-value. Dozens of statistical tests exist. One popular book is called *100 Statistical Tests* (Kanji, 1999). This fact is less intimidating when you realize that all statistical tests end in a *p*-value. It is very important to understand what a *p*-value is, when it should and should not be computed, and how to interpret it. But methods of calculating it can most often be trusted to software packages.

What Is Statistical Significance?

All that said, it remains crucial to have a firm understanding of the meaning of statistical significance. We will focus on that for the remainder of this chapter. What is meant by the question: Are the results *statistically significant*? Significance or hypothesis testing always answers this question the same way—with a *p*-value or a decision based on a *p*-value. The *p* stands for *probability*. Probability of what? We can answer this question at several levels starting with the most elementary and approximate and ending with the most precise. As your understanding of inferential statistics progresses, you will feel comfortable with the more advanced answers. If you get lost, you can revert to one of the elementary-level answers. (Don't expect to fully understand answers 3 and 4 at this point. They are explained thoroughly later in the book, especially in Chapter 8.)

Suppose someone said the following: In a sample of students at my university, I calculated the correlation between hours spent studying and grade point average to be $r = .47$. The *p*-value for this cor-

relation is $p = .03$. What does the *p*-value mean here? The following four correct answers start with the most approximate and end with the most exact answer. $P = .03$ means:

1. There's a 3% chance I'm wrong.

2. The probability that the result is due to chance (is a coincidence) is 3%.

3. A result of this size (.47) would occur by chance alone, in a sample of the size I used, 3% of the time.

4. If there were no correlation in the population, the probability of finding one this big (.47) or bigger in a *random* sample of this size would be 3%. This fourth answer is the fully correct one, but you can often get by with one of the earlier ones in the list.

The standard conventional cutoff for statistical significance is .05 or 5%. If a result is likely to be due to chance less than 5% of the time—written as: $p < .05$—it is usually said to be (statistically) significant. The actual, exact *p*-value is less commonly reported than whether it meets a cutoff score such as .05 or .01. This practice of using cutoffs rather than exact values grew up in an era when computing exact values was very tedious and generally more time consuming than it was worth. Today, with computerized computations of *p*-values that usually take less than one second, the practice of using cutoffs is increasingly challenged, and the challenge is part of a larger debate about the uses of statistical significance testing.

How Have Recent Controversies Changed Statistical Practice?

In the late 1990s and early 2000s, researchers in psychology and education engaged in very heated debates about how best to report quantitative research results. Many felt that statistical significance, *p*-values, and Type I error had been overemphasized. By comparison, confidence intervals, effect sizes, power, and Type II errors had been underemphasized. Personally, from the first day I heard about the debate, which took place at the highest levels of the psychologists' and educators' professional organizations, I found the controversy perplexing. Statistical tests, *p*-values, confidence intervals, effect size statistics, and power coefficients all provide useful information. Mathematically speaking, they are, to a very large extent, functions of one another (meaning that if you know one you can calculate another). And, given that the time-consuming work of calculating them has been fully automated, why wouldn't a researcher want to report them all? These issues are discussed in some detail in Chapter 8; here we briefly introduce them, emphasizing, as always, an understanding of the concepts behind the calculations and the jargon.

The positions on each side of the debate were not new. What was new is that in some fields those who thought that reporting statistical significance was sufficient lost the argument. As of the year 2000 all journals in psychology sponsored by the American Psychological Association and all education journals sponsored by the American Educational Research Association are committed, by formal policy, to publishing only articles that report effect size (an associational measure) as well as statistical significance. This means that in order to read articles in these journals, knowledge of significance tests will no longer suffice. And if you are planning to do quantitative research in any psychology-based field or in any of the education disciplines, you will need to include information about effect sizes, confidence intervals, and power (Type II error) as well as significance tests (Type I error). Table 1.3 helps organize our discussion of these topics by comparing Type I and Type II errors and related issues.

What Is the Difference between Type I and Type II Errors, and Why Does It Matter?

Students often find the notion of types of error and how they are related to statistical significance and power to be hard to grasp. Although the terminology is more than a little confusing, the concepts are pretty ordinary. The following analogy has been

TABLE 1.3 *Types of Inferential Error, p-values, and Power*

Type I Error	Type II Error
Definition: Reject a true H_0	Definition: "Accept" a false H_0
Example: Vending machine rejects a good dollar	Example: Vending machine accepts a counterfeit
In diagnosis: False positive ("you have cancer" when you don't)	In diagnosis: False negative ("you don't have cancer" when you do)
p-value: The probability that the H_0 is true, given the statistic (e.g., mean difference or Pearson *r*) and the sample size	*Power:* The probability of rejecting a false H_0; more generally, the sensitivity of a research design to detect relationships

helpful for many. You approach a vending machine with your dollar. Your null hypothesis (abbreviated H_0 or "hypothesis zero") is "There is no significant difference between this dollar and the population of real dollars." You insert your dollar into the slot, but the machine rejects it. That's Type I error. The machine has wrongly rejected a true dollar. If, and I'm *not* recommending this, in your frustration you cut out a dollar-size piece of paper from your notebook, you could test for another kind of error. Your null hypothesis is the same, "There is no significant difference between this dollar and the population of real dollars." You stick your crude counterfeit into the machine—and, surprisingly, it accepts your piece of notepaper! That's Type II error. The machine has wrongly accepted a false dollar. So the machine can make two kinds of mistakes; it can reject a true dollar or accept a false one. Of course, most often it does not make such errors: It usually rejects pieces of notepaper and accepts real dollars. The *p*-value is the probability of making a Type I error. Power is the probability of avoiding a Type II error.

Until the revolution in research reporting in psychology and education in the late 1990s, most research was designed to minimize Type I error, which, it was often claimed, is the worst kind. But it is easy to think of examples in which Type II error may be the more serious mistake. False negatives in diagnosis are one example (see Table 1.3). Most people would agree that although all diagnostic mistakes are bad, a false negative—that is, concluding that someone is OK when that person in fact has the disease—is worse. A false positive can have many disagreeable consequences, but is usually the lesser error. To return to the original example, the people who build vending machines are quite happy to make some Type I errors (think of how many times you've had your dollar spit back at you). Type I errors are tolerable as long as the dollar reader is sensitive enough (has sufficient power) to reject counterfeits with extremely high probability.

What is all the fuss about? Why isn't research designed in a way that avoids both kinds of error? Usually, it can't be, not simultaneously. The two kinds of error are inversely related. Reducing the chances of one increases the chances of making the other. Think of a research design as being like the vending machine. If the machine accepts almost any true dollar, even one that is faded and torn, it will be more likely also to accept counterfeits (Type II error). On the other hand, if it is very good at rejecting counterfeits, it will have an unfortunate tendency to reject lots of real dollars (Type I error). This trade-off cannot be avoided. However, as we shall see in Chapter 5, increasing one's sample size helps reduce both types of error.

The "no difference" standard of comparison used in the preceding example is the infamous *null hypothesis*. The null hypothesis is the hypothesis to be *null*ified. It is usually, but not quite always, a hypothesis of no effect or no difference. This is why significance testing is also often referred to as hypothesis testing, especially when the test is performed on data gathered in experiments. Although mathematical statisticians have drawn some distinctions between and quarreled about the two terms, it is common to use the terms *significance testing* and *hypothesis testing* interchangeably. The main practical difference is that hypothesis testers set a threshold or cutoff in advance (such as .05 or .01) and then report a yes–no decision about whether the hypothesis should be rejected or retained. Significance testers, by contrast, most often report and discuss actual *p*-values and degrees of significance. (See the discussion in Huck, 2004.) These differences aside, significance testing and hypothesis testing rest equally on the null hypothesis.

The language used to discuss null hypothesis testing is clumsy, maybe even twisted. Ordinary people do not often talk that way, and I'm convinced, nor do scientists. Could you imagine the cover of *Scientific American* announcing a special article on the decade's "Most Important Null Hypotheses We've Failed to Reject"? People can get confused when one uses double negatives. But the language of hypothesis testing often uses triple negatives. I have even seen examples of quadruple negatives: "We have not (1) failed (2) to reject (3) the null hypothesis of no (4) difference between the groups." Otherwise put, the evidence did not, *not,* <u>not</u>, **not** support the hypothesis that there *was* a difference between the groups. What could this mean? One way to work your way through the confusion is to count the number of negatives. An even number of negatives means the evidence supports the *research* hypothesis that there is a difference. An odd number means that it does not. One never uses fewer than two negatives, but even if one did (and *accepted* the null hypothesis) this would still follow the odd–even rule. The most common statements about the null hypothesis, with negatives counted, follow.

- We reject (1) the null hypothesis (2)—even, supports the research hypothesis.
- We cannot (1) reject (2) the null hypothesis (3)—odd, doesn't support the research hypothesis.
- We fail (1) to reject (2) the null hypothesis (3)—odd, doesn't support the research hypothesis.

These annoying locutions do point out one crucial fact, however. Testing for statistical significance has *no meaning whatsoever* apart from a null hypothesis about a random sample. The null hypothesis asks the following kind of question: How likely are we to find a relation *in a random sample* if there is no difference *in the population*? Or, how likely are we to find a difference of this size between two samples if the populations from which they were drawn were not different? Answering this kind of question is what significance testing is all about. If you are not studying a random sample in order to make inferences about a population, computing the statistical significance of descriptive or associational statistics makes no sense. If you are just studying some group that is of interest to you (for example, the way teachers might study the students in their classes), you need compute no tests of significance because you do not intend to generalize your findings to a population. Also, if you are studying a whole population (as university administrators might do with data about all enrolled students or city managers might do about taxpayers in their city), again there is no point

in computing p-values. You already know the population value; you do not need to make inferences about what it "probably" is.

Meaningless p-values are quite frequently computed and reported, however. Computer programs, such as SPSS, will calculate them, because the program has no way of knowing that what it has been asked to do makes no sense. This is another example, and one of the most important, of how good quantitative research is not mainly about accurate calculating. It is about good thinking. Good thinking leads to calculating things that can be meaningfully interpreted, so that one can solve problems and answer questions that matter. Computers can do our calculating for us, but not our thinking. Thinking about statistics, not computing them, will be our emphasis in this book.

Terms and Concepts to Review

Some terms will appear again in the lists for subsequent chapters where the concepts are discussed further.

Research question
Design
Measurement
Analysis

Research designs (ranked, low to high, by level of interaction with subjects/participants)
• Document analysis
• Secondary analysis of data
• Naturalistic observation
• Surveys
• Interviews
• Experiments and quasi-experiments
• Participant observation

Levels of measurement
• Nominal (for qualitative variables)
• Ordinal (for ranked variables)
• Interval (for quantitative variables)
• Ratio (for quantitative variables)

Measurement criteria for categories
• Mutually exclusive
• Exhaustive

Scales of measurement
• Discrete scales
• Continuous scales
• Qualitative scales
• Quantitative scales

Types of statistics categorized by levels of measurement
• Parametric
• Nonparametric

Types of statistics categorized by their purposes
• Descriptive
• Associational
• Inferential

Terms associated with statistical inference
• Null hypothesis
• H_0
• p-value
• Type I error
• Hypothesis testing
• Statistical significance
• Estimation
• Confidence intervals
• Type II error
• Statistical power

Discussion Questions

Most of the discussion questions at the end of each chapter ask you to consider a concept by devising your own example and then to work out the implications of applying the concept to your example. I use this kind of discussion question in my classes because students usually find that when they have worked out their own example, they "own" the concept. When you need to remember the concept and what it means in practice, you will tend to do so first by accessing your example(s).

1. Think of examples of two research questions that address a topic of interest to you. One of these should be a good research question, the other should be inadequate. Why is one question good and the other not good? Discuss what that tells you about the nature of good research questions in general.

2. What does it mean for a question to be researchable? Can you think of an important question that is not researchable? Why isn't it researchable? Can you think of an example of a question that is researchable but that is not a good research question? Why is something that is researchable not inevitably important or interesting?

3. Think of a topic or problem of interest to you and plan how you would go about doing research on it. What is your research question? What design would you use to gather evidence to answer that question? Why? Now think of another approach to *the same* problem or topic. What other design could you use? What are the advantages and disadvantages of the two designs? Would you have to change your research question, or could you investigate the same research question with a different design?

4. After deciding on the design you would use (for question 3) to collect the evidence, decide what evidence you would collect. This is a measurement issue. For example, if you surveyed people, would

you ask them yes–no questions, would you use open-ended questions and expect respondents to write sentences, would you ask them to rate things on a scale of 1 to 10, or would you use some other technique? Or, to take another example, if you conducted an experiment in which you randomly assigned participants to two different instructional groups, how would you determine which method of instruction was better? Would you interview participants? Would you test them? Would you survey them about what they thought of the instructional program? How would you decide?

5. Think of an example of research on a topic of interest to you for which it would be very important to test the results of the research for statistical significance. Now think of an example for which statistical significance would be less important or perhaps even completely inappropriate. What are the key differences between your two examples? How can statistical significance be very important for some research problems and irrelevant to others?

6. Construct an example that will help you distinguish between Type I errors and Type II errors and that will help you remember how they are related. One of the key characteristics of good research design is that it helps you figure out how to avoid errors. Type I and Type II errors are the two most important categories of errors when using inferential statistics. The example I use to help me remember (in addition to the vending machine discussed in the chapter) is the sensitivity of smoke alarms. If they are very sensitive, they will go off when you wish they wouldn't. But, if your alarm doesn't go off whenever you fry something in your kitchen, it might be too insensitive and miss a real fire. Try to construct your own example and explain how it helps you think about the problems of research design.

Self-Test

If you can answer most of the following questions accurately, you can feel confident about your understanding of the material in this chapter. If not, it would be a good idea to review the chapter. (Answers can be found in the Appendix.)

1. The distinction between qualitative and quantitative research is more a matter of measurement than of design. True or False?

2. Knowing the levels at which variables are measured is important because this influences the choice of

the appropriate test statistics and measures of association to use in analyzing the variables. True or False?

3. Measures of association are designed to indicate how likely a particular result is to be due to chance alone, that is, due to sampling error. True or False?

4. According to new standards of practice in psychology and education, it is unnecessary for researchers to report statistical results beyond those that indicate whether the findings have reached the threshold of statistical significance. True or False?

5. The null hypothesis is very often a statement that there is "no difference" between populations or groups. True or False?

6. Researchers usually hope to be able to disprove or reject their null hypothesis. True or False?

7. The purpose of statistical inference is to enable researchers to draw conclusions about samples based on knowledge of population parameters. True or False?

8. Knowing the levels at which your variables are measured is important because
   a. It determines the correct research design to use on your project.
   b. It influences the choice of the appropriate statistical technique to use in analyzing your data.
   c. If your data are nonparametric, then you know that you need to dispense with associational analyses and statistical tests.
   d. Of all of the above.

9. If one of your results is statistically significant, this means that
   a. The *p*-value obtained using a statistical test of that result is larger than a conventional cutoff for significance.
   b. You would not likely have obtained a result this large by chance.
   c. The result is large and practically significant.
   d. All of the above are true.

10. Concerning Type I and Type II error, it is accurate to say that
    a. It is generally more important to avoid Type I error.
    b. It is generally more important to avoid Type II error.
    c. Typically, reducing the probability of one increases the likelihood of the other.
    d. Type I error is the main concern of significance testing whereas Type II error is the focus of hypothesis testing.

11. Concerning the null hypothesis, it is accurate to say that
    a. Significance and hypothesis testing imply a null hypothesis, even when one is not explicitly stated.
    b. It is usually an hypothesis of no effect or no difference between groups.
    c. It is central to the process of making inferences from a sample to a population.
    d. All of the above are accurate.

12. Concerning the relation of research questions to research designs, it is accurate to say that
    a. For most research questions there is only one appropriate research design.
    b. If a question is not researchable, then only inferential techniques can be used.
    c. Various designs can usually be applied to the same research question.
    d. If a design is nonparametric, it is not possible to apply the tools of statistical inference.
    e. All of the above are accurate.

Endnote

1. Pedhazur & Schmelkin's (1991) well-known text is the inspiration for the title of this chapter and for Figure 1.1.

2

Standard Deviation and Correlation

The standard deviation (SD) and the correlation coefficient (Pearson *r*) might seem an odd couple. Most texts do not discuss them together, yet they have many things in common. Each is a powerful descriptive technique. The standard deviation is used to describe the variation in a distribution of scores. The correlation coefficient is used to describe how two distributions of scores are related to each other. Another important link between them is that one computes *r* using the standard deviations of two distributions. Most importantly, each is the basis on which much else in statistics is built. A thorough understanding of these two statistics is a key to understanding most of the other aspects of quantitative analysis discussed in this book.

Because these two are so important, this chapter devotes a bigger share of time to how to compute these statistics than does any other. Time is spent on how to calculate, *not* because it is a useful skill. Personally, I have used computers to do this work for so long that I barely remember how to calculate many statistics by hand. But SD and *r* are two big exceptions to the rule that there is not much point in knowing how to compute statistics by hand. One needs to know how, not to actually be able to do the computational work, but in order to define and understand the concepts. This chapter studies standard deviations and correlations by addressing the following questions.

1. What is a standard deviation?
2. How are the standard deviation and the variance calculated?
3. What are standard scores, and how are they used?
4. What is the normal distribution, and how is it related to standard scores?
5. What is a correlation coefficient, and how can it be interpreted?
6. How is a correlation coefficient calculated?
7. How can correlations and their statistical significance be interpreted?
8. How can correlations be used to find relations in and interpret real data?
9. What is a large correlation?
10. What is linearity, and why is it important for interpreting correlations?
11. What is the relationship between correlation and cause?

What Is a Standard Deviation?

The standard deviation (SD) is a measure of variability of a group of "scores."[1] It tells you how much the scores are spread out (high standard deviation) or are clustered together (low standard deviation). The standard deviation is a measure of how much all the scores

19

in a group of scores differ on average from the mean score. In other terms, it is a measure of the deviation from the mean or average. It is widely used in many fields to describe the variability of values ranging from the birth weights of infants to the prices of stocks and bonds. Like most of the statistics we will discuss in this book, the SD is built on the mean. Most statistical calculations are variations on a mean.

The SD—and the square of the SD, the *variance*—is fundamental to a remarkable number of statistics. If the collection of statistical techniques is like a bakery shop filled with a wide variety of breads and pastries, the standard deviation is the flour with which most of them are made. It is hard to think of a more crucial statistical concept. Yet, the basic idea is simple. Imagine that standing in front of you are three men whose average height is 6 feet; individually, they measure 5 feet 11 inches, 6 feet, and 6 feet 1 inch tall. The SD of those measurements will be low. Now imagine three others whose average is 6 feet, but their individual measurements are 5 feet, 6 feet, and 7 feet tall. Their SD will be much bigger. Finally, imagine three more, all of whom are exactly 6 feet tall. Their mean height would be 6 feet, of course, and the SD of their heights would be zero. Because those in the last group are all the same, there is no deviation from the mean, no difference between anyone's height and the average height of the group. Specifically, the first group, whose heights in inches are 71, 72, and 73, has an SD of .82 inch. The average difference of members of the group from the mean is a little less than an inch. The second group, whose heights in inches are 60, 72, and 84, has an SD of 9.8 inches. On average, the heights of the individuals in this group differ from the overall group mean by nearly 10 inches. In general, the smaller the standard deviation, the better the mean describes all the scores for a group; a large SD, on the other hand indicates that the mean is not very representative of the individuals in the group.

Of course, one would not bother to make the calculations for groups of three, but for groups of 300 or 3,000, the SD can be a very handy descriptive statistic. The purpose of a descriptive statistic is to summarize a lot of information with one number. A mean can be very good at this. For example, imagine two high schools, A and B, each with about 2,000 students. It is useful to know that the mean combined SAT score (combined scores can range from a low of 400 to a high of 1600) of the students at High School A is 1100, whereas at High School B it is 950. Knowing those two numbers does not tell you everything, but it tells you a fair amount, very economically, about SAT scores at the two high schools. If you also have the standard deviations of the scores for the two high schools, you will know quite a bit more. Say that the SD at High School A was 100, whereas the SD at High School B it was 300. This would mean that at High School A many of the students scored pretty close to the mean of 1100. Most students scored within 100 points more or less than the mean. At High School B, on the other hand, although the average score was lower (950), that is not the big story. School B's high standard deviation (300) means that students' scores differed greatly in that school. In fact these differences among students *within* School B were bigger than the differences in the averages *between* Schools A and B. Many students at High School B scored hundreds of points above or below the mean. At High School A, the students' scores tended to be fairly close to one another. High School B enrolled many students who scored unusually high *and* unusually low. All this information can be summarized in one line of type:

School A, mean = 1100, SD = 100; School B, mean = 950, SD = 300

How Are the Standard Deviation and the Variance Calculated?

People rarely compute standard deviations by hand. Computer programs that are widely available do the job very quickly and, equally important, more accurately. But knowing *how* an SD is calculated helps you better understand exactly *what* it is. The steps are simple and require nothing more than ordinary arithmetic, but the calculations for thousands of scores of students at High Schools A and B would be tedious in the extreme. To illustrate the meaning of the standard deviation, two of them are calculated in Table 2.1. One of the SDs is for the scores of five students who took Test X, and the other is for the scores of the same group of five students who also took Test Y. To repeat, it is worth paying attention to how SDs are calculated, not because you are

TABLE 2.1 *Examples of How to Compute the Standard Deviation*

	Column 1 Scores	Column 2 Minus Mean	Column 3 Deviation Scores	Column 4 Squared Deviation Scores
Test X				
Student A	25	−25 =	0	0
Student B	22	−25 =	−3	9
Student C	29	−25 =	4	16
Student D	26	−25 =	1	1
Student E	23	−25 =	−2	4
Totals	125		0	30 (sum of squares)
	Mean: 125/5 = 25			Mean: 30/5 = 6.0 (variance)[*]
			Average deviation: 10/5 = 2.0	SD: square root of 6.0 = 2.45
Test Y				
Student A	19	−24 =	−5	25
Student B	30	−24 =	6	36
Student C	14	−24 =	−10	100
Student D	29	−24 =	5	25
Student E	28	−24 =	4	16
Totals	120		0	202 (sum of squares)
	Mean: 120/5 = 24			Mean: 202/5 = 40.4 (variance)[*]
			Average deviation: 30/5 = 6	SD: square root of 40.4 = 6.36

[*]*Note:* When computing the variance of a *sample,* one should divide by the number of scores minus 1 ($n − 1$); when figuring the variance for a *population,* you use the number of scores (N). Most computer programs use ($n − 1$) by default; that is, unless you tell them to do otherwise.

ever likely to calculate one, but to make sure you clearly understand what this fundamental statistic actually is.

The steps for calculating a standard deviation are illustrated in Table 2.1: (1) Calculate the mean or average of the scores (column 1); (2) subtract the mean from each score to get the deviation scores (columns 2 and 3); (3) square the deviation scores (column 4); (4) calculate the mean of the deviation scores, which is the *variance* (column 4); and (5) take the square root of the variance (column 4).

These steps parallel those used when calculating a wide variety of statistics. First take the mean of all the scores. Then subtract the mean from each of the scores. Square each result and add them all up. This is the famous *sum of squares* (that is, the total of the squared deviation scores). Adding endless columns of squared deviation scores to get sums of squares was how thousands of unfortunate students spent much of their time in statistics courses prior to the widespread availability of personal computers.

The work involved many hours of tedious fourth-grade arithmetic to get the sums of the squares, but this work was necessary to calculate the standard deviation, the *t*-test, the *F*-test or ANOVA, correlation coefficients, and regression coefficients, among other statistics. In more specialized terms, these computational steps are how the general linear model, which is the foundation of modern statistics, is implemented.

The average or mean of the sum of the squares is the *variance* (sometimes called the *mean squares*). It is another fundamental statistic. It is not very important as a descriptive statistic in its own right, but it is crucial and more convenient for calculating other statistics, most notably in analysis of variance or ANOVA. Remember that the variance is just the square of the SD, or, looking at it the other way around, the SD is the square root of the variance. The standard deviation is often abbreviated as *s;* if so, the variance is abbreviated as s^2.

Looking at the raw scores in column 1 of the table, it is clear that if one had only the means of the scores to describe Tests X and Y, one might wrongly conclude that students' scores on the two exams were roughly equivalent. The mean of Test X is 25 and the mean of Test Y is 24. But the standard deviations are much further apart. The standard deviation for X, abbreviated SD_x, = 2.45, whereas SD_y = 6.36, which is over 2.5 times as large. The students all got roughly the same score on Text X (at least as compared with their scores on Test Y), but their performance on Test Y varied greatly.

Note that the SD is closely related to the *average deviation* (AD), also called the mean deviation and, most accurately, the mean absolute deviation (MAD). Most students find the idea of the average deviation easier to understand and remember than the standard deviation, and the two measures of deviation from the mean will often give roughly the same value. Looking at column 3 in Table 2.1, you can see how to compute an average deviation (AD). When you add up all the deviations from the mean the total is *always* zero. This is because the mean sums up all the scores, both those above and those below the mean. By definition, deviations from the mean will cancel each other out and sum to zero. But, this zero, because it is true by definition, doesn't tell you any-thing. You want to know how much deviation there was *both* above and below the mean. To get the average deviation you use absolute values, that is, numbers without the plus and minus signs. You total these and take their mean to get the AD. The problem with the AD, and the reason it is seldom used, is that it is extremely difficult to work with when using more advanced quantitative techniques. The SD is much more versatile. But average deviation is pretty close as a definition of the standard deviation.

There are some useful rules of thumb for using and interpreting standard deviations. They are also helpful for understanding what the standard deviation actually measures. It is important to note that the closer the distribution of scores is to a normal distribution, the better these rules of thumb will work.

• One SD equals how far from the mean you have to move (up or down) to cover one-third of the scores.

• About two-thirds (68%) of scores in a distribution will be between 1 SD above and 1 SD below the mean.

• Nearly all (95%) scores in a distribution will be between 2 SDs above and 2 SDs below the mean. About 99% of the scores will be plus or minus 3 SDs.

• Because most of the scores will be between 2 SDs above and below the mean, you can often make a pretty accurate estimate of the range (which is the difference between the highest and the lowest scores) of all the scores by multiplying the SD by 4. For example, if the SD is 5, the range is likely to be around $5 \times 4 = 20$.

• Because you are more likely to know the range than the SD, you can do it the other way around. If you take the difference between the highest and lowest scores and divide that by 4, this will often give you a good estimate of the SD.

Thus far in this chapter you have seen a progression of related statistics building on one another. To review, first is the mean or average. Then come the deviation scores, which you get by subtracting the mean from each score. You can take the average of the (absolute) deviation scores to get the average deviation. Next comes the all-important *variance,* which is the mean of the squared deviation scores. Finally, there is the *standard deviation,* which is the square root of the variance. It is hard to over-emphasize the importance of the mean, the deviation scores, the variance, and the standard deviation. Even in a book such as this one, designed to eliminate nearly all calculations, it has been worth spending time learning how to compute these.

What Are Standard Scores, and How Are They Used?

Standard deviations are the basis on which many familiar *standard scores* are built. For example, SAT, ACT, GRE, and IQ scores are all based on standard deviation scores. The original standard score is the *z-score.* Once you understand it, the other standard scores are just a matter of translation. Standard scores are standard deviation scores recomputed to be in convenient uniform units. Just as the standard deviation is always a measure of deviation from the mean, so too with standard scores. A series of *z*-scores computed on a set of data has a mean of 0 (the *z* stands for "zero") and an SD of 1.0. Thus, if you got a *z*-score of 1.0 on a test, this would mean you scored 1 SD above the average. On the other hand, if you got a *z*-score of −1.5, that would mean you got a score 1.5 SD below the average.

Here is an example of how *z*-scores are computed and of how they can be handy. Say you took two midterm examinations. Your total points on the first was 85; on the second you got 155. On which test did you do better? It is hard to tell without more information. One way to tell is to compute your percentage correct on each test by dividing the total possible points into your score and multiplying by 100. A percentage is a form of standard score; it allows you to compare across tests by using the same *standard* (per 100) of measurement. But if you were more interested in your *rank,* in how you compared to other students who took the tests, the *z*-scores would give you better information. Say on the first test you got a score of 85, the class mean was 75, and the SD was

10. On the second you got a score of 155, the mean was 170, and the SD was also 10. In each case, you subtract the mean from your score and divide the result by the standard deviation, as in the following.

$$\frac{\text{Score} - \text{Mean}}{\text{SD}} \qquad \frac{85 - 75}{10} \qquad \frac{10}{10} = 1.0$$

$$\frac{155 - 170}{10} \qquad \frac{-15}{10} = -1.5$$

The results tell you that your 85 was a much stronger score than your 155. Your 85 was above average; your 155 was below average. Like all other standard scores, the *z*-score tells you your rank or comparative standing in a group. It is a measure of your relative position; it does not measure your progress toward an absolute standard of achievement. Your *z* of −1.5 could be quite an accomplishment if, for example, you were a freshman taking a senior-level course. And your *z* of +1.0 might be a mediocre performance if you were a senior taking a freshman-level course.

Mostly for reasons of popular consumption, *z*-scores have been recomputed *many* different ways. The idea has been to avoid negative numbers and decimals. For example, *T*-scores have a mean of 50 and an SD of 10. So, instead of getting *z*-scores of +1.0 and −1.5, as in the above example, you would get *T*-scores of 60 and 35. To me, that is just confusing, but presumably it helps some people. Scores on the individual parts of the SAT and GRE are reported using means of 500 and SDs of 100. IQ tests use means of 100 and SDs of 15, whereas the ACT uses 20 and 5. Figure 2.1 summarizes some well-known standardized test scores and compares them with percentile rankings and IQ scores, and it does so in the context of the normal distribution (discussed in the next section). For example, you can see that a *z*-score of 2.0 is equivalent to the 98th percentile, an SAT of 700, an IQ of 130, and an ACT of 30.

What may have started out as a way to simplify things for the general public, has, I think, ended up causing more confusion than it is worth, at least to anyone who doesn't have too much trouble with decimals and negative numbers. Surely the winner of the

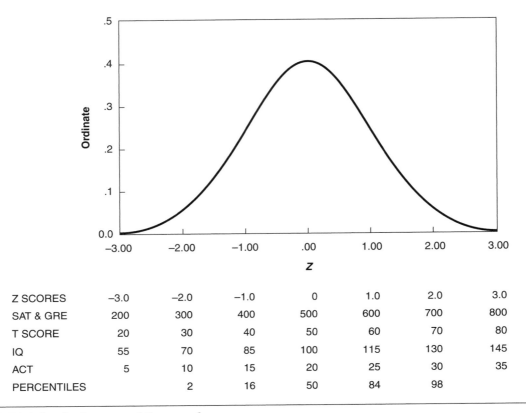

Z SCORES	-3.0	-2.0	-1.0	0	1.0	2.0	3.0
SAT & GRE	200	300	400	500	600	700	800
T SCORE	20	30	40	50	60	70	80
IQ	55	70	85	100	115	130	145
ACT	5	10	15	20	25	30	35
PERCENTILES		2	16	50	84	98	

FIGURE 2.1 *Standard scores and the normal curve*

award for the least helpful obfuscation of z-scores is the "stanine" or standard ninth. It is still widely used to report scores on achievement tests. The scale has nine values, 1 through 9. Stanines 2 through 8 are half an SD wide. Stanine 5 straddles the mean (one-quarter of an SD above and one-quarter below). Stanines 1 and 9 are, respectively, 1.75 SDs below and above the mean. In the 1970s I confidently predicted that stanines would die of terminal stupidity before the twentieth century came to a close. I was wrong. Like most social scientists, I have rarely been good at predicting the future.

To repeat, all standard scores are versions, more or less helpful, of z-scores. The z-score is a way to express scores in standard deviation units, it is the basis of many other statistics, and it is the statistic most used for describing and interpreting the normal distribution.

What Is the Normal Distribution, and How Is It Related to Standard Scores?

The normal distribution, which is depicted in Figure 2.1, is covered in more depth in Chapters 4 and 8. Here it is enough to say that the normal distribution is a *theoretical* distribution. No empirical distribution can match it exactly, but many distributions of scores in the real world in fact do approximate the normal curve very closely. The normal curve has many wonderful mathematical properties about which much is known and which enable one to solve many problems. So, if a real distribution that researchers are studying comes quite close to the normal distribution, that means that the researchers automatically know a great deal about the real distribution without further work.

The horizontal axis (called the *X*-axis or abscissa) gives the scores, in this case, standard deviation or z-scores. The vertical axis (called the Y-axis or ordinate) gives the frequency of the scores. The most common scores are toward the middle, which is the mean or a z-score of zero. The least common scores are far from the mean—and from the mode and the median, which are all identical in a normal distribution. The area under the curve gives the percent of the total scores that are between two scores. For example, the area under the curve between $z = -1.0$ and $z = +1.0$ is about 68% of the total area under the curve. The area between $z = 0.0$ and $z = 2.0$ (or the 50th and 98th percentiles) is about 48% of the total.

Many things in the real world are not distributed normally of course, such as number of years of schooling completed by the adult population in the United States or the annual incomes of members of the working population. The bulges in those distributions would not come in the middle. The means, modes, and medians would not all be the same as they are in a normal distribution. And the numbers of people at the high and low ends of the distribution would not be equal. But even in such cases, the normal curve is a very useful standard of comparison. Much work in statistics has been done devising ways to describe how an empirical distribution is or is not similar to a normal distribution. Also, the normal distribution is used in inferential statistics, even for making inferences about samples whose scores are not normally distributed. Finally note that the normal curve depicted in Figure 2.1 is one of many. This one is the *standard* normal curve (sometimes called the *unit* normal curve). That means it is measured in standard deviation units or z-scores, with a mean of zero and a standard deviation of 1.

In brief, the standard deviation (and the square of the SD, the variance) is the base on which much else in statistics in built. For example, one computes the SDs of two variables in order to calculate the correlation coefficient, r, between them.

What Is a Correlation Coefficient, and How Can It Be Interpreted?

A correlation coefficient is a measure of (statistical) association between two variables. It is a way of describing their "co-relation." It can range between −1.00 through zero to +1.00. Several varieties of correlation exist, which are used with data at different levels of measurement. Most often, when people speak of correlations they mean the Pearson r, or just r for short. The other types of correlation, such as the point biserial, Spearman, or phi, are special cases of the Pearson that were important before computers because they made hand calculations easier. Although you will still encounter them in your reading, they are of little consequence today. Some guidelines for interpreting correlation coefficients, of whatever type, are as follows:

• Zero indicates no association, meaning that knowing about one variable tells you nothing about another.

• Negative correlations indicate *inverse* relationships; that is, when one variable goes up the other tends to go down (e.g., hours of TV watching and grade point average).

• Positive correlations indicate *direct* relationships; that is, the variables tend to move in the same direction (e.g., hours of studying and grade point average).

• Positive and negative in this context refer only to the algebra of the relations. They are not evaluations. Class size and academic achievement are negatively related, but small classes and high test scores are not bad; they just move in opposite directions. Similarly, smoking rates and lung disease rates are positively related, but they are not good things. They are positive only in the sense that when one goes up (or down) so does the other.

The *squared correlation coefficient, r^2* (also known as *r*-squared), indicates how much of the variance in one variable can be explained or predicted by the variance in another. Here as elsewhere, variance measures the amount of deviation from the mean. For example, if the r^2 between years of experience and teachers' salaries were .65, that would mean that 65% of the differences in teachers' salaries could be explained by their years of experience—and that 35% could not. Another way to think about this relation

TABLE 2.2 *How to Compute the Correlation, r, of Test X and Test Y
(data are from Table 2.1, which showed how to compute the SD)*

Student	X Scores	X Dev. Scores	Divide by SD	Standard Scores (z) of X	Y Scores	Y Dev. Scores	Divide by SD	Standard Scores (z) of Y	z of X times z of Y
A	25	0	0/2.45	0	19	−5	−5/6.36	−0.79	0.00
B	22	−3	−3/2.45	−1.22	30	6	6/6.36	0.94	−1.15
C	29	4	4/2.45	1.63	14	−10	−10/6.36	−1.57	−2.56
D	26	1	1/2.45	0.41	29	5	5/6.36	0.79	0.32
E	23	−2	−2/2.45	−0.82	28	4	4/6.36	0.63	−0.52
Total									−3.91
Mean									−0.782

is that if you knew a teacher's years of experience you could guess his or her salary 65% better than if you did not. For multiple correlations (more than two variables) and in regression analysis, the comparable statistic is capitalized, R^2 (*R*-square or *R*-squared). This is also called the *coefficient of determination*.

How Is a Correlation Coefficient Calculated?

Conceptually, the correlation is the average of the products (scores multiplied times one another) of two sets of scores, when those scores are expressed as standard scores, or *z*-scores, that is, in SD units. (This will become clearer in the following example.) Because correlations are calculated using *z*-scores, they are standardized. This means that they can be used to compare the degree of association (co-relation) between variables measured in different units. For instance, imagine you wanted to compare the relation of income to education level, measured as years of schooling completed, in several countries. Say that on average for each extra year of schooling an individual earns 2,000 dollars in the United States, 31,000 pesos in Mexico, and 1,500 pounds in England. In which country is the relationship the strongest? You can't really tell, but if you compute the correlations, you would have a standard of comparison to use. Suppose that you do the calculations

and get correlations of $r = .32$, $r = .60$, and $r = .30$. Although it is hard to compare dollars, pesos, and pounds, the correlation coefficient puts them all into the same "currency," which is measured in standard deviations.[2]

The formula for *r* involves multiplying the *z*-scores of one variable times the *z*-scores of another variable and dividing the result by the number of pairs of scores.

$$\frac{(z\text{-scores of X}) \times (z\text{-scores of Y})}{\text{Number of pairs of scores}}$$

This formula tends to make more sense to people when they see its details worked out in an example. Table 2.2 takes the same scores on two tests used to compute standard deviations (in Table 2.1) and calculates the correlation between them. Again, the purpose is not to help the reader with proficiency in calculation, because no one is likely to compute a correlation by hand (and if you did, there is a better formula). Rather, the idea is to understand what it means when someone says two sets of scores are correlated.

Going through the steps described in the table, start out by using the calculations done in Table 2.1 in which the SDs for the two tests were computed. Then, divide the deviation scores by the standard deviation for each distribution to get the *z*-scores. Multiply the *z*-scores of the scores of each student on Test X times the *z*-scores of their scores on Test Y. Add up the results and compute the average or mean. That mean is the Pearson *r*. So, the Pearson *r* is the average of the products of two sets of *z*-scores. These steps lead to an answer, a correlation of −.782. To double-check my math, I calculated the correlation between these two series of scores using SPSS, the Statistical Package for the Social Sciences, which is one of several widely used computer programs. The answer SPSS gave was −.784. The difference (.002) is due to my rounding errors. SPSS carries out the calculations to more decimal places and is thus more precise. This extra accuracy does not matter here, but it can be very important for some statistics.

How Can Correlations and Their Statistical Significance Be Interpreted?

Computational details aside, the correlation of −.782 means that scores on the two tests are inversely or negatively related; that is, students who did well on one exam tended to do poorly on the other. This is important new information beyond what we learned by computing the means and SDs in Table 2.1. The r^2 is .612 (−.782 squared), which means that you can predict students' scores on one test 61% better if you know their scores on the other test.

According to the SPSS output, the significance of the correlation, −.784, is .117. In other terms, for this correlation, $p = .117$. This *p*-value is not small enough to meet any of the conventional cutoffs for statistical significance. That means this result could easily be a coincidence, due to chance alone. In other examples encountered in this text, we will see correlations *much* smaller than −.784. But many of those correlations will have greater statistical significance (have smaller *p*-values). How can that be?

This is a good time to reinforce the idea that two things go into calculating a *p*-value: (1) the size of the sample and (2) the size of the statistic, such as a correlation. First, the bigger the (random) sample the more likely it will be representative of the population. Conversely, it is quite likely that a small sample will not be typical of the population from which it

TABLE 2.3 *Sample Size and Statistical Significance of* r

Size of Random Sample	r Needed to Reach p of .05
5	.878
10	.632
15	.514
20	.444
25	.396
30	.361
100	.197

was drawn. Second, the bigger the statistic the more likely it is to be statistically significant. If you compute two correlations in samples of the same size, the bigger one is more likely to be significantly different from zero in the population. Table 2.3 lists how big a correlation has to be to be statistically significant at the .05 level given different sample sizes. As you can see, when you are using a small sample of 5 or 10, for the correlation *r* to be significant at the .05 level that correlation would have to be quite large, larger than one usually finds in the social sciences. On the other hand, with a more substantial sample of 100 cases, the correlation can be less than .20 and still be statistically significant; that is unlikely to have occurred in the sample if there were no correlation in the population from which the sample was drawn.

How Can Correlations Be Used to Find Relations in and Interpret Real Data?

Let's examine a more realistic set of data than the scores of 5 students on two tests. Table 2.4 is an actual grade book from a course with 35 students.[3] The course was designed in part to prepare students for a licensing examination (column headed License). The grade book also includes scores on two exams, a project, and a paper. In addition, two pieces of information about the students are given: gender and major area of study.

The format used in this table looks similar to what most teachers do with their grade books. Each

TABLE 2.4 *Data from Class of 35 Students*

Student	Exam 1	Exam 2	Paper	Project	License	Female	Major
1	88	89	73	74	90	0	1
2	77	79	95	92	80	1	1
3	91	89	71	75	90	0	2
4	83	82	97	95	81	1	2
5	84	85	72	90	82	0	2
6	93	94	95	79	90	1	2
7	88	87	88	77	90	0	1
8	75	76	88	89	77	1	1
9	76	77	70	93	85	0	3
10	83	81	99	90	79	1	3
11	80	84	75	74	77	0	1
12	74	75	86	90	70	1	3
13	81	80	70	70	86	0	2
14	88	89	94	77	90	1	1
15	87	86	75	75	90	0	2
16	77	78	95	94	79	1	2
17	76	74	93	95	80	0	3
18	99	100	96	81	96	1	1
19	100	100	90	80	95	1	1
20	65	80	75	85	79	0	3
21	88	83	80	96	85	0	3
22	91	96	85	71	90	0	1
23	97	95	90	79	93	1	2
24	76	80	85	98	82	1	3
25	82	84	83	90	83	0	3
26	99	95	91	82	94	1	1
27	72	77	90	89	77	1	3
28	86	84	97	74	85	1	2
29	79	76	79	88	75	0	3
30	93	96	81	81	98	0	2
31	92	94	82	75	99	1	1
32	77	75	91	84	80	1	3

row is for a specific student and each column is for a graded assignment. It so happens that this is also the way computer programs such as spreadsheets (like Excel) and statistical packages (like SPSS) require you to enter your data. The rows are for *cases* (e.g., the individual students) and the columns are for *variables* (e.g., the assignments). You should try to get familiar with this way of thinking about organizing evidence.

You use a separate *row* for each case (student, business, hospital, etc.). And each variable gets its own *column,* such as test score, profit, cure rate, etc.

The first thing to do with the data in the table is to enter it into a computer program. With easy-to-use spreadsheet-like programs, such as SPSS, this job takes most people less than 15 minutes. In this unanalyzed form, it is not easy to make out any patterns.

TABLE 2.5 *Descriptive Statistics*

	N	Mean	Standard Deviation
Exam 1	35	84.29	8.710
Exam 2	35	84.86	7.893
Paper	35	84.77	9.601
Project	35	83.23	9.947
License	35	85.14	7.109
0 = male; 1 = female	35	.51	.507
Valid *N* (listwise)	35		

Once the data are entered, however, you can instruct the computer to calculate various statistics for you, and patterns become clear. It is usually a good idea to begin with descriptive statistics, such as the mean and standard deviation. The SPSS output for descriptive statistics is shown in Table 2.5. The means and SDs for the grades on the exams, paper, project, and licensing examination are all quite close.

Note that by coding male = 0 and female = 1, we can get an "average" gender. The mean of .51 indicates that 51% of the students were female. Had we coded male = 1 and female = 0, the mean gender would have been .49, or 49%. It does not matter which is coded 1 and which is 0, but it is usually a good idea to code a dichotomous (two-value) variable, such as yes–no, that way. For obscure reasons, this is called *dummy coding,* a term you will encounter frequently when you read research articles. A clearer, but less common term is *indicator coding,* because the 1s and 0s indicate categories. When using dummy (indicator) coding, it is best to code yes as 1 and no as zero. If you code this way, you will be speaking the same language as your computer.

When I instructed SPSS to compute correlations between all pairs of variables, I got Table 2.6 as the output. Major (humanities, social science, etc.) is not included in this or the previous table because coding and doing calculations on this kind of categorical variable would be inappropriate. How to handle such nominal variables will be discussed in later chapters.

If you were the instructor of this class of 35 students, what would this table tell you? Tables such as this one are full of information. They have to be read slowly and studied to discover what they convey. It might take you only a few minutes to enter the data and a couple of seconds for your computer package to generate the table, but you could easily spend an hour or more trying to understand and interpret the results.

What Table 2.6 gives you is all the correlations between each pair of variables. Each variable (Exam 1, Exam 2, Paper, etc.) is correlated with each of the others. Our 6 variables yield 15 pairs of correlations. The first thing to note in this table is that all the information occurs twice. The correlation of Exam 1 with Exam 2 (.917) is the same as the correlation of Exam 2 with Exam 1 (also .917). If you look on the diagonal from the upper left of the numbers to the lower right, you will see a series of 1.00s. Each 1.00 is the correlation of a variable with itself (Exam 1 with Exam 1, Exam 2 with Exam 2, and so on), which will, of course, be a perfect correlation. Looking closely, you can see that the information on the upper right and lower left of the table is exactly the same. In most published tables, one of these redundant parts of the table is omitted.

The correlation of .917* comes with one asterisk. You can see from the table footnote that this indicates that the correlation is significant at the .01 level. This means that the *p*-value is less than .01. A result this size ($r = .917$) in a random sample of this size ($n = 35$) would occur by chance less than 1% of the time—if there were no correlation in the population. This footnoting system for statistical significance is common. When such footnotes are used, the actual *p*-values—here given in rows called Sig. (for significance)—are often omitted. Note that some Sig.s or *p*-values are .000. That does not mean that the *p*-value is exactly zero and that there is no chance whatsoever that the outcome is a coincidence. SPSS stops reporting the value after three decimal points. Good practice is to round up and report .000 as <.001. Finally, a published table would usually also indicate the number of subjects, $n = 35$, only once in a footnote. A stripped-down version of the Table 2.6,

TABLE 2.6   *Correlations*

	Exam 1	Exam 2	Paper	Project	License	0=Male;1=Female
Exam 1						
Pearson Correlation	1	0.917(*)	0.216	−.511(*)	0.860(*)	0.166
Sig. (2-tailed)	.	0.000	0.213	0.002	0.000	0.342
N	35	35	35	35	35	35
Exam 2						
Pearson Correlation	0.917(*)	1	0.171	−.562(*)	0.887(*)	0.144
Sig. (2-tailed)	0.000	.	0.326	0.000	0.000	0.410
N	35	35	35	35	35	35
Paper						
Pearson Correlation	0.216	0.171	1	−.007	0.043	0.792(*)
Sig. (2-tailed)	0.213	0.326	.	0.968	0.807	0.000
N	35	35	35	35	35	35
Project						
Pearson Correlation	−.511(*)	−.562(*)	−.007	1	−.519(*)	−.001
Sig. (2-tailed)	0.002	0.000	0.968	.	0.001	0.997
N	35	35	35	35	35	35
License						
Pearson Correlation	0.860(*)	0.887(*)	0.043	−.519(*)	1	0.036
Sig. (2-tailed)	0.000	0.000	.807	0.001	.	0.837
N	35	35	35	35	35	35
0 = Male; 1 = Female						
Pearson Correlation	0.166	0.144	0.792(*)	−.001	0.036	1
Sig. (2-tailed)	0.342	0.410	0.000	0.997	0.837	.
N	35	35	35	35	35	35

Note: Correlation is significant at the .01 level (2-tailed).

in a format in which such tables are often published, is given here as Table 2.7.

How do we interpret the information in this table? What you focus on in the table depends on your interests. If your course really were *only* a test preparation class, then you would mostly be interested in what correlated with the license exam score. Exam 1 and Exam 2 were highly and positively correlated ($r = .860$ and $.887$) with the license exam. You would probably want to be sure to do more of the kind of work measured by those two exams. On the other hand, the project was a disaster. It was negatively associated with score on the licensing test. People who did *worse* on the project did better on the licensing exam ($r = -.519$). And the paper didn't make much difference one way or the other on the licensing exam ($r = .043$). So maybe you would want to get rid of the paper and the project and replace them with more exams. That conclusion would be appropriate—*if* your only concern were

TABLE 2.7 *Correlations (Pearson r) for All Variables on Grade Sheet*

	Exam 1	*Exam 2*	*Paper*	*Project*	*License*
Exam 1					
Exam 2	.917*				
Paper	.216	.171			
Project	−.511*	−.562*	−.007		
License	.860*	.887*	.043	−.519*	
Gender (1 = female)	.166	.144	.792*	−.001	.036

*Note: n = 35. *p < .01.*

the licensing exam. But if you had additional goals in the course that were better achieved by the paper and the project, you would want to retain those assignments.

Or, say you are looking at the data in Table 2.7 because you are concerned about gender equity in your teaching. You could look at the correlations between gender and the five grades (for Exam 1, Exam 2, and so on) to discover that on four of the five measures, there is no significant correlation between gender and grades or, what amounts to the same thing, there is no significant difference by gender in your grading. Females did slightly better on the exams, but this difference was too small to be statistically significant. But females did much better on the paper, $r = .792$. Note that if males had been coded 1 and females zero, then the correlation would have been $r = -.792$, meaning that the males did worse on the paper. The information is exactly the same. When researchers use this 1/0 coding, called dummy coding, you have to know which variable is coded 1 and which 0 in order to interpret the results.

So, what does this positive correlation between gender and scores on the paper tell you? First, and most certainly, it tells you that if you knew the gender of a particular student in your class, you could guess his or her score on the paper 63% more accurately than if you did not, because the $r^2 = .63$ (.792 × .792). Remember that this kind of prediction required that you use the *squared r*. You can predict scores even if you cannot *explain* what caused them to vary. Explanations are more speculative and are

only suggested by the correlation. It could be that the explanation is simple. The females in your class were better writers than the males. And, if the students in the class were a sample drawn from a population, then you could conclude that the females in the population were better writers than the males. But there are other possibilities. It could be that the paper assignment was designed in such a way as to be biased in favor of females (perhaps the required topics were of more interest to females). Or, it could be that *you* are biased in favor of females and gave them higher grades than they deserved. Although it is hard for you to slant your grading in their favor on objective tests such as Exam 1 and Exam 2, you could easily have done so when grading papers. Which of these three interpretations is correct—females were better writers, the assignment was biased, or you were biased?

The statistical evidence (the correlation) does not differentiate among these explanations. The correlation tells you that you have something to explain, but it does not provide an explanation. *You* have to choose among possible explanations. This is one of the ways that *qualitative* thinking usually enters into interpreting quantitative results. You could use further statistical evidence to narrow the range of possible explanations. For example, you could argue that the project was also graded "subjectively" by you, but there was no gender advantage on the project ($r = -.001$). If you were a biased grader, one would expect the correlation between gender and the project grade to be similar to that between gender and the paper grade. Relieved you conclude, "It isn't, so I'm off the hook!" That conclusion may be a bit glib, but at least you have *some* evidence for it. In any case, *interpreting* statistical evidence is when the higher-order thinking comes in. The calculations are just the preliminary work. The statistics cannot really "prove" anything, but *you* could try to prove several things using your interpretations of the statistical evidence. Often your interpretations will lead you to calculate more statistics to try to confirm your explanations.

Because interpreting the evidence is the really crucial thing, this chapter concludes by reviewing three important interpretative problems that arise when you try to understand most correlational data: size, linearity, and cause.

What Is a Large Correlation?

How big does a correlation have to be to be strong or high? How low is weak or small? Such adjectives are *always* comparative. Sometimes rough cutoff scores for correlations are given—for example, anything over .80 is big or less than .30 is small. But these guidelines are nearly *meaningless*. There are no useful *statistical* rules for deciding about big and small or important or unimportant. Big and small make sense only in a context. A jumbo shrimp is tiny by comparison to a baby whale. Meaningful discussions of the size of correlations have to be based on comparisons. A correlation is big if it is large in comparison to what was expected. Expectations are often based on the correlations between the same variables in other studies. A correlation of .30 would reasonably be thought of as strong, *if* .30 is double what the researcher expected; the same correlation would be weak if it were half of what the researcher expected.

The practical importance of a correlation of a given size also has to be judged in terms of context, but here the context has more to do with the substantive significance of the relation being studied. Say the correlation between hours of exercise per month and years of longevity were .30 and that this correlation measured a genuine causal relationship between exercise and longevity. Longevity is important, a matter of life or death in fact. Thus if you could determine 9% of your longevity ($r^2 = .09$), you would know something of great importance, even though most textbooks would tell you that .30 was a smallish correlation and that .09 was a small effect size. Personally, if such a "small" effect size were an established fact, I'd be spending *many* more hours in the gym.

What Is Linearity, and Why Is It Important for Interpreting Correlations?

Checking to see if the relationship between variables is linear is very important when reading or calculating a Pearson r because r is a measure of linear relationship between variables. A linear relationship is one in which (1) the direction and (2) the rate of change in one variable are both consistent with respect to changes in another variable. In other words, when plotting one variable against another, the result approximates a straight line. The correlation r cannot accurately measure other kinds of relationships. Responsible use of r requires one to check and to report the results of checking whether the relation is linear. If part of the relationship is not linear, r will miss that part. Curvilinear relations are the best example. Take the case of physical strength and age. From birth children generally grow stronger as they get older and this continues into adulthood. But at some point the relationship is reversed: the older one gets the less physical strength one has. Ten-year-olds are generally quite a bit stronger than 5-year-olds, 20-year-olds are usually stronger than 10-year-olds, but 60-year-olds usually are not as strong as 20-year-olds, and after age 60, the older you are the less strong you tend to be. This relationship is very strong and very clear, but it is *not* linear. Because it is not linear it cannot be measured very well with a Pearson r. And r could even miss the relationship altogether if the early increases in strength with age were exactly balanced by the later decreases.

The correlations of exam and paper grades provide good examples. We can see what is meant

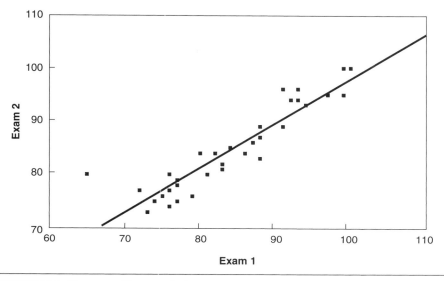

FIGURE 2.2 *Strong positive correlation*

by linear, and get a clearer understanding of what a correlation is, by looking at a *scatter diagrams* of the relations between scores on the exams and the paper. These are depicted in Figures 2.2 and 2.3.

Each dot in Figure 2.2 represents two exam scores for one student. For example, the dot on the far upper right is a student who got 100 on each exam. The dot farthest to the left, toward the bottom, represents a student who got a 65 on the first exam and an 80 on the second. The line is the regression line, discussed more extensively in Chapter 9. Here note only that this is the line that comes closer on average to all the dots than any other line that could be drawn. The dots are generally quite close to the line. Graphically speaking, the definition of a correlation is the degree to which the dots form a straight line, the degree to which the relation between the two variables is linear. Because the line moves up steeply, that means that the correlation is strong and positive. A high score on Exam 1 is clearly associated with a high score on Exam 2, and low scores tend to go together too.

As we saw earlier, the correlation between Exam 1 and the paper was much smaller and was not statistically significant. Figure 2.3 shows what a weak

correlation looks like. The degree to which the dots form a straight line is much smaller, which means that the correlation is much lower. The line does a very poor job of summarizing the relation between the exam and the paper. The relation is not linear. It is virtually nonexistent. The line is almost flat. An increase in Exam 1 scores has almost no discernable effect on scores on the paper.

By contrast, when the relation between variables is *curvi*linear, there is a relation, but it is better described by a curved line than a straight line. Hypothetical data describing the relation between strength and age are depicted in Figure 2.4. The relation is very clear. As people get older, they get stronger—up to a point. Then, as they get older, they tend to get weaker. The dots could be close to a line, but that line would be curved, not straight. The straight line in Figure 2.4 represents the Pearson *r.* It is virtually flat, sloping downward ever so slightly for a correlation of –.026. In short, there is an obvious relationship, but because it is curvilinear, the *r* misses it altogether.

One real-world example of a curvilinear relation in education is the association of parental involvement with their children's grades in school. Both low and

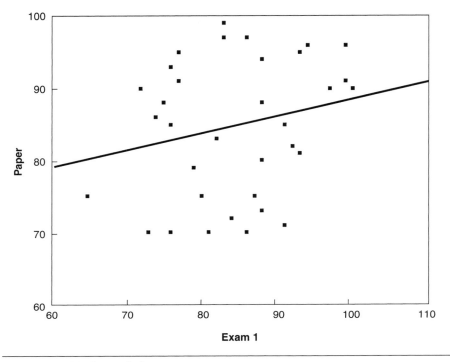

FIGURE 2.3 *Weak correlation*

high levels of involvement seem to be associated with low grades (Sui-Chu & Willms, 1996). Low involvement could contribute to low grades, but low grades can also trigger increased parental involvement. A middling level of involvement is often most strongly associated with high grades. Another good example of a curvilinear relation is that between high school grades and the number of hours that students are employed. Several studies have noted (most importantly Warren, LePore, & Mare, 2000) that there is a statistical association between grades and (1) not working at all, (2) working a moderate amount (1 to 15 hours), and (3) working a lot (more than 15 hours per week). But the association is curvilinear. Students who work a moderate amount have the highest grades, whereas those who do not work at all *and* those who work a great deal each have grades lower on average than those who work a moderate amount.

The same pattern can be seen in the relation of employment to other measures of academic achievement. For example, the percentage of seniors who said they were very likely to go to college was, respectively, 55%, 64%, and 50% (highest for those who worked some, but not a lot). For sophomores, the percentages of those who dropped out by the twelfth grade were 5.3%, 1.5%, 7.5%. Thus, the dropout rate was lowest for those who worked a moderate amount (Warren et al., 2000, Tables 1 and 2, pp. 953 and 956). The associations are strong and consistent, but a straight line does not describe them. They are curvilinear. Another national study also found nonlinear relations between the number of hours *college* students work and their grades (NCES, 2002). The Pearson *r*, because it measures linear relationships, would misrepresent these relationships by underestimating them. This is why it is so important to check to see if

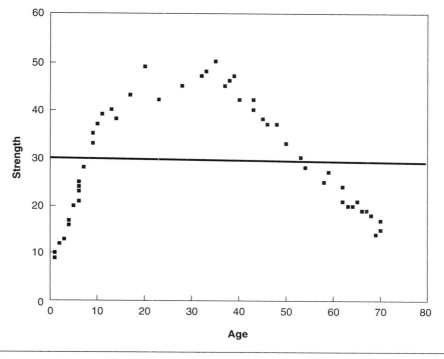

FIGURE 2.4 *Curvilinear relation*

your variables are related to one another in a linear way. Using nearly any statistical analysis software you can construct and examine the scatter diagrams that depict the relation between the two variables as was just done.

Curvilinear relations may not be all that common, but, as the preceding examples show, they are common enough that you need to take care not to overlook them. If you used a linear measure of association between employment and grades, you might be led to encourage students who work, say, 10 hours per week to cut back. This would be a *very* misleading strategy for two reasons: first, because kids who work this amount tend to have the highest grades and the lowest dropout rates. Second, and more importantly, working appears not to *cause* the statistical association. Rather it is caused by the fact that kids who worked different amounts were different *before*

they started working. For example, kids who were disaffected from and did poorly in school sought opportunities to work a lot. Low grades lead them to work more, not the other way around. Which gets us to the really crucial question: What is the relation of correlation and cause?

What Is the Relationship between Correlation and Cause?

It is common to find statements in statistics texts such as a "correlation coefficient does not speak to the issue of cause and effect" (Huck, 2004, p. 67). This usually means that the kind of research studies that typically report their data using correlations are weak designs for drawing causal inferences. These weak designs are nonexperimental. The argument is that experiments, which rarely report results using correlations (although they could), are the best designs for making causal inferences. The brief, if misleading, way of putting this is that "correlation does not equal causation." Such injunctions are based on a good principle, but they are sometimes overstated and easy to misinterpret. The good principle is that many things may be statistically associated that are clearly not causally related. This is sometimes the main thing students remember from their statistics and research methods courses. Students are so often enjoined to repeat the mantra that correlation does not equal cause that occasionally one of them comes to the silly conclusion (I'm not making this up!) that two variables that are correlated *cannot* possibly be causally related—*because* they are correlated. (The irony here is especially rich if you think about the word be*cause*.)

It is most accurate to say, I think, that correlational designs (i.e., nonexperimental research) provide weak or partial evidence about causation. Variables that are strongly linked causally will most often be strongly correlated. But the converse is not necessarily true. Many variables can be strongly correlated but not causally linked. A strong correlation between two variables *suggests* an increased *probability* that they are causally related, but by itself a correlation is usually not sufficient to make a conclusive case. If two variables are correlated you *can* correctly say that the data look as though they would if the variables were causally linked. In other words, the data are consistent with a conclusion that there is a causal connection between the variables. It is often impossible to go beyond that kind of cautious statement.

However, in many important areas of investigation, associational or correlational evidence is all that we have or will ever be likely to have. For instance, most public health advice—to reduce your risk of lung cancer, quit smoking; being overweight increases your chance of a heart attack—is based *entirely* on correlational evidence. On occasion, well-known researchers have questioned conclusions that seem all but indubitable, because the conclusions were reached using nonexperimental, correlational data.

Ronald Fisher, probably the best-known statistician in the first half of the twentieth century, and surely the most influential, publicly rejected the warnings about the health hazards of smoking. He lambasted these warnings because they were based on correlational data. Although Fisher may have been in the pay of the tobacco industry, this was not the only basis for his skepticism about the hazards of smoking. He was also making a point about the weaknesses of inferences drawn from nonexperimental research. This question is discussed in much greater detail in Chapter 6 on experimental designs, Chapter 8 on statistical inference, and Chapter 9 on regression analysis. At this point it is sufficient to say that *any and all* claims about causation should be treated with caution. Ultimately, intelligent decisions about whether variables are causally related will be made on the basis of rigorous thinking, not by blindly applying rules about the best design or method of analysis.

Finally, it is very interesting to note that the same people who warn us that correlation does not necessarily equal cause are sometimes much less likely to warn us that correlation does not equal "identity," especially when it comes to validating tests. It is often held that if two tests are highly correlated, such as two versions or parts of an IQ test, they must be measuring the same thing. A more modest and accurate claim would be to say that they are *more likely* to be measuring the same thing if they are highly correlated than if they are not. The general point is that the strength of the correlational evidence is, of course, *exactly* the same for the two kinds of claim. If a correlation provides weak evidence that A causes B, it provides equally weak evidence that A is identical to B (usually that A and B are both *caused* by the same thing, such as knowledge or aptitude). Chapter 7 discusses this measurement problem further with a review of the reliability and validity of measurements and causal claims.

The question of causation is a recurring theme in this book, as it is in most good studies of methodology. Causation is an especially important element of our next chapter, "Variables and the Relationships among Them."

Terms and Concepts to Review

Mean
Deviation score
Average deviation (mean absolute deviation)
Sum of squares

Variance
• Mean squares (mean of the squared deviation scores)

Standard deviation
Standard scores
z-score
Normal distribution
Correlation
Pearson *r*

Negative correlation
• Inverse correlation

Positive correlation
• Direct correlation

Dummy coding
Linear relationship
Nonlinear relationship
Curvilinear relationship
Causal relationship
r^2 (*r*-squared; bivariate)

R^2 (*R*-squared; multivariate)
• Coefficient of determination

Discussion Questions

As always, most of the discussion questions ask you to consider a concept by devising examples of its use or that illustrate its aspects. There is no better way to understand and remember what a concept is and how it is applied to research questions. This is as true of technical topics, such as standard deviation and correlation, as it is of broader questions of research design.

1. Think of examples of measurements of a single variable, such as heights of basketball players, populations of cities, ages of retirees, or prices of a stock. Think of one example for which the standard deviation (SD) is likely to be very high and another for which it is likely to be quite low. What do your examples illustrate about the nature of the SD?

2. Using the same examples as in question 1, consider the variances of your groups of measurements. How do variances and standard deviations differ?

3. Discuss the relation between standard scores, such as IQ scores, and the *z*-scores on which they are based. How do these scores relate to the normal distribution?

4. Correlations range from a possible low of −1.0 through zero to a possible high of +1.0. Discuss the issue of the size of correlations. Think of examples of correlations you would consider important and unimportant. How does the size of an association (correlation) relate to its importance? Can you think of a correlation that is fairly close to zero, but is nonetheless important, or one that is fairly close to 1.0, but that matters little?

5. Why is linearity important in the interpretation of correlations? What is the relationship between a correlation (Pearson *r*) and a straight line? Can you think of a relationship between two variables that is not likely to be well described by a straight line?

6. Consider the relation between correlation and cause. Do this by thinking of two correlations, both the same size, say, .80 and both computed on a sample of the same size, and which therefore have equal *p*-values, say .01. Think of one example in which a correlation of $r = .80$, $p = .01$ is likely to indicate a strong causal relation and another example in which it is not likely to do so. Reflect on what this tells you about the nature of causes.

Self-Test

If you can answer most of the following questions accurately, you can feel confident about your understanding of the material in this chapter. If not, it would be a good idea to review the chapter. (Answers can be found in the Appendix.)

1. The standard deviation can be appropriately used with data measured at any level of measurement, quantitative, rank, or qualitative. True or False?

2. The ACT scores of the entering class at a particular college have a mean of 21 and an SD of 4. From this you can conclude that about 95% of the students in the entering class would have scores that ranged between 17 and 25. True or False?

3. Consider two groups of 300 students and their scores on the same test. Group 1's scores have a mean of 70 and an SD of 5. Group 2's scores have a mean of 65 and an SD of 20. Which of the following is true of these two sets of scores?
   a. The individual student with the highest score on the test will be a member of Group 1.
   b. There will be almost no overlap in the scores of the students in the two groups.
   c. A score of 80 equates to a higher z-score in Group 1 than in Group 2.
   d. If the distribution is approximately normal, about two-thirds of the scores in Group 1 will fall between 70 and 75.

4. Concerning standard scores, it is accurate to say
   a. A standard score cannot be calculated unless the distribution of scores is normal.
   b. A standard score on a norm-referenced test such as the SAT measures one's rank rather than one's absolute level of achievement.
   c. The z-score cannot be converted into another standard score unless the distribution of scores is normal.
   d. All of the above are accurate.

5. You compute a correlation between two variables: $r = .50$, $p = .009$. About this finding, it is accurate to say
   a. By most standards, the result is not statistically significant.
   b. The relationship between the two variables is inverse.
   c. Knowing one variable enables you to predict or explain 25% of the variance in the other variable.
   d. One variable cannot be causally related to the other because they are correlated at such a low level of statistical significance.

6. A negative correlation indicates that the relationship between two variables is unfavorable or disadvantageous. True or False?

7. A correlation of 2.34 between an IV and a DV means that the DV is over two times as large as the IV. True or False?

8. When using Pearson r correlation,
   a. It is important to check for linearity, because r will overestimate a nonlinear relationship.
   b. One obtains evidence only about pairs of variables.
   c. Nonlinear relationships between variables are better measured by the r-squared statistic rather than by the simple r.
   d. All of the above are true.

CORRELATIONS OF FOUR TEST SCORES (FOR QUESTIONS 9–12)

	Test 1	Test 2	Test 3	Test 4
Test 1		.37**	.05	−.68**
Test 2			.22*	−.18*
Test 3				−.08
Test 4				

*Note: $p < .05$, **$p < .01$.

The following four questions (9–12) refer to the preceding correlation matrix.

9. Because the table is incomplete, it is not possible to examine the correlations between all pairs of tests. True or False?

10. The correlation between Test 1 and Test 3 is significant at the .05 level. True or False?

11. The strongest correlation in the table is between Test 1 and Test 4. True or False?

12. All of the correlations in the table are statistically significant. True or False?

13. Concerning the relation between the size of a correlation, the size of the sample on which it was computed, and its level of statistical significance, it is accurate to say
   a. The larger the sample, the more likely a correlation will be statistically significant.
   b. All else equal, the larger the correlation the larger the p-value.
   c. In two samples of the same size, the larger the correlation the less likely it is to be statistically significant.
   d. All of the above are accurate.

Endnotes

1. The term *scores* here is used generically to refer to any series of measurements on which one might compute a standard deviation, such as ages, incomes, or years of experience, as well as marks on a test.

2. When making such comparisons, the correlations should first be squared. An r of .60 is not two times as strong as an r of .30. After squaring r coefficients, the r^2 statistics are .36 and .09, which would show that the relation is four times as strong.

3. The data are real scores drawn from my grade books, but made more tidy for our examples here by deleting cases with missing information and combining scores from two different classes.

3

Variables and the Relations among Them

Social scientists try to explain or predict some things on the basis of what they know about other things. A special language has evolved for discussing this kind of prediction and explanation. It is so widespread that it is nearly impossible to talk about, or read works in, sociology, economics, politics, psychology, education, business, and social work without using it. Like any language, some of the less familiar terms are jargon, but the language is not merely jargon. It introduces useful concepts and ways of thinking that are widely employed in the social and behavioral sciences (and in the natural sciences too). This language of research was originally developed by researchers using statistical methods, but it is also frequently used by investigators conducting qualitative research.

Most often social scientists study *variables*.[1] Variables are things that can change or be different. The opposite of a variable is a constant. Variables have *variance*. This term is used loosely to mean an amount or degree of variety (or more technically, as in Chapter 2, to mean the square of the standard deviation). Social scientists try to explain or predict the variance in some variables by seeing how it relates to the variance in other variables. An example should help make this clear. The grades of college students vary. Everybody does not have the same grade point

average (GPA). High school students' GPAs also vary. And students' SAT scores vary; they range from 200 to 800 on each part of the test. A research question could be: Can we predict or explain college GPAs by high school GPAs and SAT scores? Note that only if these three things are variables can you use some of them to predict others. For example, if all students got the same SAT score, you could not use differences (variance) in SAT scores to predict variance in college grades.

This chapter examines the kinds of variables and types of relations among them by answering the following questions.

1. How are different types of variables related?
2. How can relations among variables be depicted?
3. How does the inclusion of effect modifiers improve understanding of research questions?
4. What is causal modeling, and how is it represented?
5. How can causal modeling be used in the example of parental involvement?
6. How can causal modeling be used in the example of student advisory programs?
7. What is the nature of causation when studying research problems?
8. What are the criteria for assessing causation?

TABLE 3.1 *Classification of Variables*

	Independent Variable	*Mediating Variable*	*Dependent Variable*	*Effect Modifiers*
Common Symbol	X		Y	
Rough Definition	Cause	Link	Effect	Influences
Other Labels	Predictor variable Explanatory variable	Intervening variable	Outcome variable Criterion variable Response variable	Antecedent variable Moderating variable Interaction effect Extraneous variable Control variable
Examples	High school GPA	Knowledge gained in high school	College GPA	Gender, ethnicity, age

How Are Different Types of Variables Related?

The kinds of variables in the preceding example about predicting grades have typical labels. The thing you are trying to explain or predict, college GPA, is most often called the *dependent* variable. It depends on others, which are called *independent* variables (in our example, high school GPA and SAT scores). An independent variable can sometimes be thought of as a *cause* and a dependent variable as an *effect*. But, in the example, it doesn't make much sense to think of high school grades or SAT scores as *causing* college GPA. Perhaps, all three variables are caused by one or more other variables, such as students' work habits or their intelligence. In that case, work habits and/or intelligence are sometimes said to *mediate* the relationship between the independent and dependent variables. Finally, although they are not direct causes, high school GPA and SAT scores might be good *predictors* of college GPA, which is why such independent variables are often called predictor variables.

Controversy about labels for variables is oddly intense. The quarrels mask deeper differences about the best ways to do research. Many researchers claim one should use *dependent* and *independent* only to describe variables in experimental research. Perhaps this is good advice, but most social scientists ignore it. Because my goal here is to discuss how social scientists in applied fields such as education, business, social work, and nursing actually work, not how some

of them think others ought to work, I have employed the most widely used labels. By far the largest number of researchers use the labels *independent variable* (abbreviated *IV*) and *dependent variable* (abbreviated *DV*). I will follow that practice in this book. These and the other most commonly used names for different kinds of variables are summarized in Table 3.1.

As can be seen, most concepts in research methods have several more or less synonymous names. This fact is one of the things that make learning the field difficult. Multiple labels were probably not created, as some have suggested, to confuse students and make professors seem more knowledgeable. The confusion of terms mostly stems from the fact that researchers in different fields invented, and sometimes reinvented, techniques. Separate inventors usually applied different labels. And there is no authority that can mandate that we clean up the mess. Language, even the language of quantitative methods, is untidy. Usage is inconsistent.

The bottom row of Table 3.1 repeats the basic model of how the variables are related in the example about grade point average (GPA). High school GPA is the independent variable, college GPA is the dependent variable, and students' knowledge (as learned in high school) is the mediating variable. Some researchers might call a variable such as students' work habits a mediating variable. But it is *not* really a good example of a mediating, or intervening, variable. Work habits do not come "between" high school and college grades, but probably come before and cause both. That is why work habits are more

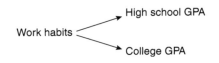

FIGURE 3.1 *Model with an antecedent variable*

accurately thought of as an antecedent variable. Work habits precede and cause both high school and college GPA, as illustrated in Figure 3.1.

How Can Relations among Variables Be Depicted?

The illustration in Figure 3.1 is called a *causal model,* which is simply a description of how the variables are related. This model is a picture or diagram. Models can also be described with formulas, and discussion of how that is done will come later in this chapter.

A true mediating variable would be something caused or affected by high school GPA, which in turn would cause (or influence) college GPA. Knowledge is a good example. High school students with high GPAs are more likely to arrive at college better prepared (have more knowledge and cognitive skills), which means they are more likely to get high college GPAs. This relationship, with knowledge as the mediating variable, is depicted in Figure 3.2.

Note that predicting and explaining can use different models. When the goal is simply to predict, we do not care about intervening variables. The *why* often does not matter at all if the goal is only prediction. For example, if someone sat on an admissions committee and were using high school grades to predict college grades, the reason why one predicts the other is much less important than the fact that it does so. But, if the goal is explanation, the intervening variables matter most of all. They tell why or how the independent and dependent variables are linked.

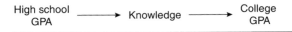

FIGURE 3.2 *Model with a mediating variable*

FIGURE 3.3 *Mediating variable with positive and negative effects*

A classic example comes from the field of health care. Many years ago it was discovered that men who had one heart attack were less likely to have a second if they developed arthritis after the first heart attack. What was it about arthritis that protected against a second heart attack? Almost no one thought arthritis directly reduced the risk of a heart attack. Arthritis was a good predictor, but until the causal link (mediating or intervening variable) was found, it had little practical significance. The answer, you have probably guessed, is aspirin. Men who developed arthritis took aspirin, which reduced their risk of heart attack. This is illustrated in the causal model in Figure 3.3.

Note the minus and plus signs over the arrows in Figure 3.3. These are used to show whether the relation is positive or negative. Arthritis increases consumption of aspirin, so that arrow is labeled with a plus. But aspirin reduces heart attacks, so that arrow is labeled with a minus sign.

The effects of school size on students' learning provide another good example. Lee and Loeb (2000) studied the effects of school size on students' academic achievement, specifically gains in mathematics test scores. Their study, like several others on the topic, indicated that students learn more in small schools. As Lee and Loeb point out, however, "it is difficult to see how the size of the school could actually influence students *directly*" (p. 23, italics added). To understand how small schools foster learning, the indirect link or mediating variable between the independent and dependent variables had to be found. Lee and Loeb suggest that smallness of schools tends to influence other things, such as teachers' attitudes toward students, which in turn influence students' learning, as in the model in Figure 3.4.

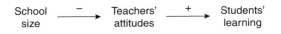

FIGURE 3.4 *Mediating variable with negative and positive effects*

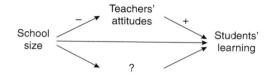

FIGURE 3.5 *Mediating variable with incomplete or partial effects*

Note in Figure 3.4 that the arrow between school size and teachers' attitudes is marked with a minus sign, because the relationship is inverse: As school size goes up, teachers' attitudes get worse (go down). The arrow between teachers' attitudes and students' learning is direct or positive, so it is marked with a plus sign.

But changes in teachers' attitudes, Lee and Loeb (2000) discovered, do not tell the whole story. This mediating variable is different than aspirin. In the case of heart attacks, no direct effect of arthritis was left after we included aspirin in the model. The "effects" of arthritis were completely explained by the effects of aspirin. But this was not the case with the effects of school size. So the model can be redrawn to include the remaining direct effects of school size, as is done in Figure 3.5.

The direct line from school size to students' learning reflects the effect that remains after accounting for the part of student learning influenced by teachers' attitudes. The arrows to and from the question mark represent the effects of as yet unidentified (known as *unspecified*) intervening variables. The missing variable(s) could be any number of things. Figuring out what they might be and figuring out whether your hunch is a good one is of the most creative and exciting parts of the research process. One variable that could explain why small schools tend to have higher student achievement is that students have more opportunities to participate in extracurricular activities in small schools, and more participation in extracurricular activities tends to be associated with higher academic achievement. Of course, that raises the question of why or how extracurricular activities promote academic achievement. Figuring that out requires suggesting other mediating variables and then finding evidence to see whether those suggestions can be supported by data.

But, for practical purposes, one might ask, why do we care about the intervening variables? Why waste time on the details? We know that smaller schools promote learning. Leave the discovery of the causal links to the researchers. Let's start reducing school size. Let's cut elementary schools in half, down to about 400 students and high schools down to about 800. But, leaving aside the question of the ideal size and whether some schools might be too small, changing school size is no easy matter. Although it might be less expensive to cut school size in half than to reduce *class* size by 50%, it would not be cheap or easy. On the other hand, if researchers could figure out what the most important intervening variables are, they might be able to get the effect without reducing school size—for example, by improving teachers' attitudes or increasing students' opportunities to participate in extracurricular activities. To return to the earlier example, we do not need to give men arthritis to reduce their risk of heart attack. Because we know the mediating variable, we can just give them aspirin.

How Does the Inclusion of Effect Modifiers Improve Understanding of Research Questions?

Effect modifiers add some very important complications to understanding the relationships among variables. In the social sciences, effect modifiers are often called *moderating variables.* Moderating variables are sometimes confused with mediating variables (Gall, Gall, & Borg, 1999, 217). Although it is true that the two can be handled with the same statistical techniques, they are conceptually quite distinct. A mediating (or intervening) variable, as we have seen, is a causal link between an independent and a dependent variable, as aspirin is the link between arthritis and reduced heart attacks. But what if the effect of aspirin were stronger for males than for females? Then the effect would be *moderated* (or modified) by gender. If the effect were stronger for younger patients than older, it would be moderated

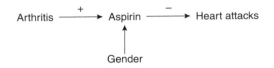

FIGURE 3.6 *Model including an effect modifier (or moderating variable)*

by age. Gender and age would be called moderators of the relation between aspirin and heart attack. In other words, gender and age influence the size of the effect of the aspirin. Sometimes a model including a moderating variable is drawn as in Figure 3.6.

Both moderator and mediator variables can be studied with either ANOVA or regression. But it is traditional to study causal links (mediating variables) with regression and path analysis. Moderating variables are more often studied using ANOVA. (See Chapters 8 and 9.)

Another complication and refinement is that moderating effects are also called *interaction effects.* Rather than saying that gender moderates the effect of aspirin, some researchers might say, "There is an interaction with gender." Although the two terms, *moderator* and *interaction*, can be used interchangeably, it is useful to keep the kinds of effect they describe distinct. An interaction effect is a *joint* effect of two or more independent variables. Drug interactions are perhaps the best-known example. Two drugs that have mild effects taken separately can be dangerously strong when taken together. To look at another example, if you are trying to lose weight, reducing the calories you consume can be effective; so can increasing the amount you exercise. Also, an interaction effect may occur between diet and exercise; those two together may add up to more than the sum of their parts. So the interaction effect is the joint or multiplier effect of diet and exercise. By contrast, a moderating effect would exist if, for example, exercise were more effective for women than for men. The same would be true if any other attribute of the people being studied influenced the strength of an independent variable's effect on a dependent variable. In the one case, moderating effect, gender modifies

a relation between exercise and weight loss. In the other case, interaction of dieting and exercise, each strengthens the other's relation to weight loss.

The final type of effect modifier is the control variable or extraneous variable. These refer to variables that might influence the relationship you are studying but that, for the purposes of your study, you are not interested in. If you were studying the effects of school size you might wish to control for the effects of community population. Small schools might be more common in rural districts. If in your study you were not interested in the effects of rural versus urban settings, you could "control for" these, which essentially means subtracting any effects they might have. On the other hand, you might be very interested in whether the effects of school size were modified (moderated) by town size. Maybe small schools foster learning everywhere, but they are even more likely to do so in urban environments. Then population would be a moderating variable. So is urban/rural a moderating or a control variable? That depends on you, specifically the purpose of your study as indicated in your research questions. Any difference between moderating and control variables is not a statistical distinction, because the statistical techniques for studying the effects of town size would be the same in either case. Your research questions and the elements of your design determine this. Statistical analyses can help you answer those questions, but the questions must come first.

What Is Causal Modeling, and How Is It Represented?

We have been drawing what are known as *causal models* of the relations among variables (Figures 3.1–3.6). A *model* is a representation of reality. Familiar examples include model cars and airplanes. These are scale models that involve miniaturization. Maps and blueprints are also scale models. Social scientists more often draw pictures or diagrams of relationships among variables rather than scale models. Another term for a model of relationships among variables is *theory*. There are some distinctions between *model* and *theory*, but for the most part they are interchangeable terms. *Theory* is used more, but *model* better captures what most researchers actually do as they attempt to make sense of things. Whichever term you use, a model or a theory is just an explanation. For such an explanation to be interesting for researchers, they have to be able to test it, that is, to compare it against some evidence.

In general in the social sciences, the idea is not to make a scale model of something you already know about. Rather, the idea is to try out different "pictures" to see which one best matches reality or tells you most about what you want to know. The value of a model is that it simplifies reality—and this is also its weakness. The question you face when building models is: Is what you gain in simplicity worth what you lose in detail? The answer is a matter of judgment, context, and knowledge of the subject being studied.

Thus far we have been drawing causal models. Drawing models is a way of thinking graphically. When quantitative researchers get ready to conduct their studies, they usually turn these pictures into equations. That process is less complicated than you might think—once you get the hang of seeing certain kinds of diagrams as equations, and vice versa.

Let's illustrate with the earlier example of the causes of differences in college GPA. Say you think (your model or theory is) that academic ability and study habits together cause college GPA. First draw a model and then see how it would be turned into an equation. Figure 3.7 includes typical symbols for variables as well as words telling what they are. Y is the usual symbol for the dependent variable. X is the symbol for the independent variable. When there is more than one independent variable, they are designated X_1, X_2, and so on.

When we change from pictures to equations (from graphic to algebraic models), the customs are different. In the pictures, the dependent or outcome

FIGURE 3.8 *Model of a formula*

variable is customarily put on the right. In equations, it usually goes on the left. Other than that the translation is pretty direct:

> Study Habits + Academic Ability = College GPA

Using the typical symbols (in parentheses in Figure 3.7) and switching the order we get

$$Y = X_1 + X_2$$

which, putting the algebra back again into graphic form, yields Figure 3.8. Y is the dependent variable (GPA). X_1 and X_2 are the independent variables: study habits and ability, respectively. It is necessary to switch from pictures to equations when testing our models (theories) with quantitative evidence. Researchers often get so comfortable with equations that they skip the graphics stage and work directly with equations when they construct their models. For people who aren't professional researchers, this may be less easily done. So, at this point, our discussion of variables and the relations among them continues by returning to the graphic approach. These graphical approaches are important not only for grasping basic concepts; they are also central to more advanced statistical techniques such as path analysis and structural equation modeling (see Part 2, especially Chapter 14).

How Can Causal Modeling Be Used in the Example of Parental Involvement?

In my research methods courses I usually have students review some research literature on a topic of their choosing. One of the most common topics

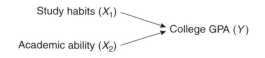

FIGURE 3.7 *Model with two independent variables*

selected by education students in recent years has been the effects of parental involvement. This is surely an important topic, but in that form, it is not yet ready to be researched. The topic, effects of parental involvement, is incomplete. One way to know it is incomplete is that you cannot yet draw a model or a causal diagram of the research topic. All you have at this point is an independent or predictor variable, parental involvement. Several questions have to be answered before beginning to do research. To start with, (1) The effect on *what*? (2) *How* does the effect work? (3) The effect on *whom*?

The first question, The effect on what? asks for your dependent or outcome variable. Let's say that it is academic achievement. By convention the dependent variable goes all the way on the right end of the causal graphic and the independent or predictor variable (parental involvement) goes on the left. The second question, How does the effect work? asks what your mediating or intervening variable(s) might be. *How* does parental involvement increase achievement? Let's say it does so, in part, because it improves students' motivation. The third question, The effect on whom? asks if there might be any moderating variables. It is not hard to imagine that the effects of parental involvement on students might well be different for 7-year-olds than for 17-year-olds. If the effects might be moderated by age, that too has to go into the model. The full model would look like Figure 3.9.

So, parental involvement increases students' motivation (arrow 1), which, in turn, increases their academic achievement (arrow 2). You don't take arrow 3 out of the model because you suspect that motivation is only part of the story, that parental involvement might increase achievement in ways you are not yet ready to specify in your model.

Age is in the diagram in Figure 3.9 because the effects of parental involvement might be influenced by age. How should this be handled when gathering evidence to test the model? That is a key design question. One way or another, you need to *control for* the effects of age. To do that you could study students of different ages to see whether the effects differed by age. Or you could simplify the research problem by confining the study to a particular age group, say, students in the early elementary grades. Then the final research question would be, Does parental involvement in the early elementary grades increase students' academic achievement by increasing their motivation to learn?

Now the model or theory and the research question are set. You are "good to go" to the next steps on the way to building a full design, such as a dissertation proposal. A further set of questions awaits. If this were your dissertation, you would need to figure out how you will turn your general concepts, such as academic achievement, into variables that you can measure. This is called *operationalizing* variables, because you determine what operations you will perform on the variables to measure them. The result is your *operational definition*. You also need to decide how to define or to operationalize involvement: What kind of involvement? helping with homework? coaching a team? bringing in cookies for the bake sale? attending PTA meetings? conferences with teachers? If you think the answer is "all of the above," that means you believe that the mediating variable works the same way regardless of the kind of involvement. You also need to operationalize the dependent variable. How will you define and measure achievement? grades? scores on standardized tests? attendance or graduation rates? A good case can be made for each of these, but your study, even if it is just a short litera-

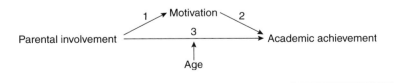

FIGURE 3.9 *Model of the effects of parental involvement, moderated by age*

ture review for a class, can get far too complicated to handle unless you make some choices and decide to refine your research question still further. You might settle on something like the following: Does parental help with homework in grades 1 through 3 improve students' grades by increasing their motivation to learn?

Many other questions could be asked. Are grades the best measure of achievement? Is motivation the most important mediating variable? How can we operationalize motivation? Although you now have a good, clear understanding of where to begin and know what you need to gather evidence about, you would still need to settle other design and measurement issues. How will you learn about parents' help with homework? Will you ask the parents, the students, and/or the teachers? (This is a *design* issue.) What questions will you ask to get evidence: Will you ask parents to estimate how many hours per week they help or will you ask them to place themselves on a scale ranging from very frequently, through sometimes, to never? (These are *measurement* issues.) Choices and decisions like these abound. The process of planning a research project, involves answering ever more specific questions about what you plan to do and how you plan to do it. The answers eventually add up to a detailed plan of work, an agenda or schedule of sorts, that is built on your choices.

How Can Causal Modeling Be Used in the Example of Student Advisory Programs?

Even when you have a good topic with most of the key questions answered, such as the example of parental involvement just discussed, you still have several options about how to achieve your goal of understanding the relations among the aspects of your topic. As an example, let's take a research question proposed by Amy, a graduate student in a research methods course: Do school advisory programs increase student academic achievement and school satisfaction through building self-esteem? Her question is important. Schools, especially middle schools, have devoted considerable resources to these programs in the belief that they will be effective. It is not only an important question but also a good question from the standpoint of research methods. Because the question states a model and does so with variables that can be defined and measured, it is likely to give a useful answer. People thinking about the effectiveness of education programs have to "decide how to decide" whether a program is working. Amy's answer about how to decide is implied in her question, but let's first look at a couple of alternatives.

One popular way to research the question about the effectiveness of advisory programs would be easy, easier than Amy's approach. You could simply ask: "Has academic achievement gone up in our school since we introduced the advisory program?" The new program was introduced in the fall. In June, let's just compare the scores on our standardized achievement tests with last year's scores. If the program has been effective, scores ought to have gone up. The popularity of this approach rests on several things. It seems to be a no-nonsense, bottom-line approach focusing on outcomes. It has the virtue of simplicity (everyone can understand it). And it costs nothing. You just look at the scores to see whether they have improved. But, say the scores *have* gone up. What does that really tell you? Not much—because it does not provide information about mediating variables. Many other things besides the advisement program could have caused achievement to go up, such as hiring some new, highly motivated teachers at the same time the program was started. Or achievement might have gone up even faster had it not been for budgetary problems that slowed down progress. In short, regardless of the answer you got from comparing last year's scores to this year's scores, you couldn't be very sure about the effectiveness of the programs. Variables, such as hiring new teachers at the same time you begin a new program, are *confounded,* which means that there is no way to determine their separate effects.

In this example, you would probably call the hiring of new teachers an extraneous variable (see Table 3.1). An extraneous variable is a variable other than your independent and mediating variables that could influence the dependent variable. One of the main purposes of research design is to control for (remove the effects of) variables that are extraneous to your research question. Hiring new faculty is not extraneous in any ultimate sense; it is extraneous only to *your* purposes as a researcher. For another researcher it might be an important independent or mediating variable. If an extraneous variable is not controlled, then it becomes a confounding variable; that is, it makes it difficult or impossible for you to say whether your predictor (independent) variable led to your outcome (dependent) variable.

The best approach for controlling extraneous variables, according to most textbooks in educational research methods, would be to conduct an experiment. Rather than introducing a program and then, after the fact, saying, "Oh, I wonder how well it's working," you could make planned comparisons. For instance, in a district with eight middle schools, you could randomly assign four of the schools to introduce the advisory program. The other four schools would not do so or would do so later. At periodic intervals you could measure academic achievement in the two groups of schools: the experimental group that got the program and the control, or comparison, group that did not. If the experimental group did significantly better than the control group, this would be pretty good evidence about the effectiveness of the program. Despite the attractions of this kind of design for program evaluation, and despite its widespread use in clinical trials, it is usually highly impractical for evaluating social and educational programs (see Chapter 15). Most researchers do not have the authority to tell schools: "OK, listen up! You in the experimental group, institute the program starting next September. And you in the control group, even if you'd like to have the program, don't start it because that would ruin my research design."

Usually, researchers have to study schools and their programs as they are, as they exist in their natural settings, in their political and social contexts, and while they are constantly changing. Studying reality on the fly, as it changes and when you have little or no control over the changes, is very common in the social sciences. More common still is studying the past, even when historical questions are no part of one's research design. For example, economists and marketing personnel might study monthly sales figures over the past 10 years to understand trends and fluctuations in the relation of sales and prices so as to make future pricing decisions more effectively. Political scientists and legislative aides could study the effectiveness of previous campaign strategies to develop their plans for the next election. Or sociologists and social workers might use data from the last two decades to examine the effects of maternal employment and family size on divorce rates so as to provide better family counseling. All work of this kind is built on the assumption that the future will be sufficiently like the past so that studying the past will help with future planning and decision making.

Of course, researchers have no control whatsoever over the past, because it has already happened. Only time travel would allow researchers to control the past. So, whether you have no control over what you are studying because what you study is already over and done with, and you are incapable of time travel, or because you do not rule the world, lack of direct control is a fact of life for most researchers in the social sciences and applied disciplines. One of the most misleading aspects of many elementary textbooks is that they proceed as though you will be able to control what you study, and that if you cannot, there is something sadly lacking in your research. In fact, such control is exceedingly rare for most researchers in the social sciences. To verify this all one has to do is review the methods used in the articles published in the major research journals in the social sciences. In brief, some questions are open to experiment where researchers exercise the control that comes with assigning subjects to treatment groups. Most questions, including many highly important ones, are not.

What do you do if you cannot conduct an experiment, because no one is going to turn over control to you, as in the school district example, so you can do your research? And assume that you want to do better than simply compare last year's scores to this year's. How do you proceed? This gets us back to Amy's question: Do school advisory programs increase student academic achievement and school satisfaction through building self-esteem? By specifying a model, which implies a theory of *how* the programs have led to improvement, Amy's question gives her a way to study the program's effectiveness, and she can be fairly sure that the answer will actually tell her something. At minimum, she will be able to say the data look like (or don't look like) they would *if* school programs increased academic achievement by fostering self-esteem and satisfaction. In other words, she could say: "*If* school programs had an effect, the data would turn out as follows; let's see if they do."

Nonetheless, as always, questions remain, and they have to be answered. In the first place, it seems that Amy has two potential dependent variables or outcomes: academic achievement and school satisfaction. Let's say she decides to focus on achievement. How could one draw a causal diagram of her question? The independent or predictor variable is the advisory program, the dependent variable is academic achievement. These are tied together, mediated by self-esteem and students' satisfaction with school. But one can model those mediating ties in three quite different ways, as shown in Figure 3.10.

It might be that achievement causes self-esteem to go up or it might be the other way around. Which is it? In order to conduct your study *you* need to decide. How do you decide? After your review of the literature and after reflection and discussion, you determine what is the most important topic. You might find that most of the research has looked at the link from self-esteem to achievement, but you think that is to miss the obvious link from achievement to self-esteem, and that's what you want to investigate.

Note, and this is really the crucial point, there is no *statistical* way for the researcher to decide which is the better model to investigate. What you can do statistically, *after* you have constructed the model and gathered evidence, is determine which model fits the evidence better. But you need the model first. Without it, you have no conception of what statistical evidence to gather and how. There is no statistical substitute, and certainly no computer substitute, helpful though these tools are, for serious thinking about research problems and how to gather evidence to solve them. Good quantitative research is not mostly about mathematics. It has much more to do with logic, knowledge of your subject, and your design for collecting evidence.

An ounce of design is worth a pound of analysis. The design, or the plan for gathering the evidence, does more to determine the quality of a research project than does the statistical analysis. Often one can fix a mistake in statistical analysis. Even toward the end of the research project one can usually go back and recompute using a different statistic. But it is hard to correct for a faulty design. As Shadish, Cook, and Campbell put it (2002, p. xvi), "in the interplay between design and statistics, design rules."

So what is a good design? There is no one answer, because the characteristics of good design depend on your research problem or question. You might be interested in a purely descriptive question, such as: What are the trends in test scores in the district in recent years? Often, however, pure description is not very satisfying. A researcher usually wants to get at the causes of things. For example, Why have test scores gone down? What has caused them to

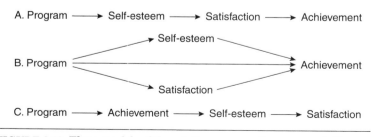

FIGURE 3.10 *Three models of the relations among the same variables*

decline? Because researchers are so often interested in causes, one of the marks of a good research design is that it enables us to come to trustworthy conclusions about causes.

What Is the Nature of Causation When Studying Research Problems?

Most research projects in education do not identify previously unknown causes. That is why naïve readers will sometimes conclude that an article reporting research was too complicated, too lengthy, and too laboriously detailed just to "prove something we already knew." The misconceptions in that phrase, "prove something we already knew," are important enough to examine in some detail. In the first place, researchers using quantitative methods *never, ever* prove anything. Except in mathematics, the word *proof* is mostly used by people, such as advertisers, who are not known for the accuracy of their claims. This is why the old saying that "you can prove anything with statistics" is doubly wrong. Honest statisticians insist that they deal only in probabilities, not certainty or proof. Of course, it is possible for dishonest people to use statistics to trick gullible people, but they can do that with words too. Deception has been around much longer than statistics. The only honest use of statistics is to help one *estimate* the *probability* that something is true.

So quantitative researchers using statistics can't prove anything, and what they tell us is *probably* true we "knew already." What's the value in that? It is accurate to say that researchers rarely come up with a cause that is completely unexpected. Indeed, the whole reason to draw models is to lay out expectations in advance. For example, not many people are surprised when they read research showing that students learn more in small classes. What researchers usually add is more detailed knowledge. *How* does reducing the number of students in the class improve learning? Are small classes more important for some students than others? How small does a class have to be before students start learning more? Will reducing class size from 35 to 25 have the same (or a bigger or

a smaller) effect as reducing the number of students from 25 to 15? Finally, and often most important, *how much* does reducing class size increase learning? Reducing class size is very expensive, more expensive than any other popular education reform. By contrast, making *schools* smaller is usually less expensive, and that reform also tends to promote student achievement. Which reform has the stronger effect on students' learning? If you can afford to do only one of them, which is the better choice? To answer such questions one needs to know the details of the kind that are usually the focus of research. *Whether* something has an effect is often less interesting in the social sciences than the questions of *how* it has its effect and the *size* of that effect.

Answering these questions involves inquiring about *causes,* although the word is not always used. Does reducing class size promote (cause) more learning in younger than in older in children? How does making schools smaller lead to (cause) academic achievement? Even though we use the idea all the time, there is no more difficult and complicated a concept than causation. Philosophers have studied it at least since Aristotle. Although promising new developments have occurred (Salmon, 1998; Pearl, 2000), controversies abound. Yet, for our purposes, the key issue can be reduced to the "problem of induction," first explained by Hume in the eighteenth century and given its classic illustration by Mill in the nineteenth century. Mill gave us the "black swan problem." No matter how many times you observe white swans, you cannot rightly infer that all swans are white. But, if you observe just one black swan, that is enough to refute the claim that all swans are white.[2] By observing white swans, you certainly have not *proved* that all swans are white. At best, you can say that your observations have *failed to refute* the claim that all swans are white. If this sounds familiar, it ought. It is the key idea behind the null hypothesis and hypothesis testing. (See Chapters 1 and 8.)

Despite the fact that philosophers and others have not solved most of the problems with causality, in order to function in daily life we usually assume that we can come to conclusions about causes. And researchers make this assumption for a living. The inconclusiveness of the ongoing discussions of causality should make us cautious and humble, but it is hard to see how, if we want to do research, we really can do anything but to assume, no matter how tentatively, that causal knowledge is possible.

What Are the Criteria for Assessing Causation?

How do we tell whether an inference about cause is worth believing? Three rules of thumb are often cited. In the language of variables we can say that an independent variable, *X*, could cause a dependent variable, *Y*, when (1) *X* precedes *Y*; (2) *X* and *Y* covary or vary together; and (3) other possible causes for *Y* are ruled out. These three criteria are *necessary* but not *sufficient* conditions. This is a key distinction. For example, to win the lottery it is necessary to buy a ticket, but it is not sufficient; for it to snow next December 25, it will be necessary that the temperature is 32 degrees Fahrenheit or colder, but that is not enough (not a sufficient condition) to make it snow.

One of the reasons it is difficult to establish causality is that there are no sufficient conditions in the social and behavioral sciences; that is, there are no criteria we could use to conclude, with complete certainty, that *X* caused *Y*. What can be said with certainty is that if the relations between variables do *not* meet the three following necessary conditions, then one can reject the hypothesis that *X* causes *Y*. If the necessary conditions are met, that does not prove causality, but one can say that one tried to disprove the hypothesis of causality and failed to do so. (It's that null hypothesis again!) The necessary conditions for causality, for *X* to cause *Y*, follow.

X *Precedes* Y

This is the clearest criterion. The cause must come before the effect. Or, to look at it the other way around, *after* cannot cause *before*. Establishing temporal order, determining the before and after, helps limit the range of possibilities. For example, gender or age could be a cause of doing well on a test, but

the opposite cannot be true. Doing well on the test won't change your gender, or make you younger. Again, before is only a necessary condition; it does not prove causality. One of the oldest logical errors is the so-called *post hoc* fallacy; *post hoc* is short for a Latin phrase meaning "after this, therefore because of this." This mistake in reasoning is remarkably easy to make. The school system hired a new superintendent last year; this year we have a budget crisis. The college raised admissions standards, and the number of applicants went down. Liability insurance premiums increased, and the number of operations in the hospital declined. *Before* is a necessary but not sufficient condition. It *could be* that the new superintendent caused the budget crisis; it *could be* that the new admissions standards caused the decline in applications; and it *might* be that increasing premiums made physicians reluctant to operate. The fallacy comes only in saying that it *must be* so.

X *Covaries with* Y

This means that *X* and *Y* change together. When one varies, so does the other. One could hardly say that *X* caused *Y* if a big increase in *X* were not followed by a change in *Y*. To say that *X* and *Y* covary is another way of saying that *X* and *Y* are correlated. For *X* to cause *Y* it must be correlated with *Y*. But what about the famous saying "Correlation does not equal causation"? It is true that correlation does not *prove* causation, but a lack of correlation comes pretty close to *disproving* it. Establishing that a correlation exists is not sufficient to show causation, but correlation is one of the necessary conditions of causation. If variables are not correlated, if they are independent (also called *orthogonal*), then they do not cause one another.

Most quantitative research studies in the social sciences, including education, business, and social work, are correlational or associational. They attempt to explain or predict relations, including causal relations, among variables by examining statistical associations among them. Because a statistical association such as a correlation is only a necessary, not a sufficient, condition for causation, we must exercise much caution when using the fact that variables covary to infer that they are causally related. Suppose, for example, that you had access to a state's educational data. Many states collect and provide to the public, at no charge, often online, huge amounts of data about many aspects of the schools and the education system. What if one could put the state's data for 100 variables into a spreadsheet or statistical package, such as SPSS, and instruct the software to compute all possible correlations[3] among them? Perhaps teachers' years of experience are positively correlated with seventh-grade girls' math achievement, and state spending on public higher education is positively correlated with the percentage of undergraduates who take more than four years to graduate. Would this mean that if schools wished to raise girls' math test scores in the seventh grade, they should hire more experienced teachers? Or can we conclude that to encourage more undergraduates to graduate on time, states should spend less money on higher education? Perhaps, but it is not very likely that these changes would have the desired effects.

If you have a large number of variables and you go trolling for correlations, chances are that you will find some coincidences, some random statistical associations. The most absurd instances of coincidences being treated seriously that I have ever heard concern stock and commodity prices. What renders them especially outrageous is that sometimes well-educated people who have passed tests and are certified financial planners make them. Stockbrokers making cold calls have interrupted my dinner with facts such as in the past decade, whenever corn futures have declined for three quarters in a row, airline stocks have surged. Now is the time to buy! In years when the NFC wins the Super Bowl, the stock market soars! While this and many other coincidences may be true of relations between trends in grain prices, football scores, and stock prices, a person would have to be more than a little naïve to make investment decisions based on such information. It is hard to determine whether these bogus claims arise from dishonesty, stupidity, or some potent combination of both, but the prevalence of such specious reasoning has given correlations a bad name.

Looking for correlations without having any particular idea to guide your search is often called a "fishing expedition." You toss in your line and hope you come up with something. Once in a while, important discoveries have been made this way. The correlation between arthritis and fewer heart attacks is one example. Trolling in medical records hoping to find a clue that could lead to better health care can be worth the time because better health care is very important. But the probability of success is very low. On the other hand, if instead of a random *fishing* expedition, you have reason to expect a specific relation among variables, and you go *hunting* in available data to see whether those particular variables are correlated, the chances of arriving at valid conclusions are higher. This is the kind of approach taken, for example, by researchers investigating the effects of school size on academic achievement. Again, what one is doing when going on a hunting expedition is seeing whether the evidence looks like it would, whether the data behave as they would, if the variables were causally related.

No Alternative Explanation for Y

The third criterion for identifying a causal relation is the most demanding. It is comparatively easy to tell whether X came before Y or whether X and Y are statistically associated. By contrast, being sure that nothing else could possibly have caused the statistical association is daunting. How could you have eliminated, controlled, or explained away *all* other possible causes, including those you don't know about? You cannot, but it is possible to use various designs to reduce the number of possible alternative causes. Also, dependent variables such as academic achievement surely have many causes; therefore, there will always be alternative explanations for them. So, the third criterion for causality is the one that is most difficult to meet. Meeting it is most often the main goal of research designs and is the main criterion used to judge the quality of designs. A good design controls for *some* (not *all* as the rule implies) other plausible explanations. The more alternative causes that can be eliminated or controlled, the better the design.

How is controlling for other potential causes accomplished? Different research designs are in large part defined by how they do this. The classic method, some would say the "gold standard," for controlling alternative explanations is the randomized experiment (see Chapter 6). Experimenters control by direct manipulation. The method is very straightforward. Get some people (subjects) together. Assign individuals by coin toss or some other random method to two groups: (1) the experimental group, to whom you give a treatment or do something (e.g., show a movie depicting violence); (2) the control group, to whom you deny the treatment (e.g., show a movie with no violence). Then you administer an attitude survey to see whether the movie affected attitudes toward methods of disciplining children including spanking. You design the experiment so that the movie viewing experiences are identical in every conceivable way (seats, lighting, time of day, and so on) except for the movie viewed. Random assignment ensures that the two groups are identical, at least within the bounds of random error. Using this design, if there is a difference in postviewing attitudes between the two groups, it is hard to think of another cause except the movie they have seen. This is the main advantage of the randomized experiment, and it is a powerful one. Experiments greatly reduce the number of potential competing causes. The main disadvantage is that there are many things we would like to study for which experiments do not work well. Random assignment and manipulation are often impossible or difficult or illegal or unethical.

Another way to control for alternative causes is statistically. Remember the second criterion. If there is no statistical association between the variables, one cannot cause the other.[4] This means that you can eliminate other possible causes by finding variables that do not correlate with the effect. Much of the rest of this book, especially in Part 2 on advanced techniques, is devoted to the many ways researchers have figured out how to do this. They are all attempts to make up for the fact that, for many things we would like to study, randomized experiments are inadequate, difficult, or impossible. Often statistical methods of control are second-best alternatives, but

many times these second-best options are all that is available. Let's continue with our example of studying the effects of violent movies on attitudes about disciplining children by spanking. The randomized experiment described above would not be too difficult to set up, but it is very artificial. People do not just see one movie; a lifetime of viewing choices is likely to shape their attitudes; and people hardly ever let someone else decide by a flip of a coin which movie they should see. To avoid the artificiality of an experiment, a researcher might survey a sample (see Chapter 5) of adults about the movies they have seen, their attitudes toward spanking, and many other variables, such as their education, gender, age, and ethnicity.

If the researcher finds a statistical association between seeing violent movies and favoring spanking as a method of discipline, can we conclude that violent movies cause people to favor spanking? Maybe. But unlike in the experimental study, it *is* very easy to think of other causes for the statistical association. Perhaps men are more likely to see violent movies and to favor spanking. Maybe people with higher levels of education are less likely to go to violent movies and are less likely to favor spanking. To find out, you would *statistically control* for gender and education. Essentially, that means you would subtract the effects of those two variables. If, after subtracting the effects of the other variables, the correlation between violent movies and spanking disappears, then that correlation is *spurious*. "Spurious" in this context means that there is an association, but it does not indicate a causal relation. On the other hand, if the relation between viewing violent movies and favoring spanking persisted after controlling for those two variables, then we could have more confidence in it. But, because it would not be terribly hard to think of other possible reasons for the association of violent movies and violent child discipline, we could not be sure. We cannot know for certain that we have included all potential causal variables. Leaving other possible causes out of the design is called *specification error.* If we commit a specification error, this means that in our model, we did not specify (identify and include) variables that might have been important. There is no statistical test for specification error. To see whether a variable is correlated and is a potential cause, one has to include it. But, if we have not included it, then we cannot measure its effects—or its lack of them. A statistical test for specification error can be conducted only if we haven't made the error in the first place!

Finally, researchers are interested not only in whether *X* causes *Y*, but also in *how strongly* it does so, particularly in comparison to some other *X*s or independent variables. Movie viewing might influence attitudes about spanking as a method of child rearing, but how one was raised—for example, whether one was spanked oneself—might be a much more important influence. If the researchers do not remember to put questions about how one was raised into the survey, they will never know. They cannot fix the omission with statistics. As always, thinking ahead about design is much more important than knowing how to crunch the numbers.

Surprisingly, once we assume that we have a cause, measuring the size of its effect can be a comparatively simple task. In following chapters we will look at statistical tools for measuring the size or strength of associations among variables. When our research design suggests that variables are causally related, we begin by using descriptive statistics to discuss characteristics of the relationship. These statistics are the subject of the next chapter.

Terms and Concepts to Review

Variable
Variance

Independent variable (IV)
• Predictor variable
• Explanatory variable

Dependent variable (DV)
• Outcome variable
• Criterion variable
• Response variable

Mediating variable
• Intervening variable

Effect Modifiers
• Antecedent variable
• Moderating variable
• Interaction effect

• Extraneous variable
• Control variable

Prediction
Explanation
Causation

Causal model
• Theory
• Equations as models or theories

Necessary condition
Sufficient condition
Operational definition
Specification error
Spurious relation
Confounded variable

Discussion Questions

1. Discuss the differences and similarities between two research questions that you construct. The first question is solely to predict an outcome (dependent variable) on the basis of information about independent (predictor) variables. In the second research question you seek to explain or understand the relations among the independent variables (IVs) and between the IVs and the dependent variable (DV).

2. Consider the differences and similarities between mediating and moderating variables. Can you think of two different research models in which the same variable would be a mediator in one and a moderator in the other?

3. Think of a research problem or question for which it would be very important to study interaction effects. Why would interaction effects be likely to matter for this research example?

4. Think of an example of a research problem for which you could, using the same variables, model it in two or more different ways. Discuss the implications of the fact that you can take the same variables and use them to construct different causal models. Hint: It is often easier to do this with traits of individuals than with other kinds of variables. For example, individuals' beliefs, attitudes, intentions, motivations, abilities, achievements, and behaviors are fertile ground for this kind of exercise looking at the possible multiple ways variables could be related—for example, attitudes could influence beliefs or beliefs could influence attitudes.

5. Think of a simple causal model. Then start listing all of the variables you might want to control. To take an example discussed in the chapter, small classes promote learning. What are all the things that might also promote learning that could have an influence on or accompany class size? For example, classes might be smaller in richer schools, so you might want to control for (subtract the effects of) schools' levels of prosperity. Small classes might be more common in small schools, so you might consider controlling for school size. Or prosperous schools, with smaller classes, might also have the funds to hire higher-quality teachers, so you might need to control for teacher quality. And so on. How would you know when to stop adding control variables? How can anyone?

Self-Test

If you can answer most of the following questions accurately, you can feel confident about your understanding of the material in this chapter. If not, it would be a good idea to review the chapter. (Answers can be found in the Appendix.)

1. A researcher reports that increasing per pupil expenditure in the district has not led to higher average scores on state achievement tests. In this case, test scores are a(an)
   a. Independent (or predictor) variable.
   b. Dependent (or outcome) variable.
   c. Mediating (or intervening) variable.
   d. Moderating variable.
   e. Interaction effect.

2. Researchers propose to study whether reducing class size has the same effects on achievement in colleges (grades 13 and 14) as in high schools (grades 9–12). In this study, grade level is the proposed
   a. Independent (or predictor) variable.
   b. Dependent (or outcome) variable.
   c. Mediating (or intervening) variable.
   d. Moderating variable.
   e. Interaction effect.

3. If students' scores on a test improve as a result of receiving tutoring, and if they improve as a result of number of hours they spend studying, and if researchers wanted to investigate the combined effects of tutoring and studying, the researchers would be looking for a(an)

   a. Independent (or predictor) variable.
   b. Dependent (or outcome) variable.
   c. Mediating (or intervening) variable.
   d. Moderating variable.
   e. Interaction effect.

4. In a study of the effects of homework on students' academic achievement, it is discovered that the effects differ by age. In this case, age is a(an)
   a. Independent (or predictor) variable.
   b. Dependent (or outcome) variable.
   c. Mediating (or intervening) variable.
   d. Moderating variable.
   e. Interaction effect.

5. If it is hypothesized that the reason smaller class sizes sometimes lead to greater student achievement is that smaller classes allow teachers to devote more individual attention to students, then teachers' individual attention is the hypothesized
   a. Independent (or predictor) variable.
   b. Dependent (or outcome) variable.
   c. Mediating (or intervening) variable.
   d. Moderating variable.
   e. Interaction effect.

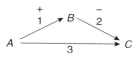

Causal diagram

6. In the causal diagram above, variable *C* is the
   a. Independent (or predictor) variable.
   b. Dependent (or outcome) variable.
   c. Mediating (or intervening) variable.
   d. Moderating variable.
   e. Interaction effect.
7. In the causal diagram above, the negative sign (–) over line 2 (between variables *B* and *C*) indicates that
   a. When the value of B declines, the value of C will decline.
   b. When the value of B goes up, the value of C will decline.
   c. When the value of B goes up, the value of C will not be affected.
   d. Variables B and C are directly (not inversely) related.
8. In the causal diagram above, variable B is the
   a. Independent (or predictor) variable.
   b. Dependent (or outcome) variable.
   c. Mediating (or intervening) variable.
   d. Moderating variable.
   e. Interaction effect.

9. Concerning the study of causation in educational research, it is accurate to say
   a. In order to prove that two variables are causally linked the researcher has to identify both the necessary and sufficient conditions for causality.
   b. If two variables are correlated (covary), this is sufficient to determine whether they are causally related and to what degree.
   c. It is easier to demonstrate that things are not causally linked than that they are.
   d. All of the above are accurate.
10. Concerning the study of causation in educational research, it is accurate to say
   a. It is easier to measure the size of a presumed causal relation than it is to establish that one exists.
   b. Specification error involves failing to include a causal variable in one's research design.
   c. A spurious correlation between two variables is a statistical association that does not measure a true causal relationship between the variables.
   d. All of the above are accurate.

Endnotes

1. Variables are sometimes called *variates* or, when one is talking about two or more of them, *covariates*.

2. This hypothetical example took on new meaning when, years after Mill wrote, a black variety of swan was discovered in Australia.

3. All correlations between 100 variables would total to 4,950 bivariate correlations!

4. In rare cases, when *suppressor variables* are at work, variables can be uncorrelated, but causally related.

4

The Uses of
Descriptive Statistics

Descriptive techniques are used in almost all quantitative research projects, but textbooks sometimes do not treat them in enough detail. Emphasis on statistical significance and hypothesis testing has occasionally led to the neglect of descriptive statistics. Such neglect is unfortunate, because descriptive statistics are one of the most important tools researchers can use to conduct meaningful analyses. They are useful substantively because many questions can be answered with descriptive techniques; graphic approaches are particularly helpful. And descriptive statistics have a key role in any quantitative research, because they are necessary to help spot problems with the data that require changes in the inferential and advanced techniques the researcher employs.

This chapter reviews some of the most important uses of descriptive statistics by addressing the following questions.

1. How do researchers use the term *descriptive statistics*?
2. How are descriptive statistics used to depict populations and samples?
3. What are measures of central tendency, and how does one choose among them?
4. How can the shape of data distributions be explored?

5. How does the theoretical normal distribution relate to actual data?
6. What do you do if data are not continuous and not normally distributed?
7. What are nonparametric statistical techniques?
8. How can descriptive statistics be used to check assumptions?
9. What are some substantive uses of descriptive (noninferential) statistics?

How Do Researchers Use the Term Descriptive Statistics?

The term *descriptive statistics* is used in at least three different ways. The first, and most common, use of the term *descriptive statistics* is to contrast it with *inferential statistics*. In this usage, anything that is not inferential is, by default, descriptive. Inferential techniques are used to come to conclusions (make inferences) about a population on the basis of information about a sample that has been drawn from the population. For example, at election time, pollsters will ask a sample of voters how they would vote if the election were held the next day; on the basis of what pollsters learn from the sample, they make inferences about the likely results of the election in the population. By contrast, if you were *not* trying to generalize from a sample to a broader population, you would be using descriptive techniques. Also, if you were studying a whole population, your statistical techniques would be noninferential, that is, descriptive. Studying an entire population is more common than one might suppose. For example, a great deal of educational data available at the state level is not sample data, but refers to the entire population of students in the state. Researchers studying a particular university or a specific school also often have data about the entire population of students at the university or school and do not need to draw inferences based on samples. And vital statistics (on births and deaths) are almost always collected for entire populations, not just samples.

A second meaning of descriptive statistics is less useful, although quite widespread. Descriptive techniques are often implicitly contrasted with multivariate statistics, that is, with statistics that study more than one variable at a time. A third usage contrasts descriptive techniques with approaches to data that try to discover causes, even when this causal work does not lead to attempts to draw inferences about a population from a sample. In these second and third definitions, which are often combined, descriptive statistics would be used to refer to the work of researchers who examine only one variable at a time and who do not discuss relations among the variables they study. Such research is unusual. I cannot think of a single published example. Because many researchers using noninferential statistics do, in fact, study causal relations among groups of variables, the second and third definitions of descriptive statistics can be confusing.

If we use the definition "not inferential" for descriptive techniques, the number of such techniques is large, and the scope of their uses is huge. Except for statistics used to compute *p*-values, nearly all statistics can be employed descriptively. Even very advanced techniques such as multilevel modeling or logistic regression (see Chapters 11 and 12) can be used to describe populations. They can be very helpful in fields such as education and public health, which rely heavily on descriptive techniques. Depending on what the researcher wants to describe, there are four different types of descriptive statistics: (1) *Measures of central tendency,* such as the mean and the median, describe the typical or middle score in a distribution; (2) *measures of dispersion,* such as the variance and the standard deviation, describe the scatter or deviations from the mean; (3) *measures of relative position,* such as the percentile or the *z*-score, describe where a particular score is located in a group of scores; and (4) *measures of association,* such as the correlation, describe how the scores in two or more distributions vary together or covary, "correlate." Each of these can be used in several ways by researchers analyzing their data.

How Are Descriptive Statistics Used to Depict Populations and Samples?

The first use of descriptive statistics in most research reports is to tell the reader about the methods used and the cases or subjects[1] studied. Who (or what) was studied? How were the cases or subjects selected? How many of them were selected? What were their characteristics? What methods were used to gather evidence about them? How was this evidence handled? These and many other questions have to be answered if the research project is to meet one of the most fundamental criteria of a good study: *It could be replicated.* Researchers need to describe what they did and how they did it in enough detail that other researchers could replicate their findings. Although replicability is crucial for advancing our knowledge, doctoral students sometimes resist a suggestion that they conduct replication studies for their dissertations. Despite unanimous agreement that the whole idea of scientific research entails replication, people are afraid they will be thought unimaginative if they do this important work. But many doctoral students would be well advised to undertake replication studies. In addition to their contributions to knowledge, replications are a type of work a novice researcher can "learn on."

Most fields in the applied social sciences desperately need replication research if they are ever to become more than a jumble of loosely related findings. One of the key differences, for example, between educational and medical research is that the latter puts much greater stress on replication. Advances in a field are much easier if researchers systematically build on, verify, and correct one another's work. Synthesizing findings into credible summaries of best practices is possible only when the works being synthesized are actually studying the same phenomena.

Because replication has an undeserved bad name, perhaps we should give it a new one. *Results verification* would be a good candidate, and it also better describes what really goes on in research of this type. Indeed, except in very particular circumstances,[2] true replication is impossible. Say you learned of some interesting results obtained last year by researchers at Stanford University who were studying cooperative learning among third graders, and you wanted to replicate it. In the first place, your study would be done at a different time (this year, not last year). Second, there is almost no chance you could study the same subjects, and, if you could, they would no longer be third graders. So, a replication study will almost always study different subjects at a different time. You study the same concepts or variables, but you change the subjects, the settings, and sometimes the methods used to measure the variables. Often the point of studying different (types of) subjects is to test the *scope* of the conclusions: "Sure that's true of Hispanic third graders in the San Francisco area, but would it hold for African American third graders in Atlanta?" At other times a replication study will use different methods of measurement: "Although they found that achievement improved using the ABC assessment, we seek to verify the achievement gains using the XYZ test." In brief, science depends on replication, or results verification. And replication depends upon detailed description.

Descriptions of an investigation's sample and population are often quite extensive, and they should be. For example, if the group about which one wants to generalize, often called the *target population,* is all the undergraduates at a university, the population's size and its other known characteristics should be

discussed in full. This would include information about the number of students at the university and features of the university at which they are enrolled, such as whether it is public or private, a research university, highly selective, located in an urban area, and so on. The gender, ethnicity, and ages of the students should also be reported as well as any other available potentially relevant information, such as their mean SAT scores and GPAs.

Among the first and most important uses of data about the population is comparing it to the *sample* data. Say that our university had 15,000 undergraduates and we selected a sample of 500 of them. Comparing data about the sample of 500 to data describing the population of 15,000 enables us to judge the representativeness of the sample. Large discrepancies are a cause for concern and a potential limitation of the study. For example, if we knew that 60% of the population was female and we found that only 35% of our sample was female, this would be a serious limitation to our ability to generalize from the sample to the population, especially about issues that might be related to gender.

Using the more technical terms to describe this work, known population data, called *parameters,* are compared with sample data, called *statistics.* For example, one might compare the mean age of the sample and of the population of university students. When a statistic is used to estimate a parameter, the statistic is often called, reasonably enough, an *estimator. Estimator* is a clearer term than *statistic* in this context, and it is used with increasing frequency. When a statistic is an *unbiased estimator* of a parameter (see Chapter 5), it is called the *expected value* and is symbolized by *E.* One expects the mean of the sample on some measure, such as number of alcoholic drinks consumed per week, to be a good estimate of the mean number consumed by the population.

Description is equally important in experimental research. First one describes how the subjects were recruited, how many were recruited, and how they were assigned to control and experimental groups. Then the experimental researchers compare the control and experimental groups in the same way that survey researchers compare samples and populations, and for the same reasons, to make sure that the two are equivalent. Typically one compares the groups' mean age, gender, ethnicity, pretest scores, and anything else that seems possibly relevant. These comparisons are especially important in *quasi-experiments*. In quasi-experiments researchers are unable to assign subjects to groups. Instead, researchers use preexisting groups, such as clients receiving particular services, and compare them to clients who are not receiving those services. Using existing groups for quasi-experiments is very common in social research and requires that researchers make every effort to determine the comparability of the groups studied. Descriptive statistics are most commonly used for this purpose.

What Are Measures of Central Tendency, and How Does One Choose among Them?

Several descriptive techniques are used for the preliminary work of comparing populations with the samples drawn from them and for comparing control groups with experimental groups. Means, medians, modes are the most common. Collectively these are called *measures of central tendency*. The standard deviation (a measure of dispersion) is also widely used in connection with measures of central tendency. It is usually best to report all four. Each can be a useful descriptive technique that conveys a good deal of information. The value of each for describing the data depends on the pattern of scores and the level of measurement. No one of them tells the whole story. Having all four available makes for a fuller, more accurate description.

In a series of scores, such as the number of correct answers on a test, the *mode* is the most common or most frequent score. The mode is often useful mainly for nominal or qualitative variables. In fact, for nominal data, such as the academic majors of our sample of 500 college students, the mode is the *only* appropriate measure of central tendency. The modal, or typical, student in the sample might be a business

major. The mode is also useful for highly skewed distributions. Suppose that we were studying the income from paid employment during the school year of the 500 students in our sample. Say 400 of the students did not work and made no money. The other 100 did work, and to make the arithmetic simple, say each earned exactly $1,000. The mean or average income for all 500 would be $200. This figure would be nearly useless for describing the group. On the other hand, the mode, which is zero, is the best single descriptor of incomes. A modal income of zero perfectly describes 400 of the 500 students.

The *median* is the middle score in a series ranked from highest to lowest. It splits the group in two, with half of the scores above and half below the median. In our example of the incomes of the 500 students, the median would also be zero. Like the mode, the median is not affected when the distribution contains a small number of extreme scores. In other terms, the median is also a very useful statistic for skewed distributions (see the following).

A common misconception can be cleared up at this point. People often say that, by definition, half the scores are above and half below average. If by average one is referring to the median, this is true, but it is only sometimes true of what most people mean by average, that is, the *mean*. For example, in our sample of 500 students, half were *not* above and half below the mean. The mean was $200. So 400 were below the mean and 100 were above. Only when the distribution of scores is symmetrical, such as in a normal distribution, is the mean the middle score. In fact, in a normal distribution, the mean, median, and mode are all identical.

The *mean* is the total of all the scores divided by the number of scores. The mean is much more important for statistics than is either the mode or the median. This is true even though the mean can be misleading as a description of some distributions. The mean, and the standard deviation from the mean (see Chapter 2), is the foundation for most advanced statistics. Recall how, in Chapter 2, we calculated a standard deviation for two sets of scores and then the correlation between them. The early steps were to (1) calculate the mean; (2) subtract the mean from each score to get the deviation scores; (3) square the deviation scores; and (4) add up, or sum, all the squared deviation scores. What makes the mean so special is the results of this fourth step, the *sum of the squared deviation scores,* known as the *sum of squares* for short. The sum of squared deviations from the mean is smaller than the squared deviations from any other statistic, such as the median or the mode. This characteristic of the mean, called the *least squares criterion,* is fundamental to the general linear model. And the general linear model is at the heart of analysis of variance and regression analysis (see Chapters 8 and 9), which, in turn, are the two legs on which modern statistics walks.

In addition to measures of central tendency, measures of association are increasingly employed for description in research reports. Typically researchers use the Pearson *r* correlation and produce a correlation matrix for all quantitative variables, as in Chapter 2 with the grades for 35 students on various exams and assignments. What the correlation matrix enables the researcher to do is to look for patterns of relationships between *pairs* of variables. In a study with many variables, the number of pairs to be correlated can quickly get very large. There were 6 variables for the 35 students and that produced 15 correlations between pairs of variables. If these were 10 variables, this would yield 45 correlations, and 20 variables would result in 190 pairs.[3] One reason a correlation matrix for all variables is very often reported in modern research is that having these data available makes it easier for other researchers to use the research to conduct a meta-analysis (see Chapter 17) or a factor analysis (see Chapters 13 and 14).

How Can the Shape of Data Distributions Be Explored?

It is very important for researchers to get to know their data and to help their readers become familiar with it too. This is why, when doctoral students ask for my advice, I strongly recommend *against* hiring someone to enter their data into a computerized statistical package. When you want something done right you should do it yourself, and no one has as strong an incentive as you do to avoid careless errors in data entry. Equally important, you learn about your evidence by tending to it. In order to be able to write about your data with intelligence, you need to get intimate with it, to handle it, to examine it, and to learn its quirks. You need to look for patterns in your data that will help you answer your questions. You need to tell your readers about the "shape" of your distributions, and you should be very critical of other researchers who do not provide this information for you. By shape of a distribution we mean how the scores or values or variables are distributed. For example, if you rank the scores from high to low, are most of them clustered toward the middle? Or are the scores spread evenly across the values? Or are there lots of high scores and lots of low scores, but very few middling scores?

It is also important to identify extreme scores or *outliers.* Outliers are usually defined as scores that are 3 or more standard deviations above or below the mean. Sometimes an outlier is just a mistake. For instance, in a study I conducted that used date of publication as a variable, I had 37 publications in 1987, 52 in 1988, 34 in 1989, and 1 in 1089. Obviously the year 1089 for a publication was a data entry mistake. I found the mistake in the course of describing my data and might not have found it had I skipped the descriptive phase of data analysis. To take another example, in a survey of college student gambling, researchers found a student who claimed to have lost over $100,000 betting on sports! If true, this was an astonishing amount of money for a college student to have lost. Even if true, the researchers should probably delete the case from their database before doing their analyses. A score this extreme can greatly influence the mean and, therefore, the standard deviation and, therefore, every statistic based on them, such as correlations and regression coefficients. Any analysis based on data with highly extreme outliers can be very misleading. On the other hand, simply discarding real data about your most interesting and unusual cases is not a step to be taken without a great deal of thought.

In general, describing and examining your data is often mostly a preliminary step before you move to the real analyses, but it can be a crucial step, and it can be more complicated than novice researchers believe. In other terms, you need to explore your data. There is even a branch of statistics called *exploratory data analysis* in which the main question is often the shape of distributions. Looking at frequency distributions is especially useful when the shape of the distribution is *not* normal. When it is normal, measures of central tendency make excellent summaries of facts about the distributions. The mean and standard distribution tell you much of what you need to know, particularly in a normal distribution.

There is, by the way, nothing necessarily normal about the normal distribution. The values of many ordinary variables do not arrange themselves into the familiar bell-shaped curve. For example, the variable years of education completed by the adult population in the United States is not normally distributed. If you graphed the number of years completed from 0 through 20 you would be unlikely to get the familiar, bell-shaped curve. The same would be true of a distribution of incomes in the United States. On the other hand, many empirical distributions do come quite close to a normal distribution. And, because the normal distribution has many well-known and handy mathematical properties, it is generally easier to interpret data when it has this form. So how do you determine whether your sample distribution is normal or pretty close to it? Several ways, both statistical and graphical, exist.

Graphic techniques are very useful, and many of the best descriptive techniques are graphic in whole or in part. The importance of graphic approaches is a reminder of how easy it is to become distracted by the disputes between the Quants and the Quals, between the advocates of numbers versus the advocates of words. We can forget that there is a third, equally useful, option: images or graphics. Words, numbers, and pictures all help us understand reality. In Kant's famous phrase, reality "is not adapted to our powers of cognition." *We* have to adapt; we should use all the tools we can, whether they are verbal, numerical, or pictorial.

TABLE 4.1   *Stem-and-Leaf Table*

	Exam 1		Exam 2
10s	*1s*	*10s*	*1s*
6	5	6	
7	23456667779	7	3455667789
8	0123346678888	8	0001234444567999
9	112334799	9	3445566
10	0	10	00

Perhaps the handiest graphic technique is the stem-and-leaf diagram. Its beauty is that it turns a listing of scores into a graphical display of their distribution. The scores of the 35 students on Exam 1 and Exam 2 (from Table 2.4) are listed here in Table 4.1. The column headed "10s" refers to the students who scored in the 60s, 70s, 80s, and so on. For example, on Exam 1, one student got a 65 (6 from the 10s column, 5 from the 1s column). One student got a 72, another a 73, another a 74, another a 75, but three students got a score of 76, another three got 77, and so on. Comparing Exams 1 and 2 we can see that more students scored in the 80s on Exam 2 than on Exam 1 and that the distribution of scores on Exam 1 is more symmetrical. If you look at the table sideways, with the 10s column at the bottom of the page, you have a bar chart of the scores; the height of the bars is determined by the number of numbers. The 1s make up the columns and the 10s the base on which they rest. A bar chart for these data will convey the same picture, but it will lose the data (the raw score for each student).

Despite these handy features, the stem-and-leaf technique is not used very frequently. Histograms are more common. I had SPSS produce stem-and-leaf diagrams and histograms for the same data from Exam 1 and Exam 2. Comparing the stem-and-leaf diagram in Table 4.1 with the SPSS output in Figure 4.1, we can see that the results do not look very similar. That is because the bases are different. Rather than having one column for the 60s, 70s, and so on, SPSS has used two (60–64, 65–69, etc.) And the his-

FIGURE 4.1 *Stem-and-leaf plots*

Frequency	Stem & Leaf
.00	6.
1.00	6.5
3.00	7.234
8.00	7.56667779
6.00	8.012334
7.00	8.6678888
6.00	9.112334
3.00	9.799
1.00	10.0

Stem width: 10.00
Each leaf: 1 case(s)

Frequency	Stem & Leaf
2.00	7.34
8.00	7.55667789
10.00	8.0001234444
6.00	8.567999
3.00	9.344
4.00	9.5566
2.00	10.00

Stem width: 10.00
Each leaf: 1 case(s)

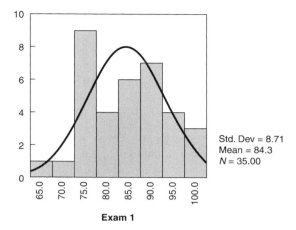

Std. Dev = 8.71
Mean = 84.3
N = 35.00

Exam 1

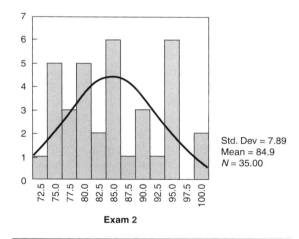

Std. Dev = 7.89
Mean = 84.9
N = 35.00

Exam 2

FIGURE 4.2 *Histograms for Exam 1 and Exam 2*

tograms for the two distributions of exam scores in Figure 4.2 give yet another picture. It is not the case that one of these depictions of the same data is right and the others wrong. It is more accurate to say that it is not easy to find an unambiguous way to graph one's data. Depending on the technique used, the results may vary considerably. And the same technique using different intervals at the base can generate quite different descriptions of the data. My advice is to explore various ways to display your data, study the results, and use those that convey the most useful information and the most informative picture of your data. No statistical tests for "most useful" and "most informative" exist. As with so much else in quantitative methods, choosing the most accurate description is more a matter of judgment than of statistics.[4]

Among the *statistical* (not graphic) summaries used to describe a distribution, the measures of skewness and kurtosis are the best known. The statistics for skewness and kurtosis for the distributions of scores on Exam 1 and Exam 2 are given in Table 4.2.

The *skewness* statistic summarizes the extent to which a graph of a distribution is symmetrical. Symmetrical distributions, such as the normal curve, are not skewed; they have a skewness of zero; the left half of the distribution is a mirror image of the right half. When a distribution is right skewed, or positively skewed, the infrequent scores are on the right

TABLE 4.2 *Skewness and Kurtosis of Distributions*

	Skewness	*Kurtosis*
Exam 1	.016	–.664
Exam 2	.375	–.985

or high side of the distribution. The skewness statistic is a positive number. Conversely, a left-skewed distribution, in which the rare values are on the low or left side of the distribution, is described by a negative skewness statistic. Scores on a difficult examination would tend to be right skewed (more low scores than high), whereas scores on an easy examination would tend to be left skewed (not many very low scores). The skewness statistics for Exams 1 and 2 are both positive but quite small. They are right skewed, but not very much.

Kurtosis is a measure of how flat or pointy a graph of a distribution is. A normal curve has a kurtosis of zero. If the kurtosis statistic is a positive number, the distribution is pointier than a normal curve. If the kurtosis is negative, the graphed distribution is flatter than a normal curve. So we can see in Table 4.2 that the distributions of scores in Exams 1 and 2 are a little less pointy and a very little less symmetrical than a normal curve. See Figure 4.2 to compare the actual distribution (bars) to what it would be (lines) if the distribution were normal. The bars extend above the lines at several points.

How Does the Theoretical Normal Distribution Relate to Actual Data?

Clearly, the normal curve is the point of reference for nearly everything. You can never know too much about the normal curve. Understanding it is central to understanding much else. The normal curve is a *theoretical* distribution. The distributions of scores in Exams 1 and 2 are real, empirical distributions. The normal curve describes a *probable* distribution that *would* result from a perfectly *random* process. Because nothing in reality is perfect, and no pro-

cess is perfectly random, the normal distribution is theoretical, not real. A classic elementary example for comparing a real and a theoretical distribution is tossing a coin. If you had a perfectly balanced coin and you flipped it with perfect fairness, this would be a random process. The result of each flip of the coin (heads or tails) would be completely *independent* of all the other flips. Perfect randomness or independence is hard to achieve. The coin might be slightly heavier on one face than the other. Or the person flipping it might be unintentionally doing so in a way that favored either heads or tails. When a process for generating scores is not perfectly random, the scores are not completely independent of one another. Then the process, and the data it generates, is *biased*. The distribution of scores from a biased process will not conform to a normal distribution. The kurtosis and skewness statistics will not equal zero.

When the process is random, each outcome will be independent of the others. The probability of getting a tail at each flip will have nothing to do with any of the other results. Say you had tossed a fair coin fairly and it came up tails three times in a row. What is the probability of getting a tail on the fourth toss? The same as on the first toss, $p = .50$, and it will be the same on every other toss. Thinking that if you've gotten tails three times running, heads is somehow "due" to come up is known as the "gambler's fallacy." Gamblers often believe this, which is one of the reasons why they tend to lose money, and why casinos are profitable businesses.

I often have students in elementary statistics classes roll dice or toss coins and record the results. In one recent class 22 students were divided into 11 teams of two students each. The teams each performed 10 coin toss experiments. They flipped a coin 10 times and recorded the number of heads. Each of the 11 teams did this 10 times for a total of 110 experiments. When we tallied the results we found that the mean was 5.04, and the standard deviation was 1.54. The mode and the median were each 5. There was some negative skewness of –.124, but it was small. Figure 4.3 gives graphs of the results. The students were pleased. They knew that, in a perfectly random process, 5 out of 10 heads would be the most frequent result. And 4s and 6s

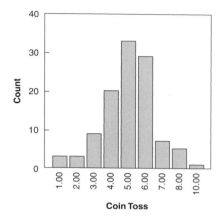

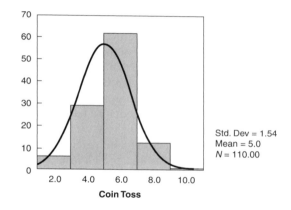

FIGURE 4.3 *Coin toss graphics*

The distribution of 110 experiments in Figure 4.3 is pointier than a normal distribution; the bars extend above the normal curve line; there are more scores in the middle and fewer at the ends. The kurtosis statistic is .988, and it has a standard error of .457. Without going into the details (see Chapter 8), a rule of thumb is this: When a statistic is two or more times as big as its standard error, then it is statistically significant at the .05 level ($p < .05$).

What does that mean in this case? The null hypothesis would be that there is no difference in kurtosis between the empirical distribution generated by the class experiment and the kurtosis of a normal distribution. We would reject the hypothesis of no difference because, from a perfectly random process, we would get a kurtosis statistic of .988 less than 5% of the time. In other words, there probably is a difference between the way these students are flipping coins and a random process. The difference makes the process biased. What is going on? My guess is that the answer probably lies in what Robert Rosenthal has called "experimenter expectation." Rosenthal has demonstrated that the results experimenters expect often influence what they get. In this case, the student coin flippers were the experimenters. They expected lots of 4s, 5s, and 6s—and they got them. Expectations do not completely *determine* all results; some experiments did result in 1s and 10s, but not many. The number of 4s, 5s, and 6s should have been large if the process were random, but not quite that large (82 out of 110 or 74.5%). Applying a perfectly random, unbiased process is no small accomplishment.

Elementary statistics books don't have as many tables in their appendixes as they once did. The tables were used to look up answers that are now provided by computer. But tables of random numbers are still valuable. Computer programs are pretty good at producing *approximately* random numbers. But because computers have to use *rules* to generate random numbers, the numbers are not truly random. If someone knew the rule the computer used, it would be theoretically possible for that person to figure out the next number the program would produce. But, a series of numbers is random only if knowing some digits (say, the first 10 in the series) tells you nothing about any

would be common too, but there "shouldn't" be many 0s, 1s, and 2s or 8s, 9s, and 10s.

What students knew was the *underlying theoretical distribution,* and they expected it to be roughly normal. So the students were delighted that their experiments turned out "right." But my impression was that the results were a little too good to be true. This impression was reinforced by the fact that my class experiments have almost always resulted in this pattern of more middle numbers and fewer high or low ones than one would expect from a truly random process. Something was amiss. One rough measure of whether the distribution was too weighted toward the center, as we have already seen, is the kurtosis.

other digits. This is similar to how knowing that the first three coin flips (of a fair coin) came up heads tells you nothing about whether you'll get heads on the fourth flip. Random is a hard, probably impossible, standard for a computer to meet. If you really want a series of random numbers, you are probably still better off using a table.

A *random variable* is one whose values are determined by a *random process,* such as flipping a coin or throwing dice or using a table of random numbers. (Just to make life difficult, and for no good reason I know of, these are also called *stochastic variables* and *stochastic processes.*) It is important to remember that the randomness in a random variable has to do with the way the values are determined or the cases are selected. Random has to do with the process, not with anything about the variable itself. For example, in our random sample of 500 college students, gender and income were random variables, because of the random process we used to select the students, not because their genders and incomes were random.

After having selected a random sample for a survey, or assigned subjects to groups randomly for an experiment, we use the normal curve (and other theoretical probability distributions) for comparison with empirical frequency distributions. In this way we can see whether the frequency distribution of a variable is close enough to a normal curve to say that it is a random variable generated by a random process, such as the number of heads in coin toss experiments. Of course, this comparison also tells us whether the frequency distribution indicates that something other than a random process has probably occurred. For example, the incomes of our sample of 500 students were not determined by a random process. Most of them had no income and 100 had incomes of $1,000. Plotting this information on a graph would not produce a bell-shaped curve—or any curve at all.

An empirical frequency distribution can never be *exactly* identical to a normal distribution. The values of a frequency distribution are discrete, not continuous. Even when the variable being measured is in theory continuous, such as age or weight, because of the limitations of precision of measurement, we must

always round off—for example, to the nearest month for age or the nearest ounce for weight. Rounding off makes a continuous variable discrete. And some variables are inherently discrete: we can get 3 heads out of 10 or 4 or 5, and so on. We cannot get 3.1 or 3.2, or 3.21, and so on. By contrast, the normal distribution is continuous; the curve describing it is smooth. Such continuous distributions are theoretical; they are mathematical abstractions that are not observed in the empirical world.

However, like many mathematical abstractions, the normal curve comes close to describing things in the world. This can be very useful. We know a great deal about the properties of the mathematical abstraction known as the normal distribution, which means that, by extension, we also know a lot about empirical distributions that are similar to the normal distribution. So, if in a study of the reading test scores of 800 third graders, we see that these scores are approximately normally distributed, we automatically know a great deal about that empirical distribution. For example, if Mary scored 1 standard deviation above the mean on the reading test, we automatically know that she scored at the 84th percentile; that is, she got a score that was higher than that of 84% of those who took the test.

There is not just one normal curve, even though we sometimes talk as though there were. The bell-shaped curve we often see is usually the *standard* (or standardized) normal curve, which has a mean of zero and a standard deviation of 1. But this is only one normal distribution among many. An infinitely large *family* of normal distributions exists, one for each value of the mean and the standard deviation. This is a family with much in common. Points of resemblance among its members are very strong. By definition, the area under the normal curve adds up to 1.0. In the standard normal distribution, the mean is 0 and the standard deviation is 1. The z-score, or standard score (see Chapter 2), is equal to the number of standard deviations from the mean. A score that is 1 standard deviation above the mean (84th percentile) has a z-score of 1. The height of the curve at any z-score (or standard deviation score) is known. For example, when $z = 0$ (i.e., for the mean), the height of the curve is .3989. The area between $z = -1$ and $z = +1$ will be about 68.2% of the total area under the curve. The scores between 2 SDs below and 2 SDs above the mean ($z = -2$ and $z = +2$) include about 95.4% of the scores. And, about 99.7% of the area under the curve is between 3 standard deviations below and 3 above the mean. This explains why the low score on standardized tests such as the SAT and the GRE is 200. The mean of these tests is set at 500, with an SD of 100. Thus, 3 SDs below the mean (or $z = -3$) is equivalent to 200. The test makers rightly concluded that greater precision for these examinations is not necessary and would be largely meaningless. It is possible on these exams to score higher than 800 or lower than 200, but the testing company does not report such scores.

What Do You Do If Data Are Not Continuous and Not Normally Distributed?

Although z-scores are ratio-level measurements, this is not true of many of the most common standard scores that are based on z-scores, such as GRE, SAT, and percentile scores. These latter three are *ordinal* measures. Percentiles provide information about the order of the raw scores, but not about the distance between them, that is, they are not interval-level measures. Because they are ordinal-level measures one should not do math on them that requires higher levels of measurement. Because standardized exam scores such as those on the SAT have many ranks, they are "approximately" interval level, and many researchers in fact treat SAT, GRE, and so on as though they were true quantitative rather than rank-order measures.

The problem with treating data based on ranks as though they were truly quantitative can be most easily seen by looking at the familiar ordinal-level grading system: A, B, C, D, and F. Is the gap between an A and a B the same as that between a C and a D? Perhaps, but not necessarily. Does a B in one course represent the same amount of learning or even the same student rank in all courses? Of course

not. A grade of B in one course might be a significant accomplishment, whereas in another it may be the average grade or even a below average grade. So it makes no sense to assign numbers—A = 4, B = 3, and so on—to these very different grades and then to average them. But this fallacious procedure is such a deeply ingrained tradition that it is an integral part of our education system. It is used to determine, at least in part, students' futures, such as their accessibility to colleges and professional schools.

Just as it is inappropriate but common to do math on grades of A, B, C, D, and F, so too with ranks such as percentile, GRE, SAT, and IQ scores. The differences between ranks are not equal intervals on any of these scales. For example, five percentile points can mean very different things. The difference between the 95th and 99th percentiles in a normal distribution is over five times as large (z-score difference of .681 versus .126) as the difference between the 50th and 55th percentile The basic rule is that the farther from the middle of the distribution, the greater the error when treating percentile ranks as equal intervals.[5]

At one time, we might have been tempted to consider these issues mainly technical matters. No longer. Understanding the meaning of and accuracy in reporting standardized test scores has become centrally important. Educational decisions about students and policy decisions about schools are being increasingly made on the basis of these test results. We will pursue some of these important issues in greater depth in Chapter 16.

What do you do when you describe your data and you learn that the data you intend to analyze are *not* normally distributed? And what do you do when studying data that are ranked (ordinal) rather than quantitative (interval or ratio)? Many statistical techniques assume that your sample data and the population from which they were drawn are normally distributed and measured on a ratio scale. If your data do not conform to these assumptions, you can have a problem. Sometimes the solution to your problem is simple enough. For example, if you want to compare sets of percentile scores or to correlate them, you can transform them into z-scores and proceed. Other transformations for data that are not normally distributed are also frequently used but can be more controversial (see Part 2 of this book). Often it is better to use what are known as nonparametric techniques.

What Are Nonparametric Statistical Techniques?

The awkward term *nonparametric* is applied to techniques that make no assumptions about population parameters and distributions (such as that these are normal). For this reason they are also sometimes called *distribution-free* statistics. Nonparametric statistics get their name from the fact that they do not use the mean and standard deviation (called parameters) fundamental in the calculation of parametric statistics. Labels aside, to decide which statistical techniques you should use, four questions are most important: (1) At what levels are your variables measured—nominal, ordinal, interval, or ratio (or as I've called them: qualitative, rank, quantitative)? (2) Are your sample data distributed normally? (3) How big is your sample? (4) How many values does your dependent variable have?

Nonparametric statistics are designed for research in which your variables are measured at low levels (nominal and/or ordinal). Nonparametric statistics are also used when the fairly stringent assumptions about the distributions of the values of variables are not met, assumptions that are especially important for significance tests such as analysis of variance (ANOVA). These two criteria of low level of measurement and nonnormal distribution are closely related. For example, when your dependent variable is dichotomous (has two values such as pass and fail), there is no sense in which individuals' scores on that variable could be normally distributed. Many points are required to make a normal curve. Dichotomous data have only two.

Among the most important measures of association for ordinal variables are gamma, Spearman's rho, and tau. For nominal data, important measures of association are the phi coefficient, Cramer's *V,* and lambda. Among the commonly used tests of statistical significance for nominal data are the chi-squared

test, the Mann-Whitney *U* test, the Kruskal-Wallis test, and the Wilcoxon test. Do not try to memorize a list of such statistics. But be prepared to consult one.

Knowing *exactly which* measure or test is best for what kind of variable or research design is not as important as knowing *that* it matters. Because it matters, you need to look it up or seek technical advice. In other words, it *is* crucial to know when and why you might have to abandon parametric measures of association (such as Pearson's *r* or ordinary regression analysis) or parametric test statistics (such as *t*-tests or ANOVA) and resort to nonparametric alternatives. In short, you *do* need to know when to look something up and/or seek advice. It is usually better to use a nonparametric measure of association and/or test of significance when data were collected at the nominal or ordinal rather than the interval or ratio level; data being studied are not normally distributed, for example, are highly irregular or skewed; the dependent variable is categorical; sample sizes of comparison groups are unequal; or samples are quite small.

Even when you have continuous data, if it is highly skewed and/or if the sample sizes are very small, you *may* want to convert continuous data into ranks and use nonparametric methods to study it. This involves discarding data and is not an action to be undertaken lightly, but it is *sometimes* the most appropriate avenue of data analysis. Also, some questions for which continuous data are available may be more accurately studied using ordinal or categorical levels of measurement. This happens when continuous measures contain socially significant breaks. Age is continuous quantitative variable, but for some purposes age should be divided into ranks. For example, in studies of voting, greater than 18 or less than 18 is more important than the difference between age 16 and 17 or between 19 and 20. To take another example, the specific number of years of schooling someone has accumulated may not be very important as a measure of education level. Much more important for many purposes are ranks such as less than high school, high school graduation, some college, and college graduation. Differences between 10 and 11 years or 13 and 14 years of schooling are generally less important than major branching points in the system of education: attend or not, graduate or not. Age and education level are examples of variables where discarding data (turning continuous data into categories or ranks) can sometimes give you a better picture of the world you are studying.

The main disadvantage of nonparametric statistics is that they are usually less *powerful.* Statistical power is a tricky concept that we will deal with in Chapter 8. Here we can just point to the analogy of a microscope. A powerful statistical test is like a powerful microscope. Using it, you can detect things you couldn't see if you used a less powerful tool. In general, nonparametric techniques are less powerful, which means they are more likely to overlook true differences between groups or to underestimate the size of associations among variables. That is why researchers often try to avoid them. But in some circumstances, nonparametric tests can actually be more powerful, especially when the values of the variables are not normally distributed.

How Can Descriptive Statistics Be Used to Check Assumptions?

Nonparametric statistics are also sometimes more powerful when variables being studied do not meet the assumptions of *linearity* and *equality of variances.* Thorough description of one's data helps one to check for the accuracy of these assumptions and thus leads to better decisions about which statistics to use.

In our discussion of correlations in Chapter 2, I pointed out that the Pearson r correlation is a measure of the extent to which two variables tend to form a straight line when plotted on a graph, that is, the relation between them is *linear.* One of the most important uses of descriptive techniques is to determine whether the relation between the variables is linear. The upper panel of Figure 4.4 is a scatter diagram of data relating the ages of 51 subjects to their scores on a test of physical strength. The result is far from a straight line. The strength scores rise sharply with age, level off a bit, and then decline steadily. Because the Pearson r measures the linear relation between

variables, it is not surprising that it is very low in this case, $r = -.03$, with a p-value of .86. This is not even close to statistical significance: You would get a correlation of that size by chance alone 86% of the time. There is clearly a strong relationship between age and strength, but a straight line (and therefore the Pearson r) does not describe it. The lower panel of Figure 4.4 shows what happens when we see how closely the data match a curve instead of a straight line. Leaving out the technical details (I used quadratic regression), it is easy to see that the match is quite close. The equivalent of the r is .95 with $p = < .001$. In this extreme case, it is easy to see the mistake: by using a Pearson r on these data we would have missed a very strong relation. A scatter plot describing the relation between the variables is often the best way to discover that a relation is not linear.

Scatter plots are also important for spotting *outliers* or extreme scores, which can greatly influence a statistic such as the Pearson r. When people think of an outlier, a score on one variable is what usually comes to mind. But bivariate outliers, which are extreme combinations of two variables, are just as important. For example, if we were studying the ages and heights of students in the first through twelfth grades, an age of 8 years would not be extreme, nor would a height of 5 feet 10 inches. But a combination of 8 years and 5 feet 10 inches would be an outlier.

Scatter plots are also helpful for testing the assumption of equality of variances, which is also called homogeneity of variances, and most portentously, *homoscedasticity*—literally, the tendency to scatter in the same way. This fundamental assumption, on which many parametric statistics are built, is not easy to grasp. But equality of variance can be fairly easily understood if you examine scatter plots made of data with and without it. The upper panel in Figure 4.5 describes a situation in which the variances in the Y variable are substantially equal at all values of the X variable. The scatter of the points above the value of 60 on the X-axis is about the same as the scatter at 80 and at 100 and so on. However, the lower panel of Figure 4.5 shows a very different situation. Here the assumption of equality (homogeneity) of variances would not be met. When the value of X is

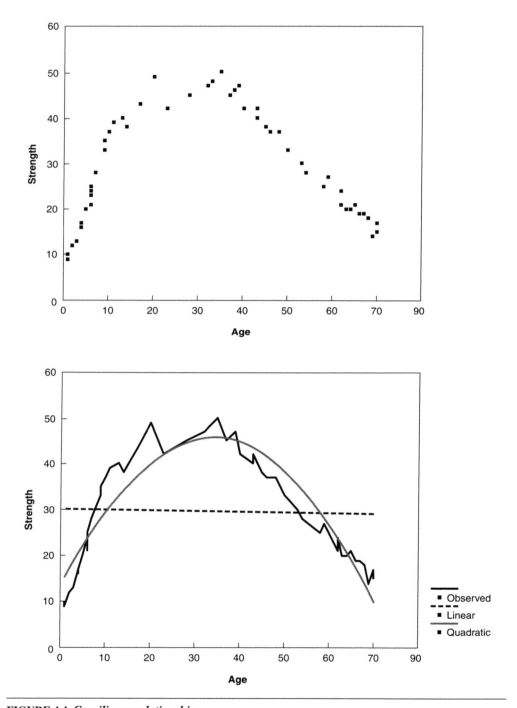

FIGURE 4.4 *Curvilinear relationship*

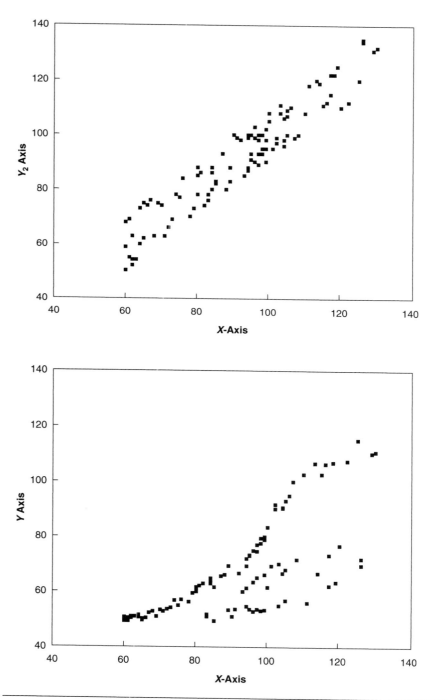

FIGURE 4.5 *Homogeneity and heterogeneity of variances (homoscedasticity and heteroscedasticity)*

60, the values of *Y* are very tightly clustered, but at *X* = 100 they are much more widely dispersed, and that difference is even greater at values of *X* higher than 100. Graphic descriptive techniques such as scatter plots help one see what various statistical tests of homogeneity of variances (such as Levene's test; see Chapter 8) report as numbers that are not always easy to interpret.

What Are Some Substantive Uses of Descriptive (Noninferential) Statistics?

To this point, we have mostly been treating descriptive statistics as a way to get ready to do something more important, such as compute a correlation or perform a statistical test. But descriptive statistics are widely used to relate substantive findings of great practical significance. Indeed, for policy research in many fields, descriptive statistics are a more informative way to report results. A pair of examples from educational research illustrates this nicely.

How do teachers and students spend their time in schools? How much is spent on direct instruction and how much is devoted to other things? In other words, how much "opportunity to learn" do students have? In an article called "Quantity Matters," Smith (2000) reports on her investigation of this question in 8 elementary schools. She and a team of researchers observed some 70 teachers during more than 300 periods of instruction in the second, fifth, and eighth grades. Note first that the research design was anthropological and observational, what many people would think of as a qualitative design. But the data gathered were quantitative, which illustrates the fact that the method of handling evidence (measurement) is not determined by the method of obtaining evidence (design). The researchers used intensive observation to gather their data and comparatively simple descriptive statistics to tell their story. They concluded that a typical student loses at least 40 instructional days (out of 180, or more than 20%). Days are interrupted, in whole or in part, by standardized testing, substitute teachers, Halloween or Christmas parties, and so on. One way to increase achievement, the authors con-

clude, would be to increase the amount of time in school spent on learning. Smith shows how this could be done either by increasing the amount of time at the schools' disposal (e.g., by a longer school day) and/or by making better, more efficient use of the time available.

A question often answered mainly with descriptive statistics is: How well are schools doing at promoting the learning of their students? Increasingly, state governments are mandating tests and holding schools accountable for the scores of their students. The reliability of scores over a four-year period (1997–2000) for all schools in Colorado was studied by Linn and Haug (2002). They used descriptive statistics (and no inferential statistics) to report their findings. Many states use a system similar to Colorado's to hold schools accountable. This year's scores are compared to last year's to see whether a school has improved, stayed the same, or gotten worse. But these scores tend to fluctuate in ways that have little or nothing to do with schools' practices or policies. This is partly because the student body changes from year to year, and these changes can lead to dramatic differences, especially in the scores of small schools. The scores change because *different students* are being measured, not because the schools are doing something different. The scores are highly unstable: "Schools that gain a lot from year one to year two will generally show a decline in year three, while those that show a decline from year one to year two will generally show a gain in year three" (p. 33). On the basis of such largely meaningless fluctuations, state policy makers can be tempted to recommend that practices in "successful" schools be imitated, even though such schools are likely to be "failures" next year. Until states begin tracking students and measuring how much individual students have learned, using student scores will be a poor way to judge schools' achievement.

These two investigations—how time is spent and how achievement is measured—are different in many respects. One is based on observations of a small number of schools whereas the other examines public data for all the schools and students in a state. But they also have much in common. They both address pressing policy issues about how to foster student learning (Smith, 2000) and how to measure whether schools are in fact fostering it (Linn & Haug, 2002). They are high-quality studies authored by distinguished researchers, and they both use fairly simple descriptive statistics to analyze their data and come to important conclusions. Novice researchers sometimes believe that they need to learn highly specialized advanced techniques before they can use quantitative methods. These two articles illustrate that simple descriptive statistics often suffice to deal with important problems. Descriptive statistics are not only preparations for higher-level work.

In sum, in addition to being important for conveying substantive information, descriptive statistics are also crucial for reviewing data distributions to determine their shape and for examining the evidence about whether a sample is representative of a population. Conscientious researchers will examine their data to determine which statistics are appropriate to use with the data. Pointing at and clicking the wrong measures and tests will produce output, but it will be misleading or meaningless. These issues about samples, distributions, and levels of measurement discussed in this chapter are particularly salient in survey research. Survey research is one of the most common designs used by professionals in applied fields, and it is the topic of our next chapter.

Terms and Concepts to Review[6]

Descriptive statistics
Inferential statistics
Measures of central tendency (mean, mode, median)
Measures of dispersion (variance, standard deviation)
Measures of relative position (percentiles, z-scores)
Measures of association (correlation)
Sum of squares
Least squares criterion
Sample
Population
Target population
Parameter
Statistic
Estimator
Expected value
Normal distribution
Standard normal distribution

Outlier
Skewness (right skewed; left skewed)
Kurtosis
Stem-and-leaf diagram
Biased
Random

Random variable or process
• Stochastic variable or process

Random numbers (table of)
Linearity

Equality of variances
• Homoscedasticity

Scatter plot or diagram
Nonparametric statistics
Statistical power

Discussion Questions

1. Think of at least two examples of research problems for which you would want to use descriptive (meaning noninferential) statistics and two for which you would definitely want to use inferential statistics. What are they key differences between your two groups of examples?

2. What can you learn from comparing the empirical distribution from data you have gathered to the theoretical distribution that is the normal curve? Why might it be important to know this?

3. Discuss the differences between a random and a biased procedure for selecting a sample from a population. Now consider the differences between randomness and bias in assigning subjects to control and experimental groups. How does using a random procedure help you avoid bias?

Self-Test

If you can answer most of the following questions accurately, you can feel confident about your understanding of the material in this chapter. If not, it would be a good idea to review the chapter. (Answers can be found in the Appendix.)

1. To describe the central tendency of the annual salary of employed adults in the United States, the median is a better measure than the mean. True or False?

2. The mean cannot be used as a measure of central tendency when the data are skewed. True or False?

3. Whenever a distribution has only one peak (is unimodal), the mean and the median will have the same value. True or False?

4. A few extreme scores (outliers) will have a bigger effect on the mean than on the median. True or False?

5. If your statistics professor tells you that "Your score on the exam was zero—your *z*-score, that is," this means
   a. You did worse on the examination than all the other students who took the exam.
   b. All the other students scored lower than you did.
   c. Your score was the same as the class mean score.
   d. The standard deviation of the scores in your class was zero.

6. Which of the following is true of *z*-scores?
   a. They can be calculated only on data measured at the ordinal level.
   b. They are expressed in standard deviation units.
   c. They are not as reliable as standard scores.
   d. Their distribution tends to be more platykurtic than the original distribution on which they were calculated.
   e. All of the above are true.

7. A distribution that is negatively or left skewed has
   a. A large number of low scores.
   b. A large number of high scores.
   c. Many scores clustered in the middle of the distribution.
   d. Few scores clustered in the middle of the distribution.

8. Which of the following is least likely to approximate a normal distribution?
   a. IQ test scores of a large group of third graders.
   b. SAT scores of the students who applied to a large university.
   c. The incomes of U.S. adults.
   d. The birth weights of all children born in Chicago last year.

9. In which of the following series of scores would the standard deviation be the largest?
   a. 1, 12, 23, 34, 45, 56, 67.
   b. 234, 235, 235, 236, 237, 237, 238.
   c. −82, −84, −84, −85, −86, −87, −88.
   d. 798, 799, 800, 802, 804, 805, 806.

10. Which of the following is true about the exam scores described in the stem-and-leaf diagram?

    ### Exam Scores for 29 Students

Stem	Leaves
4	3
5	4
6	899
7	157899
8	2222345689
9	13345667

    a. The modal score is 82.
    b. The median score is 82.
    c. The distribution is left skewed.
    d. All of the above are true.

11. How many dots on a scatter plot or scatter diagram would you need to plot the scores of 30 students on two exams?
    a. 60
    b. 15
    c. 30
    d. 2
    e. The number cannot be determined from the information given.

12. Scores on a very difficult exam would tend to be positively or right skewed. True or False?

Endnotes

1. Fields of study can be partly defined by how they label the persons or things they study. Psychologists often study *subjects*, though more recently these have come to be called *participants*. Anthropologists talk to *informants*, and survey researchers tell us what *respondents* have said. *Subjects* and *cases* have traditionally been the most generic terms. Today

these are out of fashion. Using them can lead to charges of political incorrectness, but, because there are no universally accepted alternatives, I continue to use them.

2. True replication can occur when researchers use the same database, such as the National Educational Longitudinal Study (NELS), to examine the same question using the same methods. This is done mostly when one researcher suspects that another has made a technical error.

3. To figure out how many correlations you would get, multiply the number of variables times itself and subtract the duplicates. So, if you had 10 variables, you would multiply 10 times 10 to get 100. You'd subtract 10 (the diagonal correlations of each variable with itself) to get 90. Then you'd divide the result by 2 to eliminate the duplicate correlations in the upper right or lower left of the table. So, the answer is 45. In symbols, if X is the number of variables, the number of pairs equals $(X^2 - X)/2$.

4. The box-and-whisker diagram is another useful graphic technique, and it is particularly good for comparing distributions. See Glass and Hopkins (1996) for a brief discussion.

5. Also, a raw score increase—of say 8 points—will have more effect on the percentile rank when it is toward the top or the bottom of the distribution than when it is near the middle of the distribution of scores.

6. The reader will note that several of these terms have appeared before. They will be listed again—when we look at some of the same concepts in greater depth or from a different perspective.

5

Surveys and Sampling

No form of research is more familiar to most people than survey research. It is nearly impossible to avoid. Millions of people are surveyed every year, as we all know by the annoying phone calls and junk mail. Many of the surveys we encounter are bogus. These surveys aren't really trying to learn something about respondents but are rather pretexts to get our attention and sell us something or encourage us to make a contribution. Even subtracting these phony surveys, the number and influence of real surveys is great. Governments routinely survey citizens about matters of fact, such as employment status. Businesses conduct surveys to gauge customer satisfaction or learn about the features of products customers might prefer. Educational institutions often survey their clientele about their needs. And millions of college and university students are surveyed each year when they fill out forms to evaluate their courses and instructors.

Regardless of the purpose or audience, two questions are key to assessing any survey. First, can you learn what you want to know by asking people? Second, can you generalize from what people tell you (your sample) to a broader group (your target population)? The answer to the first question has a lot to

do with the survey's quality—what you ask and how you ask it. It is a matter of design. The answer to the second question—Can you generalize?—is mostly determined by the quality of your sample, particularly its representativeness. And representativeness, in turn, is determined by the statistical properties of your sample. Well-designed questions and appropriate sampling techniques are the two components of good survey research.

When the term *survey* is used, it usually refers to a sample survey. When one surveys the entire population, as is done every 10 years in the United States, the activity is often called a *census* (of a population) rather than a survey (of a sample). For large populations, such as all persons residing in the United States, a sample survey can be better (contain less error and cost less) than a census. For example, the Current Population Survey is conducted monthly for the Bureau of Labor Statistics by the Census Bureau. Fifty thousand households are surveyed; for many questions it is much more accurate and up-to-date than the census.

Selecting a sample to study is important in all kinds of research, but modern sampling theory has mostly developed around survey research, and that is how this chapter approaches it. More specifically, this chapter examines the following questions.

1. What criteria define a good sample?
2. What are the main varieties of probability samples?
3. What can be learned from nonprobability samples?
4. How important is sample size?
5. How can surveys be designed to elicit the most valuable responses?
6. How can questions be written so they will lead to effective measurement?
7. How can responses to survey questions be analyzed?
8. When are surveys likely to be a wise design choice?

What Criteria Define a Good Sample?

Everybody knows quite a bit about sampling, if they just think it through. Applied statistics is largely a matter of common sense. Although, in the study of research methods, the common sense is made more systematic and abstract, the basic ideas usually remain clear enough. This is especially the case if we begin with examples rather than general principles.

Take the following case. You enter the grocery store and see a table displaying a batch of grapes. Atop the pile is a sign that reads "Tasty grapes. Only $1.99 a pound!" You say to yourself, "I was planning to make a lot of jelly. Maybe I'll buy the whole batch. And $1.99 is a good price—but only if the grapes really are tasty." How would you find out whether the grapes really were tasty? You would have to *sample* them, of course.

The key questions that arise in any sampling situation and that get to the heart of sampling theory are: (1) How many of the grapes would you need to taste? and (2) How would you choose the ones to taste? General answers to the questions are obvious: (1) The more you tasted, the more certain you could be that your inference is correct; and (2) the more

typical or representative the grapes you tasted, the more certain you could be of any generalizations you make about the whole pile. The grape tasting problem reveals the essence of sampling theory. The degree of certainty of generalizations from the sample to the population depends on (1) the size and (2) the representativeness of the sample. The rest is technical details, footnotes if you will. Of the two, representativeness is more important.

The same principles apply when you sample anything. If you want to know what students at a university think of a new course requirement, your sampling procedures raise the same two questions. How many students do you need to ask? How do you select them so that they are representative of all the students? Both are important, but in the following paragraphs, we will focus mainly on the more fundamental issue of how to select a sample so as to make it representative.

Sampling involves selecting a small group from a larger group and studying the small group (the sample) in order to learn about the large group (the population). This works only if the sample is representative of the population. An unrepresentative sample tells us nothing useful about the population. Sampling is important in almost all research. Most researchers sample; they select from a pool of cases or subjects. This is true whether they are choosing a single case for an ethnographic study or whether they identify a thousand respondents to answer survey questions

What Are the Main Varieties of Probability Samples?

The two main categories of sampling are (1) those methods in which researchers know the probability of choosing subjects or cases from a population and (2) those methods in which researchers do not know the probability of selecting subjects or cases from a population. The first category is probability samples. Probability samples are always preferable but not always possible. There are four main types of probability samples—random, stratified, systematic, and cluster.

Random Sampling

What is usually called a *random sample* would be better labeled an *equal probability sample,* because in a random sample each member of the population has an equal probability of being selected for inclusion in the sample. As seen in Chapter 4, a truly random process for selecting a sample takes effort. When people first learn about the importance of randomness in research, confusion often arises. In ordinary English, the word *random* connotes many things besides equal probability, such as haphazard, aimless, and whimsical. But researchers cannot achieve an unbiased probability sample taking a casual or haphazard approach to sampling. And eliminating *bias* is the chief reason for conducting random samples. A biased sample occurs when some members of the population are systematically overrepresented. Because a random sample ensures that every member of the population has an equal probability of being selected, it removes bias from the process of selection.

The rules governing random selection of a sample and random assignment of subjects to treatment groups (see Chapter 6) are rigorous. Random selection or sampling is used to maximize the sample's representativeness by eliminating bias. Although random sampling eliminates bias, it does not eliminate sampling error. Some *sampling error* will always occur. There will always be some difference between the sample and the population. But random sampling minimizes sampling error. Most important, random sampling enables the researcher to estimate both the size and the likelihood of sampling error.

Random sampling is also known as *simple* random sampling to distinguish it from other forms, especially stratified random sampling. Simple random sampling uses a process to select or assign subjects, such as flipping a fair coin or rolling balanced dice or having a computer generate random numbers to use in identifying people in a numbered list about whom data will be gathered.

A key goal of random sampling is to maximize *external validity.* External validity refers to the degree to which the results drawn from the sample can accurately be generalized beyond the subjects taking part in the study (see Chapter 7). In other terms, a measure of external validity helps answer the question: How much does information about your *sample* also provide information about your *population*?

It is also important to remember that significance testing assumes random sampling. What is being tested in significance testing is the likelihood that a result would occur in a *random* sample if no such result existed (null hypothesis) in the population from which the sample was drawn. There is no way to calculate a valid estimate of that likelihood (the *p*-value) unless the sample is random. Of course, researchers can pretend; they can act as if the nonrandom sample that they are studying has been randomly drawn from a population. Then they can calculate a *p*-value, and computer programs routinely do this by default. But the resulting number will convey little real information. Yet, this nearly meaningless measure is *very* often calculated. Researchers appear to be answering the question: *If* this were a random sample from some unknown population, what *would be* the statistical significance of my findings?

Providing answers to such hypothetical questions is very common, although researchers are not always frank about the kind of question they are actually answering. Sometimes the terms *hypothetical population* and *abstract* (not concrete) population are used when researchers want to generalize about an unknown or unspecified population. One reason this is so common is that researchers often want to generalize about *future* populations. When we sample from, say, a population of high school seniors or a population of cancer patients, we rarely want to learn *only* about them. Researchers usually also want to learn something about future populations of seniors or of patients. Future populations have *not* been sampled, because, obviously, they do not yet exist. However, statistical tests are based on the assumption that you have sampled from a real population. A statistically significant result is one that can be generalized to that real population, not to a hypothetical or an abstract or a future population.

Making inferences about a future population or about a population from which one has not sampled can be done, of course, and sometimes quite properly. Even though such inferences are not based on statistics and sampling theory, they can be valuable. For example, it is not unreasonable to assume that something learned about heart disease patients in California would be true in other states (or next year) as well. But the reasonableness of that assumption is not based on probability and sampling theory. It is based on the assumptions that hearts in California are not fundamentally different from hearts in the rest of the country, and that the human heart is not likely to change much in coming years. These kinds of assumptions would be less likely to be true about political attitudes. Attitudes, unlike human organs, are quite likely to vary by region and to change over time.

Finally, when possible, random sampling should be done with *replacement*. This means that after a case (person, school, city, whatever) has been selected, it is returned to the population before the next case is selected. If you don't replace, you won't have an equal probability sample, because the later cases selected for the sample will have a higher probability of being chosen. Think of drawing a sample from a deck of cards. The chances of drawing a particular card are 1 out of 52. If you don't put the first card you pick back in the deck, the chances of picking any of the remaining cards is 1 out of 51. If you repeat, the chances for the next card will be 1 out of 50, and so on. In practice, most sampling is done without replacement, and this is not a great cause for concern. When drawing a comparatively small sample from a fairly large population, sampling without replacement causes only minor inaccuracies, so minor that they can usually be safely ignored.

Stratified Random Sampling

To do *stratified* random sampling you first select groups or "strata" from a population and then use the techniques of simple random sampling within each of those groups. Stratifying is commonly done when researchers want to compare groups that are not equally represented in the population. For instance, if you wanted to compare the opinions of male and female nurses on some issue, a simple random sample might not produce enough males for statistical analysis. So, if your research question involved comparing males and females, you would be better off to stratify on the basis of gender. There are several ways to do this, but the general idea is that you randomly select, for example, 250 female nurses from the population of female nurses and 250 male nurses from the population of male nurses. Each group of nurses would be representative of its population, but the total sample of 500 would not be representative of the total population of all nurses. The males would be overrepresented.

Systematic Sampling

Systematic sampling is widely used when random sampling would be inconvenient, which is most of the time. The researcher selects every "*n*th" person from a list of the population, such as a telephone directory. For example, if you wanted to survey 500 students at a college, and the telephone directory contained the names of 5,000 students, you would select every tenth student. Your starting point on the list, the first student you select, should be chosen at random. You could consult a table of random numbers or use a computer program that generated random numbers or roll a pair of dice. Say your random number were an 8. Then, for your sample, you would select the eighth, eighteenth, twenty-eighth, and so forth students listed. Unless the list contains some recurring pattern, the results of systematic sampling using a random starting point will be hard to distinguish from a simple random sample. On the other hand, if the list is clustered by the date on which people joined an organization or by geography, it could be biased; using it would not closely approximate a simple random sample. Generally, alphabetical lists can be assumed to be free of this kind of bias.

A key question that comes up with systematic sampling also applies to all types of sampling: How good is the list of the members of the population? A telephone directory of college students would be an incomplete record of the population of students, for several reasons. Some students wouldn't have phones and would not be included. Others might have unlisted cell phone numbers. Still other students may have transferred into the college after the directory was printed. Others may have dropped out. Differences between the population and the researchers' list of the population—called the *sampling frame*—are one source of error. Clearly, lists vary in quality. One of the marks of a good study is that the researchers use the best possible list of the members of the population. For example, if you wanted to study the faculty members at a college, the annually published faculty directory would not be as good a list as the one you might be able to get from the college's personnel office immediately before you conducted your survey.

Cluster Sampling

Cluster sampling—also called multilevel sampling—is another method used when random sampling would be difficult or impossible. It involves randomly sampling convenient clusters of the population one or more times before using random sampling to choose individuals within those clusters. National educational databases, such as those compiled by the National Center for Education Statistics (NCES), are usually put together using cluster sampling. Say we want to measure the educational progress of all school students in the United States and are seeking to draw a representative national sample to study. No list of all 50 million school students exists. The absence of such a list makes both random and systematic sampling impossible—not just hard, impossible. But we do have lists of all school districts. Within districts we can get lists of all schools, and within schools we can get lists of all classrooms. A typical sampling strategy would be to sample first districts, then schools, then classrooms, and then students within each classroom.

We might randomly sample 300 of the roughly 15,000 districts. Within each district we could randomly select 2 schools, perhaps stratifying by level (one K–8 school and one high school). Within each school we might select 2 classes. Finally, within each class we would randomly select 10 students. This procedure would give us a sample of 12,000 students ($300 \times 2 \times 2 \times 10 = 12,000$). The technique is called a multilevel cluster sample. Such huge samples are actually fairly common. One of the newest of these is the Educational Longitudinal Study (ELS). It follows the educational careers of some twenty thousand students who were high school sophomores in 2002.

Conclusions on Probability Sampling

The main problem with cluster sampling is that each level or cluster adds to sampling error. Whenever we sample there is some difference (error) between the sample and the population. If we sample four times we build error upon error—four times. The sample of districts will not be *exactly* representative of the population of districts. And the samples of schools, classrooms, and students will not be exactly representative of their respective populations either. So even though cluster sampling is often the only reasonable alternative, it must be used with caution and then not unless it is necessary. The same is true of stratified sampling. Inexperienced researchers often rush to stratify. They tend to want to stratify on all "important" variables. But this assumes that they already *know in advance* what is important. Unlike stratified sampling, random sampling equalizes the effects of *all* variables, including those that the researcher has not thought of. So, the best general rule of thumb is to use stratification or clustering *only* when your research questions demand it. Otherwise simple random sampling or one of its approximations, such as systematic sampling, is a better bet.

The chief criterion of a good sample is that it is representative of the population. The techniques just described vary in the ways they approach that common goal. For example, it is important to note that systematic and cluster sampling aim to approximate random sampling. Stratified random sampling does not try to approximate random sampling, except within strata. Researchers need to opt for different techniques depending on the character of the populations about which they aim to generalize, called the target populations. If you want to generalize about all teachers in a large district, they are your target population. Simple random sampling or systematic sampling would work best for that population. If you wanted to generalize about all teachers in the United States, however, you would probably have to use cluster sampling, perhaps first sampling districts and then teachers within districts. If you wanted to compare male and female teachers, you would probably stratify by gender. In that case you could think of your research as having two populations from which you would sample, the population of all the male and of all the female teachers. You might also use stratified sampling for other groups, such as ethnic groups, unlikely to be found in sufficient numbers if you used random sampling. In that case you would stratify by ethnicity. This strategy is also referred to as *oversampling,* because it yields a larger sample of members of the smaller groups than would be likely if simple random or systematic sampling had been used.

What Can Be Learned from Nonprobability Samples?

All of the above examples—random, stratified random, systematic, and cluster sampling—are *probability samples.* They are called this because cases or subjects have a *known probability* of being selected. Much sampling in educational and medical research is not random or probability sampling. Many varieties of nonprobability sampling exist. The two most common are convenience samples and purposive samples.

Convenience Samples

The *convenience sample* (also known as the opportunity sample) is probably the most widely used of all sampling techniques, and it is the least justifiable. Because it is convenient to do so, professors often study students in their classrooms; researchers survey people in their hometowns. There is nothing wrong with this—as long as you are willing to confine yourself to talking only about your sample. As long as you do not try to generalize the results from your convenience sample, or do so with *extreme* caution, all is well. Inferential statistics do not make a lot of sense with convenience samples, although this almost never prevents people from computing these statistics. Researchers hardly ever want to say what they should say about convenience samples: "I studied these folks for no very good reason, except that it was easy; and there is no very good reason for you to be interested in my conclusions, because the sample is wholly unrepresentative." Such a statement would be true in most cases, but it may be too harsh in some.

Purposive Samples

Another form of nonprobability sample, and a very important one, is the *purposive sample.* This sample is gathered deliberately, with a purpose in mind, but not randomly. The cases chosen might be selected because they seem typical or perhaps because they are diverse. Purposive sampling is probably the most common form of sampling in experiments and quasi-experiments, but it is widely used in surveys too. When a probability sample is not possible, researchers can still take deliberate steps to try to make the people or cases they study "representative in a purposive sense" (Shadish, Cook, & Campbell, 2002, p. 355).

For example, Vogt and McKenna (1998) studied the attitudes of teachers and future teachers in New York State who were taking university courses. They sampled from a diverse group of universities (public and private, large and small). Although this sample was in no sense representative, it was possible to say something about how typical it was. Many of the questions on the survey were drawn from surveys of nationally representative samples; this enabled the researchers to compare the attitudes of teachers in their purposive sample to teachers in national samples and to those of the general public. In a follow-up study, a further purposive sample (Agafonov, 1999) of teachers in Russia was surveyed, and their attitudes were compared to the New York group. Because these samples were not probability samples, any conclusions comparing teachers in the United States to those in Russia had to be extremely tentative.

Even in large, well-funded national studies, purposive sampling is sometimes the only practical alternative. For example, the National Institute of Child Health and Human Development (NICHD) has conducted a longitudinal Study of Early Child Care of over 1,000 children. The children were followed from birth to age four and one-half. How were the children selected? In 10 sites throughout the United States all women giving birth during a selected 24-hour period "were screened for eligibility and willingness to be contacted again" (NICHD, 2002, p. 136). The screening criteria were extensive and seemed mostly designed to ensure that the researchers could do their work: The mother had to speak English, live within three hours of the hospital, and live in a "neighborhood [that] was not too dangerous to visit." About 5,400 mothers met the criteria. Then a stratified random sample (stratified on the basis of criteria such as education level and ethnicity) was selected. Eventually some 1,300 mothers "completed a home interview when the infant was 1 month old and became study participants." Because the goal was to be nationally representative, the sample was not ideal, but the ideal (a random sample of all children born in a particular day or month or year) was impossible. By selecting widely scattered sites, choosing all women giving birth on specific days, and then sampling from this group, the researchers constructed what is arguably the single best database for studying issues of child development. But, the "single best" was far from being a true probability sample.

A different reason to use a purposive sample is at work when researchers seek to identify members of an unusual group. For example, Lee et al. (2001) did much detective work to find public high schools in which all students and teachers were divided into subunits or "schools-within-schools." They found only 55 of these nationwide. This uncommon group was interesting because the schools-within-schools model is often recommended as a practical way to reduce the size of high schools. This example differs importantly from the first two. In the earlier examples—the New York teachers and the mothers giving birth—the researchers would gladly have used probability samples had this been possible. But in the schools-within-schools example, the researchers were not interested in making inferences from a sample to a population. Rather they wanted to find all members of a rare, perhaps pioneering, group in order to study it.

Conclusions on Nonprobability Sampling

The frequency with which convenience and purposive samples are used does not change the general rule: The more representative the sample the more accurate any generalizations inferred from it. In other terms, conclusions drawn from representative samples are often said to be characterized by "external validity." Good sampling practice reduces *threats* to external validity (see the fuller discussion in Chapter 7). A threat to external validity is any feature of a research design that would, by using an unrepresentative sample, reduce the ability to generalize from a sample to a population. For example, students studied in one state (say, Texas) might not be representative of students living in another state (such as Pennsylvania). Also, what was true of students sampled in 2004, might no longer be true of students today. These examples show that it is not always easy to specify exactly what the population is or to be sure about how broadly it is legitimate to generalize. About whom can you really draw conclusions? There is no hard and fast answer. Reasonable people can disagree. One could just as easily ask: Why *wouldn't* a conclusion about how students learn based on evidence drawn from students in Texas also be applicable to students in Pennsylvania—or anywhere in the United States?

That question raises an issue similar to the legal concept of "burden of proof." Does the researcher making a claim have to demonstrate that it is externally valid or does the skeptic challenging the claim have to show that it is *not* externally valid? In what circumstances should the burden rest more heavily on one than on the other? For example, Roderick and Camburn (1999) concluded that students who fail a course in the ninth grade are at great risk of not graduating from high school. This conclusion was based on an intensive study of students in Chicago (which is probably the most thoroughly researched urban education system in the United States). Can this result be generalized to students in other districts? No definite answer can be given, but most people would probably agree that cautious generalizations to other urban populations could be appropriate. What about generalizing to other age groups? Is what was learned about high school freshmen applicable to college freshmen? Most people would probably agree that it would be a bigger stretch to generalize from high school to college freshmen than to generalize from high school freshmen in Chicago to high school freshmen in Cleveland or Miami. But, again, this is not a statistical question.

Frequent and useful generalizations from unrepresentative samples are often made in medical research. We have learned a great deal about human diseases and how to treat them by studying laboratory animals. It would be silly to claim that the mice studied in medical experiments are a representative sample of people. In fact, they are not even a representative sample of the population of mice. As the old joke goes, in medical research, even the mice are white males. Yet we generalize from mice to people. Eventually, of course, before coming to firm conclusions about the applicability to humans of lessons learned from white mice, human testing has to be done; nonetheless, we have learned much from such unrepresentative samples.

Sometimes researchers are faced with a "trade-off between good data and low external validity" (Lee & Loeb, 2000, p. 24). This can occur when researchers have access to very deep pools of data that are not broadly representative of a population. Lee and Loeb were able to use extraordinarily rich data for the entire population of students in Chicago public schools. But what is true of Chicago might not be true of other populations, even of other urban populations, say of students in Los Angeles or Atlanta. On the other hand, nationally representative samples are often less detailed than more local ones. In other terms, the choice is sometimes between local depth and national breadth. This distinction can apply in a wide range of circumstances. It is quite similar to one way to describe a difference between quantitative and qualitative research. As Ragin (1994) put it, qualitative research tends to have good *internal* validity, or clear knowledge about subjects, because it studies a small number of cases in great depth. Quantitative researchers, by contrast, will often examine a larger number of cases, but will study them in less depth. They tend to aim for *external* validity. A similar trade-off exists between laboratory experiments and field studies. Laboratory experiments tend to be strong on internal validity because, by controlling for unwanted variance, they can make strong causal inferences. But experiments are often weak on external validity because they are usually conducted using small unrepresentative samples, and they take place in the artificially "pure" setting of the laboratory.

Epidemiological researchers can take interesting approaches to the problem of generalizing from cases studied. For example, the protection that moderate alcohol consumption offers against heart disease has been established mostly by using medical records. In one recent large study (Klatsky, 2003), the records of 128,934 patients who were members of one California health plan (Kaiser Permanente) were analyzed. Between 1978 and 1998, 16,539 of these patients died—3,001 from coronary heart disease (CHD). The sample was in no sense representative, of course, but it is still of great interest to learn that "those who had one or two alcoholic drinks a day had a 32 percent lower risk of dying from CHD than abstainers did" (p. 77). Ever since the 1960s, when computer analyses of patients' records (again at Kaiser Permanente) first revealed that abstinence was "associated with a higher risk of heart attack" (p. 76), researchers have sought explanations besides alcohol consumption. Perhaps abstainers differ from moderate drinkers in other ways that would explain the association. Such *confounding variables* could include differences in diet, exercise, or psychological traits. Although the subject has been studied many times, with samples from several nations, no such confounder has been discovered. Thus, according to Klatsky, "the available evidence satisfies most standard *epidemiological criteria for establishing a causal relation*" (p. 77, italics added).

The kind of study that would provide better causal evidence is unlikely ever to be done, for obvious reasons. To be certain of a causal relation, researchers would need to select a large random sample of nondrinkers, randomly assign them to two groups, force one group to begin drinking, compel the other group to persist in its abstinence, and then monitor their health for a couple of decades. Because we are never likely to get such studies, we will have to make do with convenience and purposive samples, including samples of medical records. If such samples are large and their findings are replicated in several settings, they can provide solid, if not quite incontrovertible, causal evidence about important problems.

How Important Is Sample Size?

What about sample size? Thus far we have mostly talked about the representativeness of the sample because the representativeness of a sample is typically more important than its size. But among equally representative samples, bigger is *always* better. The bigger the sample, the smaller the sampling error and the greater the statistical power. In other words, large samples are more likely to be representative of the populations from which they were drawn, and researchers using large samples are more likely to be able to detect true relations among variables. A little reflection makes it clear why a large sample gives a more accurate picture of a population. Say you wanted to estimate the average GPA of 50 students in an undergraduate class. You could take a random sample of 2 students, compute their mean GPA, and then try to generalize that to the population (the class of 50). But the 2 students you selected could easily be atypical, and your generalization about the whole class easily could be faulty. However, if you took a random sample of 20 students, you could have a lot more confidence in your conclusions about the whole class. Of course, if you got data from all 50 students

in the class, your "sample" would be identical to your population. In sum, the smaller your sample the less certain you can be of your findings. The practical advantages of designing your research using large samples are numerous. For example, one of the ways to make up for the increased sampling error that occurs when using cluster sampling is to increase the total sample size.

Sometimes you will read warnings in textbooks about samples that are "too" large. This is a false alarm. When samples are too large, the argument goes, it is easy to label as *statistically* significant an effect that is so small that it is not *practically* significant. But this is a problem *only* if the researcher or the reader is ignorant enough to believe that statistical significance is a measure of practical significance. Assuming no such ignorance, all else being equal, the bigger the sample the better. The price of using a sample that is too small is reduced statistical power; that is, increased risk of Type II error, which means you could fail to detect an actual relationship in a population. There is *no* comparable risk of error using a big sample. Big samples reduce Type I error also. The only price to be paid for a big sample is that it is more work to gather information from a big one than a little one, and you might conclude that the extra accuracy isn't worth the effort.

Statistical power and statistical significance are the two halves of statistical inference. As we have seen, there are two ways to make a mistake when trying to generalize from a sample to a population. The probability of avoiding Type I error is significance; the probability of avoiding Type II error is power. The two are often inversely related; that is, when you reduce the chances of one kind, you often increase the chances of the other kind of error. Another useful analogy is to think of your research as being like a smoke detector. If your smoke detector can detect even very small amounts of smoke, it has lots of power, and it won't be likely to make the mistake of missing a real fire hazard. But that means it *will* make the mistake of warning you when there is no real problem, for example, whenever you cook something. Computing statistical power is complicated (see Glass & Hopkins, 1996, for details), but the general idea is clear. *At a given sample size,* the probability of the two kinds of error are inversely related. However, and this is the fundamental point, you can reduce *both* kinds of error by increasing sample size.

The advantages of big samples are important, but, except for the tiniest sample sizes, representativeness matters more. Big cannot make up for unrepresentative. Most readers are familiar with some of the famous cases when predictions using very large samples were way off the mark. The *Literary Digest* poll predicted that Alf Landon would be elected president in 1936. This notorious mistake was made using a sample of over 2 million. The error occurred because even that huge sample was highly unrepresentative (it contained way too many Republicans). Conversely, quite small samples can be surprisingly accurate. During the 2000 election campaign between Bush and Gore, survey after survey from several different polling organizations concluded that the election was "too close to call, a statistical dead heat." And those were highly accurate predictions: Gore won the popular vote, and Bush won the electoral vote, but only by very small margins and only after several weeks of recounts and uncertainty. Those excellent predictions of dead heat were usually made using samples of around 600 respondents. How could polling organizations use information drawn from 600 potential voters to predict accurately what over 100,000,000 voters would do? The simple answer is that their sampling techniques were very good at drawing representative samples.

Usually, the pollsters said that their results were accurate, plus or minus 4%. Sometimes they added the information that they were 95% certain that the estimate was accurate plus or minus 4 points. Because the estimates of the percentage of the votes each candidate would receive overlapped, the election was too close to call. For example, if the estimate for Bush were 51% +/– 4%, his range would be 47% to 55%. If the estimate for Gore were 49% +/– 4%, his range would be 45% to 53%. These estimates overlap. Bush's lowest of 47% is lower than Gore's highest of 53%. At one extreme, the estimates tell us

that Bush would win with 55% to Gore's 45%. At the other end of the range, Gore would win with 53% to Bush's 47%. In short, too close to call. As we will see in Chapter 8, these ranges (4% on either side of the estimate) are called *confidence intervals* and the degree of certainty (e.g., 95%) is called a *confidence level.*

What if the pollsters had used larger samples? The larger the sample, the smaller the margin of error would have been (or the narrower their confidence interval). For example, had they used a sample of 1,200, then their margin of error would have been around 3%. So, to reduce the margin of error by 1% they would have had to double their sample size. This would have greatly increased their costs and reduced the speed with which they could get the answers they sought. To get the margin of error down to about 2%, they would have had to survey around 2,400 potential voters. Polling organizations almost never think that this degree of increased accuracy is worth the extra cost in time, effort, and dollars.

So how big should *your* sample be? This is not mainly a statistical question. Formulas for determining the sample size exist, but they often require information you aren't likely to have until after you've already done your survey if ever (e.g., the variance of the sample and the normality of the distribution of the population). As with so many other questions in quantitative research methods, you can inform your decision with statistics, but the choice is made on other grounds. How big a sample do you need? That depends mostly on your tolerance for uncertainty. How much uncertainty can you stand? How much of a risk are you willing to take of drawing a false conclusion? How big a margin of error will you be comfortable with? You don't need a very big sample *if* you can get by with a large margin of error. But a large margin of error means that your conclusions will be very imprecise. You risk having a low level of confidence in your findings. Statisticians can estimate your risk, but only you can decide if it is worth it.

"Worth it" is also an economic criterion. It is a waste of time and money to increase sample size to the point that you can detect things that are too small to be of interest. That would be like buying a very powerful and expensive microscope when an inexpensive, less powerful one enables you to see all that you want to see. But you do want to be able to detect important things. What is important and of interest in your area of research? This is not a statistical question. After you have answered it, then you can calculate whether you have enough power. If you decide you need more power, you can lower your significance level or increase your sample size. Another option, especially important in survey research, and discussed in the next section, is to increase your *design sensitivity* by asking better questions.

If you write a grant proposal or a dissertation proposal, especially if your sample is composed of human subjects, you will probably be expected to calculate your sample size in advance. Your calculations will be meant to tell you how big a sample you would need to attain enough statistical power to detect an effect big enough to be substantively meaningful. You need a sample that is big enough. And bigger than big enough is wasteful of your resources and your subjects' time. If the subjects are volunteers, such as schoolchildren being taken out of their classrooms, wasting their time can rightly be thought of as unethical. So you will almost certainly want to use one of the standard formulas for computing your sample size. The formulas aren't very complicated (see Kraemer & Thielmann, 1987, or Cohen, 1988). There is one big catch, however; they assume you have information that you aren't likely to have—such as the variance in your sample's dependent variable. Of course, you won't have this before you collect the sample, but in order to decide how big your sample should be, you need to have it. This puts you in the impossible situation of having to compute things on the sample you have not yet collected in order to decide how big a sample you should collect! In practice, you avoid this problem by estimating or assuming what you need from your review of the literature of similar studies. If you plug your estimates into the formula, you will get a precise number of subjects for your study, but the precision can be misleading especially if some of the assumed values are little more than "guesswork" (Berk, 2004). In brief, deciding on your sample size requires more thoughtful judgment than calculations, and you are well advised to give

up the idea that there is an unambiguous way to calculate the correct sample size. Using power analyses to compute sample size is a good thing, but it sometimes turns into a set of rules researchers follow more ritualistically than thoughtfully. See Parker and Bergman (2003) for a brief, helpful, and very reasonable discussion of this issue.

Note finally that the *proportion* of the population that your sample constitutes is less important than the *size* of your sample. In national samples of the adult population of the United States, when using a sample of 600, each person surveyed represents something like 200,000 others. On the other hand, if you used a sample of 600 to survey the undergraduates at a big university, each member of the sample might represent something like 30 students. But your risk of error in generalizing about these two populations would not differ. When a computer program, such as SPSS, computes your *p*-values and confidence intervals it does not ask you to supply the population size or the proportion of the population in your sample. The computation is made using only the sample size.

A final caution: Even a large probability sample could be unrepresentative of a population. Anything can happen in a random sample, but some things are more likely than others. The beauty of probability samples is that we know the probability that the results we draw from it are unrepresentative. We know the probability of error. That is what we learn when we compute confidence intervals, which are margins of error, and *p*-values, which are likelihoods of Type I error. In the 2004 presidential election major polling organizations (Harris, Pew, and Gallup) using very good probability samples of about 750 to 800 likely voters produced highly divergent results. As late as September, estimates of the popular vote difference between Bush and Kerry varied by as much as 17%. Some polls indicated a dead heat and others showed Bush winning by a substantial margin. Such examples should make us all cautious when interpreting the results of a single survey.

This primer on sampling is sufficient for most beginning research. Because sampling is so widely used for commercial and academic purposes, many works on the subject, from highly practical handbooks to very theoretical monographs, are available, and it is a good idea to consult one of these when you do research that involves sampling (e.g., Weisberg, Krosnik, & Bowen, 1996). Now we turn from the statistics-driven questions of *who* and *how many* to sample to the design-driven questions of *what* to ask survey respondents and *how* to ask them your questions.

How Can Surveys Be Designed to Elicit the Most Valuable Responses?

It is best to approach the questions of what to ask and how to ask it with an extended example. Let's say you want to learn about the attitudes of people served by a program—for example, patients at a medical clinic or parents with children in a school. Call it Program X. Deciding how to learn about attitudes raises questions of design, measurement, and analysis. First think about what kind of design to use. You have to decide whether to do a survey or interviews or focus groups. There is something to be said for each of these designs, but because this chapter is about surveys, let's say you decide to do a survey. Your next question is: How do you conduct your survey? Do you conduct it face to face? This was long the gold standard in survey research. On the other hand, the face to face interview is the most costly in time and resources. The least demanding technique, especially in terms of your time, would be to ask your questions by mail. Under what circumstances, with what kind of populations, would a mail survey be a good choice? Today the most common method is probably to use the telephone. How do you choose among these options?

There are several advantages and disadvantages to each method. Mail surveys, although costly in postage, are the quickest and easiest to administer to a large number of respondents. But they presume that the potential respondents are comfortable with reading and writing in the language of the survey, which for many research questions would not be a safe assumption. Face-to-face interviews are the slowest, but they have the advantage that researchers and trained surveyors record respondents' answers.

Also, in a face-to-face survey, respondents have an opportunity to ask for clarification if they do not understand some questions. Telephone surveys have some of the advantages of face-to-face surveys, and surveyors can cover much more ground on the phone than on foot. Potential respondents might find a phone call annoying, but probably no more annoying than if you showed up at their door.

Sometimes decisions about the best method are shaped mainly by practical considerations. You are an individual researcher who needs to contact a sample of over 500 respondents. A mail survey is your only practical choice. For some populations, e-mail is an attractive option that would greatly simplify contacting the sample and tallying their responses. At other times, decisions about method are (or should be) shaped mostly by the nature of the research problem and the characteristics of the potential respondents. If the survey questions require detailed answers and the population is not highly literate or is not likely to be reachable by telephone (a study of the coping skills of homeless persons, for example), face-to-face surveying is the only method that will give you insight into your research questions. As with most research designs, so too in surveys, deciding on the details of implementation often requires making trade-offs between methods that are cost effective and methods that are most effective for answering your research questions. In other words, what you can easily afford to do and what you need to do have a nasty habit of not lining up very well. Techniques of survey research are very thoroughly developed, which means that many excellent sets of guidelines and handbooks for making these choices are available to guide the novice researcher (e.g., Nardi, 2003).

How Can Questions Be Written So They Will Lead to Effective Measurement?

Let's return to our example of studying Program X. To move the discussion forward, say you decide to conduct a mail survey of a random sample of the people (patients or parents) involved in Program X. Design questions continue, but now they are linked to many *measurement* questions. What do you ask and how do you ask it?

You might ask the respondents to write a paragraph.

1. Please tell me, in your own words, what you think of Program X. (Write on the back of the page if you need more space.)

Or you could give the respondents a rating scale and ask them to come up with an overall numerical assessment of the program.

2. On a scale of 1 to 10, with 10 being high or positive, how would you rate Program X?

    1   2   3   4   5   6   7   8   9   10

(Please circle the number that best expresses your opinion.)

Which type of question is better, question 1 or question 2? One answer is: Why choose? Questions 1 and 2 provide different kinds of information. Combining the answers to the two can be very informative. If you get the same impression from the two types of questions you can be more confident about what you have learned than if you used only one type. Or, perhaps you will learn different things from respondents' answers to the two types of questions. In either case, if your resources allow you to gather your evidence more than one way, you are better off having both types of questions on your survey. You could also make your choice about type of question, not on substantive grounds about what you'd like to know, but because you believe that respondents would be more likely to answer some kinds of questions than others. Combining broad statistical approaches with in-depth methods that yield qualitative data is a good idea whenever you have the resources. For example, in one huge, ongoing study of the effects of welfare reform, administrative data on clients were combined with face-to-face case study interviews each year (Glenn, 2002), but few researchers have the resources to attempt something so ambitious.

A much more common format for survey questions, surely the most common in survey research today, is to offer respondents a series of statements to

which they agree or disagree. Typically the response options would be arranged in what is called a *Likert scale,* named for the researcher who pioneered it. This is the familiar set of choices ranging from strongly agree through neutral to strongly disagree. Returning to our example, statements for parents of children in Program X could take the following form:

3. I think that Program X helps my child learn better.

    strongly   agree   don't   disagree   strongly
    agree   know   disagree

4. Program X increases my child's positive attitudes toward school.

    strongly   agree   don't   disagree   strongly
    agree   know   disagree

5. Program X costs more than it is worth.

    strongly   agree   don't   disagree   strongly
    agree   know   disagree

6. Program X uses up instructional time that would be better spent on the basics.

    strongly   agree   don't   disagree   strongly
    agree   know   disagree

The advantages of this kind of approach have led to its widespread use in educational and other social science research. One reason is that each of questions 3 through 6 provides information about a specific aspect of Program X. By contrast, question 2 asks the respondents to give only an overall rating or score. So the Likert scale questions give specific information, but the researcher can add up the answers to the questions to get a general overall rating. And such composite rating scales tend to be more accurate than answers to single questions.

How Can Responses to Survey Questions Be Analyzed?

Several important measurement issues, leading to analysis questions, often come up when Likert scales are used in survey research. We can address them by answering questions about how to handle our Likert example questions 3 through 6.

- *What numbers should be assigned to strongly agree, agree, and so on?* Conventionally, you would assign strongly agree a 5, agree a 4, and so on to 1 for strongly disagree. Another option is to assign a zero to don't know and make agree +1, strongly agree +2, disagree −1, and strongly disagree −2. You could also make strongly agree 1, agree 2, and so on. This is probably the least important of the measurement choices you will have to make. It is mostly a matter of taste.

Note one important point, however. The responses to the statement are in a clear rank order from strongly agree to strongly disagree. But are the gaps between items in the list of responses equal? Probably not. The distance from strongly agree to agree is probably smaller than the gap between agree and don't know. In other words, your measurement scale is a rank-order scale, but the numbers you've assigned treat it like a quantitative (interval) scale. Taking rank-order data and analyzing them as though they were quantitative data is very common in survey research—controversial, but common.

- *How would you assign numbers to questions 3 and 4 compared to questions 5 and 6?* Questions 3 and 4 are positively worded. If a parent says, "strongly agree," that this program helps my child learn, he or she likes the program. But if a parent says, "strongly agree," to question 5 or 6 (costs more than it is worth), he or she dislikes the program. So you need to code the answers differently. If you have assigned 5 to strongly agree in questions 3 and 4, then you need to make strongly agree worth 1 for questions 5 and 6. This is called *reverse coding*. Using reverse coding, liking the program would get 5 points on both positively and negatively worded statements/ questions. Disliking it would get 1 point. This seems like a trivial matter, but I have worked with dozens of perplexed survey researchers who find that their results make no sense—until they realize that they need to recode the response scale for some of their questions. Fortunately, using modern statistical packages, such recoding takes only a few minutes.

- *Should the questions include neutral items such as don't know or unsure?* Measurement specialists disagree quite a bit about this. Many researchers favor having no neutral, wishy-washy options. Their argument is that by forcing respondents to take a stand, you get better answers, that is, with bigger variances. Although it is true that you get bigger variances this way, I'm not persuaded that this justifies eliminating the neutral option in questions. It seems to me that don't know or don't care are real opinions. Forcing respondents to act as though they know or they care, even when they do not, hardly seems the way to improve accuracy. Researchers get annoyed when respondents too often pick the middle response; that makes it more difficult for researchers to get statistically significant results. But nobody ever said it was going to be easy, and it is certainly no reason to twist respondents' actual beliefs.

Allowing respondents to express themselves fully is almost always a good idea, whether this means having neutral options on Likert scales or encouraging comments and leaving space for respondents to make them. Leaving room for comments has sometimes yielded important results. For example, in one survey I did of about 400 undergraduates, the second largest category of responses to a question about students' ethnicity was made up of remarks such as "none of your business," "racist question!" and "why are you asking this?" I was surprised, because I had never encountered that reaction before, but it told me a great deal about the students I was surveying.

- *Can you sum (or take an average of) the answers to questions 3 through 6 to make an overall scale? Why would you want to?* Of course you *can* do this. The real question is, Should you? Adding up the answers to Likert scales is very often done. In this case, it would allow you to turn those partial answers to questions about aspects of Program X into an overall answer. The highest possible score would be 20 (5 × 4 questions = 20), and the lowest possible score would be 4 (1 × 4 questions). Such a scale, composed of several items, has many favorable statistical characteristics. Usually, the more items in a scale, as long as they are all measuring aspects of the same thing, the better the scale is at measuring what it is designed to measure, in this case, attitudes about Program X.

• *How can you tell whether questions 3 through 6 are all measuring the same thing?* Relatively straightforward techniques help with this decision. The most commonly used test is *Cronbach's alpha.* Cronbach's alpha is a correlational measure of the reliability or consistency of the items in a scale. It tells you the extent to which people who answered some questions favorably or unfavorably about Program X tended to do so on all items. If they did not, then it is probably the case that the items are not really measuring aspects of the same thing, and the items should not be summed up to make an overall rating scale. You can still investigate the items individually, but adding their scores together is adding apples and oranges, or maybe even adding apples and baseballs. Cronbach's alpha ranges from 0 to 1.0. The usual cut-off point for a reliable scale is .70 or higher. It is not uncommon to encounter statements such as the following in reports of survey research: "The alpha for this scale was .58, which is an acceptable level for this type of measure." Don't believe it. The level of .70 is the *minimum* for reliability. Anything less and the scale isn't really a scale because its questions are not all measuring the same thing. For longer surveys with more items, more scales, and several hundred respondents, the usual method to check for reliability is factor analysis (discussed in Chapter 13).

• *If you do sum the answers to questions 3 through 6, can the resulting score be treated as an interval-level variable, or is it better to think of it as a rank-order scale?* Quantitative researchers disagree about this one too. The strict, conservative, safe answer is that you should treat your scale of 4 through 20 as a rank-order scale and use the appropriate rank-order statistics. However, the usual practice is to treat the summated rating scale as a quantitative, not a rank-order scale. This is controversial, but statisticians are more likely to object than are applied researchers. Many measures treated as interval level in the social sciences are what we might best think of as "approximately interval." A rating scale, composed of several Likert-like questions, that has

a high Cronbach's alpha seems to be more than a mere ordinal measure, but it is clearly less than a true interval measure. One alternative in the face of such uncertainty is to compute and report both ordinal and quantitative results and let the reader decide which is more appropriate.

When Are Surveys Likely to Be a Wise Design Choice?

Surveys are an extremely popular method in research on marketing, social attitudes, and education. They are popular because they tend to be efficient, that is, they can yield a lot of information at a reasonable cost in time and effort. One way to decide whether survey research is a good design choice for you is to consider the circumstances in which surveying subjects works well to answer questions. Here follow four important criteria.

When It Is Best to Get Information Directly from Individuals

Often the only efficient way to obtain information about people is by asking them. This is especially true of "subjective data"; that is, data about the subjects being studied, such as their attitudes, beliefs, or values. Do you like Program X? What *should* the main educational goal of this school be? A researcher could conceivably gather information about such questions indirectly, by studying subjects' behaviors and inferring what their attitudes and beliefs might be, but that seems a hopelessly inefficient way to obtain subjective data. You might ask people about their attitudes and beliefs in interviews or in focus groups rather than in surveys, but one way or another if you want to study people's attitudes and beliefs, you've got to ask them.

Surveys are also very useful for objective data—when these are most easily obtained from individuals. Such information as individuals' age, income, education level, marital status, and so on could possibly be looked up somewhere, but it is usually more efficient simply to ask. On the other hand, when you have access to records, as educational and medical researchers often do, using records may be the better choice. For example, asking students about their grade point averages is a quick and easy way to get the information, and studies have shown that it is quite reliable—but not nearly as reliable as getting the information directly from students' transcripts. Generally, it doesn't make sense to gather information from surveys if this can be better obtained in other ways. For example, when surveying teachers from 20 different schools, don't ask them how many students are in their school. This is public information easily available to anyone who wants it. Don't waste survey space and your respondents' time asking needless questions. Save your time and theirs for answers only they can provide.

When a Reasonable Response Rate Is Likely

Unless you have good reason to believe that a fairly high percentage of those you plan to ask to respond to your survey are likely to do so, the survey method may not be the best option for your research. Suppose you randomly select a sample of 500 potential respondents and mail surveys to them, but only 100 return a complete survey to you. You then have the problem of *nonresponse bias*. Your response rate of 20% (which is not unusually low for mail surveys) makes any generalizations about your target population quite suspect. Might the 100 who responded be a representative sample of your random sample? It is possible, but unlikely, and there is hardly any way for you to tell. One cannot compel people to participate in research, of course, and volunteers and recruits are likely to be different *in unknown ways* from those who refuse to involve themselves in research. You cannot survey those who didn't agree to be surveyed to find out why they refused, because that would involve them agreeing to be surveyed. At any rate, nonresponse bias means that you no longer have a random sample. Thus it does not make sense to use inferential statistics to compute statistical significance, because computing statistical significance is calculating how likely the findings *from a random*

sample are to be true of a population. There is nothing to stop you from computing *p*-values, of course. You could say, "Just in case the 100 who answered happen to be a random sample, here is what the level of statistical significance would be." The researcher reduced to such dubious practices is not in an enviable position. This is why, if you have good reason to suspect that you will get a low response rate on your survey, you should consider an alternative research method.

Much research has been conducted on the issue of response rates, and there are several rules of thumb useful for maximizing them. For example, guaranteeing respondents that their answers will be anonymous often helps. *Anonymity* (it is impossible for anyone to know how a specific person responded) is much better for this purpose than *confidentiality* (the researcher knows, but promises not to tell). Other ways of increasing response rates are giving respondents a small gift or entering those who respond in a lottery for a prize or asking a well-known person to write a cover letter encouraging participation, and so on. Again, if you are planning to conduct survey research, it is important to consult one of the many textbooks in the field. These provide much useful craft wisdom.

Declining response rates are a big problem in telephone surveys. The technology is much better than 20 years ago. Phone numbers are selected by random digit dialing, interviewers enter answers into a computer, and the data are automatically fed into a program that analyzes them. But for various reasons (annoyance with telemarketing, caller ID, and so on), typical response rates are down from around two-thirds to around one-third. And the population of phone owners is not representative of the general population. Some people don't have a phone and are underrepresented; others have more than one phone and are overrepresented—if and when they answer. Cell phones add another complication. Most random digit dialing does select cell phones. Depending on pending legislation, cell phone owners, a large and growing group, may be able to keep their exemption.

How big does *your* response rate have to be? The only answer is the bigger the better. Select the people in your sample randomly and then pursue them relentlessly. Big national surveys, such as those conducted by the National Center for Education Statistics (NCES), often achieve response rates of 85% or 90%. In my experience, students writing doctoral dissertations seldom do better than 40%. That means they can legitimately generalize only about the subsample who answered. Some students do get a much better rate of response, however. They sample a population whose members are, for one reason or another, eager to participate. Or they achieve unusually high response rates by using their "connections." Professionals working in clinics contact colleagues in other clinics. School principals call other principals to ask for their cooperation. In general, people who work in programs or service agencies or clinics often do well at gaining the cooperation of other people who work in similar programs, agencies, and clinics.

Another option that frequently meets with success is sampling records rather than individuals. A researcher often uses cluster sampling to do this. First, a random sample of institutions, such as schools or hospitals, is selected, and then anonymous access to a random sample of records in those institutions is obtained. Studying existing records is an important, and underused, source of very good information. Researchers using it can often achieve very high response rates, because they need to persuade a comparatively few number of individuals to give them access. And the data tend to be very reliable data, because they are not based on respondents' memory or goodwill or forthrightness.

When Respondents Are Expected to Give Reliable Information

Sometimes surveys are an unwise choice because the subject matter is so sensitive that even if you get a reasonable response rate you suspect that respondents will not be as frank as you need them to be. One much discussed problem of this sort is called *social desirability bias*. If you suspect that respondents will give you the answers they think they "ought" to give you rather than tell you what they really believe, then you could have a problem of social desirability

bias. For obvious reasons, there is not much evidence about the prevalence of this problem. People who are skeptical about the value of surveys tend to assume it is a big problem, but this assumption is hard to substantiate—or to refute. As a researcher, what would you do to find out? Imagine the kind of questions you would have to ask: "OK, question 15. When you said on question 14 that you favored Program X, were you telling the truth, or were you just telling me what you thought I wanted to hear? Tell the truth now, are you a liar?" Personally, I've found that most people who agree to answer survey questions seem eager to try to give honest answers—or to cast their "vote." And if you don't believe that your potential respondents will be truthful, why would you bother to survey them? In short, as a general rule, if you think that a particular method will not yield valid and reliable answers, then you should choose a different one.

When the Researcher Is Clear about How to Handle the Answers

This is a good criterion for judging the quality of any design, but in my experience, it is more often ignored by people when they do survey research than when they engage in any other type of investigation. In general, researchers will collect better evidence if they have a pretty good idea of what they want to do with it after they get it. Perhaps part of the problem with survey research is that it is *too* familiar. We've all seen so many surveys that it hardly seems like rocket science, and we are tempted to jump in before thinking it through.

The following scenario has become familiar to research consultants. A committee of practitioners, say at a clinic, has been pulled together to conduct a self-evaluation. One of them says, "You know, we haven't done enough to see if our clients are satisfied." Heads nod, and someone suggests, "Let's do a survey!" All agree, and they start brainstorming about what should be included. "Let's ask about how hard it is to get an appointment," says one. "What about whether the staff is courteous?" says another. "Good idea, and let's not forget parking." And so on. Twenty questions are written, printed on nice paper, and mailed to 600 current and former clients along with a postage-paid envelope to return the completed survey. After a couple of weeks, 115 responses are received, and the committee gets together to decide what to do with the stack of completed surveys. At this point, someone says, "We should hire a consultant to help us analyze all this." A consultant would probably be able to provide some help at this point, but the committee would have more likely gotten its money's worth if it had brought in a consultant *before* printing and mailing the survey. As Ronald Fisher, the inventor of ANOVA, once said, bringing in a statistician after the data have been gathered is mostly useful for conducting a *postmortem*. The statistician may be able to tell you what the research study "died of," but often not much else. Fisher's statement may be a little extreme, but there is no doubt that statistical consultants can be more useful if they help design the survey. A well-designed survey can more or less analyze itself, because a good design usually implies a plan of analysis. Before mailing out a survey, it is important to know exactly how you will tabulate the answers, and it is very helpful if you know which of your problems each item on the survey will help you solve. If there is an item on the survey that is not answering one of your research questions, delete it.

Survey research is probably the most common method used to investigate topics in the social and behavioral sciences, and, when well-designed, surveys can generate very useful information. The other major methodological option for social, psychological, and educational research, one that is less often used but more often recommended, is experiments (and quasi-experiments). Many of the most important quantitative analysis techniques in use today were originally developed for analyzing survey data. Even more such techniques were created for analyzing experimental data, which is the topic of our next chapter.

Terms and Concepts to Review

Probability samples
- Simple random sample
- Stratified random sample
- Systematic sample
- Cluster sample

Non-probability samples
- Convenience sample
- Purposive sample

Sampling error

External validity
Bias
Nonresponse bias
Social desirability bias
Sampling with replacement
Confidence interval
Confidence level
Likert scale
Cronbach's alpha

Discussion Questions

1. Suppose you worked for a survey research firm that was hired by a university to survey its students on several controversial questions. A member of the project planning committee suggests that you visit residence hall cafeterias at mealtimes and distribute your survey there. What do you think of this plan for gathering responses and why?
2. Why is probability sampling so important in survey research?
3. If probability sampling is so important in survey research, why is it often not used?
4. Think of a research question that you could answer with a survey for which you would need to use a stratified random sample. Why would a stratified random sample be better than a simple random sample or a systematic sample?
5. Think of examples of surveys that it would be best to conduct (a) by mail, (b) face to face, or (c) on

the telephone. What are the advantages and disadvantages of each method in terms of efficiency (cost, speed, etc.)? What are the advantages and disadvantages of each method for different populations of respondents?

Self-Test

If you can answer most of the following questions accurately, you can feel confident about your understanding of the material in this chapter. If not, it would be a good idea to review the chapter. (Answers can be found in the Appendix.)

1. If you are studying a population about which you know very little, and have a choice between using simple random sampling or using stratified random sampling, it is almost always better to use stratified random sampling. True or False?

2. If you read two studies, and these studies both used equally representative samples, but Study A gathered data from a sample of 50 and Study B gathered data from a sample of 200, you could be more confident about the results from Study B. True or False?

3. In planning your research, if you have a choice between making your sample larger or making it more representative, you should plan to make it more representative. True or False?

4. Nonresponse bias makes it harder for you to generalize from sample to population, but newly developed statistical analysis techniques have all but eliminated the inaccuracies stemming from this once very troublesome problem. True or False?

5. Promising respondents anonymity is usually better for increasing response rates on surveys than is promising them confidentiality. True or False?

6. If you were planning to survey a sample of all the community college students in a state, but could only get a list of the colleges, not of all the students, it would be best for you to use
   a. Simple random sampling.
   b. Stratified random sampling.
   c. Purposive sampling.
   d. Cluster sampling.
   e. Convenience sampling.

7. If you wanted to compare the attitudes of male and female engineers in a state where over 80% of the engineers were male, it would be best for you to use
   a. Simple random sampling.
   b. Stratified random sampling.
   c. Purposive sampling.
   d. Cluster sampling.
   e. Convenience sampling.

8. If you were unable to draw a probability sample, but you tried to make your sample more representative by intentionally selecting subjects from diverse groups, this would be
   a. Simple random sampling.
   b. Stratified random sampling.
   c. Purposive sampling.
   d. Cluster sampling.
   e. Convenience sampling.

9. Which of the following is definitely *not* a probability sample?
   a. The seventh, seventeenth, twenty-seventh, thirty-seventh, and so on members in a list of all members of an organization.
   b. A fair lottery used to assign students to dormitory rooms.
   c. The first 10 callers in a radio station contest.
   d. 10 names drawn from a hat.

10. Statistics calculated on data from a nonrandom (nonprobability) sample
   a. Are without value.
   b. Cannot correctly be used to draw inferences about a population.
   c. Require a larger sample size in order to be accurate.
   d. Yield smaller confidence intervals.

11. All else equal, the larger a random sample the
   a. Smaller the statistical power.
   b. Larger the sampling error.
   c. Smaller the confidence interval.
   d. Larger the *p*-value.

12. Using a probability sample eliminates all sources of bias in the sample as well as all sampling error. True or False?

13. All else equal, the bigger the probability sample the better, because the bigger the sample, the smaller the sampling error and the greater the statistical power. True or False?

6

Experiments and Random Assignment

The general idea behind experimental research procedures is simple. It is a natural way to learn. For example, in cooking we might add a teaspoon of red pepper to one batch of chili and leave it out of another. Then we taste the difference. That is an experimental design. There is nothing unusual in such a procedure; it is something we all do once in a while. The basic model involves four steps: (1) Assign subjects randomly to control and experimental groups (two equivalent pots of chili); (2) provide a treatment or intervention (the independent variable) to the members of the experimental group (add pepper to one pot); (3) provide no treatment or an alternative treatment to members of the control group (don't add pepper to the second pot); and (4) compare the outcomes on a dependent variable for the control and experimental groups (taste the difference).

This four-step procedure is a very powerful design for identifying effective treatments or interventions. The sources of its remarkable strength are (1) the use of control or comparison groups (two pots of chili, not just one) and (2) the *random assignment* of subjects to control and experimental groups—or, what can amount to the same thing, random assignment of treatments to subjects. The purpose of random assignment is to make the groups equivalent (identical chili recipe in each pot except for the extra pepper). This chapter examines the purposes and powers of experimental research by addressing the following questions.

1. What is random assignment, and why is it so important?
2. How are experimental results (size of outcomes) reported?
3. What are control groups, and why are they so important?
4. What advantage does control over the independent variables confer?
5. What are the basic types of experimental design?
6. When do ethical issues become important in experimental research?
7. What analytic tools are used to interpret experimental results?
8. What are the relations of populations and samples in experimental research?
9. When are field experiments and quasi-experiments likely to be good design choices?
10. What are the advantages and disadvantages of experimental methods?

What Is Random Assignment, and Why Is It So Important?

Random assignment might be better called *equal probability assignment,* because all members of the subject pool have an equal probability of being assigned to the experiment's groups. This feature is, of course, directly parallel to the chief characteristic of random sampling: Each member of the population has an equal probability of being selected for the sample. In both sampling and assignment, it is randomness that enables us to apply statistical theory in order to make inferences about results. Without the random component, inferential statistics are usually inappropriate. Of course, one can always use descriptive and associational statistics to study one's evidence.

The reason why random assignment is so important for experimental research is because it makes the control and experimental groups more equivalent. *Within the bounds of probability,* it ensures that the subjects' prior characteristics are equal. This is true both of the subjects' known *and* of their unknown characteristics. Random assignment reduces what are called *selection effects* or self-selection effects. For example, if the experimenter allowed subjects to decide whether to get the treatment or whether to be in the control group, the control and experimental groups would no longer be identical. Different kinds of people—volunteers and nonvolunteers—would be in the two groups. This difference could be especially important in experiments studying interventions meant to influence subjects' behavior. The two groups would be different in their behavior *before* the experiment began. It is important to remember, however, that *all* subjects are volunteers or recruits who consent to be part of a study. Fortunately, researchers cannot compel persons to participate in an investigation. We can recruit, but not draft; this means that selection effects are *always* a problem. Volunteers and recruits are likely to be different from refusers, no-shows, and dropouts. These differences may often be important, but their extent is usually impossible to determine with any precision. What random assignment does, then, is equalize groups of volunteers.

Random assignment is meant to make the control and experimental groups equivalent. They will not be exactly identical, of course. Even with cases much less complicated than people, such as two pots of chili, exact equivalence is an impossible ideal. The two pots of chili will not be identical because of small measurement errors, such as differences between "medium" onions and "large" tomatoes used

in the two batches, though the differences *might* be small enough to be unimportant. In random assignment, the lack of identity between groups stems from *random error.* By chance, cases or subjects assigned to groups will differ in various ways. Because the purpose of random assignment is to generate equivalent groups, the differences are *error.* But, because the error is random, the size and likelihood of this kind of error can be estimated (with margins of error, confidence intervals, and *p*-values), and this error has known properties. Much like random error in sample surveys, random error in experiments contrasts with *systematic error* or bias. Bias is a great source of the "threats to the validity" of research discussed in Chapter 7.

In sum, as we have seen, in research work "random" has three aspects: random *sampling,* random *assignment,* and random *processes.*[1] Random processes (such as rolling dice or flipping a coin or consulting a table of random numbers) are used to determine how random sampling and random assignment are implemented. The key concepts are *independence* and *equal probability.* In a random process, each event is independent of the others and has an equal probability of being produced. In random selection, each potential case has an equal chance of being chosen. In random assignment, each recruit has an equal chance of being placed in the experimental group. Random assignment will *sometimes* result in nonequivalent groups and nonrepresentative samples, but the special property of randomness is that we can estimate how often this is likely to happen. Randomness does not cure all ills, of course. It will not save survey researchers who ask poorly worded questions or experimenters who use inadequate outcome measures. But random assignment is crucial if you want to draw trustworthy conclusions from your experimental research.

The importance of random assignment can easily be seen in examples drawn from medical research. Dialysis patients are susceptible to a particular infection. A vaccine to treat this infection was tested in a national study of 1,798 patients (Seppa, 2002). Note that these patients were not a random sample of the general population. Rather, the target population consisted only of dialysis patients. Of the 906 patients who did not get the vaccine (control group), 26 became infected, whereas 11 of the 892 who got the vaccine became infected. In brief, two groups of around 900 were studied. One group contracted 26 infections, the other 11. What does 26 versus 11 tell us? Is it a significant difference? *If* patients were assigned to the two groups at random (or the treatments were assigned to patients at random), this is a major finding. If they were not so assigned, it would be hard to know what to make of it. The group with 26 infections may have come from hospitals with less stringent sanitary standards, or they could have been treated by less able physicians or nurses. It is easy to imagine a difference of 26 versus 11 out of nearly 1,800 being due to chance—*unless* the two groups were assigned randomly. If the patients were assigned randomly, the difference is unlikely to be due to random error.

How Are Experimental Results (Size of Outcomes) Reported?

How big a difference is the 26 versus 11 infections in the preceding example? How much was the risk of infection reduced, and how should we report that reduction? Saying that it is a statistically significant difference is important, but we are likely to be equally interested in the size of the difference. There are two common ways of computing and reporting results relating to size when the dependent variable is lowering the risk of an undesirable outcome: *absolute* and *relative* reduction of risk. Continuing with our example of infections, the method for calculating and reporting the absolute rate is as follows: Of the 906 who did not get the vaccine 26 were infected, or 2.87%. Of the 892 who got the vaccine 11 were infected, or 1.23%. The total reduction of risk was 1.64% (2.87 − 1.23 = 1.64). These figures are low because the great majority of patients in both groups did not become infected—around 97% of those in the control group versus 99% of those in the experimental group.

Relative risk reduction is much more commonly reported. The risk was reduced from 26 to 11

patients, that is, by 15 patients. The percentage of risk reduction is around 57% (15 divided by 26 = 57.7; or, more accurately, 1.64/2.87 = 57.1). Another way of reporting a finding such as this one would be to say that patients not receiving the new treatment were nearly two and one-half times (or 233%) more likely to contract the infection (2.87/1.23 = 2.33). Which of these four is most accurate: 1.6%, 57%, two and one-third times, or 233%? They are all equally accurate; they all use the same information. But a physician trying to persuade a patient to undergo a procedure or a researcher trying to get a grant or a pharmaceutical company trying to get FDA approval is less likely to be successful using the absolute method and the rate of 1.6% than the relative rate of 57%—to say nothing of the more sensational ways of presenting the data, such as 233%. (See Gigerenzer, 2002, for an extended discussion.)

Choosing the methods to report results can be almost as important as the results themselves. Consumers of research are usually interested in whether an effect is statistically significant *and* in the size of the effect, or *effect size* (ES). Investigators engaged in nonexperimental quantitative research have almost always reported effect sizes, such as correlation coefficients and standardized regression coefficients. What is newer and somewhat controversial is the emphasis on reporting effect sizes in experimental research.[2] Experimental psychologists have a long tradition of emphasizing statistical significance and hypothesis testing, sometimes to the near exclusion of measures of effect size. This greater focus on statistical significance and smaller emphasis on effect size was long true also of educational researchers who modeled their research on psychology. Over-emphasis on statistical significance can occur in other fields too (for economics, see McCloskey & Ziliak, 1996). As previously noted, as of the year 2000, the official policy of the American Psychological Association and of the American Educational Research Association is that researchers should report both effect size *and* statistical significance (and confidence intervals are also strongly recommended).

There are several effect size measures, three to four dozen, depending on how you categorize. The one most discussed in educational and psychological research, often referred to as *the* measure of effect size rather than *one* of them, is the standardized mean difference, or *d* for short (sometimes called Cohen's *d* after its creator). It is particularly suited to reporting the effect sizes of experiments and quasi-experiments. It is closely parallel in concept and computation to the *z*-score discussed earlier, and like the *z*-score, the effect size *d* allows you to make easy comparisons across studies. To obtain *d* you subtract the mean for the subjects in the control group from the mean for the subjects in the experimental group and divide by the standard deviation of the scores of all the subjects. To express it as a formula:

$$\frac{\text{Mean for experimental group} - \text{Mean for control group}}{\text{Standard deviation for all subjects}}$$

Suppose that two studies of the effectiveness of a new teaching method have been conducted and that they have used different outcome measures. Study A used a 5-point instructor rating scale and Study B used a 100-point achievement test. Say that in both cases, students taught with the new method (experimental group) did better than those taught the old way (control group). In Study A, the mean for the control group was 2.6 and for the experimental group it was 3.8; the standard deviation for the two groups together was 0.6. In Study B, the results were as follows: experimental group mean = 85, control group mean = 70, standard deviation = 20. Just from that information, it is hard to tell which study showed the bigger effect—until you convert both into a standardized measure, such as the *d* statistic. The calculations for the *d* statistic for the two studies are as follows.

Study A $\dfrac{3.8 - 2.6}{.6} = \dfrac{1.2}{.6} = 2.0$

Study B $\dfrac{85 - 70}{20} = \dfrac{15}{20} = .75$

Now it is obvious. The effect of the new method in Study A (*d* = 2.0) was much stronger than in Study B (*d* = .75), over twice as strong (2.0/.75 = 2.67 times as strong). A difference that big raises the question, Why? Maybe the new method was applied more effectively in Study A, or perhaps the outcome was measured better in Study B. Whatever the reasons for the difference, the *d* effect size statistic allows you to measure it. The beauty of the effect size *d* is that, like all standardized measures, it allows you to compare across studies. You *can* compare apples and oranges. Just convert information about them into a common unit of measurement—calories per ounce, perhaps, or grams of carbohydrates. To take another analogy: Most people would not know the answer to the question, "What is worth more: 85 British pounds, 1900 Japanese yen, or 3000 Mexican pesos?" But the answer is easy once you convert those currencies into a common one, such as dollars. The *d* statistic is a common "currency" for mean differences in experiments.

When a research study does not report results as mean differences between groups, other kinds of effect sizes beyond Cohen's *d* have to be used. The standardized mean difference effect size can be used only when the independent variable is dichotomous and the dependent variable is continuous or quantitative. This is exactly parallel to the requirements for the *t*-test, which is the usual measure of statistical significance in an experiment with two groups. The *t*-test also requires a dichotomous IV and a quantitative DV. When both the IV and DV are quantitative—for example, if the independent variable is age—*d* cannot appropriately be used. When both variables are quantitative, the typical ES is the Pearson *r*, which is also calculated using standard scores, as we saw in Chapter 2. When both the independent and dependent variables are dichotomous, then the *odds ratio* (see Chapter 11) is the typical measure of effect size. These ES choices are summarized in Table 6.1. Beyond these three—Cohen's *d*, the Pearson *r*, and the odds ratio—there is not much point in mastering a list of the different kinds of ES measures appropriate or useful in various circumstances, particularly because the list is often revised and expanded in this rapidly developing field.[3]

Looked at from another perspective, there is little new about reporting effect sizes. Some measure

TABLE 6.1 *Types of Effect Size Measures*

	Independent Variable	*Dependent Variable*
Cohen's *d*	Dichotomous	Continuous
Pearson *r*	Continuous	Continuous
Odds ratio	Dichotomous	Dichotomous

of the extent of an effect, such as average difference between control and experimental groups, has almost always been reported, even when the researchers' emphasis was on significance testing and *p*-values. Furthermore, it is somewhat bizarre to think of effect size as somehow the "opposite" of the *p*-value. ES is entailed in the *p*-value, which answers the question, What is the probability of a result *this size,* in a sample this size, given the null hypothesis? Experimental researchers have routinely reported the size of the mean difference between the experimental and control groups. The effect size "movement" has mostly added the recommendation that researchers should report *standardized* differences between experimental and control groups and that researchers should emphasize differences in size as much as the statistical significance of the differences.

What Are Control Groups, and Why Are They So Important?

Why do we need control groups? Random assignment is important only if we need to make different groups equivalent, but couldn't we just do without different groups and conduct before-and-after studies? (We taste the chili, add the pepper to it, and taste it again. What could be simpler?) Many experiments are in fact conducted in this way, but this kind of "pre–post" design with no control group is usually weaker than a randomized groups design, especially for drawing causal inferences.

Medical research again provides an excellent example of the importance of control groups. A phenomenon sometimes referred to as "your memory or your life" occurs in patients with heart disease.

Heart bypass surgery seems to lead to memory loss and other cognitive dysfunctions in a surprisingly large percentage of patients (Newman, 2001). But the cause of this result is not clear. Some researchers believe that, in the course of the operation, various particles are knocked loose, travel through the bloodstream, and lodge in the brain. Others believe that the anesthesia is a likely culprit, or at least shares some of the blame. Still others point out that "elderly patients, who used to be considered too vulnerable to undergo surgery, are now being operated on routinely," and this kind of patient is "inherently more likely to experience cognitive declines" (Guterman, 2002, p. A14). The ideal design for finding out whether surgery really did lead to mental decline, would be to conduct a controlled experiment. Heart disease patients would be randomly assigned to two groups: One would be operated on, and the other (control) group would not get the bypass; after a few years, the cognitive functioning of the two groups would be compared. Such an experiment would make it clear whether surgery indeed had caused the problem. The obvious flaw, however, as one physician pointed out, is that after a few years, most patients in the control group (no surgery) would have died and would not be available for comparison (Guterman, 2002). For similar reasons, it would be difficult to conduct an experiment to see whether anesthesia caused the problem, because performing major surgery without anesthesia is not an option, except sometimes on unfortunate laboratory animals. This is an important example. It is substantively important because hundreds of thousands of bypass surgeries are performed each year in the United States. It is methodologically important because it illustrates the beauty of control groups for identifying causes. It also illustrates something equally important: it is often difficult or impossible to use control groups.

What Advantage Does Control over the Independent Variables Confer?

We have not yet discussed a key step in an experiment: the treatment, intervention, or manipulation—in other terms, the independent variable. An element central to any experiment is that the researchers *do something to* the subjects. In other kinds of research investigators observe what happens when life provides people with different experiences. In experiments the researchers provide the experiences. (In several languages, *experience* and *experiment* are the same word.) The reason control over subjects' experiences is important is that it enables the researchers to determine *who* receives the treatment, *when* it starts, *what* it consists of, and *how much* of it is administered.

Take the much-discussed case of the effects of class size on academic achievement. Experimental researchers could, for example, decide to randomly assign students in the first grade to classes of different sizes (sizes that the researchers would determine); and they might decide that the control group, of regular-size classrooms, would each get a teacher's aide. This research has in fact been conducted in one of the few truly experimental large-scale research projects in educational evaluation (Gerber et al., 2001). By contrast, researchers using a nonexperimental design to study the same question (whether smaller classes lead to greater achievement) have to search for data. They do not produce data; they find it. They need to locate otherwise similar classes that differ in the number of students to a great enough extent that the researchers can draw some conclusions about the effects of class size. They have to make do with what they can find rather than study exactly what they are interested in (Pong and Pallas, 2001).

Nonexperimental researchers thus have no influence over variables that experimenters control: the size of the classes, the ages of the students, the length of time they are in classes, and the measures of achievement. Experimenters know that if students have been randomly assigned to small and regular-size classrooms, they can be sure, within the bounds of probability, that the two groups of classes are equivalent, and that they differ only in respect to class size. By contrast, researchers studying preexisting groups can have no such assurance. Classes of different sizes could differ in numerous respects, such as students' motivation, parents' education level, and teachers' experience. Such differences make it much more difficult to isolate the effects of class size.

What Are the Basic Types of Experimental Design?

The main types of experimental research designs have been described and summarized by many authors. Most of these descriptions derive quite directly from the classic chapter, also published as a separate booklet, by Campbell and Stanley (1963). Campbell and Stanley introduced the still widely used notation of Xs and Os for describing designs. O stands for observation and X stands for treatment (X-perimental treatment). For example, a simple before-and-after experiment without a control group would be described as in Figure 6.1.

FIGURE 6.1 *Simple pre–post design*

O   X   O

A simple example would be a pretest of students' knowledge of a subject (the first O), using a new method to teach a unit on the subject (the X), followed by a posttest of subject knowledge (the second O). However, without a control group, the researcher could not be sure that any gain in students' knowledge was due to the new method. An experiment, with random assignment (symbolized R) to control and experimental groups, would be depicted as in Figure 6.2.

FIGURE 6.2 *Basic randomized experiment*

1. R   O   X   O   (experimental group)
2. R   O   O   (control group)

By comparing equivalent groups who had and who had not received the treatment and by giving both groups the pre- and posttests, the researcher could be *much* more confident about the effect of the new method (X).

The number of possible combinations of groups, observations, and treatments is very large and adds up to many different experimental designs, each of which is suited to study a particular kind of problem or to avoid a particular type of interpretative error. For example, if researchers were worried that the observation could influence the outcome (perhaps a pretest would influence scores on a posttest), they could use the *Solomon four-group design*. The Solomon design is summarized in Figure 6.3.

FIGURE 6.3 *Solomon four-group design*

```
1. R  O  X  O
2. R  O     O
3. R     X  O
4. R        O
```

Groups 1 and 2 are the same as in Figure 6.2, but Groups 3 and 4 omit the pretest. Adding Groups 3 and 4 to the design controls for any effects the pretest has on the posttest.

This book is not the place to examine the numerous elaborations of experimental design. Researchers planning to do an experiment should consult one of the many design books available. The brief summary in Creswell (2002) is handy and informative. Shadish, Cook, and Campbell (2002) have built the original Campbell and Stanley booklet into a major comprehensive design treatise. Myers and Well (2003) and Tabachnick and Fidel (2001a) put more emphasis on the analysis techniques that are used with various designs. The field is well served by many good texts and handbooks, and a person planning to conduct experiments should consult them rather than doing the unneeded work of "reinventing the wheel." An even bigger risk to the researcher who does not consult a handbook is *reinventing the flat tire* by needlessly repeating easily avoidable mistakes. Experimental

designs provide researchers with powerful means of solving problems and answering questions. And, because the techniques for conducting experiments have been worked out with great care and sophistication, even a novice researcher who takes advantage of what is known has a high probability of doing good work using experiments.

When Do Ethical Issues Become Important in Experimental Research?

So why don't all researchers do experiments? One reason, perhaps the most important in educational experiments, is that parents are very reluctant to allow their children to be randomly assigned to valued educational resources such as small classes. In medical research as well, volunteers for clinical trials often want to be in the experimental group. That is why they volunteered, to get access to the promising new treatment. Deciding who gets access to valued educational resources or promising new medical treatments obviously raises important ethical questions. Random assignment is not only the best method for researchers interested in measuring effects; many would argue that it is also the fairest way (essentially a lottery) to determine which students or patients get scarce resources. A counterargument is that any extra resources should go to the neediest, not the luckiest. Thus, the goal of social justice can come into conflict with the goal of determining whether treatments are effective.

A related ethical question arises because researchers are morally and legally required to ensure that subjects of research are fully informed about any risks that they could incur by participating in research. The rights of research subjects were first importantly codified in the Nuremberg Code of the 1940s. Since that time, the sometimes gradual and sometimes rapid movement has been in the direction of greatly increased rights of human subjects. Whatever information subjects might need to give their *informed consent* must be provided before they receive treatment. But good research practice often requires that subjects not be told which treatment they will receive, or what the purpose of the study is, because this knowledge might influence how they react to the intervention. Finding the fine line between informed consent and good research practice often challenges researchers. Although research ethics is not, strictly speaking, a branch of research methods (ethics is neither design, nor measurement, nor analysis), the application of research methods is always importantly influenced by investigators' moral and legal obligations to the individuals who participate in research projects.

Researchers have committed some truly shameful acts. Exposing soldiers to radiation and not treating poor African American men with syphilis are two of the more notorious. Discovery of the latter abuse (which went on for 40 years, between 1932 and 1972) at least had the positive effect of leading to the National Research Act. This act gave rise to Institutional Review Boards (IRBs). These boards must approve all research involving human subjects that is federally funded or takes place at an institution receiving federal funds. It is hard to overemphasize the progress that such regulations represent, despite the fact that the rules can sometimes seem annoying to researchers in a hurry to get to work. The rules are also used fairly frequently as a pretext to avoid scrutiny. Administrators who fear evaluation will sometimes use "privacy" of patients or students to deny access to data—even when privacy can be fully guaranteed, for example, by the use of anonymous institutional records. The American Evaluation Association has published a good collection of articles on the subject of research ethics (Fitzpatrick and Morris, 1999), and the *Standards for Educational and Psychological Testing* (AERA, 1999)[4] is crucial in those fields. The best way to keep up with developments in this quickly changing area is to consult the Web site of the major professional organization in your field of specialization.

The issue of participants' rights is usually most important in experimental research because, by definition, experiments involve manipulations, interventions, and/or treatments. Although the legal and ethical issues raised by studying human subjects are important in less intrusive forms of research too, because experiments involve *doing something to* re-

search participants, the ethical and legal concerns are usually most pressing in this form of research.

What Analytic Tools Are Used to Interpret Experimental Results?

The final step in an experimental design comes when the researchers compare the outcomes for control and experimental groups in order to see whether the experimental treatment had an effect. Good practice requires that, whenever possible, investigators and subjects be blind to (not know) who received which treatment. If the investigators are blind when analyzing the results, their expectations cannot influence the results. Blind or not, the researchers try to answer two important questions about the outcomes: Was there a statistically significant effect of the independent variable? How large was it? We have already discussed the size of the effect (effect size statistic d). Here we will again review what it means for an outcome to be statistically significant. The null hypothesis is used in the comparison of the outcomes on the dependent variable for the control and experimental groups. Usually the null hypothesis is a hypothesis of no difference between the control and experimental groups. A statistically significant effect occurs when we can reject this hypothesis of no difference. Although the null hypothesis is not always the "nil" hypothesis of no difference, exceptions to the rule are fairly infrequent. The basic procedures of hypothesis testing are the same whether the null hypothesis equals zero or some other value.

Experimental researchers frequently test the null hypothesis that there is no difference between the means of the two groups on the dependent or outcome variable. For example, the null hypothesis might be that there is no difference between the mean educational achievement of students in large and small classes. The two tests most commonly used are (1) the *t*-test for comparing two groups and (2) the *F*-test for comparing three or more groups. The *F*-test is probably more commonly known as *analysis of variance*, and even more commonly known by its abbreviation, ANOVA. Conceptually, the two signifi-

TABLE 6.2 *A 2 × 3 design*

	Treatment 1	Treatment 2	Treatment 3
Men			
Women			

cance tests are parallel, and when either can be used, each will yield the same answer (*p*-value). The *t*-test can study two groups that differ on one independent variable, such as the difference in average achievement between large and small classes. ANOVA is more versatile and can simultaneously study multiple independent variables with multiple groups, such as the difference in average achievement of students: in small, medium, and large classes; in elementary and secondary schools; in rural, urban, and suburban communities. Whichever statistical test is used, the question answered is: How often would we get a difference this big between samples if there were no difference between the populations from which the samples were drawn? If it is not very likely, then the *p*-value will be small and the result is statistically significant. Another way to put it is to say that if the null hypothesis is true, the difference between the control and experimental groups should be close to zero; if the null hypothesis is not true, the difference should be far from zero.

Because many variations on the basic experimental design have been developed, so too have many versions of ANOVA been elaborated to test the statistical significance of the findings. If you are using one independent variable (IV), the ANOVA is called *one-way*. If you have more than one independent variable, the ANOVA design is called *factorial*. A *two-way* ANOVA has two IVs, a three-way ANOVA has three IVs, and so on. Although the general principle of testing for significance remains the same, the calculations and interpretations become quite complicated with more than one IV. For example, if your subjects were male and female (IV 1) and if they received three treatments (IV 2), you would use a two-way ANOVA. The design would be called a 2 × 3 design—two genders by three treatments, as

in Table 6.2. Using this design, you would first look at the average scores of the treatments to see if there were differences between men and women. Then you would examine average scores of men and women to see if there were differences among the treatments. *Then,* you would look for interaction effects; that is, whether the treatments affected the men and women differently.

Obviously, if you added another IV, things would get very complicated indeed. The best non-technical discussion is in Huck (2004); Tabachnick and Fidel (2001b) provide full details. Here we need only point out that no matter how complicated the design, the answer in an ANOVA always takes the same form—an *F* ratio. This is a ratio of the explained to the unexplained variance. Obviously the more the explained variance outweighs the unexplained variance the better. For example, an *F* ratio statistic of 14.0 means that the variance in scores in the dependent variable that you *can* explain by variance in the independent variable(s) is 14 times greater than the variance in the DV scores that you *cannot* explain by the IV(s). The *F* ratio is used to calculate the *p*-value, which, as always, tells how likely it would be for you to obtain your sample result if the null hypothesis were true of the population.

This concept of the *F* ratio, which is the ratio of explained to unexplained variance, is so fundamental that it merits a bit more discussion (see also Chapter 8). Although the exact methods of calculation need not concern us, the general idea is essential for anyone who would understand quantitative methods, especially statistical inference. Here is an example my students find helpful. I decide to do an experiment in my class of 40 students. After explaining the experiment to them and obtaining their informed consent, I randomly assign the students to two groups: Group M, whose members are all given a nice mug of warm milk, and Group E, whose members all get a big espresso. After the drinks are consumed, I begin lecturing on, say, the analysis of variance. My assistant, using a stopwatch, records the amount of time that elapses before students fall asleep. Students in Group M (warm milk) start nodding off after 7 minutes; by the eleventh minute, they are all dozing peacefully. Students in Group E (espresso) are better able to fight off sleep; they last about 20 minutes longer. The first drops off at 28 minutes. All students in both groups are sound asleep after 32 minutes. I continue lecturing. After class, my assistant and I examine the data. The milk group members took on average 10 minutes to fall asleep. The espresso group's average was 32 minutes for a difference between the groups of 22 minutes.

Is that 22-minute difference statistically significant? To determine whether it is statistically significant, we have to compare the differences *between* the groups to the differences among individuals *within* the groups. This is another way of saying we have to compare the explained variance (between the groups, explained by the drinks they consumed) to the unexplained variance (within the groups, which should be very similar because students were assigned randomly to the groups). In a successful experiment, the difference between the groups should be large because the treatments were effective. On the other hand, the differences among members within the groups should be small, because members were randomly assigned, and the whole point of random assignment is to make the groups equivalent. The *F* ratio, the basic statistic of analysis of variance (ANOVA), is the ratio of the between-group difference to the within-group differences; that is, you divide between by within to get the *F* ratio. The bigger the number, the bigger the effect of the treatment (milk versus espresso) in comparison to the differences among individuals in the groups. In other words, the bigger the *F* ratio, the more likely it is to be statistically significant (see Chapter 8 for further details). In our example the mean difference between the groups was 22 minutes. Let's say that the mean difference within the groups was 2 minutes. The ratio of between to within would be 11 to 1 (22 to 2).

Say I repeated the experiment in a different class. The between-group difference was quite similar—20 minutes—but the within-group differences were bigger. A few of the espresso drinkers fell asleep almost immediately and some of the milk drinkers heroically lasted almost as long as the espresso drinkers. Say the mean difference within the groups in this second experiment were 10. Then the ratio of between to within is 2 to 1 (20 to 10). The ratio is much smaller and the results of the second experiment are less likely to be statistically significant. These ratios (of 11 to 1 and 2 to 1) are not exactly the *F* ratios, but they are parallel to *F* ratios, and the example nicely captures the idea behind calculating statistical significance, which is done by computing the ratio of explained (between-group) to unexplained (within-group) variance. In other words, if what you can explain is a lot bigger than what you can't explain, your results are more significant than if what you can explain is small compared to what you can't explain.

Researchers should also report the *power* of their statistical tests as well as the statistical significance (*p*-value) and the effect size. This seems currently to be most often done when the *p*-value is too high and the results are not statistically significant. The researchers then look at the power of their test for a possible explanation. It has recently become more common for researchers to routinely report power. Remember that power is *the power of a test of the null hypothesis.* If you do not have a null hypothesis, statistical programs will often supply one by default (usually zero). But, if you are not trying to generalize from a sample to a population, it makes no sense to compute power, just as it makes no sense to compute statistical significance. Effect sizes are still meaningful in these circumstances, however.

What Are the Relations of Populations and Samples in Experimental Research?

What is the population to which inferences are made? In experiments, there is rarely any actual known population from which a sample is drawn. Or, if such a population is known, no one is very interested in it; it is not what is being studied. For example, the population sometimes consists of all students in a given semester, at a particular university, who are taking Psychology 101. A volunteer sample is drawn from this group. But the purpose is seldom to find out about these student volunteers. Experimenters in psychology are so well known for using unrepresentative samples, particularly their own students, that it has given rise to a well-known joke. The often-repeated quip (made originally by a president of the American Psychological Association) is that psychology can be defined as the scientific study of the behavior and attitudes of college sophomores. What can be the justification for such practices? What can be learned from studying such fundamentally unrepresentative samples? As with the laboratory animals mentioned in a previous chapter, so too with the sophomores. The general idea is to *find* an effect, a causal relationship. For the purposes of *discovery,* representative samples are less crucial. After a causal relationship is discovered, then subsequent studies can estimate the generality of the effect by studying samples that are more representative.

The typical procedure in experiments is to randomly assign subjects to groups, but the subjects who are randomly assigned are almost always drawn from a non–randomly selected sample. The conclusion of the hypothesis test, then, is that the result is unlikely if the null hypothesis of no difference is true of the population—whatever population this might happen to be. One way to think of this practice is that experimenters using random assignment of nonrandom samples essentially *create* populations—the populations of treated and untreated subjects—rather than *sample from* an actual population. The *F*-test or *t*-test then tells researchers whether they have successfully created different populations: the population of those who have received a treatment and the population of those who have received no treatment or a different treatment.

Ideally, hypothesis testing in experiments would involve first a random sample from a population and then random assignment to control and experimental groups. This ideal is rarely approached (see Table 6.3). Good quality research usually involves random assignment OR random sampling,

TABLE 6.3   *Random Assignment and Random Sampling*

	Random Sample	
	YES	*NO*
Random Assignment		
YES	Very rare	Experiments
NO	Surveys	Frequent

but rarely both. Random assignment is common in experimental research; random sampling is more often found in nonexperimental research, such as surveys.

Experiments are so powerful at uncovering causes that problems with the representativeness of populations are readily excused. Random assignment can be used to draw strong, valid causal inferences about a biased population, which is better, at least, than weak causal inferences about a biased population. We will review some examples from the psychology of learning and from experimental economics to illustrate what can be achieved with unrepresentative samples, and how representativeness can be approximated or improved upon by conducting a series of experiments.

Does using multimedia presentations of subject matter help students to learn it? The evidence from a series of four experiments by Mayer, Heiser, and Lonn (2001) suggests that just the opposite is true. When you add "bells and whistles," such as on-screen text, music, and images to catch viewers' attention, students are distracted and their understanding of subject matter is reduced. Mayer and colleagues came to these conclusions by studying four groups of 18-year-old college students taking a psychology course at the University of California, Santa Barbara. The four experiments used a total of 257 students (78, 109, 38, and 32 in the four experiments, respectively). In each of the four experiments, students were randomly assigned to control and experimental groups and were shown multimedia video clips containing different kinds and amounts of text and "seductive details." In all tested circumstances, students with the more elaborate presentations had lower levels of understanding as measured by a test immediately following the presentations.

The limitations of the research are clear. College students from Santa Barbara, California, are not representative of the general population, perhaps not even of college students in Iowa or Texas. On the other hand, there isn't much reason to assume that college students in different states learn differently. But what about 18-year-olds who are not college students? And would the results be the same for high school students or nurses or lawyers? The researchers might wish to examine the generality of their findings by seeing whether they could duplicate them with other samples drawn from other groups, such as elementary students—or their teachers. That would not be the same as testing their findings with a representative sample of the population, but such *purposive sampling* (see Chapter 5) would enable the researchers to be more confident that their results could be generalized beyond Santa Barbara.

Another limitation, typical of most experiments, is that the treatment was restricted in its range. Students viewed a very short multimedia presentation in a laboratory and then were tested on their understanding of the subject matter. Would experiments in a different setting, such as long-term learning in a classroom, give the same results? And what if the focus were on memory rather than understanding? And would the multimedia "distracters" have the same effects outside the laboratory, such as when watching television? These questions can all be answered, little by little, by conducting additional experiments. Persuasive research findings are often built up by a long series of related studies in which a network of questions is addressed one strand at a time.

An excellent example of how a series of experiments can be used to establish ever more convincing conclusions occurs in an article asking whether praise for intelligence—compared to praise for effort—has negative effects on children's learning and on their motivation to learn (Mueller & Dweck, 1998). In brief, yes; if you want children to try hard, to be interested in learning new things, and to achieve their full

potential, praise them for their effort rather than their ability. That is a striking conclusion. How did the authors' arrive at it? They conducted a series of six experiments; the later experiments built on the earlier ones. The subjects totaled about four hundred 10-year-old fifth graders in a small midwestern town and a large northeastern city. The ethnicity of the children ranged widely from experiment to experiment. For African Americans the range was from 8% to 76%; for Hispanics, 8% to 31%; for European Americans, 2% to 84%. Thus, although the students were in no sense a random sample of fifth graders, the authors' purposive sampling ensured that no obvious cultural or regional differences accounted for the outcomes. Because the authors obtained similar results with different populations of children, the generalizability of their findings was greatly enhanced.

The experimental procedure was roughly as follows. Children were given a cognitive task to perform. Regardless of how well they did they were told either: Good job! You must be very smart (experimental group 1); or good job! You must have tried very hard (experimental group 2); or good job! with no reason for the success suggested to the child (control group). Then the children were given a second, much more difficult set of problems, on which they naturally did much less well. After students did poorly on the second set of tasks, they were told of their performance. Then differences between the two experimental groups—praise for ability and praise for effort—were measured on several dependent variables. The differences were large and statistically significant. Children praised for their effort were more likely to persist in and get better at solving more difficult problems, and they wanted to learn new things. By contrast, the children praised for their ability mostly wanted "to continue to look smart" (p. 37). Each of the five subsequent studies following the first experiment was designed to investigate alternative explanations for the findings and/or to examine the effects of types of praise on different dependent variables. For example, when given the opportunity to misrepresent (lie about) their scores, three times as many children praised for intelligence inflated their scores as children praised for effort

(38% versus 13%). Such differences, found in the six experiments, occurred among boys and girls in urban and rural schools and in different ethnic groups. This example shows how a carefully designed series of experiments can increase the generalizability of findings and enhance the validity of causal conclusions drawn from them, even when the samples are not randomly drawn from a population.

Our final example comes from the interdisciplinary field of experimental economics. Like many experimental fields, it has been built largely on findings about university students. The basic idea is to observe subjects playing games that simulate aspects of economic behavior that interest researchers. Because researchers cannot experiment directly on the economy, they do the next best thing and experiment on undergraduates. For example, the *ultimatum game* is used to study cooperation, fairness, and altruism. It is a two-person game. The first person is given a sum of money (say $10). He or she is free to offer any part of that money to the second player (say $3). If the second player thinks the offer is fair and accepts the offer, the players each keep the amounts (in this example, $7 and $3). If the second player turns down the offer ("You can keep your crummy 3 bucks"), neither player gets anything. Many players will turn down "insulting" offers and would rather get nothing than to be unfairly treated. (Other researchers have found similar reactions among capuchin monkeys.) That seems economically "irrational" if one assumes, as classical economics has long done, that economic exchanges are motivated only by self-interest. Many fascinating relationships have been suggested by examining the results of this and similar economic simulation games.

What would happen if researchers expanded their experiments and brought their games to traditional, nonindustrialized cultures? Would they find levels of cooperation and notions of fairness in these societies similar to those of undergraduates in developed nations? Only purposive sampling among other cultures can resolve the issue and enrich our understanding of the universality (or lack thereof) of cultural norms. In a series of studies in 15 "small-scale societies," in nations such as Tanzania, Mongolia, and Peru, Henrich et al. (2001) found a great deal of variety from one society to the next. The amounts that the first player offered and the amounts that the second would accept tended to be lower in these small, traditional societies than in campus labs. More important, the amounts varied markedly among societies, suggesting that notions of altruism, fairness, and selfishness vary greatly with social conditions. This seems to challenge the assumption of some economists that self-interest is the universal motivator of economic actions and the equally universalistic assumption of some geneticists who believe that norms of altruistic and selfish behavior are a product of evolution. Experimental economics was importantly advanced because anthropologists and economists took their college lab experiments into more field-like settings.

When Are Field Experiments and Quasi-Experiments Likely to Be Good Design Choices?

Experiments can be done in a laboratory or in the "field." Each type of locale has certain advantages. Studies conducted in natural settings, in the field, have the advantage of not requiring researchers to generalize from the artificially pure world of the laboratory to the messy real world. But the mess can cause big problems for researchers. So much is typically going on in the real world that it is hard for researchers to be sure about what they are studying. For example, imagine if the study of praise for intelligence versus effort, discussed earlier, were to be conducted in real classrooms with real teachers. The researchers could train 20 teachers in how to use the two techniques of praise for effort versus for ability. The teachers could be instructed to select, randomly, half of their students to be praised consistently for their intelligence. The other half would be praised consistently for their efforts. After some period of time, perhaps a week, the students would be tested on the same outcome variables used in the experiments.

The problems that could arise in setting up such a field experiment are numerous. How many teachers would be willing to do this? Among those who were willing, how many would be able to pull it off and *randomly* select students in their classrooms to teach differently and then to remember to do it *consistently*? How many principals would allow experimenters to come into their schools and disrupt the normal flow of instruction? And how many parents would sign consent forms? By contrast, principals and teachers would usually have less trouble allowing researchers to use an empty room as a "lab" and giving them permission to "borrow" some kids for a 30-minute learning experiment. Finally, in the short, researcher-conducted experiment, the researchers could have more confidence that the students would be randomly assigned to the two praise groups and that the different kinds of praise (treatments) would be administered consistently.

One of the big advantages of a field experiment is that real practicing professionals, not researchers, administer the experimental treatment. Ultimately, most researchers are interested in how well the treatment would work in the real world, not in the artificial world of the laboratory. But, when researchers rely on others to administer the treatments, as they generally must and should in a field setting, they need to have some way to assess the *treatment fidelity*. Assurance that treatment that was *intended* for the clients, or students, or patients was the treatment they actually *experienced* is crucial in field research. Qualitative observations of the practitioners administering the treatment are often the best way to accomplish this check. Likewise, *manipulation checks,* which investigate whether the intervention is strong enough or consistent enough that it has the intended effect, are important in both laboratory and field research. But they are absolutely essential in field experiments, in which investigators often have only limited control over the way the treatment, manipulation, program, curriculum, or whatever is implemented. It is usually a good idea to do a manipulation check in a pilot study, when you are doing a "dry run," and to check again for treatment fidelity during the course of the actual study.

Field researchers, whether doing experiments or not, are guests. Even if they merely want access to records, this will require the permission of a school or hospital board or other officials for whom delivery of services, not the facilitation of research, is and should be the top priority. Such officials naturally resist research efforts that would disrupt the work of their organization. That is one reason so many field experiments are not "randomized trials," which tend to cause greater disruption for the school or clinic or agency. To minimize disruption *quasi-experiments* are used. Quasi-experiments are almost certainly more common than true experiments in field research. In quasi-experiments, researchers do not assign subjects to groups; rather, they use preexisting groups such as classrooms. They then randomly assign *treatments* to these non–randomly assigned groups. If researchers can assign neither subjects to groups nor groups to treatments, then, by most definitions, the investigation is not experimental in *any* sense of that term. But no terminology police exists to prevent the misuse of terms. Nearly all methodologists agree (this is rare) that quasi-experiments are a second-best alternative, especially when one is interested in making causal inferences. But most researchers would also agree that quasi-experimental evidence is better than no evidence at all.

By definition, a *quasi*-experiment is an experiment "in some degree" or is a research procedure "having some resemblance to" a true experiment. The big difference is the researchers' lack of control over the experimental situation; the researchers are working in a field setting in which they are more or less welcome partners. Because researchers do not control the research setting the way they control the laboratory, complex designs (e.g., factorial designs with several independent variables) are harder to implement. And, because researchers cannot assign subjects to groups, they have to use groups that have already been formed, such as schools, or classrooms,[5] or hospitals. The problem with this is that, without random assignment, researchers run a serious risk of comparing nonequivalent groups.

To reduce problems associated with using nonequivalent groups, researchers try to match groups, such as classrooms, on variables that could influence outcomes on the dependent variable. For example, researchers might try to pick classrooms of the same size, taught by teachers with similar levels of education and experience, attended by students with similar ethnic backgrounds, and so on. When doing this *matching*, one should focus on characteristics of the groups that are likely to have an important effect on the outcome variable. Matching is difficult. Don't waste your effort matching groups on irrelevant variables. How do you know which variables are relevant? You don't *know*, but a review of previous research on the subject allows you to make an educated guess.

To see whether the matching has been successful, it is vital to administer a pretest to the experimental and control groups (which are often called *comparison groups* in quasi-experiments). Pretest scores on the dependent or outcome variable are a measure of how equivalent the groups are. Quasi-experimenters whose groups have scores that are very similar can be more confident in their comparisons. This is one of those cases, more common than beginning researchers imagine, in which a *lack* of statistical significance (no significant difference in the scores of experimental and comparison groups) is a *good* thing.

Pretests are important even when researchers have been able to use random assignment. Among the many reasons pretesting is important is *attrition*. In all but the shortest experiments, subjects drop out. To compare groups it is crucial to know whether those who dropped out from the different groups were the same or different on the dependent variable. You hope they were the same, but if they weren't, at least you can make statistical adjustments for the differences—but you can do this only if you have pretest scores.

What Are the Advantages and Disadvantages of Experimental Methods?

An article by Derry et al. (2000) reporting on a quasi-experiment on students' statistical reasoning contained a very important discussion of the limits of experimental data. The researchers pointed out that experiments

> differ from everyday tasks in important ways.... Students were aware that they were being inter-

FIGURE 6.4 *Advantages and disadvantages of experiments*

Advantages

- Controls are very strong because of random assignment to groups.
  - With random assignment it is reasonable to assume that any preexisting differences among subjects are evenly distributed (within the bounds of probability) between the groups.
- The "purity" of the laboratory environment ensures that "contaminating" influences are kept to a minimum.
- Great (not perfect) certainty of identifying causal effects and eliminating other possible explanations.
- Strong on *internal* validity; that is, assurance that you are studying what you mean to study.

Disadvantages

- Much of what interests us cannot be studied experimentally.
  - Many variables cannot be manipulated—or it would be unethical to do so.
  - Experimental treatments are short term (often less than two hours).
  - Treatments must be mild (not harmful).
- The purity of the laboratory environment is unrealistic/artificial.
- Weak on *external* validity; that is, they have a limited ability to generalize to a population.

viewed in connection with a statistics course.... Hence, observed changes in pre- to post-course propensities...may not parallel changes.... associated with real-life experience. (p. 764)

These conclusions are apt, but they probably did not invalidate students' *gains* in statistical reasoning, because the students were in an experimental setting during both the pretest and the posttest. But the authors' statement does underscore the *artificiality* of the typical experimental situation, which is the source of many of the strengths *and* the weaknesses of experimental designs. Table 6.4 briefly summarizes these.

As Figure 6.4 indicates, in general, the advantages and disadvantages of experiments are fairly balanced. But researchers do not do research *in general;* they investigate specific problems. For some of these problems experiments are clearly the best choice; for others, experiments are just as clearly impossible. At any rate, the advantages of experiments are formidable. By random assignment of cases to control and experimental groups, experimenters are able to eliminate the effects of (to control for) other variables in which they are not interested. Experiments can do this to a degree unsurpassed by other methods. When the experiments are conducted in a laboratory setting, this further reduces worries about *confounding variables,* that is, variables that make it difficult or impossible to come to conclusions about relations among the variables of interest in a study. In short, experiments are especially good at ensuring *internal* validity—that is, studying what you intend to study—and they are particularly apt at identifying causal effects.

Many ingenious experimental designs have been devised to increase internal validity. Most of the problems you are likely to encounter have been encountered before, and many techniques have been developed to reduce their impact. To get the greatest benefit from your experimental efforts, take the time to learn the tricks of the trade that veteran experimenters are happy to share with readers willing to consult their works. Good resources include Shadish, Cook, and Campbell (2002), Pedhazur and Schmelkin (1991), and Myers and Well (2003).

The disadvantages of experimental designs are equally formidable. Chief among them is that there are too many things about which we need to know that we cannot study experimentally. If we are interested in the effects of poverty on children's ability to learn in school, we obviously cannot assign children at random to impoverished and middle-class groups. The purity of the laboratory environment allows researchers to isolate the effects in which they have a particular interest. But real-world effects are not isolated; they are all mixed together with other effects. In other terms, the beauty of an experiment is that it is artificially pure, but that is also, for some research problems, a source of weakness.

Experimenters have to have more respect for subjects' rights than does the real world. Experimental treatments must generally be mild (not harmful) and of short duration. People cannot usually be isolated in a laboratory for more than an hour or so. In sum, experiments tend to be weak on *external* validity—that is, the ability to generalize from a sample to a population—for the simple reason that most of them are not conducted on samples from scientifically interesting populations.

Experiments are recommended much more often than they are conducted. This is perhaps nowhere truer than in education research. Textbooks are usually written as though most future educational researchers will become experimenters and as though most practitioners will be reading the results of experimental research. But, with the important exception of research in cognitive psychology and learning theory, the vast majority of published research in education is not experimental.[6] The situation is just the opposite in medical research (with the significant exception of epidemiology). Difficult as they are to implement in many circumstances, many more experiments could be done in educational research. Slavin (2002) pointed out that new federal mandates promulgated in 2001 seem close to *requiring* experimental research for federally funded investigations. It took federal legislation, following the thalidomide scare of the 1970s, to mandate clinical experimental trials for drugs. Similar regulations are increasingly common for federally funded educational research, and they may lead to more experiments. If so, Cook (2002) would be pleased. He reviewed the arguments adduced by educational policy researchers for not conducting experiments and found most of them wanting. Cook may underestimate some of the practical difficulties of conducting experiments in schools, especially for researchers not working on fully funded government-sponsored programs, but he is surely right to point out that the cost of ineffective evaluations of educational programs and policies can be very high. Millions or even billions of dollars could be wasted on ineffective programs, to say nothing of the potential educational damage to students. Choosing research methods and finding effective ways to learn about important questions is not merely of academic interest. Well-conducted research in education, medicine, and social services can lead to immediately practical results.

When researchers choose designs to use in their studies, it is important that they consider the designs' strengths and limitations, their costs and benefits, as this and the previous chapter have done with surveys and experiments, respectively. Although no one method is best for investigating all problems, certain problems are easier to address with one method rather than another. The advantages and disadvantages of different research methods can be most thoroughly discussed using the concepts of reliability and validity. The reliability and validity of research methods are the subjects of our next chapter.

Terms and Concepts to Review

Experimental group

Control group
• Comparison group
• Solomon four-group design

Random assignment
Random process
Independence
Random error

Systematic error
• Bias

Selection effects/bias
• Self-selection effects/bias

Quasi-experiment
Matching

Manipulation check
Treatment fidelity
Internal validity
Absolute differences/rates of change
Relative differences/rates of change
Effect size (ES)
Cohen's *d*
Informed consent
Institutional Review Boards (IRBs)
t-test/*t* ratio

F-test/*F* ratio
• Analysis of variance (ANOVA)
• One-way ANOVA
• Factorial ANOVA
• Two-way ANOVA

Discussion Questions

1. Think of a research topic important to you and design two studies to learn more about it. One of the studies should be experimental, the other nonexperimental. Compare and comment on the strengths and weaknesses of your two designs.
2. Why is random assignment so important in experimental research? How is random assignment similar to and different from random sampling?
3. Reflect on what can be learned by using control groups by designing two research studies on the same question, one that employs control groups and one that does not. What do you gain by using one or more control groups? Are there any disadvantages to doing so?
4. Discuss the role of research ethics, particularly the requirement that subjects give their informed con-

sent to any procedure. Think about one of the designs you created to answer a previous discussion question (in this or an earlier chapter), and plan how you would ensure that subjects were given informed consent. Would providing informed consent limit the research in any way?
5. Discuss the role of populations and samples in the design and analysis of experimental research. How do these concepts differ between experimental and survey research?
6. What are the comparative advantages and disadvantages of laboratory experiments and field experiments? Think of a research problem that would be better studied in a laboratory setting and another that could be most effectively studied in the field. What general principles can you draw from your examples?

Self-Test

If you can answer most of the following questions accurately, you can feel confident about your understanding of the material in this chapter. If not, it would be a good idea to review the chapter. (Answers can be found in the Appendix.)

1. Random assignment is important for experimental research because it eliminates sampling error. True or False?
2. Selection effects can be greatly reduced by allowing subjects to decide whether they would like to be placed in the control or the experimental group. True or False?
3. Because experimenters control the delivery of the independent variable, they can have greater assurance about the causal effects of that variable than can researchers using nonexperimental methods. True or False?
4. In two experiments the results were as follows. Experiment A: mean score of the control group (CG) = 30; mean score of experimental group (EG) = 45; overall SD for the scores of the two groups = 15. In Experiment B, the CG mean = 100, the EG mean = 125 and the overall SD = 25. What can you conclude about the two experiments?
   a. Random error was greater in Experiment B.
   b. The effect size was the same in the two experiments.
   c. Experiment B had greater power and less sampling error.
   d. Experiment A was more vulnerable to selection effects.
   e. All of the above are true.
5. Experiments tend to be stronger on internal than on external validity. True or False?
6. In quasi-experiments, researchers randomly assign subjects to control and experimental groups, but rather than manipulating treatments, they use the treatments the groups are already receiving. True or False?
7. The greatest strength of experimental designs is their ability to provide evidence about conclusions that are high in external validity or generalizability. True or False?
8. The advantage of random assignment is that it equalizes (within the limits of probability) the characteristics of members of the control and experimental groups. True or False?
9. The null hypothesis in an experiment is usually that there is no difference between the population and the sample, whereas in nonexperimental research the null is states that no difference exists between the control and experimental groups. True or False?
10. The *t*-test and the *F*-test (ANOVA) are both used to test the statistical significance of the effects of categorical independent variables. True or False?
11. The statistical power of the results of an experiment can be raised by increasing the sample size. True or False?

Endnotes

1. Experimental researchers also use the term *random variable*. The values of a random variable are not controlled or fixed by the researcher, as the doses in a medical experiment would be. The opposite of a random variable is an experimental variable, also called an independent variable.

2. As we will see in Chapter 17, effect size measures are also central to meta-analysis.

3. The journal *Educational and Psychological Measurement* often publishes articles on the subject.

4. This volume is jointly sponsored by the American Educational Research Association, the American Psychological Association, and the National Council on Measurement in Education.

5. Sometimes students in a school are assigned at random to classrooms, and researchers can make use of this random assignment by the school to improve their research designs.

6. By my count, less than 5% of the articles published in the *American Educational Research Journal (AERJ)* in the three years 2000, 2001, and 2002 reported original experimental research. By most accounts the *AERJ* is the most prestigious and representative general journal in educational research. In some journals, such as the *Journal of Educational Psychology,* the figure for experimental studies is higher, but in others, such as *Sociology of Education* or *Educational Evaluation and Policy Studies* or *Educational Administration Quarterly,* the rate is much lower than 5%.

7

Reliability and Validity

Once you have determined your research question, choosing the methods to employ in your research is your most important decision. The choice is complicated because it is really a series of interlocking decisions. You need to decide about (1) the overall design, (2) the measurement techniques, and (3) the analysis procedures. Perhaps the most useful way to go about picking among your options is to use the concepts of reliability and validity to organize your thinking. Selecting any method involves trade-offs. Even the best alternative usually has some disadvantages compared to other methods that might be used. Increasingly recommended is combining methods; for example, surveying a large sample and then interviewing a small subsample. This is generally good advice, but multimethod research does not avoid the choice problem; it actually exacerbates it by multiplying the number of possible choices (Vogt, 2002b). Faced with a huge menu of choices, each to some degree influenced by others, researchers can resort to checklists to help them be more confident that they have not overlooked something important. Such checklists are usually structured around the concepts of reliability and validity.

Reliability and validity are important aspects of all research designs and measurement techniques.

Although the basic concepts are simple, they have been greatly elaborated by researchers and methodologists. Reliability and validity are often discussed together, but they are quite distinct. They have in common that they are important, in varying degrees, to planning and to judging the worth of all research. Invalid research is pointless. Unreliable approaches to research will also have little if any value. This chapter examines the main issues related to reliability and validity by discussing the following questions.

1. What is reliability, and how does it relate to operational definitions?
2. What are the main measures of reliability?
3. What is Cronbach's alpha, and how is it used to assess measurement scales?
4. Why does the reliability of measurements matter?
5. What is validity, and how is it related to reliability?
6. What are the main types of validity, and how are they assessed?
7. What if you use existing measures of variables?
8. What are threats to validity, and how can they be used for assessment?

9. What are the main threats to validity in research?
10. Why is a negative approach taken by focusing on threats and problems?

What Is Reliability, and How Does It Relate to Operational Definitions?

Reliability refers to *consistency* of either measurement or design. How consistent will multiple measurements of the same thing be? Is the design such that different researchers using it to study the same phenomena will arrive at the same conclusions, or at least the same evidence? In other words, reliable research can be replicated, at least approximately. Reliability, and therefore replicability, is greatly helped by clear *operational definitions* of the variables or constructs being studied. An operational definition consists of the criteria researchers use to identify or measure a variable. For example, if researchers wanted to study college juniors, they could define them as those students with two or more years of college, but less than three years; or juniors could be defined as students having completed 60 to 90 credit hours. The two definitions would categorize many, but by no means all, students the same way. Think of the examples of a student beginning his third year but with only 57 credit hours completed, or a student in her fourth semester who, by taking a heavy course load and attending summer sessions, had earned 63 credit hours after one and a half years. Depending on the operational definition used, each of these students could be classified as a junior—or not. The definition the researchers used could importantly influence findings about juniors, because the different definitions would produce different groups of students; hence, they could come to disparate conclusions about the same topic. Forms of research that do not use clear operational definitions pay a price in reliability. Sometimes qualitative researchers and naturalistic observers will gladly pay the price of reduced reliability, especially in the early exploratory stages

of their research, if they believe that by so doing they can increase the validity of their research.

What Are the Main Measures of Reliability?

There are several forms of reliability, and they can usually be measured quite precisely, because consistency tends to be easy to define and to gauge. The usual measurements are *reliability coefficients*. These range from 0.0, for results that are completely inconsistent, to 1.0, for measurements that are entirely consistent. Reliability coefficients are nothing more than correlation coefficients (see Chapter 2). Among the best-known and most important types of reliability is *inter-rater reliability,* or the extent to which two or more raters or judges agree. To what extent do different radiologists reading X-rays diagnose patients the same way? To what extent do different observers of children's play agree on what counts as aggressive behavior? Say that two judges of aggressive behavior worked with a scale ranging from a high of 5 to a low of 1. They each rated the same 50 subjects. The coefficient for their inter-rater reliability would be the correlation between their two sets of ratings of the same subjects. If they agreed substantially on their ratings, the coefficient would be high, perhaps around .80 or .90. The coefficient would be low if their level of agreement were low.

Another type of reliability is *test-retest reliability,* or the degree to which two administrations (or versions) of a test give the same results. If scores of individuals or average scores of groups vary markedly from one test to the next, the change may be attributable to problems with test reliability rather than to changes in the people being tested. Finally, and perhaps most importantly, *internal consistency reliability* is the degree to which different parts of a test or items in a test intended to measure the same thing in fact do so. *Split-half* reliability, for example, is often measured by computing the correlation between scores on the odd-numbered items with scores on the even-numbered items. By dividing the questions in two and correlating individuals' scores on the two halves, you get an assessment of the consistency of the questions, an indication of whether they are measuring the same thing.

What should you look for in reliability coefficients? Although they all differ in their details, and you may need to consult more technical manuals for a full interpretation, they all have several traits in common. Reliability coefficients are built on data such as scores on a test or answers to a survey. Researchers use the data about the consistency of subjects' scores to evaluate the quality of the measure. The several different kinds of reliability all are correlational in nature. Best practice, but unfortunately rare practice, is to use *all* the reliability checks that are appropriate for a particular investigation and to report them all. Because one kind of reliability is not necessarily related to another, all the different types relevant to the particular study should be calculated and reported. For example, a test could be internally consistent (reliable) when given to a sample from one population, but not consistent across populations.

What Is Cronbach's Alpha, and How Is It Used to Assess Measurement Scales?

Cronbach's alpha is the mother of all split-half reliabilities. If you calculated the split-half reliability of all possible halves of a set of measures and then took an average of all the coefficients, the result would be the Cronbach's alpha. (The actual formula is easier to use than this would suggest; easier still, of course, is using a statistical package.) *Cronbach's alpha* (also known as alpha and coefficient alpha)[1] is the measure researchers typically use when they want to see whether several items that they think measure the same thing are correlated. It is almost certainly the most widely reported reliability statistic. For example, you might write eight survey questions to probe students' attitudes about the fairness of their school's policies. You think each of the questions measures a different aspect of one central concept, fairness, and that together the eight questions add up to a good overall index of

students' attitudes on the issue. The questions (items) could be scored from 1 for completely unfair to 5 for completely fair. Although you might want to study the answers to each of the items separately, you also want to look at them together to get an overall measure of students' perceptions of fairness. You could compute the mean score for answers to the eight questions or you could add the scores on the eight items to get an overall score. The lowest possible score would be 8 ($8 \times 1 = 8$) for a student who thought that all policies were completely unfair. The highest would be 40 ($8 \times 5 = 40$) for a student who answered completely fair on each question. But are your questions all measuring the same general construct of fairness? Does it really make sense to add them together into an index or a scale of fairness? To determine this you could use Cronbach's alpha.

Like all the other measures of reliability, Cronbach's alpha ranges from zero when the measures are totally inconsistent[2] to 1.0 when the items correlate with one another perfectly. An alpha of .70 or higher is often considered satisfactory for most purposes. This cutoff is used because if the alpha were any lower, the R^2 or "coefficient of determination," or percentage of variance explained, would be less than 50%: $.70 \times .70 = .49$ (see Chapter 2). The computer output for the Cronbach's alpha gives you an overall reliability coefficient for your scale and also tells how each item contributes to the total score. It does this by indicating what the reliability coefficient *would be* if the item were deleted. Usually, deleting any item will lower a scale's reliability, but sometimes deleting an item will improve the reliability. This means that answers to that item do not correlate well with answers to the other items. That could be because you have made a coding error, but if you decide that no error was made, you would almost always remove the item from your index. For example, a colleague and I recently computed the Cronbach's alpha for seven questions about college students' attitudes toward affirmative action. We believed that the seven questions could be summed to make a scale. To test that belief we used data from 240 students who answered the questions to compute a reliability analysis.

TABLE 7.1 *Reliability Analysis for Seven Items in a Scale*

Item Number	Alpha If Item Deleted
Q20B	.6597
Q20C	.6498
Q20D	.6384
Q20E	.6417
Q20G	.7414
Q20M	.6876
Q20N	.6874

Note: Alpha = .7011.

An abbreviated version of the results is in Table 7.1. The alpha, indicated in a footnote, is over .70, although not by much. This is what I would call a minimally reliable scale. We can use the questions as a group, as a scale. However, look closely at Item Number Q20G. The "alpha if item deleted" is .7414. This means that by throwing out the item, the scale would be better. All the other items in the scale are good; that is, if any one of them were removed, the alpha would go down to .6597, .6498, and so on. After this analysis and discarding item Q20G, there no longer is a seven-item scale with an alpha of .70, but a six-item scale with an alpha of .74—a modest improvement, but a change it would be careless to omit. It is important to remember at this point that the reliability measure says nothing about students' attitudes (whether they favored affirmative action, did so strongly, and so on). The reliability measure tells the researcher only whether the individual subjects answered the questions consistently enough that their answers form a cluster that can meaningfully be studied together. If Jennifer is opposed to affirmative action, do her answers to all the questions show that consistently? If Sean advocates affirmative action, does he do so on all questions? If Jennifer and Sean and all the others answering the questions do not do so consistently, this is an indication of problems with the *scale,* not with the people answering it. That is what we are assessing with Cronbach's alpha, which is a measure of internal consistency reliability.

A related way to accomplish the end of seeing whether items that you think "should" hang together in fact do so is *factor analysis* (see Chapter 13). Factor analysis is another correlational technique, but it is much more computationally sophisticated and carries the analysis well beyond the first step of Cronbach's alpha. With a factor analysis you might find that, although you thought you were measuring one thing, in fact you were measuring two or more. For example, in a study of teachers' attitudes about appropriate dress in high schools (Vogt & McKenna, 1998), the alpha for seven questions was .73. My coauthor and I were hoping that the seven questions would enable us to tap into a general liberal-to-conservative set of attitudes about proper dress, a perennial issue in high schools. Although the alpha for the scale was satisfactory, it was not spectacular, so we also did a factor analysis and found, to our surprise, that the seven questions formed two quite distinct clusters: One measured attitudes about uniforms, and the other dealt with questions about appropriate "civilian" clothing. It turns out that the teachers who favored strict dress codes did not necessarily favor uniforms, and vice versa. The two sets of attitudes were quite independent. Had we not used factor analysis to look more deeply into the reliability of our scales, we never would have known this.

Why Does the Reliability of Measurements Matter?

The consistency or reliability of scales or other measures matters because it largely determines the possible accuracy of your measurements. Low reliability of your measurements could lead you to miss a relationship between variables that in fact existed. Imagine trying to measure the correlation between height and weight of children. For your measuring instruments you have a good tape measure. But to measure weight you have only a cheap bathroom scale that gives sharply different readings (sometimes too high, sometimes too low) depending on where exactly individuals stand on it when weighing themselves. The inconsistency of the weights would lower any correlation between height and weight. If the scale were bad enough, you could miss a strong relationship between height and weight altogether. If your scales are "attitudes toward affirmative action," measured adequately but not well, and "level of education," also measured adequately but not well, any correlation between these two would be *lower* than if they had been measured more accurately. Again, note that this statement says nothing about the direction of the relationship between the two variables. The correlation could be negative or positive. Whatever it is, you will *under*estimate it with inconsistent (unreliable) scales.

Note that if measures are biased but consistent (reliable), the correlation between them could still be strong and would be unaffected by the bias. If the bathroom scale measured everyone 25% high and the tape measure underestimated everyone's height by 10%, the correlation of height and weight would be the same as it would be with perfect measures of height and weight. Reliable measures are consistent, but they are not necessarily accurate or valid.

Ultimately, reliability or consistency in measurement matters because it partly defines accuracy in measurement. To the extent that measures of variables are unreliable they will lead to underestimates of differences between groups and to underestimates of associations between the variables. For the sake of illustration, imagine that academic achievement were totally determined by academic aptitude. Then perfect measures of aptitude and achievement would be perfectly correlated, $r = 1.0$. But no measurement device is perfect. Let's say that a measure of aptitude had a reliability coefficient of .90 and a measure of achievement had a reliability coefficient of .80. Here the important reliability would be test-retest reliability; that is, how consistent are the aptitude (or achievement) scores from one measure to the next? These hypothetical coefficients of reliability—.90 and .80—are very high, much higher, at any rate, than I usually encounter in social science research. They are probably higher than, say, the SAT as a measure of aptitude and surely higher than grades in courses as a measurement of learning.

What do reliability coefficients of .90 and .80 mean for a correlation between those two variables? If one variable *totally* determined the other, the *highest possible* correlation between these perfectly related variables would be .85.[3] When reliability coefficients for variables are lower, the upper limit for correlations between them declines accordingly. That is why reliability matters. Typically one reads in the research literature that a reliability coefficient of .70 is satisfactory, and I've seen many claims that .50 and .60 indicate acceptable reliability. These are very low standards. For example, what if you have a reliability of .72 for one scale and .65 for another? The highest possible correlation between these two would be $r = $ .68, even if these two scales were *perfectly* associated, co-related. Even if one totally determined the other, the highest possible correlation between them would be .68. So unreliability leads to error in the variables you are measuring *and* to error in any association you calculate of those variables with others.

Do females have less knowledge of this subject than males? Your estimate of any such difference will be reduced to the degree the test is unreliable or inconsistent. Is there a correlation between attitudes toward free speech and support for affirmative action? Your estimate of that correlation will be too low to the degree that attitudes and support are measured unreliably. And think of how imperfectly variables such as knowledge and attitudes are measured. Unlike height, weight, age, or gender, the definitions of knowledge or attitudes or beliefs or motivation are not self-evident; they are often controversial. Without clear definitions measurement is inherently unreliable, and unreliable measurements of variables lead to invalid claims about them.

What Is Validity, and How Is It Related to Reliability?

It is often said that *validity* refers to the truth or accuracy of the research. This is an apt description when talking about valid inferences or conclusions drawn from evidence. But when talking about design or measurement, it is probably better to say that assessments of validity speak to the *relevance* of the design or the measurement. More specifically, validity means the relevance of the design or measure for the question being investigated or the appropriateness of the design or measure for coming to accurate conclusions. A valid research design tells researchers what they want to know about their subject. Does the experiment really test the variables the researchers mean it to test? Do the survey questions truly inquire about the beliefs, attitudes, or opinions that the researcher wishes to study? Are the ethnographers observing what they think they are observing? Is the evidence gathered really pertinent to studying the causal links of interest to the researcher?

The questions just asked are all examples of *internal* validity; they pertain to the accuracy or relevance of the study's results for the question being studied. *External* validity, on the other hand, refers to whether these results can be generalized beyond the subjects studied. In other terms, to what degree does information about your sample also provide information about your population? We have discussed external validity in Chapter 5 on sampling and will do so again in Chapter 8 on statistical inference from samples to populations. In this chapter the focus is more on internal validity.

Validity and reliability are related but distinct. A completely unreliable measure, one that gives a different answer every time you use it, will not be valid; it cannot be accurate or relevant. But mere consistency (reliability) is no guarantee of validity. If you are using an inappropriate or irrelevant measure, the fact that your answers are highly correlated from one inappropriate measure to the next does not save you. The misinterpretation of aptitude and achievement tests provides a familiar example of invalidity. No matter how reliable aptitude tests are, they are not valid measures of achievement. Simply, an aptitude test measures how easy it *would be* for you to learn something in the future. It does not measure whether you have actually learned it. Actual knowledge is measured by an achievement test, which measures what you have already learned in the past. You might have high aptitude for calculus, and the aptitude test by which this was determined might have a very high

reliability, but this does not mean that you know any calculus at all. If you have never taken a calculus course, you probably won't know anything about calculus despite your high aptitude. Someone with average aptitude who has studied calculus for a year will surely know much more than you do, regardless of the fact that his or her aptitude is lower than yours. No matter how often aptitude tests are reported in the news media as if they measured learning, they are invalid measures of academic achievement.

This example brings us to perhaps the most important conclusion about validity. Tests or other measurements are not valid or invalid in any absolute sense. Tests are not inherently valid or invalid. Validity is determined by the *use* to which a measurement is put. What might be a perfectly fine measure of one thing, such as a test of knowledge of how to compute correlation coefficients, might be quite invalid when used to assess understanding of when and how correlational techniques should be applied to research problems.

What Are the Main Types of Validity, and How Are They Assessed?

Another important difference between validity and reliability is that validity is often more a matter of judgment than statistics. This is particularly the case for one key type of validity, *content validity,* which gauges the degree to which the content of a test or survey matches the content it is intended to measure. Judgment is most often the only feasible way to assess content validity. The typical procedure is to assemble a panel of experts to judge the relevance of the test items to the content the test is meant to measure. The experts' judgments are used to validate the measure and often lead to numerous revisions and improvements. For example, if you wrote a general test on organic chemistry, it would be wise to have several expert chemists read it to see whether they agreed that the test actually covered the most important aspects of the subject. Even if you are yourself an expert, the scrutiny of other experts almost inevitably leads to greater validity.

FIGURE 7.1   *Types of validity and methods of assessing them*

1. Content Validity
Question: Is the instrument measuring what it is supposed to measure?

Method: Obtain experts' opinions.

2. Criterion-Related Validity
Question: How closely is the measurement related to something that, were it valid, it ought to relate to (the criterion variable)?

2a. Method: In *predictive validity* one uses the measure to predict something; for example, the predictive validity of the SAT might be measured by its correlation with college GPA.

2b. Method: In *concurrent validity* the researcher correlates one measure with another thought to be valid; for example, if a new version of the GRE were valid it ought to correlate with the old version—assuming the old one were valid.

3. Construct Validity
Question: How well does the measuring instrument measure the concept (construct) of interest?

3a. Method: In *convergent validity* one calculates the extent to which the measure correlates positively with some other test that presumably measures the same thing.

3b. Method: In *discriminant validity* the researcher calculates the extent to which the measure correlates negatively with another test that measures the theoretical opposite of the thing being measured. For example, a measure of managers' democratic leadership style ought to correlate negatively with, or diverge from, a measure of authoritarian leadership style. At the minimum, the two ought not to correlate positively.

Although much assessment of validity depends on expert judgment, there are several quantitative approaches to validity that yield validity coefficients, each of which is associated with a different kind of validity. As with reliability statistics, most of these validity coefficients are correlations. Indeed, when you use expert judges to assess content validity, you usually measure the inter-rater reliability of those judges by correlating their judgments. In addition to content validity, two other main types are often discussed, and each of these two types itself has two variants. Psychologists who study learning theory would not be surprised that people have difficulty keeping these types of validity distinct. First, they are mostly measured the same way (by correlation coefficients). Second, unlike the various kinds of reliability, the plain English meanings of the labels for validity are obscure. And third, most of them begin with the letter *c*.

In addition to content validity, already discussed, the other two main types are criterion-related validity and construct validity. Figure 7.1 briefly lists the question each kind of validity addresses and indicates the main methods used to gather evidence to assess that type of validity.

As we have seen, content validity is most often ascertained by expert judgment. *Criterion-related validity* is usually measured with a correlation coefficient. A *criterion variable* is another term for a *dependent variable*. To measure criterion-related validity, one correlates the measure of a variable, usually an independent variable, with the criterion of interest. Some measurement instruments derive their validity from their ability to predict an outcome or criterion. For example, if the Medical College Admissions Test (MCAT) is valid, scores on it ought to correlate with grades in medical school. It is important to note, however, that with this kind of measure, when the predictor leads to a self-fulfilling prophecy, the correlation between the predictor and the outcome will almost always be quite modest. In this example, that is because would-be medical students with low scores on the MCATs don't get to go to medical school. Only quite high-scoring students are admitted. This means that there is not much variance in the scores of medical school students. And when an independent variable (such as the MCATs) has little variance, it cannot be very effective at predicting variance in another variable, such as grades in medical school. If students with low MCAT scores were admitted to medical schools, they would probably get low grades, and that would strengthen the correlation between MCATs and grades, but we will never know for sure, because low-scoring students do not get admitted.

There are two types of criterion-related validity, *predictive* validity and *concurrent* validity. The main difference between them is a matter of time. Predictive validity involves computing a correlation coefficient with a future criterion, such as whether an employment screening test predicts successful job performance. Concurrent validity correlates two measures occurring at the same time or very close in time; it is used to compare different rating scales of the same criterion.

Construct validity concerns the question of whether the instrument is actually measuring what one intends it to measure. The thing one is trying to measure is called the *construct,* which is another term for *concept.* Constructs get their name because our understanding of them comes from our mental "constructions." We build up, or construct, our knowledge of the thing out of observations and reasoning about those observations, because we cannot measure it directly. Height and weight are comparatively easy to measure—but what about the constructs of pain, or of normal rate of development, or of intelligence, or of social class? Furthermore, constructs are socially constructed—and contested. Reasonable people can and do disagree about what is normal and how to define intelligence or what is meant by middle class.

What construct validity involves, then, is correlating one (perhaps contested) measure of a construct with another. In *convergent* validity one is looking for a positive correlation. For example, if researchers develop a new rating scale for measuring mental retardation, they might be encouraged if it correlates strongly and positively with an older, established measure. But a critic of the old measure, one who thinks that the old measure is flawed, is not likely to be impressed by a new measure that correlates highly with the old measure. For the critic, the strong correlation shows only that the new measure suffers from some of the same problems as the old. In the *discriminant* validity version of construct validity, one

is looking for a negative correlation. For example, measures of creativity and conformity would probably be expected to diverge, not converge. Individuals high in one ought to be low in the other. If so, this would be an indication of the discriminant validity of the two measures.

Defining and measuring constructs and assessing their relationships with other constructs is the essence of science. Of the types of coefficients discussed here, construct validity coefficients are the least likely to settle an issue and eliminate disagreements. Indeed, disagreements about constructs, and the adjustments in operational definitions and measurements they generate, are how researchers make progress in their understanding of complicated problems and issues. The several types and measures of validity reviewed here are all aimed at assessing one thing: whether we are studying what we mean to study when we conduct research. That is essentially the definition of construct validity. In fact, many measurement specialists today say that construct validity is the whole of validity (see Thorndike, 2005). If this unified understanding of validity is correct, the coefficients and types of validity covered in this section are all various ways of judging construct validity, that is, the usefulness of our constructs as applied to research problems.

What If You Use Existing Measures of Variables?

Many researchers use existing measures (instruments) of variables rather than design their own. Whenever well-regarded instruments exist in your field, it usually does not make sense to construct your own unless your research question truly demands that you do so.[4] Existing instruments have often been tested for validity and reliability, and coefficients indicating the results of those tests are generally published along with the instrument. What do you do about reliability and validity when you are using an established instrument (that is, when you use a test or scale for which published reliability and validity figures already exist)? You still *must* compute your own. Even when you are using a well-established measure, it is important to compute and report coefficients based on *your* data from *your* sample. This is especially the case when the population being studied is different from the population originally studied to make the reliability estimates. For example, a measure of leadership style developed in the United States *might* work quite nicely in another nation, but one cannot just assume this. In a study of the effects of leadership style in Thailand, Sennum (2002) found that her U.S. instrument worked well, but it worked even better after she conducted a Cronbach's alpha analysis and discarded two items that lowered the reliability of the instrument with her sample. By discarding the two items and thus raising the reliability of her scale, Sennum also made her instrument more valid for use in the Thai context. Whenever researchers use an established instrument, they should first conduct a brief *psychometric* study of the reliability (and if possible the validity) of the instrument for their sample/population. Once reliability (and validity) have been established, and any interesting and important differences with previous research noted, then it is appropriate to go ahead and use the instrument.

Perhaps the practice of skipping this fairly obvious step of computing reliability coefficients for one's own data dates back to the days before computers when the computational demands of such work were heavy. Today there is no excuse. Checking on the reliability of the instrument for the population or sample you are studying takes little more than a few mouse clicks. Whatever the reason researchers sometimes skip this step, doing so is bad practice. As an alert reader you should not trust research reports that fail to report reliability and validity coefficients, and, of course, you should always report them in your own research.

Finally, it is crucial to remember that nearly all the measures of reliability and validity discussed here are correlations, most commonly Pearson's *r*. All the cautions that apply to the interpretation of correlations apply here also. As discussed in Chapter 2 on correlation, writers of research methods texts frequently warn against the assumption that a correlation is evidence of a causal relation. But some of those same authors rou-tinely assume that a correlation is a cause in matters of reliability and validity. Are the scores on two versions of the test highly correlated? That is be*cause* they are measuring the same thing. Correlation may not prove cause, but it doesn't prove the identity of constructs either. In my view there tends to be too much caution about cause in the first instance and too little in the second. It makes no sense to be skeptical in the one case (causal links between variables) and gullible in the other (reliability coefficients).

What Are Threats to Validity, and How Can They Be Used for Assessment?

In addition to calculating validity (correlation) coefficients, which is mostly a measurement approach to validity, validity can also be discussed in terms of design. This is usually done by discussing all the *things that could go wrong* when you carry out a research design: What features of your research design could prevent you from drawing valid conclusions from your findings? Since the 1960s, when Donald Campbell began writing about the subject, these things that could go wrong have usually been called *threats to validity*. They have been summarized in various ways. Because such summaries are widely available in nearly every beginning or intermediate text, I'll keep my account here focused on some of the threats likely to be most important in applied research settings.

Discussing research designs by listing threats to validity has become very popular, and the list of threats has grown to over two dozen. Four major categories of threat are now commonly used. (1) Threats to *external* validity involve problems that make it hard to draw trustworthy conclusions about populations based on evidence about samples. (2) Threats to *construct* validity occur when there are problems with the measures the researcher uses to study the construct or concept, as when the researcher uses an inadequate operational definition. (3) Threats to *statistical conclusion* validity occur when poor choices are made in the selection of statistics to use in the analysis of the data. For example, threats to statistical conclusion validity occur when the data seriously violate the statistical assumptions of the technique being used or when the statistic is used in such a way that it has low statistical power. (4) Finally, threats to *internal* validity pertain to mistakes that can lead to errors in reasoning about cause and effect.

Threats to validity can be roughly categorized as design, measurement, or analysis errors. Threats to internal validity, or mistakes about causation, and threats to external validity, or mistakes that make it hard to generalize the findings of the study, arise from and are most easily reduced by paying attention to research *design*. Threats to construct validity mostly have to do with errors made through poor operationalizations or definitions used in *measurement*. And threats to statistical conclusion validity refer to possible errors in *analysis*. In the rest of this chapter, we will focus mostly on threats to validity that arise out of problems with design.

The subject of threats is usually treated narrowly, in which case the threats are listed as a quick checklist that researchers might use. But it is also possible to treat the subject broadly and for considerations of threats to validity to become an extended treatise on research methodology. Cook and Campbell's 1979 book, *Quasi-Experimentation: Design and Analysis Issues for Field Settings,* is the best known of these. That book has been revised and extended by Shadish, Cook, and Campbell in their *Experimental and Quasi-Experimental Designs for Generalized Causal Inference* (2002). I strongly recommend that this volume be consulted by any serious researcher undertaking a major research project. Threats to validity should be systematically reviewed and pondered prior to deciding how to proceed with one's investigation and again after the data have been collected when deciding how to interpret the results of one's efforts.

What Are the Main Threats to Validity in Research?

In what follows, I have tried to find a middle ground between a scant checklist and a treatise. All of the threats are more likely to be a problem when research is done in natural settings (field research) rather than in a laboratory. The laboratory greatly reduces the danger from each of these threats, but often at the cost of studying effects in an artificially pure environment. The chief threats to validity that arise in applied field research are self-selection effects, volunteer effects, attrition, history effects, maturation effects, and communication among subjects.

Self-Selection Effects

Self-selection effects are probably the most important of the threats to validity in nonexperimental research. If subjects are not randomly assigned to the groups that interest the researcher, this means that they assign themselves, so to speak. And they are not likely to do so randomly. For instance, comparing the effects of attending public and private schools is very difficult, because the people who attend the two different kinds of schools are likely to be different *before* they enroll. Those prior differences are confounded with the effects of the schools. Similar problems occur in trying to gauge the effects on students of attending two-year versus four-year colleges or taking courses online versus in traditional classrooms. The comparison groups are likely to have been different in important ways before they began their studies. Elective surgery provides another good example: What are the effects of cosmetic surgery on patients' perceived sense of psychological well-being? The psychological states of potential patients who choose the surgery, and who can afford it, are almost surely different from those who cannot afford it or choose not to have the treatment. Separating the effects of prior differences from the effects of programs, practices, and treatments can be attempted using statistical controls, but the methods for doing this are far from foolproof.

Similar problems arise in survey research when some members of the sample choose not to respond or are not home when the pollster calls. And even if researchers manage to draw an unbiased sample, their research usually involves asking respondents what they *would* do—if the election were held tomorrow, which candidate *would* get your vote? A few respondents might intentionally deceive the pollsters; others, who answer honestly, could change their minds by Election

Day; still others could forget to vote. Even a large and perfectly random and representative sample will not eliminate such sources of error. Rather than struggle to make samples ever larger and ever more representative, survey researchers adjust their estimates in light of what they know about respondents' likely behavior. For example, they might use regression techniques (see Chapter 9) and give less weight to the responses of categories of potential voters whose past behavior indicates that they are less likely to vote. Such adjustments are one way to deal with threats to validity arising from self-selection effects, nonresponse bias, and similar problems.

Volunteer Effects

A related kind of self-selection effect is the *volunteer effect*. People cannot usually be studied without their prior consent, but those who give their consent are likely to differ in important ways from people who do not consent. It is sometimes possible to study people without their consent, for example, by observing their behavior in public places or by using anonymous institutional records. The latter has been very important in medical research and has considerable potential in education research as well. Businesses study customer behavior, sometimes by offering discounts to customers who use their "membership" cards. Such cards are really behavior tracking cards used to determine which customers are likely to purchase particular products under particular conditions. The accuracy of the conclusions based on these cards is limited to the extent that customers forgo the discounts rather than use the cards. People who do not use the cards may simply be careless or they might be wary of having their behavior tracked. Whatever the reason some customers do not use the cards, their behaviors cannot be used by companies to plan sales strategies.

Education research almost always requires the use of volunteers. College students who are willing to try taking a course online are almost surely different in important ways from those students who resist online courses. Or the children whose parents sign consent forms to allow their children to participate in a study, are almost surely different from parents who refuse to volunteer their children, and they are also probably different from those who just don't get around to signing the necessary forms. It is usually *impossible* to study these differences directly, because doing so would require that the nonvolunteers agree to be studied, in which case they would be volunteers.

Attrition

Attrition effects occur when subjects drop out of a study. They might move to a new location, or perhaps they become annoyed with the researcher. Attrition is another form of self-selection effect, but involves self-selecting *out,* not in. Attrition is often called *mortality,* perhaps originally because of the short life span of laboratory rats. But *attrition* is a better term than *mortality* for educational research and even for most medical research in which, fortunately, subjects do not often die during the course of the investigation. Educational research has its limitations, but subjects usually survive the experience. Whatever it is called and for whatever reason it happens, when some of the people being studied leave before the end of the research project, it is hard to know what their outcome measurements might have been had they not left. People who leave or otherwise drop out are not likely to be a representative sample of the original sample. Perhaps the independent variable was having its greatest (or its smallest) effects on those for whom we have no outcome data. We cannot directly determine whether their departure made a difference, because, for obvious reasons, there is no way to compare what happened when they stayed to when they went. However, if pretest data have been collected, then it is possible to see whether the leavers differ from the stayers on an early measure of the dependent variable. If the pretest scores of those who leave the study do not differ markedly from the sample as a whole, their departure is less cause for worry. If their scores are markedly different, one can attempt to make some statistical adjustments. In either case, having the pretest score is crucial. Most researchers who include pretests of the dependent variable in their design do not do so with the attrition problem in mind, but help with interpreting the consequences of attrition is an added benefit of pretesting.

History Effects

History effects are oddly named. They do not refer mainly, as their name might suggest, to events in the past. They refer to events that occur during the course of a study that make it difficult to interpret the results. When a study involves the passage of a considerable period of time, the validity of the study can be jeopardized by events over which the researcher has no control. For example, in a one-year study of the effects of a curriculum reform on academic achievement in a school district, many other things that might influence academic achievement are sure to happen in the course of the year. Those other things are the history effects. The state might liberalize charter school legislation, the voters in the district could defeat a school tax referendum, or the school board could dismiss the superintendent. Such events make it difficult to attribute any changes in academic achievement to the curriculum reform. Change could just as easily be due to the district's history. Or, in a study of the effect of new auto exhaust emission regulations on air pollution levels, other developments that could influence air quality (population growth, a new factory) could make it difficult to isolate the effects of the emission regulations. If a new factory raises pollution while the exhaust controls are lowering it, the net effect could be no change even if the exhaust controls worked quite well.

One way to guard against the potential threats to the validity of history effects is to take frequent measurements of the outcome variable rather than just one measurement at the end of the study. In this way, researchers can see if the confounding event's timing (the new factory starts belching fumes) coincides with a change in the outcome variable.

Maturation Effects

Like history effects, *maturation effects* arise because of the passage of time. But in this case the change that occurs is due to the individual development of participants in the research, not to external events. One common example happens when researchers investigate the effects of attending college. They might study college freshmen and then follow up with them again years later. Changes between, for example, freshmen and seniors are attributed to the effects of college. But as people age from 18 to 21 they are likely to change regardless of whether they go to college. Without a comparison group of same-age people who did not go to college, the effects of maturation are confounded with the effects of attending college. In this example, as in many research designs, having a comparison group is crucial to making valid inferences. Deciding against having a control or comparison group is just about the *worst* design choice you can make. More than most design errors, not having a comparison group seriously reduces your chances of being able to interpret your results accurately. Control or comparison groups are useful for reducing many threats to validity, not only maturation effects.

Communication among Subjects

Communication among subjects and the problems this can raise for researchers takes many forms. The group not getting the experimental treatment may try harder. This is sometimes called the "John Henry effect." Or, those not receiving the treatment may become demoralized and give up. In a training program, if some people being studied are enthusiastic about what they have learned, they may pass it on to others. This could greatly reduce the measurable effects of the program, because some of the people in the comparison group, who supposedly did not get the training, actually did get it, although indirectly. Professionals naturally talk with one another about their practice, and that is good for the delivery of professional services, but it is not good for researchers trying to identify the most effective practices. One solution is to introduce the new technique into different settings, such as different schools or different hospitals. Say you have six institutions agreeing to participate. You could introduce the new technique by randomly assigning half the practitioners in each setting to receive the training. The other half would be the control group. Or if communication among subjects were a big worry, you could randomly assign three of the hospitals or schools to receive the training. The other three would serve as a control group. People working in different institutions would be less likely to communicate than those working in the same institution. Which design is better? It depends on the particular study. The bigger the communication threat, the more it makes sense to assign institutions, not individuals, to control and treatment groups. On the other hand, if the six institutions differed greatly among themselves, you might be better off accepting the risk of communication. Communication could be less a threat to understanding your study than having your control and experimental group institutions be very different. Your decision is best based on your knowledge of the settings and the people in them, not on following a methodologist's recipe. Finally, of course, as with history effects, the longer the study lasts, the greater the likelihood that communication among subjects will influence your results.

Why Is a Negative Approach Taken by Focusing on Threats and Problems?

In closing, it is crucial to note that the presence of these threats is the rule, not the exception to the rule. That is why researchers focus on threats. Like travelers preparing for a journey who pack rain gear, a first aid kit, and extra clothing, they try to anticipate problems that could come up. It is by no means the case that only a few poorly designed research projects are subject to these problems of selection, attrition, history, and the rest. The threats are ubiquitous. And, to make things worse, the fact that all these threats to validity are listed separately here and in most texts does *not* mean that they actually occur separately. Maturation, history, self-selection, volunteer, attrition, and communication effects are *all* likely to occur, to one degree or another, in *all* research, es-

pecially nonexperimental research that extends over any considerable period of time. And when they occur simultaneously, they can interact; that is, their *joint effects* can be greater than their separate individual effects. It would be hard to overestimate the importance of these problems for all research. The threats are not occasional; they are perennial sources of invalidity. The limitations sections of research reports should address, if only briefly, the degree to which these threats limit the researchers' confidence in the findings and the steps the researchers took to reduce them. Knowledgeable readers can work out much of this on their own, but they should not have to do so. It is always better for the writer to discuss, frankly and explicitly, where the reader should be cautious in the interpretation of results of a research report.

When reporting results, probably the most used and discussed statistics are inferential. Researchers generally want to make inferences about populations, not merely to describe their samples. Thus far in this book we have looked at some of the most common ways of making inferences and have focused mainly on what statistical significance means. The next chapter will examine statistical inference more closely and look not only at what one answer (the p-value) means but also a bit more closely on how one arrives at it. Knowing how one arrives at the answer, of course, enhances understanding of what the answer means. Also discussed will be a form of inference touched on only lightly so far: estimation with confidence intervals. Estimation and significance testing are closely related, siblings perhaps. Many readers, if they react as most of my students do, will find estimation with confidence intervals much more appealing than her "twisted sister," statistical significance testing.

Terms and Concepts to Review

Reliability
Operational definition

Reliability coefficients
- Interrater
- Test-retest
- Internal consistency
- Split-half

Cronbach's alpha
Factor analysis
External validity

Internal validity
- Content
- Criterion-related
- Predictive

- Concurrent
- Construct
- Convergent
- Discriminant (divergent)

Threats to validity
- Self-selection
- Volunteer

- Attrition
- History
- Maturation
- Communication among subjects
- Interaction among threats (joint effects)

Discussion Questions

1. How are reliability and validity related? Think of a measurement that is reliable but not valid. Can you think of a measurement that is valid but not reliable? Why or why not?
2. Why does measurement or scale reliability matter? What are the consequences of using unreliable scales? How can you evaluate the reliability of a scale or other measurement instrument? What steps can you take to improve measurement reliability?
3. Sketch a research design or return to a design you have used to answer a previous question. Briefly discuss how you would try to assess and improve on the design's measurement properties, specifically its content, criterion, and construct validity.
4. Building on the design you used in question 3, talk about the main threats to validity you would face in trying to implement that design. Give particular attention to how you could go about reducing the seriousness of those threats.

Self-Test

If you can answer most of the following questions accurately, you can feel confident about your understanding of the material in this chapter. If not, it would be a good idea to review the chapter. (Answers can be found in the Appendix.)

1. To increase the reliability of your research design, you should avoid the use of operational definitions. True or False?
2. Cronbach's alpha is used to measure the validity of the measurements in experimental research. True or False?
3. Unreliable measurements of your variables will lead you to underestimate the size of any associations among them. True or False?
4. If the measures you use to study your variables are reliable, then they will be, by definition, valid as well. True or False?
5. If, in your research, you are using a well-known measure of a variable, one with published validity and reliability coefficients, you should nonetheless compute all relevant reliability and validity coefficients for your data. True or False?
6. In your research's limitations section, you should point out any potential threats to the validity of your findings and how these affect the trustworthiness of your conclusions. True or False?
7. If budgetary problems force you to cut back on your research study, usually the most effective approach would be to eliminate the control group, because this can be done with least harm to your ability to interpret your results. True or False?
8. If you are checking the validity of your measuring instrument by correlating your subjects' scores on it with their scores on another instrument that measures the same thing, you are most likely investigating your instrument's
   a. Content validity.
   b. Criterion-related validity.
   c. Construct validity.
9. If you judge the validity of a test, such as the SAT, by investigating how well it predicts an outcome, such as college grades, you are most likely studying the test's
   a. Content validity.
   b. Criterion-related validity.
   c. Construct validity.

10. If you ask a group of experts to review the items on your test to make sure that your test is valid in its coverage of the subject, you are most likely investigating your test's
    a. Content validity.
    b. Criterion-related validity.
    c. Construct validity.
11. In the course of a study of the effects of a campus-wide multicultural awareness program, the campus police are accused of using excessive force in arresting four African American men. Which of the following threats to validity is most likely to be important in this example?
    a. (Self-) selection
    b. Attrition
    c. History
    d. Maturation
    e. Subject interaction
12. You want to study the effects of a district's magnet school program by comparing the academic achievement of students attending and not attending magnet schools. Which of the following threats to validity is most likely to be important in this example?
    a. (Self-) selection
    b. Attrition
    c. History
    d. Maturation
    e. Subject interaction
13. You plan to study the importance of family background on students' development in a school district where students have a high mobility rate. Which of the following threats to validity is most likely to be important in this example?
    a. (Self-) selection
    b. Attrition
    c. History
    d. Maturation
    e. Subject interaction
14. A friend in your research methods class tells you she is going to include the following item on a survey she is writing: "Please indicate your marital status by circling the appropriate number. Are you 1 Married or 2 Divorced?" What advice should you give her about writing survey questions and coding data?
    a. The item is good except that she should code Married 1 and Divorced 0.
    b. The item is flawed because the choices do not exhaust all the possibilities.
    c. Despite the item's flaws, the choices have the merit of being mutually exclusive.
    d. She would do better to ask: "Are you married, Yes or No?"
    e. All of the above would be good advice.

Endnotes

1. A similar measure, once widely used, is the Kuder-Richardson 20 or K-R 20, but because it can be used only with items scored dichotomously, it is less versatile than Cronbach's alpha.

2. It is possible, though rare, to get a negative number when computing one of the correlations that constitute reliability coefficients. Because the idea of being "less than *completely* unreliable" is theoretically incoherent, some texts advise converting negative coefficients to zero. A wiser choice would be to report and try to interpret any such negative coefficients. They sometimes indicate that an item has been miscoded. Compare with discriminant validity, discussed later.

3. The formula for determining this is to multiply one reliability coefficient times the other and take the square root of the product: $.90 \times .80 = .72$, the square root of which is .85.

4. Many guides to measurement instruments exist. Among the most widely used in education and psychology are the ETS Test Collection, the ERIC Test Locator, and the *Mental Measurements Yearbooks*. See McMillan (2004) for an overview.

8

Statistical Inference

Researchers usually want to generalize beyond their samples. Statistical inference, in its various forms, is how they do this. There has been a lot of controversy about the best way to make inferences from samples to populations. Whomever you read (including me) on the topic will be presenting a controversial position because there is no position that is not challenged by knowledgeable persons. My view is that much of the controversy is pointless. The answer to the question "What's the best approach?" can only be "It depends." The various approaches to inference are more or less useful depending on one's research questions and data. With the general conclusion "It depends" in mind, this chapter discusses the two main approaches. One set of data, already familiar to readers, will illustrate the two approaches. You can compare for yourself the strengths and weaknesses of the two methods of analysis. The chapter reviews the main issues pertaining to statistical inference by addressing the following questions.

1. What are the controversies about statistical inference?
2. How is statistical significance related to the importance of research findings?
3. How does estimation with confidence intervals compare to statistical significance?

4. How can computer output for *t*-tests and confidence intervals be interpreted?
5. How can computer output for ANOVA be interpreted?
6. What are standard errors, and how are they used in statistical inference?
7. What is statistical power, and why is it important?

What Are the Controversies about Statistical Inference?

One of the main controversies involves cutoff points for defining when a statistic is or is not significant. The conventional cutoff for statistical significance is .05, or 5%. If a result is likely to be due to chance less than 5% of the time—the familiar $p < .05$—it is said to be statistically significant. But other values, especially .01, are also common. In an earlier example, our obtained value was $p = .03$. This would be significant if the cutoff were $p < .05$, but it would not be significant if it were $p < .01$. Clearly, the cutoff point—known as the *alpha level*—is arbitrary. It is a matter of convention, convenience, and tradition. Dissatisfaction with the cutoff approach, which involves a yes/no decision about statistical significance (hypothesis testing), has been one source of the controversies of the late 1990s and early 2000s about the best methods of inference.

Imagine a weather report that gave only cutoffs and did not report actual temperatures. Say the standard cutoff for "significantly cold" is 30 degrees. The prediction for tomorrow morning is for significantly cold weather, that is, less than 30 degrees. You get up in the morning, look out your window at your thermometer and you see that it is 31 degrees. Your conclusion probably would not be "Whoa, they were *way* off, it's not significantly cold." Nor, the next morning, if the temperature were 29, would you be likely to say, "Yikes, what a change from yesterday! Today it's *significantly* cold." Obviously, using such a cutoff point can produce false dichotomies. For example, if the cutoff point or alpha level is .05, a difference between $p = .048$ and $p = .052$ leads to a distinction between "significant" and "insignificant," but it is also clearly a distinction without a meaningful difference. (For a counterargument, see Chow, 1996.)

For that reason, among others, many people argue that hypothesis/significance testing,[1] because it uses arbitrary pass points, should be abandoned in favor of simply reporting actual *p*-values. The other main option, to be discussed later in this chapter, is reporting confidence intervals and confidence levels. The two approaches are not so very different, and neither makes the null hypothesis go away. Statistical significance is the degree to which the data contradict the null hypothesis. Are the sample data *sufficiently* different from what they would be if the null hypothesis were true? If so, we can reject the null hypothesis. What's *sufficiently*? One definition is "falling outside the confidence interval." The dispute between advocates of significance testing and proponents of confidence intervals is also related to the use of effect sizes, which already has been discussed (in Chapter 6). My personal preference is to report on and interpret all useful statistics: *p*-values and effect sizes and confidence intervals. Only if a shortage of ink and computer time reached crisis proportions, or if we still had to compute the statistics by hand, could a case perhaps be made that we should pick the best method and only report on the results of using it. However, even if we did have to pick the one best method, it would not be the same for all problems.

How Is Statistical Significance Related to the Importance of Research Findings?

Another reason some researchers are annoyed with the standard methods of reporting statistical significance is that they think these methods detract attention from the size of effects. There is no doubt that statistically significant findings can be so small that they are insignificant for practical purposes. For instance, in a recent article, Karen (2002) reports that after controlling for "all other variables, women are *significantly* less likely than men to attend selective colleges" (p. 198, emphasis added). One could easily be led by these words to believe that women were *importantly* less likely to attend selective colleges or that there was a *large* difference in selectivity between the colleges men and women attend. But closer examination reveals that *significant* here can only mean statistically significant. Women on average attended colleges where the mean SAT score of the students was 13.5 points lower than the colleges men attended. This is 13.5 out of a total of 1,600 SAT points, which, by any measure except *statistical* significance, is a very trivial difference. Given the possible confusion of substantive and statistical significance, careful writers should always specify which one they mean, as awkward as it sometimes is to insert adverbs and adjectives, such as *statistically* significant or *substantive* significance.

Looking at things the other way around, it is also true that statistically *non*significant findings can be substantively very significant. One area in which this is the case and statistically nonsignificant findings can be signs of social progress is in measures of bias and discrimination. When no statistically significant differences are found between men and women or between minorities and nonminorities on some measures, this can indicate dramatic change from the none-too-distant past. Nonetheless, the naïve assumption that statistical significance is necessary for substantive significance is remarkably resilient.

Here are a few examples of recent work in which most or all of the results were statistically nonsignificant, yet quite interesting and important.

- Employment during high school had no long-term effects on grades in academic courses (Warren et al., 2000).
- On only a few subtests were gender differences found in either question format or content in high school science achievement tests; that is, most differences were not statistically significant (Hamilton, 1998).
- Fleming and Garcia (1998) found few significant differences between African Americans and Whites in correlations of SAT scores and college grades.
- No consistent effects, negative or positive, of maternal employment on children's development were detected (Harvey, 1999).
- Comparing college students' evaluations of professors, researchers found virtually no statistically significant male–female differences (Centra & Gaubatz, 2000).
- No significant differences were found between elementary school classes with and without teacher aides (Gerber et al., 2001).

In each one of these articles, the big news was "no difference," because the expectation (sometimes a stereotype) might have led one to believe that a difference was likely. Yet the authors of these articles had a tendency to linger over the rare and tiny differences (which were statistically significant) and to underemphasize the overwhelming evidence that differences were small exceptions to the rule of no difference. Of course, a finding of no difference is not *statistically* significant. But, researchers often seem uncomfortable saying that their findings aren't significant, even when this lack of statistical difference/significance is a very important result. Old habits die hard.

What is one to do about all this? One option, and one that is fast becoming the norm, is always to report an effect size along with the statistical significance. A related option, and one that statisticians have long argued for, is to report confidence intervals and levels. Neither effect sizes (ESs) nor confidence intervals (CIs) directly eliminate the foolishness of automatically equating statistical *in*significance with a lack of importance. But both ESs and CIs provide information that can help bring careless researchers to their senses. Despite the tendency of proponents of the various methods to treat significance/hypothesis testing on the one hand, and estimation and confidence intervals on the other, as opposites, the two approaches are closely related. They have overlapping historical origins and are based on the same information (see the later section on standard errors). The difference lies mainly in the way the information is reported. The disputes center on the question of which forms of reporting are most effective in specific circumstances.

How Does Estimation with Confidence Intervals Compare to Statistical Significance?

To repeat, there are two broad categories of statistical inference, two ways of inferring conclusions about populations based on data from samples: (1) estimation with level of confidence and probable margins of error (confidence intervals) and (2) hypothesis testing and statistical significance. The *p*-values already encountered several times in these pages are a way to report statistical significance, but they are closely related to confidence intervals and levels. As we have done in the past, it is best to define something complex by a method of successive approximation, that is, to start simply with each approximation getting a little more complicated and a little more accurate.

Say you measure something in two samples and find that the mean difference between them is 107 points. *Here is the first and simple approximation:*

You can either ask, (1) "What is the probability that I'm wrong?" This is the significance-testing approach; or (2) "How confident am I that

I'm right?" This is the confidence-interval approach. The two are closely related, roughly mirror images of one another. If you're 95% confident that you're right, then the probability that you're wrong will be 5% ($p = .05$). If you're 99% confident, then the chances you're wrong are 1%. The parallelism breaks down at this point, however, because one is *not* "probably wrong" and "confident of being right" about the same things.

Here, as the *second approximation,* are the kinds of statements that could be made using the two methods, plus a variant. (1) *Statistical significance:* "If there were no difference between the populations, the chances of finding a difference this big (107) in a sample of this size would be less than 5%." (2) *Exact p-value:* "If there were no difference between the populations, the chances of finding a difference this big (107) in a sample of this size would be 3%." (3) *Confidence levels/intervals:* "In samples of this size, one can be 95% confident that the true value of the difference between the populations is between 87 and 127 (107 plus or minus 20)." Where does the plus or minus 20 come from? It is calculated using the standard error (see discussion later in chapter).

The differences among the three statements are clear. The first two are versions of the statistical significance approach. The first says that it is unlikely that the population value is zero. The second provides more specific information about *the degree to which* it is unlikely that the population value is zero. The third gives you an estimate and a range of possible values in the population. The third statement, about confidence levels and intervals, is clearly more informative. As will be seen in more detail later, the confidence-interval approach gives you all the information the *p*-value gives you—plus more. It also has the attractive property of not requiring one to speak in double and triple negatives.

It is instructive to look at how the statements overlap. If you have the third statement, the confidence interval, you can skip the first, because the first is implied in the third. However, the confidence-interval approach does not give you the exact *p*-value of the second statement. So, statement 3 also gives you 1, but not 2. Statement 2 gives you 1, but not 3. Of the three, only statement 1, about statistical significance, is redundant because it is implied, either in statement 2 (exact *p*-value) or in statement 3 (confidence interval). But statement 1, the least informative one, has long been, and continues to be, the most frequent way to report the results of inferential statistics.

Statistics textbooks often spend hundreds of pages on statistical inference and describe many ways to determine statistical significance by hypothesis testing and/or to compute exact *p*-values and/or to set confidence intervals. This is useful information, but it is among the topics reluctantly omitted in this book. In order to have time to discuss advanced and specialized techniques, a quicker way must be found to address statistical inference. In the remaining pages of this chapter, rather than explain dozens of ways to calculate *p*-values and confidence intervals, and rather than discuss the probability theory on which the calculations are based, the focus instead will be on a few examples of computer output reporting on significance levels and confidence intervals. We will let the computer do the computing and spend our time interpreting the computer output. Learning how to read the computer output is a useful skill, and it is also one of the most effective ways to understand the concepts behind the output.

How Can Computer Output for t-*tests and Confidence Intervals Be Interpreted?*

Chapter 2 used an example of a grade book with scores on exams, a paper, and a project for 35 college students. There was also information about the students' genders and their academic majors. A correlation matrix for all of the variables showed that there was a small and statistically *in*significant correlation between gender and scores on Exams 1 and 2 are a substantial and statistically significant correlation between gender and grades on the paper. Tables 8.1, 8.2, and 8.3 examine the same data. But here the question has changed. When doing correlations the question was: What are the *associations* between

TABLE 8.1 *Descriptive Statistics: Males and Females on Exam 1 and Paper*

0 = male;1 = female	N	Mean	Standard Deviation	Standard Error Mean
Exam 1				
1.00	18	85.6667	9.78594	2.30657
.00	17	82.8235	7.41818	1.79917
Paper				
1.00	18	92.0556	4.70884	1.10988
.00	17	77.0588	7.03092	1.70525

gender and scores, and are those associations statistically significant? Now the question is: What are the *differences* between the average scores for males and females, and are those differences statistically significant? These two questions are, of course, two versions of the same inquiry. First, when doing the correlations, we asked: How much are the students alike? Second, when computing the *t*-tests, we will ask: How much do they differ?

Tables 8.1, 8.2, and 8.3 display SPSS output for the *t*-test and ANOVA for our two relationships: (1) between gender and the exam grade and (2) gender and the paper grade. The *t*-test and ANOVA are by far the most widely used tests of statistical significance. And, because SPSS automatically computes confidence intervals when computing *t*-tests and ANOVAs, it gives everything necessary to compare the *p*-value approach to the confidence-interval approach.

Table 8.1 simply reports the average scores for males and females on Exam 1 and on the paper. The 18 females, who are coded 1.0 (males are coded .00), got an average score of 85.66 on Exam 1. Males got an average of 82.82. On the paper females averaged 92.05, the males 77.05. What the *t*-test is designed to tell the researcher is whether these mean differences are statistically significant. Are they big enough that they are unlikely to be a coincidence? Would you get a mean difference this big if there were no difference in the populations from which these 35 students were drawn?

Table 8.2 provides the answers to those questions. It is a big table and gives a lot of additional information as well, which will take some time to work

thorough. Start by looking at the upper half of the table, the part reporting on Exam 1. First, in columns 1 and 2, we see *Levene's test for equality of variances*. This concept of equality of variances was reviewed briefly in Chapter 4, and it is a tricky concept. Here it is enough to say that if the test gives a statistically significant result (< .05), the null hypothesis of equal population variances is rejected and you use the second row, called "Equal variances not assumed," for the *t*-test.[2] The significance for this test, which is a *p*-value, is given in the second column, called "Sig." Because .077 is bigger than .05, you can use the first row, though in this case there is very little difference between the two rows.

The third column is the *t*-statistic; it is used to determine the *p*-value. The fourth column gives the degrees of freedom (df), which is closely related to the number of cases. Degrees of freedom is another of those concepts that is crucial if you are doing computations by hand or planning to become a professional statistician (see the brief discussion in Chapter 11). But it is less central for our immediate purposes. In the fifth column you get the "answer" about statistical significance. SPSS labels the *p*-value as "Sig." The *p*-value is .342, which is bigger than .05. This means that the difference between males and females on Exam 1 is not significant at the .05 level; you could expect a difference of this size in a sample of this size 34.2% of the time. The mean difference is given in the sixth column. It is 2.8432 (that is, 85.66 minus 82.82, from Table 8.1).

The significance test in column 5 is two-directional, termed "2-tailed" by SPSS. A two-direction

TABLE 8.2 *Independent Samples Test: Mean Differences between Males and Females on Exam 1 and Paper*

	Levene's Test for Equality of Variances		t-test for Equality of Means						
	Column 1 F	Column 2 Sig.	Column 3 T	Column 4 df	Column 5 Sig. (2-tailed)	Column 6 Mean Difference	Column 7 Standard Error Difference	Column 8 95% Confidence Interval of the Difference	
								Lower	Upper
Exam 1									
Equal variances assumed	3.323	.077	.964	33	.342	2.8431	2.94863	–3.15590	8.84218
Equal variances not assumed			.972	31.565	.338	2.8431	2.92528	–3.11870	8.80497
Paper									
Equal variances assumed	3.331	.077	7.454	33	.000	14.9967	2.01195	10.90340	19.09007
Equal variances not assumed			7.371	27.742	.000	14.9967	2.03463	10.82723	19.16623

approach tests the hypothesis that there is a difference between females and males, but it does not specify which one is bigger. The one-direction (one-tailed) approach tests whether the average score of a specific group is larger. Usually, the two-direction (often called nondirectional) approach is better; it is always more conservative, that is, it is a harder test to pass. The mean difference has to be twice as big for a two-direction test to pass muster as statistically significant.

The seventh column, labeled "Std. Error Difference," is the standard error of the difference between the female and male average scores. The *standard error* (SE) is one of the more difficult concepts to understand in basic statistics (see the discussion later in the chapter). Leaving out the probability theory on which it is built, the SE is a kind of standard deviation; it provides an estimate of how much *sampling error* one is likely to get in a sample of a particular size. Remember that the sampling error is the difference between the population value and the sample value. So the SE answers the question: By how much is the sample value likely to miss the population value? The standard error gives you an estimate of the sampling error; it tells you how much error you are likely to have if you use the sample to estimate the population. The standard error (SE) in this example is 2.9486 points. Rounding off, the mean difference between males and females is 2.8 in the sample. The standard error is 2.9. That tells you that if you use that sample mean to estimate the population mean, you are likely to be wrong by 2.9 points. In brief:

Estimate = 2.8   Probable error = 2.9

Clearly this is not a very accurate estimate, which is why the difference between male and female students is not statistically significant.

Note that the *t*-statistic, which is used to determine the *p*-value, is computed by dividing the mean difference (that is, 2.8) by the SE of the difference (that is, 2.9). So the *t*-statistic is a ratio of an estimate to its likely error. You get the *t*-value by dividing the actual difference by the average probable error. If a difference is statistically significant, it will be bigger than the estimate of error (SE), usually at least two times bigger. The *t*-statistic is just the sample statistic divided by its probable error.

Finally, the confidence interval (CI) is given in column 8. What it tells you, rounding off, is that you can be 95% certain that the true value of the difference in the population is somewhere between *minus* 3.2 and *plus* 8.8. You get these lower and upper bounds by taking the estimate of 2.8 and adding 2 SEs for the upper bound and subtracting 2 SEs for the lower bound. The SE of 2.9486 times 2 equals roughly 6.0. So, 2.8 +/– 6 gives you –3.2 and +8.8. This is a very wide range of scores. Using the sample mean difference to estimate the population mean difference, the estimate is that the population of females got 2.8 points higher. After constructing the CI, you can be 95% sure that the real value is somewhere between females getting 3.2 points *lower* and 8.8 points *higher*, which means you we can be sure of almost nothing. You can be 95% confident that females in the population scored higher—or maybe they scored lower!

Another complication to be addressed is that some writers about statistical methods claim that this way of describing confidence intervals—"we can be 95% confident that the true value in the population is between . . ."—is not technically correct. They claim that we should say something more complicated, "if we were to take an infinite number of random samples of this size, in 95% of them the mean would be between. . . ." Which of these should you use? The substantive differences between the two statements strike me as minor. The first way of putting it—"95% confident that the true value"—strikes me as more direct, and it is used by distinguished scholars (e.g., Cohen et al., 2003). The second way of putting it—"if we were to take an infinite number of random samples . . . 95% of them"—is insisted on by equally distinguished scholars (e.g., Huck, 2004). In this book, I will use the first, because of its greater simplicity. But be forewarned, if you use the first, occasionally you will encounter fastidious scholars, advocates of the second, who will be disappointed in you.

Whichever way you choose to express it, the CI gives you the range *and* the cutoff for statistical significance of a particular *p*-value. You know that a difference is not significant at the .05 level, if the 95%

TABLE 8.3   *ANOVA: Mean Differences between Males and Females on Exam 1 and Paper*

	Sum of Squares	df	Mean Square	F	Sig.
Exam 1					
Between groups	70.672	1	70.672	.930	.342
Within groups	2508.471	33	76.014		
Total	2579.143	34			
Paper					
Between groups	1966.286	1	1966.286	55.560	.000
Within groups	1167.886	33	35.390		
Total	3134.171	34			

CI includes zero. In this case, the low end of the interval is −3.2 and is below zero, whereas the high end of 8.8 is above zero. Because the CI includes zero, you can be 95% confident that the real difference might be zero. You cannot reject the null hypothesis of no difference; the difference might well be zero.

Having laid this groundwork by looking at the mean difference on Exam 1, we can now look more quickly at the male–female mean difference on the paper. In column 5, we see that the Sig., or *p*-value, is .000, which is short for < .0005. This figure of .000 does not truly mean zero. All it indicates is that SPSS does not give more than 3 decimal points in computing *p*-values (more than 3 decimal points would be a silly level of precision for a *p*-value). Good practice when you obtain a *p*-value of .000 is to round it up to < .001. At any rate, by nearly any imaginable cutoff score, this difference is statistically significant. The mean difference between male and female mean scores is 14.99 points. A difference this big between male and female averages would occur by chance alone less than 5 out of 10,000 times (< .0005).

Now look at columns 6 and 7, the mean difference and the standard error. The difference in the sample, which is an estimate of the difference in the population, is about 15 (14.99). The sampling error is about 2 (2.011); as always, the SE is an estimate of how far off the estimate is likely to be. So the estimate of the difference is much larger than the typical error, about 7.45 times larger in fact—which is the value of the *t*-statistic. Again, the *t*-statistic tells you

how many times larger the estimate is than the likely error of the estimate.

Using the CI to look at the same data you would say the sample estimate of the population value is 15. You can be 95% confident that the true value in the population is between 11 and 19. That is, the true population value is likely to be between 2 SEs above and 2 SEs below the sample mean. Because the CI ranges from 11 to 19 and does not include zero, this finding is statistically significant at the .05 level.

In sum, there are two ways of expressing a statistical inference. Using this example, we can say either (1) the difference in the sample is 15 points, and it is very likely to be between 11 and 19 points in the population; or (2) the difference in the sample is 15 points, and a difference that big or bigger would be unlikely if there were no difference in the population. I prefer the first statement. It seems to me more direct and to convey more information. But, a choice between the two is not mostly a matter of right and wrong. It is also in part a matter of taste and tradition.

How Can Computer Output for ANOVA Be Interpreted?

Table 8.3 looks at the same data, but uses analysis of variance (ANOVA) to do so. Anything you can do with a *t*-test, you can also do with an ANOVA—but the reverse is not true. At any rate, the two ways of measuring statistical significance are conceptually similar, though computationally fairly different. Notice, however, that they give the same answer. In Table 8.3, the Sig. (*p*-value) for Exam 1 is .342 and for the paper it is .000—exactly the same as the *t*-test (in Table 8.2). One final similarity can be seen by comparing the *F* statistic and the *t*-statistic. For the mean difference on the paper, the *F* = 55.56; the *t* = 7.45. If you square the *t* you get the *F;* take the square root of the *F* (55.56), you get the *t* (7.454).

In moving from looking at differences in mean scores by gender to differences by academic major, ANOVA and the *t*-test are no longer equally useful. In talking about academic major, the cases (students) are classified into three groups: those who study the natural sciences, the social sciences, and the humanities. The *t*-test can handle only two groups at a time. You could compare two at a time, but this would be cumbersome and would raise other problems that it is better to avoid. But ANOVA can simultaneously handle three or more groupings of cases in the independent variable. ANOVA is more versatile than the *t*-test. So we use ANOVA to study the independent variable (academic major) with three groups. Looking at three dependent variables (Exam 1, the paper, the project), you will have to conduct three ANOVAs. The question now is: Are there significant differences in the mean scores of the students majoring in the three subject areas in the dependent variables on Exam 1, the paper, and the project? The SPSS output for answering these questions is given in Tables 8.4 and 8.5.

Table 8.4 gives the means on each of the three dependent variables (scores on Exam 1, the paper, and the project) for each of the three categories of the independent variable (using the abbreviations of the table: *natscis, socscis, humas*). Each of these means is accompanied by its standard deviation, standard error, and 95% confidence interval, but we will not examine those now. Rather the discussion will concentrate on the *differences* in the mean scores (DVs) of the different groups (IV). For that analysis, consult Table 8.5, which reports the ANOVA output.

Let's move to the last column of Table 8.5 to get to the "bottom line," the "final answer." The column

headed "Sig." again gives the *p*-values. For Exam 1 and the project there are statistically significant differences among the groups (*p* = < .000 for Exam 1 and *p* = < .001 for project). But the differences among the group means are not statistically significant on the paper (*p* = .425). By chance alone, you would get mean differences that large 42.5% of the time.

Note the important fact that ANOVA does not tell you *which* mean scores of which groups are significantly bigger than others. It tells you only that one or more of the group means is significantly different from one or more of the others. Sometimes it *seems* clear where the difference lies, but often it is not. For example, look at the mean scores (in Table 8.4) on the project. Leaving off the decimals, they are for the three academic majors: 76, 82, and 90. It might be that each score is significantly different from the other two, but perhaps only the highest and lowest are significantly different. ANOVA tells you *only* that *some* difference in mean scores is significantly different. To find out which, you need to do further testing, known as *post hoc* (Latin for "after this") testing, which is also called making *multiple comparisons*. There are several ways to conduct such tests or make such comparisons, and a researcher using ANOVA will probably want to pursue this question in some depth to decide which of the *post hoc* tests is best to use (see the discussions in Huck, 2004, and Glass and Hopkins, 1996).

Although picking the multiple comparison test to use can be a complicated decision (the version of SPSS I'm using at the moment gives over a dozen options), acting on your choice is simple. With a few mouse clicks you instruct the computer software to make the comparison tests, and the output tells you which among all the possible pairs of comparisons is statistically significant. The software also reports the confidence intervals. Table 8.6 gives the output for the data using one of the more popular multiple comparison tests, Tukey's honestly significant difference (HSD). All possible comparisons are made for each of the dependent variables. As an example of how to read the output, let's look at the first two rows for Exam 1. The mean difference between the natscis and the socscis is 2.16, the standard error (2.873) is

TABLE 8.4 *Descriptive Statistics for Exam 1, Paper, and Project for Students Majoring in the Natural Sciences, Social Sciences, and Humanities*

	N	Mean	Standard Deviation	Standard Error	95% Confidence Interval for Mean		Minimum	Maximum
					Lower Bound	Upper Bound		
Exam 1								
natscis	12	89.2500	8.43289	2.43437	83.8920	94.6080	75.00	100.00
socscis	11	87.0909	5.92376	1.78608	83.1113	91.0705	77.00	97.00
humas	12	76.7500	5.89491	1.70171	73.0046	80.4954	65.00	88.00
Total	35	84.2857	8.70960	1.47219	81.2939	87.2776	65.00	100.00
Paper								
natscis	12	87.7500	7.77087	2.24326	82.8126	92.6874	73.00	96.00
socscis	11	83.0000	11.83216	3.56753	75.0510	90.9490	70.00	97.00
humas	12	83.4167	9.08003	2.62118	77.6475	89.1858	70.00	99.00
Total	35	84.7714	9.60112	1.62289	81.4733	88.0695	70.00	99.00
Project								
natscis	12	76.8333	10.46929	3.02222	70.1815	83.4852	50.00	92.00
socscis	11	82.2727	9.06742	2.73393	76.1811	88.3643	70.00	95.00
humas	12	90.5000	4.27466	1.23399	87.7840	93.2160	84.00	98.00
Total	35	83.2286	9.94717	1.68138	79.8116	86.6455	50.00	98.00

TABLE 8.5   *ANOVA: Mean Differences on Exam 1, Paper, and Project for Students Majoring in the Natural Sciences, Social Sciences, and Humanities*

	Sum of Squares	df	Mean Square	F	Sig.
Exam 1					
Between groups	1063.734	2	531.867	11.231	.000
Within groups	1515.409	32	47.357		
Total	2579.143	34			
Paper					
Between groups	163.005	2	81.502	.878	.425
Within groups	2971.167	32	92.849		
Total	3134.171	34			
Project					
Between groups	1135.323	2	567.661	8.150	.001
Within groups	2228.848	32	69.652		
Total	3364.171	34			

bigger than the mean difference, and therefore the p-value (Sig.) is high, .735—clearly not statistically significant. The confidence interval ranges from −4.90 to +9.22. It contains zero, which also means that the mean difference between natscis and socscis is not statistically significant. Looking at the next row and the next comparison, between the natscis and the humas, we see a different story. Here the mean difference is 12.5 and the Sig. is .000, which rounds up to $p < .001$, and the confidence intervals range from 5.6 to 19.4—a statistically significant difference. In brief, ANOVA in Table 8.5 reported that *some* statistically significant difference or differences existed, but it didn't indicate which ones. The multiple comparisons in Table 8.6 specify *which* differences are significant.

At this point, more important than these details about the example is getting a basic idea of what ANOVA is in general and of how a researcher using ANOVA determines whether there is a statistically significant difference between/among groups. Returning to Table 8.5, you can start to conceptualize what is meant when you conclude that there is a statistically significant difference between group means. Consider the information for project under the column labeled "Mean Square." As mentioned in Chapter 2, the mean square is another term for the variance. Whatever you call it, mean square or variance, it is the mean of the total squared deviations from the mean. What matters for determining statistical significance with ANOVA is whether the average difference (MS) between the groups is bigger than the average difference within the groups. Differences *between* the groups would be clearest if everyone *within* each group got exactly the same score (no variance, zero standard deviation, no mean square) but the group averages were very different.

Imagine that there were only nine students, three in each group. You could be pretty sure of a real difference among them if the scores were as follows.

Natscis	76	76	76	mean = 76
Socscis	82	82	82	mean = 82
Humas	90	90	90	mean = 90

The students in each group are all alike, but the group averages are different. But what if the groups had the same means but the scores of the individual students were as follows?

TABLE 8.6 Multiple Comparisons of Differences in Table 8.5 Using Tukey's HSD

Dependent Variable	(I) major	(J) major	Mean Difference (I-J)	Standard Error	Sig.	95% Confidence Interval Lower Bound	Upper Bound
Exam 1	natscis	socscis	2.16	2.873	.735	-4.90	9.22
		humas	12.50*	2.809	.000	5.60	19.40
	socscis	natscis	-2.16	2.873	.735	-9.22	4.90
		humas	10.34*	2.873	.003	3.28	17.40
	humas	natscis	-12.50*	2.809	.000	-19.40	-5.60
		socscis	-10.34*	2.873	.003	-17.40	-3.28
Paper	natscis	socscis	4.75	4.022	.473	-5.13	14.63
		humas	4.33	3.934	.520	-5.33	14.00
	socscis	natscis	-4.75	4.022	.473	-14.63	5.13
		humas	-.42	4.022	.994	-10.30	9.47
	humas	natscis	-4.33	3.934	.520	-14.00	5.33
		socscis	.42	4.022	.994	-9.47	10.30
Project	natscis	socscis	-5.44	3.484	.277	-14.00	3.12
		humas	-13.67*	3.407	.001	-22.04	-5.29
	socscis	natscis	5.44	3.484	.277	-3.12	14.00
		humas	-8.23	3.484	.062	-16.79	.33
	humas	natscis	13.67*	3.407	.001	5.29	22.04
		socscis	8.23	3.484	.062	-.33	16.79

*The mean difference is significant at the .05 level.

Natsics	96	76	56	mean = 76
Socscis	64	82	100	mean = 82
Humas	80	90	100	mean = 90

It would be much harder to conclude that there were important differences between the groups in this second case. The pattern is far from clear. For example, the "natscis" group had the lowest overall mean, but one of the students in that group outscored most of the students in the other two groups. So, in this case the variance within the groups is large in comparison to the variance between them. Therefore, the differences between the groups are not likely to be statistically significant. It would be hard to claim that academic major made a difference when the scores of the students in the different majors showed no consistent pattern.

This notion of differences within groups being small in comparison to differences between groups is absolutely central to the logic drawing conclusions from experiments. A researcher can be confident that the treatment had an effect if all the members of the experimental group improved, whereas none of the members of the control group did. If each group is internally very similar, but the differences between them are great, you have a statistically significant difference between them.

Looking again at the mean square column for the project in Table 8.5, the MS (the variance) within the groups is fairly small (69.65) in comparison to the variance (MS) between the groups (567.66). In fact, the MS between the groups is 8.15 times as big as the MS within the groups. And 8.15 is, of course, is the F statistic. That is the question the F statistic or the F ratio answers: How much more variance is there between the groups than within them? The within-group variance is often called the *error variance*. And that brings us back to the parallels with the t-test. The t-test is a ratio of an estimate to probable error. The F-test is a ratio of the differences attributable to the independent variable (group membership) to the differences not attributable to the independent variable. In both cases, the researcher compares a sample value to an estimate of its likely error to draw inferences about populations. Studying the details of the ways that these comparisons of estimates and errors are made raises numerous very intricate problems. But the general principle is the same: Compare the size of what you can explain to the size of what you can't explain; if what you can explain is a lot bigger than what you can't, the result is statistically significant.

The same principle is used to examine the mean differences between two overlapping groups. We have looked at mean differences between genders and among majors, but what about different genders in different majors? Perhaps males who major in the humanities do significantly better (or worse) on the dependent variables than female humanities majors. In other terms, is the effect of major moderated by gender? Or, in still other terms, is there a significant interaction between major and gender? To find out you would conduct a *two*-way ANOVA. There are two independent variables, not only one as in the examples in Table 8.3 (in which the IV was gender) and Table 8.5 (in which the IV was major). In Table 8.7 there are two IVs: gender and major together. For this example, the grades on the project are the DV. First look at the effects of gender controlling for the effects of major, which is called the "main effect" of gender. Then examine the effects of major controlling for the effect of gender, that is, the main effects of major. Looking at the Sig. column of the table, we see that there is no significant main effect of gender ($p = .424$). There is a significant main effect of major ($p = .002$).

Last, look at the interaction of gender and major. As discussed in Chapter 3, an interaction effect is a joint effect of two variables. The presence of an interaction effect means that the total effects of two variables adds up to more than the sum of their individual effects. In other terms, an interaction effect is a multiplier effect. The test for a significant interaction is shown in the row labeled GENDER * MAJOR, which means gender *multiplied times* major. Here the Sig. or *p*-value is .779, which is clearly a nonsignificant result. One is likely to get a result of this size due to sampling error alone about 78% of the time. The conclusion is that effects of major are not influenced by differences in the gender composition of the majors.

TABLE 8.7 *Two-Way ANOVA: Tests of Between-Subjects Effects*
Dependent Variable: PROJECT

Source	Type III Sum of Squares	df	Mean Square	F	Sig.
Corrected Model	1218.310*	5	243.662	3.293	.018
Intercept	228703.904	1	228703.904	3090.792	.000
GENDER	48.721	1	48.721	.658	.424
MAJOR	1154.756	2	577.378	7.803	.002
GENDER * MAJOR	37.374	2	18.687	.253	.779
Error	2145.862	29	73.995		
Total	245809.000	35			
Corrected Total	3364.171	34			

*R-squared = .362 (adjusted R-squared = .252).

What Are Standard Errors, and How Are They Used in Statistical Inference?

The general procedure used to make statistical inferences is based on interpreting standard errors (SEs), which are derived from *sampling distributions* (to be discussed shortly). Examples of standard errors have already been presented and used. In the ANOVA of students' scores, the SEs *of the means* of the students in the difference academic majors were used (Table 8.4). In the *t*-test example, the SEs *of the mean differences* between make and female students were shown (Table 8.2). Any statistic can have an SE (for example, Chapter 9 will discuss SEs of regression coefficients), but the SE of the mean is the easiest place to start. Standard errors of the mean are fairly easy to compute and to use to construct confidence intervals or conduct hypothesis tests.

For instance, recently on the first day of class, I gave the students a pretest of their knowledge of the subject matter in one of my courses. Possible scores ranged from 0 to 500 points. There were 25 students in the class, and their mean score on the test was 240. The standard deviation was 35. That is all the information needed to compute the SE of the mean. Because I was teaching one of several sections of a course to which students were more or less randomly assigned, it seemed reasonable to draw some infer-

ences from my class (the sample) to the population (students in all of the sections). The first step was to compute the standard error. To do that, divide the standard deviation by the square root of the number of students. That's it. The formula is

$$\text{Standard error} = \frac{\text{Standard deviation of the sample score}}{\text{Square root of the sample size}}$$

Remember that the standard deviation was 35. The square root of the number of students (25) was 5. And 35/5 = 7. So the standard error (SE) was 7. With that information, I was ready to draw inferences about the population. The mean in my class was 240. So my estimate was that 240 was also the mean for the population, that is, for all the students in all the sections. But, sampling error must always be taken into account, because the sample (my class) will not exactly match the population. The standard error (SE) is an estimate of the sampling error. We can use the SE to construct a confidence interval (CI). To get the 95% CI, use the estimate (the sample mean) plus or minus 2 SEs. In this case, the CI ranges from 240 minus 14 (7 × 2 = 14) to 240 plus 14—that is, 240 − 14 = 226; 240 + 14 = 254. Assuming that my class was a random sample, I can say: Had this test been given to all students in all sections, I can be 95% confident that the mean would have been between 226 and 254.

So the SE is an estimate of likely sampling error, and it is easy enough to use. But what *is* it really? The SE differs from most of the statistics discussed in this book. Generally statistics are hard to compute but comparatively easy to understand, at least in general terms. Just the opposite is true of the SE: It is easy to compute but hard to understand. The definition of the standard error is brief: It is the standard deviation of the sampling distribution. You are already familiar with the standard deviation, but what is a *sampling distribution*? It is a *theoretical* or *hypothetical* distribution, not a real empirical distribution. It describes what *would* happen were one to take repeated *random* samples. One doesn't actually have to do it, because randomness, plus some statistical theory, enables one to know what *would* happen if it were done. Suppose that instead of taking one sample of 25 students (my class), I *randomly* selected an *infinite* number of samples of 25 students and gave them the pretest. Plotting the mean scores of each sample on a graph would result in a normal curve. Computing the standard deviation of those mean scores results in the standard error. What the SE estimates is how much the mean *would* vary from sample to sample. In other words, it estimates sampling error. You can use that estimate to make statistical inferences, such as constructing confidence intervals.

One final point about the standard error and sample size. This example makes it clear why sample size matters in statistical inference. Because the square root of the sample size is the denominator in the equation for the SE, the bigger the sample, the smaller the standard error. The smaller the standard error, the more accurate the inference from the sample to the population. In our original example, the sample size was 25 and the square root of that is 5. Dividing 5 into 35 (the standard deviation) results in an SE of 7. But what if my class, the sample, contained 100 students? The square root of $100 = 10$. Dividing 10 into 35 results in 3.5, so the size of the error is cut in half (from 7.0 to 3.5), but the sample size had to be quadrupled (from 25 to 100) in order to do that. Is the extra effort of quadrupling the sample size worth the gain in precision? That depends on how much

you value precision, which, as always in matters of values, is not a statistical question.

What Is Statistical Power, and Why Is It Important?

As discussed briefly in Chapter 1, statistical power is the converse of statistical significance. Statistical significance measures the probability of rejecting a true null hypothesis—that is, one that shouldn't have been rejected (Type I error). *Statistical power,* by contrast, is the probability of retaining (or not rejecting) a false null hypothesis—one that shouldn't have been retained (Type II error). Statistical power is influenced by the sensitivity of a test or of a design. A powerful test or sensitive measuring instrument is not likely to miss a real relationship among variables. Rather, a powerful test's or instrument's errors are likely to be *false positives*. To reduce the number of false positives, you have to increase the chances of making a *false negative* decision. Think of a psychological test for dyslexia or a blood test for cancer. If the test is very powerful, it will miss almost no true cases, but it will also tend to produce false alarms or false positives. Tests less likely to produce false alarms are likely to miss a bigger proportion of true cases—of dyslexia, cancer, or whatever is being tested for. Clearly, information about a test's power is very important for interpreting diagnostic and research results.

As with estimation and confidence intervals, professional research organizations and scholarly journals strongly recommend that investigators report power along with statistical significance. And as with confidence intervals, the advice is still more often given than followed. I would guess that readers of research reports will, in coming years, encounter rapidly increasing numbers of estimates with confidence intervals, but they will probably see reports of power increase more slowly. Part of the reason is that although the concept of power is clear enough to most people (on the analogy of, for example, the power of a microscope), power coefficients are harder to compute and interpret. Statistical packages do not routinely produce power coefficients by default, although some packages will do so as an option for some tests.

As a researcher, you would surely want to know whether your test (of the null hypothesis) is powerful enough to uncover an important relationship, one that is big enough to matter. You want to be able to detect the smallest relationship (such as a difference in sample means) that is substantial enough to be of interest. (The calculations are too technical to review in this book; see a specialized statistics text—e.g., Hinkle, Wiersma, & Jurs, 1998—for details.) As we have seen, you can increase your statistical power by increasing your sample size. How big should you make your sample in order to increase your statistical power? Although there is no invariably correct answer to this question, the advice of Glass and Hopkins (1996, p. 266) is very reasonable: "Take the largest sample that is practical and then determine if this sample size has adequate power for detecting a difference large enough to be of interest."

This chapter quickly reviewed statistical inference, both the confidence-interval approach and the statistical significance approach. Though the use of confidence intervals is often strongly recommended, it still is not widely practiced in many fields. Inference without intervals is much more common. This review of significance tests has been limited to one variety of the *t*-test and one type of the *F* test (or ANOVA). Although these two are by far the most commonly used, many other statistical tests exist. Different tests are used with particular research designs or with specific types of data (see Chapter 11 for examples). If you intend to do quantitative research, you will almost certainly conduct significance tests and construct confidence intervals. My advice is *not* to begin by surveying the range of possible statistical tests that you *might* use in your research. There are dozens of them. It is not efficient to learn many techniques in advance *in case* you should ever happen to need one. Rather, I recommend beginning your research by asking an important research question and designing a plan to gather good evidence relevant to answering it. Once you know your design and the kind of evidence it will yield, *then* you will want to investigate the kinds of statistical inferences relevant to your work. If you have a good grasp of the meaning and uses of statistical inference, you can learn (or look up) the specific applications when you need to know them.

Clearly, the subject of statistical inference is a complicated and controversial one. For many researchers, being able to make valid statistical inferences is their chief goal, the main reason they do research. For other quantitative researchers it is important, but only as a sort of screening device. Such researchers believe that for a result to be important, it may often be *necessary* that it be statistically significant, but its statistical significance is very far from *sufficient*. Many of the researchers in this latter group, which assigns a less prominent role to statistical inference, are practitioners of the art of regression analysis, which is the subject of the next chapter.

Terms and Concepts to Review

Effect size (ES)
Confidence interval (CI)
Confidence level
Exact *p*-value

Statistical power
- False positive
- False negative

Levene's test for equality of variances
t-test/ratio

2-direction *t*-test
- 2-tailed *t*-test
- Nondirectional *t*-test

Standard error (SE)
Sampling distribution

Mean square (MS)
- Variance

MS within groups
MS between groups

F ratio/test
- ANOVA

Discussion Questions

1. If you had to choose between using estimation with confidence intervals and measures of statistical significance, which would you choose and why? Which would you rather read in a research report by someone else?

2. Discuss the effects of increasing sample size on *p*-values, confidence intervals, standard errors, and power. What happens to each of these as sample size increases and decreases?

3. Describe in general terms what the standard error is. How is the standard error used in statistical inference?

Self-Test

If you can answer most of the following questions accurately, you can feel confident about your understanding of the material in this chapter. If not, it would be a good idea to review the chapter. (Answers can be found in the Appendix.)

1. The standard error is an estimate of sampling error. True or False?

2. As the size of samples increases, standard errors will decrease. True or False?

3. A confidence interval (CI) is an estimate of the range within which a population value is likely to be located. True or False?

4. If you were estimating population values with your sample data and using confidence intervals to discuss your estimates, you would need a wider interval (bigger margin of error) with a 99% confidence level than with a 95% confidence level. True or False?

5. Statistical significance tells you only about the probability of getting a particular result; it does not tell you whether that result is "significant" in any other sense of the term. True or False?

6. Statistical significance is a measure of the likelihood of making Type II errors. True or False?

7. If in the course of your research you have to choose whether to emphasize Type I or Type II error, you can use one of several statistical formulae or software routines for deciding. True or False?

8. Statistical power is the ability of a statistical test to detect relations between/among variables. True or False?

9. The smaller your sample, the less likely you are to be able to detect relationships among your variables. True or False?

10. Confidence intervals give researchers more information than do significance tests. True or False?

11. Statistical significance, power, and effect size are unrelated concepts. True or False?

12. In order to use ANOVA to study a continuous (quantitative) IV, a researcher would have to divide that variable into categorical or rank-order groups, such as low, medium, and high. True or False?

13. To assess statistical significance, ANOVA compares the variance within groups to the variance between groups. True or False?

14. In an ANOVA, the bigger the within-group variance, the more likely a treatment is to be statistically significant. True or False?

15. The *F* ratio is obtained by dividing the average variability between treatment groups by the average variability within treatment groups. True or False?

16. If you are conducting a study with two IVs and you want to test for the presence of an interaction effect, you should use one-way ANOVA. True or False?

Endnotes

1. There is also a distinction between significance testing and hypothesis testing that some experts think is still important. It arose out of a historical debate between the inventors of various inferential techniques. See the series of comments and replies in *The American Statistician, 57* (3), 2003, 171–182.

2. Note that this is another of those occasions on which it is *good* to get a *statistically* nonsignificant result.

9

Regression Analysis

Regression analysis is oddly named. People who first hear of it are often surprised at what it involves. It has nothing to do with the common meaning of returning to an earlier or a lower stage or declining to a previous level, such as a 10-year-old who starts wetting the bed and sucking his thumb. And it certainly has nothing to do with séances and reincarnation. If we named regression for its main uses, we would call it *prediction* analysis or *explanation* analysis. In the social sciences (with the possible exception of psychology) it is by far the most widely employed method for studying quantitative evidence. It is especially useful for helping us to explain relations among multiple variables.

Regression analysis got its name by historical accident. The nineteenth-century statistics genius (and eugenics crackpot) Francis Galton is responsible. In his study of the heights of several thousand men and their sons, he noticed that very tall fathers tended to have sons who, when they reached adulthood, were tall; but they were somewhat *less* tall than their fathers. Galton called this "regression toward mediocrity." The modern statistical term for this widespread phenomenon is *regression toward the mean.* For example, when students are tested more than once on the same subject, those who get very low scores on the first test will often get somewhat higher (closer to the mean) scores on a second test. And students who get very high scores will be likely, upon being retested, to

get somewhat lower scores. In other words, extreme scores will often move (regress) toward the mean. To understand regression analysis, this chapter starts with this fact of regression toward the mean and proceeds to investigate the forms and functions of regression analysis by addressing the following questions.

1. What is regression analysis?
2. What are the basic questions that regression answers?
3. How does one read the output of a regression analysis?
4. What is a regression equation?
5. How are regression and correlation related?
6. Are regression and ANOVA antagonistic methods?
7. How can regression be used to analyze real data?
8. What are the uses and the limitations of regression analysis?

What Is Regression Analysis?

Regression happens when the independent variable does not totally predict or explain the dependent variable. In the case of Galton's study of the nineteenth-century sons' heights, the regression toward the mean

145

occurred because other factors besides their fathers' heights—most obviously, their mothers' heights and grandparents' heights—also determined the sons' stature. If sons were always exactly as tall as their fathers, there would be no regression. Were there no regression, a father's height would perfectly predict his son's height.

In the case of retesting students on the same material, regression toward the mean may occur because of measurement error. For example, some part of a very high (or very low) score on the first test may be good (or bad) luck. When students are retested, good or bad luck is likely to change. This means that the common practice of selecting subjects for an experiment or for a program because they have extreme scores on a test almost guarantees regression toward the mean. For instance, if a school decides who is eligible for a new remedial curriculum by selecting those with the lowest scores, some of the improvement of those students is likely to be due, not to the program, but to regression toward the mean. Be that as it may, the less regression toward the mean, the better one can predict or explain a dependent variable. The more regression toward the mean, the less well one can predict or explain. By analyzing regression to the mean, it is possible to determine the degree to which information about some variables can be used to predict or explain others.

When reading research that uses regression analysis, you will often encounter the expression *regress on*. This means "explain by" or "predict with." For example, "We regressed tenth-grade test scores on class size and on eighth-grade test scores." This means that the authors explained variance in the tenth-grade scores (the dependent variable) by variance in class sizes and in eighth-grade scores (the independent variables). So again, by quirk of history, we are saddled with very unhelpful terms: In a world that valued clarity of expression, *regress on* would not mean explain by or predict with—but it does. Unfortunately, there is nothing to be done about such odd jargon except to try to demystify it. Because it is widely used, one has to learn it if one wants to read discussions of quantitative research.

What Are the Basic Questions That Regression Answers?

Many varieties of regression analysis exist. Although the technical complexity of some of the advanced forms of regression analysis is high, all forms, even the most advanced, *always* ask some version of one basic question: *How much better can I predict (or explain) a dependent variable (Y) if I know an independent variable (X)?* This is *the* fundamental fact about regression. Regardless of the complications we will encounter when studying the subject further in Part 2 of this book, the goal in regression analysis is always to answer a form of, or an elaboration on, this question.

Problems on which regression is used usually have more than one independent variable—labeled $X_1, X_2, X_3, \ldots$ When there is more than one independent variable, we are doing *multiple* (or multivariate) regression analysis.[1] Using multiple regression analysis, two main questions can be answered:

1. Taking all the Xs (independent or predictor variables) together, how much better can we predict Y (the dependent or outcome or criterion variable)? For example, if you know students' high school grades *and* their SAT scores, how much better can you estimate their college grades? Here the main emphasis is on putting together the evidence from all the independent variables to make the best or most efficient predictions of the values of the dependent variable, as admissions committees might do.

2. How much better can we explain Y if we know X_1—while *controlling for* (statistically subtracting or eliminating the effects of, or taking into account) X_2, $X_3, \ldots$? For example, how much does class size affect math achievement after taking into account (controlling for) teacher quality, expenditure per pupil, and students' prior math achievement? Here the emphasis is usually on studying the relative importance of the independent variables, as might be done when one wanted to understand the factors that contributed most to student learning.

In sum, when using multiple regression there are three kinds of issues: (1) the total contribution of all the independent variables together; (2) the comparative importance of different variables; and (3) the role of a particular independent variable separate from the effects of the other independent variables. Although these are distinct issues, the mathematics involved is the same. Our interests as researchers determine whether we focus on predicting by using all the IVs together or on explaining the separate effects of the independent variables. The questions researchers ask of regression analyses are shaped by the goals of their research, not by the technicalities of computations.

How Does One Read the Output of a Regression Analysis?

Regardless of what questions we use regression to address, the answers are always expressed the same way. The three most important numbers for interpreting the results of a multiple regression analysis are (1) R^2, or the percentage of variance in the dependent variable (Y) explained by the independent variables, that is, $X_1, X_2, X_3...$; (2) the regression coefficients, b and beta; and (3) the statistical significance of the regression coefficients.

R^2

R^2 is an estimate of the total variance in the dependent variable predicted by or explained by or associated with *all* the independent variables taken together. Readers of the results of a regression analysis often start out by looking at the R^2, because it gives an overall measure of how much of the variance in the study's dependent variable can be predicted or explained. If the R^2 in a study of the effects of high school GPA and SAT scores on college GPA were .32, that would mean that 32% of the variance in college GPA is accounted for by (or associated with, or predicted by) the two independent variables taken together. It *also* means that 68% is not. Put another way: R^2 tells you how much better you can

guess the dependent variable if you know the independent variables. Better than what? Better than the average or the mean. If you had to guess a student's GPA and knew nothing at all about that student except the college he or she were attending, your best guess (the guess that would on average be closest to the actual value) would be the mean GPA for all students at that college. But, if you knew that student's high school GPA and his or her SAT scores, you would be able to make a better guess. In this hypothetical example, you could guess, on average, 32% better. This is the kind of guess (prediction) admissions committees make.

The Regression Coefficients **b** *and Beta*

A *regression coefficient,* usually symbolized b, is a number that answers the question: What happens on average to a dependent (or outcome) variable when the predictor (independent) variable goes up by 1? For example, if every 1-point increase in high school GPA were associated with three-tenths of a point increase in college GPA, the regression coefficient for high school GPA would be .3. This means that on average one would expect students with high school GPAs of 3.0 to have college GPAs .3 higher than those with high school GPAs of 2.0.

Regression coefficients can vary dramatically in size even when the strength of the relationship they express is similar. For example, say we were studying the relation between years of schooling completed and annual income. If we found that on average for every year of education completed expected annual income went up by $1,200, then the regression coefficient for this relation would be 1200. Consider our two examples of regression coefficient: .3 and 1200. One is thousands of times bigger (4,000 times bigger to be precise) than the other. Does the bigger one describe a stronger relationship? Not necessarily, and surely not one that is thousands of times stronger. The difference in the size of the regression coefficients has to do with the size of the variables and how they are measured. The highest GPA is 4. The highest income in the sample might be $400,000. That is why a regression coefficient dealing with income will almost inevitably be larger than one dealing with GPA. Even the same variable, measured on a different scale, can yield regression coefficients that are very different in size. Consider the effects on some measure of health, such as cholesterol level, of amount of exercise per week—measured in hours, minutes, or seconds. Say that for each additional hour of exercise, cholesterol went down an average of 4 points. For each minute it would go down .067 point and for each second, .001 point. The coefficient *b* measured in minutes would be 60 times smaller than the one for hours, and the one for seconds would be 3,600 times smaller, but the strength of the effect of exercise would be *exactly* the same.

In a regression equation discussed later, we will see a hypothetical value of .3 for high school GPA and .004 for every SAT point above 500. What matters more for predicting college GPA? We cannot tell by comparing the *unstandardized* regression coefficients. Differences in the size, or measurement scale, of the variables mean that ordinary regression coefficients cannot usually be compared directly. But *standardized* regression coefficients can be. The standardized regression coefficient has already been discussed by another name—the Pearson *r* correlation. Correlation is a special case of regression, and the Pearson *r* is a standardized regression coefficient between two variables. In fact, the reason correlation is abbreviated *r* rather than *c* is that the *r* originally stood for *regression* (a name that was popularized by Galton's younger colleague Pearson). In any case, a standardized regression coefficient, usually symbolized *beta,* answers the same question as an ordinary regression coefficient, but it does so in standard deviation units, that is, as *z*-scores (see Chapter 2 for a review). When using standardized coefficients, the (slightly revised) question the coefficient answers is: *For every 1 standard deviation increase in an independent variable (*X*), how many standard deviations of an increase can be expected in the dependent variable (*Y*)?*

Using standardized coefficients has the great advantage of comparability among coefficients. But this is sometimes offset by the disadvantage that these coefficients can be hard to interpret. For ex-

ample, knowing that a 1 SD increase in years of education is associated with .37 SD units of income is pretty obscure compared to saying that 1 year is associated with $1,200. The standardized coefficient *beta* is more effective at communicating some results and the unstandardized *b* is better at others. Researchers often report both.

In sum, in *multiple* regression analysis, a regression coefficient, whether standardized or not, answers the following question[2]: For every one-unit increase in an independent variable, what change is expected in the dependent variable—*controlling for (taking into account) the effects of all the other independent variables*? In the example of the high school GPA, SAT scores, and college GPA, the regression coefficient for high school GPA is reported after "subtracting" (or controlling for or holding constant) the effects of SAT. And the reported coefficient for SAT is the effect of SAT minus the effect of high school GPA. What the subtracting or controlling does is eliminate "double counting." High school GPA and SAT scores each help predict college GPA, but they are not independent; that is, the two IVs can also be used to predict one another. By controlling for this overlap, multiple regression identifies the unique or independent contribution of each predictor (IV) to the outcome (DV).

The Statistical Significance of Regression Coefficients

The statistical significance of regression coefficients can be dealt with quickly, because it means the same thing as the statistical significance of any value or measure of a variable. A statistic is significant if it is unlikely to have been obtained by coincidence. More specifically, statistical significance answers the question: How likely would we be to get a result (regression coefficient) of this size (or bigger) in a sample of this size, *if* the coefficient in the population were zero? For an individual regression coefficient, this is computed using the *t*-test and, as always, statistical significance is reported using *p*-values. Confidence intervals (see Chapter 8) can also be computed for regression coefficients. Although reporting confidence

FIGURE 9.1 *Moving from a verbal description to a regression equation*

1. predicted college GPA = average college GPA + high school GPA + SAT score
2. dependent variable = intercept or constant + independent variable 1 + independent variable 2
3. $Y' = a + b_1X_1 + b_2X_2$
4. $Y = a + b_1X_1 + b_2X_2 + e$

intervals would be good practice, it is not often done with regression coefficients. Rather, statistical significance is the usual inferential technique. As always, the smaller the *p*-value, the greater the statistical significance. As with any other assessment of statistical significance, of course, *statistically* significant does not necessarily mean big or important. In the terms of multiple regression, the coefficient for a variable can be highly (statistically) significant without increasing R^2 by very much. Finally, in regression one also tests the statistical significance of an entire set of independent variables and their relation with the dependent variable. This test is conducted with an ANOVA (also known as *F* test). What is tested is essentially the overall R^2 for the regression equation. More specifically, the *F* test for the whole model tests the null hypothesis that all the coefficients equal zero in the population (Allison, 1999).

What Is a Regression Equation?

As seen in Chapter 3, relations among variables can be described using equations. In published research using regression analysis, one often encounters equations. They summarize how the researchers have designed their study. At first, regression equations look formidable and mysterious, especially to those who have little math background. But the basic concepts are easy enough to understand by looking once more at our familiar example. Say you sit on an admissions committee that uses high school GPA and SAT scores to predict students' likely college GPA. Knowing students' likely college GPA helps you decide whether to admit them. We can move from describing this task in sentences to describing

it in a formula in the four easy steps described in Figure 9.1.

1. The first step says to estimate a student's college GPA start with the average college GPA. In the absence of any other knowledge, the average would be the best guess. Then add to that guess the other information available. One might conclude, for example, that because a particular student's high school GPA and SAT scores are quite a bit higher than average, she will have a higher college GPA than average.

2. The second step basically repeats the same information as in step 1 but describes it with more general labels. Predicted college GPA is now called the dependent variable. High school GPA and SAT score are now named independent variables 1 and 2. Average college GPA has been *replaced* by the intercept (also called the *constant* and the *Y-intercept*).

The *intercept* is what the value of the dependent variable would be if the values of all the independent variables were zero. Although the intercept is necessary to use the equation, it often has no substantive meaning in multiple regression. For example, it is inconceivable that we would receive applications for college admission from students with 0.0 high school GPAs and SAT scores of 0.

3. The third step replaces the verbal labels with letters. *Y* is the usual symbol for the dependent variable. Note that a *prime* mark ' is added to the *Y* (sometimes a circumflex ^ called a *hat* is used instead). This mark is merely a reminder that the value is an estimate. *X* is the usual symbol for an independent variable. Because there are two independent variables, they are called X_1 and X_2. The letter *b* is the symbol for the unstandardized regression coefficient.

So step 3 translates as follows: To estimate *Y*, take the intercept (*a*) and add to it the value of X_1 times the regression coefficient (b_1) for X_1 *plus* the value of X_2 times the regression coefficient (b_2) for variable 2.

Let's see how to use the equation to make an actual prediction. Say that the value of *a* is 2.0, and the value of b_1, or high school GPA, is .3. The value of the average SAT score, or b_2, is .004. In the case of SAT, which is a standard score with a mean of 500, the value could be calculated on points above 500. A student applies for admission. She has a high school GPA of 3.0 and an SAT of 600, which is 100 points above the mean of 500. What would be the estimate of her college GPA? Putting these numbers into the formula yields:

$$Y' = 2.0 + (.3 \times 3.0) + (.004 \times 100)$$

or

$$Y' = 2.0 + .90 + .40$$

or

$$Y' = 3.30$$

This means that the estimate of the student's probable college GPA is 3.30.

Let's take another student, one with a high school GPA of 2.0 and an SAT score of 400, or 100 points *below* 500. For this student the figures would be

$$Y' = 2.0 + (.3 \times 2.0) + (.004 \times -100)$$

$$Y' = 2.0 + .60 - .40$$

$$Y' = 2.20$$

So the estimate of this second student's college GPA is 2.2. Obviously, all else equal, a college would be more eager to admit the first student than the second. She would have a higher probability of success at college.

4. The fourth step in Figure 9.1 is a more general version of the regression equation, but it has little practical value. The prime mark is removed from the *Y* and the letter *e* is added, which stands for error. It indicates that the estimates will never be exact. Estimates will be off for many reasons. First, the independent variables are never perfect predictors of the dependent variable. Second, the IVs are never perfectly measured. And third, there are almost always other influences on the dependent variable that are not included in the equation; for example, in this case, the students' level of effort, social support, and financial resources could all influence their college GPAs. The letter *e* thus stands for all the measurement errors and all the omissions and reminds us not to forget those. This *error term* is mathematically necessary, because, without it, the equation would wrongly assert that high school GPA and SAT were the *only* determinants of college GPA.

Where do the values for *a*, b_1, and b_2 come from? It is clear where the values of X_1 (high school grades) and X_2 (SAT scores) for individual students originate. They come from the students' applications. When my students ask where *a*, b_1, and b_2 come from, I say, "The computer gives them to us." If they are dissatisfied with that answer, I begin to explain. Typically, after a couple of minutes, they say, "Oh, never mind." So, I will be very brief. The intercept, *a*, and the regression coefficients, b_1 and b_2, are computed using the applications and grades of students who attended our college in prior years. One might, for example, take a random sample of 2,000 students attending our college over the last four years and then compute the intercept and regression coefficients for that sample. The process is similar, though more complicated, to computing correlations between variables; many sums of squares are involved (see the example in Chapter 2). Once the intercept and coefficients are computed, they would be used to make a formula (regression equation), which we would then use to predict likely grades of future applicants.

When using the formula to *predict* the likely GPAs of this year's applicants, we *assume* that the future will be like the past; that is, what was true of students, their SATs, and their GPAs in past years will continue to be true of them in coming years. Of course, this kind of assumption, like any assumption about the future, can easily be wrong. And, it is not a matter of statistics; it is an assumption about the level of stability in the world. Afterward, next year, we can check to see whether the assumption was true this year, but we can only compute statistics on past data. Future data do not yet exist, so it is impossible to plug them into computer programs.

To use the formula to *explain* (not only predict) the dependent variable, college GPA, with, for example, an eye to developing programs to help students in academic trouble, one would want to add many more variables than background variables such as high school grades and SAT scores. Of probable interest would be variables pertaining to students' experiences in college, such as their majors, whether they worked off campus, whether they lived in residence halls, and so on. One might learn that students who majored in a particular subject and worked and lived off campus had, on average, lower college GPAs. Counselors might use this information to good effect. Regardless of the use one puts them to, explanation or prediction, the regression coefficients and the way they are computed are the same. One can get a general idea of those computations and what is involved in regression analyses by comparing them to correlation.

How Are Regression and Correlation Related?

Correlation and regression analysis are often discussed together. This makes good conceptual sense because they are related techniques. One common abbreviation is *MRC*—for multiple regression and correlation (Cohen et al., 2003; Keppel & Zedick, 1989). The biggest difference between the two is that correlation coefficients do not imply a causal direction; regression coefficients do. The correlation between variable *A* and variable *B* is exactly the same as between *B* and *A*. But with regression analysis, using *A* to predict *B* is *not* the same thing as using *B* to predict *A*. Using SAT to predict GPA is not the same as using GPA to predict SAT, and the regression coefficients for the two predictions will be different (the

correlation is the same). The relation of two variables in a correlation is called *symmetric,* whereas that between two variables in a regression is called *asymmetric.* Graphically, the difference can be shown as follows, with the arrows representing the direction of cause or prediction:

Correlation: $A \leftrightarrow B$

Regression: $A \rightarrow B$ OR $B \rightarrow A$

Discussing regression and its relation to correlation is most easily done with *bivariate* examples—that is, relations involving only two variables, one independent and one dependent—and that is how we will begin. However, virtually all regression analyses are multiple or multivariate, using two or more independent variables and sometimes multiple dependent variables too. By contrast, correlations are almost always computed for variables two at a time. Forms of multiple correlation[3] exist, but they have been largely supplanted in the research literature by regression analysis.

Conceptually, the relation of correlation and regression can be grasped most easily by using a scatter diagram. Figure 9.2 is a scatter diagram for the scores on Exam 1 and Exam 2 for the 35 students in the example encountered several times already. The line drawn through the dots is the *regression line.* It is the line that comes closest to the dots. The angle of the line, known as its *slope,* is described by the regression coefficient, *b.* The correlation coefficient, *r,* measures how close the dots are to the line. In simple terms, then, we have the angle of the line through the dots and the distance of the dots from the line. You can't get the line that comes closest to the dots unless you have the dots, and you can't measure the distance of the dots from the line without the line. Correlation and regression are thus closely dependent on each other—roughly like the relation of the chicken and the egg.

Figure 9.2 represents the correlation of Exam 1 and Exam 2. The regression line moves upward from left to right, which means that the correlation and the regression coefficients are positive. The dots are quite close to the line, which means that the correlation is

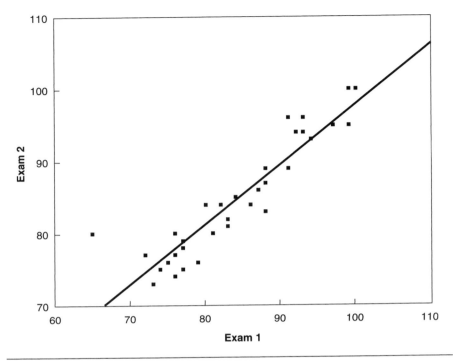

FIGURE 9.2 *Correlation of Exam 1 and Exam 2 with regression line*

strong—r = .917 in this case. Figure 9.3 depicts the correlation between Exam 1 and the project. Here the regression line moves down from left to right, which means that the correlation and the regression coefficient are negative (when the scores for Exam 1 go up the scores on the project go down). The dots are quite a bit farther from the line, so the correlation is not as strong—r = −.511 in this case.

Looking at the regression lines in Figures 9.2 and 9.3 shows another way to see what a regression coefficient is. Our original question answered by the regression coefficient was: For every 1 unit increase in the independent (or X) variable, how much of an increase do we get in the dependent (or Y) variable? Translating this into graphic terms, the same question is: For every one unit of movement to the right on the horizontal (or X) axis of the graph, how much does the regression line move up on the vertical (or Y) axis? The regression coefficient is a ratio of movement up (in the dependent variable) divided by move-

ment right (in the independent variable). Increase (movement rightward) in the independent variable is sometimes called the *run,* whereas increase in the dependent variable is called the *rise.* Using these terms, the regression coefficient, $b,$ is the rise divided by the run, or the ratio of the rise to the run. If the regression coefficient is negative, this means a movement to the right on the X axis is followed by a movement down on the Y axis. The slope is downward from left to right.

Are Regression and ANOVA Antagonistic Methods?

Oddly, regression analysis has often been seen as competing with ANOVA. Newton and Rudestam (1999) refer to regression and ANOVA as the "big two" families of statistical analyses, and point out that these two have sometimes developed in com-

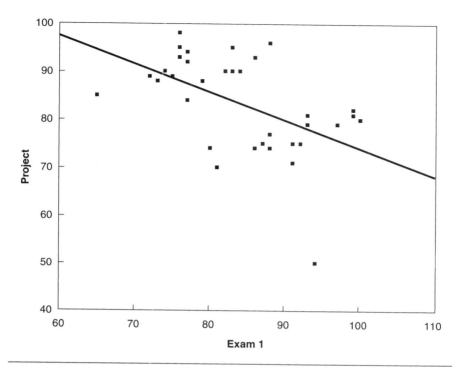

FIGURE 9.3 *Correlation of Exam 1 and Project with regression line*

parative isolation from one another. The notion that the two are in competition has much more to do with traditions of research in various fields than it does with statistics, because both are built on the same *general linear model.* Researchers in different disciplines have traditionally reported their quantitative results in different ways. ANOVA approaches have been prevalent in psychology and psychology-dominated disciplines such as education. Regression approaches are preferred in most other social science disciplines, including economics and economics-dominated disciplines such as business. Regression is also dominant in sociology and political science. Yet regression and ANOVA are routinely paired. For example, when one wants to test a multiple regression equation for statistical significance, one does so with an ANOVA. Or, when one conducts an analysis of covariance (ANCOVA) in order to improve on an ANOVA, regression techniques are used to adjust for a control variable before performing the ANOVA. Ul-

timately, the statistical differences between the two approaches are not fundamental. Anyone who has ever calculated them by hand can attest to the fact the most of the grunt work is the same.

It is perhaps easiest to see the similarity of the two methods by comparing their bivariate cousins, that is, the Pearson r and the t-test, and referring to earlier examples. Recall that in previous chapters (Table 2.5) the Pearson r between Exam 1 and gender was computed. Later, a t-test of the mean difference between males and females on Exam 1 was conducted (Table 8.2). The mean for females was about 85.6 and for males it was about 82.8, for a mean difference of 2.8. Using the t-test for equality of means it was concluded that the male–female difference in scores was not statistically significant (p = .342). The Pearson r between gender and scores on Exam 1 was .166. SPSS produced a t-test of the correlation coefficient; examining this, we found the correlation to be statistically insignificant (p = .342).

It is no coincidence that we got the same *p*-value for each. The two questions asked by the analyses are mirror images of one another: (1) What is the difference by gender on test scores, and is it statistically significant? (2) What is the similarity (co-relation) between gender and test scores, and is it statistically significant? The answers are that the average difference between the genders is small and that the correlation of gender and test scores is small; and neither is statistically significant—and they are insignificant to *exactly* the same degree.

Is it better to report the mean difference or the correlation? Once again, the only reasonable answer is: It depends. I'd say that for the relation of gender to test scores, the mean difference is more revealing. On the other hand, to talk about the relation of scores on two exams, such as Exam 1 and Exam 2, the Pearson *r* conveys more useful information. If the independent variable is dichotomous, like gender is, a *t*-test of the difference between the means often most directly provides the information one would want. But if the independent variable is quantitative, to use a *t*-test or an ANOVA, information would have to be discarded. For example, if Exam 1 is the independent variable and Exam 2 is the dependent variable, to do a *t*-test would require converting the scores on Exam 1 into two groups, high and low. Then one could see whether there was a significant difference in the average scores on Exam 2 between those who scored high and those who scored low on Exam 1. Clearly, this would be a very inefficient way to look at the relation of the two exams. Most of the information about Exam 1 (the specific scores) would have to be discarded to use the *t*-test.

Although there is no one best approach for all problems, the regression/correlation approach is more versatile in the range of problems it can handle. Anything you can do with ANOVA you can do with regression, but the reverse is not true. The advantages of regression over ANOVA fall into four categories.

1. As with the *t*-test, so too with ANOVA, the independent variables must be categorical; if the independent variables are quantitative, they have to be converted into categorical variables, for example, by clustering quantitative scores into high, medium, and low. In regression analysis, the independent variables can be either qualitative or quantitative.

2. The number of independent variables (IVs) that each method can comfortably handle varies greatly. With ANOVA when one has three or more IVs, the analyses become quite complex. For example, with three IVs, the three-way ANOVA tests for 3 main effects and 4 interaction effects. In my experience, most novice (and many experienced) researchers find it easier to interpret the results of a regression analysis on the same data. Regression analyses can easily handle 10 or 15 independent variables. Studying that many independent variables with ANOVA would be nightmarishly difficult.

3. Regression coefficients give the researcher a measure of the *size* of the effect of the independent variable on the dependent variable, and they do so controlling for the other independent variables. ANOVA tells the researcher only whether *somewhere* among the independent variables and their interactions *something* is statistically significant. But ANOVA does not say *which* variable is significant or how big its effect is.

4. In ANOVA, the dependent variable (DV) must be quantitative. In the typical form of regression, the DVs are also quantitative, but regression techniques exist for handling categorical DVs, most importantly, logistic regression.

In sum, when using regression analysis the researcher can handle both qualitative and quantitative data for either independent or dependent variables. Also, many people find results of regression analyses easier to interpret, especially in problems containing many independent variables. Dealing with three or more IVs using ANOVA is extremely complicated.

For example, Young and Shaw (1999) studied 25 independent variables. Each was an item on a questionnaire about college professors' teaching. The questions asked whether the professors were enthusiastic, well organized, open to students' questions, available outside of class, and so on. A sample of 912 students answered these questions. The students also answered a question about the overall effectiveness of the college and university teachers they rated. Students were asked to agree or disagree on a nine-point scale with a statement saying that compared to other professors, this one is "extremely effective." This overall effectiveness question was Young and Shaw's dependent variable. The authors wanted to learn which among the 25 characteristics of teachers (well prepared, knowledge of subject matter, enthusiasm, etc.) were the most important determinants of students' overall ratings of teacher quality. Which ingredients of good teaching (concern for student learning, being well organized, having a sense of humor, etc.) most importantly determined students' overall rating of effectiveness? The researchers found that 7 of the 25 independent variables together explained 87% of the variance in the dependent variable; that is, the R^2 was .87. Adding the other 18 independent variables to the equation increased the explained variance (or R^2) by only one percent. Of the 7 IVs, none was a *sufficient* determinant of an overall rating of effectiveness. Any one of the traits—such as being well organized or concerned for students' learning—was not enough. Nor was any one of the traits *necessary,* though having a good rating on 5 or 6 of them did seem to be necessary. But it did not always have to be the same 5 or 6. Being weak in one or two areas, even those areas that were very important determinants of the overall ranking, could be offset by excellence in other areas. In sum, there was no one single way to be judged an effective college teacher.

Causation is like that in the social sciences. Many different independent variables can contribute, and in varying degrees, to the same effect. Multiple regression analysis enables us to identify variables that contribute to an outcome and to measure the comparative sizes of their contributions. To understand how regression is used in research to solve problems and make decisions, it is best to turn to a concrete example. The question investigated is whether a particular university discriminated against its female professors in the salary it paid them. Did males earn more for no other reason than they were male?

TABLE 9.1 *Average Salary and Years of Experience for a Sample of 50 Faculty Members*

Female = 1	N	Mean	Standard Deviation
Salary			
1	22	44281.82	6061.874
0	28	62967.86	15534.861
Years			
1	22	8.59	5.704
0	28	14.46	6.552

How Can Regression Be Used to Analyze Real Data?

A random sample of 50 faculty members was drawn from a public university; the data are real, not hypothetical.[4] The sample includes 22 women and 28 men. The average salary for the women was about $44,300; for the men it was around $63,000, a difference of almost $19,000. Those numbers make a *prima facie* case for gender discrimination in salary. But as Table 9.1 summarizes, women faculty also had fewer years of experience on average than did the men (about 8.5 versus 14.5), a difference of about 5.5 years.

So, are the differences in salary wholly explained by the differences in years' experience? If experience explains only part of the salary difference, how big of a part? In other words, if men and women had identical years' experience, would their salaries be identical? These are the sorts of questions that regression analysis is meant to help with. Indeed, among the best-known uses of regression analysis in public policy questions has been in gender discrimination cases.

In our example, the outcome variable is salary; the predictor variables are gender and years of experience. The SPSS regression output for the data about these 50 faculty members follows in Table 9.2. The answers we seek are mostly found in the column headed *B*, the regression coefficients. Look first at the bottom row of the column, the row for years'

TABLE 9.2 *Regression Analysis: Salary, Gender, and Years' Experience of 50 Faculty Members*

Model		Unstandardized Coefficients		Standardized Coefficients		
		B	**Standard Error**	**Beta**	**T**	**Sig.**
1	(Constant)	49034.54	4209.13		11.650	.000
	Female = 1	−13028.27	3443.22	−.425	−3.784	.000
	Years experience	963.29	253.82	.426	3.795	.000

Notes: Dependent variable: Salary; R-squared = .52.

experience. The regression coefficient is 963.29. This means that, on average, 1 year of experience (the predictor variable) was worth $963.29 in salary (the outcome variable).

In these data gender is coded: female = 1, male = 0. This is usually called, for no good reason, *dummy coding*. (I prefer *indicator coding,* because 1 and 0 merely indicate membership in a group, but this term is less widely used.) Putting our conclusion in the terms used in the previous examples is odd: For every one-unit increase in gender, salary goes down about $13,000. We know it goes down because the coefficient is negative. The conclusion from this regression analysis is: Females earn on average $13,028 less than males, *even taking into account differences in years of experience*. The raw difference, without taking experience into account, was about $19,000. Regression analysis indicates that some of that difference was due to a difference in years of experience, but much of it was not. If men and women at this university had identical years of experience, their salaries would probably still differ substantially. Remember that these conclusions apply first to a sample. Because it was a random sample, they *probably* apply to the population, too. How probably? Look at the column for "Sig." for the row Female = 1. It indicates that if there were no difference between men and women in the population, the probability that a result this big would occur in the random sample are extremely remote (Sig. = 000).

That's the kind of answer you can get with regression analysis, but what *is* regression analysis really? To trust the results, it is important to under-

stand where they come from. Elaborating on our earlier discussion, the basic idea of regression analysis can be shown graphically. Figure 9.4 is a scatter diagram of the salaries and years of experience of our 50 faculty members. Each dot represents one faculty member. For example, the dot on the far lower left is a person with about 2 years of experience and making about $31,000. The highest paid individual (around $98,000) has about 20 years of experience.

The *line* is what is crucial for understanding regression analysis. It summarizes the *average* relation between experience and salary; it is the line that comes closest, on average, to all the dots. It is the *regression line*. The slope or angle of the line gives you the regression coefficient. Looking at the line, you can see that for every one unit the line moves to the right on the horizontal axis (experience, the predictor variable) the line moves up about $1,000 on the vertical axis (salary, the outcome variable). That $1,000 is the regression coefficient (B = 963 in Table 9.2).

The point at which the line crosses the vertical axis is called the intercept or constant. Technically, the intercept is the value of the outcome (dependent) variable when all the predictors (independent variables) are zero. Because the line crosses the vertical axis at about $39,000, that means that a person (both sexes, male and female averaged together) with no years of experience would make on average about $39,000. To estimate what the salary of someone with 5 years of experience would be, you would add $5,000 ($1,000 for each year of experience) to the $39,000. This would give you an answer of $44,000, which, eyeballing the line, looks about right.

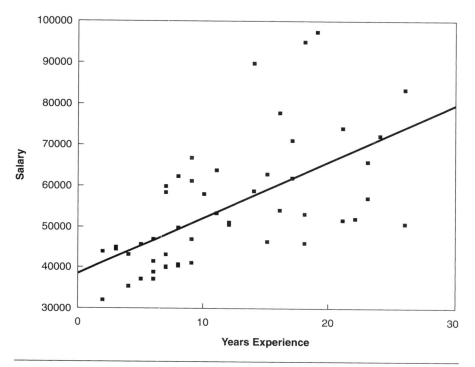

FIGURE 9.4 *Scatter diagram with regression line: years of experience and salary*

Returning to the regression results in Table 9.2, in which both gender and years of experience are studied, the intercept (called constant) is different; it is $49,034. Remember that the intercept is the value of the dependent variable when *all* the independent variables are zero. In this case, a male (coded 0; females are coded 1) with no experience would make on average $49,034. What would be the estimate that a female with zero years' experience earns? On average, $49,034 *minus* $13,028, or $36,006. To see how to get these figures, let's look at the regression equation. As seen in Figure 9.1, the generic regression equation is

$$Y = a + b_1X_1 + b_2X_2$$

In this case, Y is salary, a is the intercept, X_1 is gender, and X_2 is years of experience. Each b is a regression coefficient. So, putting in the values from the table, we get

$$Y = 49,034 + (-13,028 \times X_1) + (963 \times X_2).$$

To estimate the salary for any particular individual, we insert that individual's values on X_1 and X_2. Let's take the example of a female with 6 years of experience. Plugging in the numbers we would get 49,034 (the intercept) minus 13,028 (female) plus 5,778 (963 × 6 years of experience) = 41,784. We could thus estimate the salary for anyone as long as we knew his or her gender and years of experience. How much better could we estimate salary by knowing gender and years of experience? Go back to Table 9.2 and find the R^2. It is .52, which means we could predict 52% better; 52% of the differences in individuals' salaries are explained by gender and years of experience—and 48% of those differences were not explained by those two variables. Which of the two variables is the stronger explanation of salary differences? Here is where the beta coefficients come into play. As standardized coefficients they allow us to compare gender, which ranges from 0 to 1 with years' experience, which ranges from 2 to about 30. The two betas are virtually identical. The negative sign just means that the lower-paid group was coded 1. If we had coded males 1 and females 0, the coefficients (both standardized and unstandardized) would have been positive. The identical betas mean that the two variables made an equal contribution to the determination of salary. And are the variables statistically significant? Because this is a random sample from a population, it makes sense to compute statistical significance. The two coefficients are significant at the same level, which is given in the table under "Sig." as .000 (SPSS stops reporting after three decimal points).

What Are the Uses and the Limitations of Regression Analysis?

Can you use regression analysis to prove that there has been gender discrimination? Not really, but you can use it to refine your knowledge about such questions. In our example, you can say that *some* of the female–male salary difference ($5,658) *is associated with* differences in years of experience—and that the rest is not. That $5,658 is the difference between the male and female salaries without and with years of experience controlled: $18,686 – $13,028 = $5,658. So about 13,000 of the difference is left unexplained.

What other variables besides years of experience might account for the salary disparity? That is *not* a question for statistical analysis. The answers come from reasoning about knowledge of how universities work. It might be that women teach more and that teaching is undervalued, or they might publish less and publishing is overvalued, and/or women might be concentrated in lower-paying fields (evidence about that will be reported later). All of these, some of them, or none of them could be a full or partial explanation. We could put each of these into the set of predictor variables (making them X_3, X_4, and X_5) and recompute the male–female difference. If the salary difference got smaller as we added predictor variables, that means the additional predictors might be part of the explanation.

HOWEVER, each of these predictors (experience, publications, etc.) can be either an explanation for apparent, but not real, gender discrimination OR an explanation of *the mechanisms by which discrimination is carried out.* For example, the difference in years of experience could itself be due to gender discrimination: If women are discriminated against in the hiring and tenure process, they will accumulate fewer years' experience. Even assuming that paying according to years of experience were a perfectly equitable thing to do, if opportunities to accumulate years of experience were not made available equitably, if it were easier for males to accumulate years of experience, then experience would be a method to discriminate by gender. It would be a subtle means of discrimination because it is indirect. The discrimination could be more subtle still. Women are, of necessity, the childbearers. If they have children, and our species survival obviously depends on this, that will make it more difficult for women to accumulate years of experience. Salary schedules based on years of experience thus incorporate a biological necessity in a way that disadvantages females and advantages males.

A debate about how much of the difference in years of experience reflects discrimination cannot be *settled* by statistical analysis. Regression analysis can, however, set some parameters. What can be said after this regression analysis is that about 30% of the male–female salary difference at this university ($5,658) is explainable or predictable by years of experience—whether years of experience constitute discrimination directly or indirectly, wholly or partly.

That form of analysis will be the same with any variable. (We will add more variables and carry this analysis further in the next chapter.) Any variable that can be adduced can be a nondiscriminatory explanation for the male–female salary gap or it can reveal a mechanism by which discrimination is instituted. We want to include all important variables, but how do we know which variables to include in our list of predictors? How can we tell what kinds of relations to postulate among those variables? The answers to those questions are *never* statistical. No statistical techniques, however refined, can replace thought. Statistical analyses help researchers find patterns in evidence. There are no formulas for figuring out what evidence to gather, what patterns to look for in that evidence, and what interpretations make most sense of the patterns one finds.

Statistics helps one to be a creative researcher in roughly the same way that knowledge of grammar helps one be a creative writer. Each is a very helpful tool.

This discussion of regression analysis concludes Part 1 of the book and our review of basic quantitative research methods. These techniques are basic in the sense that all of the more advanced techniques covered in Part 2 build on them. But the advanced topics in Part 2 will not be more difficult than the basic concepts of Part 1. Rather, they will mostly be more specialized variations on already familiar themes.

Terms and Concepts to Review

Regression to the mean
Regress on
Regression equation

Regression coefficient
• Slope coefficient
• Unstandardized regression coefficient, *b*
• Standardized regression coefficient, beta: β

Intercept, *a*
• *Y* intercept
• Constant

Regression line
Slope
Run and rise of regression line
R^2

Discussion Questions

1. Consider a research topic of interest to you. How could you could study it using regression analysis? What would your research question(s) be?
2. Using the same topic from question 1, identify your dependent and independent variables. How would you decide which independent variables to include in the regression? How could you tell whether you had left out any important variables?
3. Using the same example of a research topic, discuss how you could investigate that topic using methods other than regression analysis, especially ANOVA. What would your research question(s) be? How would your research question(s) differ if you studied your topic with ANOVA as compared to when you studied your topic with regression analysis?
4. Think about this chapter's closing example about possible gender discrimination in salaries? Do you think it likely that women were discriminated against? Why or why not? Could someone make a reasonable case that although there was a large salary difference between men and women, this does not prove that the difference was due to discrimination?
5. Again, thinking about this chapter's closing example, ask yourself: What other information would I want to have in order to be more certain about my conclusions? Could evidence gathered in the study of other variables be so persuasive that might it convince someone who, on the basis of less evidence, had come to a conclusion opposite to yours? What might that additional evidence be?

Self-Test

If you can answer most of the following questions accurately, you can feel confident about your understanding of the material in this chapter. If not, it would be a good idea to review the chapter. (Answers can be found in the Appendix.)

1. Regression analysis is a more versatile technique than ANOVA; using regression one can do anything that can be done with ANOVA, but the reverse is not true. True or False?
2. Multiple regression is used for problems with two or more independent variables. True or False?
3. If you read a research report that states "We regressed employees' income on their years of experience," you can most accurately conclude that
   a. Income was the independent variable.
   b. Years of experience was the independent variable.
   c. There probably is no independent variable because this phrase refers to a correlation.
   d. The researchers tried to predict years of experience by income.
   e. All of the above are true.

4. When reading the results of a regression analysis, the *intercept* (also known as the constant and *a*) tells you
   a. The z-score for the dependent variable (DV).
   b. The strength of the relationship between an independent variable (IV) and a DV when the effect of all the other IVs has been controlled.
   c. The size of the DV when all the IVs are zero.
   d. The steepness of the incline of the slope.

5. The *coefficient of determination* (symbolized R^2)
   a. Tells you how much better you can predict the DV if you know the IVs.
   b. Is the main method used for testing the statistical significance of a regression equation.
   c. Is the most important of the coefficients in a regression equation.
   d. Gives you the effect of the IVs on the DV expressed in standard deviation units (z-scores).

6. Which of the following IVs might best be coded as a *dummy variable* in a regression analysis in which the DV was college GPA?
   a. Age
   b. High school GPA
   c. Class rank
   d. Gender
   e. Mother's education level

7. Comparing regression analysis (RA) to analysis of variance (ANOVA), it is accurate to say
   a. In ANOVA the independent variables (IVs) must be categorical, or categorized, and the dependent variables (DVs) continuous.
   b. In RA, the IVs may be either categorical or continuous.
   c. One RA can more easily handle a large number of IVs than can one ANOVA.
   d. ANOVA is for comparing means from different samples, whereas RA is for measuring the degree of association of IVs with DVs.
   e. All of the above are accurate.

8. A researcher conducts a study of the relation of poverty rates (*Y*) and the percentages of the population who are foreign born (*X*) in 500 U.S. counties. Poverty rates are measured as the percentage of the population in each county living in poverty. The regression slope (or *b*) is .30. This means
   a. 30% of the variance in poverty rates is explained by percentage foreign born.
   b. A 1% higher level in the percent foreign born is associated with a poverty rate that is 0.3% higher.
   c. The regression leaves unexplained 70% of the variance in poverty rates.

d. The intercept is .70.
   e. All of the above are true.

9. In a large university the mean salary for male faculty is $68,000; for female faculty the mean is $52,000, a difference of $14,000; a *t*-test shows this difference significant at the .01 level. Regressing salary on years of experience and gender (male = 1, female = 0), the coefficient *b* for gender is $1,300, with a *p*-value of .23. This means
   a. The salary difference between men and women is explained by the fact that men have more years of experience.
   b. The *t*-test is a more accurate measure of gender bias than is the regression coefficient.
   c. The regression coefficient, *b,* for years of experience will be bigger than the *b* for gender.
   d. The *p*-value for years of experience will be bigger than the *p*-value for gender.
   e. All of the above are true.

10. The GPAs of a large sample of students, the dependent variable, is regressed on gender (female = 1, male = 0) and on hours spent studying. The intercept, *a,* for this equation is 1.37, significant at the .01 level. This means
   a. When we find GPAs higher than 1.37, these are unlikely to be attributable to chance.
   b. Males who spent zero hours studying would, on average, have GPAs of 1.37.
   c. Females have on average GPAs 1.37 points higher than males.
   d. The R^2 for this equation is likely to be above .37.

11. A psychologist at the university health clinic believes that students who are overweight are more likely to become depressed. He collects data from his files and regresses depression (measured with a 10-point self-report scale) on overweight (yes = 1, no = 0) and gender (male = 0, female = 1). The coefficients for overweight and gender are both significant at the .05 level. This indicates
   a. That being overweight causes depression even after controlling for the effects of gender.
   b. That females who are overweight are more likely to become depressed than males who are overweight.
   c. That males who are overweight are more likely to become depressed than females who are overweight.
   d. Very little about causes of depression; it is just as likely that being depressed could lead to becoming overweight.

12. In a study of the effects of gender (female = 1, male = 0) on high school math achievement (MathAch, a

50-point test), controlling for differences in course selection, a sample of 10,000 students was drawn from a national database. The coefficient *b* for gender was .72 and was statistically significant (*p* = .000). This means that,

a. Because of the *p*-value of .000, none of the variance in the dependent variable can be attributed to variance in the independent variables.

b. Given the average difference by gender (seven-tenths of a point), the statistical significance of the coefficient was due more to the sample size than to its substantive significance.

c. Over 70% of the variance in the dependent variable can be attributed to variance in the independent variables.

d. To interpret the meaning of the coefficient, one would also need to know the *Y*-intercept, *a*.

e. All of the above are true.

13. In the study described in question 12, the data were analyzed in stages. First, math achievement was regressed on gender; the coefficient for gender was negative—*b* = –4.38. Then course selection (operationalized as "took an elective math class" yes = 1, no = 0) was added to the equation resulting in the positive coefficient for gender—*b* = .72. Both coefficients for gender were significant at the .000 level. This means that

a. Scores on the MathAch test were lower for females, but not after controlling for the fact that fewer of them took an elective course.

b. If all the variables were measured without error and if the two independent variables accounted for all the variance in MathAch scores, then if girls took the same math elective courses as boys, their average scores would go up about 5 points.

c. There was still a statistically significant gender difference even after controlling for course selection differences; after controls the females'

average on the MathAch test was higher than the males' average.

d. Most of the differences in scores on the MathAch test in this sample are attributable to differences in course selection.

e. All of the above are true.

14. In the study described in questions 12 and 13, the researcher finds that the correlation between IQ scores and MathAch scores is .43 for the boys and .20 for the girls. This means

a. Boys have higher average IQs than girls.

b. Girls have higher average IQs than boys.

c. The correlations between MathAch and IQ provide no information about the correlation between gender and IQ.

d. The regression coefficients (the *b*s) have to be different for boys and girls because correlation coefficients (the *r*s) are different for boys and girls.

e. A correlation between gender and IQ would not reveal which group had the higher average IQ.

15. As a first step in a regression analysis with 4 independent variables and 1 dependent variable, studying 100 elementary school students, a correlation matrix and scatter plots for each pair of variables is prepared. Which of the following is most accurate?

a. 25 bivariate correlations will be calculated.

b. Each scatter plot will contain 100 points.

c. Each scatter plot will contain 400 points.

d. 400 bivariate correlations will be calculated.

e. 16 bivariate correlations will be calculated.

16. If you wanted to study the relation between students' scores on an IQ test and their scores on a reading comprehension test, the best statistic to use would be

a. One-way ANOVA.

b. Four-way ANOVA.

c. Independent samples *t*-test.

d. Dependent samples *t*-test.

e. Pearson's *r*.

Endnotes

1. Statisticians differ on the question of what is properly called *multiple* or *multivariate*. Some insist that *multiple* and especially *multivariate* should be reserved for situations in which there are two or more dependent as well as two or more independent variables. Those who advocate this stricter definition seem to have lost the nominalist battle. For examples, see Allison (1999) and Berry and Sanders (2000).

2. Coefficients for more complicated forms of regression analysis (logistic regression and multilevel modeling) will be considered in Chapters 11 and 12.

3. With *partial correlations* one calculates the correlation between two variables after controlling for or "partialing out" the effects of one or more other variables. Another variant is the *semipartial correlation*. See Cohen et al. (2003).

4. Because the data are from a public university, they are public. But in return for easy, computerized access to this information I promised the officials that I would keep confidential the identity of the university and all participants. The university is not one at which I have been employed.

II

Advanced Methods

After having reviewed basic quantitative research techniques in Part 1, it is time to move to more advanced methods in Part 2 and to specialized applications in Part 3. Surprisingly, these advanced methods and special applications may often be easier to understand than were the more basic topics discussed in Part 1. Although we will be reviewing some of the most sophisticated techniques commonly used in applied research, readers who have a good grasp of the material in Part 1 should find many of these advanced methods familiar. Rather than introducing dramatically new concepts, Part 2 will instead be exploring variations and elaborations on themes discussed in Part 1.

There is one very big difference between the topics discussed in Part 1 and the subjects covered in Parts 2 and 3. Except for some computer applications, most of the material in Part 1 could have been learned quite well from a good textbook written in 1950. By contrast, nearly all of the techniques discussed in Parts 2 and 3 were not yet invented in 1950. And those that were invented were not used extensively because the computational demands were too great in an era in which there was no alternative to hand calculations. Logistic regression (Chapter 11), multilevel modeling (Chapter 12), structural equation modeling (Chapters 13 and 14), item response theory (Chapter 16), and meta-analysis (Chapter 17) were invented and developed into well-wrought tools in the

1970s, 1980s, and 1990s, and they are still undergoing refinement. A main failing of most intermediate-level texts written for professional practitioners is that these newest, most frequently used, techniques are not covered and are often not even mentioned. My goal in Parts 2 and 3 is to help correct that failing.

The five chapters of Part 2 of the book deal with advanced topics in the correlation/regression family of techniques. This family of techniques contains the most widely used forms of analysis employed in applied quantitative research in education and other professional fields, particularly research involving nonexperimental designs. It is also very much a modern, post-1950s set of techniques. Most of the methods of statistical analysis discussed in Part 1 were developed for the analysis of small samples and a limited number of variables. The methods were designed for researchers who would do their calculations by hand. Researchers needed to know the formulas and the formulas had to be simple so that they could be applied to a comparatively small number of cases and an even more limited number of variables. By contrast, factor analysis, multiple regression, multilevel modeling, and structural equation modeling require large data sets and can be applied to problems with dozens of variables. These are methods that are wholly impractical, if not quite impossible, without the use of advanced computer programs. Indeed the method of analysis is often known by the brand name of the computer program with which it is most commonly conducted. HLM for multilevel modeling and LISREL for structural equation modeling are the best-known examples.

Advanced methods of data analysis, which allow researchers to investigate problems in more of their richness and complexity than has ever been possible before, also require advanced methods of statistical inference. These advanced methods of assessing statistical significance will be addressed as required along the way, as they occur in the discussions of the techniques, such as logistic regression and structural equation modeling. In general, statistical inference is of less concern in the five chapters of Part 2. Because the advanced techniques discussed there are *large-sample* techniques, significance testing becomes less . . . , well, significant. That is because with a large sample, almost any nonzero effect, no matter how small, will be significant, statistically. Significance testing is essential for assessing the generalizability of *small* samples. That is where it is truly important. If we make an estimate based on a small sample, we want to know how confident we can be that the result will fall within a particular range (confidence interval) or what the probability (*p*-value) is that a sample result of a particular size could have been obtained if the population statistic were zero. As discussed in Chapter 8, with very large samples, standard errors will be very small; therefore the *p*-values will routinely be so low that they are often of little interest.

Part 2 begins by resuming the discussion of regression, the basic concepts of which were presented in Chapter 9. Chapter 10 looks more deeply into the method and how it can be used to analyze more complicated research problems. Of particular concern will be *regression diagnostics,* a rapidly developing field, which is made up of a cluster of techniques, many of them new and most graphical, that researchers can use to diagnose potential problems with the data before committing themselves, prematurely, to conclusions. Another emphasis will be reviewing several examples of actual research results with an eye to learning how to decipher the sometimes quirky ways these are presented. The relation of regression analysis and ANOVA will also be examined in more depth, particularly as these two methods are applied to the study of interaction effects. Chapter 10 will continue expanding on the "plain-vanilla" form of regression, called ordinary least squares, or OLS. With that review as a foundation, you will then be prepared to tackle the more advanced regression-based techniques. The discussion in Chapter 10, although based on the original and comparatively simple type of regression—ordinary least squares or OLS—is fully relevant to the consideration of more advanced forms. The assumptions, issues pertaining to causal inference, and diagnoses of potential problems with distributions, which are most easily reviewed by studying OLS regression, are wholly applicable to the more advanced versions discussed in the remainder of Part 2.

When dependent variables are not continuous, but are instead categorical or nominal, many of the regression techniques discussed thus far cannot be used—at least not correctly. Earlier chapters covered how to handle categorical *independent* variables. What is unique about Chapter 11 is that it deals with the special problems that arise when the *dependent* variable is categorical. It begins, by way of introduction, with the limits of the traditional means of studying categorical variables. Then it considers an important group of methods using the odds of categorical events. Logistic regression, discussed in Chapter 11, is one of these odds-based methods. It has become the technique of choice to use when the dependent variable is categorical or nominal, such as pass/fail, or graduate: yes/no, or bankruptcy: yes/no. It is called "logistic" not because it has military origins, but because, before they are analyzed, the scores on the outcome variables are transformed using natural logs—of odds. Logistic regression does not violate assumptions that would be violated if one used OLS for a categorical dependent variable, and this is why it is widely used. Although the coefficients are hard to interpret, they can be transformed into odds or probabilities. Then they can be used to give clear answers to questions such as: How much does a one-unit increase in an independent variable—say, grade point average or profit margin—influence the probability of a categorical dependent variable, such as graduating or bankruptcy?

With multilevel modeling (MLM), also known as hierarchical linear modeling (HLM), we move, in Chapter 12, to an entirely new level of complexity. The mathematical foundations of MLM are very demanding. Fortunately, with the development of more user-friendly computer programs, the topics discussed in Chapter 12 are within the range of readers of this book. This is fortunate because many substantive problems can be correctly approached only by using MLM. When the independent variables are "nested" within one another—such as students within classes, classes within schools, and schools within districts—the effects of the variables are confounded. Multilevel techniques enable researchers to estimate separately the effects of variables at the various levels—such as classroom, school, and district effects—on an outcome variable such as students' academic achievement. Multilevel modeling is rapidly becoming the "gold standard" in regression studies—when the data are extensive enough that it can be used.

Factor analysis, reviewed in Chapter 13, is important in its own right. It is also a fundamental building block of structural equation modeling (discussed in Chapter 14). Factor analysis is a correlational technique that can be used to greatly enhance the quality of the measurement of complicated variables. Factor analysis carries Cronbach's alpha (discussed in Chapters 5 and 7) several steps further. Not only does factor analysis indicate the extent to which the items in a scale hang together to form *one* reliable measure of a construct, it also determines whether there is more than one cluster of distinct items that are highly intercorrelated. These clusters are called factors. The scores on items within a factor are strongly intercorrelated, but the separate factors are minimally correlated. Numerous techniques (rotations) are used for distinguishing clusters of items from other clusters. Factor analysis is a very computationally demanding statistical technique, but *interpretation* of the factors has much more to do with intelligence and creativity than with calculations.

Path analysis begins the final chapter of Part 2. Examples of path analysis have already been seen in Chapter 3 in the discussion of the relations among variables. Path analysis can be thought of as regression analysis with causal diagrams. Each of the arrows in the causal diagram is labeled with a standardized regression coefficient. The coefficient indicates the strength and direction (positive or negative) of the relation between the variables. Path analysis is particularly useful for comparing the direct and indirect effects of independent variables on a dependent variable. The younger, but *much* bigger offspring of path analysis, structural equation modeling (SEM), is also discussed in Chapter 14. SEM combines the techniques of factor analysis and path analysis. The variables are examined with factor analysis to improve the quality with which the variables are measured. The relations (structures) among the variables are then computed/estimated with regression analysis. Like MLM, structural equation modeling is among the most advanced techniques that can be used—when the data are rich and the sample is sufficiently large.

Structural equation modeling (SEM) and multilevel modeling (MLM) are especially apt topics for the final chapters of this section on advanced techniques. Each is comprehensive; each incorporates nearly all the techniques discussed earlier in this book; each is built on and synthesizes the entire field of quantitative methods; each allows one to look at complicated research questions with greater precision than was possible only a couple of decades ago; and each is very extensively used in the modern research literature. Finally, although they have tended to be developed in isolation from one another (e.g., with sociologists being more interested in MLM and psychologists being more likely to use SEM), an active area of methodological research will probably eventually be successful in integrating the two.

After having studied the chapters in Part 2, readers should be ready to tackle most published research reports in education and similar professional fields. Part 2 covers, albeit quickly, the advanced techniques routinely used in such publications. Of course, these advanced quantitative methods are very complicated. Individual specialists spend careers understanding and developing just one of them. But you should have enough background, after having completed Part 2 of this volume, to begin reading advanced research in your field. Building on the minimum necessary base supplied in this book, with practice you can hone your skills and thus have access to research that remains closed to many otherwise knowledgeable professionals.

10

Back to Regression

Regression is the backbone quantitative data analysis in the social sciences and related disciplines. It is an essential tool for *prediction,* in which case the focus is on the outcome (dependent) variable, and for *explanation,* in which case the focus is on the predictor (independent) variables. It is probably the most widely used method of data analysis in the social sciences, especially in nonexperimental research. Chapter 9 provided a close look at the basics of regression. Here we build on that base by continuing to use the example of gender equity in professors' salaries to show the nuts and bolts of investigating a question with regression analysis. To this example are added several others from published research reports. These examples constitute the chapter's principal means of addressing the following important questions.

1. How do researchers decide which variables to include?
2. How can multi-category independent variables be handled?
3. What happens when the independent variables are highly correlated?
4. What happens when there are missing data in regression analysis?
5. What can be done when the data violate assumptions?
6. What tests can be made for interaction effects?
7. How are regression and ANOVA related?
8. How can regression be used to predict the likely results of a change?
9. How is ordinary regression related to advanced methods?

How Do Researchers Decide Which Variables to Include?

How do researchers decide *which* independent variables to include in a study and *how many* should be put in the equation? The answer is that researchers should include all the variables that are important predictors/explainers of the dependent variable. But this is a paradox. One of the main purposes of regression analysis is to determine *whether* an independent variable is important. In order to determine whether a variable is an important predictor/explainer and should be included, you've got to include it. Obviously, researchers have to have some *prior* knowledge of what to include. They get this prior knowledge from their theories, from their review of previous research, or from their hunches about how the world works. Generally speaking, it is a much more serious error (called a *specification error*) to exclude an independent variable that is importantly associated with the dependent variable than it is to include an independent variable that turns out not to be important. If you exclude an important predictor (independent) variable from the list of predictors in a regression model, doing so will result in overestimating the coefficients for the variables that are in the model. So, if you leave something out, not only do you miss the opportunity to collect information about it, you also run the very great risk that your estimates for the variables you do include will be biased upward. There is no more serious error in regression analysis studies than what is sometimes called LOVE—left-out variable error. Note well that this is *not* a statistical error; it is a design error, a mistake in thinking about the question being studied, not a mistake in calculation.

Most regression studies probably omit some important predictors. For example, in the study of the salaries of 50 professors, in which regression was used to look into the issue of whether salaries were awarded in a discriminatory way, the outcome or dependent variable was annual salary. The predictor variables were the professors' gender and years of experience. A large gender gap in salaries was found (men averaged nearly $19,000 more). This gap was partly explained by years of experience. In other words, one reason women earned less at this university was that they had fewer years of experience, but even after controlling for years of experience, the gap remained substantial (around $13,000).

We also concluded that explaining the gap was not justifying it. Even if the entire salary gap could be explained by adding more predictor variables, this is not to say no discrimination existed. It is just as logical to conclude that we had found the channels through which discrimination flowed. Among the other variables and relationships that might be important to investigate are whether women were disproportionately to be found in lower-paying fields, whether they were less likely to be promoted, and whether some of the lack of years of experience and promotions was due to their child-rearing obligations. When I originally gathered these data, I attempted to learn about all three: fields of teaching, promotions, and child rearing. Information about the first was easy to obtain, limited information was available about the second, and I could find no way of gaining access to information about the third. This is not an unusual example. One of the criteria researchers use to "decide" what to include is to "choose" to include information that is available to them. The world is not set up for the convenience of researchers.

An analogy might be helpful for understanding the issue of *model specification,* that is, deciding which variables ought to be included. The independent variables in a multiple regression can be thought of as storytellers. The "story" is the dependent variable. Each of the storytellers knows only part of the story. Even when they put their parts together, they usually do not know the whole story. (If they knew the whole story, the R^2 would be 1.0.) And many of their stories overlap. When the stories overlap, each storyteller gets to tell *only* the part of his or her story that has not already been told. Obviously, the order in which the storytellers speak is important. Whoever speaks first gets to tell all that he or she knows. Those who speak toward the end will often have little to say by the time their turn comes around. So how do researchers decide which independent variable to include first, which storyteller gets to speak first?

One common approach is for researchers to put the independent variable that is the main focus of the study first. The effect of this *focus IV* is then estimated to its fullest; this storyteller gets to tell all that it knows. In the case of the 50 professors, we put gender first because that is the focus of the study. Other independent variables are then added either as controls or as mediators. The distinctions among independent, control, and mediating variables are important. Independent variables, as we have seen, are the presumed causes. Controls are variables that researchers want to eliminate as alternative explanations. Mediators are links between the independent variable (cause) and the dependent variable (effect). Although these are clearly distinct concepts, statistically they are equivalent in a regression analysis. What makes them distinct is not the way they are computed, but rather the way they are interpreted; that is, the way researchers handle them to answer their questions. By putting predictor variables into an

TABLE 10.1   *Effects of Participating in Sports in High School on Grades in English*

	Focus IV Only	*With Controls*	*With Controls and Mediators*
Regression coefficient for sports participation	.219**	.073**	.047*
R squared	.012	.525	.528

*p < .01.
**p < .001.

Source: Based on Broh (2002), Tables 1 and 5.

equation in different orders, the researcher can investigate the roles they play as mediators or controls.

As an example, consider Broh's (2002) study of the effects of extracurricular activities on high school academic achievement. Broh first estimated the effect of *participating in interscholastic sports in high school* (the independent variable) on *English grades* (the dependent variable) in the senior year.[1] The regression coefficient, *b,* was .219, which, because the DV was standardized, translates into about 22% of a standard deviation. Broh then introduced a large group of control variables such as parents' education level, gender, ethnicity, and, most importantly, students' English grades in the sophomore year. These controls or other explanations of senior grades in English were introduced to see whether, after subtracting their effects, there still remained an effect of the focus IV, in this case, participating in sports.

When Broh added a large batch of *control variables,* this raised the R^2 from .012 to .525, that is, from a trivial to a substantial level. The total variance explained went up. But, the coefficient for participating in sports was reduced from .219 to .073, a reduction of about two-thirds. Nonetheless, the smaller coefficient remained statistically significant. After controlling for a wide range of potential alternative explanations, participating in sports still had a statistically significant and positive (albeit tiny) effect on grades in English. Often this kind of result is described by saying that the effect persists "net of" other variables. *Net of* means after other variables have been controlled, after their effects have been subtracted.

The author's next step was to try to explain *how* participating in sports raised grades. Doing so

involved looking for *mediating variables.* The regression coefficient had been reduced to .073, or about 7% of a standard deviation, by the addition of the control variables. If it could be reduced still further by adding causal links or mediators, this would constitute evidence of *how* participating in sports had a positive effect on grades. Among the important mediating variables Broh introduced were interactions with parents and teachers. One idea the author tested is that students who participated in sports might be more likely to talk to their parents and teachers about school, and this extra interaction could lead to better grades. After adding these mediating variables to the regression equation, the coefficient was reduced still further, to .047, a reduction of about one-third (see Table 10.1). This means that about one-third of the sports effect could be explained by its association with mediators such as increased interaction with parents and teachers.

Note that adding controls, such as earlier grades, to the equation (X^2, X^3, X^4, etc.) reduces the importance of the focus independent variable. It explains *away* the association. But adding mediators, such as interaction with teachers, to the equation (X^5, X^6, etc.) explains the association between the focus IV and the DV, but does not explain it away. While the coefficient goes down in each case, with the controls this *reduces* the importance of the focus IV, whereas with the mediators, this *helps understand* how the focus IV operates to bring about its effects. Again, this means that the difference between a control and a mediator is in the logic of causal inference—not in the statistical techniques, which are identical.

As can be seen in Table 10.1, when you add more variables to the regression analysis the *R*-squared statistic will usually increase. Sometimes, when the added variable has no effect, it will stay the same. Although this is a complicated topic, it is generally right to say that for the same sample, the ratio of explained variance to total variance in the dependent variable cannot really decrease when you add another independent variable. The *adjusted R*-squared could go down, because this statistic adjusts (downward) for the number of independent variables. To return to our earlier analogy, adding more storytellers (independent variables) gets more of the story (*R*-squared) told, but after the first several have had their say, additional ones will often have little to add.

How Can Multi-Category Independent Variables Be Handled?

Categorical predictor variables are easily analyzed using regression analysis. More complicated techniques are required when the outcome variables are categorical, and these are discussed in our next chapter. Here the focus is on categorical predictor or explanatory variables. Nothing unusual is required when a variable has only two categories such as male and female: You code one of them 1 and the other zero. This is called *indicator coding*—or more often, but less clearly, *dummy coding.* It is useful to think of the variable as yes = 1, no = 0, as in female, yes or no, as in the earlier study of gender differences in salary at a university.

Another important variable in the study of salary is academic rank. Has the faculty member been promoted to a higher rank? Because a salary increase generally accompanies a promotion, rank is an obvious variable to include in our list of explanations for variation in salaries. The ranks at this university, as at most others, are assistant, associate, and full professor. If promotions are based on merit and adding them to the list of explanatory variables reduces the male–female salary gap, the amount of the reduction decreases the amount we can attribute to discrimination. On the other hand, if the promotion system were biased against women, the reduction would be due to a mediator variable; rank would be one of the ways in

which discrimination is institutionalized. Whichever interpretation, mediator or control, regression analysis measures it. So, we add one more variable, academic rank. Unfortunately, when I collected the data, I was able to obtain only one piece of information about the professor—was the professor a full professor, yes or no? This limitation is not grave because in the pay structures of most universities the rank of full professor is very important for determining salary. It is an optional promotion. Many professors do not attain the rank of full professor. It is not at all uncommon for half of the professors with 20 years' experience to be full and the other half to be associate. So another indicator (or dummy) variable has been added to the equation: full professor: yes = 1, no = 0.

Of course, professorial rank is a rank-order variable. Had I had information on all three of the ranks (assistant, associate, and full), the data could have been coded in two different ways, either as categorical data or as interval-level data. Specialized techniques exist for ordinal predictor variables, but they are not often encountered in regression analysis. In any case, treating ordinal variables as categorical is a conservative strategy; that is, it is likely to underestimate the size of the effects of the predictors. By contrast, treating ordinal variables as interval-level data is a risky strategy. It assumes that the intervals between the ranks are equal, which they tend not to be in this case, and runs the risk of overestimating the effect of the predictors. Here, as elsewhere, I recommend computing the coefficients both ways and reporting and interpreting the results of each.

What if you have a true categorical predictor, but one with more than two categories? Then you use a series of indicator variables or dummy-coded variables. For example, we know the colleges in which our professors taught. Remember that we wanted to see whether some of the difference between men's and women's salaries was due to the fact that women were overrepresented in lower-paying fields and underrepresented in higher-paying fields. Our 50 professors taught in four different colleges[2]: Business, Education, Humanities, Natural Sciences. The original data set (available as Table 10.2) has one variable for college in which these are coded 1, 2, 3, and

TABLE 10.2   *Data Set for Study of Professors' Salaries*

Female	College	Years' Exp.	Salary	Full Prof	Busn Dum	Ed Dum	Huma Dum	Nat Dum
0	1	3	44900	0	1	0	0	0
0	2	7	39800	0	0	1	0	0
1	2	**21**	51700	1	0	1	0	0
1	3	18	46000	0	0	0	1	0
1	**3**	2	32000	0	0	0	1	0
0	4	11	63700	0	0	0	0	1
1	**2**	8	40700	0	0	1	0	0
0	1	26	83300	1	1	0	0	0
0	4	18	94900	1	0	0	0	1
0	2	12	50600	0	0	1	0	0
0	1	17	61900	0				
1	2	9	47000	0				
1	4	4	**43000**	0				
0	2	23	**57000**	**0**				
1	2	7	40100	0				
0	2	16	54000	0				
1	1	10	58000	0				
0	4	8	62200	1				
0	2	9	41100	0				
0	1	7	58300	**0**				
1	3	4	35500	0				
0	1	9	61100	1				
1	3	6	37000	0				
1	3	6	38800	0				
0	1	14	**89700**	1				
0	4	15	62800	0				
0	2	**11**	53300	0				
0	1	9	66700	1				
1	3	8	40200	0				
1	1	2	43800	0				
0	2	16	77700	1				
1	3	7	43000	0				
1	4	5	45600	0				
1	3	6	41300	0				
1	2	22	52000	1				
0	4	24	72200	0				
0	4	21	74100	1				
0	**2**	18	53200	0				
0	4	19	97300	1				
0	3	26	50700	0				
1	4	12	51000	0				
1	2	15	46400	0				
1	3	8	49700	0				

(continued)

TABLE 10.2   *Continued*

Female	College	Years' Exp.	Salary	Full Prof	Busn Dum	Ed Dum	Huma Dum	Nat Dum
0	1	7	59800	**0**				
0	3	5	37100	0				
0	4	23	65900	0				
0	4	**17**	71100	1				
0	4	14	58700	0				
1	1	6	47000	0				
1	4	3	44400	0				

Note: Missing data (see pp. 175–179) are indicated in bold.

4, respectively. As with all categorical variables the numbers are only labels, just identification numbers. To turn these labels into data you can use for regression analysis, you create four new dummy/indicator variables. Each college is coded in the same way the variable for female or for full professor was coded. Business is coded 1 if yes, the professor does teach in that college, and 0 if not. The same coding is then used for each of the others. These variables are then put into the regression equation. They replace the old college variable coded 1, 2, 3, 4. I've shown how to do this coding for the first 10 cases (professors) in Table 10.2.[3] Because the first professor is in Business, the column Busn Dum is scored 1 and all others for that professor 0. The second professor is in Education, so Ed Dum is coded 1 and all others in that row 0, and so on.

Because a series of dummy variables has been used, when doing the regression, only three need to be included in the regression, not all four. Indeed, one of the colleges *must* be excluded and become the comparison group (also called reference group or excluded group). If Education is made the excluded, reference, or comparison variable, it does not appear in the table, except by implication. For each of the other colleges, the regression coefficient will indicate how much more or less, on average, professors from that college earn compared to professors in the College of Education. So now we have all our variables, salary plus the four independent variables: gender, years of experience, college, and full professor. The variables have been coded and are ready for analysis.

If a university determined professors' salaries by gender that would clearly be discriminatory. You could make a case, however, that experience, college, and rank were equitable grounds on which to allocate salary. Skill and knowledge increase with years of experience, rank is an assessment of peers' and supervisors' assessment of contribution to the institution, and field of study (college) reflects market forces. This is assuming of course that these three are not the mechanisms of discrimination. Mechanisms of discrimination or explanation for fair differences? This is not a question that can be answered statistically. It is a matter of logical inference. The size of a relation can be estimated with regression analysis; its exact nature can be decided only by a process of reasoning about evidence. Let's use Table 10.3 to study the size of the relations among the variables.

The format of Table 10.3 is a common one for presenting the results of a regression analysis. It contains four models. A model is a list of the independent variables that are used to explain the dependent variable. In proceeding from model 1 to model 4, each model gets longer (adds more storytellers). The *B*s and betas are unstandardized and standardized regression coefficients. The asterisks on each *B* coefficient tell whether it, and its corresponding beta, is statistically significant. The results from the first two models have already been seen in Chapter 9. Here, in model 1 we are reminded that on average, women earn $18,686 less than men. In model 2, we see that, on average, each additional year of experience adds $963 to a professor's salary and that, even after con-

TABLE 10.3 Regression Analysis: 50 Professors' Data

	Model 1		Model 2		Model 3		Model 4	
	B	BETA	B	BETA	B	BETA	B	BETA
Constant/Intercept	62,968***		49,035***		38,483***		39,670***	
Independent Variables								
Gender (Female = 1)	−18,686***	−.609	−13,028***	−.425	−7,596*	−.248	−6,972**	−.227
Years' Experience			963***	.426	1,090***	.482	773***	.342
College[a]								
Business					14,009***	.381	10,842***	.295
Humanities					−751	.020	314	.009
Natural Sciences					13,365***	.394	11,499***	.339
Full Professor (Yes = 1)							13,683***	.384
Adjusted R-squared	.358***		.498***		.670***		.790***	

[a]Education is the excluded reference/comparison group.
*$p < .05$.
** $p < .01$.
*** $p < .001$.

trolling for male–female differences in years of experience, women still earn $13,028 less than men.

We add our variables for college when we move to model 3. The model contains 3 new rows, one each for Business, Humanities, and Natural Sciences. What happened to Education? It is the comparison group, just as men were for the variable gender. So the coefficient *B* for Business means that business professors in this sample earned an average of $14,009 more *than Education professors,* and the asterisks indicate that this difference is significant at the .001 level. Humanities professors earned $751 less than Education professors (the coefficient is negative), but this difference is so small that it is statistically insignificant. And, professors in Natural Sciences earned $13,365 more than professors in Education. How do Natural Sciences and Business compare? That information is not available in this table. To get it, all you would have to do is recode your dummy variables and make either Business or Natural Sciences the excluded or comparison group. Finally, and most important, what about the coefficient for the target variable, gender? It is now, in model 3, $7,596, which is considerably reduced from model 2. This means that when adding the college in which the professors taught to the list of variables, the male–female salary gap drops to $7,596. This means that a considerable proportion of the difference is due to the fact that men and women are concentrated in different colleges.

The "final answer" comes in model 4 in which all our storytelling variables get to speak. The coefficient for each variable is the annual salary attributable to that variable, after controlling for all the other variables in the model. When rank is added, we see that controlling for gender, years' experience, and college, full professors made on average $13,683 more per year and that this difference was statistically significant. Women, even after controlling for these other variables, still made on average $6,972 less than the men.

How good of an explanation is this regression analysis? Might we be leaving out many other important variables? This question cannot be answered with certainty, but it is possible to say that our four explanatory independent variables in model 4 do ex-

plain a large percentage of the variance in professors' salaries. We can see this by looking at the adjusted R-squared, which is .790 for model 4. This is in general a high percentage in the social sciences, although not striking for salary studies. Is it time to draw conclusions? Not quite. Before making judgments about the extent and origins of gender discrimination at this university, careful researchers would investigate several other aspects of their statistical models, including the question of how the independent variables are related and the possible effects of missing variables.

What Happens When the Independent Variables Are Highly Correlated?

Before conducting any statistical analysis, it is important for researchers to examine their data for problems that could spoil the analysis. Carefully examining the data is especially important when using multiple regression analysis (MRA), because MRA deals with several variables simultaneously, and problems with any one of them could invalidate the results. One of the first potential problems to check for is highly correlated predictor variables. To return to the storyteller analogy, when two storytellers know essentially the same thing, they are redundant, and one can be excluded for the sake of efficiency. Even if efficiency in prediction is not a major concern, highly correlated predictors cause big problems for the analysis. The source of the problems is technical, having mostly to do with matrix algebra (see Tabachnick & Fidel, 2001a).

To see how correlated predictors can cause trouble, let's return to the data about the 35 students' scores on various exams and assignments. The multiple regression problem will be predicting scores on the licensing exam. The first step in this analysis is to examine the bivariate correlations between the predictor variables. Generally any two predictors correlated more strongly than .70 should be sources of worry and those correlated higher than .90 are cause for alarm. The term used to describe the problem of highly correlated predictor variables is *multicollinearity.* SPSS, like most statistical packages, produces a group of *regression diagnostics,* which enable the researcher to detect multicollinearity and other data problems before these problems distort the analysis. One of these is the *tolerance,* which is the proportion of the variability of one predictor that is *not* explained by the other predictors in the equation. In other terms, each of the predictors is regressed on the other predictors to discover what proportion of the variance in each predictor can be explained by the remaining predictors; the tolerance is 1 minus that proportion. Like the R^2, the tolerance ranges from zero to 1.0. In any case, rules of thumb vary, but any predictor having a tolerance less than .20 is almost surely a problem. A related statistic is the *variance inflation factor,* usually called the *VIF.* It is computed by dividing the tolerance into 1.0. The lowest possible VIF is 1.0 when there is no multicollinearity. A tolerance of .20 would produce a VIF of 5.0, which is another good rule-of-thumb cutoff number that indicates potential difficulties with the analysis.

So what does all this mean for our attempt to predict scores on the licensing exam from scores on the other exams and assignments? As seen in Chapter 2, the correlation between Exam 1 and Exam 2 was .917 (see Table 2.7). When Exam 1 and Exam 2 are included along with other variables (paper, project, and students' gender) in a regression, the tolerance for the two exams were .154 and .146—too low. Also the VIF statistics were 6.48 and 6.86—too high. What should be done? There are three solutions: (1) Delete one of the redundant variables; (2) do the regression twice using only one of the redundant variables in each; and (3) combine the two redundant variables into a new variable and then use it instead of the original variables. I think the third solution is best, because it retains the most information, but in many regression problems it will make little difference which you choose.[4] The only thing not to do is to do nothing. If you have multicollinearity, the only truly unsatisfactory option is to ignore the problem.

In brief, whenever predictor variables in a multiple regression are correlated, and they almost always are, the correlations indicate that they contain redundant information. It is necessary to subtract this redundant information so that it will not be counted twice. That is what controlling for the influence of other predictors is all about. Multiple regression is very efficient at such subtracting—except in the face of high degrees of multicollinearity. This is why conscientious researchers routinely check for it.

What Happens When There Are Missing Data in Regression Analysis?

Although the two data sets we have repeatedly analyzed in this book, the grades of the 35 students and the salaries of the 50 professors, are real data from real students and professors, they are unrealistically tidy. For pedagogical reasons, I have cleaned up what we have used here. When data were missing for a student or a professor, I deleted that case; this left a subset of the original data for which we have complete information.

What would happen if some of these data were missing? To find out, I used a table of random numbers (Glass & Hopkins, 1996 p. 620) to select 3 data points for each of the 4 independent variables—salary, gender, college, and rank. In that way I selected a total of 12 out of 200 pieces of data. Then I deleted these. The data set is in Table 10.2; the deleted data are indicated in bold type. To see how much difference the missing data made, I then recomputed several statistics using this slightly reduced data set. Because the missing values were selected at random, I assumed, they probably would not make too much of a difference. At least, when one has missing values one *hopes* (you almost never know) that they are missing at random, because this provides the fewest possibilities for bias.

So what happened when 6% (12 out of 200 pieces of data) of the data were missing at random? Looking at comparisons of means, there is little difference, as is shown in Table 10.4. The mean difference between men and women in salary declines by about a thousand dollars, but the difference is still highly significant. Years of experience also are largely unaffected; the difference increases by less than one year and is slightly more significant (*p*-value declines from .002 to .001).

TABLE 10.4 *Comparison of Means with Full Data Set and with Missing Values*

	Salary, Full Data	Salary, Missing Data	Years' Experience, Full Data	Years' Experience, Missing Data
Men	62,968	61,667	14.46	14.46
Women	44,282	44,010	8.59	7.80
Total	54,746	53,641	11.88	11.43
Difference	18,686	17,657	5.87	6.66
Significance of difference (*p*-value)	.000	.000	.002	.001

The potential importance of missing values becomes clearer when we look at our multivariate analysis. Tables 10.5 and 10.6 present the regression results in SPSS format for the full data set and for the data set with the 12 (out of 200) missing values. Table 10.5 repeats model 4 from Table 10.3 and adds some information, most importantly confidence intervals for the coefficients. The method used to handle the missing values in Table 10.6 is *listwise deletion*, which means that if a case is missing one or more values it is deleted from the list of cases. It is very instructive to compare the two tables. Most of the differences between the two tables do not seem large at first glance, but the conclusions one would be likely to draw differ *dramatically*. A typical way to put the results from Table 10.5, using the full data set, would be to say: "Even after controlling for the effects of differences in years of experience, academic rank, and the colleges in which they were employed, female professors still made nearly $7,000 per year less than males, and this difference was highly statistically significant ($p < .01$)." By contrast, a reasonable summary of Table 10.6, with 6% missing data, would be: "No significant differences ($p = .28$) were found between the salaries of female and male professors, after controlling for the effects of differences in years of experience, academic rank, and the colleges in which they were employed." In other words, the key conclusions about whether the evidence indicates that the university is guilty of gender discrimination are *diametrically opposed* depending on which data set is used! An example such as this one should leave us much more humble about the certainty with which we announce our results.

Why the big difference? How could so few missing values completely change the conclusion? One reason is the small sample size. Fifty cases is enough for many bivariate analyses, but it is not adequate for multiple regression. In the chapter on sampling I stressed the importance of large samples. The larger the sample the smaller the sampling error and the more stable the estimates. When samples are large, estimates are less likely to be influenced by a couple of unusual cases or a few missing values.

How large does a sample need to be before you can trust it? There is no hard and fast answer. Even when using formulas, they are only rules of thumb. One formula for the minimum sample size in a multiple regression, for the overall prediction equation (the R^2), is 50 plus 8 times the number of variables. Because there are 4 variables in this study, the minimum is $50 + (8 \times 4) = 82$. For estimating individual variables while controlling for others, the formula for the minimum sample size is 104 plus 1 for each additional variable. In this case that is $104 + 4 = 108$. If you want to make inferences about both the overall equation and individual variables, Tabachnick and Fidel (2001a, p. 117) recommend using both formulas and picking the higher number. So one reason that the estimates were so unstable is the small sample size. A good sample size would have been 82 at minimum, and 108+ would have been better. We had 50, and fewer than that after the missing data were deleted.

TABLE 10.5 *Regression: Full Data Set*

Model	Unstandardized Coefficients		Standardized Coefficients			95% Confidence Interval for B	
	B	Standard Error	Beta	t	Sig.	Lower Bound	Upper Bound
1 (Constant)	39670.136	3524.017		11.257	.000	32563.279	46776.993
Female = 1	-6972.394	2432.887	-.227	-2.866	.006	-11878.778	-2066.011
YRSEXPC	773.212	183.147	.342	4.222	.000	403.861	1142.563
BUSNDUM	10841.808	3041.328	.295	3.565	.001	4708.385	16975.231
HUMADUM	313.793	3018.543	.009	.104	.918	-5773.679	6401.265
NATSCDUM	11499.211	2712.714	.339	4.239	.000	6028.503	16969.920
Fullprof = 1	13683.126	2685.093	.384	5.096	.000	8268.120	19098.133

Note: Dependent variable: Salary.

TABLE 10.6 *Regression: Missing Data with Listwise Deletion*

Model		Unstandardized Coefficients		Standardized Coefficients			95% Confidence Interval for B	
		B	Standard Error	Beta	t	Sig.	Lower Bound	Upper Bound
1	(Constant)	35647.679	3894.394		9.154	.000	27682.749	43612.608
	Female = 1	−3071.031	2792.336	−.099	−1.100	.280	−8781.999	2639.938
	YRSEXPC	879.392	192.459	.396	4.569	.000	485.769	1273.015
	BUSNDUM	10027.057	3540.660	.270	2.832	.008	2785.595	17268.519
	HUMADUM	472.863	3311.027	.014	.143	.887	−6298.947	7244.674
	NATSCDUM	15228.791	3367.919	.441	4.522	.000	8340.624	22116.959
	Fullprof = 1	12801.695	3191.575	.344	4.011	.000	6274.192	19329.197

Note: Dependent variable: Salary.

It is easy to see that missing data can be a real problem. Several strategies exist for replacing missing values with estimates. None is fully satisfactory. Table 10.7 uses *mean substitution* to replace missing values. Whenever a value is missing the computer substitutes the mean value for that variable. Better techniques use regression, with the missing data as the dependent variable, to estimate the missing values, but no technique can fix the problem of small sample size and, ironically enough, missing data tend to be less of a problem with large sample sizes. At any rate, as seen in Table 10.7, even with mean substitution to "fix" the problem of missing data, the coefficient for our focus IV, gender, is still not statistically significant. Again, in sum, just a few missing pieces of data can sometimes radically change conclusions. In actual research, one knows when data are missing, but one doesn't know, as we do here, what the conclusions would be if one were not missing data.

The best way to address the missing value problem is *not* to make statistical adjustments after the problem has come up. Rather, the best approach is to design your research in a way that minimizes the number of missing values in the first place. For example, getting data from records will often enable you to obtain more complete data than would otherwise be possible, for instance, in a survey. Or, in a survey, respondents are less likely to skip questions when the questions are clearly written than when they are obscure. Or, in an experiment, participants are less likely to drop out if they are paid for their time. The term *missing values* usually refers to bits of data omitted from otherwise complete cases, but what about people who drop out or who never respond? The ultimate sources of missing data, of course, are a low response rate in surveys (and consequent nonresponse bias) and refusal to participate in experiments (see the discussion of attrition in Chapter 7). Whatever the source of your missing information, something needs to be done about it. When you write up your research, you need to be explicit about what you have done to avoid missing data, what you did to handle it when you got some anyway, and how much the missing data is likely to limit the solidity of your conclusions. You should do all this in your research,

and you should expect the authors of the articles you read to be equally forthcoming. If they aren't, trust them less.

What Can Be Done When the Data Violate Assumptions?

Like most statistical techniques, regression is based on several assumptions about the data and variables being analyzed. Chief among these assumptions is linearity. Like correlation, regression is an accurate method only when the association between the variables is linear. Linearity can be checked with a scatter diagram. If you look at the points on a scatter diagram they will tend to cluster around a straight line when the relation between the variables is linear. When the relations are not linear, several options are available. Some analyze the data differently; others transform the data to make it linear (see Chapter 11).

To check for linearity the most direct method is to plot a scatter diagram for the dependent variable with each independent or predictor variable. So if you have 20 independent variables, you will want to examine 20 scatter plots. (With the right keystrokes and mouse clicks, most statistical packages will produce all 20 at once.) What do you do when one or more of your variables departs from linearity? The common solution is to transform it. This is comparatively easier when one is transforming the dependent variable because, in regression problems of the kind we are studying, there is only one dependent variable. With multiple independent variables, transformation procedures are more complicated and consequences of the transformations are harder to interpret. That is because the independent variables in a multiple regression all influence one another. Nonetheless, when data depart from linearity, they are routinely transformed. Perhaps the most common transformation is the logarithmic transformation (see Chapter 11). Like many things that are routinely done, transforming data is more complex than is realized, and some researchers have issued strong cautions. Before engaging in transformations to make your data more linear, it is crucial to review an advanced text (e.g.,

TABLE 10.7 *Regression: Missing Data with Mean Substitution*

| Model | | Unstandardized Coefficients | | Standardized Coefficients | | | 95% Confidence Interval for B | |
		B	Standard Error	Beta	t	Sig.	Lower Bound	Upper Bound
1	(Constant)	37554.560	3736.778		10.050	.000	30018.630	45090.490
	Female = 1	-3994.232	2603.555	-.135	-1.534	.132	-9244.801	1256.336
	YRSEXPC	824.129	187.190	.378	4.403	.000	446.625	1201.633
	BUSNDUM	7561.831	3164.631	.217	2.389	.021	1179.744	13943.918
	HUMADUM	-566.128	3217.268	-.016	-.176	.861	-7054.368	5922.112
	NATSCDUM	12911.344	2858.076	.401	4.517	.000	7147.485	18675.204
	Fullprof = 1	13248.880	2704.451	.392	4.899	.000	7794.835	18702.926

Note: Dependent variable: Salary.

Johnson & Wichern, 2002, Chap. 4) to decide whether to do it and also to select the proper method.

One of the biggest ways data can depart from linearity is caused by the presence of *outliers* or scores with extreme values. Screening your data for outliers is one of the easiest forms of cleaning up your evidence before using it. An outlier constitutes an *influential observation,* if its removal will importantly change a statistic such as a regression coefficient. Many analysts routinely recommend that any outlier be removed from the data to be analyzed, especially if it qualifies as an influential observation. This is sometimes good advice, but it should be followed only with caution, and the researcher should always tell the reader that outliers have been removed. Also a justification should be offered. Before removing it, before discarding data, the researcher should be able to make a strong case that an outlier is an uninteresting fluke rather than an important counterexample.

One common source of outliers is errors in data entry. A colleague once told me about a problem he encountered during his dissertation research. He found a negative correlation between IQ test scores and achievement test scores. This surprising result was due to *one* outlier, which in turn was due to a typo—the data for a student who had an IQ of 55 was mistakenly entered into the computer as 555. That one error changed the conclusion from a finding of a strong positive correlation to a weak negative one. So one reason to check for outliers is to find typos. Other outliers are less easy to detect or correct. This is especially true of multivariate outliers, which are scores on combinations of variables that are patterned in unusual ways. A simple example would be in a study of the weight of children aged 7 to 17; a child aged 16 would not be an outlier, nor would a child who weighed 70 pounds be an outlier, but a 16-year-old who weighed 70 pounds would be. Advanced statistical techniques, such as the *Mahalanobis distance,* can be used to identify multivariate outliers. Deciding what to do about them is less easy.

There are several assumptions, besides linearity, at the foundation of regression analysis. If you are using regression descriptively to analyze a population and are not planning to make inferences from

a sample to a population, most of the additional assumptions are not very important. But linearity is always important even for noninferential work. The other assumptions, those that are important for making inferences, are important because violations of those assumptions increase the standard errors (see Chapter 8) and thereby decrease the accuracy of any inferences made about a population.

Most of the other assumptions that need to be checked have to do with the *residuals,* or errors of prediction. A residual is the difference between the predicted score for a case in a regression and the actual score. Each individual case has an actual score. The regression equation provides a predicted score for each individual case. The prediction is virtually never perfect. The gap between the two is the error, or the residual. These residuals are at the heart of multiple regression. For example, the multiple *R,* which is then squared to obtain the all-important R^2, is simply the Pearson *r* calculated between the scores and the residuals.

If you are doing a multiple regression, particularly if you are generalizing from a sample to a population, it is irresponsible not to check all of the assumptions about residuals and to report the results of that work to your readers. They cannot be reviewed in detail here, but it is important to touch on the main points briefly. Again, you will need to consult a more advanced volume—such as Tabachnick and Fidel (2001a) Chap. 4 or Berk (2004, Chap. 9) or Fox (1997, Chap. 12)—to do this work when you undertake a multiple regression. So what are these assumptions about the residuals? (1) Residuals have a linear relation with the predicted outcome scores. (2) Constant or equal variances or (if you must) homoscedasticity of residuals. (3) Residuals are independent of one another (they are not correlated with one another). (4) Residuals are independent of the predictors (not correlated with the predictors). (5) The mean of the residuals is zero. (6) The residuals are normally distributed. The first two of these, linearity and constant or equal variances, are the most important for statistical inference, that is, for computing *p*-values and confidence intervals. The last, normality, is sometimes the least important; violations of this

Dependent Variable: Salary

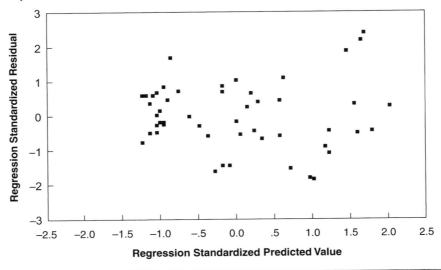

FIGURE 10.1 *Scatter plot of predicted values and residuals*

assumption often do the least damage. Fortunately one visual check of the residuals enables researchers to determine whether these assumptions have been met. Figure 10.1 is a scatter plot of the residuals or error scores and the predicted or outcome scores all of which have been converted into *z*-scores. The data are from the 50 professors file with salary as the outcome variable and gender, rank, and years of experience as the predictors.

The predicted values are on the *X*, or horizontal, axis and the residuals are on the *Y*, or vertical, axis. If the assumptions of linearity, equal variances, and normality are met, the pattern of the points on the scatter plot will be roughly rectangular. If normality is met, the number of points above and below zero on the *Y*, vertical, residual axis will be about equal, as they are in Figure 10.1 If the assumption of linearity holds, no obvious nonlinear pattern in the data points will be evident. So far so good. But in looking at the consistency or equality of variance assumption, at the low end of the predicted values (around *z* = −1.0) the points are clustered fairly tightly, but moving to the higher values on the horizontal axis (*z* = 1.5 to 2.0) the spread is much greater. Is that increasing

variance big enough to invalidate the analysis? One rule of thumb is that problems are serious when the highest spread of the residuals is about three or more times as wide as the narrowest (Fox, 1997). Here the ratio is about 2 to 1, not 3 to 1, so it is probably safe to proceed with the analysis.

What Tests Can Be Made for Interaction Effects?

Researchers can check for *interaction effects* using regression, but when doing so they have to specify the interactions they want to test. In ANOVA the statistics for interaction effects are computed automatically, by default, in most statistical packages. This is not done in multiple regression, in large part because multiple regression problems usually have many independent variables. For example, if a statistical package automatically computed regression coefficients for interaction, and if you had 12 independent variables, which is not an unusual number in regression, you would have a huge number of interactions to be checked by default—66 bivariate interactions and many more multivariate interactions.

In multiple regression (MR) you specify the interactions you think might be important and check for those. This is part of the process of model specification, discussed earlier. The interaction calculated in regression is closely parallel to how it is done in ANOVA, except that in regression you have to select the interactions you want to investigate. For example, if your research problem had six IVs, either ANOVA or MR would yield six main effects. In ANOVA these main effects are *p*-values; in regression they are regression coefficients. As always, each coefficient tells you the effect on the DV of a one-unit increase in the IV, while controlling for the effects of all the other IVs. In addition to the six main effects, there would be fifteen potential bivariate interactions (and more multivariate interactions). Assume that your literature review on your topic suggested that important interaction effects might occur between variables 2 and 3 and variables 4 and 6. To check for interactions you would need to create new variables to enter into the regression. You would create one by multiplying variable 2 times variable 3 and the other by multiplying variable 4 times variable 6.

A typical format regression output is shown in Table 10.8. The first column names the IVs, the second gives the coefficient, and the third tells whether it is statistically significant. If you were interested in the interactions of IVs 2 and 3 and 4 and 6, you would just create new variables by multiplying the values of IV 2 times the values of IV 3 and IV 4 x IV 6. You would then add those new variables to the list of IVs in your regression. The coefficients would go into the rows named Vbl 2*3 and Vbl 4*6 in the table (in such cases an asterisk is often used as a multiplication sign). If the coefficients for 2*3 and or 4*6 were significant, then that would indicate a significant interaction of those variables with the dependent variable. As with ANOVA, if you have significant interaction effects, then interpreting the main effects of the interacting variables becomes tricky at best.

In sum, testing for interaction in multiple regression is usually more complicated than doing so in ANOVA, for two reasons. First, ANOVA problems

TABLE 10.8 *How to Use Regression to Test for Interaction Effects*

Vbl Names	Coefficients	p-val of Coef.
IV 1		
IV 2		
IV 3		
IV 4		
IV 5		
IV 6		
Vbl 2*3		
Vbl 4*6		

usually have many fewer variables. Second, independent variables in ANOVA must be categorical, and interactions of categorical variables are easier to interpret than the interactions of the continuous predictor variables often found in multiple regression. In any case, it is important to check for interactions. Omitting an important interaction is a specification error, one that is potentially more serious than other LOVEs (left-out variable errors). By not examining your data for interactions, you run the risk of LOVE, of having left out the interaction variable.

How Are Regression and ANOVA Related?

The preceding section makes clear a point made several times in this book: Regression and ANOVA can handle many of the same problems. Generally regression is more flexible, but ANOVA is still preferred by many researchers. For the past three or four decades statisticians have increasingly emphasized that ANOVA is a subset of regression, a "species" of which regression is the "genus." Continuing the analogy, the general linear model would be the "family." ANOVA can be seen as a kind of regression for use when the IVs are categorical and that reports limited information—statistical significance, but not effect size. Although ANOVA is increasingly being replaced by regression, especially for complex research questions, the two are versions of the same approach. The choice between the two is to some extent a matter

TABLE 10.9   *Three-Way ANOVA*

Source	Type III Sum of Squares	df	Mean Square	F	Sig.
Corrected Model	9030495668.254*	11	820954151.659	12.191	.000
Intercept	94425762533.611	1	94425762533.611	1402.241	.000
FEMALE	913578797.329	1	913578797.329	13.567	.001
FULLPROF	1262229489.120	1	1262229489.120	18.744	.000
COLLEGE	556414776.151	3	185471592.050	2.754	.056
FEMALE * FULLPROF	201770781.671	1	201770781.671	2.996	.092
FEMALE * COLLEGE	284496822.744	3	94832274.248	1.408	.255
FULLPROF * COLLEGE	102877642.027	2	51438821.013	.764	.473
FEMALE * FULLPROF * COLLEGE	.000	0	.	.	.
Error	2558888531.746	38	67339171.888		
Total	161445610000.000	50			
Corrected Total	11589384200.000	49			

Note: Dependent variable: Salary.
*R-squared = .779 (adjusted R-squared = .715).

of taste and tradition. The two were already compared in Chapters 8 and 9. Here we add just a few more points about more advanced types of analysis.

Chapter 8 looked at ANOVA problems with one IV, known as one-way ANOVA. The college variable had four categories or groups, but it is still *one*-way ANOVA, because it is one variable, college, with four categories, Business, Education, Humanities, and Sciences. If there were two IVs two-way ANOVA would be used; with three IVs three-way ANOVA would be required; and so on. Let's conduct a three-way ANOVA using the data on gender equity in a university. Salary is a continuous DV so it can be used for ANOVA as well as for ordinary regression. The categorical IVs are gender, college, and rank. To include years of experience as an IV in ANOVA we would have to discard information, that is, to make that continuous variable categorical (for example, by coding it 1–3 = few, 4–9 = some, and 10+ = many).

Table 10.9 gives the three-way ANOVA output produced by SPSS. Salary is the DV and female, full prof., and college are the IVs. Looking at the "Sig." column, which gives the *p*-values, we see that female is significant at the .001 level and full prof. is significant at the .000 level, that is, $p < .001$. College would have been

statistically significant if we had used a cutoff of .10 for significance ($p = .056$). None of the interactions—female * full prof., and so on—are statistically significant. Comparing this to the earlier regression tables, such as Table 10.5, we see that the regression output is fuller. For instance, for full prof. we see not only that that variable is significant at the .001 level but also that on average, after controlling for other variables in the equation, full professors made $13,683 more than those who had not reached that rank.

If we conclude that the differences in the mean salaries of the colleges are statistically significant, ANOVA gives only the overall *p*-value. To see *which* colleges were significantly different from which, you would need to turn to a multiple comparisons analysis, such as the one in Table 10.10. Several such comparison tests exist for ANOVAs when IVs have more than two categories. Table 10.10 uses the most common test, the Tukey. The results show that college 1 and college 2 are significantly different, as are college 1 and 3, but college 1 and 4 are not, and so on. The results of an ANOVA are much more interpretable when such comparisons are made; these comparisons are often called *post hoc* tests, because they come after (post) the ANOVA has been conducted.

TABLE 10.10 *Post Hoc Test, Multiple Comparisons*

(I) B = 1, E = 2, H = 3, N = 4	(J) B = 1, E = 2, H = 3, N = 4	Mean Difference (I-J)	Std. Error	Sig.	95% Confidence Interval	
					Lower Bound	Upper Bound
1	2	10989.61(*)	3306.310	.010	2107.29	19871.93
	3	20290.91(*)	3499.069	.000	10890.75	29691.07
	4	-3460.39	3306.310	.723	-12342.71	5421.93
2	1	-10989.61(*)	3306.310	.010	-19871.93	-2107.29
	3	9301.30(*)	3306.310	.037	418.98	18183.62
	4	-14450.00(*)	3101.593	.000	-22782.35	-6117.65
3	1	-20290.91(*)	3499.069	.000	-29691.07	-10890.75
	2	-9301.30(*)	3306.310	.037	-18183.62	-418.98
	4	-23751.30(*)	3306.310	.000	-32633.62	-14868.98
4	1	3460.39	3306.310	.723	-5421.93	12342.71
	2	14450.00(*)	3101.593	.000	6117.65	22782.35
	3	23751.30(*)	3306.310	.000	14868.98	32633.62

Note: Dependent variable: Salary. Tukey HSD.
*The mean difference is significant at the.05 level.

One widely used technique combines the methods of ANOVA and regression. It is called *ANCOVA,* which is short for analysis of co-variance. ANCOVA is like ANOVA with a preliminary step in which the researcher uses regression to control for the effects of a continuous variable—called a covariate. For example, if you wanted to compare the effects of three different reading programs, but were unable to assign students to them at random, you could try to equalize the groups by first controlling for students' scores on a verbal ability test, which would be your covariate. Then you would conduct the ANOVA. What ANCOVA does is adjusts the group means to what they would have been had subjects had identical scores on the covariate. This adjustment makes it more difficult to find significant differences in the group means, because some of the between-group variance has been eliminated. That means that if a statistically significant difference is found it is more likely to be meaningful, because the variance attributable to the covariate has been controlled (or partialed out). Although ANCOVA can be an improvement over a simple ANOVA, it strikes me as a clumsy, last-ditch attempt to hold onto an antiquated format—the ANOVA format for testing the statistical significance of mean differences. Regression provides *exactly* the same information about statistical significance as ANCOVA plus additional information about effect sizes. Why not just use regression, which is the more efficient technique, in the first place? These are "fighting words" for some of my colleagues. While the choice seems clear to me, you should be aware that asserting a preference will sometimes provoke dissent and controversy.

How Can Regression Be Used to Predict the Likely Results of a Change?

If relations are found among variables in a current sample and generalized to a current population, how reasonable is it to generalize these findings to a *future* population—which, strictly speaking, does not yet exist? This is largely a question of what we know about the stability of variables and the relations among them.

Medical research done on last year's patients will probably be relevant for next year's patients. But what about our salary example? What would be the likely effects of independent variables if, for example, the university got a new president or a board of trustees determined to eradicate salary discrimination? In my experience authors of research reports using regression analysis often make very large inferential leaps about the future. They take sample data from the past, and data are *always* from the past, and use it to generalize about future populations. Which of such generalizations are reasonable and which are not? This is one of the most difficult questions researchers, and especially those using research to make practical decisions, have to make.

These problems can seem fairly abstract. Let's review and expand understanding of them by examining another good example of the use of regression analysis. Gamoran and Hannigan (2000) inquired whether a popular reform—"algebra for all"—would be likely to have positive outcomes for students. To study the question, they compared the tenth-grade math achievement of students who did and who did not take algebra. They used the National Educational Longitudinal Study (NELS) to compare achievement gains from with eighth- to tenth-grade math achievement tests. The key policy question this article tries to answer is "What would happen if all students took algebra?" (p. 249). Gamoran and Hannigan's use of regression analysis to try to answer this question includes some crucial methodological points. They are difficult points, but they are too important to skip.

First, if the difference in eighth-grade knowledge between those who did and did not take algebra were too large, then one could not reasonably compare the two groups. The two groups would be separated too much by prior differences. One needs to be able to compare *similar students* with dissimilar educations and achievement levels. As Gamoran and Hannigan (2000) put it:

> If there is no overlap in the achievement distribution between those who did and those who did not take algebra, then there is no real comparison group of otherwise similar students, and one cannot draw meaningful conclusions about the effects of algebra. (p. 248)

Second, when conducting a regression analysis, the relations among variables in samples that actually exist are examined. This information is then used to draw inferences about populations from which the samples were drawn. This is when regression is used to describe or *explain*. But in this example of policy research Gamoran and Hannigan are also using regression to *predict*. To answer the question "Should all students take algebra?" we have to assume that the future will be like the past. In this case, that means assuming that knowledge of differences in tenth-grade math achievement in 1990, when the NELS measurements were taken, can guide us in the 2000s.

Third, and even more important in this case, a large *counterfactual* has to be postulated: What if *all* students in the sample take algebra? If all students take algebra, would the benefits that *some* students now get by taking it extend to all of them? Changing the system to require algebra for all students could change the relations among the variables. As Gamoran and Hannigan (2000) put it,

> we can be fairly confident about the benefits of taking algebra if one student shifted from the no-algebra to the algebra-in-high-school category, but it is hard to predict the effects of moving all students in the no-algebra category into high school algebra. (p. 249)

To deal with this question, Gamoran and Hannigan (2000) had to do further analyses. They needed a way to estimate what the relations among the variables would be in the new situation in which all students took algebra.

> Opening access to algebra for all students would increase the heterogeneity of the algebra-taking group. We can simulate the difference that might make by comparing the effects of algebra in more heterogeneous and less heterogeneous populations of algebra takers. (p. 250)

What they found by conducting this "simulation," this approximation of what things *would* be like, is that the more mixed the population of the students, the bigger effect taking algebra. This is further good evidence that the reform algebra for all would be likely to have a positive effect on math achievement. Algebra seemed to be of most help to students with the weakest backgrounds. As with many educational reforms (small class size is another example), this one has the pleasing effect of seeming to be most beneficial to those who are most in need of help. All this presumes, it must be repeated, that relations found in the past with a sample from one population, will be applicable to future populations.

Such complicated adjustments as those employed by Gamoran and Hannigan in their simulation are often necessary when researchers want to increase their confidence about their conclusions. The mathematics behind such adjustments are usually no more complex than computing any other regression coefficients. The key elements helping researchers decide what would be useful to compute are having a good working knowledge of the analysis technique and having a nuanced understanding of the variables being studied and the likely relations among them. This returns us to one of the most important themes in this book: What matters most for good research is depth of understanding of the subject being studied combined with careful thinking about how to gather and interpret evidence. The statistical techniques are powerful tools, but they are not the driving force behind good research. Clear thinking about the problem tells you which coefficients to compute. Computing them mostly requires pointing and clicking to activate a software routine. If inferences about the likely result of changes for the future, such as algebra for all students, are accurate they will be built of a synthesis of statistical methods *and* substantive knowledge of the variables *and* rigorous logic.

How Is Ordinary Regression Related to Advanced Methods?

Discussions about regression in this chapter and in Chapter 9 have concentrated on the type called *ordinary least squares,* or *OLS, regression.* This original type of regression analysis is most closely linked to the Pearson *r* correlation. When using scatter diagrams to illustrate correlation and regression, we have seen that the regression line is the line that comes closest to the points that form the scatter diagram. The method for calculating closest uses the *least squared* distance of the points from the line, which is the source of the name *least squares regression.* As we have seen, for this method to work properly important assumptions must be met, especially linearity, independence of observations, and equality of variances. When these assumptions are not met, other more advanced techniques are available. The most important of these advanced techniques are the topics the remaining chapters of Part 2. Logistic regression (LR), discussed in Chapter 11, is used when the dependent variable is dichotomous, such as pass or fail. Multilevel modeling (MLM), discussed in Chapter 12, is used when the independent variables are nested, such as individual children, within classes, within schools. Structural equation modeling (SEM), discussed in Chapter 14, is used to study relationships among dependent and independent variables that are measured in several ways. A key element of SEM is factor analysis, which is reviewed in Chapter 13. SEM essentially combines the measurement benefits of factor analysis with the effect size techniques of regression analysis.

Although ordinary least squares regression was the original form and was once the most commonly used, today in research journals a reader is more likely to encounter one of the three advanced and comparatively new methods that will be reviewed in the next chapters. Despite the sophistication and technical complexity of logistic regression (LR), multilevel modeling (MLM), and structural equation modeling (SEM), the basic question one tries to answer with these advanced regression methods remains the same as in ordinary (OLS) regression analysis: How much better can we predict or explain a dependent variable when we have information about one or more independent variables? The next chapter on logistic regression starts by looking at what you do when you want to predict or explain a dependent variable that is categorical rather than continuous. This is a job that cannot be handled by ordinary least squares (OLS) regression, but is easily accomplished by logistic regression.

Terms and Concepts for Review

Model specification
• Specification error
• Focus IV

Dummy coding
• Indicator coding
• Comparison or reference group

Multicollinearity
• Tolerance
• VIF (variance inflation factor)

Missing values
Outliers
Interaction effects

Regression assumptions
• Linearity
• Residuals

ANOVA
ANCOVA
OLS regression
Control for Hold constant
Net of
Specification
• Model specification
• Specification error
• Focus IV

Discussion Questions

1. In a survey in which attitude toward a proposed new tax reform is studied, one of the predictor (independent, explanatory) variables is income. The mean annual income of the 80 respondents is $50,000. One respondent has an income of $600,000. How could this one outlier change the regression coefficient describing the association between income and attitude toward the reform? Could it make the

coefficient bigger? Smaller? Could it change the coefficient's sign? Why or why not?

2. Consider two research designs on topics of interest to you. Each design involves predicting what will happen in the future. One of your designs should deal with a problem wherein predictions can be made with fairly little risk of being wrong. The other should address a problem wherein prediction is much less certain. What are some of the key features of the two problems/designs that account for their different levels certainty in prediction? Can you generalize from these examples to talk about the problems of using data to make predictions?

3. How would you try to ensure that a research project you designed was not hampered by the specification problem called LOVE (left-out variable error)? What could you do to reduce the risk of omitting something really important?

4. Why is it important to check your data for missing values? What can you do to avoid the problem? What can you do to fix it when it occurs?

5. Explain how you could analyze the same data from one research project using both regression analysis and ANOVA. How would the main conclusions that you could draw from the data differ depending on the method of analysis you used? How would they be the same? For the research problem you are imagining for this question, decide which of the two methods would be most practical for your purposes.

6. Examine Table 10.3, especially the row labeled "Adjusted R-squared." Why does this statistic increase as we move from model 1 to model 4? What does the size of each R^2 and its increase indicate?

Self-Test

If you can answer most of the following questions accurately, you can feel confident about your understanding of the material on this chapter. If not, it would be a good idea to review the chapter. (Answers can be found in the Appendix.)

1. Modern statistical packages, such as SPSS and SAS, have largely automated the issue of handling specification errors and reduced them to a minor problem. True or False?

2. If researchers compute a regression coefficient for a variable after controlling for the effects of all the other variables that they or any other researcher imagine could be important, and if that regression coefficient is statistically significant, this can be taken as proof of a causal relation between the predictor and the outcome variables. True or False?

3. Researchers must use fundamentally different statistical techniques when employing regression analysis to study mediating, moderating, and control variables. True or False?

4. When an independent variable in a multiple regression is categorical, researchers can study its effects by using the techniques of dummy (indicator) coding. True or False?

5. Dummy coding is appropriate only when categorical variables have exactly two categories. For categorical variables with more than two categories, different coding schemes must be used. True or False?

6. When a categorical variable has only one category, dummy coding is especially appropriate. True or False?

7. Missing data can importantly influence the outcomes of quantitative analysis, especially when the size of the sample being studied is small. True or False?

8. Highly correlated independent variables are indicated by a low tolerance statistic, and steps should be taken to address this problem before conclusions are drawn from the data. True or False?

9. Multiple regression analysis assumes that the relations among the variables are linear. If they are not perfectly linear, then multiple regression cannot be used. True or False?

10. Like measurement errors, outliers always reduce the size of associations (such as correlation and regression coefficients) between variables. True or False?

11. Interaction effects can be studied with either regression analysis or analysis of variance. True or False?

12. ANCOVA combines techniques of ANOVA and regression analysis. True or False?

13. Using multiple regression to analyze data from a large, representative national sample eliminates most of the problems associated with drawing conclusions that pertain to future samples. True or False?

Endnotes

1. Our discussion here reports on only parts of Broh's study. She also examined the effects of participation on math grades and test scores and obtained generally similar results.

2. These "colleges" are really clusters of departments, rather than colleges strictly speaking. In order to preserve confidentiality, I've not used the exact structure of the colleges and schools at this university.

3. Other forms of coding for categorical variables exist, but they are much less widely used than dummy (indicator) coding. See Cohen et al. (2003) for a discussion of contrast and effects coding.

4. The interested reader who uses the data from Table 2.4 to do the calculations will find that a regression predicting the scores on the licensing exam, using exam 1, paper, project, and gender as the predictors, gives an R^2 of .735; using the same variables but replacing Exam 1 with Exam 2 yields an R^2 of .773, a small difference. Also the tolerances and VIFs for Exam 1 and Exam 2 when used separately are very acceptable: .694 and 1.44 for Exam 1 and .656 and 1.525 for Exam 2.

11

Methods for Categorical Variables

Contingency Tables, Odds, and Logistic Regression

When variables are categorical, particularly when *dependent* variables are categorical, special techniques need to be used. Obviously, the values or scores on categorical variables cannot be distributed normally, because the normal distribution is continuous. Most techniques for continuous variables studied thus far require computing means of the scores on variables. The *t*-test and ANOVA, for example, compare mean differences. Regression examines the mean change in a dependent variable (DV) for a one-unit change in an independent variable (IV). Of course, the idea of computing the mean for categorical variables—such as religion or ethnicity—is ridiculous. In short, if our techniques require normal distributions and means (or mean-based statistics such as the standard deviation and the variance), they cannot be properly used with categorical variables.

The most common technique used when both the IV and the DV are categorical has historically been the chi-squared test for statistical independence. This chapter examines that test in some detail because it is very easy to understand and doing so helps lay the groundwork for more modern techniques. The chi-squared test, which is a test of relative frequencies, has increasingly been supplanted by various odds-based methods, but many of the basic principles of studying categorical variables can best be examined initially by reviewing simpler methods. That review will serve as an introduction to the advanced techniques with which this chapter concludes. The chapter organizes discussion of the issues involved in studying categorical variables according to the answers to the following questions.

1. How is the chi-squared test used to study categorical variables?
2. What are the limitations of the chi-squared approach?
3. How can odds and odds ratios be used to study categorical variables?
4. How can log-linear methods improve analysis of contingency table problems?

TABLE 11.1 *Contingency Table: Marginals (Totals), and Expected Frequencies (in Parentheses)*

	K–8	*9–12*	*Totals (marginals)*
Men	*(180)*	*(120)*	300
Women	*(420)*	*(280)*	700
Totals (marginals)	600	400	1,000

5. How do discriminant analysis and probit regression compare in the analysis of categorical dependent variables?
6. What is logistic regression, and how is it used?
7. Which methods work best for what sorts of problems?

How Is the Chi-Squared Test Used to Study Categorical Variables?

To illustrate the use of the chi-squared test, suppose a random sample of 1,000 K–12 teachers is drawn: Seven hundred of these teachers are female (and 300 are male); 600 of the teachers teach in K–8 schools (and 400 teach in grades 9–12). Putting that information in a *contingency table*—so called because the idea is to see if the value of one variable is contingent on another—results in Table 11.1.

Are these two variables (gender and grade level) *independent*? That is, do they have nothing to do with each other? Or are they dependent or contingent upon each other? Are men and women in the sample distributed proportionately across the grade levels of teaching? If we thought that gender preferences or hiring practices influenced (caused) who was hired for the different grade levels, we would *not* expect the two variables to be independent. Of course, the grade level at which a teacher teaches cannot cause his or her gender, but that knowledge is not statistical. As usual, causal inferences are more a matter of logic than statistics. Statistical data merely provide evidence that supports or fails to support causal inferences.

If gender and grade level were independent, what would be the number in each cell? This can be easily calculated, which is one of the attractive features of the chi-squared test.

• To compute the number for each cell, you multiply the totals for each variable and divide the product by the total number of subjects. For example, to get the number of male K–8 teachers you would expect if the variables were independent, you would multiply 600 K–8 teachers times 300 men and divide that by 1,000, which is the total number of teachers: $600 \times 300 = 180,000/1,000 = 180$. The answer, 180, is called the *expected value*. It is what you would expect if the variables gender and grade level taught were independent.

• In a 2 × 2 table such as this one, you need to compute only one cell this way. All the others are determined as soon as you know one; the others can be computed by subtraction. In this example, if you know that men in K–8 = 180, then women in K–8 must equal 420 (600 minus 180), which also means that women in 9–12 must equal 280 and men in 9–12 must equal 120. When you know one number, the values of the other cells in the table are determined.

• In other terms, in a 2 × 2 table, there is only one *degree of freedom,* or *df*. A degree of freedom is the number of variables and/or values that are free to vary.

• When the IVs and DVs are categorical, the number of *df* is determined by the number of categories.

TABLE 11.2 *Contingency Table: Observed Frequencies*

	K–8	9–12	Totals
Men	95	205	300
Women	505	195	700
Totals (marginals)	600	400	1,000

• When at least one of the variables is continuous—as, for example, the DV is in a *t*-test or an ANOVA—then the *df* is determined mainly by the *N* of cases. For example, for a *t*-test, the number of degrees of freedom is the number of cases minus 1: *N* – 1. So a *t*-test on 30 cases would have 29 *df*, that is: 30 – 1 = 29. By contrast, the *df* for two categorical variables, each with two categories, equals 1, even if the *N* of cases = 1,000.

The way to tell whether gender and grade level of teachers are independent is to compare the *expected* frequencies with the *observed* frequencies, that is, the ones actually in our sample, as in Table 11.2. The numbers in the cells of Tables 11.1 and 11.2 clearly are not the same, but are the differences between them big enough to be statistically significant? That's what the *chi-squared test* tells you. The formula for computing the chi-squared statistic is as follows:

$$\frac{(\text{Exp val} - \text{Obs val})^2}{\text{Exp val}} \quad \text{or} \quad \frac{(E - O)^2}{E}$$

Starting with the upper left cell of Tables 11.1 and 11.2 and using the formula produces: $(180 - 95)^2$ divided by 180, or 7225/180 = 40.14.

• You do the same for each cell, and add up the results. The total is the chi-squared statistic. If you did the math for this example, the total would be 133.3. You then consult a table to compare this against what you would need (the so-called *critical value*) to achieve statistical significance. Table 11.3 is a very abbreviated version of a table of critical values for the chi-squared statistic.

• The degrees of freedom for this example equals 1, which gives you the row to use. If you were using the significance level of .05, you would use the first column of the table: the critical value at 1 df with a significance level of .05 = 3.8. Because the calculated chi-squared statistic (133.3) is much bigger, you can say that gender and grade level are not likely to be statistically independent.

• In other terms, the association of gender and grade level is statistically significant. As always, this means that if there were no association between the two variables in the population, the chances of getting a chi-squared value this big or bigger in the sample would be less than 5% ($p = < .05$).

• Finally, note three facts about the chi-squared statistic and how it is judged to be statistically significant: (1) The more the observed values differ from the expected values, the bigger the chi-squared statistic. (2) The larger the *df*, the larger the critical value needs to be to reach significance. (3) The lower the significance level, the larger the critical value needs to be to reach significance.

Let's look at a slightly more complicated problem. If we had asked respondents about their political party identification (and if each of them responded), the contingency table would look something like the marginals and the expected frequencies in Table 11.4.

TABLE 11.3 *Abbreviated Table of Chi-Squared Critical Values*

Significance Level	.05	.01	.001
Degrees of Freedom			
1	3.8	6.6	10.8
2	6.0	9.2	13.8
3	7.8	11.3	16.3

TABLE 11.4 *Contingency Table: Party affiliation × Gender (Expected Values in Parentheses)*

	Republicans	*Democrats*	*Independents*	*Totals*
Men	*(105)*	*(165)*	*(30)*	300
Women	*(245)*	*(385)*	*(70)*	700
Totals	350	550	100	1,000

The expected frequencies if the two variables were unrelated are calculated the same way as before. For example, for male Independents: 300 × 100 = 30,000/1,000 = 30; and for female Republicans: 350 × 700 = 245,000/1,000 = 245. Note that once you have these two values (or any other two), you can compute the remaining four cell values by subtraction. In short, this problem has 2 degrees of freedom. If you determine any two values, plus the totals or marginals, the other four values in the table are no longer free to vary. The observed frequencies are displayed in Table 11.5.

As is virtually always the case when comparing expected and observed frequencies, the match is not perfect. But are the numbers *different enough* to be statistically significant? Are the genders significantly different in their party affiliations? To find out, use the same formula, of course:

$$\frac{(E - O)^2}{E}$$

For example, for male Republicans the calculations would be $(105 - 116)^2/105 = -11^2/105 = 121/105 = 1.15$. After computing the statistics for the other five cells, you would add up the totals to get the chi-squared statistic. You would then consult Table 11.3 to see if the difference between the observed and expected frequencies was great enough to be statistically significant. If you worked out the example, you would find that the chi-squared statistic was about 3.8. To see whether this was significant at the .05 level, we would again look in the first column of Table 11.3. This time there are 2 df, so we would look in the *second* row for the critical value to find the value of 6.0, which is larger than 3.8. This means that the chi-squared statistic was *not* large enough to be statistically significant.

What Are the Limitations of the Chi-Squared Approach?

What if you wanted to look at all three variables (gender, grade level taught, and party affiliation) at one time? You could make a contingency table with 12 cells, one each for male Republicans teaching in K–8, female Democrats teaching in 9–12, and so on, as illustrated in Table 11.6. And you could compute the chi-squared statistic and compare it to the critical value in the same way. If you added just one more variable most people would find the resulting table too complex to interpret. For example, adding the variable years of teaching experience,

TABLE 11.5 *Contingency Table: Observed Frequencies and Party Affiliation by Gender*

	Republicans	*Democrats*	*Independents*	*Totals*
Men	116	151	33	300
Women	234	399	67	700
Totals	350	550	100	1,000

TABLE 11.6 *Contingency Table: Party Affiliation by Gender by Grade Level Taught*

| | Republicans | | Democrats | | Independents | | |
	K–8	9–12	K–8	9–12	K–8	9–12	*Row Totals*
Men							
Women							
Column totals							

divided into three categories—less than 5 years, 5 to 10 years, and more than 10 years—would require a table of 36 cells. You still could do the computations, but it would be hard to make sense of the results.

As with ANOVA, so too with the chi-squared test of statistical significance. A statistic that exceeded the critical value would mean that at least one of those 36 cells contained a relationship that was not statistically independent, but the test gives no indication of which one. Clearly, the chi-squared test could be cumbersome when studying a problem that required looking at the relations among several variables. Furthermore, when one of those variables is continuous, such as years of experience, the chi-squared approach, like ANOVA, requires that you discard data by making it categorical—for example, by turning both 11 years and 25 years of experience into "more than 10."

The chi-squared test was once the main way to deal with contingency table problems. Its popularity was in part due to the fact that it is easy to compute by hand. It is still useful when dealing with bivariate problems. To recall, *bivariate* refers to relations between two variables; *multivariate* refers to relations among three or more variables. Today, the chi-squared test has been largely supplanted by tables of odds and odds ratios, which have been transformed by taking their natural logs. Odds ratios have replaced chi-squared tests particularly when the research problem is multivariate. Computing odds and taking their logs is no small step. The calculations are more technically demanding. Worse yet, the results are less intuitively clear. To see why most researchers consider it a step worth taking, let's look at one more example.

The National Assessment of Educational Progress (NAEP)—also known as "the nation's report card"—is clearly the single best source data we have on educational achievement in the United States. The NAEP reports periodically on achievement at various grade levels using huge, representative national samples of students. Tables 11.7 through 11.10 give the mean scores in public high schools on the twelfth-grade national mathematics exam.[1] Table 11.7 looks at the mean scores of the national samples of twelfth graders in 1996 and 2000 categorized by whether the students were male or female and by the highest education level of either parent. The test is scored

TABLE 11.7 *Mean Twelfth-Grade Math Scores by Student Gender and by Highest Education Level of Either Parent, 1996 and 2000*

	Year	< HS	HS Graduate	Some College	College Graduate
Males	2000	277	289	303	313
Males	1996	287	293	304	314
Females	2000	279	286	296	310
Females	1996	278	294	300	312

TABLE 11.8   *Mean Twelfth-Grade Math Scores by Student Ethnicity and by Highest Education Level of Either Parent, 2000*

	< HS	HS Graduate	Some College	College Graduate
White	281	294	306	316
Black	265	265	276	281
Hispanic	276	277	288	291
Asian	303	*	315	328

*Insufficient data.

on a 500-point scale with 300 as the mean; the standard deviation is 50. We can see that the differences between the years were small, although the trend downward was consistent. Also the differences between males and females were very modest in most categories, typically 2 or 3 points on a scale of 500 points. But the differences in mean scores by parents' education level were substantial—about 10 times the differences by gender.

In Table 11.8 we drop gender and year because their effects are small and focus on parents' education level. We replace gender with ethnicity and study only the more recent scores. Both variables in Table 11.8 appear to have an effect on math scores. Both parents' education level and student ethnicity seem to influence math scores. Which matters more? It is not easy to tell. And the relation of ethnicity and scores may be spurious; ethnicity may be a proxy for poverty. To investigate that, Table 11.9 reports on at a standard measure of poverty, students' eligibility for free or subsidized school lunch. When we look at both student poverty and parents' education level, it is again hard to tell which has the greater potential influence. However, it is clear that the increase in mean math scores by education level is stronger and

more consistent for the nonpoor than the poor. Poor students' scores go up with each increase in parental education level, but at only about one-third the rate nonpoor kids' scores increase.

Finally, what if we compare the effects of ethnicity versus those of poverty? The scores of these categories are compared in Table 11.10. Again, it is hard to tell which matters more. Poverty and its absence have effects of different sizes in different ethnic groups—28 points for Asians and 7 points for Blacks. More important in disentangling the influence of these variables is the fact that they themselves are related. Poverty varies by ethnic group. Thus, although the publicly available data about the National Assessment of Educational Progress allows researchers to examine the potential effects of hundreds of variables with just a couple of mouse clicks, doing so soon becomes frustrating. The reason is that one can look at only two independent variables at a time in this way.

To get a clear concept of the comparative influence of these variables on math scores, it is necessary to put them all together in one analysis and look simultaneously at the effects of year of exam, gender, poverty, ethnicity, and parents' education level. To

TABLE 11.9   *Mean Twelfth-Grade Math Scores by Student Poverty (Eligibility for Lunch Program) and by Highest Education Level of Either Parent, 2000*

	< HS	HS Graduate	Some College	College Graduate
Poor (eligible)	276	275	286	288
Not poor (not eligible)	279	290	302	314

TABLE 11.10 *Mean Twelfth-Grade Math Scores by Student Ethnicity and by Poverty (Eligibility for Lunch Program), 2000*

	Whites	Blacks	Hispanics	Asians
Poor (eligible)	294	269	277	297
Not poor (not eligible)	309	275	286	325

do this in a contingency table would require a table with 128 boxes or cells—for example, one for Hispanic males in 2000 whose parents were high school graduates and who are not poor, another for White females in 1996 who were poor and whose parents had less than a high school education, and so on. Finally, to make the tables true contingency tables with frequencies (not mean scores) in each cell, the mean achievement scores would need to be converted into categories. The three most common categories for these kinds of data are "does not meet," "meets," or "exceeds" standards. Adding those three categories would push the required number of cells in the table to 384. This could be simplified by ignoring variables that made little difference (gender and year), but we would still need 96 cells (4 parent education levels, times 4 ethnicities, times 2 economic levels, times 3 math score levels). A table with 96 cells would befuddle most attempts at interpretation.

In short, the contingency table method is severely limited, particularly if one wants to study the effects of more than a handful of independent variables on a dependent variable. A table of 384 cells, or even 96, is too unwieldy to be useful. Besides, a thorough analysis of the origins of differences in math scores would need to include many more variables than the five we have looked at (year, parent education level, ethnicity, gender, and poverty level). A researcher would also likely be interested in, for example, the courses students took, their high school tracks, the number of AP courses offered by their schools, the size of their schools and classrooms, the schools' per pupil expenditure, the qualifications of their teachers, and so on.

Finally, as seen before with other methods of significance testing, the results of a chi-squared test on a cross tabulation give researchers evidence about how unlikely the null hypothesis is, but they say little about the size of the association between and among variables. In sum, to improve on the chi-squared approach, two things are required: (1) a way to talk about degrees of association or effect sizes in contingency tables, and (2) a way to handle problems with more than a few variables.

How Can Odds and Odds Ratios Be Used to Study Categorical Variables?

The most useful ways to handle the problem of measuring and communicating the size of an effect in contingency tables employ odds, odds ratios, and relative risk ratios. The main improvement of these statistics over the chi-squared approach is that they provide measures of the strength of the associations. Indeed, the beauty of odds is that, when expressed as single numbers (e.g., 4 to 1 = 4), they can be directly compared. They are in a sense standardized measures of association.

An odds can be calculated for a dichotomous (two-value) variable by dividing the probability of something occurring (of Yes) by the probability of it not occurring (of No)—such as meets standards, yes/no. Yes and No are often called *success* and *failure*, but these can be misleading labels for many contingency table problems. In epidemiology, the usual label is *case/noncase*. Because yes/no is the most generic, if not the most common, label, it will be used here.

To study the odds and odds ratio approaches, let's use the same teacher data. Teaching in K–8 schools is called Yes. Not teaching in K–8 is then

TABLE 11.11 *Male and Female Teachers by Grade Level Taught (Proportions/Probabilities are in Parentheses)*

	K–8/Yes	9–12/No	Totals
Men	95 (.3167)	205 (.6833)	300
Women	505 (.7214)	195 (.2786)	700
Totals	600	400	1,000

called No, of course. In our table, No is equivalent to teaching in grades 9–12. The information from Table 11.2 is repeated in Table 11.11, but the *proportion* of teachers has been added in each cell, which is also the *probability*. (Also, if you move the decimal points two places to the right, you have the *percentages* in each category.) Note that the proportions or probabilities always add up to 1.0 (as percentages will sum to 100). When you have two mutually exclusive categories, the probability of one of them will always be 1 minus the probability of the other. For example, because the probability of men being Yes equals .3167, this means that the probability of No for men is 1 – .3167 = .6833. Although these proportions are informative, they are used here as a step on the way to additional measures.

When computing *odds,* one can use either the raw numbers or proportions (or percentages). Using the numbers, the odds of Yes (teaching in K–8) for men are 95/205 = .4634. For women, the odds of Yes (K–8 teaching) are 505/195 = 2.590. The *odds ratio* is simply a ratio of two odds.[2] So the odds ratio (OR) of women to men in K–8 teaching is 2.590/.4634 = 5.589. What this means is that the odds of women in the sample being K–8 teachers are 5.6 times the odds of men being K–8 teachers. If the sample were representative, you could draw conclusions (make inferences) about the odds and odds ratios in the population.

Another way to handle this kind of dichotomous data, and one that is very widely used in medicine, is called the *relative risk ratio.* Here the concepts of success and failure make more sense,

because *risk,* by definition, is the probability of something one wants to avoid. Let's say we took two random samples of 100 students each at a particular university to measure the graduation rates of male varsity athletes and of elementary education majors. These two categories are not mutually exclusive, of course, though there tends to be little overlap. What has to be mutually exclusive in the analysis are the categories Yes/graduate and No/Not graduate. Even here, "Failure" isn't necessarily an appropriate label for all cases of No, because some university students leave before graduating so as to pursue highly successful professional careers. John McEnroe in tennis and Bill Gates in software are two famous college dropouts that most people wouldn't think of as failures.

Our hypothetical samples are described in Table 11.12. The male varsity athlete odds equal .67, which is obtained by dividing Yes by No, that is, 40/60 = .67. The elementary education major odds = 75/25 = 3.0. The odds ratio is 3.0/.67 = 4.5, which means that the odds of an elementary education major graduating are 4.5 times greater than those of a male varsity athlete. The odds ratio for not graduating is calculated the same way: Odds for athletes = 60/40 = 1.5; odds for education majors = 25/75 = .33; odds ratio 1.5/.33 = 4.5. This means that the odds of an elementary education major graduating *or* an athlete *not* graduating are 4.5 times as great. Typically, one divides the smaller odds into the larger to get the odds ratio (OR), but the same information is conveyed if you do it the other way around. The OR of .22 (.33/1.5 = .22) means that the odds of not graduat-

TABLE 11.12 *Graduation Rates for Two Samples of Students*

	Yes/Graduate	No/Not Graduate
Male varsity athletes	40	60
Elementary education majors	75	25

ing for the education majors are .22 or 22% of those for the athletes. Finally, note that 1.0/.22 = 4.5.

Be careful to remember that, although they are built on the same information and can be easily converted into one another, odds and odds ratios are *not* the same as probabilities and probability ratios. The *probability* of an elementary education major graduating is only 1.875 times greater, not 4.5 times greater. And, the relative risk ratio (risk of not graduating) is .60/.25 = 2.4 times less, not 4.5 times less.

Which is a "better" way to report the difference? They amount to several ways to talk about the same data: probability and the odds of graduating; probability and odds of not graduating; the odds ratio of two groups graduating, and the relative risk of two groups not graduating. Although all of these are mathematically equivalent, because they are all ways of expressing exactly the same information, they do have different rhetorical impacts. Choice of which to use is often mostly a matter of taste, but more advanced methods of analysis rely heavily on odds. Odds, probabilities, and ratios of odds and probabilities have different uses as the bases of analytic techniques. Of these the odds and the odds ratio have become dramatically more prominent in recent years, especially in the social sciences.

It is hard to overemphasize the importance of *relative* ratios or rates. Let's start with the relative risk ratio of suffering a heart attack of two groups: Group A has a risk of .05 and Group B has a risk of .005. The absolute difference between them is .045, which seems small, but the *relative* risk is 10 times

greater for A than for B.[3] Take two additional groups: Group X has a risk of .490 and Group Y has a risk of .445. The absolute difference is exactly the same: .045, but the *relative* difference for X and Y is trivial. X is 1.1 times more likely to suffer a heart attack than Y, whereas A is 10 times more likely than B. Odds ratios yield a similar picture. The odds ratio for Groups A and B is 10.47, which means that the odds that members of Group A will have a heart attack are 10.47 times greater than that of Group B. And for X and Y the odds ratio is 1.2. This example illustrates an important feature of the relationship between probabilities and odds. At the upper and lower limits of probability (*P*), such as probabilities for A and B, the odds will change greatly with only a small change in *P*. In the middle range, such as the probabilities for X and Y, a small change in the probability (*P*) produces a small change in odds and odds ratios.

Probabilities, of course, range from zero, when something is completely improbable, to 1.0 when it's a sure thing. When something is equally likely to happen or not happen, the probability or *P* = .5. By contrast, when the probability of two events is equal, the odds, or *O*, equal 1.0. And the range of odds is infinite, up from 1 when the probability is greater than .5 and down from 1 when the probability is less than .5.

The formula for an odds is:

$$\text{Odds} = \frac{P}{1 - P}$$

For example, if the probability of graduating is .8, the probability of not graduating is 1 − .8 = .2.

$$\frac{.8}{.2} = 4 \text{ (or 4 to 1), which is the odds.}$$

If you know the odds, you can get back to the probability with equal ease. The formula is:

$$P = \frac{\text{Odds}}{1 + \text{Odds}}$$

If the odds is 4, then

$$P = \frac{4}{1+4} = \frac{4}{5} = .8$$

As for odds, when there is no relationship the odds ratio = 1. When there are more cases in category Yes than in No, the OR is greater than 1. When there are more cases in category No than in category Yes, the OR is less than 1. An OR of 4 is the inverse of an OR of .25 and they indicate the same degree of association.

Although all these techniques are complicated in some senses, the complications stem mostly from the large number of ways there are to measure the same relationships. Each of the methods is simple enough, and each rests on nothing more than elementary arithmetic (addition, subtraction, multiplication, and division). The mathematical complexities come with the more advanced methods, which use odds and probabilities to study multivariate problems.

How Can Log-Linear Methods Improve Analysis of Contingency Table Problems?

Log-linear methods use odds and odds ratios to handle contingency table problems with a higher degree of precision possible than with the chi-squared approach. The greater precision and more powerful statistical tests are achieved through transforming the odds and odds ratios by taking their natural logs. The reason for doing that is to turn rank-order data into linear data. Hence, the name: log-linear methods. By taking the logs of the values, the data are made linear. Log-linear methods allow for the study of interactions (much like two-way ANOVA) when all the variables are categorical (ANOVA requires a continuous dependent variable). And log-linear methods make it possible for researchers to deal with contingency table chi-squared type problems, but with the statistical power of regression analysis.

Although these advantages are formidable, we will nonetheless deal fairly briefly with log-linear

methods. Instead, logistic regression methods will be covered more thoroughly because they are more widely used. Their greater use is in part due to the fact that they are designed for research problems in which there is one dependent variable and several independent variables, and research questions very often take this form.

Before examining logarithmic transformations, here is a brief review of the issue of transformations more generally. Although transforming data may seem very complicated, especially to the more math averse among us, the basic ideas can be stated clearly. It is important to take the time to understand transformations, because they open the way to powerful methods of quantitative analysis.

What is the purpose of logarithmic and of other transformations? Mostly transformations are used to make distributions of scores easier to work with or to allow one to use a wider range of statistical analysis techniques. Such manipulations are possible because one can multiply or divide series of scores by a constant without affecting statistics computed on the series of numbers. A familiar example is transforming proportions into percentages by multiplying by 100. If 7 of 10 students answer a question correctly, the proportion of right answers is 7 out of 10, or 7 /10 = 0.70, which, when multiplied by 100, equals 70%.

But any number could be used, not just 100. For example, if you took the two sets of test scores in the earlier correlation example (Exam 1 and Exam 2) and doubled all the scores (multiplied each score by 2), so that 80 became 160, 90 became 180, and so on, you would have "transformed" the two sets of numbers. If you then recomputed the correlation *r* between the two sets, the coefficient would be *exactly* the same. That would also be true if you multiplied each score by 6 or 33 or any other number, or if you divided each score by 10 or any other number. But why would you do that? You wouldn't, because those transformations would simply make for more tedious calculations. However, some transformations greatly expand our opportunities to analyze data well. Depending on the shape of the distributions of the scores, if, for example, they are curvilinear or skewed (see Chapter 4), we might want to take the square root of each score or to take the log of each score. The log transformation is extremely important in modern methods of test construction and analysis (studied in Chapter 16) as well as in the particular regression techniques that are the focus of this chapter.

What are logarithms and how/why are they used in applied statistics? A *logarithm* is an exponent of a base number indicating the power to which the base number must be raised to produce another number. That abstract definition can be made clear by examples. For example, the log of 100 *in base 10* is 2 because 10^2 (10×10) equals 100. The log of 1,000 is 3 because 10^3 ($10 \times 10 \times 10$) equals 1,000. The log of 50 is 1.69897 because $10^{1.69897}$ (which is 10 multiplied by itself 1.69897 times) equals 50. The "antilog" turns the relation around. Thus, in base 10, antilog 2 = 100, antilog 3 = 1,000. But, you might well ask, why would you ever do such a thing? When invented some 300 years ago, logarithms were an enormous time-saver. They greatly eased the burden of calculations. Rather than multiply and divide large numbers, researchers could simply add and subtract their logs. Since the 1970s or so, with widespread availability of calculators and computers, logs are rarely used to simplify calculations, but they are still very important in statistics.

Base 10 logarithms (sometimes called *common* logs) are probably most familiar to most people, but they are not the most frequently used in applied statistics. Rather, the base *e* log or *natural* log is much more often used in research reports. The natural log is usually abbreviated *ln* for "log, natural." In base *e,* 100 equals 4.60517 because *e* multiplied by itself 4.60517 times equals 100. The natural log of 1,000 is 6.9078 and the natural log of 50 is 3.912. What is *e,* and why is it used? Sometimes called the "universal constant," *e* is an irrational number (like pi) that has many mathematical uses and is one of the building blocks of calculus. The value of *e* is 2.718281…. The natural log (base *e*) has some mathematical properties that make it preferable to the common log (base 10), although in many instances either can be used to equal effect. Indeed, in my research, whenever I have compared the two logarithmic transformations, the outcomes were very similar, nearly indistinguishable.

Again, what is gained by transforming data? Usually we make it open to more types of analysis. For example, correlation and regression are built on the assumption that scores are linear, not highly skewed, and measured at the interval or ratio level (that is, that they are quantitative, not nominal or rank ordered). Transformations can perform little miracles. They can make crooked distributions straight and lopsided (skewed) distributions symmetrical. A very widespread use of such transformations is with nominal (or qualitative or categorical) data. By taking the natural log of the odds of categorical and ordinal scores in a distribution, they can be rendered linear and interval. Then we can use techniques that it would otherwise be impossible or inappropriate to use. More specifically, one takes the log of the *odds* of each categorical score, such as right/wrong, pass/fail, survive/perish. A basic grasp of the procedure is so important for modern analytic techniques that this chapter will examine it briefly.

The easiest way to take the log of an odds (or *logit*) is with a handheld calculator. For example, if the probability of graduating for boys is 80%, the odds is 80 divided by 20, which equals 4. Entering 4 and pushing the "ln" button on your calculator, you find that the natural log of 4 is 1.3863. If the probability of graduating for girls is 90%, then the odds are 90 to 10, or 90/10, or 9, and the ln of 9 = 2.1972. When the odds are less than 50:50, the log of the odds or *logit* is negative. For example, the log of 20 to 80 is *negative,* −1.3863, the log of 10 to 90 = −2.1972. Also an odds of 50 to 50 = 1, and the log of 1 = 0. So a negative log odds, or *logit,* is less than 1.0 and a positive log odds, or logit, is greater than 1.0 (or greater than 50:50).

Log-linear methods, like logistic regression, use the natural log of odds, known as the *logit*. Let's perform the *ln* transformation using data from Groups A and B and their odds and odds ratios of a heart attack.

- The odds for Group A: Yes/No = .05/.95 = .0526
- The odds for Group B: Yes/No = .005/.995 = .00503
- The OR for A to B: .0526/.00503 = 10.46
- The logit of the OR: 10.46 = +2.349
- The OR for B to A: .00503/.0526 = .0956
- The logit of the OR: .0956 = −2.349

The output of log-linear analyses produces results that look more like a correlation matrix than regression. Log-linear methods deal with associations between pairs of variables, but, and this is a big advantage, they can do so while controlling for the effects of other variables. As with correlations, log-linear methods are used when there is no clear independent and dependent variable, which in essence means that all variables are treated as dependent on all the other variables. Log-linear methods are more powerful techniques than simple frequency tables or tables of odds. Still, even when you transform odds by taking their logs, you ultimately cannot avoid some of the problems encountered with any contingency tables or correlation matrices. Chiefly, the number of cells multiply rapidly, almost uncontrollably, as you add variables.

As seen in Chapters 9 and 10, it is possible to do much better than the contingency table or crosstabs method allows by using multiple regression analysis (MRA). MRA enables you to examine the (1) *total effects* of a large number of independent variables on a dependent variable, without needing to discard data, *and* to examine the (2) *conditional effects,* that is, the effects of any one of the variables while controlling for the effects of the others. However, the kind of MRA studied thus far—ordinary least squares (OLS) regression—is not appropriate when one is studying a categorical dependent variable (DV). OLS regression is built on assumptions about the distribution of the dependent variable that simply cannot be true when it has two categorical values such as Yes and No.

There are three main ways to handle research questions with a categorical DV and several IVs. If your DVs were continuous and normally distributed, you would use OLS. If not, one of the following options can be selected: discriminant analysis, probit regression, or logistic regression. Each of these can be an effective way to deal with categorical dependent variables, and each has its advocates. Often the outcomes of analyses using different methods are very similar, but some techniques are clearly more appropriate and more effective in particular circumstances. Even though logistic regression has become the most widely used, we need to briefly review the other two methods, because they remain important in some fields, and because understanding them helps to put logistic regression in context.

How Do Discriminant Analysis and Probit Regression Compare in the Analysis of Categorical Dependent Variables?

Discriminant analysis was the first and long the favored means of treating problems with a categorical DV—such as college graduation, yes/no—and several continuous, quantitative IVs, such as parents' income, high school grades, SAT scores, and so on. Discriminant analysis (DA) helps researchers identify the boundaries between (to discriminate between) cases, such as students who are and who are not likely to graduate. Rather than find the best *line* that summarizes the relation between continuous variables, as in OLS regression, one uses DA to find the best *cutoff score*. In OLS regression analysis, the question is: How much better can I predict your score on a continuous DV if I know your scores on these IVs? By contrast in DA, the question is: How much better can I guess your group (graduate/nongraduate) if I know your scores on these IVs? In regression you find the equation that minimizes the errors in prediction of scores. In DA you find the equation that minimizes errors of classification—or, in other terms, the equation that minimizes errors in the prediction of group membership.

Discriminant analysis (DA) is a form of regression analysis used when the DVs are categorical (the categories have to be mutually exclusive, of course). The idea of DA is to classify or categorize cases using information about IVs. Say the dependent variable is college graduation and that the average rate of graduation is 50%. In the absence of any other information, your best guess for any individual (case) would be 50%. How much better could you predict the classification of cases if you had information about several variables, such as parents' income, students' SAT scores, and their high school GPAs?

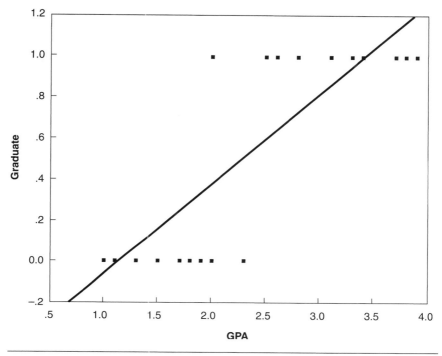

FIGURE 11.1 *Relation of GPA to probability of graduating*

Discriminant analysis produces a weighted combination of IVs in an equation. This equation, which is equivalent to a regression equation, is called the *discriminant function*. The equation (function) is used to determine whether the particular cases meet a cutoff score for making it into one group or another. Each case gets a score by having the equation applied to its data. The value being computed with the equation is usually symbolized L, which is directly parallel to the Y in a regression equation. The L either is or is not above the cutoff score, and that determines the classification of the case.[4]

Two disadvantages of discriminant analysis have led to it being replaced by the probit and logit regression methods. First, it works only with continuous IVs, whereas probit and logistic regression can work with any combination of IVs, categorical or continuous. Second, and more important, discriminant analysis requires important assumptions be true

of the IVs (e.g., equality of variances), assumptions that are unlikely to be met in real data sets. This restriction does not apply to probit and logistic (or logit) regression analysis.

Probit regression, like discriminant analysis, is used when the dependent variable (DV) is categorical. Remember that with OLS regression the idea is to find a straight line that most closely approximates the actual data. When the DV is categorical, a straight line will not fit the data unless all cases fall into the same category. To see why, let's take a simple two-variable problem with a categorical variable: college graduation, yes/no as the DV. Grade point average at the end of the freshman year is the IV. The data form two separate straight lines when the DV = 1 (graduate) or 0 (not graduate). The data depicted in Figure 11.1 show the characteristic shape often encountered when the DV is categorical. The horizontal axis depicts GPA at the end of the first year of college and the vertical whether the students graduated three years later: yes = 1, no = 0. Nearly all students with very high GPAs graduated and almost all those with very low GPAs did not. A straight line can be fitted to these data, as is done in Figure 11.1, but it misses the point—most of them anyway. However, there are *curves* that come quite close to approximating the kind of data depicted in Figure 11.1. One is the logit curve and the other is the probit curve.

Probit is short for *probability unit*. To conduct a probit regression analysis, one first needs to transform the categorical DV. The probit and logit provide roughly equivalent (though mathematically quite different) ways of doing this. Given our already extensive coverage of the normal curve in this book, most readers will probably find the probit approach easier to understand (or, maybe I'm projecting because it has always seemed to me to be more intuitively obvious and easier to understand). For regressions with dummy DVs, the logit and probit approaches almost always give very similar results (Agresti, 1996). However, logit or logistic regression is much more widely used, so we will examine it in greater detail. Our analysis of probit regression is intended merely to set the context for logistic regression.

In brief, leaving out lots of technical details (see Pampel, 2000, for an introduction), one transforms the probabilities of the DV (e.g., of graduating) into *z*-scores, using the *cumulative standard normal distribution* (CSND) to do this. If you remember the normal distribution depicted in Chapter 4 and the corresponding percentile scores, the concept is easy to understand. A score that is 2 standard deviations below the mean ($z = -2.0$) would fall in the 2nd percentile and would have a cumulative frequency or probability of 2%. A score 2 standard deviations above the mean ($z = +2.0$) would be in the 98th percentile and have a cumulative probability of 98%, and so on. To picture what the cumulative standard normal distribution looks like, imagine that you have cut a vertical line through the middle of a standard normal curve. The CSND looks like the left-hand side of your bisected normal curve (see Figure 11.2).

Details aside, the questions you answer with probit regression are variants (in probability units) of the questions you answer with any regression analysis. Those questions in probit regression language are: (1) What is the change in the probability of the DV being 1 (e.g., yes, graduate) for a one-unit change in an IV? (2) What is the change in the probability of the DV being 1 (yes) for a one-unit change in an IV, while controlling for the effects of the other IVs? (3) What is the cumulative effect of all the IVs together on the probability of the DV equaling 1 (yes)?

What Is Logistic Regression, and How Is It Used?

Our final method is the one that has come to be the most widely used. Like log-linear methods, it uses odds and their logarithmic transformations (logits) as its unit. As seen earlier, log-linear methods can be applied when all variables are categorical and when no distinction is made between IVs and DVs. By contrast, *logistic regression* is used when there are IVs and a categorical DV. The two methods are closely related. They are strictly equivalent when all variables are dichotomous. Some authors consider one a special case of the other, but not all agree on which is the general and which the special case. Be that as it may, logistic regression is more flexible and is more frequently encountered in research reports.

Usually, the DV in a logistic regression is dichotomous or binomial. But the DV can have multiple categories, in which case it is called *multinomial* logistic regression. For example, in diagnoses in medicine or special education, the ordered categories in the outcome variable might be mild, moderate, and severe. Additional techniques are required when the multinomial DV's categories are ordinal or ordered, but reading the output poses few special problems. The special techniques, although more complicated, do not differ in principle from the two-outcome case (see Harrell, 2000, and Menard, 2002). As done with

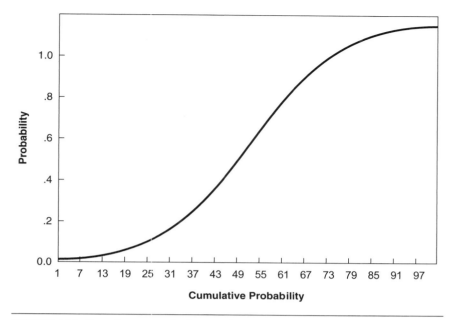

FIGURE 11.2 *Cumulative standard normal distribution (CSND)*

OLS regression, the general principles involved in all forms of logistic regression can be established by studying the two-outcome case and generalizing to more complicated cases as necessary.

Logistic regression is used for exactly the same kinds of problems as probit regression. Return briefly to Figure 11.1, where the freshman grade point averages are plotted on the horizontal axis. On the vertical axis is the probability of graduating, yes = 1, no = 0. In logistic regression one uses the *odds* of graduating, not the *probabilities,* but the need for a curve, rather than a straight line, is the same. The curve needed is roughly S-shaped (see Figure 11.2). It has that form because an increase in the score at the extremes of the distribution has much less influence than scores in the middle. In our example, the odds of a freshman with a 1.1 GPA graduating three years later are not much improved if the GPA goes up to 1.2 or 1.3. The curve rises slowly. The same is true at the other end of the GPA range. A student with a freshman GPA of 3.5 is very likely to graduate. Another student with a

3.6 might be somewhat more likely to graduate, but not much more. Not many with GPAs of 1.1, 1.2, or 1.3 will make it; nearly all with 3.5, 3.6, or 3.7 will. It is in the middle where we would find that comparatively small increases in the independent variable are likely to have a big effect on the odds, or probability, of graduating. That's what the curve, whether a cumulative probability curve or a logistic curve reflects: slow increase until some threshold, probably around 2.0 in this example; then more rapid increase to around 3.0 where the curve flattens out again. A straight line does not fit the distribution, but the S-shaped curve does.

Once we have the logistic curve that fits the distribution, logistic regression works the same way that the more familiar ordinary (OLS) regression works. You use it to address the same kinds of questions: First, how much of a change in the DV is associated with a one-unit change in an IV (controlling for the other IVs)? Second, what is the total effect on a DV of all the IVs taken together? The only difference is that in logistic regression the DV is expressed in different units. The dependent variable in a logistic regression is the log of the odds or *logit*. This is arrived at by dividing the probability of Yes by the probability of No to get the odds.[5] Then one takes the natural log (*ln*) of the resulting odds. This transformed odds is usually symbolized by the letter *L*. (This is not the same *L* as in discriminant analysis. The same letter is used here and elsewhere, because there are many more techniques than letters to label them with.) Only the DV is thus transformed. The IVs all stay in their original units (years, dollars, GPA, etc.) as they do in ordinary regression.

So in ordinary regression one might say: What is the expected change in *Y* for a one-unit change in *X*? In logistic regression, the equivalent question would be: What is the expected change in *L* (the log of the odds or logit) for a one-unit change in *X*? Remember that the dependent variable, *L,* is the log of the odds (not the probability) that Yes will occur. The DV could be log of the odds of yes graduate, or yes change jobs, or yes attend college, or yes survive surgery, and so on. An important caution needs to be mentioned at this point. It applies generally when we have to depend on computer software to do our calculations for us. Be sure you are clear about what is being calculated. In this case, SPSS gives the log of the odds (logit) of Yes or 1. SAS, an equally well-known program, gives the logit of No or 0. The two outputs provide the same information. It doesn't matter what program you use—unless you are unaware of the difference.

The results of a logistic regression are presented in tables in a couple of different ways and are discussed in the text of articles as odds *or* as odds ratios *or* as probabilities. This is partly a matter of the taste of the writer, because, as we have seen, it is easy enough to move from logits to odds to probabilities and back again. Different statisticians give different advice about how wise it is to do this. Talking about results in terms of logits (logs of odds of Yes) is probably most accurate, but it is also pretty obscure to most people—unless they are a lot more familiar with natural logs of odds than I am. Talking in terms of probabilities might be less accurate, but it is most

meaningful (easiest to understand) for most readers. My advice in this as in other similar situations is to report results in all meaningful ways. Readers usually benefit from seeing the results expressed in different measurement units or *metrics*. (See Liao, 1994, for a thoughtful discussion.)

It is easiest to discuss different methods of reporting by looking at a few published examples of research using logistic regression. "Who goes to graduate school?" was the question addressed by Mullen, Goyette, and Soares (2003) in their study of influences on the educational careers of a large group of college seniors. Their study used multinomial logistic regression because they did not simply study graduate school: yes or no. Rather their DV came in five categories: none, master's, MBA, professional, doctoral. However, the coefficients in their tables are read the same way whether the DV has two categories or five. In this article, as in many others, the regression coefficients are presented in columns labeled *Exp(B),* which is short for the exponent of the regression coefficient *B*. For example, the influence of parents' education level on entering a doctoral program was reported as: Exp(B) = 1.20. This means that for every one-year increase in parents' education level the odds that a college senior would enter a doctoral program increased by 20%. In logistic regression, the Exp(B) is an *odds ratio*.

One source of confusion for many readers of logistic regression is that an Exp(B) coefficient showing *no effect is expressed as 1.0.* By contrast, in ordinary (OLS) regression, a coefficient indicating no effect would be zero. This oddity, as it were, arises from the fact that we are dealing with odds. If the odds of the DV being Yes (graduating, for example) are unaffected by the DV, the odds will be 1 to 1 or 50:50—or, expressed as a single number, 1.0. For instance, if gender has no effect on the odds of graduating, the Exp(B) of the coefficient for gender will be 1.0. On the other hand, if the Exp(B) for, say, honors students is 2.0, that means that the odds of honors students graduating are twice as large. In other words, the odds are 2 to 1.

To return to the example of likelihood of entering a doctoral program: Mullen and colleagues (2003) gave the Exp(B) as 1.20, which meant that the odds were 20% higher (1.2 to 1) for each year of parental education. And that was a statistically significant difference. As always, the reader should ask how big the effect is as well as how much the results tend to refute the null hypothesis (are statistically significant). In this case, Mullen et al. point out that because very few college seniors enter doctoral programs (around 3% of the total), the absolute effect of a 20% increase is quite small: "The large odds ratios here represent only small absolute increases in the overall probability of entering" doctoral programs (p. 157). If the probability of going on to a doctoral program is about 3%, then the odds of entering a doctoral program are 3/97 = .031. The Exp(B) of 1.20 means that the odds (*not* the probability) of entering a doctoral program go up by 20%. A 20% increase means that the odds go up from .031 to .037—a small change indeed.

In my view, the Exp(B), or odds ratio, approach is the clearest way to present the results of a logistic regression, but it is not the only one. For example, in a study of teacher turnover, Ingersoll (2001) reports the results of his logistic regressions using the unstandardized regression coefficient *b,* not the exponent of the coefficient *b.* As with any regression coefficient, this one indicates what the effect is on a DV of a one-unit change in the IV. In logistic regression, the effect on the DV is expressed in logits. This means that the reader needs to do a little work before interpreting the coefficients, because in their original form, the coefficients in logistic regression seem to me to defy interpretation. For example, Ingersoll shows that support by administrators for teachers is important for keeping teachers from quitting and leaving for another school. The coefficient *b* for that effect is −.26. Ingersoll summarizes by saying that a one-unit increase in administrative support "is associated with a 23% difference in the odds of a teacher departing" (p. 518). How do you get from a *b* of −.26 to "a 23% difference in the odds"? Basically, you have to compute the exponent of *b* yourself. Enter −.26 into a calculator and then push the e^x button. The result is .77. When administrative support is increased by one unit, the odds of leaving are .77 of what they would have been if administration support

had not been increased. To say that the odds are 77% of what they would have been is the same as saying they are 23% lower than they would have been—because 1.0 minus .77 equals .23.

Note that the negative coefficient −.26 is interpreted the same way as a negative coefficient in ordinary regression. It is negative because an *increase* in administrative support *lowers* the odds of teacher turnover. The relationship is inverse. On the other hand, an increase in student discipline problems raises the odds of teachers departing. The coefficient *b* is .39. Enter .39 into your calculator, hit the e^x button. You get 1.48, which means that the odds of a teacher leaving a school go up 48% (odds of 1.48 to 1) with every one-unit increase in student discipline problems. It is possible to transform the odds into a probability, in which case the results could be presented as the probability, not the odds, of a DV being 1 or Yes. Some researchers report their logistic regression findings this way, whereas others caution that doing so is an unwise practice. Regardless of the method of explicating the results, they are all initially calculated using the natural log of the odds (logit) of the DV being Yes.

What about the appropriate coefficient of determination, the equivalent of R^2 in OLS regression? As already seen, the R^2 statistic estimates the percentage of variance in the DV explained by all the IVs taken together. As such, it is often one of the first things a reader looks at when examining the results of an ordinary (OLS) regression, but there is no exact equivalent in logistic regression. There are approximations—often referred to as pseudo-*R*-squared[6]—but statisticians have not yet reached a consensus about which of these is preferable—or whether any one of them is useful enough to be reported. The differences between them can be substantial. For instance, let's return to the earlier example of faculty salaries, gender, college, rank, and years of experience from Chapters 9 and 10. Rather than have salary as the dependent variable, we might be interested in whether an individual had reached the rank of full professor. Our DV in a logistic regression would be full professor: yes/no. Our independent variables could be gender and years of experience. SPSS

TABLE 11.13 *Logistic Regression Predicting Full Professor Rank*

	B	Standard Error	Wald	Df	Sig.	Exp(B)
Step 1(a)						
FEMALE(1)	1.133	.899	1.590	1	.207	3.106
YRSEXPC	.121	.059	4.136	1	.042	1.128
Constant	−3.543	1.047	11.450	1	.001	.029

Note: Variable(s) entered on step 1: Female, yrsexpc.

reports two versions of the R^2 statistic: "Cox & Snell R Square," which in our example equals .177, and "Nagelkerke R Square," which is always larger. For the same data it equals .264. The uncertainty about which coefficient of determination to use or whether to use it leads many researchers to use none or, more frequently, to report them but not say much about them. They are not crucial interpretive tools as is the R^2 is in OLS regression.

The logistic regression output for the odds of having attained the rank of full professor is shown in Table 11.13. Gender and years of experience are the predictors (IVs). In the column headed "Sig." we see that years of experience is statistically significant (p = .042), but gender is not (p = .207). When we look at the Exp(B) column to get the size of that effect by examining the odds, something is odd. The odds ratio, the Exp(B) for female, is 3.1. The odds of a female being a full professor are 3.1 times as high in this sample as the odds for a male. However, this is not statistically significant. The odds ratio for years of experience, on the other hand, is only 1.1, but it is statistically significant. How can that be? The oddity is due to the way the IVs are measured or scaled.

This scaling problem comes up in any form of multiple regression, but the effects are sometimes aggravated in logistic regression. Female has only 2 values: 1 and 0. A one-unit increase in this variable captures its entire effect. But years of experience has 30 values in our sample, from 1 year to 30 years. A one-unit increase in this variable measures 1/30, or about 3% of the total effect. So the effect of a one-unit increase in years of experience will almost al-

ways be smaller than a one-unit increase in gender. The coefficient for experience would be smaller still if we used months of experience, and smaller still if we used weeks of experience. It would be bigger if we used decades of experience instead of years. What if you want to compare the size of the effects (not only their statistical significance) of variables that are scaled differently? One approach is to scale the two variables the same way (to standardize them). In this case you could multiply the coefficient for years by 30, because the range for years is 30 times bigger than for gender. If you did that for the regression coefficients (column headed B in the table), you would multiple .121 times 30 and compare the result for the B for female. Years would equal 3.6 while female equals 1.1, so you could say that the effect of years of experience on the odds of being a full professor is roughly three times as strong as the effect of gender.

One final point about this example. Logistic regression, not ordinary linear (OLS) regression, is used for the research, because the relation between years of experience and full professor, yes/no cannot be linear, it cannot be well described by a straight line—unless all professors in the sample are full professors (or none of them are). Rather the relationship will be described by an S-shaped curve. The curve expressing the odds of becoming a full professor will at first increase gradually with years of experience, then go up rapidly, and then level off. The odds of making it to full professor don't go up much as you move from 1 to 2 years of experience—at most universities they would be nil. And the odds don't improve much as you move from your twenty-seventh to your twenty-eighth year of experience. If you haven't made it by your silver anniversary, you aren't ever likely to do so. Years of experience tends to have the most important effect on the categorical dependent variable in the middle of the range of experience, probably from about 10 to 20 years at most universities. That makes the relation between attaining the full professorship and years of experience an ideal candidate for logistic regression. By contrast, the relation of years of experience and salary is quite likely to be linear, and salary is a continuous variable, so studying years and salary we would use the original, simpler, form of regression, ordinary least squares (OLS).

Methods of significance testing are very different and more complicated in logistic regression as compared to ordinary (OLS) regression. As already seen, in OLS regression *t*-tests are used to assess the statistical significance of each individual coefficient. ANOVA is used to test the entire regression equation for statistical significance. Neither of these is appropriate for logistic regression (nor are they appropriate for log-linear methods or for probit regression). Rather, what is used is a general category of approaches known as *maximum likelihood estimation* (MLE), which in turn is part of what is known as generalized linear models. The general linear model is made even more general (generalized) and applicable to a wider range of research problems, such as those when the dependent variables are categorical. In any case, when you read or produce the results of a logistic regression you will often find (e.g., in the SPSS output in Table 11.13) that the individual coefficients are tested with the *Wald statistic*. The whole model (the effect of all the IVs taken together on the DV) is assessed with the log likelihood test. You will see this listed at the bottom of the regression table as -2 LOG L or -2LLR or -2LLF or -2 log likelihood. These are all abbreviations for exactly the same test.[7]

Maximum likelihood estimation and the generalized linear model are highly technical subjects, well beyond the scope of this book, and it is not easy to find nontechnical discussions of these topics. However, researchers reading and perhaps even conducting logistic regression research can "get by" with very little of such knowledge. Regardless of the method of statistical inference, the results are the same: *p*-values and confidence intervals. The methods of calculating the *p*-values and CIs may be taken "on faith." If you are one of those people taking things *on faith* in order to *get by*, you ought to feel quite nervous. But you shouldn't let that keep you from reading research; and you can even cautiously conduct research using these methods, especially if you have access to an expert who can help you over the rough spots and check your work when necessary.

Which Methods Work Best for What Sorts of Problems?

Contingency tables analyzed with the chi-squared test are no longer state of the art. The good news is that now there are much better analytic tools. The bad news is that most of these are harder to understand. In this chapter we have reviewed a handful of new techniques with an emphasis on logistic regression.

The relation of log-linear and logit methods is roughly parallel to the relation of the Pearson *r* correlation and OLS regression. Both logistic regression and OLS regression require a dependent variable (DV). By contrast, the Pearson *r* and the log-linear methods do not. The correlation between *X* and *Y* is the same as between *Y* and *X*, but this is not true of regression. You do not get the same coefficient when *X* is the independent variable (IV) as when *X* is the DV. Nonetheless, the two pairs of methods are closely related. Just as OLS regression and the Pearson *r* are siblings, so too are the log-linear and logit regression pair.

This chapter has looked at several methods for dealing with categorical variables, particularly regression for categorical *dependent* variables. It is not always the case, however, that OLS regression has to be abandoned when the dependent variable is categorical. Especially when the categories are a set of *ordered* categories, and it is particularly the case when it can be assumed that the gaps between the ranks in the ordinal scale are "fairly" even, which means that the ordinal scale is close to an interval scale. Say, for example, that a dependent variable has

TABLE 11.14   *Analysis Techniques and Measurement Levels of Variables*

Analysis Technique	IVs	DVs
Chi-squared contingency tables	Categorical	Categorical
Log-linear analysis	Categorical	Categorical
t-test	Categorical	Continuous
ANOVA	Categorical	Continuous
Pearson *r* correlation	Continuous	Continuous
OLS regression	Either	Continuous
Discriminant analysis	Continuous	Categorical
Probit regression	Either	Categorical
Logistic regression	Either	Categorical

answers to a question scored on a Likert-like scale with the following values: 7 = totally agree, 6 = agree strongly, 5 = agree, 4 = don't know, 3 = disagree, 2 = strongly disagree, 1 = totally disagree. Should this scale be treated as categorical or continuous? Is it an ordinal or an interval scale? It is probably somewhere in between, not merely ordinal, but not quite interval either. When is it "reasonable" to assume that the gap between, say, strongly agree and agree (from 5 to 6) is pretty much the same size as that between don't know and disagree (from 2 to 3)? The answer is not directly statistical (which is why I have put "fairly" and "reasonable" in quotation marks). The answer depends more on the researcher's knowledge of the subject and the context in which the question is being asked. The simplicity of OLS regression and the comparative ease with which its results can be communicated would make me reluctant to give it up in a context in which it could be appropriate. To help with the decision, I would return to the regression diagnostics described in Chapter 10. If those diagnostic tests indicated that the problems with OLS regression were "fairly" minor, I would use it rather than probit or logistic regression for an ordinal dependent variable. As is often true, the choice is made by using one's judgment, not simply by applying a rule.

Table 11.14 summarizes some of the characteristics of the range of analytic choices discussed in this chapter, puts them in the context of other familiar measures, and outlines which method to use when—given the nature of your variables.

The chi-squared test for contingency tables and log-linear methods of analysis are designed for circumstances in which all variables are categorical and it often does not make sense to differentiate between independent and dependent variables. The chi-squared test has the advantages of being familiar and generally easy to understand. But it is less powerful than log-linear methods and gives no effect size. Both the chi-squared and the log-linear methods can have problems with rapidly multiplying numbers of cells as variables are added.

I have included the *t*-test and ANOVA here for completeness. These tests of significance are used for comparing means. Because means can be computed only on continuous variables, the DVs must be continuous in either the *t*-test or ANOVA. On the other hand, the IVs must be categorical or, if they are continuous, they must be categorized. In that sense, discriminant analysis is like ANOVA stood on its head. Discriminant analysis requires continuous independent variables and a categorical dependent variable; ANOVA works with a continuous dependent variable and categorical independent variables.

Both the Pearson *r* and OLS regression require continuous DVs. These workhorses of modern quantitative analysis are thus inapplicable in cases in which the DV is categorical.[8] When the DV is categorical, one must use either contingency table methods of the chi-squared test or log-linear methods or one of the three regression-based approaches discussed in the chapter: discriminant analysis (DA), probit regression

(PR), or logistic regression (LR). DA was once the method of choice. Today, PR and LR are more widely seen in the published research literature in most fields. Neither require the assumptions about distributions required in DA, and both are much better than DA at accurate estimates when the number of cases in the categories of the categorical dependent variable are very uneven—such as the preceding example of entering doctoral programs: Yes = 3%, No = 97%.

Although PR and LR usually give nearly identical answers to most analysis questions, we have focused more on LR because of its greater use in most research contexts. LR works like any other regression and answers the same sorts of questions, but the units of measurement are different and more difficult to interpret. Logs of odds just do not make as much sense as years of experience or dollars of salary or other natural units of measurement. On the other hand, the odds ratio approach—Exp(B)—yields a readily interpretable measurement of the effect of independent variables.

Finally, LR (like PR and log-linear methods) requires a very different approach to significance testing of the coefficients and the whole equation. This approach is known as maximum likelihood estimation (MLE). However, as with all methods of statistical inference, MLE methods end up in *p*-values or confidence intervals, and whether the inferences are built on classical statistical methods or on MLE, the results are conceptually identical.

Finally, the general overall form and function of regression analysis is the same whether it is ordinary least squares OLS regression or logistic regression or probit regression. The two questions answered take the same general form: (1) What is the effect on a dependent (or outcome) variable of a one-unit change in an independent (or predictor) variable, when controlling for all the other independent variables? (2) What is the effect on an outcome variable of all the predictor variables taken together? Although the measurement units used to report the effects of the predictors on the outcome variables vary (*z*-scores, logits, probits, or natural units), the basic form of the questions asked, and of the answers provided, by regression analysis remains the same.

Our next chapter, on multilevel modeling (MLM), extends the range of problems that can be investigated with regression even further. Over the past two decades, researchers have developed techniques that can handle "nested" variables, variables that are located within other variables. For example, an individual lives in a neighborhood; the neighborhood is nested within a town, which is nested within a state, which is nested within a region. The environmental conditions that an individual experiences are in part due to the conditions in the neighborhood, but each broader context, each higher level of analysis has its effect too. What multilevel modeling does is provide researchers with new tools to investigate the separate effects of variables at different levels. Because nested variables are the rule, not the exception, these are very important tools. Our next chapter examines them.

Terms and Concepts to Review

Contingency tables
- Marginal frequencies
- Expected frequencies
- Observed frequencies

Chi-squared test
- Critical values

Degrees of freedom (*df*)
Odds
Probability
Odds ratio
Relative risk ratio

Log-linear methods
Logarithms
- Base 10 log
- Natural log
  - *ln*
  - *e*

Transformations
Logarithmic transformations
Logit
Discriminant analysis

Probit regression
- Cumulative standard normal distribution (CSND)

Logistic regression
- Logit
- Exp(B)

- Pseudo-*R*-squared
- Maximum likelihood estimation (MLE)
- Wald statistic

Discussion Questions

1. Think of a research question that requires you to use a categorical dependent variable. Can you think of a research question wherein the variable could be measured either on a continuous or a categorical scale? If so, which would you choose, and why?

2. Why is it inappropriate to use ordinary least squares (OLS) regression to study the relationship between a categorical dependent variable and one or more independent variables?

3. What does it mean to transform a variable? Why do researchers need to transform variables? What is gained thereby? Is anything lost?

4. If one researcher concluded that the *probability* of getting a disease was double for subjects who smoked at least a pack of cigarettes per day, and another researcher, studying the same question with a different sample, reported that the *odds* were three times higher, which researcher found the greater risk? How can you tell?

Self-Test

If you can answer most of the following questions accurately, you can feel confident about your understanding of the material in this chapter. If not, it would be a good idea to review the chapter. (Answers can be found in the Appendix.)

1. If you were using the chi-squared test for independence, and the observed and the expected frequencies in a contingency table were almost identical, this would indicate a very high level of statistical significance. True or False?

2. The chi-squared test of independence indicates statistical significance but gives no direct evidence about effect size. True or False?

3. If a researcher reported data using relative risk ratios, another researcher could recompute and report the same data using odds ratios. True or False?

4. Neither the chi-squared test for independence nor log-linear methods for contingency tables require researchers to specify which variables are dependent and which are independent. True or False?

5. If the independent variables in a planned regression analysis are categorical, the researcher should use discriminant analysis, probit regression, or logistic regression rather than OLS regression. True or False?

6. Logistic regression and probit regression are designed to handle the same kinds of research problems and usually produce very similar results. True or False?

7. The odds describing the association between two variables provides the same information as the odds ratio describing the association between those two variables. True or False?

8. When the logistic regression coefficient Exp(B) is 1.0, this means that the variance in the dependent variable is wholly accounted for by the variance in the independent variable. True or False?

9. If the Exp(B) in a logistic regression were reported to be .40, this would mean that a 1-unit increase in the independent variable is associated with a 60% decrease in the odds of the dependent variable being Yes or 1. True or False?

10. If the Exp(B) in a logistic regression were reported to be 2.70, this would mean that for a 1-unit increase in the independent variable, we can expect a 270% increase in the odds of the dependent variable being Yes or 1. True or False?

11. If the Exp (B) in a logistic regression were reported to be 1.55, this would mean that a 1-unit increase in the independent variable is associated with a 155% increase in the probability of the DV being Yes or 1. True or False?

Endnotes

1. Tables 11.7 through 11.10 were constructed from data available on the Web site of the National Center for Educational Statistics (NCES): http://nces.ed.gov.

2. The odds ratio is usually abbreviated as OR, and for no good reason, in more advanced texts and research reports, as the Greek letter theta, θ.

3. When Vioxx was pulled off the market in 2004, the risk of heart attack or stroke for those who took the drug was reported as 3.5% versus 1.9% for those who took a placebo. This is an absolute difference of 1.6%, but the relative risk was nearly double (3.5/1.9 = 1.8).

4. Discriminant analysis can also be conducted using standardized coefficients (in z-scores). As with OLS, this helps when comparing the importance of predictors.

5. More commonly this is described by saying you take the probability of Yes or success, symbolized P, and divide it by $1 - P$ to get the odds. The formula for the logit would then be $L = ln[P/1 - P]$.

6. The R-squared statistic in OLS regression refers to the amount of variance explained. Variance is deviation from the mean. Because there is no mean, we cannot compute the deviation from it—hence, any such estimate is *pseudo*.

7. The basic likelihood ratio or function has to be multiplied by -2 in order to produce a statistic that can be tested with a chi-squared distribution with the degrees of freedom equal to the number of IVs.

8. There is a wide variety of bivariate correlations to use when variables are categorical and/or ordinal, such as Kendall's tau and Cramers' V. Most of them are direct analogues of r.

12

Multilevel Modeling

Multilevel modeling (MLM) is one of the two most widely employed statistical methods used in published social and behavioral research. The other is structural equation modeling (SEM). These two methods are the topics of our final three chapters in Part 2. Each has become a mature analytical technique quite recently, and each was simultaneously invented by researchers working in different fields. For that reason, each has several different names. For instance, multilevel modeling is also called hierarchical linear modeling (HLM), as is one of the most popular software packages for conducting it. Structural equation modeling (SEM) is frequently referred to as LISREL, that is, by the name of the first popular software for undertaking SEM.

The needs these two methods satisfy became possible to meet, mostly since the 1990s, with the development of computer memory and speed and the software written to take advantage of them. Using MLM and SEM, researchers are more able to study real-world complexity. Prior to the availability of these analytical models, many statistical techniques were pitifully inadequate to describe the intricacies of the problems typically encountered in research. The advantages of the two methods led to dramatic growth in their use in social and behavioral research.

For example, Harwell and Gatti (2001) reviewed all the articles published in the mid-1990s in three of education's most prestigious and widely cited journals: *Sociology of Education,* the *American Educational Research Journal,* and the *Journal of Educational Psychology.* They found that in these three key journals "more than 85% of the studies reporting empirical results used hierarchical linear modeling (HLM) or structural equation modeling (SEM), although ANOVA-based procedures were also used" (p. 109). Obviously, anyone wanting to read educational research in these journals—and at least one of these journals is almost certain to be an important source for nearly any research topic in education—will need to be familiar with these methods. The same considerations apply in sociology and psychology and only somewhat less so in economics and political science.

Multilevel modeling is probably the best generic label for our topic in this chapter. But it is not the most common label. In sociology and education it is hierarchical linear modeling (HLM). At least four other labels are used for multilevel modeling (MLM). *Random effects models* and *mixed effects models* are common terms in economics. Two other terms are *random coefficient regression models* and *covariance components models.* All of these terms make sense. Each describes an important feature of this group of methods. But the multiple labels are a source of considerable confusion, particularly because the different names for identical techniques tend to vary across disciplines. To uncover the world of multilevel analysis, which is somewhat obscured by multiple less-than-clear names, this chapter will answer the following questions.

1. What kinds of research questions require the use of multilevel analyses?
2. What technical analysis problems give rise to the need for multilevel models?
3. How does multilevel analysis work in practice?
4. How can MLM be applied to concrete research problems (six examples)?

What Kinds of Research Questions Require the Use of Multilevel Analyses?

Many research problems are inherently multilevel problems. One research problem important in the development of multilevel methods was investigating the causes of students' academic achievement. Indeed, multilevel analyses grew up in large part out of a debate among researchers, dating back to the 1960s, about how to study the effects of schools on learning. It is easy to see how the influences on a student's academic achievement operate at several levels. Think of the components of, say, an individual student's math learning in the eighth grade. Most obvious are the student's individual characteristics, such as personality traits, talents, parental support, and so on. But, the outcome variable, academic achievement, is also influenced by other kinds of factors, by contextual or higher-level factors. At the second level, a student's learning is shaped by variables operating in the classroom, such as the size of the class and the teacher's knowledge and skills. A third, higher level, would be the school-level variables, such as per pupil expenditure (PPE). Differences in PPE are sufficiently large that they almost surely have an ef-

fect. For example, in Illinois in 2004, the difference per pupil between the highest and lowest spending district was over $15,000 ($20,173 versus $4,829 per pupil). An analysis that ignored higher-level variables such as class size or PPE would likely be missing important variables and thereby committing a specification error. Another common metaphor is to say that variables are "nested." Individual student variables are nested inside classroom variables, which, in turn, are nested within school-level variables. So differences in achievement can be influenced by differences among individuals, differences within classes and between classes, and differences within schools and between schools. Variables at all levels probably contribute to individuals' academic achievement to *some* degree. What MLM is designed to do is help researchers to estimate to *what* degree, to sort out the size of the contributions of the variables at the different levels.

Consider another example. How long is a patient likely to survive after heart bypass surgery? Variables at the individual level include the condition of the patient (age, weight, and so on). Second-level variables would relate to the quality of the surgeon, indicated by such variables as years of experience, board certification, and the like. A third level would be the hospital's sterilization procedures and its comparative freedom from infection. All levels matter. An otherwise healthy patient operated on by a competent surgeon could be killed by a hospital-based infection. Surviving surgery is a different kind of research problem than academic achievement. In part because survival is an all-or-none variable, good quality is necessary at all levels. By contrast, in the math learning example, in which the outcome is a continuous variable, excellence at one level might more easily compensate for deficiencies at another. Perhaps individual talent can make up for a crowded classroom; or a dedicated teacher could overcome the problems arising from a small budget for books and equipment. What MLM allows one to do is to go beyond speculating on and trading anecdotes about the important of such differences. Using MLM one can measure them. With MLM one can, for example, examine the effects of differences in expenditures per pupil while controlling for student talent and teacher quality.

Most aspects of the world are multilevel, and so too must our analyses be. For instance, when program evaluators (see Chapters 15 and 16) use individual outcomes to evaluate program outcomes they are doing multilevel work. Variables about the individuals being served by the program are at level 1. The outcome variable, student achievement, is also measured at level 1, but evaluators are focused on level 2, the program variables. Such relationships can be thought of as layers arranged in a hierarchy with the upper levels including the lower. *Nested-variables problems* might be another good term to describe this frequently characteristic structure found in research phenomena. Whether they are thought of as layered or nested or in concentric rings, variables so arranged operate in context. What goes on at the lower levels is influenced by the higher. The outer rings of the circle influence the inner, and the inner rings influence the outer. Indeed, lower-level outcomes can be constitutive of higher-level outcomes. For example, one of the influences on an individual student's learning is the level of learning of the students in his or her class and school, but the measure of the level of learning of the class or the school is simply the pooled measurements of individual students' learning levels. Often these pooled individual variables are referred to as *context* or *composition* variables.

What Technical Analysis Problems Give Rise to the Need for Multilevel Models?

It is easy to concede that everything is in a context. What's the problem? Why don't we just measure contextual variables in the ordinary way? We have already seen, have we not, examples of multilevel analysis that were handled quite nicely with *ordinary least squares (OLS) regression*? For instance, think of the ongoing example of the 50 professors and their salaries. Variables were measured at the individual level (gender, years of experience, and rank) and one variable measured at a higher or group level (college). We took care of this nicely enough by entering a variable for college and measuring its effect while controlling for the effects of the other (individual-level) variables. Was there something wrong with that procedure? Admittedly it is a common approach, but it is flawed. Explaining why clarifies the need for multilevel regression.

Briefly, the problem is that when individual-level and group-level variables are entered in the same equation, assumptions of ordinary least squares (OLS) regression are violated. OLS regression assumes that the observations of individual variables are independent. But when individuals are grouped, the observations are no longer independent.[1] When observations are not independent, this can inflate Type I error rates. In other words, it can lead us to reject null hypotheses when we should not do so; we could conclude that a particular result (such as a difference in salary) is quite unlikely to be due to chance, when it may in fact be fairly likely to be due to chance.

Think of what happens when observing a particular professor. Individual-level observations of the professor (such as gender) are not independent of group-level observations (college). Why? Some colleges have a higher proportion of women and some have a lower proportion. Professors in particular disciplines (such as Humanities) earn less, *and* they have more women. Women earn less regardless of college, but they are clustered disproportionately in colleges in which professors earn less—regardless of gender. Using OLS we cannot correctly sort out the effects of these confounded variables. Using MLM we can.

In OLS regression one can appropriately add predictor variables almost at will, as long as the sample is large enough, but *only* as long as the variables are independently measured, which means they cannot be nested. Why can't we control for nested variables, just as we control for independent variables measured at the same level? The reason is that in controlling for variables we use their means. The question being answered is: What is the effect of one predictor (say gender) on an outcome (salary) controlling for another predictor (years of experience)? To do that you use the mean years of experience; the question more precisely stated is: What is the effect of gender on salary—assuming that all professors had the same number of years of experience; that is, if all had the mean number of years? If all had the same number of years of experience, the mean number, there would be no variance or deviation from the mean. That is an acceptable assumption as long as the two predictors are measured at the same level. But when they are not measured at the same level, this raises big problems, especially when the main research question involves sorting out the effects of the two levels.

Sorting out the effects of levels in education was one of the chief problems that motivated two of the pioneers of MLM/HLM, Anthony Bryk and Stephen Raudenbush, in the late 1980s and early 1990s (Raudenbush & Bryk, 2002). Their problem was to figure out how to measure and to assess the relative importance of within-school variance (level 1) and between-school variance (level 2) in the study of academic achievement. If OLS regression is used for this problem, to control for variables at each level it must be assumed that the variance at one of the levels or the other is zero. To study within-school effects (such as individual students' differences in tested ability) while controlling for between-school effects (such as per pupil expenditure), it must be assumed that there is no variance in the between-school effects. That is how we control: We assume no variance about the mean because all are at the mean. In the same way, if we focus on between-school effects (per pupil expenditure) and control for within-school effects (students' tested ability), we have to assume that all students have the mean tested ability. In other words, we have to ignore level 1 variance. When the whole idea is to measure *both* level 1 and level 2 and compare their effects, we do not want to have to assume that the effects of one or the other are zero. For multilevel problems, OLS regression requires that we assume away the very thing we are trying to study.

Variables at the same level, such as individual student-level variables, might be and usually are related. In that sense they are not independent. But the kind of independence that matters for deciding whether multilevel analysis is needed is whether the variables are independently *measured*. A student's tested knowledge and her parents' socioeconomic status (SES) are likely to be related, but the measure-

ment of one and the measurement of the other are independent: We give the student a test; we ask the parents about their occupations and incomes. One measure does not influence the other measure. But what about the student's achievement test scores and the test scores of the students in her class? These cannot as easily be measured independently because students with similar achievement tend to be clustered in the same classes. Students in the same classroom are likely to be more similar than students selected at random, particularly given tracking. If one ignores this group-level effect, as one has to do when including it in an OLS regression, this increases the chances of incorrectly finding statistical significance for level 1 variables—because we assume away the influence of level 2 variables.

Overestimates of the effect of level 1 variables have long been a problem, with potentially great policy implications, in the study of educational effects. Such overestimates have led some policy analysts to conclude that what schools do doesn't matter; achievement all boils down to student-level variables, such as the students' tested ability, their SES, and so on. By contrast, school-level variables such as expenditures and teachers' salaries or teacher certification are held to be irrelevant. In short, in the past, potentially important effects of school-level variables were assumed away by the statistical analysis techniques of OLS regression. The effects of an individual having a high level of ability *and* of being educated in a high-ability classroom are impossible to distinguish correctly using OLS regression methods. That is what multilevel regression is for. How do we separate out the effects of levels in multilevel regression?

When one wants to measure the effects of a new variable in OLS regression, one adds a new *term* to the regression equation. In *multilevel regression,* if the new variable is at a higher level, one adds a new *equation* to the first equation. By so doing one can measure the effect of a variable or variables at a higher or a grouped level. What do you do with the two equations? Basically you mix them together into one, which is where the label *mixed effects model* comes from. More specifically, "the intercept and slopes in the level-1 model become the outcome

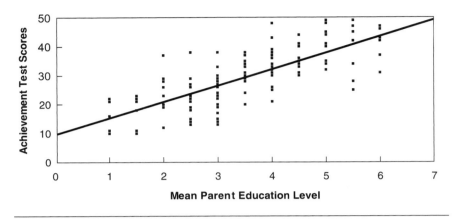

FIGURE 12.1 *Scatter diagram for all schools*

variables at level 2" (Raudenbush & Bryk, 2002, p. 31). Explaining that one sentence fully will require a few paragraphs and an extended example.

Everything about multilevel models, including the equations, tends to look formidable to the inexperienced reader. The notation is quite different from OLS regression. Although level 1 predictors are indicated by *X*s as they are in OLS regression, level 2 predictors are symbolized with *W*s or sometimes *Z*s. The regression coefficient at level 2 is usually a gamma, not a beta or a *b* (these still show up at level 1). Despite such differences, the basic idea behind regression analysis is still the same, regardless of whether the variables are nested. Complications arise from the greater intricacy of the problems being investigated, but we still want to answer versions of the same two questions: (1) What is the effect on the outcome variable of a one-unit increase in a predictor variable, while controlling for the effects of the other predictor variables? (2) Taking all the predictors together, how much better can we predict (or explain) the outcome? The mathematical substratum is more complicated when studying multilevel models, and the notation at first seems strange, but conceptually MLM is only an extension of OLS regression. If you remember the concepts discussed in Chapters 9 and 10 and make some additions and adjustments, it is possible to get a handle on MLM. Regardless of whether OLS regression or multilevel regression is used, we are still trying to explain vari-

ance in outcomes by variance in predictors. MLM enables us to divide that variance (to "partition" it) among two or more levels.

How Does Multilevel Analysis Work in Practice?

Understanding how the analysis works is most easily achieved by seeing an example. Say there is a sample of 5,000 students in 100 schools, 50 students randomly selected from each school. We are interested in the effects of parents' education level on students' achievement; achievement in this case is measured by scores on a 50-item test. Also of interest are school-level effects, such as per pupil expenditure (PPE) and school size. We would first conduct an ordinary least squares (OLS) regression for all the students. Parents' education is measured by a 6-point scale ranging from 1 = eighth grade or less, 2 = less than high school graduation, 3 = high school graduation, 4 = some college, 5 = college graduate, 6 = graduate or professional degree. The relationship between parents' education and students' scores is depicted in Figure 12.1, which is a scatter diagram with a regression line. The correlation between the two variables is high, $r = .75$. The slope or regression coefficient is $b = 5.6$. This means that, on average, for every one-unit increase in parents' education level, scores on the achievement test are 5.6 points higher.

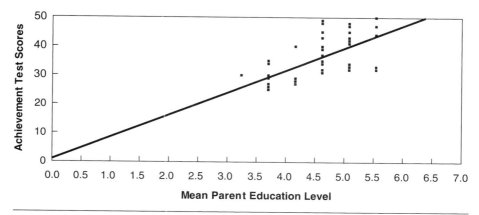

FIGURE 12.2 *Scatter diagram for School A*

In order to investigate the question of whether there are any school-level effects on this relationship between parents' education and students' achievement, we begin the multilevel analysis with familiar techniques. We conduct the OLS regression 100 times, once for each school, using the 50 students in each school to do this. That will yield 100 regression coefficients (slopes) and 100 intercepts. Remember that the intercept is the mean value of the outcome variable when the predictor variable is zero. What interests us in this analysis is whether the intercepts and/or the slopes differ among the schools. Figures 12.2, 12.3, and 12.4 show the scatter diagrams including the regression lines for 3 of the 100 schools.

The differences among the schools are quite striking. The slopes and intercepts vary considerably. Indeed, if the slopes and intercepts did not vary between schools, there would be no need to conduct a multilevel analysis. In School A, Figure 12.2, the parents have very high education levels and the students' scores are quite high. The regression (slope) coefficient is also high (7.1) and the intercept is around 1.0. By contrast, the parents of students in School B, Figure 12.3, have low levels of education, and their children score at correspondingly low levels on the achievement test; the regression/slope coefficient remains strong: 5.7, which means that for every one-step increase in education level students' scores on

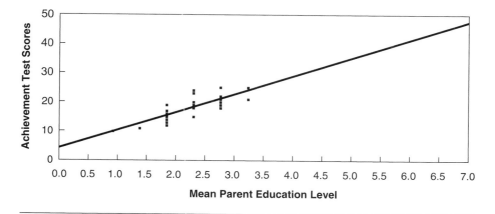

FIGURE 12.3 *Scatter diagram for School B*

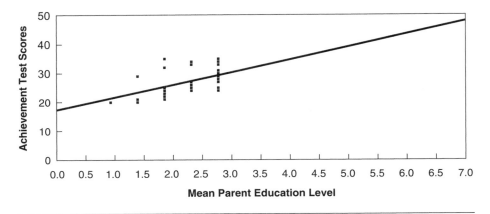

FIGURE 12.4 *Scatter diagram for School C*

average go up 5.7 points. Figure 12.4 paints a very different picture of things in School C. Here the parents' education level is as modest as in School B, but the students do much better on the achievement test, almost as well as the mean for all 5,000 students in whole sample. School C's advantage over B can most easily be seen by comparing the intercepts, the average score on the test for students if their parents had no education. In School C this is 17.3, whereas in School B it is a mere 4.4. There are clearly important differences between the schools, which are summarized in Table 12.1. School C is doing a much better job than B in promoting its students' academic achievement. And School C is much more egalitarian too, because the effect of parents' education is less pronounced there ($b = 4.0$). Important differences

such as these lead to the need for a multilevel regression analysis. What is it about School C that accounts for its comparative success? Is it per pupil expenditure, school size, teacher qualifications, or some other school-level variable? Because there is great variance among the schools (in means, slopes, intercepts, and percent of variance explained), we have to examine school-level variables to try to explain it.

In an actual analysis, we probably would not examine 100 slopes, intercepts, and *R*-squared statistics. Rather, to determine how much of the total variance in the outcome variable (student achievement) is attributable to variance between the schools, we would use the *intraclass correlation* (ICC). This widely used statistic can be described in many ways. Basically, it measures the degree to which members

TABLE 12.1   *Students' Achievement Scores and Parents' Education Levels: Comparison of Slopes and Intercepts for Three Schools*

	Mean Achievement Test Score	*Mean Parent Education Level*	*Correlation of Score and Level*	*Adjusted R-Squared*	*Intercept*	*Slope (Regression Coefficient)*
All schools	29.6	3.5	.75	.57	9.8	5.6
School A	35.7	4.9	.64	.40	0.9	7.1
School B	18.0	2.4	.83	.67	4.4	5.7
School C	26.6	2.3	.53	.26	17.3	4.0

of the same category (such as classrooms) are more similar to one another than to members of other categories. It is calculated by dividing the variance between the groups by the total variance in the sample. If the ICC were, say, .30 this would mean that 30% of the variance in students' scores was attributable to between-school variables, and the remaining 70% was not. Whether 30% of the variance is enough to merit a multilevel approach is a matter of judgment, although 30% would usually be judged more than sufficient. Multilevel analysis would have to be used to study school-level variables, because individual-level variables cannot be reasonably used to explain school-level differences. An appropriate analysis would have to study the variance at two levels.

Multilevel analyses can in theory have any number of levels, but the most common number is two. Probably the main reason that multilevel analyses are very often two-level analyses is that it is quite rare to have large enough sample sizes to study more than two. Sufficiently large sample sizes are more of a problem for the variables measured at the higher levels. For instance, if the 100 schools of our example were in 100 separate districts, we could not do a district-level analysis. One school per district would obviously mean that there could be no between-school variance in a district. Except in large urban school systems, there is usually an insufficient number of schools per district. Or, if the 100 schools were divided among 4 districts, 25 schools per district, you would be able to calculate the slopes and intercepts for each district, but a set of 4 slopes/intercepts would be far too small for further analysis. One of the reasons that researchers using MLM so often use large national or international data sets is that only these are large enough for the requirements of multilevel modeling. You could, however, use dummy coding techniques (discussed in Chapter 10) to include the 4 districts in an analysis; this is limited because it measures only overall-district level effects, not variables at the district level, but it is better than nothing.

To recap: The early steps of MLM are briefly as follows. First one conducts an OLS regression of the relation of students' scores to parents' education for each of the 100 schools. The result is a regression coefficient or slope for each school and an intercept for each school. These slopes and intercepts become new outcome (dependent) variables for the analysis of school-level (level 2) effects. One then uses level 2 predictors to try to understand what is behind the level 2 variance. So in the next, level 2, equation, the intercepts and slopes would be the outcomes. School size and per pupil expenditure (PPE) would be the level 2 variables with which we tried to explain the level 2 variance in the intercepts and slopes. If there is little variability in the slopes, the researcher can "fix" the slopes. This means that they can be set to zero variance, which is what OLS regression does. The researcher then focuses only on the intercepts in the level 2 analysis.

It is important at this point to remember the parallels with OLS regression. Multilevel regression is an extension of one-level OLS regression, not something radically new. Although multilevel regression does not require the researcher to assume that the measurements were independent of one another, it still assumes linearity. If researchers expect that a relation they are studying is nonlinear, they may investigate this by introducing an exponential term into the equation, just as is done in OLS regression. (See Chapter 10 for a review of regression assumptions.) If relations among the variables are nonlinear because the dependent or outcome variable is not continuous, then the techniques of logistic regression (see Chapter 11) can be applied in MLM. The issue of sample size is important in any kind of analysis, and it can be especially crucial in multilevel regression, because the sample has to be adequate at all levels of the analysis. In our example, enough students in each school are needed to estimate the slopes and intercepts; we had 50, which is not quite enough using the criteria discussed in Chapter 10. We also need enough schools; we had 100, which does meet the one of the cutoffs suggested in Chapter 10. By contrast, if the sample were all 5,000 students attending three high schools we would have plenty of students to compute the slopes and intercepts for each school, but the sample size would be only three for the level 2 variables. We would not be able to use the slopes and intercepts to estimate the effects of school-level variables. Rather, if there were important differences among the three schools (discovered by including them in the regression as dummy variables), it would be better to investigate those differences using case study methods.

How Can MLM Be Applied to Concrete Research Problems (Six Examples)?

Instead of discussing methodological issues abstractly, it is more helpful to continue with an overview of multilevel models by examining actual examples of how they have been used in recent research. This highlights the kinds of problems to which the models can be applied and you get some practice interpreting results of multilevel analyses. In what follows, I have used examples from educational research, because the use of MLM is so widespread there, and because there is considerable overlap in the issues that appear in one field. This "redundancy" helps individuals trying to learn new concepts.

It is easy to find examples of MLM in the educational research literature. Indeed, when searching for articles applying regression analysis to use in my classes, I have often found it difficult to locate regression studies that did *not* use multilevel regression. In the more advanced research journals, studies using simple OLS regression analyses are comparatively rare. OLS regression is a still very common in dissertation research, which typically deals with simpler problems and smaller samples. A researcher who plans to write a dissertation, and who does a review of the literature in preparation, will find that published regression-based studies very frequently employ MLM (usually called HLM in the education journals). Here follows a brief examination of six examples to illustrate the kinds of analyses that can be done and to show how to read the output.

Example 1: Why Do High School Students Flunk Courses?

The transition to high school can be difficult for students. In some urban systems nearly half of first-year high school students fail one or more courses. Roderick and Camburn (1999) examined this problem among 27,612 high school freshmen in 73 Chicago high schools. They specifically wanted to investigate the extent to which the course failure problem was attributable to student characteristics and the degree to which it was due to school characteristics. Their dependent variable was categorical: fail a course, yes/no. Because their outcome variable was categorical, they used the log odds (logit) of failing. This shows that multilevel regression can be combined with logistical regression (see Chapter 11) when the outcome variable is categorical. Using multilevel regression, the authors were able to establish that the course failure rate varies widely among schools even after adjusting for differences in students' background characteristics, including their prior achievement levels. Individual-level differences explained "only about a third of the across-school variance in the proportion of students failing courses" (p. 337). The rest was undoubtedly attributable to school-level variables. This finding has potentially important policy implications. Educators have often focused on individual student characteristics and concentrated their efforts on individual student remediation to address the problem of likely course failure of students deemed to be "at risk." Roderick and Camburn's research findings suggest that to reduce the problem of course failure, it would be at least as helpful to address differences among schools as differences among students. We should also be identifying at-risk schools, not merely at-risk students.

Example 2: Can School-Wide Curricular Reforms Promote Student Achievement?

The effectiveness of school-level reform efforts was the focus of a study of over 200 Chicago elementary schools. The particular reform variable studied was whether and how much these schools had moved in the direction of increased instructional program coherence, a change believed to be important for fostering student academic achievement. The outcome variable was student's scores on achievement tests. As always in multilevel models, the outcome variable was measured at the lowest level, the innermost circle or nest. Individual student variables constituted level 1 of the analysis. Level 2 was the year, and level 3 included school-level variables. In short, students, who were the unit of analysis, were nested within years and years were nested within schools. The basic research question was: Did movement in the direction of instructional program coherence lead to improvements in academic achievement? Briefly, yes: "Schools that showed substantial improvement in coherence achieved average . . . [test] scores that were almost one fifth of a year higher," that is, the equivalent of about two additional months of school learning per year (Newman, Smith, Allensworth, & Bryk, 2001, p. 306). Then, using an approach that shows the potential compatibility of data-intensive research with case study work, Newman and colleagues used the results of this three-level MLM to identify particularly effective schools for more detailed ethnographic study, especially for inquiring into *how* certain schools were able to increase the coherence of their academic programs.

Example 3: Do Schools Create the "Learning Gap"?

How much does school learning matter? An extra two months per year of the previous example seems substantial, but what effects does it have, particularly on students from different backgrounds? There is ample evidence that schooling has quite positive effects, particularly for students most in need of instruction, that is, those of lower socioeconomic status (SES). To investigate this issue, Alexander, Entwisle, and Olson (2001), like Newman et al. in the previous example, studied learning over time; they followed the same children in order to do so. Using a well-known database from Baltimore's schools, they used MLM to do "growth curve modeling." This technique will be briefly discussed again when we study issues pertaining to student assessment (in Chapter 16). Here we can note that growth curve modeling is a value-added approach. If one has data from students over time, rather than merely school-level mean data, one can use MLM to estimate learning *trajectories* for individual students. Learning over time was the outcome variable in this study. Level 1 was within-

person growth over the five years of the study. Level 2 brought in between-person variables. These variables enabled the researchers to measure differences in achievement that varied in relation to individuals' traits. The researchers were particularly interested in SES. To accommodate the fact that growth curves are often curved rather than linear, Alexander et al. included an exponential term in their model, which means that they could check for curves, for nonlinear growth, just as one can in OLS regression (see Chapter 10).

Alexander and colleagues (2001) studied early elementary schooling in Baltimore. It is no surprise to learn that Baltimore, like other large urban school systems, lags well behind much of the rest of the nation in mean levels of academic achievement. And the achievement gap between low-SES and high-SES children widens as they get older, a fact that is widely believed to be an indicator of school failure. Some even say that the schools *cause* the gap to widen. That inference seems reasonable when we consider that the longer students are in school the wider the gap gets. To investigate, Alexander et al. used the summer break to design a "natural experiment." The differences between the summer months and the school months are equivalent to control and experimental conditions that can be used to measure learning in the two seasons, as long as measurements are taken both at the end of one school year and at the beginning of the next. The researchers studied some 700 students in 20 schools. They collected achievement data for five years and four summers. Note here that, like most growth curve models, the level 2 data are not school-level data. If one wanted to introduce that, one would need to add a third level to the analysis. But with only 20 schools Alexander and colleagues could not do this. Rather, for them, level 2 was comprised of the individual-difference variables that have constituted level 1 in most of our other examples.

The conclusions from this study were clear. Upper-SES students arrive in the first grade ahead of their lower-SES classmates. During the school year lower-SES children move forward at about the same pace as the upper-SES children. The gap does *not* increase. Rather, lower-SES children fall behind in the *summers,* especially in verbal skills. So, in September, upper-SES children return to school ahead of where they were the previous June; lower SES children are slightly behind their previous level. The gap that widened over the summer does *not* grow during the school year; it remains about the same, but it expands again in the next summer season. These results about the achievement gap are specific to family SES. At least in Baltimore, the achievement gap is an SES gap. Any differences in achievement by ethnicity/race are entirely attributable to an SES gap between racial/ethnic groups.

Example 4: Do Small Schools Promote Learning?

A commonly suggested avenue of reform is making schools smaller, because there is some evidence that smaller schools can be more effective than larger ones at encouraging academic achievement. It is important to note a key fact about this evidence, like much regression evidence: Even though we have data indicating that small schools might enhance achievement, we do *not* have any evidence that transforming big schools by making them smaller will have the same effect. Does it seems reasonable to compare currently big to currently small schools and use any differences to conclude that *changing* school size would have the same effect? This is not a statistical question; it involves an inference, but not a statistical inference. Be that as it may, the small school effect has been mostly examined for high schools. Lee and Loeb (2000) studied the small school effect using as their data some 23,000 students in 264 Chicago elementary schools. The reader will have noticed the prominence of Chicago in these examples. There are two reasons. First, data about Chicago are probably richer and more readily available to researchers than for any other major urban educational system. Collecting the data and making them available to researchers was part of the school reform movement in that city. Second, one of the most important pioneers of MLM, Anthony Bryk, teaches at the University of Chicago and has been importantly involved in conducting research on the Chicago data.

The question examined by Lee and Loeb (2000) using this very rich data source is one you have already encountered as one of the examples of mediating variables in Chapter 3: If smaller schools are more effective, how does smallness lead to more student learning? Lee and Loeb concluded, you may remember, that part of the reason for the small school effect is that teachers in smaller schools had attitudes more conducive to student learning than did teachers in larger schools. The attitude difference was the key mediating variable. Our question here is: How did the authors use MLM to come to that conclusion? Their outcome variable at level 1 was student math achievement growth from the sixth to the eighth grade, a value-added measure (see Chapter 16). At level 2 their outcome measure was teacher attitudes. As is often the case when researchers undertake MLM, Lee and Loeb did their study because they were particularly interested in the higher-level variables. They assumed that individual-level outcomes would be different in different higher-level groups, such as big and small schools. As a researcher, if you are not interested in higher-level effects, there isn't much point in MLM, except to control for overeager generalizations about the size of individual-level effects.

As with any multilevel analysis, Lee and Loeb's first step was to partition the variance in the outcome variable (gains in students' achievement scores) into within-school variance and between-school variance. This was done with the intraclass correlation (ICC), discussed earlier. Only the between-school variance was used to study the effects of school-level characteristics. In brief, the findings indicated that small schools (compared to either medium or large schools) in grades 6 through 8 were more effective, even after controlling for a large number of variables both at the individual and at the school level. The gains in academic achievement in small schools were about half a standard deviation greater. To put this in perspective, the effect size (ES) for score on the test for all students the previous year was about 1.7 SDs. Small schools mattered, but they weren't a miracle; they increased learning by about one-third.

Example 5: Do Small Classes Increase Academic Achievement?

A reform even more popular than reducing school size to improve achievement is reducing *class* size. Pong and Pallas (2001) examined this problem ideally suited for study with multilevel models. They used data from the 1995 Third International Math and Science Study (TIMSS). The outcome variable was eighth-grade math achievement; the two levels of their study were the individual student level and the classroom level. Their target predictor variable was class size. They studied the relation between class size and students' math achievement in nine nations: the United States, France, Germany, Iceland, Canada, Australia, Singapore, Hong Kong, and Korea. This means they conducted their two-level regression nine times, once for each of the countries. They could not do multilevel modeling with the countries as a third level because the *N* of 9 was too small. As with all multilevel analyses, the first step was to partition the variance into within-class and between-class variance, with the between-class variance becoming the focus of the level 2 analysis. Class size varied widely both within and between the nations. The Far Eastern countries in the study had class sizes as much as double those in the United States. On the other hand, the between-class variance (as measured by the ICC) was much lower in the Far East. The between-class variance was 52% in the United States, which was the largest of the nine countries studied. The variance between classes was only 6% in Korea, which had the lowest variance of the nine nations. The effect of class size was measured by comparing the lowest and highest quintiles within each country with the middle 60% in each country. After controlling for all of the variables in the model, there was a significant relation between class size and achievement in only three countries: the United States, Singapore, and Hong Kong. However, the United States was the only one where achievement was greater in smaller classes. In the United States, the lowest quintile of classes in terms of size (6 to 18 students) scored about 20 points higher on the TIMSS test. By contrast, the lowest quintile (smallest classes) in Hong Kong scored about 32 points *lower* on the exam, and the highest quintile (biggest classes) in Singapore, students in the biggest classes, scored an average of 22 points *higher*. In the Far East, students did worse in small classes and better in large ones.

Small classes fostered learning, but only in the Unites States. More important than the class size—and it was more important in *all* countries—was the effect of classroom socioeconomic status (SES), that is, the average SES ranking of the other students in an individual student's class. Indeed this was a more important influence on achievement than the student's own SES. Attending a math class in which the other students had high SES backgrounds was consistently more important, even in the United States, than studying math in a class with a small number of students.

Example 6: What Are the Effects of School Budgets on Student Learning?

Reducing class size is very expensive, probably the single most expensive reform of the currently popular reform ideas. Although it seems to have a modest benefit for students in the United States, many other countries would probably see little improvement from devoting resources to making classes smaller. Much of the purpose of regression modeling, whether multilevel or not, is to compare the likely outcomes to the likely costs. With money enough, there is a nearly limitless number of genuinely good things one could do. By estimating the size of the effects of various reforms, regression analysis can provide useful evidence for policy makers who need to choose among various good things. Our final illustrative study investigates the effects of per pupil expenditure on rates of improvement in academic achievement. For her database, Elliott (1998) used the National Educational Longitudinal Study (NELS) and census data about per pupil expenditures. Her outcome variable was gains in math and science achievement test scores from the eighth to the tenth grade. Table 12.2 reports on a portion of her results. We will use the table mostly as an example of the format found in many MLM studies and as a review of some of the concepts already discussed.

The upper section of Table 12.2 is read much like any other regression table. Each coefficient is a *gamma* rather than a *b* or a beta, but the coefficients are interpreted the same way. The question answered is: For every one-unit increase in a predictor variable, what happens to an outcome variable? For example, in equation 1, the figure .94** for eighth-grade math achievement means that for every 1 point higher on the eighth-grade math test,

TABLE 12.2   *Gain in Math Achievement from Eighth to Tenth Grade (in IRT Theta Scores)*

	Equation 1 *(gammas)*	*Equation 2* *(gammas)*
Predictor Variables		
Student-Level Variables		
Intercept	50.21**	50.22**
Eighth-grade math achievement	.94**	.94**
Parents' SES	.89**	.88**
Ethnicity (1 = Minority)	−.75**	−.76**
Gender (1 = Female)	.00	−.01
Track (General is comparison group)		
Vocational	−1.36**	−1.37**
Academic	.85**	.85**
School-Level Variables		
Per pupil expenditures (in thousands)		.20*
Urban school		−.53
School size		.00
Percent free lunch		.01
Percent LEP		.09
Percent special education status		−.03*

Model Summary

	Total Variance	*ICC*	*Residual Variance*	*ICC*	R^2	*Residual Variance*	*ICC*	R^2
School-level	24.06	.37	4.49	.18	.81	4.33	.18	.82
Student-level	41.09		20.14		.51	20.16		.51

Note: N = 6,318 students nested in 708 schools.
*p < .05.
**p < .01.

Source: Elliott (1998), pp. 234–235.

tenth-grade scores were .94 point higher, clearly a large effect. The indicator or dummy variables are also interpreted in the familiar way. Students in the general track (not listed) were the excluded or comparison group. Students in the vocational track scored on average 1.36 points lower and students in the academic track .85 point higher than students in the general track—after controlling for other variables. The coefficient of zero for gender, means

there was no measurable difference between males and females, and so on.

In equation 2 in Table 12.2, school-level variables were added: per pupil expenditures (which was the one Elliott was focusing on) plus a group of school-level control variables. Here you see that, controlling for all the other variables in equation 2, increasing per pupil expenditure by $1,000 was associated with scores that were on average 0.20 point higher. This is a statistically significant coefficient, but it is small. To increase scores on average by 1 full point, schools would have to raise expenditures by $5,000 per pupil, which is an amount nearly as big as many school budgets.

The differences between an OLS regression table and a multilevel regression table are also important. In MLM, the intercept is the mean for the higher-level units; in this case it is the mean achievement level for all schools. Very often in OLS multiple regression, the intercept is not substantively important and not easily interpretable. But in MLM the intercept is a key statistic. Most of the other differences in interpreting an MLM table are in the lower part of the table, called "Model Summary." The ICC reported there is the intraclass correlation. In an equation without any control variables, often called the *null model*, the ICC was .37. This indicates that 37% of the variance in students' test scores was between schools. This is a substantial ICC. Even much smaller ICCs can have an important effect on estimation and especially on statistical inference; that is, standard errors, *p*-values, and confidence intervals (Cohen, West, & Aiken, 2003). The remaining 63% is explained by school-level variables.[2] In moving to equation 1, the ICC drops to 18%, which means that 18% of the variance in that equation is due to between-school variance. The R^2s in Table 12.2 are interpreted roughly the same way as the R^2 in OLS, but there are two levels. So equation 1 accounts for 81% of the between-school variance (81% of the 18%), whereas equation 1 accounts for 51% of the within-school variance (51% of the 82%). Finally, notice that adding more variables in equation 2 makes very little difference to the overall explanation. Adding per pupil expenditures and the school-level controls increases the R^2 by 1%, from .81 to .82.

These six examples illustrate the ubiquity of multilevel problems. They are central to most program evaluations, notably in education in which school-level changes are instituted with the specific goal of bringing about student-level outcomes (see Chapters 15 and 16). Multilevel methods allow researchers to study evidence both about individuals and about the groups they are in—simultaneously, with each level of variables controlling for the others. Researchers can study "how variables measured at one level affect relations occurring at another" (Raudenbush & Bryk, 2002, p. 8). Before the development of nested variable analyses, the effects of variables at different levels had to be studied as separate problems and could not easily be linked. Actually, there was an alternative: fallacious reasoning. Either one could commit the *ecological fallacy* of treating group phenomena as though they held for individuals, or one could commit its logical opposite, the so-called *fallacy of composition,* in which information about individuals is presumed to hold true for groups. More technically, if you use a one-level analysis for a two-level problem, you have either got to disaggregate the level 2 data or aggregate the level 1 data. Neither is ideal although both are still fairly common (Luke, 2004), despite their tendency to encourage fallacious reasoning about data.

Although multilevel methods have been state of the art among researchers for at least a decade, they are still not widely known outside the fairly limited circles in which researchers communicate. But the kinds of problems multilevel methods help solve are important enough that researchers and practitioners will need to find a way to bridge the gap between them.

The same kind of gap needs to be closed between researchers and practitioners in understanding the final advanced method considered here, structural equation modeling (SEM). It too is crucial for the appropriate analysis of many problems. Indeed, the techniques of SEM are sometimes combined with those MLM. SEM, which sits, along with MLM, at the top of the quantitative methods "food chain," is the subject of our next two chapters. SEM is sometimes referred to as confirmatory factor analysis; it is used to test and confirm theories. It is built on a foundation of exploratory factor analysis, which is used to explore the data, not to confirm theories. Exploratory factor analysis is treated in Chapter 13; confirmatory factor analysis (also known as SEM) is investigated in Chapter 14.

Terms and Concepts to Review

Multilevel modeling (MLM)
- Hierarchical linear modeling (HLM)
- Mixed effects models
- Random effects (or coefficients) models
- Covariance components models

OLS regression
Multilevel regression
Independent observations
Level 1 variables
Level 2 variables

Regression coefficients
- *b*
- Beta
- Gamma
- Regression slopes
- Intercepts
- Intraclass correlation (ICC)

Discussion Questions

1. Think of a research problem that would be best addressed using multilevel analysis. How many levels would you need to study your research problem? What problems, if any, would you encounter in trying to get enough data to conduct a multilevel analysis?

2. Why shouldn't multilevel problems be studied with one-level methods? Why can't a researcher simply use one-level methods to study various levels one at a time?

3. Can you think of a research topic that has no multilevel components? Are there any research designs in which analysis at one level typically would pose no problems?

4. Have you encountered in your reading any research reports that use one-level analyses, but that should have used multilevel models? What are possible effects on the conclusions? What might change if the one-level analysis used to study the problem had been supplemented with a multilevel analysis?

Self-Test

If you can answer most of the following questions accurately, you can feel confident about your understanding of the material in this chapter. If not, it would be a good idea to review the chapter. (Answers can be found in the Appendix.)

1. To study a multilevel problem using regression analysis, a researcher should study each of the levels of the variables one at a time with separate OLS regressions. True or False?

2. Because individual differences are small in most areas of research, when confronted with multilevel problems (individuals = level 1; groups = level 2), researchers can concentrate their attentions on the level 2 variables and not control for differences in level 1 variables. True or False?

3. The assumption that variables are independently measured is mainly important for multilevel models, not for OLS regression models. True or False?

4. If variables at the same level are related (correlated), it is inappropriate to apply any form of regression analysis, multilevel or one level. True or False?

5. Although multilevel regression is more complicated than OLS regression, it addresses the same types of questions, such as: What is the effect on a dependent variable of a one-unit increase in an independent variable, when controlling for all the other independent variables? True or False?

6. The intraclass correlation (ICC) is used to measure how much of the total variance in a sample is attributable to variance between the level 2 units. True or False?

7. Most MLM research addresses problems that involve variables at three or more levels. True or False?

8. Researchers using multilevel regression do not have to worry about outliers and the assumption of

linearity, so important in OLS regression. True or False?

9. In MLM as in OLS regression, to generalize correctly from sample to a population, and to compute *p*-values and CIs, the sample must have been randomly drawn from the population. True or False?

10. Most research using multilevel models has concluded that variables at the higher levels routinely have little or no impact on the level 1 variables. True or False?

Endnotes

1. This means that the error terms (prediction errors, residuals) will not be independent or uncorrelated.

2. The ICC is calculated as follows: The total variance is 65.15 (24.06 + 41.09); 24.06/65.15 = .37; 41.09/65.15 = .63.

13

Factor Analysis

Factor analysis (FA) is used to find patterns in the correlations among variables. The patterns are used to cluster the variables into groups, called factors. The factors can then be treated as new composite variables. Factor analysis can be and has been used to explore patterns among any set of correlated variables. Gould (1981), in what is still one of the best nontechnical introductions, explained how he used it in his biological studies of variations in the measurements of snails. But, as Gould's discussion makes clear, factor analysis had its origins in the testing and measurement of human psychological characteristics. In the social sciences, it is most widely used in the study of knowledge, abilities, beliefs, and attitudes.

Let's return to the test scores of the 35 students. The correlation matrix (see Table 2.7) showed that Exam 1, Exam 2, and the licensing exam were all highly correlated with one another. Students who did well, or poorly, on one of these almost always did well, or poorly, on the other two. Scores on those three tests would constitute a factor, because they were highly intercorrelated. By contrast, grades on the paper and on the project did not correlate highly with this group of three. They would not be part of the factor. To take another example, say you wrote a 20-item survey on student attitudes about education. Each of the 20 items

would be a variable. After a large number of students answered the survey, you could use factor analysis to inquire whether some subgroups of the 20 items could be clustered and whether these clusters were measures of the same underlying attitudes. The 20 questions might be measuring fewer than 20 distinct attitudes. The questions might cluster into groups of items, such as attitudes about the curriculum or about teachers or about other students or about social life in school. Factor analysis could tell you whether and how the items clustered together by showing which questions were answered in the same ways by respondents. The items *within* each group (factor) would correlate highly with one another. On the other hand, different factors (groups of items) usually do not correlate highly with one another.

The advantages of factor analysis are considerable. If your 20-item survey can be structured into 4 distinct clusters of items, analyzing of the results of your survey will be easier and more meaningful. Rather than juggling 20 variables, you can examine the relations among 4. For example, you could assess whether your "scale" (or factor or group of items) on student attitudes toward the curriculum is related to your scale on student attitudes toward the school's social life. Furthermore, and most important of all, when your conclusions about the curriculum, social life, and so on are based on multi-item scales rather than on single items, they will be more reliable (less subject to measurement error) and perhaps more valid. In brief, factor analysis is widely used to construct tests and other measurement instruments such as attitude scales. Researchers use factor analysis to try to find relations among measurements—and to explain them.

Much of the pioneering work on factor analysis was conducted by researchers studying various ways to measure mental ability. One reason that factor analysis has always been very controversial is that the field of intelligence testing has been and still is a very contentious one. Testing for mental ability is a good example with which to begin. Is there one general mental ability, intelligence, or are there several types? Do smart people tend to be pretty smart at everything or are there different kinds of "intelligences," with some people being good at one kind of mental ability (say, spatial reasoning) and others good at other kinds (say, verbal reasoning)? Factor analysis provides correlational evidence that one can use to discuss such issues. But factor analysis cannot *resolve* such questions. Factor analysis is a technique we can use to find patterns in data. The conclusions we draw will be based only in part on the data. Analyses of patterns in the data leave much room for interpretation.

Our conclusions almost always depend on considerations *in addition to* data analysis. This is true of all statistical techniques, but it is most glaringly obvious and undeniable in the case of factor analysis. Factor analysis involves selection from a large array of techniques and usually includes much trial-and-error work and re-reanalysis. For many of my colleagues, that makes factor analysis is too "squishy" and subjective, and they avoid it when possible. For others, the highly interpretive nature of factor analysis is one of its main attractions. They like having to interact with their data, to read the output and, on the basis of what they learn, to redo the calculations using a different analysis technique or a different set of assumptions. The contrast with the tradition in hypothesis testing could hardly be stronger. As we have seen (Chapter 8) in hypothesis testing, the problem is

structured to produce a one-word answer: statistically significant, yes/no. In traditional hypothesis testing, examining the results and deciding whether you need to recalculate is tantamount to "cheating." The difference is heightened by the fact that, unlike in most other associational techniques, in factor analysis, hypothesis/significance testing plays little or no role.[1] Regardless of whether one is or is not happy with the interpretative and iterative character of factor analysis, this character makes it hard to summarize. As in previous chapters, the discussion will be built around the answers to a series of questions.

1. What is factor analysis, conceptually?
2. How is factor analysis (FA) related to principal components analysis (PCA)?
3. How do I select the method of analysis?
4. How do I begin the analysis and determine the number of factors to use?
5. How do I identify (extract) the factors?
6. How do I fine-tune the factor solution to make it more interpretable?
7. How do I interpret the output of a factor analysis?

What Is Factor Analysis, Conceptually?

There are two broad categories of factor analysis: *exploratory factor analysis* (EFA) and *confirmatory factor analysis* (CFA). As their names indicate, they differ in purpose. Exploratory FA focuses on *finding* structures (patterns) of correlations in the data. It is used most often in the early stages of research in an area to *construct* measurement scales. EFA asks: What is the structure of the items? Confirmatory FA, by contrast, inquires: Does a hypothesized structure fit the data? CFA is a key component of structural equation modeling and will be discussed extensively in Chapter 14. This chapter begins with exploratory factor analysis, which is used to help researchers find patterns of correlations among data, and after detecting them, to discover ways of describing and explaining them. The distinction between exploratory and confirmatory is not absolute. One usually has some idea how things might turn out even when exploring, and one occasionally discovers something unexpected when confirming. Perhaps the most important distinction between the two is that exploratory factor analysis tends to occur earlier in the process of research on a topic, whereas confirmatory factor analysis usually occurs later, only after considerable exploratory work has helped identify patterns to test.

Factor analysis is a correlation-based technique. Initially what is analyzed is a correlation matrix[2] of the kind first discussed in Chapter 2. Because factor analysis is based on correlations, all the things that have to be true of the data to make correlations valid analytic tools also need to be true of factor analyses. Most importantly, as seen in Chapter 2, to use Pearson r correlations in a meaningful way, the variables must be continuous, and the relations between them must be linear.

Because factor analysis analyzes correlation *matrices* it uses matrix algebra to do so. Matrix algebra is a complex set of computational techniques that allows one to do math on matrices such as correlation matrices—for example, to multiply two matrices by each other or to divide one into another (Namboodiri, 1984). Because the work of matrix algebra with large data sets is so complex, factor analysis was not commonly used by applied researchers for several decades after it was invented, until the availability of computers to do the computations. Indeed, factor analysis did not become a popular analytic technique until powerful desktop computers and easy-to-use statistical packages became widespread.

Terms often used to describe what is being analyzed in factor analysis are *indicators* and *constructs*. For example, indicators would be the items on a test; constructs would be the topic or "domain" a group of the items measured. Related terms are *observed variables* and *latent variables*. The observed variables are what you can actually see and measure. They add up to the operational definition of the latent variables, which is what you are really interested in, but cannot measure directly. For example, on an intelligence test the indicators or observed variables are the answers to test questions. The construct, the latent variable, is intelligence. Intelligence is a construct. It cannot be measured directly in the way that, for example, height or weight can.

I remember several questions from IQ tests I've taken. One went something like this: "If you were walking along headed north and made a right turn, walked 100 yards, made a left turn, walked another 100 yards and made another left turn, in what direction would you be headed?" Another question asked you to listen to a series of numbers—for example, 3, 4, 2, 9, 9, 8 read to you by the examiner, and then to repeat them—backwards. If you did this successfully, the length of numbers was increased—for example, 6, 6, 8, 2, 1, 4, 9, 7—and so on until you were unable to repeat the series correctly or until you reached some upper limit. Finally, many questions just asked for the definitions of words. No one of these items (definitions of words, figuring out your direction, or remembering strings of numbers) *is* intelligence. But they all could be *indicators* of intelligence. They might be indicators of one general mental ability or perhaps indicators of different kinds of mental ability. What factor analysis helps researchers do is determine which indicators (test items) cluster together in a consistent or reliable way, indicating that they are probably measuring the same thing (see the discussion of reliability in Chapter 7). If people who can define lots of words are also quite likely to be able to determine the direction in which they are headed, and to remember/repeat long strings of numbers, perhaps these are all indicators of one thing—one factor, one construct, one latent variable. If not, if for example people who are good at repeating a series of numbers are no more likely to have big vocabularies than people who are not good at repeating numbers, then the two items are not reliable (consistent) measures of the same construct. In sum, exploratory factor analysis is commonly used to assess the reliability of scales, to determine whether the items in a scale consistently measure the same thing.

How is Factor Analysis (FA) Related to Principal Components Analysis (PCA)?

Because factor analysis is a general term describing a large group of techniques, when using factor analytic approaches to study actual data, the researcher is confronted with many choices of technique. Part of the

TABLE 13.1   *Variables in PCA and FA*

	Item/Indicator	Factor/Component/Construct
PCA	IV or predictor variable	DV or outcome variable
FA	DV or outcome variable	IV or predictor variable

complexity of factor analysis is that you have to make all (or most of) the choices before you can begin. It is hard to do factor analysis a little at a time. The first major choice is whether to use factor analysis (FA), properly speaking, or *principal components analysis* (PCA). Experts disagree, sometimes vehemently, about which of the two is better to use for particular kinds of analysis problems. General, nonmathematical descriptions of the two techniques are parallel. Components and factors are conceptually, but not computationally, similar; they both relate constructs to items/indicators. Because PCA is easier to explain, very often elementary descriptions of FA in textbooks are really descriptions of PCA. And while the two can occasionally produce quite different results, in my experience, in exploratory work, the factor structures frequently look pretty much the same regardless of method. As a general rule of thumb, the larger the number of items/indicators, and consequently the bigger the correlation matrix, the more likely the results of a PCA and an FA are to resemble one another.

Another way to distinguish between the two is to think of PCA and FA as regressions. The roles of the independent variables (IVs) and dependent variables (DVs) are reversed in the two regression methods. One way to differentiate PCA and FA is to note that in PCA the items/indicators are considered IVs and the factors/components are DVs. The opposite is true for FA, because the factors are the IVs and the items the DVs, as illustrated in Table 13.1.

Figure 13.1 illustrates the same concepts graphically. The convention is to use circles or ovals for components, factors, constructs, or latent variables. Boxes are used for indicators, items, and observed variables. As can be seen in the figure, the main difference between PCA and FA is the direction of the causal arrows. In PCA they move from the items to the component, whereas in FA they point from the factor to the items. In factor analysis we think of the underlying trait as *causing* the observable variables, as intelligence might cause the correct answers to questions. In principal components analysis, the observed variables are components of the latent variable, as heart rate, blood pressure, and lung capacity are *components* of health. Health does not cause lung capacity in the way that intelligence causes or enables one to answer a question correctly. A correct

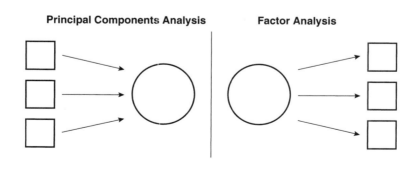

Principal Components Analysis   **Factor Analysis**

FIGURE 13.1 *Principal components analysis and factor analysis*

answer is not a component of intelligence in the way that lung capacity is a component of health.

An Extended Example

The clearest way to discuss factor analysis is to present an example showing a typical sequence of steps analyzing data. At each step I'll explain the choices I confronted as a researcher, explain why I made the choices I did, and then discuss how to interpret the output. The example illustrates the range of choices confronting a researcher using factor analysis and the kinds of thinking that goes into making them. No example can cover the topic fully, but this one provides, I believe, a useable introduction.

The example data are drawn from a survey of teachers and teacher education majors concerning their attitudes toward diversity and toward high school students' rights. The survey and its analysis focused on several issues, such as whether teachers' attitudes differed from those of the general public and whether different methods of studying their attitudes (quantitative and qualitative) would yield different results (Vogt & McKenna, 1998). In this example I'll focus on a subset of data made up of survey responses of 276 undergraduates in 9 classes at 4 separate colleges. I'll particularly address the "dimensionality" of those attitudes. Did the respondents' attitudes tend to be of a piece (one dimension)? If so, the answers would reveal a general positive/negative spectrum on all issues. Or did students' answers vary by type of diversity and category of student rights? If so, the factor analysis would identify clusters of questions that students tended to answer in a similar way; each of these clusters would be distinct from the other clusters. These clusters would be the factors.

The dimensionality of attitudes is a question often discussed in political and social psychology, but it is one that is largely unresolved and that continues to be studied extensively. See Vogt (1997) for a general overview. In that book I argued that there were some theoretical considerations and some empirical evidence that would lead us to expect to find three general categories of attitudes toward diversity. The categories would be defined by the *targets* or objects of the at-

titudes. Although respondents' attitudes could in part conform to an overarching liberal/conservative spectrum, we could also expect that they would vary depending on whether the attitudes were directed toward political, social, or moral groups. The question I was trying to answer with the survey was whether attitudes sorted out on a general liberal/conservative spectrum, or whether they clustered in some other ways.

The survey contained 43 questions that covered a wide range of political, social, and moral beliefs and actions. Many questions were drawn from national surveys. Others were written by the researchers; they were based on controversial events, as reported in the national and local news media, that had occurred in high schools in the United States. in the late 1990s. The review of this example will be structured around the answers to this chapter's remaining questions. Each question asks how a researcher can take the steps needed to conduct a factor analysis.

How Do I Select the Method of Analysis?

The main thing one is looking for initially in a factor analysis is the *common variance* of the items. This is the amount of variance that the items have in common with other items after they have been clustered into factors (or components). If part of the variance in a specific item is not shared in common with other items, this is referred to as its *specific variance*. Finally, no items or clusters of items are ever measured perfectly. There is also measurement error, so each item will have an *error variance* associated with it. How can these types of variance be calculated: (1) the variance that items have in common with other items, (2) the variance that is unique to particular items, and (3) the variance that is simply a matter of measurement error? The two main approaches are principal components analysis (PCA) on the one hand and several varieties of factor analysis (FA) on the other. Which of these two methods should be used to find the factors, to *extract* them from an analysis of the correlation matrix in our example?

PCA and FA make different assumptions about the data analysis problem, about the nature of the variance in the items. The principal components approach assumes that the components are totally uncorrelated (they are *orthogonal*). The items are treated as though they are measured without error and as though they have no specific variance or variance that is not shared with the other items. These are large assumptions and, in the context of my particular survey example, highly unrealistic ones. The measurement of attitudes is notoriously error filled and the clusters of items that form attitude scales are quite likely to be associated. At least researchers would like to be able to test for this. The assumptions of PCA are too badly violated to use it to study my survey responses. The same is likely true of most problems in the social sciences. Therefore, for the analysis of this example, one of the methods of factor analysis, not principal components analysis, needed to be chosen.[3] To illustrate using these data, I selected *principal axis factoring* (PAF), which is the method most commonly used for exploratory analyses and therefore the one readers are most likely to encounter.

Because FA is so computationally intense, the only realistic way to do it is by computer program. As with other examples in this book, I have used SPSS. Other programs exist of course, such as SAS. I have not used others because our goal in this book is not to teach keyboarding, but rather to address the basic ideas and to learn how to read typical output. For the problems we analyze in this book, differences in the software are fairly inconsequential. The various brands provide largely the same options and answers. I'll briefly describe the SPSS commands I used and then move to interpreting the output before turning to the next step in the analysis.

How Do I Begin the Analysis and Determine the Number of Factors to Use?

To conduct a factor analysis in SPSS researchers have to begin by making several choices and specifying how they want the program to do the computations. The choices have to be made up front and they are interconnected. This means that you need to know how you want to do everything before you can do anything. The choices and specifications I made

for the example are sketched, but not explained fully, in this and the next paragraph. I need to use a jumble of unfamiliar terms to explain what I did. Their meanings will become clear in the remainder of the chapter. To start the analysis in SPSS, I issued the following commands: first, *Analyze,* then, *Data Reduction,* then, *Factor.* This got me to the factor analysis menu. And it is a full menu of choices that you must make in order to do a factor analysis. First is *Extraction,* where SPSS asked me to specify the method. As just mentioned, I selected *Principal Axis Factoring* (PAF) over principal components analysis (PCA), because it is more appropriate to the kinds of questions being examined and because PAF is the method readers are most likely to encounter. Then I specified that I wanted to *Extract Eigenvalues Over . . .* 1.0. (Again, I realize that eigenvalues have not yet been explained; they will be shortly; I am following the order the choices dictated by the software.) Then the software asked me, *Number of factors?*

I remember the first time I encountered this question. My reaction was: How am I supposed to know? The whole idea of a factor analysis is to tell me how many. Although it is true that you use factor analysis to determine the number of factors, it is helpful to specify a number to get started. Ultimately, the best method for deciding how many factors is trial and error (this statement causes some colleagues to gnash their teeth). I recommend running the analysis a few times with different numbers of factors and choosing the one that is of most help interpreting your substantive questions. Although I expected three factors to emerge (describing political, social, and moral attitudes), for the theoretical reasons outlined earlier, I doubled that number and specified six. The exact number did not matter; it was just to get the analysis rolling so I would have some output on which to base my subsequent decisions, and if necessary, change the number after I had looked at the results. I also asked for a *Scree Plot.* Then, within the *Options* box, I asked the program to *Sort by size* to make the output easier to scan, and to simplify the output, to *Suppress absolute values less than . . .* I said, .40.

What a mouthful! I wasn't kidding when I said that factor analysis requires readers to make many choices before the computer can do the preliminary work. Now that the decisions and specifications have been made in the two previous paragraphs, let's see what the result is.

Those specifications yielded enough output to get the analysis under way. Conducting a thorough factor analysis generates a large amount of output. Most of the output has unusual sounding labels. Let's begin with the *eigenvalues* and the *scree plot,* for these point to the answer to the question, How many factors? The output in Table 13.2 gives what is needed to begin. The first column, called "Factor," indicates that there are 43 factors, one for each question in the survey. The next three columns are called "Initial Eigenvalues." Focus first on the columns headed "% of Variance" and "Cumulative %" (of Variance). Percent of variance is a familiar concept from our discussions of regression analysis (Chapters 9 and 10). The first factor explains 18.651% of the variance. The second factor adds a little over 8% for a total of about 27%; the third factor adds another 6% for a total of about 33%, and so on down to the last factor (number 43), which brings the total variance explained to 100%. So, if I used all 43 factors, I would be able to explain 100% of the variance in respondents' answers, but would have gained nothing over just looking at the items one at a time. What I was looking for is a smaller number of factors consistent with an explanation of a good-size chunk of the data. All 43 factors together fit the data perfectly, but give no ability to summarize, because the summary is as long as the items summarized.

Each additional factor improves the explanation of the all the variance in the answers, but each additional factor complicates the picture. Deciding how many factors you should use is like asking how big you want your map of your city to be. If it fits in your wallet, that's OK for a general overview, but it leaves out too much detail for most purposes. On the other hand, a map as big as the living room rug will have all of the detail you would ever be likely to want, but it will be too awkward to use. So you pick a middling size and trade off some detail for some simplicity. There is no exactly right size. The same is true in factor analysis. The two most common rules of thumb deciding how many factors to use are (1) only use factors with eigenvalues greater than 1.0; and (2) using a line graph of the eigenvalues (called

a scree plot), use the point where the line levels off to separate the useful from the un-useful factors. Here I will apply these two rules of thumb to the data one at a time.

What is an *eigenvalue?* An eigenvalue is a measure of the amount of variance in all the items or variables that is explained by a factor. The general idea is closely parallel the amount of variance explained by the variables in a regression analysis (see Chapter 9). Adding factors works the same way as adding variables to a regression equation. (You may remember the analogy of the multiple storytellers used to describe that process.) At any rate, the total variance in a given group of variables is equal to the number of variables. In the example, there are 43 variables (items), so the eigenvalues for all 43 items will total to 43. The eigenvalue for the first factor in Table 13.2 is 8.020. If you divide 8.020 by 43 you get 18.651, which is the number in the % of Variance column. An eigenvalue of 8 for a factor means that the factor accounts for as much of the variance as would 8 variables/items on average. A variable with an eigenvalue of 1.0 would explain $\frac{1}{43}$ of the variance, roughly 2.3%. An eigenvalue of 1.0 means that the factor explains no more than a typical item. If it explains no more than that, it seems reasonable to ignore it when trying to summarize. In Table 13.2 there are 13 factors with eigenvalues greater than 1.0, which together explain 66.9% of the variance. So I might consider using 13 factors in this case. But that strikes me (you see where the judgment comes in) as too many factors. The reduction from 43 to 13 is OK, but not good enough.

Perhaps the second criterion will be more helpful. Figure 13.2 is a line graph of the eigenvalues from Table 13.2. This line graph is called a scree plot. Looking at the shape of this line, you can get an answer by "eyeballing" and finding the point at which the line abruptly levels off, which is to say, where the gains in percentage of variance explained become small. Using this criterion, it looks to me as though the answer should be 4, because that's where the line begins to level off. Looking more closely, I might want to add the next two points for a total of 6, and maybe also the next 3 for a total of 9. So I conducted the analysis three times—with 4, 6, and 9 factors specified. I finally picked 4 as the number of factors. That number

TABLE 13.2 *Total Variance Explained, Six Factor Solution*

Factor	Initial Eigenvalues			Extraction Sums of Squared Loadings			Rotation Sums of Squared Loadings(a)
	Total	% of Variance	Cumulative %	Total	% of Variance	Cumulative %	Total
1	8.020	18.651	18.651	7.508	17.461	17.461	6.214
2	3.632	8.447	27.097	3.089	7.184	24.645	3.138
3	2.727	6.341	33.438	2.193	5.100	29.745	2.682
4	2.284	5.312	38.751	1.774	4.126	33.871	3.485
5	1.771	4.117	42.868	1.213	2.821	36.692	1.933
6	1.682	3.911	46.779	1.070	2.489	39.181	3.202
7	1.507	3.504	50.282				
8	1.444	3.357	53.639				
9	1.384	3.218	56.857				
10	1.138	2.647	59.504				
11	1.114	2.591	62.096				
12	1.046	2.432	64.528				
13	1.021	2.374	66.901				
14	.931	2.164	69.065				
15	.888	2.064	71.129				
16	.868	2.018	73.147				
17	.822	1.912	75.059				
18	.752	1.750	76.809				
19	.691	1.606	78.415				
20	.662	1.539	79.954				
21	.651	1.514	81.467				
22	.625	1.454	82.921				
23	.560	1.302	84.223				
24	.543	1.263	85.486				
25	.536	1.247	86.733				
26	.501	1.166	87.899				
27	.474	1.103	89.002				
28	.455	1.058	90.061				
29	.446	1.038	91.099				
30	.434	1.010	92.108				
31	.386	.899	93.007				
32	.364	.847	93.855				
33	.346	.804	94.659				
34	.333	.774	95.433				
35	.296	.688	96.121				
36	.282	.656	96.777				
37	.260	.605	97.382				
38	.249	.579	97.961				
39	.245	.569	98.530				
40	.188	.437	98.968				
41	.174	.405	99.372				
42	.143	.332	99.705				
43	.127	.295	100.000				

Note: Extraction method: Principal axis factoring.

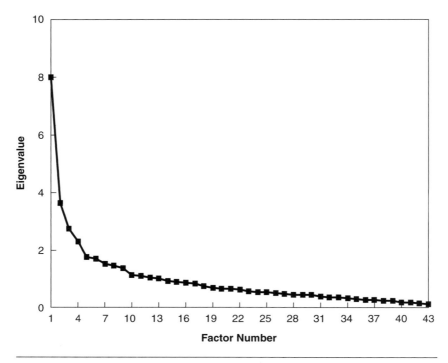

FIGURE 13.2 *Scree plot*

seemed to me a good trade-off between simplicity and total variance explained. Adding the fifth and sixth factors and then adding the seventh, eighth, and ninth did not help enough (subjective judgment again) with my substantive task of explaining the dimensionality of these students' attitudes. There is no statistical rule for making this decision. Researchers have to decide on the basis of what is most helpful with the kinds of explanations they wish to make.

How Do I Identify (Extract) the Factors?

Now I was ready to move closer to "the answer," to uncovering a pattern of clusters of items that can be used to interpret how people's attitudes hang together—or fail to do so. Table 13.3, the factor matrix, gives the initial look at the patterns in the answers to the questions. The first column gives the question number and an abbreviation for what it is

about. In the first row, Q38APPRO is question number 38, which asked about approval (SPSS limits you to eight letters). In the column for factor 1, we see the number .688 for this question. This is its *factor loading.* Each question is sorted into factors and each gets a factor loading. For example, factor 4 is composed of two questions (Q18DATE and Q3MARRY); they have factor loadings of .536 and .484, respectively.

What is a factor loading? A factor loading is a correlation (Pearson *r*) of a variable with a factor. A factor is comprised of a cluster of items (questions). What is the correlation of each item with that cluster? Those correlations are the factor loadings.[4] Factor loadings less than .40 are usually considered too small to be important. Like all such rules, this one is somewhat arbitrary. Some researchers use .30, others .50, but .40 is probably most common. The reasoning for eliminating items with small loadings is as follows. Because the loading is a correlation, squaring the correlation gives you the percentage of variance in the item associated with the factor. If less

TABLE 13.3 *Factor Matrix*—Unrotated*

	Factor			
	1	*2*	*3*	*4*
Q38APPRO	.688			
Q11RMVBK	.685			
Q10RMVBK	.682			
Q6GYWRNG	.662			
Q39BAN	.654			
Q9TCHHS	.617			
Q22ORGNZ	.612			
Q8TCHCOL	.604			
Q7GYSPK	.567			
Q20GYTCH	.560			
Q21ACEPT	.543			
Q42DAUGH	.540	−.420		
Q19RULES	.458			
Q5LAWAGT	.410	−.405		
Q34PUNSH	.402			
Q32CODE				
Q31REMOV				
Q37LTRS				
Q43SAMSX				
Q24SPECH				
Q41PROM				
Q40NOTFY				
Q17FREPR				
Q36OFFPR				
Q27DEROG		.502		
Q28OFNZV	.405	.468		
Q26DRESS				
Q35PRIOR				
Q30EFFCT				
Q12RACSP				
Q29UNFRM				
Q2IMPWH				
Q13TCHCO		.407	.543	
Q14TCHHS		.425	.534	
Q15RMVBK			.478	
Q16RMVBK			.466	
Q25PRESS			−.427	
Q23EDIT			−.427	
Q1IMPBL				
Q18DATE	.488			.536
Q3MARRY	.423	−.404		.484
Q4DINNER				
Q33TCHRS				

Note: Extraction method: Principal axis factoring.
*4 factors extracted; 7 iterations required.

than 16% (.40 x .40 = .16) of the variance in an item is associated with the factor, most researchers conclude that the item should not be part of the factor. Using this reasoning, I instructed SPSS not to list loadings less than .40 in the table. By eliminating unimportant numbers, we make the table easier to read.

Examining Table 13.3, we see that factor 1 has loadings over .40 for 18 of the questions, which are labeled with the original eight-character abbreviations I had used in SPSS. Q38APPRO refers to question number 38, which asks about whether the respondent approves of a topic for a school assembly; it has a loading of .688. Q11RMVBK and Q10RMVBK refer to questions 11 and 10, which concern whether respondents think a book should be removed from a public library and a high school library. Those two items have loadings of.685 and .682, respectively. The general idea in a factor analysis is to look at the substance of the questions comprising the factors to see if the factors make sense. Can the questions be understood as being about a common factor? Do they constitute a latent variable? Do they all seem to be about the same thing?

Now look at factor 4, which has only two loadings greater than .40. They are Q18DATE and Q3MARRY. Question 18 is, "Do you approve of interracial dating during high school?" Question 3 is, "Do you approve or disapprove of interracial marriage?" It is not too surprising that respondents' answers to these two questions should cluster. But note that these two questions also fit into factor 1 and question 3 is negatively loaded onto factor 2. Factor 2 has positive and negative loadings and is called a *bipolar* factor. Bipolar factors are often hard to interpret. A negative loading is interpreted like any other negative correlation or regression coefficient. For example, take three common measures when you get your annual physical: good cholesterol level, bad cholesterol level, and blood sugar level. Perhaps these three could add up to a construct or latent variable, call it "blood problems." If those three measures did add up to one underlying construct, and if bad cholesterol level and blood sugar had positive loadings, then the measure for good cholesterol would load negatively. So a bipolar factor does not in and of itself signal a

problem. Much worse in terms of clarity of interpretation is when items appear in more than one factor. Most of the second factor's items also load on (are correlated above .40 with) other factors. In short, at this point the factors are still somewhat too complex to interpret; they are not really distinct. This is where the factor analyst brings in *rotation*.

How Do I Fine-Tune the Factor Solution to Make It More Interpretable?

A person who has a good basic grasp of correlation and regression usually has little trouble understanding factor analysis. The terminology is weird (eigens and screes, for example), but the concepts are ordinary. That changes when we get to rotation, which is very hard to describe in a nontechnical way. Originally, rotation involved plotting variable scores on graph paper and then turning (rotating) the axes of the graph to try to find a better fit. The goal of this exercise when Thurstone (1947) first explained it is has not changed: to produce greater clarity, to generate factors that are more closely related to their variables and more distinct from one another. Rotation helps the researcher reach the ideal solution in which the variables load heavily on one factor, but hardly at all on the others. After rotation, the correlations among the items in a factor are raised, but the correlations among the factors are lowered. In short you get more clearly distinct clusters of variables (items). Rotation does not affect the total variance in the set of variables, but it does change how the variance is distributed among the factors.

Rotation involves looking at the same data from different angles. The data are not changed; their interpretation is rearranged. In that sense, rotation is a kind of transformation. The correlation matrix is transformed using matrix algebra. Without an extended discussion using matrix algebra, it is hard to explain rotation, but an analogy (suggested by one of this book's reviewers) may prove helpful. You have seen several examples in this book of correlations between two variables and how they can be represented by a scatter diagram and a regression line that summarizes the pattern of the data points (see, for example, Figures 12.1 through 12.4). Factor analysis works more with a three-dimensional problem. Rotation involves looking at the same data from different angles in three-dimensional space. The analogy is imagining that scores for individual questions, the data points, are like stars scattered across space. Some areas of space have very few stars, whereas others (galaxies such as the Milky Way) have dense clusters. With factor analysis, straight regression lines are drawn or rotated through this three-dimensional space until they cut through the densest clusters of scores. The number of factors is the number of intersecting regression lines. To make the fit better, the intersecting regression lines are rotated until they best align with the most scores. So far so good, but there are different methods of rotation.

So, to proceed with the factor analysis and rotate the factors so as to make them more interpretable, one more decision remains. What method of rotation should be used? There are two general categories of rotation: *orthogonal,* or uncorrelated, and *oblique,* or correlated. The question you have to ask yourself is: Does it make sense to assume that the factors will be completely uncorrelated? If so, you should use an orthogonal rotation. If not, you should use an oblique method.[5] To return to the analogy, in orthogonal rotation, the intersecting regression lines will be at right angles and will only be allowed to go through clusters of stars (scores) that are wholly distinct. In oblique rotation, the regression lines are allowed to go through clusters of scores that overlap somewhat. In either case, the scores aren't changed. They are fixed in space, but the regression lines are moved around, which means that the factor loadings (regression coefficients) and the patterns of factor loadings change.

For my problem, where I suspected that the factors might be related, oblique rotation makes more sense. In general I would argue that except in very special circumstances, oblique rotation is almost always the better choice. That is because an oblique method of rotation can result in an orthogonal solution (in which the factors are uncorrelated), but the opposite is not true. In an orthogonal rotation, the factors are *forced* to be uncorrelated. At any rate, I used an oblique method of rotation called "direct oblimin." The results are given in Table 13.4, in the pattern matrix.[6]

How Do I Interpret the Output of a Factor Analysis?

Table 13.4 shows our four factors after rotation. The first factor contains 11 questions with loadings of .754, .720, and so on. This first factor was fairly easy to interpret. It concerned homosexuality. The 11 questions asked whether same-sex relationships were wrong or not, whether homosexuals should be allowed to be teachers, and so on. This does *not* mean that all respondents answered the questions the same way, though there was a strong liberal trend among the undergraduates I surveyed. What it does mean is that each individual surveyed tended to answer all 11 questions in the same way: If he or she answered one in a conservative way, he or she would have a strong tendency to answer the others that way. The same was true, of course, for individual respondents answering questions in a liberal way. What makes the questions a cluster is that most individuals tended to be consistent in the way they answered, whether they were consistently liberal or consistently conservative or consistently neutral on this issue.

Another 10 questions (factor 2) concerned freedom of expression for high school students. To me this factor seemed to combine two disparate sorts of freedom of expression, but in the minds of the college students responding to the questions, they were one. The two areas were freedom of the press and freedom of dress. People who supported freedom of the press tended to support freedom of dress—and those who didn't support the one didn't support the other. It is interesting to note that high school teachers saw freedom of press and dress as two distinct factors, not one.

Factor 3 was composed of five questions borrowed from a national survey called the General Social Survey. The questions concerned a racist, in the

TABLE 13.4   *Pattern Matrix*—After Rotation*

	Factor			
	1	*2*	*3*	*4*
Q9TCHHS	.754			
Q8TCHCOL	.720			
Q10RMVBK	.699			
Q7GYSPK	.669			
Q39BAN	.636			
Q11RMVBK	.620			
Q38APPRO	.611			
Q22ORGNZ	.587			
Q21ACEPT	.535			
Q6GYWRNG	.515			
Q20GYTCH	.499			
Q43SAMSX				
Q24SPECH				
Q37LTRS				
Q40NOTFY				
Q28OFNZV		.596		
Q25PRESS		.572		
Q35PRIOR		.537		
Q23EDIT		.532		
Q34PUNSH		.521		
Q32CODE		.517		
Q27DEROG		.511		
Q26DRESS		.485		
Q30EFFCT		.415		
Q31REMOV		.400		
Q29UNFRM				
Q36OFFPR				
Q33TCHRS				
Q14TCHHS			.711	
Q13TCHCO			.707	
Q16RMVBK			.635	
Q15RMVBK			.613	
Q12RACSP			.439	
Q18DATE				.812
Q3MARRY				.776
Q42DAUGH				.726
Q4DINNER				.485
Q5LAWAGT				.481
Q19RULES				.429
Q41PROM				
Q1IMPBL				
Q17FREPR				
Q2IMPWH				

Note: Extraction method: Principal axis factoring. Rotation method: Oblimin with Kaiser normalization. *Rotation converged in 10 iterations.

TABLE 13.5   *Factor Correlation Matrix*

Factor	1	2	3	4
1	1.000	.267	.087	.268
2	.267	1.000	.127	.048
3	.087	.127	1.000	.117
4	.268	.048	.117	1.000

Note: Extraction method: Principal axis factoring. Rotation method: Oblimin with Kaiser normalization.

words of the question, "a person who believes that blacks are genetically inferior." This individual evoked a very strong and usually negative response. Even respondents generally in favor of freedom of expression tended to make an exception here. People who would allow a homosexual to be a teacher or to have a book in a public library would not necessarily afford a racist the same liberties. If so, if individuals had answered questions about homosexuals and racists consistently (e.g., supporting freedom of speech regardless of the speaker), those questions would have formed part of the same factor, probably factor 1.

Another six questions (the fourth and final factor) concerned interracial dating and intermarriage. Individual undergraduate teacher education majors tended to have consistent beliefs and attitudes about these issues. Note that although factors 3 and 4 were both about race, they were not closely related. Answers to the questions making up factor 3 (about the rights of a racist) and factor 4 (about the rights of people of different races) were *not* strongly related. This can be seen in the correlation matrix among the factors in Table 13.5, where the correlation is listed as .117. This low correlation means we cannot use answers to factor 3 to predict answers to factor 4, or vice versa. The r^2, or percent of variance explained, is only a little over 1% (.117 x .117 = .014). While I might have thought of the two sets of questions as being in the same "realm," that of race relations, the respondents appear not to have thought of them that way. Among these respondents the answers formed distinct clusters. These distinct clusters indicate that the survey respondents understood the issues covered by the two clusters of questions to mean different things, to be different issues.

Finally, looking at Table 13.4, we can see that about one-quarter of the questions fit into no pattern whatsoever. They had factor loadings of less than .40 and were not listed. We have also seen that the four factors taken together explained less than half of the variance. Those four clusters accounted for less than half of the differences among individuals' answers. This means that there was a lot of variety in the ways respondents answered the survey questions. For about one-quarter of the questions there was no discernable pattern. For the remainder of the questions, the patterns, though clear, were not very strong. Over half of the variance in respondents' answers was not explained by the four factors.

Because it yielded four factors, the factor analysis told me that I needed to *investigate* people's patterns of beliefs and attitudes, not simply assume that I knew what these were. If these results are typical, if what I learned in surveying undergraduates turns out to be true also of other populations, I can no longer assume that conclusions about any aspect of attitudes and beliefs pertaining to intergroup relations will tend to transfer to other aspects. For example, knowing what people think about gay rights will not be of much help in guessing what they might think about interracial dating. Those who assume there is a general liberal/conservative continuum that is useful for describing people's attitudes on all issues may be assuming too much—if these data patterns hold for other groups.

On the other hand, I learned some things beyond the fact that the structure of people's attitudes might be more complicated than I had thought. Four distinct scales have been identified that no longer have to be treated as separate variables, but can rather be united in an analysis of political and social beliefs and attitudes. Let's see how it works by taking the fourth factor, the one having to do with interracial dating and marriage. I can now treat this as a scale that will give good answers about how folks think about the cluster of issues described by the items. To investigate the reliability of that scale, I conducted a reliability analysis with SPSS to illustrate, which is shown in Table 13.6.

The individual questions in this survey were coded 1.0 for a liberal response, 0 for a neutral response, and −1.0 for a conservative response. These

TABLE 13.6   *Reliability Analysis for Scale Identified in Factor 4*

Statistics for Scale

Mean	Variance	Std Dev	N of Variables
4.8315	5.4414	2.3327	6

Item-Total Statistics

	Scale Mean if Item Deleted	Scale Variance if Item Deleted	Corrected Item—Total Correlation	Squared Multiple Correlation	Alpha if Item Deleted
Q3MARRY	4.1124	3.3557	.7100	.6195	.7512
Q4DINNER	4.0262	3.8978	.4599	.2614	.8156
Q5LAWAGT	3.8839	4.6820	.5250	.4497	.8055
Q18DATE	4.0674	3.5142	.7640	.6163	.7392
Q19RULES	3.8764	4.8456	.4701	.4244	.8149
Q42DAUGH	4.1910	3.2228	.7084	.5489	.7533

Reliability coefficients. 6 items.
Alpha = .8135.

were added together for the six questions to produce a scale in which the highest possible score was 6.0 and the lowest possible was −6.0. That's how you turn items into a scale; you add them together and treat the result as one entity. The mean on this scale was 4.8, which indicates that the undergraduates were quite strongly concentrated on the liberal end of the spectrum. However, there was a good deal of variety in the answers, as can be seen by the standard deviation of 2.3. Our concerns at this point are with the reliability or internal consistency of the scale, not how the group scored on it. Did individuals who answered it in a conservative *or* a liberal way, tend to do so consistently? The answer is yes. That is what the alpha of .8135 tells us. This is the *Cronbach's alpha* discussed in Chapter 7. It indicates the internal consistency of the scale. These six questions can reasonably be treated as one variable. The column "Alpha if Item Deleted" shows that there is no item which, if deleted, would greatly improve the scale. Three of the items, if deleted, would make it noticeably worse. Eliminating Q18DATE, for example, would lower the alpha to .7392, which is a serious reduction in reliability.

This extended example has shown how factor analysis is a way to try to find patterns of relations among variables, which can then suggest associations among things in the world. More than most statistics, these correlational statistics, which are used to *discover* patterns, require interpretation. Merely reporting them is insufficient. You have to reason about your evidence, not simply record it, if you are to use it effectively to solve problems and make decisions. This is nowhere more true than with exploratory factor analysis. Even deciding what to name the factors, once the analysis has identified them, is a highly subjective process. Factor analysis can be a powerful exploratory tool. But it is exploratory; it gives the researcher an early, crude approximation of the structures that might exist among variables. It does not test the statistical significance of relations among variables. Rather it can be used to suggest questions to investigate and hypotheses to test in subsequent analyses with new data.

Factor analysis is used to "find" variables, as it were. Having found clusters of indicators that constitute variables, one can then use other techniques to explore relations among them. Chief among these techniques is regression analysis. In our next chapter, on structural equation modeling (SEM), we will see how factor analysis is used to assess the reliability of measurements of constructs; then the relations among the constructs are studied with multiple regression.

Structural equation modeling integrates factor analysis and regression analysis into a new more powerful analytic technique. It has become the method of choice of researchers whose data are rich enough to benefit from it.

Terms and Concepts to Review

Factor analysis
- Exploratory factor analysis (EFA)
- Confirmatory factor analysis (CFA)

Principal components analysis (PCA)

Sources of variance in factor analysis
- Common variance
- Specific variance
- Error variance

Factor extraction
Principal axis factoring (PAF)

Eigenvalues
- Scree plot

Factor pattern matrix
Factor structure matrix
Factor loading

Rotation
- Orthogonal
- Oblique

Cronbach's alpha reliability

Discussion Questions

1. Think of something of interest to you that has several components or aspects. It is often easiest to do this if you think in terms of an ability, such as ability to write well or play tennis or diagnose problems. If you had several measurements of this same thing, how could you use factor analysis to tell whether it was in fact one thing?

2. Using the same example as in question 1, would you do better using principal components analysis, in which the measured variables are *components,* or factor analysis in which the measured variables are *indicators*?

3. Why is it that methods of statistical inference are seldom if ever applied to factor analysis? Why do you see no *p*-values and confidence intervals in this chapter? What would it mean for the results of a factor analysis to be statistically significant or not significant?

4. Think of a course you have taken, one that had an objective final examination. Could you use factor analysis to assess the reliability of the examination? How? What would it mean to say that a factor analysis found the examination to be reliable—or unreliable?

Self-Test

If you can answer most of the following questions accurately, you can feel confident about your understanding of the material in this chapter. If not, it would be a good idea to review the chapter. (Answers can be found in the Appendix.)

1. By using factor analysis researchers usually can end controversies about how to cluster test items into measurement scales. True or False?

2. A factor is a cluster of correlated variables. True or False?

3. A group of items on a test or on attitude scale forms a factor when *each individual* tends to answer questions in the same way—for example, correctly or opposed. True or False?

4. A group of items on a test or on attitude scale forms a factor when all examinees (respondents) tend to

answer questions in the same way—for example, correctly or opposed. True or False?

5. Exploratory FA focuses on finding patterns of correlations in the data whereas confirmatory FA is used to test (confirm) theories about how variables are clustered. True or False?

6. Factor analysis can be used to assess the reliability of a measurement scale. True or False?

7. An eigenvalue indicates the percentage of the total variance in a group of variables that is explained by a factor. True or False?

8. When doing a factor analysis the goal is always to find a number of factors that maximizes the total variance explained. True or False?

9. A factor loading is a correlation of an item or variable with the cluster of items that constitute a factor. True or False?

10. Once the computer program has identified the factors and their eigenvalues and the loadings of the items, the researcher's interpretive problem is largely solved. True or False?

11. Factor rotation is used to more clearly distinguish the factors from one another. True or False?

12. When using oblique rotation the factors must be uncorrelated, whereas with orthogonal rotation the factors are assumed to be correlated. True or False?

Endnotes

1. When FA is a component of structural equation modeling (SEM), then testing models for goodness of fit to a hypothesized structure is a key part of the analysis. See Chapter 14.

2. For computational reasons, a covariance matrix is more often used. For our purposes, the difference need not concern us, because our computations will be done "behind the scenes" by computer software and because a covariance is a kind of correlation; it is an unstandardized Pearson *r*.

3. I also did the analysis of the 43 items using PCA (results not shown here). The general patterns of relations among the items were quite parallel using the two methods. Different though they are, in this case, they did not lead to markedly different conclusions.

4. Technically, factor loadings are regression coefficients; the items are regressed on (explained by) the factors. This

means that each item in turn is treated as a DV and the other items as IVs to arrive at the loading.

5. To examine this and related issues more deeply see Thompson (2004); he generally prefers PCA and orthogonal rotations, because they tend to be more parsimonious. By contrast, Pett et al. (2003) favor PAF and oblique rotation.

6. Note that major authorities disagree whether one should use the factor *pattern* matrix, as I have in Table 13.4, or the factor *structure* matrix. I believe that factor pattern matrix is more appropriate for factor analysis with oblique rotation. Good practice will often involve producing and inspecting both, but experts disagree with one another even about this.

14

Structural Equation Modeling

Structural equation modeling (SEM) combines several techniques with which you are already familiar. Indeed, it integrates virtually every quantitative method discussed so far in this book into a new and analytically powerful whole. Because of its integration of elementary techniques into an advanced whole, SEM provides a fitting conclusion to this part of the book. Specifically, SEM uses regression analysis (see Chapters 9–12) for measuring the relations among variables. It employs factor analysis (see Chapter 13) to improve the measurement of the variables. And causal modeling (see Chapter 3) is combined with regression to yield a way to picture and test regression models called path analysis. So, although SEM is the most advanced analytic method studied in this volume, it is built almost entirely out of elements that you have already encountered.

Structural equation modeling is a *confirmatory* method. Indeed, it is often called *confirmatory factor analysis* (CFA). What *confirmatory* means is that in order to use SEM you have to have a model or a theory or at least a hunch to test. You can tinker with or adjust the model to make it work better, but you have to start with one. What you do is propose a model, collect sample ,data, and then test the model on the data to see how well your model worked, that is, to see how closely the sample data fit into the model. The major question answered by an SEM analysis is: How closely does the proposed model of the way we think things work in the popula-tion match the empirical data gathered in the sample? One hopes that any differences between the empirical sample and the theoretical population model will be small and *not* statistically significant. A lack of statistical significance, when testing for differences between the model and the sample, is evidence that the model may be an accurate portrayal of reality. This chapter discusses SEM by addressing the following questions.

1. What is a model, and how can one be built?
2. How is factor analysis incorporated into the model?
3. How are the results of a full measurement and structural model calculated?
4. How can what has been learned be used to interpret actual research results?
5. How is SEM used in causal inference?

What Is a Model, and How Can One Be Built?

So, what is a model (or theory), and how do you build one in order to test it? We talked about models in Chapter 3, in the discussion of the relations among variables. Let's start with one of the examples we used there when discussing possible ways to depict how variables can be related. In Chapter 3, we proposed a

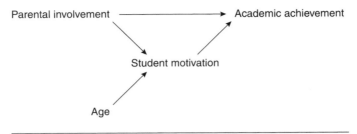

FIGURE 14.1 *Model of effects of parental involvement*

model to account for the tendency of parental involvement with a child's schooling to increase the child's academic achievement. That model is redrawn as Figure 14.1. It specifies that parental involvement increases student motivation, and that motivation increases achievement. It also states that the model in general and student motivation in particular vary depending on students' ages. This model can be tested with a form of regression analysis called *path analysis.*

As with all regression analyses, path analysis asks one form or another of a basic question: How much better can you predict or explain variance in an outcome variable if you have data about one or more explanatory variables? Our outcome here is academic achievement and our explanatory (or predictor) variables are parental involvement, student motivation, and student age. But our model in Figure 14.1 is not a simple regression model. What makes it special is that it proposes a *pattern* of relationships among the variables. This is pattern is called a *structure.*

A simple regression model, one that postulated no structure among the variables, is shown in Figure 14.2. Here involvement, age, and motivation all influence achievement, but no relationships are proposed for *how* the explanatory variables are related to one another and to the outcome. Figure 14.2 has no structure. It claims: All these things influence the outcome—*somehow.* By contrast, Figure 14.1 proposes a structure of the relationships among the explanatory variables and the outcome variable. It says: Here is *how* the variables influence the outcome. Obviously, we are using the same variables in the two models or figures, but we are proposing something much more specific in Figure 14.1: a structure. This is the structure of the structural equation model (SEM).

The structure can also be depicted as an equation, one that directly translates the figure into terms a software program can use to test the model. In the not too distant past, one had to be able to write the equation to conduct the analysis, but today several of the SEM software packages (such as LISREL, Amos, and EQS) allow you to draw a picture of the model on the screen and then, without further ado, conduct the analysis. The program turns the graphic model into an equation for you (see Kline, 2005, for a thorough review). It is nonetheless useful to know at an elementary level how figures can be translated into equations (or equations can be translated into figures). Consider just two of the explanatory variables (involvement and motivation) and their relation with the outcome (achievement) in Figures 14.1 and 14.2. In the structureless model, Figure 14.2, the equation is

$$\text{Achievement} = \text{Involvement} + \text{Motivation}$$

In the structural model depicted in Figure 14.1, the equation is

$$\text{Achievement} = \text{Involvement} + \text{Motivation} + (\text{Involvement} \times \text{Motivation})$$

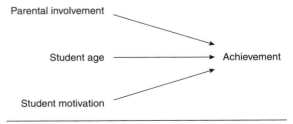

FIGURE 14.2 *Simple regression model of the effects of parental involvement*

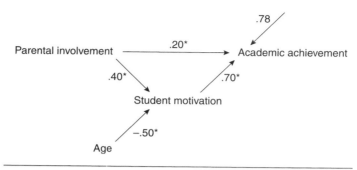

FIGURE 14.3 *Path analysis model of effects of parental involvement*
Note: p < .05.

What that means is that Figure 14.1 proposes that involvement influences achievement directly *and* it does so indirectly, by its effect on motivation.

What do you do with the model in Figure 14.1? How do you use evidence to see whether what has been proposed might be true? You use the structural form of regression analysis called path analysis. Each one of the arrows in the model is a path, a path of causal influence. What you need to do is compute a regression coefficient for each one of those arrows. The regression coefficients in a path analysis such as this one are usually standardized; that is, they are in *z*-score units. There are four arrows, so you will compute four coefficients. Say you collect data from a representative sample of the students and their parents in a school district. Parents are asked: How many times per month do you usually confer with teachers, help with homework, attend PTA meetings, and so on. Their answers are tallied to produce an "involvement score." From students you collect data about their ages and their scores on an achievement test. You also have them answer the questions on a 10-item scale that measures their academic motivation. The results of this analysis might produce a path diagram, with coefficients, such as the one in Figure 14.3.

What is added now in the model are the standardized regression coefficients, which are usually called *path coefficients* in a path analysis. These regression coefficients are read like all others: For each 1 standard deviation (SD) increase in the predictor variable, what happens to the outcome variable? So the figure .20 means that for every 1 SD increase in parental involvement, achievement goes up two-tenths of a standard deviation. For every 1 SD increase in students'

age, motivation decreases (the coefficient is negative) by half an SD, and so on. We see that involvement increases motivation (.40) and motivation increases achievement (.70). Because these are standardized coefficients we can compare them directly and conclude, for example, that the direct effect of involvement on achievement (.20) is only half as large as the effect of involvement on motivation (.40).

One of the great advantages of path analysis is that we can use it to assess the strength of *indirect* effects. We can examine the effect of involvement *through* motivation, that is, the indirect effect of involvement. To calculate this effect, you simply multiply the two coefficients: .40 for involvement on motivation times .70 for motivation on achievement, which equals .28 (.40 × .70 = .28). This means that the indirect effect of parental involvement (.28) is stronger than the direct effect (.20). An even stronger indirect effect is that of age on achievement. First, we see that, in this sample, when age goes up motivation goes down. This is a negative effect (−.50). To measure the indirect effect of age on achievement, we multiply the coefficients: −.50 × .70 = −.35. For every 1 SD increase in age, achievement goes down by about one third of a SD. Finally, note the .78 on the arrow coming from outside the model and pointing at the dependent/outcome variable of achievement. This is the *residual* term or *error* term or *disturbance* term (all mean essentially the same thing). It is usually labeled *D* for disturbance, but also labeled *U* for unanalyzed component. However labeled, it tells you how much of the variance in the outcome is *not* explained by the predictor variables in the model.

In some respects, a path analysis is a structural equation model (SEM). In path analysis the researcher provides a picture or a model or a structure of how the variables are related to one another. Next, this is tested with sample data. If the sample is representative, then the relations suggested by the structures in the model are likely to be true of the population. Some researchers call their path analysis results SEM results, but most reserve the term *SEM* for a more elaborate set of methods. Path analysis can be thought of as the original form of structural equation modeling. It is appropriate to use path analysis, rather than the more elaborate version of SEM, when we have only one measure of each variable, as in the current example. Also, the variables should be observed directly, that is, they should not be latent variables; this is not so clearly the case in our example. Most researchers would not call a simple path analysis, such as the one shown in Figure 14.3, an SEM. Generally, the label *structural equation model* is reserved for work that combines a structural model with a *measurement model*, such as the example in Figure 14.4. Testing the measurement model requires the use of factor analysis.

How Is Factor Analysis Incorporated into the Model?

The discussion of factor analysis in Chapter 13 introduced the distinction between *latent variables* and observed variables. This distinction is labeled a few different ways in research reports. Some variables can be measured quite directly: Height, age, income, and years of schooling are examples. These are the observed variables, which are also called *manifest variables* and *indicators*. Whatever they are called, it is generally easy to measure them, and there is comparatively little dispute about the validity and reliability of the measures. They are low-inference measures. Latent variables, on the other hand, have to be measured indirectly using measured or indicator variables to do so. Their measurement requires a larger degree of inference, and their reliability and validity are more often open to question. Latent variables are variously called constructs, unobserved variables, and factors. They include variables such as intelligence, health, and self-esteem. These must be measured indirectly, and, rather than using one measure for each latent variable, it is usually wise to use several (at least three is the typical recommendation). Together, the several indicator or observed variables comprise the composite or latent variable or factor. When we want to use factor analysis to refine the measurements of the variables in a path analysis, and simultaneously to examine the strength of the relations among those variables, we turn to structural equation modeling, or SEM.

To see what this involves, let's continue with the example of the influence of parental involvement on academic achievement. Figure 14.4 presents a structural equation model of the same set of variables. The structural equation model adds a new dimension to the path model in Figure 14.3. Comparing the two figures we see that the inner core of the figure—the path diagram composed of the relations among involvement, motivation, age, and achievement—remains the same. This inner core is called the structural component of the model, or the structural model. The additions to the diagram, the parts that radiate out from the core, constitute the measurement part of the model, generally called the measurement model. So, SEM combines a structural model and a measurement model.

Look first at involvement. Involvement is now a latent variable that is measured indirectly by the four indicators to which the arrows point. Note that the arrows point from the latent variables to the measured variables. Because involvement is a latent variable or factor, it is now symbolized by an oval. The measured indicators are symbolized by boxes. This convention of using boxes and ovals is all but universal. It makes it easier for readers to sort out what is going on in these complex models. Returning to Figure 14.4, the first boxed variable is homework help. It is one indicator of parental involvement; so is talking with the student about school. Two others are included: conferring with teachers and participating in community efforts to support the school. Those four boxed indicators are how we propose to measure the latent variable, parental involvement.

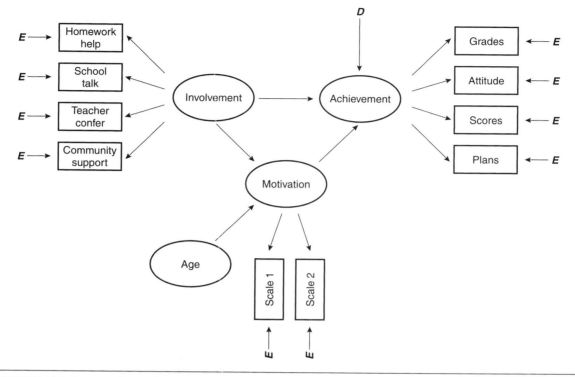

FIGURE 14.4 *Structural equation model of the effects of parental involvement*

The figure shows that we propose to measure achievement by another four indicators: grades, attitudes toward learning, state test scores, and plans for further education. There are two indicators (two different tests) of motivation. Indicators of age are not needed, because age can easily be measured directly. It is not a latent variable.

Once the model has been drawn and the sample data collected, an SEM software program is used to conduct an analysis. Among the results of that analysis is information about how strongly each of the indicators is related to its factor or latent variable. The numbers that will appear over the lines from the factor (latent variable) to the indicator will be factor loadings. As seen in Chapter 13, a *factor loading* is a correlation of an indicator variable with a factor. Our factor called parental involvement is measured by a cluster of indicators. The correlations of each of the

indicators with that cluster are the factor loadings. The direction of the arrows is important. Because SEM uses factor analysis, not principal components analysis, the arrows point from the factor to the indicators (compare Figure 13.1). Conceptually, this direction of the arrows means that the general concept or trait, involvement, *causes* the indicators. Involvement leads the parents to help with homework, to talk with their children about school, and so on. Helping with homework does not cause involvement; it is an indicator of involvement.

Motivation is measured by two scales rather than one as in the original path model. Achievement is measured by four indicators: grades, students' attitudes toward education, students' scores on standardized tests, and their educational plans. Another striking feature of Figure 14.4 is all the *E*s. Each of the indicator variables has an *E* pointing to it. This

E stands for error, specifically measurement error. There were no such measurement error terms in Figure 14.3, the simple path model. There was surely of plenty of error because no measure is perfect, but there was no error *term,* no way of controlling the error. The crucial advantage of SEM over simple path analysis is that, because it adds multiple indicators of variables, it provides a method for estimating the amount of error (essentially the reliability) of the measurement of the latent variable. This is a big improvement over simple path analysis, which has to proceed, by assumption, as though the variables are measured without error. Finally, in Figure 14.4, achievement has an arrow pointing to it labeled with a *D*. This *D* stands for the disturbance term, which is what the error term is called in the structural part of the model. It is the part of the model *not* explained by all of the variables taken together.

SEM is a correlation and regression-based technique. Most of the assumptions that need to be met and cautions that pertain for correlation and regression are discussed in Chapter 10, but we need to briefly mention them again here. For example, data need to be screened for the presence of outliers. Outliers can always pervert an analysis, but SEM is especially sensitive to their effects. Also, as in multiple regression, it is assumed in SEM that the relations between the variables are linear and that the explanatory variables are not too highly intercorrelated. If we find that assumptions are violated, the same solutions are available as in multiple regression more generally. For example, when two explanatory variables are highly correlated (multicollinearity), one variable can be eliminated, or the two variables can be summed to make a new composite variable. For dealing with nonlinear effects, one can create a special squared variable to measure curvilinear relations. When the relations between the explanatory variables and the outcome variable are nonlinear because the outcome is categorical, a logistic regression type of approach (see Chapter 11) is available for SEM. Finally, there is one assumption important for multiple regression and path analysis that is not necessary for SEM—that is, the assumption of no correlation between the residuals (errors) and the causal variables.

SEM calculates these correlations and incorporates them into the model.

In our discussion of factor analysis, we learned that it is a correlation-based technique. The main data employed by factor analysis is the correlation matrix of the variables in the study. This is also true of SEM. Because of that, researchers can often conduct interesting studies using only the correlation matrices in published studies; they do not need the original raw data. This raises the possibility of many opportunities for interesting reanalysis of data. Indeed, if the researcher begins with raw data, the first thing the SEM software will do is create a *correlation matrix,* which it then uses to conduct the analysis. This statement needs one qualification. Rather than the correlation (Pearson *r*) matrix, SEM uses the matrix of *covariances.*[1] As you will recall from Chapter 2, the Pearson *r* is a standardized measure of association; that is, it is expressed in standard deviation units. The covariance is simply an unstandardized Pearson *r,* or what amounts to the same thing, the Pearson *r* is a standardized covariance. A correlation, we saw in Chapter 2, is the mean of the product of the *standardized* deviation scores of two variables. The covariance is simpler; it is the mean of the product of the deviation scores; they have not been standardized, but remain in their original units. Because it builds on covariances, SEM was once commonly (and still sometimes is) referred to as analysis of covariance structures. By extension, factor analysis might be thought of as analysis of correlation structures.

How Are the Results of a Full Measurement and Structural Model Calculated?

It is important to reemphasize that in structural equation modeling, the researcher has to specify a model. This means choosing the particular variables that are important to understanding a problem and describing how those variables are related. In some sense this is true of any research, at least implicitly, but it is an unavoidably prominent and explicit part of SEM. That is because SEM provides a test of a whole model, which means that unless you have an explicit model to test, you cannot do SEM. How is the model tested? In the simple path analysis version of SEM, without a measurement model, the researcher can use OLS regression to calculate the path coefficients and the R^2 statistic for indicating the *goodness of fit*. Goodness of fit measures tell you how well the data match the model or, in other terms, whether the data in the sample came out the way they ought to have if the model you proposed before you collected the data really did describe how the variables are related.

For full structural equation models, such as the one in Figure 14.4, other techniques are required to calculate the path coefficients and to assess the goodness of fit. First discussed here will be the methods of estimating the path coefficients, then the methods of judging the goodness of fit. For the path coefficients, *maximum likelihood (ML) estimation* is used. Although for a simple path analysis ML and OLS methods will yield similar results, for the more complex models of SEM, only ML methods will work.

ML methods are particularly required when the path model (the structural part of the SEM diagram) is *nonrecursive*. A model is called nonrecursive when it has a feedback loop among the variables. The terms *recursive* and *nonrecursive* are widely used in SEM, and are the source of some confusion. Oddly, given its meaning in ordinary English, a *recursive*[2] model is one is which all the arrows in the structural part of the equation point in one direction; it is a model without a feedback loop. In any case, for recursive path analysis models without a measurement model, OLS methods work well enough. Most SEM problems contain a measurement model, and many are nonrecursive. For these research problems maximum likelihood methods of estimation are the preferred alternative. Other alternatives exist, especially generalized least squares (GLS), but ML is the most widely used and is the default option in most SEM programs. "It would be no exaggeration to describe ML estimation as the motor of SEM" (Kline, 2005, p. 112).

So, what is maximum likelihood estimation (MLE) and what do we get by using it? MLE is used to provide estimators in SEM models,[3] not to construct models. Model construction is done by the researcher. What MLE does is compute the coefficient and its statistical significance for each of the arrows in

the model. By contrast, in exploratory factor analysis, there are no good statistical tests to indicate whether an item is a statistically significant indicator of a latent variable or factor. That is because in exploratory factor analysis, there are no hypotheses to test. The ability to test the coefficients for significance is one of the big advances of SEM. In other terms, it is one of the advantages of confirmatory factor analysis over exploratory factor analysis.

Although the path coefficients and their levels of statistical significance are fairly easy to interpret, the calculations required to obtain them via MLE are very complex and computer intensive. Unlike OLS approaches, which seek coefficients that minimize the squared distance of the sample values from the mean *of the sample,* MLE calculates the most likely population values—given the sample values. MLE yields the (unobserved) population parameter estimates that are most likely to have been true of the population given the (observed) covariance matrix of the sample data. MLE is an "iterative" (repetitive) approach, a trial-and-error method, that involves cycles of recalculation, each one getting closer to the solution. MLE "systematically searches over the different possible population values, finally selecting parameter estimates that are most likely (have the 'maximum likelihood') to be true, given the sample observations" (Eliason, 1993, p. v). The researcher specifies some initial values for the population parameter (some programs will do this for you), and the software compares the covariance matrix of these starting points with the sample covariance matrix. The "fit" or similarity of the two matrices is not likely to be good on this first attempt, so the program changes the starting values in a direction that improves the fit. The process is repeated, each time moving the population estimates closer to agreement with the sample statistics. The number of repetitions is usually set by the program at around 30, but the researcher can increase this number if necessary. If everything goes well (and fairly often things do *not* go well), the program arrives at a point at which successive iterations will not improve the estimate. At this point, MLE is said to have "converged" on a solution (Loehlin, 2004).

The next question is: How well does the overall model fit the sample data? This can be a particularly important question when you have more than one model and you want to compare them, and researchers want to know about the goodness of fit even when examining only one model. The usual first step is to compare the sample covariance matrix to the estimated population covariance matrix and to use the chi-squared test of statistical significance. Of course, this is a test for significant differences; the null hypothesis is that there is no difference between the two. This means that when testing for fit you hope to be able to *accept* or *retain* the null hypothesis, not reject it. A nonsignificant chi-squared test indicates an acceptable fit; it means that there is no significant difference between the population data estimates and the sample data. The chi-squared test is usually the first and most common test; however, it is widely acknowledged to be a crude test. Because of its inadequacies, many other fit indexes have been developed, perhaps too many. As Thompson (2004) points out, "there are dozens of fit statistics, and . . . [their] properties are not completely understood" (p. 127). A research article will usually report on three to six of them (see Kline, 2005, for a comparative overview). Although the fit indexes provide useful information about the adequacy of the fit for an overall model, a good overall fit does not mean that all components of the model fit equally well. Also, an overall fit index does not necessarily mean that the predictive value of the model is high. To determine the predictive strength of the model, one examines the disturbance term for the outcome variable (the arrow marked with a *D* in Figure 14.4). This can be used to make a judgment about whether the unexplained part of the variance is too large for the purposes of the research problem being investigated.

How Can What Has Been Learned Be Used to Interpret Actual Research Results?

At this point in our discussion of structural equation modeling, an extended example is more instructive than further review of general principles. Enough ground has been covered and the basics of SEM have been reviewed sufficiently to be ready to examine

some research reports using the method. Our main example addresses the question: Does self-esteem foster learning?

A widespread belief in our society is that self-esteem in children leads to many positive outcomes, including better performance in school. By extension, low self-esteem leads to negative outcomes, perhaps because it discourages effort. The evidence for the importance of high self-esteem for academic achievement has always been thin (Baumeister, Campbell, Krueger, & Vohs, 2005), but this has apparently had little influence on some parents' and teachers' commitment to self-esteem as a solution to educational problems. Another psychological construct, and one that is somewhat related to self-esteem, is *locus of control.* Belief that one has some control over and responsibility for the course of one's life is called *internal* locus of control. Psychologists often find that this belief *does* have an influence on outcomes such as academic achievement. By contrast, persons with an *external* locus of control believe that their lives are controlled from the outside, and any efforts they might make would be a waste of time. Persons with an internal locus of control believe that their efforts can be efficacious, which is why the construct is also sometimes called *sense of self-efficacy.* How much do these psychological traits influence academic achievement? If high self-esteem promotes achievement, psychological interventions raising it could have a positive effect.

Structural equation modeling proved to be very helpful in addressing these questions in a study conducted by Ross and Broh (2000). They used data from a longitudinal study of a nationally representative sample of 8,802 teenagers in the eighth, tenth, and twelfth grades (the National Educational Longitudinal Study, or NELS). With this rich data set they were able to examine the effects of parental social support, and students' self-esteem and their locus on control on their academic achievement. After fitting the model with SEM techniques, they measured its fit with five fit indices. All indices indicated adequate fit. Their hypotheses, design, and results are all shown in Figure 14.5 (Ross & Broh, 2000, Fig. 1, p. 279). Not shown in Figure 14.5 are additional controls in the

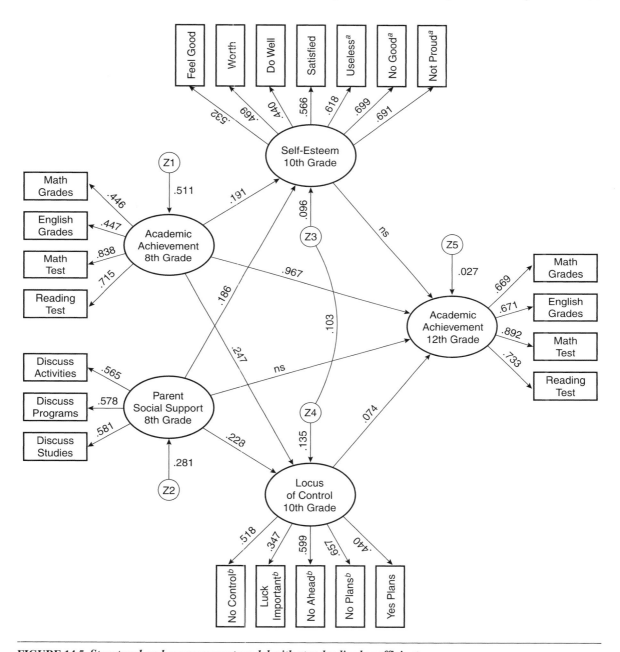

FIGURE 14.5 *Structural and measurement model with standardized coefficients*

Note: [a]Coded so that higher values equal higher self-esteem, and [b]coded so that higher values equal a high sense of control. All paths significant at $p < .05$ except for those labeled ns.

Source: Ross & Broh (2000), p. 279. Reprinted by permission of the American Sociological Association.

model, which included parents' education, family income, and students' gender and race. By close study of this model, we can review most of the concepts related to SEM that need to be examined.

First consider the five variables indicated by ovals. These constitute the structural model. The relations among them, the structure of their relations, is indicated by the arrows connecting them. Represented by the oval on the far right, academic achievement in the twelfth grade is the dependent or outcome variable. Briefly, the researchers wanted to see whether parental support in the eighth grade influenced self-esteem and locus of control in the tenth grade, and whether these, in turn, influenced achievement in the twelfth grade. Academic achievement in the eighth grade, indicated by the oval on the upper left, is included as a control to see whether there is still an effect of parental support, through self-esteem and locus of control, on twelfth-grade achievement after its effects have been subtracted. The numbers on the arrows are standardized coefficients, which means that their sizes can be compared directly—for example, .20 indicates an effect twice as big as .10.

The five variables of the structural model are latent variables or constructs. They are not measured directly; rather they are measured indirectly by the indicators shown in the rectangles. Academic achievement is measured by four indicators: math and English grades and math and reading tests. Self-esteem was measured by seven survey items, whereas locus of control was measured by five survey items. The numbers over the arrows pointing from the latent variables to the indicators (from the ovals to the rectangles) are factor loadings, which show the degree to which the factor (latent variable) is reflected in the scores of the indicator.

Each of the latent variables has an arrow pointing to it labeled Z. These Zs are the disturbance terms, or error terms, that is, estimates of the amount of the variance not explained by the model. The disturbance term labeled $Z5$, the one for the final outcome variable, is a remarkably small .027, which indicates that the model is very powerful. Virtually all the variance in the final outcome variable, academic achievement in the twelfth grade, is explained by the

model. The model is as powerful as it is for predicting twelfth-grade achievement mainly because it includes eighth-grade achievement as an explanatory or control variable. The arrow running directly from eighth-grade achievement to twelfth-grade achievement has a coefficient of .967. This means that every 1 SD increase in eighth-grade achievement was associated with 97% of an SD increase in twelfth-grade achievement, which is a nearly perfect association. Given the strength of that link, it is, as Ross and Broh (2000) note, "surprising that any social psychological attribute could have an independent effect" (p. 280). By controlling for prior achievement, they have definitely provided a "stringent test" of the other variables in the model.

What are the conclusions of the study as depicted in Figure 14.5? Read the figure from left to right, and look first at the arrows leading from eighth-grade achievement and parental support. Academic achievement in the eighth grade tends to foster increased self-esteem and increased internal locus of control in the tenth grade, with the effect on locus of control being somewhat stronger. The same is true of parental social support in the eighth grade. Parental support promotes both, but the coefficient for locus of control is somewhat larger than for self-esteem. Now move to the two variables in the middle. Notice the curved line connecting self-esteem and locus of control. Its coefficient is .103, indicating that esteem and locus of control are related. The line is curved because the authors are not postulating a direction of causality. Indeed, this line makes their model nonrecursive, because it contains at least one self-reinforcing relationship. The key findings in the study are seen in the arrows from self-esteem to achievement and from locus of control to achievement in the twelfth grade. This is what the authors set out to learn. Self-esteem is not associated with increased achievement. Only locus of control has a statistically significant influence on achievement.

This is a finding with potentially important policy implications. If a school system wishes to help improve achievement through psychological counseling programs, it would seem that focusing on internal locus of control would be more likely to produce success than would attempting to foster self-esteem. At this point, we might wonder why self-esteem does not have the widely expected effects. One reason is a potential measurement problem: The studies I know of that have found no effect have treated self-esteem as a linear variable in a regression model. The question addressed is: What is the effect of a one-unit increase in self-esteem on academic achievement? It could be that very low self-esteem actually is deleterious for achievement. But that does not mean that incremental increases between, say, medium and high levels increase achievement incrementally. My suspicion is that too little *or* too much self-esteem could have a negative effect on achievement. To investigate this we would probably need to use measures of self-esteem more nuanced than the seven-item scales in the NELS and to use regression techniques that could measure a curvilinear relationship. More important, however, than speculating about why self-esteem does not have the promised effect is building on knowledge of the psychological traits that do seem to be effective. Internal locus of control or as it is also called, sense of self-efficacy, routinely shows up as important in studies of achievement (for experimental results, see Mueller & Dweck, 1998). Students do better when they have learned how to make their efforts pay off, for example, by developing effective study habits, and they do better when they understand that personal *efforts* (not merely personal *worth*) have a potential for achieving outcomes.

As this example suggests, the measurement components of SEM are particularly attractive to researchers interested in the study of psychological traits and conditions. For example, in a study of the behaviors of cocaine-dependent outpatients, self-efficacy did not have an effect on abstaining from cocaine use—after controlling for previous behaviors (Wong et al., 2004). On the other hand, self-efficacy was found to be importantly linked to the development of interests in children (Tracey, 2000).

The measurement features of SEM have also been attractive to researchers not primarily concerned with the examination of personality traits. In an interesting study of graduate department rankings, Paxton and Bollen (2003) used SEM to sort out the

components of the ratings by the National Research Council (NRC) and *U.S. News and World Report.* Both organizations use reputational measures, that is, judges are asked about how they perceive the quality of the graduate departments. But there are important differences in the two methods. The NRC asks a representative sample of faculty to rank 50 biggest departments in a discipline, whereas *U.S. News* asks department chairs and directors of graduate programs to rank all graduate departments. How much do these methodological differences in the two rating systems matter, and, more broadly, how reliable are the rankings?

Paxton and Bollen construct a measurement model to answer these questions. The latent variable is perceived department quality, that is, rank. The indicators are the scores given by NRC raters and by *U.S. News* raters. In addition, three measures of departments' scholarly productivity are used as indicators. Other variables, such as the department's size and whether it was located in a private university, were added as controls. The study does not really include a structural model because the relation of latent variables to one another is not examined: For example, does perceived department quality lead to career success for graduates? Rather, Paxton and Bollen focus on the reliability of the measures of departmental quality. They conclude that although there are only small measurement, or *random,* errors in the ratings, some 20% to 30% of the final ranking is due to *systematic* error or bias. This "nonnegligible portion of the ratings" attributable systematic error arising from differences in measurement method, is a cause for concern, especially given how seriously these rankings are taken by the departments and those who deal with them. No one ever thought that the rankings were perfect. Indeed, some people believe that they are so arbitrary as to be useless. What the measurement model in SEM provides is an estimate of the *size* of the imperfections in the measurements. Of course, they are imperfect, but *how* imperfect are they? Depending on the department, measurement error and systematic error together account for between 20% and 40% of the total variance in the rankings.

How Is SEM Used in Causal Inference?

Structural equation modeling (SEM) has both causal and measurement components. There is not much point in doing SEM, especially the structural model part, unless one is going to propose a causal model. And there is little reason to use SEM measurement models unless there is a degree of uncertainty in the way at least some of one's variables are measured. It seems to me that researchers are hardly ever *un*-interested in cause, and in the social and behavioral disciplines researchers can rarely be so certain of the measurement qualities of their variables that they can dispense with a method that brings improvements to measurement. These two phenomena, an abiding interest in cause and great imperfections in measurement, help explain the popularity of SEM.

Like other correlational and regression techniques, such as multilevel modeling (MLM), SEM is often used on nonexperimental data, but this is more a matter of custom than necessity (Shadish, Cook, & Campbell, 2002). Allowing the choice of research methods to be shaped by custom and tradition does not seem the best practice. Traditions can develop quickly. There is a tendency, I believe, for multilevel modeling to be more popular among sociologists and economists and for SEM to be more attractive to researchers in the various psychology-based disciplines. This is unfortunate, because the two analytical methods are complimentary in important ways. A latent-variable measurement component can be added to multilevel models, and a hierarchical component can be incorporated into structural equation models (see Heck, 2004, for an example). Although originally developed and still developing somewhat separately, it is possible "to integrate the strengths of the two modeling frameworks." (Bauer, 2003, p. 136). I suspect that in the not-too-distant future, many aspects of MLM and SEM will be synthesized into a broader model or researchers will come to realize that they are versions of the same model—much as they did with ANOVA and regression.

Be that as it may, can we really derive valid causal conclusions using correlational methods, no matter how advanced? It is true correlational evidence only suggests cause. A correlation may be a coinci-

dence. Two correlated variables may be caused by a third. It is even possible, in the presence of a suppressor variable, for the causal relation of two variables to be hidden by a third so that the correlation coefficient of a true cause and effect is close to zero. But a multivariate model, built upon a theory, and one that fits sample data that is gathered *after* the model was constructed, is considerably less likely to be a coincidence than is a mere bivariate correlation. And the presence of common causes and/or of suppressor variables can be examined and adjusted for—if we have the wit to include them in our models. My advice? Develop a model. Use sample data to test it and refine it. Then test it again using independently collected sample data. If your conclusions hold up under that second round of testing you may be justified in making decisions and taking action on the basis of those conclusions.

Causal inference is not statistical inference. Justifiable causal inference arises mainly from the quality of the design and the data and only incidentally from statistical technique. But techniques that allow one to examine the structures of relations among variables (SEM) and to study nested variables without violating regression assumptions (MLM), are huge improvements in the investigation of topics that cannot be studied experimentally. For the many possibly important causal variables not subject to manipulation by researchers, and for the many social situations that preclude random assignment to control and experimental groups, these methods do much to help us improve the quality of our causal inferences.

Having reviewed quantitative research methods from the most elementary, such as means and standard deviations through the most advanced, such as MLM and SEM, we are now prepared to examine how these are applied to particular types of research problems. This is done in Part 3. The chapters of Part 2 have focused most heavily on the analysis aspects of our three foci of design, measurement, and analysis. In Part 3 the emphasis will fall more heavily on research designs. The areas of application discussed in Part 3 are program evaluation (Chapter 15), individual assessment (Chapter 16), and synthesizing research results (Chapter 17). The full range of analysis techniques reviewed in Parts 1 and 2 reappear in the applications of Part 3.

Terms and Concepts to Review

Causal modeling
Model testing
Confirmatory factor analysis (CFA)
Path analysis
Structure
Structural model
Measurement model
Path coefficients
Indirect effects
Disturbance term
Latent variables

Measured variables
• Indicator variables
• Manifest variables

Factor loading
Correlation matrix
Covariance matrix
Recursive model
Nonrecursive model
Maximum likelihood estimation (MLE)
Goodness of fit

Discussion Questions

1. Draw a causal model (path diagram) of the relations among the variables in a research problem of interest to you. (Chapter 3 provides several examples in addition to those in this chapter.) Which of the variables in your model or path diagram would benefit from a measurement model and which would not? Why?
2. For the latent variables in your model in question 1, how would you build a measurement model? What measured variables would you use to construct your latent variables?

3. If all of the variables in one of your causal models could be measured directly—if they were variables such as age, years of experience, days absent, and salary—would you need to use the measurement model features of SEM? Why or why not?
4. Although structural equation modeling is built around the techniques of correlation and regression, researchers who use it tend, nonetheless, to make strong claims about the causal relations among variables. To what extent are those claims justifiable? Why?

Self-Test

If you can answer the following questions accurately, you can feel confident about your understanding of the material in this chapter. If not, it would be a good idea to review the chapter. (Answers can be found in the Appendix.)

1. Structural equation modeling combines path analysis and factor analysis into a new, more powerful method. True or False?
2. As with any method employing factor analysis, SEM is an exploratory method that seeks to discover patterns of relationships among variables rather than to test hypotheses about them. True or False?
3. Path analysis provides the structural component of SEM, whereas factor analysis provides its measurement component. True or False?
4. By definition, the indirect effects in a path model must always be smaller than the direct effects. True or False?

5. Latent variables in SEM are indicated by circles or ovals, whereas measured variables are indicated by squares or rectangles. True or False?
6. One of the main advantages of SEM is that it uses its measurement models to improve the reliability of the variables studied in the structural model. True or False?
7. Powerful SEM software, such as LISREL or AMOS, enables the researcher to simply enter a data file into the program and have the program generate the model that best fits the data. True or False?
8. The method most often used to estimate the coefficients in structural equation models is maximum likelihood estimation (MLE)? True or False?
9. As in any regression technique, the overall fit of the model to the data, the percentage of the variance it explains, is assessed with the R-squared statistic in SEM. True or False?

10. Levels of statistical significance have no role to play in a confirmatory method such as structural equation modeling. True or False?

11. In the overall model test of goodness of fit using the chi-squared test, the researcher hopes to obtain a nonsignificant result. True or False?

12. Because it is a correlational technique, structural equation modeling should not be used to test causal relationships among variables. True or False?

Endnotes

1. The covariance matrix is sometimes called the variance-covariance matrix. The variances are on the diagonal of the matrix. The covariances fill the other cells.

2. Most people find this terminology counterintuitive. They expect "recursive" to refer to something that repeats itself, as a feedback loop would. Unfortunately, in this context, it means just the opposite.

3. MLE is also the main estimation technique for statistical significance in logistic regression (Chapter 11) and multilevel models (see Chapter 12).

Part III

Specialized Applications

An overview of quantitative research designs, measurement considerations, and analysis techniques is provided in the first two parts of this book (Chapters 1–14). Here, in Part 3, attention is turned to specialized applications of the methods reviewed in the first two parts of the book. It is especially informative, in a book such as this one, in which the intended readers are practicing professionals, to examine how general research methods can be used to understand work in applied professional settings. Three specific applications of research methods are addressed in Part 3. First, program evaluation is considered in Chapter 15. Then, testing and individual assessment are reviewed in Chapter 16, and methods for literature reviews and meta-analyses are discussed in Chapter 17. With some exceptions, these chapters do not introduce new methods. Instead, we look at how familiar quantitative methods from the first 14 chapters can be applied to the specific problems of evaluating programs, assessing individuals, and summarizing research.

It is important to review specific applications of research, because seeing how methods can be applied, and how they have to be tailored to fit specific research problems, provides a deeper understanding of "generic" methods. We have already considered applications in Chapters 5 and 6 on survey research and experimental research. Surveys and experiments are not analytic techniques; they are categories of research design in which multiple analytic techniques are used. Surveys and experiments appear in books

such as this one more often than other applications such as evaluation and testing, but that is more a matter of tradition than logical necessity. The basic point is that we better understand any set of methods when we see how they can be applied to, and how compromises sometimes have to be made when they are addressed to, different categories of research problem.

Program evaluation is discussed in Chapter 15. Program evaluation investigates the effectiveness or impact of interventions and social programs. One engages in program evaluation research to learn which aspects of a program are working and which are not. Program evaluators sometimes give advice about how to improve a program; at other times they help to determine whether a program should be continued or terminated. But program evaluation does not use unique research methods. Instead, it mostly applies well-known methods to a specific class of problems. So why include it in a text on research methods? Because program evaluation is the single area of research application that most links researchers to professional practitioners. For example, when I ask students to think of a research topic of interest to them and discuss how they would apply a given concept or method to it, at least three-quarters of the time their examples involve program evaluation. This is true whether their field is social work, nursing, business, or education. Research methods for professionals means, if you ask the professionals, program evaluation.

The applications of research methods made by evaluators are also particularly appropriate to review because they can be quite challenging. Program evaluation is particularly interesting to methodologists, because doing it right is so very hard. It is always conducted in applied field settings in which the number of confounding variables is potentially huge. Control over the variables can be weak to nonexistent. All of the challenges of applying program evaluation make it instructive to those who would learn about research methods. Finally, because there is probably no quantitative method that has not been used by program evaluators, reviewing it provides an instructive way to think about the entire realm of quantitative research methods.

We move from evaluating programs to assessing individuals in Chapter 16, most importantly their knowledge, skills, abilities, characteristics, and traits. This means that the focus will be on measurement, specifically the reliable and valid application of measurements. Two issues confront us: constructing good tests and using them wisely. Individual assessment has become increasingly important in applied research today, in part because program evaluation has become so central, particularly in government-sponsored and - mandated programs. The link between program evaluation and individual assessment is strong. Individual assessments are now increasingly required to be a main component (sometimes the only component) of a program evaluation. For instance, federal education grants supporting school programs must usually be evaluated by assessing the learning of the children in the programs. Comparatively new techniques such as item response theory are at the heart of the quantitative side of individual assessment. These modern testing methods have been erected on a foundation of the kind of model building we have discussed in the earlier chapters of this book, particularly logistic regression models. Modern measurement methods are widely used by specialists in testing and measurement, but are generally not well understood by other members of the professional public. The chapter provides an overview that professionals can use to orient themselves to this rapidly developing area.

Meta-analysis is presented in Chapter 17. This formidable sounding technique is simply a way to systematically conduct quantitative reviews of research literature. Also called *research synthesis*, meta-analysis builds directly on a technique discussed in earlier chapters, the effect size (ES) measure. More importantly, it builds on the classic literature review, and the first half of Chapter 17 is devoted to examining that foundation. From a researcher's perspective, the point of a literature review, whether a meta-analysis or a traditional review, is to help researchers base their work on what is already known. One tries to learn from the past, including past mistakes. But meta-analysis can be even more important from a practitioner's perspective. Sometimes it leads to new findings, not merely summaries of old ones. For instance, the conclusion that there is no statistically significant difference in the effectiveness of radical mastectomy compared to the less invasive procedure known as a "lumpectomy" was first firmly established through a meta-analysis.

Reviewing of the research literature on a subject is not really a research method. It is a crucial first step before applying any research method. To improve one's chances of learning something new, one benefits from summarizing what is already known about a subject. Although the methods of constructing such summaries are usually fairly rudimentary, one has to understand highly sophisticated methods in order to read research on most topics before summarizing it, whether via a meta-analysis or using more traditional methods. In short, reviewing research literature applies a limited number of research methods, but it requires extensive knowledge of them if it is to be conducted intelligently.

Different kinds of research applications tend to have different goals and to be aimed at different audiences. It is very instructive to think about how all the general principles learned in the early chapters of this book are translated into different areas of application. Random assignment, sample size, control groups, reliability, validity, statistical inference, causal modeling, correlation, regression, and the rest can take on a new immediacy when we address how they are used in specific realms of application. That is the purpose of the third, and final, part of this book.

15

Program Evaluation

Research is undertaken for different purposes. This usually means that it is written with different readers or audiences in mind. The first 14 chapters of this book presented research methods as "all-purpose" tools, more or less universal in their use. Although this is fairly accurate, and the tools are quite flexible, they do vary in their application to research in different settings, when aiming at different goals, and as written for different audiences. For example, we will see that one thing that varies greatly as the settings, goals, and audiences differ is the nature of the challenges of objectivity in research, that is, conducting research that is fair, accurate, and free of bias. This chapter is the first of three to examine research methods, problems, and issues as they vary when applied to different ends and end users. We begin with research designed to evaluate programs.

Evaluation and *assessment* are sometimes used interchangeably, but there is a handy distinction. *Evaluation* usually means *program* evaluation, and *assessment* usually refers to assessment *of individuals.* Of course, the two are very closely linked, because the increasingly preferred method to evaluate programs is to assess the individuals who have been in the programs to see how the programs have affected them. In any case, program evaluation involves various methods of investigating the efficiency, effectiveness, and/or impact of organized interventions meant to bring about change. Organized interventions, or programs, can vary greatly in pur-

pose and scope. Naturally, the research methods used to evaluate them will vary accordingly.

Understanding evaluation research does not involve learning new techniques in research design, measurement, or analysis. Rather, *evaluation research* applies techniques already discussed in this book, but it does so in the context of specific purposes and audiences. Evaluations can be done using surveys, experiments, interviews, observations, or examination of documents and records. Methods of quantitative analysis of evaluation data can include descriptive, associational, or inferential statistics. Some evaluations might compare group means with a *t*-test. Others might use regression to measure outcomes while controlling for confounding variables. What makes evaluation research distinct is the problems to which these familiar techniques are applied, the goals of the research, and the audiences for whom the research reports are written. If your primary audience is a group of research specialists, you will write differently than if your main audience is decision makers, a policy board, or legislators trying to determine whether to expand, continue, revise, or terminate a program.

A final distinguishing characteristic of evaluation research is that evaluation studies can be much harder to conduct than most other kinds of research, for two reasons. First, evaluation researchers tend to have less control over the variables and, second, research is rarely the main purpose or goal of

TABLE 15.1   *Kinds of Research Categorized by the Goals of and Audiences for the Research*

Goals	Typical Questions Answered	Common Audience
1. Basic	How do things work?	Other researchers
2. Policy	What should we do?	Policy makers
3. Applied	How should we do it?	Policy implementers
4. Evaluation	How well did we do it?	Program officers
5. Action	How can we best promote our cause?	Oneself

the program being evaluated. Typically a program has been created according to some design of what people think will work to help solve a problem. In a researcher's eyes, the problem the program addresses is the dependent variable, and the program's components are the independent variables. Thus the key components of the research design have usually been decided before the evaluation researcher arrives on the scene. Usually, for most program implementers, evaluation is an afterthought or, sometimes, a dangerous intrusion into the work of the program. Program personnel are likely to believe that evaluations use resources that could better be devoted to doing the work of the program.

Different Goals and Audiences for Research

Understanding evaluation research is aided by seeing how it compares to other general types of research, as defined by their goals and audiences. Table 15.1 lists five types: basic, policy, applied, evaluation, and action. Listed next to each type is a central question it asks and, following that, an audience to whom the research report is often directed. These are not hard-and-fast distinctions. Rather they are tendencies, but they do help capture important differences of emphasis among how researchers conduct their work, the aims of their investigations, and the uses for which the research is intend.

Basic research is sometimes called *pure* in the sense that it is research "for its own sake." If basic research is defined strictly as work that is exclusively

for its own sake, then it is a very small category in the social sciences, and it is an even smaller category in applied fields such as education, business, or medicine. Basic research is also sometimes called *theoretical*, mostly to distinguish it from the other four categories of research listed in the table, all of which have some practical aim. It is hard to think of much social science research that is truly pure, that is, that has no practical applications or envisions no practical applications. Furthermore, it is often claimed that "pure" research is *ultimately* the most practical. The really big discoveries, the ones that have led in the long run to cures for disease or to amazing technological advances, have been disproportionately based, so the argument goes, on the efforts of pure, theoretical researchers. At minimum, basic research tends to be "practical" in the sense that most people who do it expect to get something out of their work: It might be a promotion; it might be recognition; but research is rarely conducted exclusively for private pleasure, to satisfy the researcher's idle curiosity.

Another criterion used to distinguish basic research from the other types, at least ideally, is that it is *value free,* or objective. There probably can be no such thing as completely objective, value-free social science research. But different degrees of objectivity are obvious to readers of research reports. Objectivity is a difficult and distant goal, but one that can be approached. I for one would not conclude, as some have, that our research findings are *only* expressions of our values. If that's all there were to it, research would be a waste of time. It may be most accurate to conclude, as Max Weber did a century ago, that to engage in basic research is not to be value free; rather, it is to set the values of science above other values, such as political, social, ethnic, and religious values. Most textbooks in quantitative methods are written as though basic research were everyone's goal and other researchers were always the intended audience. This is not likely to be true for the professionals and future professionals who are the intended audience of this book.

Policy research is directed toward deciding what to do. It is often conducted by people working for agencies, such as the World Bank, the Council of Economic Advisors, state education departments, and so on. Much policy research is done by economists and political scientists. Questions of objectivity bedevil this kind of research much more than basic research. Do policy makers pay attention to policy research if it does not agree with what they already wanted to do? Can a researcher—following the rules of evidence and good reasoning about evidence—truly make an *objective* contribution to decisions about what to do? One typical answer is to claim that researchers and policy makers operate in different worlds, that researchers are from Venus and policy makers are from Mars, by which Birnbaum (2000) means that they engage in different kinds of work with different agendas. Rather than researchers trying to answer specific policy questions or policy makers hiring researchers to work on specific issues, they should each "do their own thing," which can eventually have a positive effect. "What is important is not that individual studies affect individual decisions, but that scholarly work over time influences the systems of knowledge and belief that give meaning to policy" (Birnbaum, 2000, 127). Policy decisions are hardly ever made solely on the basis of research findings, and one could even argue that in a democracy, they shouldn't be. But research commissioned by public and private agencies increasingly tends to inform debate about policy and probably sometimes improves the quality of decisions.

Applied research focuses on how to accomplish goals once the goals have been determined, perhaps by policy research. Many famous social scientists (Max Weber and Herbert Simon among the most noteworthy) have said that although one cannot

scientifically determine goals or ends—which means that *policy* research is inherently unscientific—one *can* scientifically investigate the means for achieving particular ends. The key is *if–then* reasoning. *If* this is your goal, *then* here are some likely consequences of pursuing it using these means. But even research on means or methods of achieving goals is not easy. Take the example of how to invest in the stock market. The end or goal is clear: Make more money. There has probably been more well-funded research done by social scientists and "rocket scientists" (Derman 2004) on this subject than on any other topic. And the problem seems simple as compared to many others that social scientists pursue. The outcome variable is easily measured (in dollars or other currency). The categories of outcome are simple: Stock prices can go up, down, or stay the same. And the range of choices meant to influence outcomes is also quite small; one can buy, sell, or hold. Yet, despite this apparent simplicity and notwithstanding the easily operationalized variables, the results have been remarkably disappointing. Conclusions have been based as much on faith or "irrational exuberance," as on evidence (Shiller, 2000). Occasionally some of us are "fooled by randomness" (Taleb, 2001) into believing that this or that stock analyst has discovered the secret to how the market works, but the evidence is thin to say the least. In short, focusing on means rather than ends does not simplify the problem of producing useful knowledge quite as much as is sometimes claimed.

Both applied and policy research investigations are sometimes pursued by methods based more on a theoretical approach rather than on gathering evidence. The general theoretical approach is most often called *rational choice theory,* but other terms, such as *decision analysis* are also common. The idea is to state some postulates and then *deduce* conclusions. Two general categories of such studies exist. The *normative type,* most favored by economists and political scientists, focuses on what you *should* do if you want to make a good decision—"good" meaning helping you get to your goals. Through careful thinking and elaborate mathematical modeling, economists and game theorists have identified rules of decision making that they claim no sane person would willingly violate, especially if the stakes were high (Becker, 1993). By contrast with the normative variety of decision research, the *descriptive type* is often experimental and examines how people actually make their decisions. Sometimes they make them rationally, as they "should" or are expected to according to the normative theory, but often they do not (Kahneman & Tversky, 2000). The implications of patterns of departures from rational choice may then form the basis of revised theories, which might be used to guide further policy and applied research.

Action research can best be thought of as applied research directed toward furthering one's personal goals. Of the forms of research discussed here, action research is most difficult to generalize about, because there is no set of commonly accepted practices. The term was probably invented by Kurt Lewin in the 1940s (Lewin, 1946), who also gave us two of the most famous social science quotations related to the goals of action research: "Nothing is as practical as a good theory," and "the best way to understand something is to try to change it." Action research is often undertaken by practitioners (psychologists, teachers, social workers) to investigate ways to improve their own practice. Thus the researchers often are their own audience in the narrowest sense of the term.

Generalizability or external validity is not typically a big concern for this type of action researcher, that is, the kind who wants to try out a procedure to see whether something can be learned that would improve actions in a given area. From another perspective, although action researchers may not be interested in generalizing their own research to other settings, they are sometimes led to undertake their research projects because they do not trust the generalizability of the research of others. It is easy to imagine someone saying: "I know there are 10 or 12 studies of program X that indicate that it is likely to be effective, but I won't believe it will be effective *here* until we test it out *here*. We *may* be like those other places in which it seems to have worked, but we may not." It is certainly easy to understand this kind of practitioner caution.

People who have been educated according to the methods of basic research, which is the most common standard in courses and textbooks, tend to be uncomfortable with action research. It often looks to them as though action researchers already "know" the answer before they gather the evidence. And action research is most often written up as case histories, which are frequently criticized as merely anecdotal. Because action research usually focuses on gathering local data to improve local practice, it is not often concerned with external validity and, consequently, the precautions usually taken to ensure external validity are usually absent. Finally, there is the "cheerleading" problem. Action researchers tend to be committed advocates for particular practices or programs, and they sometimes may find objectivity a difficult or even an objectionable standard. In my experience, students taking an action research approach to doing their doctoral dissertations have the greatest problems with objectivity—or the greatest problems persuading their dissertation committees that their conclusions rest on something beyond their personal opinions. One does not have to be uninvolved to be objective, but passionate commitment to a particular goal makes viewing it objectively very hard for most people. This quick review of the problems and criticisms of basic, policy, applied, and action research has set the stage for our consideration of program evaluation research.

Problems and Criticisms of Evaluation Research

All of the criticisms of action research just discussed have also been leveled at evaluation research: It is anecdotal, narrowly local, and unconcerned with external validity, and it has major problems with objectivity. Indeed, thinking about all forms of research other than basic research raises common themes and issues. Clearly, policy, applied, action, and evaluation research can be mutually supportive. Evaluation research and policy research are especially likely to be closely linked. Policy makers often commission evaluations in order to determine what sorts of programs were most effective so as to decide what ought to be done next (Gueron, 1997). Of course, the results of evaluation research are only one of the determinants of policy. If voters like a program the fact that evaluations show it to be ineffective might be far from decisive, to say the least. For example, despite rigorous evaluations—by the Surgeon General and the National Academy of Sciences—showing that children who participate in the DARE program in elementary school are just as likely to use drugs later in life as children who do not participate (Zernike, 2001), this program continues to be very popular and receive substantial funding.

Of the main forms of research, evaluation is the most likely to be contractual research. The researcher is hired for a specific purpose. That means that evaluators almost inevitably cede to their employers the right to set the research topics, choose the methods, and define what counts as important. The broad elements of the design, though usually not the details, are taken out of the evaluators' hands. This unusual relationship between the researchers and their "subjects" leads to a major reason objectivity is difficult in evaluation research: The researchers' subjects may also be their employers. The researchers' contract extension might even depend on the program getting a good evaluation, because a bad evaluation might lead to the elimination of the program. Objectivity is difficult enough in research in which investigators are not entangled in policy decisions; it becomes doubly so in policy research tied to evaluation research in which a negative evaluation may offend or abolish one's employer. These difficulties make objectivity all the more precious for being rare.

Related to the researchers' lack of control over the variables is their lack of control over the pace of the investigation. I have often found the power of deadlines to be overwhelming in evaluation research. By contrast, when I have conducted basic research intended for publication in a journal read mostly by other researchers, I have usually continued with the work until I was sure the research and my report of it were as good as I could make them. It might take a year—or three or four—but I'd hold onto the work until I was pretty sure I had it right. But, in evaluation research, strict deadlines are common. The evaluation might have to be finished by the required date

set by the funding agency or by the end of the fiscal year. Deadlines mean that evaluation researchers have to design their projects to be completed in the time allowed. In my experience, a deadline can be quite refreshing. Otherwise I might linger over an interesting problem long past the point of diminishing returns. But, I've also been faced with quite literally impossible tasks as an evaluator and been reduced to employing designs that in any other context I would have rejected as too flawed to even consider. And I am not alone in this.

The converse of the short-deadline problem in evaluation research is the long-term program problem. Evaluation research is usually "before-and-after" research, and studies occur over an extended time. All research takes time, but program evaluations can extend over the life of a program, which can be years or decades long. Evaluation research studying long-term programs is often complicated by outside events that intervene and influence the results. A previous chapter discussed this problem as the *history threat* to the validity of research. So, paradoxically, sometimes evaluation researchers are confronted with an uncommon pair of difficulties: Deadlines that are too short to do a good job are combined with programs that are so long that history threat is a major worry. One situation in which these problems are especially likely to be conjoined is when the program plan does not include an evaluation plan at the outset. Rather, people managing the program remember, or are reminded, about doing an evaluation when it is "too late." Last-minute evaluations are especially likely to be too late to obtain *baseline data*—that is, a *before* to compare to an *after*. Equally likely, when evaluation is an afterthought, it is usually too late to establish a *control group* to compare to those who received the program's services.

Some of the problems and strengths of evaluation research have to do with its origins in and its continuing links with government-sponsored programs. Evaluation research got its beginnings mostly as a consequence of government activism. For the past several decades, all educational and social service programs receiving federal funds have had to undergo formal evaluations. Thus as federal funding has expanded, so too has evaluation. In the last decade or so, the standards for program evaluation, especially for federally funded programs, have been raised considerably. The turning point was the Government Performance and Results Act (GPRA) of 1993. In this legislation Congress required federal agencies to evaluate their work. The idea was that evaluations would lead to improved programs and would help to justify continued funding. In the words of the act, a program evaluation is "an assessment, through objective measurement and systematic analysis, of the manner and extent to which federal programs achieve intended objectives" (U.S. Congress, 1993). This law and its subsequent interpretations by government agencies have greatly increased the emphasis put on *outcomes* as the means to judge the effectiveness of programs.

Process and Outcome: Formative and Summative Evaluations

Two questions need to be addressed in most evaluations in order for them to be useful for program improvement, accountability, and decision/making Both are very important: (1) What did the recipients of the grant do? Or, what were their *processes*? (2) What were the effects of doing what they did? Or, what were their *outcomes*? Information about processes and about outcomes are both necessary. Neither is sufficient (Mohr, 1995). Despite the GPRA, most evaluations in education tend to be much stronger in their review of processes than in their collection of evidence about outcomes. This overemphasis on processes and underemphasis on outcomes reduces the value of evaluations. A main trend, perhaps *the* main trend, in contemporary evaluation work is the insistence that outcomes be clearly defined and that evidence be systematically gathered about them. Related to that emphasis is a growing belief in the importance of *measurable* outcomes. More generally, the question is: How can we be better informed about whether programs are accomplishing their goals? In the absence of objective indicators of outcomes, there is no standard against which to measure a program's achievement and no way to distinguish success from failure.

Information about processes, which evaluation reports have traditionally supplied in abundance, continues to be crucially important. If one wants to learn from an evaluation, it does little good to have evidence *that* a program achieved some of its goals without also knowing, and in some considerable detail, *how* it did so. If we want to build on success and learn how to avoid problems, we need, in roughly equal parts, information about both processes and outcomes.

The categories of *process* and *outcome* are closely related to a widespread division of labor in evaluation research between *formative* and *summative* evaluation studies. Summative evaluations are similar to external audits; they focus on the program's product or final outcomes and are conducted at the end of a project or program cycle. In short, summative evaluations are focused on outcomes. By contrast, formative evaluations concentrate on processes. These investigations are done in the early and middle stages of a program. They focus on the intermediate steps in the program's interventions. The idea is to learn how to reform or fine-tune the program to make it work better. When doing this kind of research, evaluators are supposed to help programs, not only to judge them.[1]

As discussed earlier, all research methods can be and have been used in evaluation studies. That is why evaluation is more defined by the purpose of the research or the audiences for the research than by any particular methods. Often, evaluation manuals will be context-specific, for example, "how to evaluate the use of technology in schools" (Quinones & Kirshstein, 1998). Focusing on purposes, audiences, and contexts does not simplify description of evaluation research, because the purposes for which evaluation research are undertaken and the audiences to which it is addressed are multifarious indeed. Program evaluations may try to do many things. They tend to occur in stages, which can be thought of as a program's *life cycle*.

A Program's Life Cycle

Thinking in terms of the life cycle of a program, the typical stages of a project, helps situate project evaluation, which tends to follow those stages. The main purposes of evaluation research and the main activities, in rough chronological order, are as follows.

- Evaluations help program implementers to judge whether the program's objectives are aimed at the problem. Does the new program to bring services to an underserved area focus on the most pressing problems there?
- Evaluators often assess whether the program is being implemented as specified. Are the implementers of the program doing what the writers of the proposal promised they would do? If not, are the changes clearly designed to further the goals of the program?
- Evaluators also sometimes help participants gain a clearer understanding of what they are doing. Do the official goals of the project match the actions of those implementing it? Are members of the implementation team all "on the same page"?
- Sometimes evaluation research uncovers unintended consequences (positive or negative) of the program. Does the graduation exam lead to higher dropout rates?
- Evaluators are sometimes expected to gather data to assist managers to make decisions about aspects of the program, often about how to allocate resources among the program's components.
- Evaluators usually offer suggestions about how to improve programs. Only when they are conducting a final "audit" of a completed program do evaluators have little to say about how to improve programs. In short, nearly all evaluation is formative.
- Evaluators try to measure the program's success at achieving its objectives. This is sometimes called *effectiveness*. This work, and that described in the next two points, is often thought of as the heart of evaluation.
- Evaluators sometimes measure outcomes per unit of cost. In contrast to effectiveness, this is called *efficiency*. The question is not only whether the program achieved its goals but also whether it did so at a reasonable cost. For example, how great was the cost per graduate?

Were otherwise similarly effective programs more economical (efficient)?
- Finally, evaluators help make decisions about whether to continue or renew funding. They do not often make such decisions themselves. Rather they write reports that officials in charge use to inform their decisions.

This list makes it clear that there are very different kinds of evaluation. Naturally, different types of people will be concerned about the results of the various stages of the evaluations. These groups are often called, in the jargon of evaluation research, *stakeholders*. A stakeholder is anyone who is interested in and/or may be affected by the findings of an evaluation. This would include persons receiving the services, persons delivering the services, program managers who want to improve the services, and external funders who want to know that they are getting value for money.

One final type of stakeholder group, at least potentially, is composed of basic researchers. Mark Lipsey, whose work we will encounter again in Chapter 17 on meta-analysis, makes a persuasive case that thousands of program evaluations constitute building blocks out of which something of more general relevance could be built. Using the techniques of meta-analysis, it should be possible to move from particular studies of how specific program interventions worked to a general theory of social intervention. The idea of such an intervention theory would be "to describe...common forms and processes in ways that reveal which differences are important and which are not" (Lipsey, 1997, p. 9). But, because of the high degree of specialization common in research, with basic researchers having little interest in evaluations and vice versa, the potentially rich data source constituted by thousands of program evaluations will probably not be exploited to the extent it could be.

Twenty Concluding Tips

As noted earlier, this chapter is unique in this book in that it introduces no new research designs, measurements, or analyses. Rather, it examines how investigators have used the familiar research tool kit to work on a particular type of problem in a particular type of context. Appropriately, the conclusion to this chapter is also distinct as compared to the other chapter conclusions in this book. It consists of a series of recommendations—rules of thumb, tricks of the trade. Like the rest of this chapter, the list takes research methods out of a somewhat idealized world and moves them into the less tidy world of applying research to practice in context. Hence, the following tricks of the trade. And, evaluation research is a "trade." It is one of the few commercially viable means researchers in the social and behavioral sciences have of making a living in a "business" context. Many, perhaps most, evaluation researchers are salaried professionals, but evaluation research is probably one of the few types of research in which a substantial proportion of the investigators are fee-for-service professionals (others include survey research and statistical consulting). At any rate, here are 20 tips for working with clients, customers, or stakeholders on program evaluations.

1. For an outside evaluator, a key early task is to convince program practitioners that they have a vested interest in a frank, objective appraisal of the strengths and weaknesses of their programs. Many program implementers have to be persuaded of the wisdom of the old rule that "in order to do better you'd better know how well you're doing."

2. If you are an evaluator working with strangers, some clear understandings about the evaluation work are crucial. Is it to be formative or summative or both? Are the clients really interested in your assessment of their program or are they expecting you, because you work for them after all, to be an advocate? Sorting this out might require an awkward discussion early in the course of establishing a relationship with a client, but it is worse to put it off. You need to ask about how much professional judgment you will be able to exercise and how much independence you will have. And you need to decide before you begin which answers you will be comfortable with. For example, would you be willing to be an advocate? For a mediocre program?

3. Tie the evaluation work to the research literature in the field. Programs should have been designed and

built on knowledge gleaned from research findings. And knowledge gathered about program effectiveness in the final evaluation can be used to expand and revise that research knowledge. In other terms, a good review of the literature, including a meta-analysis when appropriate (see Chapter 17), is as important for a program evaluation as for any other form of research.

4. Try to "get in on the ground floor." My most satisfying evaluation work has occurred when I was part of the team designing the program. This made it easy to plan for better evaluations, which were more useful for program participants (formative) and external funders (summative). Integrating evaluation into the design from the beginning helps program implementers focus on the need for evaluation and increases the likelihood that sufficient resources will be devoted to conducting the evaluation.

5. Always include objective performance indicators that are clearly related to the intended outcomes of the project. At least some of these performance indicators should be in the form of quantitative measures.

A note for educators: It is extremely ill-advised, for example, to "blow off" the demand for objective data on student achievement. The politicians funding large projects increasingly require this, and there is an unusual degree of consensus among politicians of various stripes that nothing will substitute for such data. If satisfying this demand means, as it often will, using standardized test scores of greater reliability than validity, so be it. It is far better to be in the position of explaining the limitations of conclusions drawn from such data than it is to have no data to explain. One really shouldn't expect to get by with a few dismissive remarks about standardized tests and try to compensate for the lack of quantitative indicators by pointing to a pile of portfolios. Portfolios tend to be strong on descriptive validity but weak on reliability, whereas the opposite is true of standardized tests. A good evaluation system will incorporate the strengths of each.

6. When the final outcomes data are not easily available, evaluators can at least collect data on intermediate outcomes, that is, steps in the direction of the ultimate outcomes. For example, in one program designed to enable and encourage students to transfer from two-year to four-year colleges, when data on transfers were not immediately available, the program used indirect indicators, including an increase in the number of students who requested that their transcripts be sent to baccalaureate institutions. Note that intermediate outcomes are outcomes, and citing them is not the same thing as the common practice of defining "success" merely as making an effort or by asking participants whether they felt good about the program. The key difference in this example is that although requesting a transcript does not guarantee transfer, it is a *necessary* step in that direction.

7. When outcomes data are difficult to access, one alternative, especially in the short run, is to study more easily available data about mediating variables that the research literature strongly indicates lead to the outcomes of interest. For instance, increased student attendance, because it tends to increase opportunities to learn and time on task, is usually associated with increased student achievement. Thus, a program could use attendance rate as a proxy measure for achievement—at least temporarily. Indeed, attendance might be a desirable outcome even apart from its influence on achievement. The search for such mediators and proxies is time well spent.

8. An emphasis on objective outcome indicators is not to say that all programs in the same category must aim for identical outcomes or identical means of assessing them. Flexibility within a category of programs can be a strength. Even less does it make sense to say that all programs have to use the same processes to achieve their outcomes. Given the parameters of a grant program, individual grants will naturally have similar outcomes measured in similar ways. But it is less expected they will all employ identical means, or even means of evaluation, because here is where experimentation can lead to learning about what is an effective program process (Cook et al., 1992). Useful evaluations must attend to inputs and processes, for these are the causal links in the chain of events that lead to program outcomes.

9. For similar reasons, it must be stressed that outcome measures need not all be quantitative. Even

when one does use quantitative summaries, one needs also to employ qualitative interpretations to make sense of them. As long as they are reliable, replicable outcomes, whether they should be quantitative, qualitative, or a mix of the two is a decision that ought to be made on the basis of the nature of the program—not on an ideological position emerging from the War of the Quants and the Quals.

10. For larger projects, external evaluations should often be combined with internal evaluations, which are now the standard practice for most grants. There is a natural division of labor between these: Internal evaluations tend to be process oriented and formative, and external evaluations tend to be outcomes oriented and summative. This is *not* to suggest replacing internal with external evaluations. This would be to "throw out the baby with the bathwater" and lose the rich knowledge about processes that program insiders are so often able and eager to provide. Qualitative, narrative research about how the program was implemented is crucial for producing knowledge of the contextual variables (e.g., local politics) that facilitated and/or restricted program implementation. Without this contextual knowledge, others thinking about following the program's lead will not know whether what was learned might apply or how to make it apply in their context.

11. A corollary to the importance of obtaining outcomes data is the fundamental importance of collecting baseline data—particularly, of course, when the goal of the program is to increase the incidence of a desirable outcome or improve a rate. It is obviously impossible to measure improvement without having a standard of comparison. You can't tell how far you've gone unless you know where you started. If you don't check your odometer before you leave, you won't know the length of your trip. Baseline data will not be appropriate for some programs, but it will be for most. One of the most important things evaluation researchers do is remind program implementers of this fact.

12. Whether the evaluation work is formative or summative, internal or external, an attitude of *instructive helpfulness* is often an appropriate one for an evaluator to strike. Sometimes evaluators are familiar with many programs and can offer useful advice. For example, many less experienced program personnel whose programs are supported by grants would find it very worthwhile to learn what veteran grant writers usually know: It is much easier to obtain subsequent funding if your previous efforts have been rigorously evaluated and have resulted in persuasive outcomes data. Collecting outcomes data can be an investment in the future. For example, today's outcomes data can be tomorrow's baseline data on which to build subsequent requests for funding.

13. Collecting useful outcomes data can be demanding. For example, comparison group data is almost always crucial, but it is not easy to obtain. The temptation to omit comparison group data and use a simple pre–post design should be resisted; this is a weak design, and it is especially weak for evaluating a long-term program. Comparisons of different implementations are often highly informative. But comparing different implementations does not eliminate the need for control groups. For example, if one is measuring the effects of a teacher education program and is using student learning as the outcome variable, a persuasive evaluation will require comparing the achievement gains of the students taught by teachers who participated in the program with those who did not. Teachers' unions will sometimes resist this. That puts those who commissioned the evaluation in the position of deciding which they value more: avoiding trouble with the union or obtaining a high-quality evaluation. Evaluators would naturally have a preference, but the decision is not usually theirs.

14. Systematic use of the evidence and findings of other researchers can be very helpful for comparison group data. If evaluators cannot compare program effects to a true control group, they can sometimes compare program outcomes to outcomes in the research literature. Finding "virtual" control groups can provide key evidence in evaluations of programs for which comparison/control group data are not available.

15. The unit of analysis should usually be individuals served by the program. When evidence of client improvement is needed or when evidence of student achievement is required, the data should be collected at the individual client or student level. Aggregate data introduces measurement error. For example, school-level data might be appropriate when programs aim to change entire schools, and classroom-level data can be useable if the membership of the classes is relatively constant. But generally, when one is interested in individual outcomes, one needs information about individuals, not group averages. Of course, programs are often reluctant to release records about individuals, usually citing privacy concerns. It should not be too difficult to address these concerns by using identity codes.

16. The cost of evaluating a project increases with its complexity, probably even more than the cost of evaluation increases with its size as measured by overall budget. Complex programs, with long causal chains and/or many partners, naturally require more effort to evaluate. How much more? Any numbers would be crude estimates, but it is almost certain that the percentage of the budget for evaluation will be more than the program wants to spend, especially after people involved with delivering the program find that the funding wasn't as full as expected and that delivery of the project's programs will be more costly than was initially estimated.

17. In a large, complex project, it is better to concentrate centrally a considerable portion (perhaps half) of the evaluation resources. It is not wise to diffuse them over the project elements. The evaluation process requires both knowledge of the "local" units and central direction of the entire process. Meetings of the subproject evaluators will usually not be enough to achieve this overall coordination. These unit representatives will often be deeply involved in other work and "paid" for their efforts, if at all, with small amounts of reassigned time. Without substantial central coordination of the necessarily limited efforts of local unit team members, accomplishments of the evaluation group might be disappointingly few.

18. Consistent staffing of the evaluation group is important. Large, complex programs often have high turnover rates of project personnel. The more complex the project, the harder it is for new staffers to get up to speed, especially as the project tends to be a moving target. If evaluation is to be a significant goal of the program, then resources and personnel need to be precisely identified earlier rather than later in the process. Evaluation personnel need to be established project members, not merely temporary consultants.

19. Completeness in an evaluation, as in any research, is, of course, an impossible standard. Thus the evaluators will need to devote considerable attention to the question: How shall we be incomplete? Which project goals and outcomes will be rigorously researched and which will be covered lightly and more impressionistically? Evaluators need to decide which parts of the causal chain are crucial to achieving the project's goals so as to conduct interim, formative evaluations of those. These decisions are in part made by interpreting of the requirements of the funding agency, but they are also and more importantly made by bargaining.

Who should be at the table when such bargaining occurs? One answer—the expansive, inclusive, democratic answer—is any and all stakeholders. This can be a recipe for never deciding, for never paring down the list of matters to be investigated. Regardless of how unwieldy the list of potential stakeholders in a publically funded project, someone will always think of another group that has been left off the list. And, in my experience, it is very rare for it to be decided at evaluation meetings that "no, actually, that group isn't important enough to be included." The list of evaluation decision makers and bargainers needs to include all groups who are *actively and substantially* involved in implementing parts of the program. In a complex partnership program, this will be a formidably long list. Adding to it unnecessarily can dramatically increase the slowness of the decision process, sometimes to the point of immobility.

20. Most textbooks do not even imagine attempting to evaluate programs as complex as the majority of those with which I have been involved. And I do not believe my experience is wildly atypical. If one

took seriously the recommended rules of procedure in even the best of such texts (e.g., Mohr, 1995), most evaluators of complex projects would despair of ever coming to any reasonable conclusions. But evaluations need to be undertaken, if for no other reason than to satisfy the legitimate demands of funding agencies. And funders do seem able to judge complex programs somewhat effectively, to say that some programs are doing better at accomplishing their objectives than others.

Program Advocates, Researchers, and Implementers

What kind of evaluation leads to (at least partly) valid judgments? I think what is in fact used, and perhaps what should be used in many circumstances, is what I call *advocacy controlled by the rules of evidence* (ACRE). Evaluators make the best case for the programs they evaluate, but it is a case based on evidence, publicly available evidence, and on recognized rules of inference from evidence. As with the cases made by the prosecution and the defense in legal trials, juries, using advocacy-based evidence, can often make good (not to say perfectly accurate) decisions. Adjudicating program evaluations may operate at a slightly "higher" level than the typical jury trial. More technical expertise may be available to people more knowledgeable about how to weigh it, but the process is not fundamentally different. In our current state of knowledge, or in any likely future state of knowledge, we probably can do no better.

Program implementers and program evaluation researchers have similar *long-term* goals. They both wish to use knowledge to improve practice. But they usually have different *short-term* goals and tactics. Their natural long-term unity is impaired by short-term tensions. Program implementers tend to focus on the delivery of services. Program evaluation researchers tend to be more interested in acquiring knowledge about how to deliver services. It is hard to do both well—simultaneously. Part of the reason that it is hard to deliver and study the delivery of services at the same time is that good *program* design may not be compatible with good *evaluation* design. Experiments are usually touted as the gold standard for evaluation designs, but experiments and random assignment of subjects are often not a good way to deliver services. Flexibility and the opportunity for professionals to exercise their judgment are often crucial for effective program implementation. But such flexibility adds up to not sticking to the protocol. It often ruins the research. Flexibility generates confounding variables.

Almost everyone agrees that evaluation is important. It's hard to know how to do better if you really don't know how well you are doing. Learning how to reduce the short-term tensions and better achieve the long-term goals on which we are largely agreed will benefit both program implementers and evaluators, and thereby the people being served by the programs, which, of course, is the whole point.

Educational program evaluation is an interesting case because it is very public and recent changes have come about as a result of national politics (see Chapter 16). Educational program evaluation is still largely in a state of development comparable to evaluations in the Food and Drug Administration before the 1970s when the thalidomide scare led to reforms.[2] Imagine, for example, what it would be like if antibiotics were developed and dispensed as many education programs are. Different groups of researchers and practitioners could create, often in ignorance of one another, many ostensibly different treatments for infections. Some of the medicines would be very similar, but they would have different brand names. Advocates of particular medicines might have a vested interest in stressing differences that weren't

very important. Others might try to ignore differences among diseases that were important. This chaos in the production and use of medicine would have negative consequences for treatment of illness. Medical practitioners would have limited knowledge about how *specific* antibiotics worked against *particular* types of infection or which worked best with different kinds of patients. Many antibiotics work *to some extent* on many different infections; and often any of several antibiotics can reduce the dangers of an infection. But for particular diseases, some antibiotics work much better than others, and no medicine works equally well on everything and for everyone. If antibiotics were developed as most education programs are, patients might not have much confidence in the medical profession, because the average treatment effects would tend to be small. Because effective and ineffective treatments would be administered almost hit or miss, successes and failures could come close to canceling one another out on average.

Most education programs in the United States today are not effectively evaluated. This remains true despite the accountability movement that culminated in 2001 with the No Child Left Behind Act. The key feature of that act is using standardized test scores to judge whether schools, teachers, and students have "met standards." This is not the same as a program evaluation, because it gathers *no evidence* about programs, only about outcomes. Nonetheless, educational evaluations increasingly use student scores on standardized tests as their ultimate outcome variable. That means that the quality of evaluations is importantly shaped by the techniques, reliability, and validity of standardized tests. This is the subject of our next chapter.

Terms and Concepts to Review

Basic research
Policy research
Applied research
Evaluation research
Action research
Objectivity
Processes

Outcomes
Formative evaluation
Summative evaluation
(Cost) efficiency
Effectiveness
Stakeholders

Discussion Questions

1. Think of a program you know about and how it could be evaluated. Your first question is: What general design would you use (survey research, quasi-experiment, documents analysis, etc.) and why? How would the design you chose be better to evaluate the program than others?

2. Using the same program and design as in question 1, discuss what evidence or data you would gather. How would you decide what evidence would be most pertinent to your program evaluation? Assuming that you did not have enough time (you never do) to gather all evidence that could possibly be relevant, how would you decide to rank the importance of the evidence so that you gathered the most important evidence first?

3. From whom would you gather the data—clients/customers, program officers, those who implement the program on a day-to-day basis, members of the community? How would you make this decision?

4. What kind(s) of data would you gather and how would you make this decision?

5. Imagine that you were working in the program you have been using for questions 1–4. While you are partly responsible for program evaluation, you are also helping to implement the program. What would you do if, in the course of your preliminary evaluation work, you concluded that some aspect of the program were badly flawed?

Self-Test

If you can answer most of the following questions accurately, you can feel confident about your understanding of the material in this chapter. If not, it would be a good idea to review the chapter. (Answers can be found in the Appendix.)

1. Investigators conducting evaluation research have had to develop many new statistical and methodological techniques. True or False?

2. Basic research is distinguished from other types of investigation mostly by the extent to which its audience is composed mainly of researchers. True or False?

3. Program evaluation research is more likely than other kinds of research to be contractual; that is, researchers are hired to conduct a specific piece of research in a certain way by a given deadline. True or False?

4. Traditionally, program evaluation research in education has focused on processes much more than on outcomes. True or False?

5. Formative evaluations tend to focus on processes whereas summative evaluations are concerned mainly with outcomes. True or False?

6. Outcomes data are important for determining whether a program attained its goals; process data are important for determining how it did so (or why it failed to do so). True or False?

7. Processes can be thought of as mediating variables that link program interventions with program outcomes. True or False?

8. Program implementers and program evaluators often have conflicting short-term goals because the best design for an effective program evaluation is often not the best design for program implementation. True or False?

9. Most educational policies, programs, and institutions in the United States are not effectively evaluated. True or False?

10. The accountability movement as evinced in the NCLB Act cannot be said to mandate program evaluations, because it collects no evidence about programs. True or False?

Endnotes

1. Some people working in the field think the term *evaluation* refers to work that is mostly summative. For those colleagues, the term *assessment research* focuses on formative issues. The labels do not matter as long as the concepts remain clear.

2. The first randomized clinical trial of a drug was probably a test of the use of streptomycin for tuberculosis. The results were published in the *British Medical Journal* in 1948.

16

Test Item Analysis, Individual Assessment, and Accountability

This chapter moves from evaluating the performance of programs to assessing the performance of individuals—and back again. The two subjects are closely tied, because assessments of the performance of individuals are often used to evaluate the performance of programs and institutions, such as schools or hospitals. As with the other chapters in Part 3, our emphasis is on seeing how methods reviewed in Parts 1 and 2 are applied to particular realms of professional practice.

The subject of this chapter has two main parts: (1) the construction of valid and reliable tests and (2) the fair and intelligent use of tests for institutional accountability. Although they are closely linked in practice, the two aspects of our subject are very different. The methods of constructing and scoring tests, and of testing the tests for reliability and validity, are quite intricate and require considerable statistical background. Controversies are not absent from this first, more technical, part of our subject, but they are minor in comparison to the political battles that occur over the *appropriate use* of individual assessments, especially in the context of education. Employment tests are another area in which controversies abound. However, because tests for selecting personnel are less in the public eye, and are less thoroughly re-

searched, educational testing will be used for the main examples in this chapter. Questions about appropriate use in education concern whether and how to hold schools, teachers, and administrators accountable for student learning. This is the essence of the standards and accountability movement, which is probably the most important political development in U.S. education in the last decade. It is likely to remain important for several more years, at least. Hence, questions concerning the proper use of tests are of great *practical* significance. (By contrast, *statistical* significance almost never comes up.)

We will start out with the technical and somewhat less contested aspects of the subject. A brief overview of test theory will provide insight into the very specialized world of measuring tests' reliability and validity and assessing individuals' knowledge, skills, and abilities. Then we will look at the uses of tests and measurements to evaluate the performance of programs and schools. In short, the first section of the chapter will examine the issue of how to construct good tests. Then the second section will consider how to use them wisely.

Confusion sometimes arises because the same test may be used for several, quite different, purposes. For instance, a popular test, such as the Iowa Test of

Basic Skills (ITBS), is used for placing individual students in particular programs, for deciding which students get promoted and which get held back, for evaluating the work that a school has done in meeting learning standards, and even for *instructional* purposes. This last is very important. Teachers need to assess their students' progress if they are to adjust their instruction to enhance student learning. Such assessment might occur through formal, standardized testing or in many other ways, but pedagogy seems inconceivable without some means of ascertaining what students have learned. Although that kind of diagnostic assessment is beyond the scope of this chapter, by no means do I wish to suggest that politically based pressures for accountability are more important than assessment focused on improving individual student learning. Quite the opposite. The main point to remember is that testing for accountability is very different from testing for instructional purposes, even when the same examination is used for the two distinct ends.

Test Theory, Classical and Modern

One of the most important educational uses of statistics is constructing, revising, and interpreting tests, especially "objective" tests, such as multiple-choice and true–false tests. Objective tests are not necessarily the most important kinds of assessments, but objective testing is where quantitative methods, the subject of this book, have the greatest contribution to make. The reliability and validity of tests are the main concern here. Reliability and validity were first discussed in relation to survey research in Chapter 5 and again in Chapter 7. Reliability and validity as applied to survey research are closely analogous to reliability and validity in testing research. Indeed, the two realms of research deal with equivalent problems: Standardized tests are, in essence, surveys of student knowledge. So it should come as no surprise that many of the common techniques for measuring reliability were first developed in testing research and later applied to surveys, and that the mutual borrowing between the two areas of research continues

today. The research on testing and the development of techniques to improve the reliability and validity of tests (whether measuring knowledge in education or measuring attitudes in questionnaires) has grown rapidly in recent decades both in amount and in technical difficulty.

Item response theory (IRT) and *Rasch modeling* are methods widely used by testing specialists, especially on standardized tests, but they are only dimly understood by most educational practitioners. IRT and Rasch methods are computationally quite complex, but with a bit of patience, it is possible for a practitioner to get a general idea of what is involved. Rasch modeling (named after its founder Georg Rasch) and IRT were first developed at about the same time (1960s) and deal with similar problems. The IRT strand grew up more in the United States, and the Rasch strand more in Europe. Continental differences between the two continue, but there has always been a great deal of crossover. Sometimes the two are considered conflicting methods. On the other hand, Embretson and Reise (2000), among others (including me), treat Rasch models as a subcategory of IRT models, but this is controversial. Squabbles among researchers aside, having a general understanding of Rasch/IRT is essential for any professional whose work involves assessing individuals. Testing remains, however, one of those areas in which it is very difficult to dispense with the services of a specialist. Using the information contained in the following pages, the reader will not be able to engage in Rasch/IRT analyses. Learning to use these methods would require reading a book, not merely a chapter. But this chapter does provide an introduction that helps make clear the uses of such analyses.

Most practitioners and even many test constructors still base much of what they do on *classical test theory*. It is easy to understand, but has long been thought of as no longer anything like a state-of-the-art approach to constructing and evaluating tests and test items, especially for large, repeatedly offered standardized tests. However, the classical and modern approaches have much in common. Many advocates of IRT believe it contrasts sharply with classical test theory (CTT), but I see IRT as a logical extension of older techniques, one that applies modern statistical methods, such as logistic regression and structural equation models, to perennial, classical problems of testing. In any case, in both the classical and the modern approaches, the individual *items,* or test questions, and their relations to individual test takers' achievement levels, are the focus of analysis. In both the classical and the modern approaches, the goal is to answer three kinds of questions. (1) Are the items valid? Are they really measuring what those who constructed the test intended them to measure? (2) How difficult are the items, especially as compared to the other items and to the total test score? (3) How well do the items "discriminate" among those taking the test? How clearly do the items enable us to distinguish among test takers who know the subject well and those who do not?

The second and third questions (difficulty and discrimination) are mostly a matter of reliability or consistency. Quantitative techniques of measurement have a great role to play here. The first question, validity, is more complicated, and it is often less open to quantitative analysis. As already discussed (see Chapter 7), the question of validity frequently is *not* a statistical question. Rather, one typically determines whether a group of test items is appropriate and whether it covers the subject (often called the "domain") adequately by asking experts to review the items. These expert judgments are frequently summed and analyzed quantitatively, but statistical analyses usually play a smaller role in studying test validity than in studying the reliability of test items.

Rather than discuss these issues abstractly, I will use a few simple examples from assessments of my students. Because the examples are nothing special, quite routine really, they help introduce in a concrete way what can be a highly abstract subject. When I give an "objective" exam in a course, I use bubble sheets and machine scoring, even when the class is small and this saves little if any time. The "op-scan" machine probably makes fewer mistakes than I would, and that's good, but the most important reason I use the system is because when doing so it is very easy to obtain analyses of the test items. The testing service at my university, as at most universi-

ties, will compute a little item analysis that I can use to help understand the test results better.

This analysis contains a few indicators, most of which are used in both classical and IRT approaches to testing. The first is a *difficulty index,* which is the proportion of the students who got a question right. If there are 20 students in the class and 18 get an item correct, then the difficulty index is .90. If all students answered it correctly it would be 1.0, and if none did it would be 0.0. The difficulty index is another example of a confusing label, because it is clearly an "easiness index." The higher the score the easier the item. To add to the confusion, some people actually call it the easiness index. And few test specialists even reverse the measurement and report the number *missing* the item and thus compute a true difficulty index. Thus, although the concept is clear, we practitioners need to take care with the labels so that we can be certain that we know what is being reported when.

So, what can we learn when looking at this difficulty/easiness index? What does it tell us? Items with difficulty indexes at or very close to 1.0 *may* be bad items. If every student can get them right, even students who missed most other questions, these items do not really "test" students' knowledge of the subject. Also, questions that very few test takers get right, with indexes close to zero, are suspect. If only 20% of the students answered a question correctly, this could indicate a bad question. But not necessarily. Hard questions are *not* bad questions by definition.[1] Indeed, a hard item could be a good question. That would be the case if the students who knew the subject well usually answered the hard question correctly whereas those who did not know the subject well got it wrong. But how do you know that? How do we move from *difficulty* to *discrimination*?

If an item is working as it ought, it should discriminate between those who know more of the subject matter and those who know less. In classical test theory this is determined by computing a correlation between the individuals' scores on the item (correct = 1, incorrect = 0) and the individuals' total test scores. These correlations (called *point-biserial correlations*) for each question are called the *discrimination indexes,* but, maddeningly, some testing centers call them "validity." If you get a negative correlation for any particular question, that is a sign of big trouble with the item. A negative correlation means that people who did well on the test did poorly on that question and people who did poorly on the test did well on the item. In general, for each item, you would expect positive correlations between individuals' scores on the items and their scores on the test. Positive correlations do not necessarily demonstrate validity, but they are in indication of it. Bad items *could* correlate positively with total scores—on bad tests. Also, a good test item could correlate poorly with the total scores if it assessed students' knowledge of a subject differently from most of the other items on the test. Test theory as described here is built around the assumption that all the items are measuring the same subject—often called *domain* or *construct*. Factor analysis and structural equation modeling (see Chapters 13 and 14) are often used to test such assumptions about the domain(s) being measured.

Items on my tests usually get low discrimination indexes; that is, they correlate quite weakly with total scores. I mention this because the reasons for it indicate important features of testing and the kinds of choices individual instructors might make when constructing tests and interpreting item analyses. First, my test items do not always correlate strongly with total score, because my tests do not measure just one domain. Rather they typically measure half a dozen domains, such as understanding the advantages of different survey designs, reading results reported in regression tables, and reasoning about confidence intervals. Such domains are not necessarily related. Students who do well answering questions from one domain do not always do well on another. In short, an item from one domain is not as likely to correlate with a total score compiled from several domains.

A second reason my test items tend to correlate weakly with total scores is that many of my test items are answered correctly by most or all students. The difficulty/easiness index for many of my items is at or near 100%. This is by design. I write such questions to test students' mastery of the subject matter, and I use these questions especially to assess knowledge of subjects that are absolutely fundamental to under-

standing the field. This makes sense because it helps me achieve what I consider an important educational goal, but it does not help me obtain high point-biserial discrimination scores. Typically about one-third of my test questions are mastery questions of this sort; I intend and hope for all students to succeed by answering them correctly. A correlation measures the association of the variances in two variables. Answers to mastery questions have little or no variance. Therefore they correlate poorly with total scores. If I were mainly concerned about validity as measured by the correlations of the items and the total scores, then I would aim to write only questions on which the percent correct ranged between, say, 40% and 60%. Then the correlations between the items and the total scores would be much higher.

My testing center computes one more measure of discrimination, which it calls validity, but is more accurately referred to as a second discrimination index. It is an instructive way to see how such indexes can be used to distinguish among items that are good at differentiating those who know the subject and those who do not, and an instructor can easily calculate it by hand. For each item, the scores of the students who scored highest on the total exam are compared to those of the lowest-scoring students. For example, if a class has 20 students, the highest scoring 5 will be compared to the lowest scoring 5. So, on question 28, if 4 out of 5 of the high-scoring group answered correctly, their proportion correct would be .80. If, in the lowest scoring group, 1 out of 5 answered question 28 correctly, their proportion correct would be .20. Subtracting the low group's proportion from the high group's proportion—that is, .80 minus .20—yields a discrimination index of .60. This indicates that question 28 did a good job in helping to distinguish among—and to define—the low-scoring and the high-scoring groups. This discrimination index can theoretically range from 1.0 through zero to −1.0. Scores below zero will tend to be quite rare and would indicate potentially serious problems with the item. For instance, if all the high-scoring students answered question 17 incorrectly and all the low-scoring students got it right, the discrimination index would be −1.0. This actually happened on one of my exams. The item was a true–false question. All the low-scoring students answered the question correctly, while all the high-scoring students got it wrong. I couldn't believe it! What happened? The answer was simple. I had made a clerical error in the answer key. After I corrected the error, the discrimination index became +1.0.

Together, measures of item difficulty and of item discrimination provide evidence about which test items are good ones and which are not. Note that there is a kind of circularity here. A good item is one that the strong students get right and the weak students get wrong. Strong students are those who get many items right. Weak students are those who get many items wrong. This circularity is unavoidable and need not be a cause for concern, especially if the pool of students who are used to define the difficulty of items is a large one and an appropriate one.

Applications of Rasch and IRT Models: Examples

Both classical and modern test theory use the statistics just reviewed: (1) the proportion of examinees answering each item correctly, called the difficulty index; (2) the correlation between the answers to an item and the total score, called the discrimination index. They do quite different things with these two, but the building blocks are the same. Modern test theory ratchets up the level of analysis, sometimes to a breathtaking degree, but it starts with much of the same data.

To illustrate the fairly simple techniques of looking for patterns that lie behind IRT, I'll use an example drawn from a midterm examination in one of my classes. This will provide just a taste of the technical details of the beginning of an analysis that pushes beyond classical test theory to modern approaches. There is no way we can go beyond that "taste." Like most subjects that are treated in one chapter in this book, entire courses are devoted to testing. Indeed, entire doctoral programs and professional careers are spent on it. Yet it is true that the most important concepts can be described in fairly nontechnical terms.

The example uses 15 questions drawn from a test given to a class of 11 students. It closely parallels the model Georg Rasch used in 1960 to describe his method (see the excellent discussion in Bond & Fox, 2001). For this illustration I chose the fifth, tenth, fifteenth, and so on, through the seventy-fifth questions from the exam. That means, in the terms of sampling design, the questions were a "systematic sample" of the items on the exam. The 1s in the cells of Table 16.1 indicate questions that were answered correctly. Zeros indicate questions that were answered incorrectly. The table first orders the *items* by how difficult they are. Question 70 was most difficult, so it is listed first at the top. Question 5 was the second most difficult; it is listed second, and so on to the easiest questions ending with Question 75. Then the *students* are ordered according to their total scores. Students U and N got 14 of the 15 correct; they are listed first, starting at the left. Students X and P got 13 right, and so on over to Student V on the far right who answered 6 questions correctly. If you arrange items and students this way, you can do a quick eyeball assessment of the test items. If you draw a diagonal line from the upper left of the table to the lower right, you should find that most of the zeros are above that line. What that means is that, as expected, the students *weak* on this subject matter got most of the *difficult* questions wrong. Conversely, there should be very few zeros on the lower side of the line, for such zeros would indicate the anomaly of easy questions missed by strong students.

Modern test theory usually does not work with percentages or proportions correct. Rather modern item analysis uses the *odds* of getting an item correct. The dependent variable for an item analysis is dichotomous: correct, yes/no. When this type of variable is the dependent variable in a regression, the proportion yes/correct is transformed by taking the log of the odds of yes/correct (see Chapter 11). So, in addition to giving the raw score and the percent correct, Table 16.1 also reports the *odds*. For example, Students U and N each answered 14 of the 15 correctly. As reported in the table, they each got a score of 93.3%. Also reported, and ultimately more important for modern techniques, the *odds* of Students U and N getting any item right were 14 to 1, or 14:1. The odds of Student M answering an item correctly were 8 to 7, and for Student V the odds were 6 to 9.

TABLE 16.1 Ordering Test Items by Difficulty and Student Score: Early Steps in Item Analysis

Question	STD U	STD N	STD X	STD P	STD Q	STD R	STD T	STD W	STD S	STD M	STD V	sum	odds	log odds
Q70	1	1	0	0	0	0	0	1	0	0	0	3	3:8	−0.98
Q5	0	1	0	1	0	0	1	0	0	0	1	4	4:7	−0.56
Q65	1	1	1	1	1	0	0	0	0	1	0	6	6:5	0.18
Q35	1	1	1	1	1	1	0	1	0	0	0	7	7:4	0.56
Q40	1	1	1	1	1	1	1	0	1	0	0	8	8:3	0.98
Q45	1	1	1	0	1	1	1	1	0	0	1	8	8:3	0.98
Q60	1	1	1	1	1	1	1	0	0	1	0	8	8:3	0.98
Q10	1	1	1	1	1	1	0	0	1	1	1	9	9:2	1.50
Q30	1	0	1	1	1	1	0	1	1	1	1	9	9:2	1.50
Q15	1	1	1	1	1	1	1	1	1	1	0	10	10:1	2.30
Q20	1	1	1	1	1	1	1	1	1	1	0	10	10:1	2.30
Q25	1	1	1	1	1	1	1	1	1	1	0	10	10:1	2.30
Q50	1	1	1	1	1	1	1	1	1	0	1	10	10:1	2.30
Q55	1	1	1	1	1	1	1	1	1	1	0	10	10:1	2.30
Q75	1	1	1	1	1	1	1	1	1	0	1	10	10:1	2.30
sum5–75	14	14	13	13	13	12	10	9	9	8	6	122		
Odds	14:1	14:1	13:2	13:2	13:2	12:3	10:5	10:5	9:6	8:7	6:9	122:43		
log odds	2.64	2.64	1.47	1.47	1.47	1.39	0.69	0.69	0.41	0.13	−0.41	1.04		
% right	93.3	93.3	86.7	86.7	86.7	80.0	66.7	66.7	60.0	53.3	40.0	73.9		

Note: 1 = Correct answer; 0 = Incorrect answer.

Odds are very important in modern statistical analyses, and, as we saw in see Chapter 11, they are usually transformed by taking their natural logs.

So Table 16.1 not only reports odds in addition to percents; it goes one step further. It takes the *log* of the odds (*log* is short for *logarithm*). It does this to transform the odds into something more useable, the log of the odds (called the *logit*). What is the purpose of this and other transformations? Transformations are used mostly to make distributions of scores easier to work with or to allow one to use a wider range of statistical analysis techniques. In the specific example we are considering here, we do these transformations by taking logs, because distances between odds and percentages are *not* interval measures. They are ranks. By taking the logs of the odds of scores, the ranks become true quantitative, interval-level measures on which it is appropriate to use techniques such as correlation and regression. For example, the distance between 80% and 90% is *not* an interval measure. However the distance between the log odds of 80 to 20 (or 4:1), which is 1.3863, and the log odds of 90 to 10 (or 9:1), which is 2.1972, is an interval measure. That means we can appropriately use it in correlation, regression, and other statistical techniques requiring interval-level data.

On Table 16.1, question 70, which 3 students got right, is not necessarily three times more difficult than question 10, which 9 students got right. However, the log of the odds for question 70 (−0.98) and question 10 (1.50) are interval-level measures. It would be appropriate to use these transformed variables in methods of analysis such as correlation and regression. Let's take a few more examples from Table 16.1 to see how the calculations are done. Student T answered 10 questions correctly and 5 incorrectly. The odds of this student answering any question correctly are 10:5, which is 10 divided by 5, which equals 2. If you enter 2 into your calculator and press the *ln* (for *log, natural*) button, you get 0.69. For student M you would divide 8 (number correct) by 7 (number wrong) and then push the *ln* button to get a log of the odds, or logit, of 0.13. You'd do the same thing for the items. For question 5, 4 students answered it correctly and 7 got it wrong, so the odds are 4:7, which is

the same thing as 4 divided by 7, which equals 0.571. The ln of this is −0.56. For question 15, which 10 got right and 1 got wrong, the calculations are 10/1 = 10, ln = 2.30.

To repeat, the raw test results give use rank-order data: Question 70 was the hardest, question 5 was the second hardest, and so on. By taking the logit of these data, we can transform rank-order data into interval-level data. And that means we can do regression analysis on the data without violating statistical assumptions on which these techniques are based. This is how measurement specialists using modern methods of data analysis, such as item response theory (IRT), go about their work. They use regression analysis. The dependent variable in the regressions is the odds of answering a question correctly. But before doing regressions, the ordinal-level data are "rescaled," into *logits,* to make them interval-level data. The potential uses of IRT in such rescaling work are very broad because many variables in education and the social sciences are ordinal, although they are often inappropriately treated as though they were interval (Harwell & Gatti, 2001).

The main purpose of all this transforming work, which makes item response theory possible, is finding accurate measures of item difficulty and item discrimination. If, rather than using 15 questions and 11 students, as in Table 16.1, item difficulty and discrimination were calculated for hundreds of items using the performance of thousands of examinees, we could be quite confident in our assessment of the range of difficulty of the items and of their ability to differentiate among examinees at different levels of proficiency. This kind of information about item difficulty and discrimination is used widely in testing and research on testing. For example, Newman et al. (2001), in a study of the effectiveness of educational programs, used item response theory to equate four years of scores on state-level achievement examinations. IRT produced a "score, in logits, for each student that could be compared to other students' scores regardless of the form or level of the test that they took" (p. 303). This enabled meaningful comparisons of the effects on achievement scores of different types of educational programs.

There are two basic formulas (and many elaborations of them) used in IRT. They involve logistic regression. Because we are already familiar with the basic form of logistic regression (from Chapter 11), it is instructive to briefly review the formulas IRT researchers use and to explain a little of the jargon that accompanies them. The first formula is the original, as devised by Rasch. The dependent variable is the log of the odds of answering a particular question correctly. The two independent variables are the item difficulty (called *beta*) and the trait scores (called *thetas*) of the individuals who took the test. The trait score or theta is the estimate of, for example, how well individuals know the subject matter being tested. A verbal version of the formula is:

> Formula 1: Logit of an item = Trait score minus Difficulty

Formula 1 is often referred to in writing about tests as the *1PL model*. This stands for *one-parameter logistic* model. Formula 2 is called the *2PL model*, meaning *two-parameter logistic model*. Formula 2 adds to Formula 1, a measure of item discrimination, the point-biserial correlation discussed earlier. This is called *alpha*. A verbal version of Formula 2 is:

> Formula 2: Logit of an item = Item discrimination times (Trait score minus Difficulty)

But wait! You have probably noticed that you need to know the trait score to do the item analysis. However, the whole idea of testing is to obtain the trait score, a measure of knowledge, skills, abilities, and so on. Where does the trait score come from? How is it calculated? *Maximum likelihood estimation* (MLE) is the method used. As seen in Chapter 14, MLE is an iterative (trial-and-error) method that uses information from a sample to estimate the most (maximum) likely value. In the context of testing, the sample is composed of the responses to test items, particularly given their difficulty. The value being estimated is the trait level. So the question is: Given this person's pattern of responses on difficult and easy items, what trait level is most likely? Or, in other terms, What trait level is most likely to have yielded this individual's pattern of responses? It all seems pretty abstruse, but the practical applications are many.

For example, if you have taken the Graduate Record Exam recently, or the law school or medical school admissions tests, you have experienced IRT directly. These tests are now given using *computer adaptive testing* rather than paper-and-pencil tests. The general procedure is to have the examinee begin with questions at a middling level of difficulty. If you answer correctly, the computer program selects more difficult questions; if you answer these correctly, the computer selects still more difficult questions continuing the process until you reach a level at which you start answering questions incorrectly. Then easier questions are selected until you start answering correctly again. In this way the program hones in on your level of knowledge or skill. Testers using computer adaptive testing can determine your level of knowledge or skill more precisely and more efficiently than they can using traditional pencil-and-paper tests. In addition to being more precise, these tests are often shorter because they can dispense with the questions that are far below and those that are far above an examinee's level of knowledge. You don't have to waste your time answering questions that are too hard for you—or too easy for you. No two people taking a computer adaptive test are likely to get exactly the same questions or even the same number of questions. Most experts believe that using IRT methods and giving different people different tests is a more accurate and therefore fairer method than having everyone take exactly the same test. This differentiation is possible because it is possible to determine equivalent levels of difficulty of individual test items. This conclusion seems paradoxical. Should not *equal* treatment be *identical* treatment? Yes and no. Equality can be assured by making sure that examinees have an opportunity to answer questions of *equal levels of difficulty.* They need not be the same questions.

Knowledge of levels of difficulty also enables testing agencies to prepare equivalent test forms. All states are required to administer achievements tests to comply with the No Child Left Behind legislation. This legislation mandates that all students' yearly progress be measured. For security reasons, testers cannot use the same test year after year. Also, knowledge changes, perhaps especially in the sciences. Given the need to make changes for the purposes of test security and because of differences over time in what counts as knowledge in a field, how does one know that changes from this year to the next do not result in the new version being harder—or easier? An old adage in testing is: *If you want to measure change, don't change the measure.* Now you *can* change the measure and still measure change. While changing the specific questions, you keep the level of difficulty the same. This is the most immediately practical application of IRT methods. They are widely used to equate difficulty levels by private and governmental agencies writing standardized "objective" tests, that is, tests on which the answers generate categorical variables, such as right/wrong.

We cannot pursue further the technical details of how test methods make it possible to equate the difficulty levels of tests. Instead, turn your attention to the question: Even if the tests are *reliable* measures of student learning, how can they be or should they be used, if at all, for holding schools accountable for students' learning, or lack thereof? This question raises issues of *validity*. Is using individual tests to gauge institutional performance a valid application of these tests? When focusing on the application of test theory to decision making, you move from the fairly tidy technical world of tests and measurement, to the messier world in which researchers and professionals interact with politics. Studying this interaction is instructive for anyone who wants to conduct or to understand social research as it is actually done, rather than as it would be done in a world designed for the convenience of researchers. Real research in real contexts entails making many more awkward compromises than textbooks usually discuss.

How Tests of Students Are Used to Evaluate Schools and Teachers

The methods of constructing tests and interpreting scores discussed in the first half of this chapter are designed for measuring *individual* achievement. This is true whether the tests are criterion-referenced or norm-referenced. *Criterion-referenced tests* measure individual performance against a criterion—or standard—of achievement in a specific domain of knowledge: Can this student calculate the area of a triangle or not? *Norm-referenced tests* measure individual performance according to how the individual ranks in comparison to members of a *norming* group: How does this student rank as compared to others who have taken the test?

For major norm-referenced tests, the norming group is often a large group that is broadly representative of the population for whom the test is designed—such as students in the third grade or college seniors planning to go to graduate school. For criterion-referenced tests, the measure is one of degree of mastery, and the comparison is with a fixed standard of performance. For norm-referenced tests, the measure is some form of ranking in comparison to the norming group, such as a percentile rank or one of the many versions of the *z*-score. In either case, the outcome of the test, what the score tells you, is how the *individual* performed on it—as compared to a standard or compared to the performance of others.

A very different set of questions is raised when we pool the scores on these individual tests and use them to evaluate schools or programs. For the last decade or so, pooling individual tests to evaluate institutions or programs has gone under the name of accountability, and that is how it will be referred to it here.

Many people object to the standardized testing that accompanies the accountability movement. Often they object most especially to objective tests, such as multiple-choice or true–false tests. These opponents feel that the tests are not valid, that they are not good tests. My belief is that those who would challenge the accountability movement by attacking objective tests are fighting the wrong battle—or the less important one. The tests are imperfect to be sure. All measures are imperfect, whether they be multiple-choice questions, essay questions, or portfolios. Standardized tests can be good measures of the extent to which students have gained knowledge in specific fields. Opponents of the accountability movement would, in my view, do much better to focus on the dubious ways the tests have been used. The *uses* of tests for accountability are more open to much more fundamental criticisms.

This is not to say that objective, standardized, short-answer tests are valid for measuring everything. For many things, they are quite invalid methods of measurement. If we wished to determine how well someone could play the piano, or perform surgery, or write a computer program, we would not want to use multiple-choice tests. These tests are most appropriate for measuring specific kinds of knowledge and skills, such as reading comprehension or interpreting statistical tables. They can be quite useless for measuring some kinds of performances, such as playing a sonata.

The key point is that measurement error is unavoidable. I take that back. There is one way to avoid it. Don't measure. Don't judge. Don't assess. But if you measure or judge or assess, some error is inevitable. Errors of assessment are inevitable regardless of the method of assessment. I think that many of the standardized tests are quite good at measuring what they are designed to measure. So my approach in the next section will be to assume, at least for the sake of argument, that the tests are pretty good at measuring what they were designed to measure, that is, individuals' knowledge and skills. Given that assumption, how *valid* are they for measuring the performance of institutions and programs in conveying that knowledge?

The accountability movement has many components. We will take as our main example the legislation known as the No Child Left Behind (NCLB) Act. Its salience is so great, and it represents so significant a change in educational evaluation in the United States, that we can use it to address most important aspects of the subject of the valid use of individual assessments to evaluate institutions and programs.

Provisions of the NCLB

The legislation known as No Child Left Behind (NCLB) was signed into law in 2002 by President Bush with strong bipartisan support in the Congress. The NCLB is part of the reauthorization of the federal government's Elementary and Secondary Education Act (ESEA), first passed in 1965 and subsequently reauthorized every several years. The law is long (several hundred pages) and complicated. The following summary gives the minimum necessary to pursue our topic, which is the use of individual standardized tests for institutional and program evaluation.

The first thing to note about the NCLB is that the basic ideas and practices behind it are not really new. Testing for accountability has been an increasing trend in federal education legislation (see the discussion in Chapter 15). What is novel about the NCLB, this most recent reauthorization of the ESEA, is the greatly increased scope and intensity of the legislation. Individual standardized tests are used to evaluate schools and state education systems to an extent heretofore unheard of. The reauthorization of the ESEA in 1994, enacted under President Clinton, had many of the same provisions as the 2002 NCLB Act, but they were less extensive and less rigorously enforced.

According to the NCLB Act, states must, if they wish to continue to receive federal education funds, test all public school students in reading and mathematics 6 times, once each in grades 3 through 8 and then once more at some point in grades 10 through 12. This testing system must be fully in place in the 2005–2006 academic year. Beginning in 2007–2008, states must also test all students in science at three levels, at least once in grades 3 through 5, once in grades 6 through 9, and a last time in grades 10 through 12. All of these tests must be standardized (the same for all students in the state) and criterion-referenced. The criteria to be used are the states' curriculum goals. Schools and states must use the tests to demonstrate that they are making *adequate yearly progress* (AYP). What is adequate? The law defines *adequate* as improving at a rate rapid enough to bring *all* students up to a level of proficiency by the 2013–2014 academic year. For example, if in May 2006, 60% of the students in the eighth grade in a school were proficient, the school would have 8 years (until May of 2014) to bring the other 40% up to proficiency. The required rate of improvement would be 5% per year (40% divided by 8). If a school does not progress at this rate for two years in a row, it will be labeled "in need of improvement." With each successive year the school fails to meet its targets, the label is increasingly less pleasant and the consequences for the school become increasingly harsh.[2]

These daunting standards are accompanied by rigorous means of enforcement. It is hard to imagine *any* standard that has ever been achieved by 100% of students. Furthermore, even if a school is making adequate yearly progress (AYP) *on average,* it also has to do so for students in each of four categories, that is, for students who are (1) economically disadvantaged, (2) from major racial/ethnic subgroups, (3) disabled, and (4) with limited English proficiency. So even if a school is making adequate progress on average, if it is not doing so for students in one or more of these categories, it will be judged not to have met its targets, to be in need of improvement, because it has left some students behind. It was already the case, as early as 2004, that some suburban schools, widely regarded as excellent, had failed to meet their target with one or more category of students and have felt the sting that labeling can bring.

How to Measure Proficiency and Adequate Yearly Progress

The difficulty of the test and how it is scored will importantly influence how likely students—and therefore schools—are to perform well on it. Clearly if one state has an easy test and another has a hard test, differences in *proficiency* between the states will be mainly a reflection of how hard the tests are. States are largely free to set their content standards as they wish. Most states, pressed by the NCLB legislation, have set rates of improvement never before attained anywhere. That does not necessarily mean that these rates of improvement needed to reach 100% proficiency by 2014 are impossible, but it surely means that they are highly improbable. This is true even in states that have set comparatively easy targets. It is dramatically truer in states with demanding targets. And the range of difficulty on the state tests is wide. For example, Colorado's standards have been set in such a way that about 80% of its elementary students in mathematics are called proficient. The state has a little over 10 years to reach the goal of 100% pro-

ficient. So it needs to add about 2% per year to the ranks of the proficient. By contrast, Massachusetts has determined that about 20% of its elementary students are proficient in mathematics. It needs to move its students into the proficient category four times as quickly as Colorado. Is it really the case that students in Massachusetts are far behind students in Colorado? No. In fact, the best data we have from nationally administered tests is that Massachusetts students are actually slightly ahead (Linn, 2003a).

Other states with comparatively easy targets include Texas and Louisiana. When we read in the paper, as eventually we surely will, that schools in Louisiana are flourishing and their students are learning at an acceptable rate while those in Massachusetts are "failing," I suppose some people will be convinced. But anyone who knows about the quality of education in the two states will doubt the superiority of Louisiana schools. Such comparisons between states are meaningless because the definitions of *proficient* are so wildly different as to make honest comparison impossible (Linn, 2003b). *Within* states reasonable comparisons are feasible as states develop standardized state-wide exams. It is not impossible to compare students' progress across states, but that can be done only if students in different states are given the same test with the same grading scale.

National standards are available. The National Assessment of Educational Progress (NAEP), also called The Nation's Report Card, has measured academic achievement in the United States. since the 1970s. The NAEP has become a sort of national benchmark, and this role is strengthened by the NCLB. If students in a particular state do well on the state test used for NCLB reporting, but not on the NAEP, that would probably raise a red flag. Because of this role, the NAEP, which has always used large samples, has greatly increased its sample size in order to have enough cases to make state-by-state comparisons of NAEP and NCLB state tests. Because of the NCLB legislation, all states now participate in NAEP; this was not the case prior to the NCLB Act. With all states participating in 2005, about 1.2 million students in grades 4, 8, and 12 were selected by the NAEP for testing in math, reading, and science.

Cut Scores

The NAEP tests are scored in standard deviation or *z*-score units. These are transformed in the usual ways to eliminate decimals and negative numbers. The scales vary from exam to exam. The twelfth-grade math exam is typical; it has a mean of 250 and an SD of 50. As of 1990, the NAEP started reporting cut scores for various levels of achievement. These were and still are labeled advanced, proficient, basic, below basic. To count as proficient a student has to score very high—in the norm-referenced sense of high. For example, the NAEP governing board set the raw score level at the 88th percentile (Linn, 2003b) for proficiency in mathematics. By this definition, nearly 90% of twelfth graders were not proficient in math. As this example makes clear, cut scores are judgmental, not statistical. The NAEP's standards and cut scores are set by its governing board composed of a broadly representative group of individuals reflecting the political mood of the administration in power when they were appointed.

It is fine to have high standards, even impossibly high standards, meant to encourage one to try one's best—as long as such goals are understood to be ideals, not practical goals that all can attain. When one sets such standards for high-stakes testing and when failure to attain the standards will result in severe sanctions for schools, then standards ought to be more realistically set. Does anyone honestly believe that all twelfth-grade students will soon be able to achieve at the level recently attained by the top 12% of high school students? A more reasonable approach might have been to pick the median level of achievement, the 50th percentile, as the baseline measure of proficiency.

Sometimes criterion-referenced standards with cut scores make good sense. Licensing exams are case in point. If a certain minimum level of knowledge and skill is necessary to be a safe driver, one who does not greatly endanger others by being on the road. We should not relax standards to get a driver's license, even if that means that 5% or 10% of those who would like a driver's license cannot get one. Licensing for the medical profession is another example. Anesthesiologists, for example, should be rigorously screened. Even if the examination is very, very difficult, and many would-be anesthesiologists cannot pass, that is as it should be, because it is necessary to keep incompetents from killing off patients. Determining minimum levels of competence for drivers and anesthesiologists may not be easy, but it is easier than finding reasonable levels of consensus about how much math everyone *needs* to know or how well everyone *needs* to be able to read. Needs in order to do what?[3]

All systems of grading that turn raw scores into ranked categories *discard information.* This is true whether the categories are A, B, C, or advanced, proficient, basic. Say that the cut score to be called proficient is 70 on a test. Three people take the test and they earn scores of 69, 71, and 88. Obviously the first two scores are very similar and are probably within the exam's margin of error, which means if the same two people took the test again next month, the one who passed might fail and vice versa. On the other hand, the difference between 88 and 69–71 is probably real and important. Cut scores are clearly necessary in licensing where the focus is on the minimum knowledge and skills needed for safe practice. But it is less clear what societal goal is served by cut scores for measuring academic achievement. When estimating how much students have learned, I would rather keep than discard information. Again say that the cut score is 70 and we have two schools. One school moves its student average from 80 to 83. This is progress, although modest progress, and the school may be rewarded and held up as a model for others to imitate. A second school moves its student average from 55 to 65. This school has moved its students much further than the first and has, by most measures done a better job, but because it failed to reach a threshold, it could be labeled "in need of improvement," and sanctions will be applied.

Value-Added Methods

How should we measure improvement? The NCLB Act mandates the use of levels, such as *proficient* and *advanced,* and requires that all students become proficient by 2014. This requirement is generally interpreted to mean that using the average rate of pass/proficiency scores by grade. If a school has three fifth-grade classes, the average pass rate for those three classes has to reach a predefined target. For example, if in 2006 60% of fifth graders were proficient, and the school needs to make adequate yearly progress (AYP) of 5% to reach the goal of 100% by 2014, then 65% of 2007's fifth graders will need to score at the proficient level or above; 70% of 2008's students will need to score at that level. If the scores from one year to the next go up the requisite amount, adequate yearly progress has been attained.

Note that when using this method, we are *not* comparing the same students. What Heather and Erica and Robert and Juan and all the other fifth graders knew at the beginning of the year is not being compared with what they knew at the end or with what they will know by 2014. By 2014, these students will be in college or the labor market. Rather, the students who happened to attend the fifth grade in our school this year are compared with those who will happen to attend the fifth grade next year. This is *not* an estimate of the amount that the school increased students' learning. Using this method of measurement we *do not know* how much valuable learning the school added to students' store of knowledge, because that was not measured. Progress cannot be measured by testing students in a particular grade only once at the end of the year. This gives us an "after" but no "before" with which to compare it. This shortcoming—an after with no before—is what motivates adherents of the *value-added* approach.

Advocates of this approach point out that public schools have little control over who attends them, and that the characteristics of the students before they enter is one of the main determinants of their scores. Especially in small schools where the number of students at each grade level is low, a relatively small migration of students in or out can sharply influence the results. In order to hold schools accountable, say proponents of the value-added approach, we should measure the effects schools have on students, not which schools got lucky in the demographic draw.

A big problem with the value-added approach, which measures the learning of individual students, is that it is more difficult to compute. By contrast, mean grade-level proficiency scores are easy to calculate. They can often simply be read off of the state's "report card" Web site. Keeping track of students to see how much they have learned, on the other hand, can be tricky. One big problem is mobility (see the discussion of attrition in Chapter 7). Some of our fifth graders were not in our school in the fourth grade, so we won't know their "before" scores. And some of the fourth graders who benefited from our instruction, and for whom we should be able to claim credit (or get blamed), have moved to another school, which will reap the benefits (or the blame). One alternative is testing twice per year, at the beginning and at the end, but many educators would rightly resist this. They believe that too much instructional time is already spent on testing rather than learning. However, with standardized state tests mobility should pose no problem—at least for students who do not move out of state. What is required to make a value-added approach work is a way to trace students and their scores. Several states have developed student identification numbers that will allow them to track students' achievement as the students move from school to school.

There are multiple value-added methods for measuring student growth. They have in common that they follow the scores of individual students. The simplest method is to compute raw "gain scores" by subtracting an earlier score, say at the end of the fourth grade, from a later score, say at the end of the fifth grade. The concept of gain scores is sound and is what the value-added approach is all about, but simple subtraction of last year's raw score from this year's raises measurement problems. Experts agree that it is much better to use regression techniques to control for earlier achievement rather than merely subtracting it from later achievement. If the tests are first made equivalent using IRT methods, then analysts can use regression in which the pretest (last year's score) is a control variable. This approach also makes it possible to incorporate other control variables that are known to influence student achievement, such as parental income and education level. By using regression techniques to control for important variables, analysts could compute "expected rates" for each student and for each school. An expected rate would be a kind of prognosis. Then schools could be evaluated on the basis of whether they did better than their expected rate. Did a particular school "beat the odds" or fail to live up to expectations? Most measurement specialists would probably prefer this kind of approach to assessing student learning and schools' contributions to it, but measurement specialists do not often make educational policy (see Lissitz, 2005).

Value-added approaches are not merely high on measurement specialists' wish list. Although still in fairly early stages of development, the value-added approach is a practical reality in some places. For example, data are collected by student (not by class-level group) in Chicago. This makes it possible to separate student-level effects from school-level effects. Some states, including Tennessee, Pennsylvania, and Colorado, have developed or are developing the needed systems of information retrieval. By following individual students' progress, and following students from year to year, the student data are not nested in and are not confounded with the school data. That makes it possible to measure the separate contributions of school-level and individual-level variables to academic achievement (see the discussion of multilevel models in Chapter 12).

The main pioneer and advocate of value-added methods is William Sanders of the SAS© Institute, a company that makes one of the better-known software packages for statistical analysis. Several other scholars are working on some of the complicated measurement problems that value-added approaches involve. This should come as no surprise given the scope and potential impact of the NCLB legislation. The measurement issues are more intricate than is sometimes realized. For example, it is comparatively easy to use IRT and other scaling methods to make tests comparable at the same level—to make the third-grade reading test equivalent in difficulty to last year's third-grade reading test. But such scaling *across* years is more complicated, which means that value-added methods are tricky when they span more than one year. Furthermore, some subjects lend themselves more readily than others to value-added methods. Reading is probably the easiest skill to work with because it tends to vary less with grade level.

For example, suppose a particular sixth grader is in the 99th percentile of sixth graders in terms of her reading skills. It might then make sense to say that she reads at the tenth-grade level. She could probably read a tenth-grade text book. But such an inference in mathematics is less likely to be valid. Were our student equally ahead of her class in sixth-grade math, it would not follow that she would know geometry and trigonometry. This kind of comparability problem is more pronounced in secondary and higher education. The higher the grade level the more complex the problems when value added is measured vertically (see Lissitz & Huynh, 2003, for details). For example, how do we measure value added in high school science if in the tenth grade students study biology, in the eleventh chemistry, and in the twelfth physics?

Perhaps the most conceptually sophisticated method of value-added measurement of student achievement is what is known as *growth curve modeling*. The cruder group mean method, which compares one year's class mean to another's, is roughly like comparing group pictures of whole classes—*different* whole classes. This obscures individual learning. By contrast, growth modeling is like examining an ordered series of individual portraits taken at regular intervals so that one can measure and understand change. Like other value-added approaches, the growth modeling approach works with individuals and takes into account their starting points. (Growth curve models can be built using either MLM or SEM; see Chapters 12 and 14.) What this approach can add is a way to see how the starting point influences the growth curve. Perhaps in one school students with low starting scores learn more quickly than other students, whereas in other schools, they learn more slowly than the average rate (Seltzer, Choi, & Thum, 2003). In the first case the schools would be narrowing the achievement gap. In the second, the school would be leaving students further behind. An assessment aimed at leaving no child behind would do well to focus on and give credit to schools that reduced initial differences in achievement.

Another interesting development is to use value-added methods to assess teacher quality. The Tennessee Value-Added Assessment System (TNVAAS) estimates the effects of individual teachers on individual

TABLE 16.2   *Simpson's Paradox: Scores of Students, 2005 and 2006*

| | 2005 | | 2006 | |
	Group A	Group B	Group A	Group B
	80	60	81	62
	78	65	79	67
	82	55	83	57
	75	58		64
	85	62		60
				63
				61
Group mean	**80**	**60**	**81**	**62**
Overall mean		70		67.7

students' scores on Tennessee's standardized NCLB test. Although this has some problems, mainly that it does not control for variables that influence student progress (such as parental education level) over which teachers have no control, it is a pioneering effort that may be imitated in other states.

Despite many technical problems that need to be worked out, the value-added system has two chief virtues that make it superior to the main alternative of using group mean proficiency rates. In the first place, it is a more *valid* measure because it measures what we presumably mean to measure, which is progress in students' learning. Second, it is more *reliable* because it avoids the kind of volatility in scores that can occur when comparing the same grade levels in successive years rather than comparing the same students in successive years. In a study of three years of educational testing in the state of Colorado, Linn and Haug (2002) found that the data for individual schools was subject to a great deal of random fluctuation. Many of the year-to-year differences were not attributable to school variables. Rather, much of the change from year to year was due to random variation and measurement errors. In Colorado, schools that improved between the first and second years of measurement generally declined in the third year. By contrast, schools that declined from the first to the second year usually improved in the third year. This kind of fluctuation was especially likely to occur in small schools where small sample sizes made estimates unstable.

In brief, value-added methods are complicated and the technical details of applying them are far from completely worked out, but the advocates of value-added methods are addressing the complications—rather than exacerbating them as the method of mean grade-level proficiency does.

Simpson's Paradox

Would value-added methods really make a difference in the scores that are reported and the way schools are held accountable for student learning? The answer is almost surely yes. The first reason that value-added methods would make a difference is the prevalence in education of something called *Simpson's paradox.* This potentially widespread phenomenon is difficult to define but easy to illustrate. The paradox occurs when the direction of the values for groups taken individually is reversed when the groups are merged.

Table 16.2 gives an example. The scores of one teacher's two classes of 10 students in two different years are presented. Students are in two groups, A and B, one of which scores substantially higher than the other. In the first year, the 5 students in Group A score a mean of 80 and the 5 students in Group B get a mean of 60. In the second year, both groups raise their averages somewhat, to 81 and 62. The teacher can perhaps be proud of this modest accomplishment. Also, more good news, the gap between the groups narrows

TABLE 16.3 *NAEP Mathematics Scores for Students in Nebraska and New Jersey*

	Whites	*Blacks*	*Others*	*Total*
Nebraska	281	236	259	277
New Jersey	283	242	260	271

slightly. But the overall average goes *down* from 2005 to 2006! That's the paradox: Both groups do better, but the overall mean of the two groups combined goes down. The reason is that in the second year there are 2 fewer students in the high-scoring group and 2 more in the low-scoring group. What this illustrates is that seemingly minor changes in demographic composition can make a big difference in scores, especially in small schools and classes.

Simpson's paradox can make a difference in large-scale comparisons too. Wainer and Brown (2004) point out that whenever one makes comparisons among groups that were not formed by random assignment, there is a possibility of a mistake due to Simpson's paradox. They illustrate with NAEP eighth-grade math scores for two states, Nebraska and New Jersey. The Total column in Table 16.3 gives the mean for the whole state. The other columns give the mean for each group. Again we see what at first blush sounds impossible. *All* groups scored *higher* in New Jersey than in Nebraska, but the score for all groups combined is *lower* in New Jersey. The reason is the same as in the previous example—differences in the proportions of high-scoring and low-scoring groups. Which state's school system does better? If you were a parent deciding where to send your kids, New Jersey would be the better choice. Whatever your group, kids from that group did better in New Jersey than in Nebraska, even though the overall mean for Nebraska was higher.

The NCLB addresses some of these problems because it *disaggregates* scores by group, but it still deals with means of groups and subgroups rather than with individuals' scores as would be needed to take a value-added approach. Raudenbush (2003) compares the effects of using the group mean approach with the value-added approach using large national databases that contain both overall means for schools and students'

individual scores. If the value-added approach were used, the assessment question could perhaps be: "Are the schools adding value faster than they did last year?" For an individual student it could be: "Is he or she improving fast enough to attain and maintain proficiency by 2014 or by the twelfth grade, whichever comes earlier?" Schools would be judged by how well they were moving students toward the goal of proficiency.

In any case, our question is: Does using value-added scores to measure educational progress produce a result different than using group mean scores? Raudenbush found at least one huge difference. Although high-poverty schools usually have mean achievement levels much lower than other schools, the value added by high-poverty schools is essentially the same. High-poverty schools actually do quite well if one takes into account the starting points of the students with whom they are working. By contrast, if one does not take into account the starting points of students, the measurement of proficiency may be little more than ratifying that some students were more proficient than others *before* the school had an opportunity to affect their achievement levels. On the other hand, curriculum and school policy can make a difference. In my state, Illinois, the single most important determinant of individual students' proficiency on the eleventh-grade state math test is the number of math courses students take, even after controlling for students' ethnicity and their parents' income. This has led some high schools to increase the number and intensity of the math courses students must take in order to graduate.

Measuring individuals' educational achievement is very complicated and fraught with the kinds of technical problems illustrated by Simpson's paradox. It is more complicated still to use the results of individual tests to assess the accomplishments of teachers, schools, districts, and states as the NCLB legislation requires. Even assuming that the individual tests are appropriate measures of individual achievement, it is no simple matter to use them as valid measures of teachers and schools.

It is important to remember that this chapter has discussed only standardized tests in which right/wrong answers are appropriate. It is clear, of course, that in many cases such tests would not be appropriate. No one would advocate assessing the proficiency of piano students by giving them multiple-choice tests rather than have them perform on the piano. But for measuring knowledge and skills in relatively defined domains, such as reading and mathematics, standardized tests are satisfactory if not ideal.

Techniques used to develop and interpret standardized tests, such as IRT methods, are very complex. And methods of measuring improvement—for example, regression methods for assessing individual achievement growth—are also demanding. Some evaluators insist that a good system of evaluation and assessment is *necessarily* transparent to educators, parents, and policy makers. Personally, I believe that although transparency is definitely desirable, it should not trump quality and best practices. If my physician told me, "Well, Mr. Vogt, there is a better treatment available, but because most of my patients have trouble understanding it, I don't use it," I'd switch physicians in a big hurry. It is irresponsible for educators to use inferior methods because the general public has trouble understanding them. In a democracy, public schools are and should be controlled by the public, but that does not mean that professionals should dumb down their work.

Most members of the general public rightly expect the professionals to whom they trust their well-being to base professional practice on the most up-to-date expert knowledge in the field, even when that up-to-date knowledge is not easy for the nonexpert to understand. And many members of the general public undoubtedly also understand that the knowledge evolves, and consequent best practices change. Indeed, all fields of professional endeavor are built on a more-or-less rapidly changing and expanding base of knowledge. For example, Ioannidis (2005) has documented substantial change in the findings of recent research in clinical medicine. Keeping up with the changes in the intellectual basis of one's professional practice requires a knowledge of how to review and synthesize the research literature in one's field. The methods for doing so, which have also evolved considerably in recent years, are the subject of our next chapter.

Terms and Concepts to Review

Item response theory (IRT)
Rasch modeling
Classical test theory (CTT)
Item difficulty

Item discrimination
• Point biserial correlation

Computer adaptive testing
• Odds

Log of the odds
• Logit

1 PL model
• One-parameter logistic model

2PL model
• Two-parameter logistic model

Maximum likelihood estimation (MLE)
Criterion-referenced test
Norm-referenced test
NCLB
NAEP
Adequate yearly progress (AYP)
Cut scores
Value-added methods
Simpson's paradox

Discussion Questions

1. Think of a test you have taken recently. Do you believe it was norm-referenced, criterion-referenced, or neither? Why?

2. Referring to the same test as in question 1, do you think that IRT, CTT, or neither was used in the interpretation of the test results? Why?

3. Discuss the similarities and differences of item difficulty and item discrimination. Is it possible for a test item (question) to be high in one but low in the other? How?

4. The advantages of computer adaptive testing are that the test can be adapted to and more precisely measure the "trait level" of the person taking the test. Can you think of any disadvantages?

5. If you could change one thing about the NCLB Act, what would it be? How did you choose? Why?

6. Compare the relative merits of cut score methods and value-added methods of reporting the results of tests. Can you think of a circumstance in which cut scores would be appropriate and value-added methods would not?

Self-Test

If you can answer most of the following questions accurately, you can feel confident about your understanding of the material in this chapter. If not, it would be a good idea to review the chapter. (Answers can be found in the Appendix.)

1. The difficulty index (also known as easiness index) is the proportion of examinees who answered an item correctly. True or False?

2. If an item's difficulty index is close to 1.0 or to zero, this is one indication that it may be a bad item. True or False?

3. A negative correlation between an item and the total score on all items would mean that lower-scoring students did better on that item and higher-scoring students did worse. True or False?

4. Mastery questions on exams, which test whether students have met the standard for the topic typically have difficulty indexes of about .50 or 50%, because students have only two possibilities: meet standards or not. True or False?

5. If all students taking a test answered 75% of the items correctly the odds of any individual examinee answering correctly would be 3:1. True or False?

6. The *logit* of an item is calculated by taking the log of the odds of answering that item correctly. True or False?

7. Log transformations are used in testing to make nonlinear distribution linear. True or False?

8. Item response theory makes it possible to determine the levels of difficulty of items and in that way equate the levels of difficulty of different versions of a test. True or False?

9. Standards-based tests should usually use norm-referenced and not criterion-referenced scoring. True or False?

10. The NCLB legislation mandates that separate achievement tests be used for economically disadvantaged students. True or False?

11. States are locked into federal standards and have almost no choice about how to measure adequate yearly progress (AYP). True or False?

12. Statisticians and measurement specialists are largely in agreement about the technically best methods to determine cut scores for such categories as basic and proficient. True or False?

13. Using cut scores necessarily entails discarding information. True or False?

14. Using value-added measures, our best evidence indicates that high-poverty schools are much less effective than limited-poverty schools at improving student achievement. True or False?

15. When using value-added measures, statisticians are largely in agreement that it is better to subtract earlier achievement scores from later scores to arrive at a gain score than to use regression to control for prior achievement. True or False?

16. Because of Simpson's paradox, it is impossible for the mean score of the total group to decrease when the scores of all the subgroups increase. True or False?

Endnotes

1. Creators of national standardized tests often aim for items with a difficulty index between 40% and 70%.

2. The same rules apply to the school districts and to the states, but for simplicity's sake we will focus here on their consequences for individual schools.

3. And this is to say nothing of whether there ought be equally rigorous exams in other subjects, such as history or economics or ecology.

17

Reviewing, Critiquing, and Synthesizing Research

One of the first steps in basing your professional work on the up-to-date and changing knowledge in your field is to do systematic searches of the research literature in your areas of practice. When you review research for professional purposes, you usually hope for a strong degree of consensus among researchers about the likely outcomes of approaches and interventions. Reviewing the research is also the first step in preparing to conduct research of your own. You need to see what others have already done on the topic. There is not much point in doing research on a problem that has been largely resolved. This differs from a search to inform professional practice, in which you look for the clear guidance that resolution can bring. Other than this difference—practitioners look for solutions and researchers look for unsolved problems—the two processes of finding, critiquing, and synthesizing research results are essentially the same.

Although the *literature review* is conceptually the first step in a research project, and should inform professionals from the outset of their careers, it doesn't appear in this book until the last chapter. That is because this preliminary step requires a good deal of prior knowledge. Until one has substantial general background information about research methods and terminology, such as that provided in the previous chapters, it is difficult to read literature with understanding.

The process of reviewing, critiquing, and synthesizing is largely the same whether you plan to stop when you have learned what the state of the art is in research on the problem or whether you intend to do further research on the issue yourself. The general idea is to find, summarize, organize, and apply existing research knowledge to your question. Your problem might be that you have a practical decision to make and you want first to inform yourself about the research relevant to it. Or your problem could be more oriented toward further research, as when you are preparing to write a dissertation. The procedures can be somewhat abbreviated when you are reviewing research in preparation to make a practical decision (see Haller & Kleine, 2001, for some suggestions), but the basic techniques for finding research and the principles and logic for summarizing it do not differ between professional and research reviews. In this chapter, I will focus more on the longer kinds of reviews typical of those aimed at preparing for further research; professional practitioners may want to truncate the process somewhat. In either case, seeing how researchers have addressed your problem can be of great help to you in deciding the best strategy to use in tackling it yourself. Equally important, your research review can help you avoid unsuccessful approaches.

The most fundamental point, regardless of the purpose of your literature review, is that a literature review should be taken as seriously as any other kind of research. A literature review should be replicable—in two ways. First, your search techniques should be replicable. To be replicable, they have to be stated. You need to tell your readers what you searched for, where you searched, and how you searched. Another researcher, trying to follow in your footsteps should be able to arrive at the same or a very similar list of research reports. Second, and this is a tougher standard, another researcher using your procedures should come up with roughly the same general conclusions. As with any other research, if two investigators using the same data (research reports in this case) and the same methods of analyzing the data do not draw similar conclusions, the discrepancy raises important questions about the quality of the research.

There are four common ways that writers of literature reviews put together their findings about the individual research reports they have surveyed.

1. The researcher can generate a *boring list.* This method of exposition essentially involves the author saying, "In the first study I read it said . . . , in the second study I read it said . . . ." That is just typing up your notes, and it is never acceptable. No one would seriously advocate a boring list, but that is in fact what many novice reviewers of the literature produce. A list of summaries of research reports needs to be analyzed and synthesized before it qualifies as a review. Without such analysis and synthesis, it is no more than a pile of summaries.

2. The researcher could write an *impressionistic summary*—perhaps after being inspired by a visit from the muse of literature reviews. This can occasionally be a good approach, but only if you are certain that your work will be brilliant and creative. Absent that level of self-assurance, however, it is better to have a method.

3. The researcher can conduct and construct a *systematic review,* proceeding with all the care that one would use in organizing and summarizing any other type of data. That fact that one's "data" in lit-

erature reviews are research reports, does not give one license to be sloppy.

4. Finally, one can conduct a *meta-analysis,* also known as a *research synthesis.* A meta-analysis is essentially a subset of number 3, the systematic review. A meta-analysis differs from other systematic reviews in that it uses quantitative techniques for summing up the findings of the research reports, but the basic principles of good practice are the same for all systematic reviews.

For obvious reasons, I will address only the final two ways writers of literature reviews present their findings: the systematic review and the meta-analysis. Despite the persistence of the boring list and the impressionistic summary, neither practice leads to reliable literature reviews.

How to Find Research to Review

Whether you do a systematic review or a meta-analysis, two preliminary steps are required. First, you need to find the research reports to review. Second, you need principles for deciding what to include in and what to exclude from your review. Ideally, you might want to find and review everything relevant. This is sometimes possible in a field that has not been extensively researched, but you will usually have to settle for a selection from a vast field of research reports. If there is a potentially huge body of research literature on your topic, you will need to define your topic very precisely to limit the scope of your search. A complete review of all relevant literature may still be beyond reach. Even after careful delimitation of your topic, it will often still be necessary to settle for a sample of the best and most recent research reports addressing your research problem. That will especially be the case if you are doing a less exhaustive review either to make a practical decision or to write a term paper. In the case of term papers, I have my students include a brief statement about where they searched for research literature, how they searched, what they found, and how they selected among what they found. Here follows a typical example drawn from a term paper that required students to review at least 10 articles on a subject of interest to them. It is a nice example of the *minimum* necessary: "I looked in ERIC for published articles; I used the search terms *cooperative learning* and *academic achievement*. I found 47 articles; in this paper, I review the 10 most recent ones that use standardized tests to measure achievement."

Your search strategy will vary depending on the stage your research is in. Literature reviews for big projects such as dissertations are often done three times. First, you review in an exploratory way to get the lay of the land on your topic and make your decisions about how you will do your study. Such early literature reviews illustrate what is known as the "paradox of inquiry." To know what to look for, you have to have a good conception of your variables and how they are related, but one of the main purposes of looking is to get a better understanding of your variables and how they are related. If you don't start your literature review until you've decided on your design in all its details, you will be stuck in the same position as the famous fictional fool, Simplissimus, who refused to go into the water until he had first learned how to swim. In research, like everything else, you've got to start by getting your feet wet.

The second literature review is the big one. Once you've decided on what you will study and how you will study it—your question, your design, and your variables—then you are ready to return to the literature for a much more targeted search. You will want to look very closely at the work of researchers who have investigated the same variables and who operationalized their variables the way you have decided to do. In the pages that follow, I will concentrate mostly on the first and second phases of the literature review. These are done before your research is conducted, but there often is a third phase. It is not at all unusual to do a final review of the same and additional sources *after* you have conducted your study. In that case, the goal is to help you interpret your results. Revisiting the literature can often provide clues to help you interpret a puzzling result. Because this third review is actually quite common, it is useful to keep a photocopy of every article that has played

a major role in your literature review. The literature review process tends to be iterative. It is rarely a one-shot task; you usually need to reexamine the research literature on your topic from time to time in the course of a research project. Re-reviews are even more essential, of course, in professional practice. Knowledge changes (Ioannidis, 2005).

In the first phase of your literature review you should probably begin with secondary sources, such as well-known textbooks. Although your goal is to do your own review and synthesis of the *original* research on your topic, it is very useful to see how others have reviewed and summarized it. Start with a few recent intermediate or advanced texts with chapters on your topic. Specialized encyclopedias and handbooks, when available, are also helpful at this stage. If you find these sources too difficult, and need to work with an elementary text, you may not be ready to do research on the topic. You should try to investigate a topic about which you are already quite knowledgeable so that you have a pretty good idea about how to frame your research questions. It is usually more effective to build on your strengths rather than to start from scratch. Remember, too, that such secondary sources are more likely to be out of date. Research articles provide the most recent work in your field.

Go talk to a reference librarian. Usually librarians are pleased to be asked interesting questions and eager to use their considerable skills to help you. Surprisingly perhaps—despite or because of the wonderful resources for electronic searches—librarians have become even more essential in recent years. That is because electronic search tools are in a period of rapid development. Unless you are a complete novice, don't bother to read a book about how to use the electronic resources for searching the research literature. Whatever you read will probably be out of date by the time you read it. It has been my experience for many years that every time I go to a research library, the tools for finding research have been transformed. What I used last semester is no longer available, but something better is.

Despite all the change, there are some consistently important sources, although methods of access to them continue to evolve. In educational research one of the most important databases is ERIC (Educational Resources Information Center), which is actually a cluster of databases in which you can search. As good as ERIC sources are, and they are enormously helpful, they are *not sufficient* for most topics, nor is *any* other single source. ERIC's structure is evolving, not necessarily in a good direction, and its future is uncertain. But even if all were well with ERIC, it would not be enough for a large project such as a thesis or a dissertation. That is because many topics are researched in disciplinary isolation. Psychologists, sociologists, and political scientists working on highly similar subjects sometimes know surprisingly little about one another's efforts. Generally, in education research, one has to supplement ERIC searches with searches in three other data sources: *PsycINFO, Sociological Abstracts (Sociofile),* and *Dissertation Abstracts.* For most topics in education, if you have searched in these three plus ERIC, you can be comfortable that you've covered the basics. Each of the four is available in various formats: hard copy, CDs, and online. Talk to your librarian to learn what is most accessible for you. See Chapter 3 in McMillan (2004) for a good introductory review.

Be sure also to take special note of literature reviews on your topic. These can be very helpful. Most research reports will include brief literature reviews that can help you orient your thinking. And nearly all will contain reference lists that are another source of works on your topic. These lists tend, however, to be rather dated, but they provide one very helpful clue. If in reading the references for articles on your topic you note that there are one or two articles that are always cited, these "classics" provide you with another search strategy especially helpful for finding the most recent work on a topic. If you find such a classic reference, let's call it Jones (1986), look it up in a citation index (the *Social Science Citation Index* is a good example). If everyone working on your topic cites Jones (1986), then searching in a citation index to learn who cites this work will give you a list of everyone working on your topic.

You can sometimes do most of your search for research reports on your subject without going to a library, and you can get a fairly large proportion (not all) of the actual reports online. This is particularly the case if you have Internet access to the library's resources. Online sources unavailable to you as an individual may be available through your library, which pays the subscription fee so that patrons can gain access. Indeed, it may someday be possible to be a good researcher and write a top-notch dissertation without ever entering a library, but in my view, we are not there yet. If you limit yourself only to what is available online, you risk seriously compromising the quality of your work. Even when you could do much of your searching from your home or office, you can usually do some aspects of it better on the spot. More important, libraries are also a good place to meander in your field, to skim books, and to thumb through recent numbers of relevant research journals. You will probably discover that two or three journals publish many of the articles on your topic. If so, it is often very helpful to check the contents of those journals, especially the recent issues that may not yet have been indexed in databases. Much of this wandering can be done virtually, electronically. But not all of it. In my experience, even after a thorough electronic search, one can gain new insights and understanding of a field by "hiking" around in it. Exploring electronically is like looking at a field from a spy satellite. Even at the highest magnifications, it just doesn't "feel" the same as being on the ground and getting dust on your boots.

Ultimately your preferred methods (more than one is usually needed) of searching are a matter of taste. However you meander, physically or electronically, it is advisable to leave a trail of bread crumbs so you can find your way back to the interesting things. Keep a record of what you see (some search engines make it easy to do this). Enter the field like a naturalist. Carry a journal, a lab notebook, a diary—or whatever you want to call your record of what you've done. You will probably find that from time to time it will be very helpful to be able to reconstruct your travels through the literature. This happens more frequently than you might imagine, and, as the old Chinese proverb has it, the strongest memory is weaker than the palest ink. Finally, don't forget to hunt for researchers, not only for the reports they write. Send e-mails to authors of studies you find interesting. A surprisingly high percentage will respond and be glad to help. Ultimately, there is no better way to get up to date on your topic than to talk to the people who are actively engaged in doing research on it.

Despite the potentially great advantages of searching for sources on the shelves of a well-stocked research library, electronic searches are absolutely crucial. Hard-copy versions of good data sources are still sometimes held by libraries, but for most searches they are dramatically inferior to the electronic versions. Many kinds of topics can be effectively searched *only* electronically—because of the word *and*. The connector *and* allows you to specify what you are looking for with increasingly precise descriptors. For example, you might be looking for information about college graduates, (and) who are female, (and) who received financial aid, (and) who majored in engineering, and so on. Each additional descriptor narrows your search and focuses it more precisely on what you are really looking for; this enables you to use *multivariate* criteria for defining your search. Another handy search tool for focusing on your search is *not*, as in: education, not elementary. The word *or* is the opposite of *and* in searching. Whereas *and* gives you the narrowest search, *or* gives you the broadest, as in: schools or colleges. (Connectors, such as *and, not,* and *or,* are called *Boolean* after the inventor of a form of symbolic logic using them.)

Once in a while you will have the opposite problem: Your focus will be too narrow. After running your topic through *PsycINFO, Sociofile,* and other sources, you won't be able to find research on your topic. This is especially the case if your object of research is new—or if it has a new name. We are especially good in management research and education research at dreaming up new names for old concepts. We have cellars full of old wine, in old bottles, but with new labels. One sees this most often, perhaps, in the case of interventions that are products being sold to businesses or schools by profit-making firms. The most effective way to handle a search in which you find that there is "no research" on a topic

is to think in terms of variables, not their labels. The new label usually has an older name. Or the concept can be described more generally. In either case you'll probably find ample research on it. It is a rare topic indeed that has not been investigated. There is a real art to discovering the right generic descriptor (rather than a specific brand name) for a variable. Fortunately, most databases include a thesaurus to help you find the terms you need to search effectively. Again, my advice is to talk to a reference librarian if you need to find and to learn how to use the thesaurus for your database. Even modest research libraries will often have a reference librarian who specializes in your field and who can help you identify the key search terms for your topic. Sometimes, of course, there really is no research on your topic. If that is true, your literature review has given you one of the strongest of all justifications for your research, presuming your topic is important: We do not yet have any research-based knowledge about this topic. By contrast, such a lack of research on a topic would, of course, be disappointing to a professional seeking research guidance.

So far, we have talked only about searching in scholarly sources. But general Internet search engines can also be very helpful. Of course, the Internet is awash in trash—everything from pornography vendors to political extremists, to say nothing of pictures from my family reunion. Like every other new information technology since the invention of printing, the Internet can be used for good or ill, or just for fun. Truly crucial sources for research are available in the Web sites of government agencies (see Chapter 4 of McMillan, 2004, for an overview of education sites). And, increasingly, this information is available *only* online. My favorites among these government sources include the National Center for Educational Statistics (www.nces.ed.gov), the National Institutes of Health (www.nih.gov), and the U.S. Census Bureau (www.census.gov). They contain crucial information, most of which is available only online. Most states also have Web sites where they provide large amounts of the most up-to-date information. Also, an increasing number of research journals are available only online. Finally, it is often useful and fun to use commercial search engines—such as Google or Yahoo—to investigate your topic. It is particularly instructive to search using the same keywords in several search engines. One often finds remarkably little overlap on the "same" subject, which ought to lead to some caution when making claims about the thoroughness of one's searches.

What to Look for When Reviewing Research Reports: A Checklist

To read, critically analyze, and then synthesize the research literature you have gathered, it is often useful to use a checklist of questions to ask of every research report you examine. There are too many things to cover to trust your memory to think of checking them all. An important bonus of this approach is that after you've gone through your checklist with each research report, and you reach the point where you want to synthesize what you have found, a checklist gives you a way to organize your notes according the answers to a common set of questions.

To suggest how you might construct your own checklist, I have provided the one I use as an example. I use it quite specifically as a checklist, as a guide to make sure I don't forget anything important. I also use it in a different form as a template to organize my notes. Every question on the list is not equally pertinent for every article or for every topic. If you use the checklist, you may need to supplement some questions, delete a few, or add new ones for your particular purposes, but this list is a place to start. To repeat, answering a checklist of questions almost automatically produces a preliminary organization for your notes. This organization will make it easy for you to pull together all of your information about mediating variables (question 9) or sample size (question 17) or statistical significance (question 20), and so on. Being able to organize the findings of your literature review is the key to a systematic analysis, whether your goal is to find out what works in an area of practice or to build your own research on it.

Figure 17.1 presents the checklist. Following the table, I briefly discuss some points raised by the

questions on it. Because a good checklist will naturally try to ask about all important things, discussing the checklist in the table will involve raising, if only briefly, most major issues in research methods.

General Questions

1. *What is the hypothesis or the research question, if any, guiding the research?* Answering this question first can save you a lot of time. It tells you whether this article should be on your list of those that you need to review. Sometimes it is not clear what the authors of the article were investigating. If you cannot figure it out, it could be because you lack the needed background, but it also could be because the authors themselves do not have a clear conception. Not all published work is valuable.

Note that *research questions* or statements of research objectives have largely replaced formal hypotheses (and especially null hypotheses) in introductions to research reports. The difference is mostly a matter of style. Conventions vary by discipline, author, and time period. What does not vary is the reader's need for a clear understanding of the purpose of the research.

2. *Why do the authors believe it is important to investigate this hypothesis/question?* In addition to situating the research in the context of the problems it addresses, answering this question can help you determine whether an article truly is relevant to the research you plan. Articles ostensibly about the same subject might not really be about your topic or issue. If you are interested in the effects of academic achievement on self-esteem, your search could easily turn up research on the effects of self-esteem on achievement—clearly a different topic, in which you might or might not be interested.

3. *What methods did the authors use to collect evidence? What was their design?* This question needs to be asked at a couple of levels. Most generally, what research design, broadly speaking, was used? Was it an experimental study, an ethnographic study, a sample survey, a secondary analysis of data, a document analysis, and so forth? Within each of

FIGURE 17.1   *Checklist of questions to ask when critiquing the typical quantitative* research report*

A. First, and in General

1. What is the hypothesis or the research question, if any, guiding the research?
2. Why do the authors believe it is important to investigate this hypothesis/question?
3. What methods did the authors use to collect evidence? What was their design?
4. Were the methods appropriate to address this problem/question?
5. What are the main findings or conclusions of the article?
6. Are the conclusions convincing?

B. Questions about the Variables

7. What is the dependent or outcome variable (OV)?
8. What are the independent or predictor variables (PVs)?
9. Are any mediating or intervening variables identified?
10. Should these or any other mediating/intervening variables have been studied?
11. Are any control variables considered?
12. Should other control variables have been examined?
13. Does the article discuss the possible moderating variables and interaction effects? Should it?
14. How are the variables defined and measured; that is, how are they operationalized?
15. Are the definitions and measurements of the variables appropriate for this study?

C. Questions about the Sample/Subjects

16. Who is studied and are the subjects appropriate given the goals of the study?
17. How many are studied and is this enough for the purposes of the study?
18. Is the sample representative of a population? How broadly can the conclusions be generalized?

D. Questions about the Conclusions

19. Are the findings *statistically* significant?
20. Are the findings *scientifically* significant?
21. How big are the effects discovered?
22. Are the findings *practically* significant?
23. Are the conclusions really supported by the evidence cited in the article?

E. Finally and Implied in the Answers to the Above Questions

24. How could the research have been improved?
25. What questions or problems does the article leave unanswered?
26. How could you go about doing a better job?

---

*One would want to ask roughly the same sorts of questions about qualitative articles, but much of the terminology would tend to be different.

Note: For other discussions of these and related points, see Gall, Gall, and Borg (1999, pp. 516–524); Stern and Kaloff (1996, pp. 144–156); Haller and Kleine (2001, Chap. 3); and Meltzoff (1997, pp. 164–166); Light and Pillemer (1984, Chap. 6).

those categories you will want to specify further. For example, what kind of experiment was conducted, a true or a quasi-experiment, a within-groups or between-groups experiment, and the like?

4. *Were the methods appropriate to address this problem/question?* Even if the method was well-executed, that still leaves the question of whether it was the right sort of approach for the particular problem studied. For example, if a survey were used, might interviews or focus groups have been more likely to provide evidence pertinent to answering the authors' questions?

5. *What are the main findings or conclusions of the article?* What do the authors say they learned in their study? Are the findings clearly and concisely stated? If so, this will be of great help to you. The art of reviewing literature is in part the art of summarizing. You will typically review dozens of studies, but you will not want your summaries of conclusions to run to dozens of pages. So you need to be able to give the nub of the matter in less than a page. Sometimes the authors will help you by providing a concise account of their conclusions (usually in the abstract). Often you will have to construct that summary yourself—sometimes because your interests might be different than those of the report's authors. You may want to make different use of their work than they have.

6. *Are the conclusions convincing?* You will want to answer this in more than one way. First you will want to record your overall "feeling" for the persuasiveness of the article. Most of the rest of the questions on this checklist help you to explain why you might or might not find the conclusions convincing. But even though you will explain your assessment of the article via your answers to the following questions, you are also likely to have a more visceral and less analytical first reaction to it. It is good to record this reaction. One of the most common sources of a good research topic is an investigator's annoyance with a well-known article in an important journal. Irritation can motivate the reader to look very closely at the research. When a research report gives you pleasure, analyze those reactions too; they help you discover what you value in research. First, trust your instincts. Then, scrutinize them. There is nothing wrong with *starting* with gut feelings—as long as you use them to give you the energy to engage your mind.

Questions about the Variables

7. *What is the dependent or outcome variable (OV)?* The answer to this question is often a very straightforward and clear one. If it is not, that could be because the article is descriptive and does not have an outcome (or dependent) variable strictly speaking. As with question 1 (what is the hypothesis/ question?), answering this one helps you focus your attention sharply on whether a given research report is really one you want to analyze extensively. If you want to study, for example, the causes of dropping

out a counseling program, you'll want to review articles in which dropping out is the outcome variable. However, you probably don't want to review articles on the *consequences* of dropping out, in which case dropping out would be the predictor (or independent) variable. However, some portions of an article not directly relevant to your research could be useful in a limited way—for example, a good operationalization of a variable might be found in an article that was not otherwise relevant.

8. *What are the independent or predictor variables (PVs)?* In addition to recording the PVs studied in the research report, you have to decide about the ones that you are really interested in. It is helpful to make an inventory of all the PVs (or independent variables) that have been suggested in all of your sources as related to your outcome variable (OV). Then you need to decide how to handle this list. If your OV is dropping out of college, do you want to look for any and all possible factors that lead to dropping out? Or are you more focused and do you want to look only at the effects of one particular variable on dropping out? If so, all the other predictors on your list could still be important, but as control variables. You need to look at variables in which you aren't interested so as to be able to control for them, to "eliminate them as suspects," as the police say; they are alternative explanations for your findings.

9. *Are any mediating or intervening variables identified?* If a mediating variable is identified, this is often the main point of the article. Mediating variables are the links between predictors (PVs) and outcomes (OVs). In our earlier examples, we saw that arthritis was linked to reduced heart attacks by aspirin, which was the mediator. Small schools were linked to higher student achievement by improved teacher attitudes; the attitudes mediated the effect of school size. The mediator is the message in many research reports.

10. *Should these or any other mediating/intervening variables have been studied?* Sometimes your critical analysis of a research report will lead you to believe you have discovered an important potential mediator that has been omitted. Such discoveries are one of the ways in which your literature review becomes active and creative. An omitted mediator may become the variable in which you take a special interest and want to study. Often you will discover mediators of interest by reflecting on the possible relationships among the variables in your inventory of all predictors (see question 8).

11. *Are any control variables considered?* First you need to note what the control variables are in each study. Then, as with the predictor (independent) variables, it is helpful to make a list of all the control variables used in the studies you review. Then you can compare the variables controlled in the studies. This can often enable you understand seemingly discrepant findings. If one study shows a significant relation between *X* and *Y* and a second study does not, this could be because the second study has controlled for a variable omitted in the first. For example, a relationship between class size and student achievement might be influenced by the age of the students and/or their socioeconomic status (SES). Young children and low-SES students, some studies have shown, both benefit much more from small classes. Finally, because another researcher has used a variable as a control, it does not follow that you must. Indeed, you could use that variable as a predictor, in which case information about another author's control variable (e.g., a regression coefficient) is directly relevant to your predictor variable.

12. *Should other control variables have been examined?* It is almost always possible to think of other control variables that could have or should have been examined. When an article suggests that one variable influences another, it is usually possible to say, "Yes, but isn't that just because. . . ." What follows *because* in the sentence is a control variable. Yes, the students in the new program learned more, but isn't that just because their teachers were enthusiastic volunteers? Often the greatest weakness of a nonexperimental study is that the authors have not considered what seems a crucial control variable. The same can be true of experimental studies. We hope that random assignment to experimental and control groups will automatically equalize all potential control variables, including those we don't know about. And, if the sam-

ple is fairly large, we can usually count on that form of control to do the job. But if the sample is not large and/or if it is an unrepresentative convenience sample, control variables can be important in experiments too. It is in this circumstance that pretests can be so important in experimental research (see Chapter 6).

13. *Does the article discuss possible moderating variables and interaction effects? Should it?* An interaction effect occurs when two variables *jointly* influence a third, as when the joint effects of two medicines produce an unexpected result. A moderating variable is one that *modifies* a relation between other variables. Gender, age, and ethnicity are probably the most common moderators. Just as when there are obvious control variables that ought to have been considered, the authors should explain what they have done about possible but omitted interaction effects and moderating variables. As we have seen (in Chapter 9), the statistical examination of a moderating variable and of a control variable generally involves the same technical analysis procedure, such as including it in a regression equation. For example, if we study the effects of participation in an educational program on student learning, do we get the same results before and after *controlling* for student gender? If not, student gender may *moderate* the relationship between program participation and student learning.

14. *How are the variables defined and measured; that is, how are they operationalized?* Very often studies presumably about the same thing define and measure that thing so differently that really there is no reason for thinking that the same thing is being studied. A difference in the findings of two studies may stem from the fact that they have measured their variables differently. Say one study measures the effects of parental SES on student achievement by using parents' education level and students' grades. Another defines SES as income and achievement as SAT scores. Are they really measuring the same variables and the same relationship? Even if parents' education level and income tend to be fairly well correlated, they are not the same thing, nor are students' grades and SAT scores. Each may be an indicator of the same underlying variable. Perhaps the two measures of parental SES and the two measures of student achievement should be combined. Or if one is your target predictor variable, the other should be controlled. For example, what is the effect of parents' education level after controlling for their household income (or vice versa)?

15. *Are the definitions and measurements of the variables appropriate for this study?* Depending on the purposes of a study, different operationalizations of variables might be appropriate. You will at least want to be able to categorize the studies you use in your literature review according to how they made these key decisions. To understand the works in your literature review you need to know not only how the variables were *labeled* (e.g., student achievement), but also how such variables were *defined*. It surely matters whether student achievement was measured by class rank or GPA or ACT scores or "met standards" on a state test. Each of these is an indicator of student achievement, but each measures it differently. If a conclusion holds even when several different indicators are used, this does much to substantiate the conclusion. But if it differs when different indicators are used, this provides continuing challenges for researchers.

Questions about the Sample/Subjects

16. *Who is studied and are the subjects appropriate given the goals of the study?* The most accessible subjects are not always the most relevant. For example, if the subject is attitudes toward the risks of unemployment and the subjects are college students, who are not in the labor market at the time they are surveyed, the mismatch may be so great that the study is of little use.

17. *How many are studied and is this enough for the purposes of the study?* Is the sample big enough for generalization, for statistical power, for statistical significance? Often these are technical questions, but sometimes less so. Do we really want to decide about how variables are related among individuals on the basis of a study using the people in two towns—even if the number of individuals studied is technically sufficient for statistical power?

18. *Is the sample representative of a population? How broadly can the conclusions be generalized?* This is the point to which questions 16 and 17 are leading you. Were enough of the right sorts of people or schools or cities studied that you can be confident about the applicability of the conclusions? Even if appropriate subjects were studied, and even if many of them were studied, if they aren't a representative sample, one should be wary of using information about them to generalize beyond the sample to a population.

Questions about the Conclusions

19. *Are the findings* statistically *significant?* Unless the authors have made an arithmetic error, this is just a matter of reading off the *p*-values. But there is still some judgment involved. Some authors will use $p < .10$, others $p < .05$, and others $p < .01$ as the cutoff at which significance is declared. Although .05 is the conventional level, it is just a convention, and you may wish to judge whether it is appropriate (either too strict or not strict enough) in each case.

20. *Are the findings* scientifically *significant?* Do the conclusions make a genuine contribution to the knowledge that other researchers might use to further their work? Note that this is a separate question from the issue of whether the conclusions can be directly applied to a practical problem. Most research articles are cluttered with the word *significant*, especially in their concluding paragraphs. Readers need to use great caution when interpreting this adjective.

21. *How big are the effects discovered?* You want to compare the size of outcomes as well as their statistical and scientific significance. Statistically significant effects can sometimes be quite small. Measures of *size* include measures of association such as correlation coefficients and the widely used effect size statistic based on standardized mean differences. But *big* and *small* are relative. Reducing the incidence of some problem in a state by a mere 1% may mean saving thousands of people from its effects.

22. *Are the findings* practically *significant?* Practical significance, like size and scientific significance, is also a matter of judgment. Practical significance tends to be determined by the size of effects. Whether a particular size of effect is big *enough* to make an *important* difference is *not* a statistical question but is one of judgment about the context in which the conclusion is applied. An effect size (ES) of 0.1 for the effects of an inexpensive cancer treatment can be very important practically, because treating cancer is a matter of life or death. On the other hand, an ES of 0.1 for a costly SAT coaching course would probably be considered a trivial effect by knowledgeable people.

23. *Are the conclusions really supported by the evidence cited in the article?* Readers who have carefully examined the evidence as presented by the authors are sometimes shocked to find what the authors have had the audacity to conclude. Even if the authors get a little exuberant in the concluding paragraphs, good authors of good articles in good journals give the reader the data and the means to check their work, to judge the evidence to see whether it supports the conclusions. The whole reason we go through the previous questions about operationalizing variables, representative samples, effect size, and the rest of it is to be able to check. This is also why you need considerable background before you can do your literature review. Otherwise, as a reviewer, you might be limited to merely reading the discussion section in which authors tend to speculate freely and use overblown adjectives. A literature review that skips the evidence is not sufficient as a basis for further research.

Finally and Implied in the Answers to the Above Questions

24. *How could the research have been improved?* If your literature review is providing the context for your research, this question is key. If you find a perfect study on your topic, there isn't much point in you continuing. But no study is perfect—at least I have not yet encountered one. No study can examine all aspects of a question. The authors of research reports will often, and should usually, discuss the limitations of their work. When the authors are candid, descriptions of research limitations provide you with important guidelines about what needs to be done in your field.

25. *What questions or problems does the article leave unanswered?* Again, this provides you with direction for your research and limitations for applicability in professional practice. The imperfections could merely be that the study needs to be extended. The article could be excellent, but you might wish to see if the conclusions hold in different settings or with different subjects.

26. *How could you go about doing a better job?* The relevance of this question is obvious. Answer it, and you have the nub of your research design. As with limitations, many authors give you their assessment of what research needs to be done in the future. In fact, it is quite rare to read a research report that does not end with a call for further research. Some of these statements are ritualistic, but others offer serious advice about research needs on a topic.

Conclusion to Checklist Review

What do you do with your answers to the questions on the checklist? The answers tend to be short and provide you with a way of categorizing the reports in your review. I usually put the questions in a table format, reformatting the checklist as a grid, so that there is room for the answers to the questions. Each research report gets a table or grid, which serves as a cover sheet; each cover sheet has 26 rows, one for each question. This is a useful approach when the number of research reports is fairly small. For larger, more complicated studies, I use a spreadsheet program, such as Excel. Here, each article is given a row and each question is answered in a column. This is a more flexible approach, and one that facilitates handling a large number of articles. It is also possible to insert other notes into the spreadsheet, although I find that I often do not need more detailed notes when I have answered my checklist questions thoroughly. If I find that I need to take notes on topics not covered in the original checklist, I add more questions to the checklist. This is of course much easier with a spreadsheet program than a hard-copy table.

However you organize your answers to your checklist questions about the research reports you have read, you will be in a good position to develop some strong conclusions, even if some of the articles disagree, as they almost surely will. In the first place you should be clear *what* they agree and disagree about. Second, you will also have extensive evidence about *why* studies might come to different conclusions. Perhaps they used different methods or operationalized variables differently or used different controls. Perhaps they studied different settings or kinds of subjects. Say you've reviewed 25 studies, and 16 of them have claimed that *X* is associated with *Y*, but 9 say that it isn't. Have they operationalized variables differently—for example, is academic achievement defined as grades or scores? Or have they included different control variables—for example, is the effect different in those studies that controlled for SES? Or did they study different subjects (college students, males, etc.)? Or did they use different designs (experiment with random assignment versus quasi-experiment)? Or were the studies conducted in different settings (public versus private institutions)? You will be in a position to observe these things, even before you have undertaken any of your own research. You will have an overview of research on the topic. You will be quite likely to know something *new* before you even begin to gather data. The authors of individual studies will often not have your broader perspective. In brief, you should finish your literature review as the possessor of a rare kind of expertise.

What to Include (and Exclude) and How to Write It Up

Reading all of the research reports you unearth is often a formidable task. Writing a review of that research can be equally daunting. For one thing, it is not always easy to distinguish between research reports that provide interesting background for your project and those that are really essential to your research or your practice. You will almost certainly have read and taken careful notes on many works that

do not make it into your final review. Cutting these irrelevancies, which may represent days of work, is painful. Remember that the goal of the review is to establish the rationale for your research, or to learn something useful for your professional work, not to show how much homework you have done. Good reviewing means summarizing and eliminating—data reduction, if you will. But save your notes! You may find that after you have done your research you need to revisit some of this earlier work.

Writing up your literature review can often be the most conceptually demanding part of a project. Doing it well requires that you have a good grasp of the entire field and the methods used to study it. You need to have mastered your sources if you are to be able to do the kind of radical summarizing that is necessary. For example, most of my students in research classes have difficulty when I limit them to 1,000 words (about 4 typed pages) to summarize one article. A good literature review will often discuss 50 articles and other sources. At 4 pages each, that would get you to 200 pages. You do not want to write, and no one wants to read, a 200-page literature review. That would be too unwieldy for research or practice. To twist a famous quotation from Pascal, a noted seventeenth-century philosopher and contributor to statistical theory, "Excuse me for writing such a long lit review; I did not have the time to write a short one." If you have devoted sufficient time to master your subject, you can often write a *comparatively* short research review. The more drafts you write the shorter they can get. That is because you learn to generalize about your findings, not merely list them.

One way to approach the writing-up problem is to think of your research review as a history of your subject. Professional researchers often see their work this way; they think of their investigations very explicitly in terms of what has gone on before. Your literature review could help you see your work that way too. You will often encounter this historical approach in your reading and will see phrases such as the following: "The problem was originally understood as . . . then, with advances in the field, . . . what is new about the current research is that we have. . . ." One reason for the popularity of this historical approach is that it can leave the reader eager to read the study. After having been given this "running start" in the past, the reader is ready to jump into the future. Substantively and rhetorically the whole point of the literature review is to prepare first yourself and then your readers for what is to come. Some researchers dislike this historical approach; they prefer to organize conceptually rather than temporally. The historical approach is an option, probably more appropriate for research than for informing professional practice. There is no one best way.

One of the most helpful methods for learning to write good research literature reviews is to reflect on those you read. As you read research reports you will inevitably be reading literature reviews too—generally very short ones. Try to learn from these examples. Volumes published in the series, *Annual Reviews,* cover some 30 fields, several of them in the social sciences, including sociology, psychology, political science, public health, and anthropology. Another annual is the *Review of Research in Education.* It and the quarterly *Review of Educational Research* are devoted exclusively to research reviews. Among the techniques that can be appreciated by reading examples in such publications is the excellent use that can be made of tables to summarize findings. Creswell (2002, pp. 39–41) recommends constructing a physical "map" of the literature that will enable you to picture the relations among the research reports on your topic. Constructing such a map is more than an exercise to help you with your thinking. You may well want to use it when writing up your final review and to help your readers with their thinking about your topic.

As should be obvious from all that has been said here, writing your review using only the discussion sections of the research reports is insufficient. Especially when reviewing quantitative research, use numbers, not adjectives, to summarize the results. Numbers are more precise and take up less space. Knowing that two studies found a significant correlation between SAT scores and GPAs is one thing. Knowing that one found a correlation of .30 and the other of .50 tells you much more. Give the effect sizes, the correlation coefficients, and the mean dif-

ferences. Don't just say "big"; say *how* big. Don't merely say that a result was statistically significant; tell the reader at which level it was significant and, if available, give the actual *p*-values. Information about effect sizes is important for research; it is indispensable for professional practice.

If you write your review well, you will be leading your readers to see the research problem as you have come to see it as a result of your review of the research. When your readers move to the methodology section of your paper or thesis, they will not be surprised at how you have decided to investigate your topic. They will, in fact be expecting your approach, because your review should have led them to expect it, to see the research question in your terms. This is a difficult standard, but if you can attain it, it indicates true mastery of your subject.

In a review aimed at discovering the best professional practices, the review is the end of the research process. For researchers, the review is a prelude to a bigger project. Sometimes, however, researchers find that their review is important enough to become its own end, not merely a lead-in to another research project. This is especially the case for research reviews that employ the techniques of meta-analysis.

Introduction to Meta-Analysis or Research Synthesis

Everything I have said above about systematic literature reviews applies—perhaps at a somewhat heightened level of intensity—to meta-analysis. A meta-analysis is simply a systematic review that uses quantitative techniques to summarize quantitative results. I use a checklist of questions, such as that in Table 17.1, whether I am reviewing quantitative or qualitative research. Most often I review a mixture of the two on any given topic. Meta-analysis might better be called *research synthesis,* and it is thus called by many researchers, especially in biomedical research. Whatever one calls it, the basic idea is to develop quantitative summaries of the findings of quantitative research reports. In addition to calculating an effect size for each individual research finding, one can calculate an overall average effect size for all research findings. Doing this adds a new dimension to reviewing and summarizing research, but it does not change its nature fundamentally. Apart from the technical issues concerning how to do the calculations, the important questions remain the same as in any review of the research literature. And the technical issues involved with meta-analysis are often not highly complicated. Meta-analysis does not use many new techniques; rather, well-known measures are applied to new kinds of investigations—in which research reports are the unit of analysis. Readers wishing to conduct a meta-analysis will probably want more detail than can provided in this overview, although we will touch on the basics. Our focus, as always, is more on the conceptual than the computational aspects of our subject. If one understands the concepts one can easily find out how to do the calculations, but the reverse is less often true. My students' two favorite sources for the further computational details are the books by Light and Pillemer (1984) and Lipsey and Wilson (2001).

Meta-analysis was independently invented, at about the same time (1970s), by Robert Rosenthal and Gene Glass. Its techniques have developed rapidly since that time. Among the most important consequences of the emergence of meta-analysis has been its effect on all research reviews, regardless of whether they use the techniques of meta-analysis. The presence of meta-analysis has ratcheted up standards for all literature reviews. In the past, researchers too often treated the research studies they were reviewing in ways they would have been ashamed to treat any other kind of evidence. Too often (not always) articles to review seemed to have been chosen casually, based on no particular plan. Such evidence appeared to have reflected little more than the convenience or biases of the researchers. Today, most researchers would agree that research reviews should be conducted with as much care as, and they "should be just as replicable as any other piece of scientific work" (Cook et al., 1992, p. viii). And that is true regardless of whether the reviews are meta-analyses.

One useful way to think of meta-analysis is to see it as "a form of survey research in which research reports, rather than people, are surveyed" (Lipsey & Wilson, 2001, p. 1). Extending this analogy, traditional reviews, those that do not employ quantitative means of summarizing findings, are more like interviews. Just as it would be silly to say surveys are the "right" way and interviews are the "wrong" way to obtain evidence, so too with narrative and quantitative summaries of research. Each has advantages and disadvantages. Surveys, like meta-analyses, gather the same information from a large number of respondents with the goal of being able to summarize their responses quantitatively. They tend to be strong on external validity or generalizability. Interviews, by contrast, tend to probe in more depth with fewer informants and in ways that can vary from informant to informant. They tend to be better at exploring individuals' meanings and being certain that the respondents' meanings are clear. This can be thought of as a kind of internal validity. But because interviews inevitably use smaller, and usually unrepresentative, samples, they tend to be weak on generalizability. What matters more, depth or generalizability? Deciding on the best approach for your research review is as complicated as any other choice of method for a research project; it always involves trade-offs. Are you going to survey your sources or will you interview them? I usually advocate the kind of mixed-method approach advocated by Light and Pillemer (1984).

Should you do a meta-analysis for your research review? If you are conducting a literature review and it is not a meta-analysis, you probably need to explain why. It is the state of the art in reviews of quantitative research. I would even go so far as to say that the burden of proof is on you to show that a meta-analysis would not be better, not only than a traditional literature review, but than a small-scale study you are planning. In short, if you are not doing a meta-analysis, you should have a good reason. There are, however, many strong reasons why a meta-analysis would not be a good choice.

What are some reasons you would *not* do a meta-analysis? One is that another meta-analysis has recently been done on this topic. The readily analyzable topics tend to get snapped up, in part because meta-analysis is a powerful technique, and using it requires no human subjects review (IRB). Probably the main reason not to do a meta-analysis is that the number of quantitative studies on the topic is insufficient. Or, even if an apparently adequate number of studies exists, they might not be appropriate for one reason or another. For example, it is not uncommon for research reviews to conclude that studies of a subject are so flawed that is it not possible to come to any clear conclusions (see Mattingly et al., 2002, for an example). A final reason not to do a meta-analysis, of course, is that if everyone did only meta-analyses, we would eventually run out of works to synthesize. We could delay the inevitable by doing *meta*-meta-analyses, but ultimately, someone will have to undertake the original research studies that are the foundation on which we build.

My estimate is that for most of the topics that doctoral students consider, well over three-quarters will *not* be suitable for a full meta-analysis. Usually, there will not be enough studies investigating the same variables, measured the same way, and researched with the same methods. However, within a broader review of the research literature, more limited meta-analytic work—what we might call mini-meta-analyses—on a subset of research reports can often be conducted. Within a general review of several dozen reports, one is likely to find one or more clusters of a few studies for which it is possible to pool data in ways that meet the requirements of meta-analysis. When that kind of opportunity presents itself, my advice is to be pragmatic and use the tools. Looking at things the other way around, I would also recommend a similar sort of pragmatism when conducting full meta-analytic studies. In the course of a meta-analysis, one is very likely to find studies not appropriate for statistical summary. But these should not merely be discarded. If they contain relevant evidence, the fact that they will not fit into the statistical summary should not lead to their disqualification. For example, a case study investigating a single instance of a relationship in depth will usually not contain meta-analyzable data, but it may provide indispensable insights into *how* statistically associated variables are related. Another example is that studies using multivariate regression are extremely difficult

to pool, because different studies seldom use the same set of predictor variables. But skipping them would also seem ill-advised.

Narratives versus Numbers in Research Reviews

Not surprisingly, the ideological posturings of the quant/qual battle occur too in the realm of research reviews. As elsewhere, here too, the quant/qual distinction obscures more than it clarifies. Some reviews are better done with narratives, some with numbers, and many can benefit from various combinations of the two. Nonetheless, proponents and opponents of meta-analysis have sometimes turned their disputes into another episode in clash between the Quants and the Quals. However, as Light and Pillemer (1984) put it, "The pursuit of good science should transcend personal preferences for numbers or narrative" (p. 143).

The truly heated polemics between the antagonists and protagonists of meta-analysis have cooled since the 1980s. Extreme accusations on both sides have died down. One of the most common accusations was that meta-analysts think that they can take bad studies and, merely by adding them up, produce good ones. This is the famous GIGO criticism: garbage-in, garbage-out. No one would claim that meta-analysis can turn garbage into gold. In my reading, authors of the typical meta-analysis are extraordinarily careful to cull out the garbage before they synthesize findings. Often huge searches reviewing hundreds of research reports yield only a few dozen that are appropriate for synthesis. GIGO is certainly true, but it applies as much to narrative reviews as to numerical ones. Generally, meta-analysts make their selection criteria explicit. This gives readers the evidence they need to decide whether what has been synthesized is garbage. In general, bad practice in meta-analysis is bad practice in any kind of research review.[1]

The meta-analytic retort to such criticism has often been to claim that traditional narrative reviews turn gold into garbage. Good studies are thrown together in ways that mostly reveal the biases of the reviewers. Research reviews in which reports are selected and summarized according to no clear plan or are chosen and discussed as dictated by the biases of reviewers are the origin of much garbage. This also is a good criticism. Of course, not many people would seriously argue for slanted reviews. Guarding against bias is as important in meta-analyses as it is in traditional narrative reviews. In sum, the principles of good work when reviewing research literature transcend the format for stating the conclusions. They apply whether the conclusions about the research being summarized are expressed numerically, verbally, or graphically.

Comparing Apples, Oranges, and Clones in Research Reviews

What should you include in your review of the research? What can reasonably be summarized under the same rubric? These are problems for all research reviews, but they are made more explicit, and are thus more controversial, in meta-analysis. Some answers to these questions may to stem from one's disposition. The research world seems divided between "splitters" and "lumpers." Splitters are fond of saying that you can't compare apples and oranges. To do so ignores important distinctions. Lumpers might say of course you can: Apples and oranges are both fruits that grow on trees, unlike strawberries; both are rounder than plums and firmer than peaches. If apples and oranges were exactly alike there would be no point in comparing them; there is no point in comparing clones.

The lump/split distinction has parallels with the quant/qual divide. Advocates of qualitative measurement, given their stress on individual distinctions, tend to be splitters. Advocates of quantitative measurement, with their emphasis on variables that transcend individual examples, are more likely to be lumpers. As usual, these distinctions are overdrawn. Narrative reviewers can sometimes bring together (lump) a broader range of studies—precisely because narrative reviews can more easily accommodate different operationalizations of variables. And numerical reviewers often spend much time on the narrative

descriptions of design; only in that way can they be sure they are summarizing comparable studies.

Most broadly, the question is: How much detail can you afford to sacrifice in order to make a generalization? If you are not willing to sacrifice any detail, to ignore any differences, you can't generalize at all. Inevitably, generalizations are only generally true—which is why we call them generalizations. On the other hand, if you overlook crucial differences, your generalizations will be foolish. Finding a reasonable middle ground requires much wisdom. The most reasonable answer to the question, "How broadly can we generalize?" is usually a pragmatic one. Does the generalizing help you learn what you are trying to learn? Is your research question best addressed by lumping or splitting? Do you want to study a general variable such as academic achievement? If so, it might best be measured by combining indicators such as grades, class rank, and scores on standardized tests. Or, are you interested in the distinctions between aspects of achievement? In that case you would rightly resist lumping them.

Populations and Samples in Meta-Analysis

Once you have decided on your general definitions of variables, on which predictors and outcomes you want to study and how you want to measure them, how many and which studies do you need to include to do a meta-analysis? If your population is all the research done on a topic, how do you define that population? If you sample from that population, how should you do so, or should you? These are the key questions in meta-analysis. They can be extremely complicated and challenging for researchers, much more so than how to calculate a typical summary statistic used in a meta-analysis, such as an effect size. Usually it is not hard to look up how to calculate a particular statistic. It is much harder to look up how to think about these issues.

The most typical answer by meta-analysts to the question of what to study is use a "total sample," which means, use the population. Include everything, at least initially. Begin with the broadest sample possible. Be relentless in your search. Leave no stone unturned. Meta-analysts point out that many of the studies you find will eventually have to be excluded because they do not meet technical criteria, usually because they do not provide enough information to enable quantitative summary, so you had better begin by conducting a very thorough and inclusive search.

One pragmatic way to answer the question, "How many is enough?" has been suggested by Rosenthal (1979). After you have done an initial meta-analysis on the sources you first found, it is possible to calculate the number of contradictory research reports you would need to discover before you had to change your conclusions. How many research studies with divergent conclusions would you have to find before you would need to alter your summary conclusion? If you would have to find a very large number of such studies, and if you had originally done a thorough search, then your sample size is probably sufficient and your conclusions are probably sound.

The emphasis on thoroughness in searching has led most meta-analysts to advocate hunting extensively for unpublished as well as published research reports. The rationale for this is that published sources may be a biased sample of all the research on the subject. This concern has been supported by some research that indicated that studies reporting *statistically* significant findings are more likely to get published. If that is true, then otherwise good research in which no significant difference among variables was found or no significant difference between groups could be discerned (in other terms, in which the authors were unable to reject the null hypothesis), would be underrepresented in the population of studies.

There are actually two or three categories of unpublished research. The first category is made up of work that, while unpublished, is publicly available. We might call these "quasi-published." This would include, for example, dissertations indexed in *Dissertation Abstracts* and conference papers indexed in ERIC and similar citation guides. I think meta-analysts are right to be systematic in their search for these. The main reason is that dissertations and conference papers have been reviewed by other researchers before becoming available. The arguments for pursuing other categories of unpublished research, truly unpublished research, that is not publically but only privately available, strike me as less persuasive. The authors of unpublished research may not have believed their work to be interesting enough to submit for publication. I see no reason to challenge their self-assessments. Or, unpublished works could have been submitted for publication by their authors, but rejected by publishers. Such rejected work *could* have been rejected because of some sort of publication bias, but it also could have been rejected because it was of low quality. My work as an editor and reviewer for journals makes me think that the latter explanation is much more likely.

Although a large number of good-quality unpublished studies on a topic *may* exist and may differ systematically from the published ones, the possibility strikes me as quite remote in most areas of research. You should note, however, that the majority of meta-analysts disagree with me. Their argument is that a valid survey of a population cannot leave out part of the population. You can *sample* from the *whole* population (although meta-analysts seem reluctant to do this too), but even the most technically correct sampling from an unrepresentative part of the population will not yield a representative sample.

True enough, but what is the "population" in a meta-analysis? It is all the research reports on a subject. Is excluding the unpublished part of the population of research reports really parallel to excluding parts of other populations? There seem important differences. Surely if we were surveying all surgeons and omitted those who worked in HMOs, we would be making a mistake. That is because HMO surgeons are an important and a *knowable* part of the population of all surgeons. But the population of unpublished studies is in principle an unknown and unknowable quantity. How many unpublished studies are there? How could anyone possibly know? Assertions about the unknowable are risky at best. One might rightly *assume* (not know) that such privately conducted research, which is available only in the authors' file drawers, would be more common in nations with repressive political regimes. Or extensive unpublished research could exist on highly controversial topics for which limited publications outlets exist. While this seems logical, direct evidence is necessarily meager.

There is another difference, and a much more important one, between the population of research reports and other populations, such as the population of all surgeons or all cities above a certain size or all Presbyterians. Even if one obtains all research reports—public, private, published, quasi-published, and so on—about a population of research reports, one does not necessarily have an unbiased population of research subjects. One cannot necessarily generalize from this population of research reports to "the truth" about a subject. This population of reports, even if complete, can be biased in the sense that the researchers who wrote the research reports can be biased. This population is only what happens to have been studied about a topic. *It does not represent the topic; it represents researchers' work on the topic.* Indeed, a literature review, even a meta-analysis, is often designed as much to find parts of a topic that have *not* been studied as well as to sum up what is already known. For example, in the not-too-distant past, public opinion research in the United States routinely excluded African Americans. They were not surveyed about their opinions. Medical research on some conditions did not include women in the subject pool. Even a total population of this research would be a biased representation of the potential domain of knowledge in the field. If you take a representative sample of the population *of studies,* but, if most or all of their samples *of subjects* are nonrepresentative convenience samples, your sample is representative of the population of studies, but not of a population of subjects.

To take another example of the difficulty of identifying or conducting a census of "the whole" population of research reports: Do you consider studies reported in languages other than English? If your research review excludes these, the bias is potentially very large (much larger, probably, than if it excludes unpublished work). Scholars once learned languages to get access to sources, but this seems pretty rare these days, at least for native English speakers. Conscientious researchers should at minimum inquire whether their topics are studied extensively by researchers writing in languages they do not read.

Given the near impossibility assembling or even knowing the *true* population of research reports on a subject, what is to be done? In my view it is best simply to say that the *population* for the meta-analysis is the publically available research on a topic (this would include unpublished works such as dissertations and papers presented at conferences, which I've called "quasi-published"). In the limitations section of the review, one would then have to admit that this method of selection might have omitted something important. In short, I would define the population of research for the purposes of meta-analysis as the publically available research reports on a topic written in languages I know how to read. Unless one has some strong independent reason to believe that a treasure trove of unpublished material exists, that should suffice. It will have to do. Now that meta-analysis is a fully accepted research technique, researchers no longer have to pursue fugitive literature well beyond the point of diminishing returns.

Once we have settled on the population, realizing that it will imperfectly coincide with the true population, and that it will imperfectly represent the potential domain of knowledge in the field, should we do a census of the whole population, however defined? Or should one sample from it? That depends on many things, but one point can be stated with certainty here: As always, there is no point in using inferential statistics unless one has sampled from a known population. Practitioners attempting to base their professional work on up-to-date research will naturally sample the most recent research. This makes sense, but enough important articles have been unearthed, "rediscovered" long after they were first published, to remind us that this is not an infallible strategy.

Quantitative Techniques in Meta-Analysis

So once you've decided all the tricky questions about populations and samples, what are the methods for quantitatively summarizing the results of research?

TABLE 17.1   *Meta-Analysis Techniques and Measurement Levels of Variables*

Analysis Technique	Predictor (Independent) Variables	Outcome (Dependent) Variables
Odds ratio	Categorical	Categorical
Standardized mean difference	Categorical	Continuous
Pearson *r* correlation	Continuous	Continuous

As always in this book, we will concentrate on general principles rather than the technical details. Although the reader wanting to conduct a meta-analysis may wish to consult a guide, such as Lipsey and Wilson (2001), we can cover some of the basics here.

Before meta-analysis, if researchers attempted quantitative summaries of the literature, they usually used the method of *vote counting*. If you had 35 studies of a subject and 8 said yes, significant effect, and 27 said no, no significant effect, the outcome was clear. But is it? What if the 27 were small convenience samples with too little power to detect significant effects and the 8 were large probability samples? In such cases, even when the vote is very lopsided, merely counting studies is a very poor way to summarize. The development of meta-analysis has been focused on devising better means of summarizing the results of quantitative studies.

The key statistics for meta-analysis are various effect size (ES) measures. Indeed, the early history of meta-analysis, in the 1970s and 80s, overlaps that of the great effect size debate in psychological and educational research. Many of the protagonists were the same: Robert Rosenthal, Jacob Cohen, and Gene Glass. They argued that not only was it important to identify whether a result was statistically significant, but the size of the effect mattered as much if not more. Confidence intervals were also important in this debate, but at its vortex were effect size statistics. As we have seen, effect sizes are standardized measures that that can be used to summarize and compare quantitative results across studies. Many textbooks talk about effect size (ES) as though there were only one effect size statistic. In fact, several such statistics are available for the use of someone undertaking a meta-analysis. An even broader range is available for general purposes (Kirk, 1996).

The ES measure usually referred to as *the* effect size is the "standardized mean difference," sometimes called Cohen's *d,* after its inventor. As seen in Chapter 8, to compute this you subtract the mean of the control group from the mean of the experimental group and divide the standard deviation (SD)—either the SD of the scores of the control group or the SD of the scores of the control and experimental group combined (Lipsey & Wilson, 2001). Or, in symbols,

$$ES = (M_e + M_c) \div SD$$

where M_e and M_c are the means of the experimental and control groups, respectively.

The other two effect size statistics used most extensively in meta-analysis are the Pearson *r* correlation, discussed in Chapter 2, and the odds ratio, reviewed in Chapter 11. Table 17.1 lists the three most common ES measures used in meta-analysis and the types of variables for which they can be used. The selection of the appropriate statistic depends on how the variables to be summarized are measured.

In theory, one could also use as ES measures, standardized regression coefficients when the outcome variables were continuous (see Chapter 9). Some have recommended using the adjusted *R*-squared statistic for talking about overall regression effects. Logistic regression coefficients (see Chapter 11) could be used when the outcomes were categorical. But these regression-based effect sizes would work only when the same predictors were used, when the same number of predictors was used, and when they were all measured the same way—a very rare circumstance except in some replication studies. Generally, meta-analysis is hard to use with regression studies that include multiple predictor variables.

In such studies, the typical procedure is to examine the bivariate correlations among the variables in the study rather than the regression coefficients.

As with any standardized measure, so too with effect size measures: The gain in comparability is somewhat offset by losing the ability to report in natural units. Effect sizes, like z-scores, are in standard deviation units. But most people do not naturally think in standard deviation units. Mean differences are easier to understand than standardized mean differences. To say that the treatment group scored 5 points higher on the scale is pretty clear. To say that the ES is .33 seems less so. Regression coefficients can also be in natural units. We might say that for every year of experience workers earn an extra $800 in salary; this is straightforward. Saying the correlation between salary and years' experience is $r = .45$ can seem too abstract. Abstraction is the price we pay for comparability. Although ES statistics are useful for comparing studies, they are better known in meta-analysis for summarizing studies to come up with an overall mean ES.

One of the key advantages in a meta-analysis is that pooling studies results in a larger sample size and therefore more statistical power. Small effects could be more easily discernable with a meta-analysis. Meta-analysis can also identify effects that were substantial but missed because the sample sizes were too small. This advantage of meta-analysis has been especially important in experimental research, which tends to have small sample sizes. One of the most striking instances of this advantage of meta-analysis occurred in the area of breast cancer research. The benefits of the drug tamoxifen and the similar survival rates of lumpectomy and mastectomy patients were only demonstrated through meta-analytic techniques summing the results of previous work (Hunt, 1997).

When pooling studies to derive this meta-analytic benefit, one has to take into account the fact that the studies have different sample sizes (otherwise one is vote counting). That is because the real focus of interest is not the studies but rather the subjects studied. Thus, when you combine effect sizes into an overall average you have to weight the studies in order to give the large studies more emphasis in your summary. Otherwise a study with 60 subjects could

count as much as a study with 1,000. Weighting studies can also be done for the quality of the design, but this is controversial. But, in one sense, this controversial practice is actually very widespread. When studies that do not meet design criteria are eliminated from a review, they are given a weight of zero. So in meta-analysis, as in most research, *first* much qualitative judgment is involved. *Then* you use statistics.

Meta-analysis can also result in a combined p-value for the studies summarized. In most meta-analyses, this p-value will not be very revealing. The combined sample sizes tend to be very large, which means that fairly trivial effects can yield a significant p-value. As Glass put it in an interview, "Statistical significance is the least interesting thing about the results. You should describe the results in terms of measures of magnitude—not just, does a treatment affect people, but how *much* does it affect them? *That's* what we need to know" (Hunt, 1997, pp. 29–30, emphasis in original).

Texts on meta-analysis (e.g., Lipsey & Wilson 2001) often suggest hiring coders to help with the meta-analysis. When using such coders, it is very important to train them well so that they all use the same criteria. That is good advice, but better advice, I think, is to do the coding yourself if at all possible. You could also trust coauthors because they too would have a vested interest in the accuracy of the work. As discussed previously when discussing data entry, the use of hirelings is probably not good practice if you are serious about your work. Legend has it that Ronald Fisher, probably the greatest twentieth-century statistician, when doing agricultural experiments, cleaned out animal cages himself rather have to worry that the hired help would do the work inconsistently or in a way that could bias the results. This caution and the practice of doing your own data gathering and data entry seem to me especially appropriate in a meta-analysis. The "respondents" in a meta-analysis are not anonymous subjects picked by random digit dialing. They are important documents written by professional colleagues. They should be treated with care and respect.

Meta-analysis is largely a descriptive technique. You describe the population of studies. As with all descriptive studies, merely reporting a mean without first examining the distribution of individual scores is risky, and it is just as risky when the means are mean effect sizes. It is very important to study measures of dispersion and the shapes of the distributions of effect sizes. You don't want to use only the mean to describe your data if your data are bimodal or curvilinear. The full range of descriptive techniques (see Chapter 4) should be considered, including graphics. Scatter diagrams are especially useful in this regard (Light & Pillemer, 1984). For example, say you have 50 studies and have calculated the ES for each of them. You can plot the ESs against any other continuous variable, such as their dates of publication or the ages of their subjects. The idea of this work is, as always, is to help you to discover important patterns. If effect sizes are stronger for more recent studies or in studies using younger subjects, discovering this can be extremely revealing about the nature of the topic.

Finally, if you want *your* study to be meta-analyzed someday, you need to report some of your data quite fully. Means, standard deviations, exact *p*-values, Pearson *r*s and *N*s are among the most important statistics needed by the meta-analyst. They are important because they are the statistics that meta-analysts most often use to compute effect sizes. When authors do not make some of this data available, it is sometimes possible for meta-analysts to calculate the missing information. But authors should make it available in their publications, or if space constraints keep them from doing so, they can offer in a footnote to make full range of data available. Providing access to what meta-analysts need to write their syntheses is increasingly considered a matter of professional ethics.

The Goals of Research Reviews

Reviewing the research of others is fundamentally important. It can be an end in its own right or the indispensable first step in preparing to conduct your own research study. Although this chapter discusses traditional narrative literature reviews and meta-analytic reviews separately, they are two means of approaching the same goals. Whether the review is narrative or quantitative in orientation, Light & Pillemer (1984) conclude that "by capitalizing on study-level variation" research reviews "show their strongest advantage over even the most carefully executed single study" (p. 45). Others have emphasized finding not variation but similarities among the studies reviewed. Meta-analysis, says Hunt (1997), enables one to "discover patterns in the seemingly hopeless jumble of dissimilar findings" (p. 13).

In either case, not only do research reviews enable you to discover new things, they prepare you to discover still more in your research. Setting about their work innocent of a thorough grounding in what others have done has sometimes facilitated the work of geniuses, but for the rest of us it mostly results in mediocre rehashes of projects that have already been carried out more effectively by someone else.

Once you have assembled your studies for review you will want to compare and contrast them according to a broad range of criteria. Reviewing some of the main points in the checklist in Figure 17.1, we can see that among the things you'll want to examine are:

- *Settings.* Are results different or similar across settings, such as public and private schools?
- *Participants.* Do the ages or genders of participants in the research moderate some of the findings?
- *Research design.* Do laboratory experiments yield results different from or similar to those of field experiments?
- *Publication date.* Do more recent studies show stronger or weaker effects?
- *Analysis techniques.* How do studies using different analysis techniques (e.g., contingency tables with chi-squares versus log-linear analyses) compare?
- *Control variables.* If one study controls for ethnicity and another does not, do their outcomes vary?

There is much more to a good quality research review than most beginning researchers (and many veterans) realize. It is almost never time ill-spent. For many professional practitioners, the results of a research review on a topic can be much more useful than the results of *any* individual study. A meta-analysis or other research review will probably on average take about the same amount of time and effort as conducting your own small-scale study. A research review may be a better choice for you. But be forewarned. People who do research reviews often get the urge to do their own study, to investigate the topic the *right* way. That is particularly the case when they suspect that the setting in which they work or their research subjects are different from those that have been researched by others. Should you get the urge to conduct your own investigation, you may wish to return to Chapter 1 on research design, measurement, and analysis.

Terms and Concepts to Review

Literature review
Systemic review
Meta-analysis
PsycINFO
Sociological Abstracts (Sociofile)
Dissertation Abstracts
ERIC

Citation index
Boolean connectors
Vote counting
Population in a meta-analysis or other research review
Quasi-published research reports
Effect size measures in meta-analysis

Discussion Questions

1. If you were reviewing the research literature on a topic, how would you decide whether to do this using the tools of meta-analysis or those of a traditional narrative literature review?
2. Think about a review of research literature that you might conduct on a topic of interest to you. How would you know at what point you had reviewed a sufficient number of research reports?
3. Say that you have searched thoroughly for original research on your topic and that you have been successful, finding and obtaining copies of a total of 40 articles and book chapters directly relevant to your topic. How would you begin to organize this material to tackle the practical tasks of reading, assimilating, critiquing, and summarizing these sources?
4. What would you do if you entered search terms into programs such as ERIC or PsycLit only to learn that

these programs could find nothing on your topic? Assuming that research actually existed on you topic, what strategies could you use to find it?
5. Assume you have conducted a thorough and successful review of the research on a question and have summarized the results, either quantitatively, qualitatively, or with some mixture of quantitative and qualitative summaries. What do these results tell you and what are the limitations on any conclusions you might draw?
6. Under what circumstances might you decide that it would be better to devote your time to a thorough and systematic review of the research on a topic, rather than conducting your own original research? Conversely, when would it be more productive to use research reviews only as background to set the stage for your own original research?

Self-Test

If you can answer most of the following questions accurately, you can feel confident about your understanding of the material in this chapter. If not, it would by a good idea to review the chapter. (Answers can be found in the Appendix.)

1. The literature review section of a research report is the place where the author is expected to speculate freely about the subject to be studied. True or False?
2. After researchers have completed the literature review for a project, it is usually best for them to

focus on their own data and pay little attention to the conclusions of other researchers. True or False?

3. When searching for research literature to review, it is usually sufficient to use any one of the major databases, such as ERIC or *Education Abstracts.* True or False?

4. The advantage of electronic searches for research literature is that, unlike hard-copy versions of the same databases, they allow the researcher to use multivariate criteria for searching. True or False?

5. If the literature for your subject is vast, it is acceptable practice to review only the conclusions of the research reports and to assume that the conclusions are supported by the evidence. True or False?

6. If the articles reviewed in your literature review come to different conclusions, you should base your research on those that support your research hypothesis. True or False?

7. You should plan to include in your literature review summaries of all the articles you have read even if it subsequently turns out that they are not directly relevant to your subject and the way you will investigate it. True or False?

8. When summarizing quantitative research reports for a literature review, you can safely leave out the various coefficients and other quantitative indicators; it is usually enough to know whether the results were statistically significant. True or False?

9. Meta-analysis is an approach to literature reviews that uses quantitative techniques to summarize the results of quantitative research. True or False?

10. Good practice in meta-analysis tends not to be radically different from good practice in all systematic literature reviews. True or False?

11. The *population* in a meta-analysis is all the research reports that have been produced on a subject. True or False?

12. The *population* of studies in a meta-analysis is not necessarily representative of a subject, because the studies could have omitted key aspects of the subject. True or False?

13. The effect size measure in meta-analysis must be reported in the original (or natural) measurement units, not using z-scores or other standardized measures. True or False?

14. By combining the results of several studies in a meta-analysis, researchers often increase sample size greatly, which, in turn, increases statistical power and the generalizability of the results. True or False?

Endnote

1. See Chapter 13 of Shadish, Cook, and Campbell (2002) for a systematic review asserting the advantages of meta-analysis over traditional reviews. For a history of the early debates, see Hunt (1997).

Appendix

Answer Key for Self-Test Questions

The answers identified in this Appendix are not the "truth" in any ultimate sense of the term. Rather, they indicate what is *true according to the text.* Because the text addresses controversial questions, reasonable people might disagree with some of the listed answers.

Chapter 1
1. T
2. T
3. F
4. F
5. T
6. T
7. F
8. B
9. B
10. C
11. D
12. C

Chapter 2
1. F
2. F
3. C
4. B
5. C
6. F
7. F
8. B
9. F
10. F
11. T
12. F
13. A

Chapter 3
1. B
2. D

3. E
4. D
5. C
6. B
7. B
8. C
9. C
10. D

Chapter 4
1. T
2. F
3. F
4. T
5. C
6. B
7. B
8. C
9. A
10. D
11. C
12. F

Chapter 5
1. F
2. T
3. T
4. F
5. T
6. D
7. B
8. C

9. C
10. B
11. C
12. F
13. T

Chapter 6
1. F
2. F
3. T
4. B
5. T
6. F
7. F
8. T
9. F
10. T
11. T

Chapter 7
1. F
2. F
3. T
4. F
5. T
6. T
7. F
8. C
9. B
10. A
11. C
12. A

13. B
14. B

Chapter 8
1. T
2. T
3. T
4. T
5. T
6. F
7. F
8. T
9. T
10. T
11. F
12. T
13. T
14. F
15. T
16. F

Chapter 9
1. T
2. T
3. B
4. C
5. A
6. D
7. E
8. B
9. A
10. B

11. D
12. B
13. E
14. C
15. B
16. E

Chapter 10
1. F
2. F
3. F
4. T
5. F
6. F
7. T
8. T
9. F
10. F
11. T
12. T
13. F

Chapter 11
1. F
2. T
3. T
4. T
5. F
6. T
7. F
8. F
9. T

10. T
11. F

Chapter 12
1. F
2. F
3. F
4. F
5. T
6. T
7. F
8. F
9. T
10. F

Chapter 13
1. F
2. T
3. T
4. F
5. T
6. T
7. T
8. F
9. T
10. F
11. T
12. F

Chapter 14
1. T
2. F

3. T
4. F
5. T
6. T
7. F
8. T
9. F
10. F
11. T
12. F

Chapter 15
1. F
2. T
3. T
4. T
5. T
6. T
7. T
8. T
9. T
10. T

Chapter 16
1. T
2. T
3. T
4. F
5. T
6. T
7. T
8. T

9. F
10. F
11. F
12. F
13. T
14. F
15. F
16. F

Chapter 17
1. F
2. F
3. F
4. T
5. F
6. F
7. F
8. F
9. T
10. T
11. T
12. T
13. F
14. T

References

AERA (American Educational Research Association). (1999). *Standards for educational and psychological testing.* Washington, DC: Author.

Agafonov, A. (1999). *Is tolerance an important concept for Russian teachers? A cross-national perspective.* Unpublished master's thesis. State University of New York, Albany, NY.

Agresti, A. (1996). *An introduction to categorical data analysis.* New York: John Wiley.

Agresti, A., & Finlay, B. (1997). *Statistical methods for the social sciences* (3rd ed.). Upper Saddle River, NJ: Prentice-Hall.

Alexander, K. L., Entwisle, D. R., & Olson, L. S. (2001). Schools, achievement, and inequality: A seasonal perspective. *Educational Evaluation and Policy Analysis, 23*(2), 171–191.

Allison, P. D. (1999). *Multiple regression: A primer.* Thousand Oaks, CA: Pine Forge Press.

Bauer, D. J. (2003). Estimating multilevel linear models as structural equation models. *Journal of Educational and Behavioral Statistics, 28*(2), 135–167.

Baumeister, R. F., Campbell, J. D., Krueger, J. I., & Vohs, K. D. (2005). Exploding the self-esteem myth. *Scientific American, 292*(1), 84–91.

Becker, G. (1993). *Human capital* (3rd ed.). Chicago: University of Chicago Press.

Berk, R. A. (2004). *Regression analysis: A constructive critique.* Thousand Oaks, CA: Sage.

Berry, W. D., & Sanders, M. S. (2000). *Understanding multivariate research.* Boulder, CO: Westview.

Birnbaum, R. (2000). Policy scholars are from Venus; Policy makers are from Mars. *The Review of Higher Education, 23,* 119–132.

Bond, T. G., & Fox, C. M. (2001). *Applying the Rasch model: Fundamental measurement in the human sciences.* Mahwah, NJ: Lawrence Erlbaum.

Broh, B. A. (2002). Linking extracurricular programming to academic achievement: Who benefits and why? *Sociology of Education, 75,* 69–91.

Bruner, J. S. (1977). *The process of education.* Cambridge, MA: Harvard University Press.

Campbell, D., & Stanley, J. (1963). *Experimental and quasi-experimental designs for research.* Chicago: Rand McNally.

Centra, J. A., & Gaubatz, N. B. (2000). Is there gender bias in student evaluations of teaching? *Journal of Higher Education, 70,* 17–33.

Chow, S. (1996). *Statistical significance.* Thousand Oaks, CA: Sage.

Cohen, J. (1988). *Statistical power analysis for the behavioral sciences.* Mahwah, NJ: Lawrence Erlbaum.

Cohen, J., Cohen, P., West, S., & Aiken, L. (2003). *Applied multiple regression/correlation analysis for the behavioral sciences* (3rd ed.). London: Lawrence Erlbaum.

Cook, T. (2002). Randomized experiments in educational policy research: A critical examination of the reasons the educational evaluation community has offered for not doing them. *Educational Evaluation and Policy Analysis, 24*(3), 175–199.

Cook, T. D., & Campbell, D. T. (1979). *Quasi-experimentation: Design and analysis issues for field settings.* Boston: Houghton Mifflin.

Cook, T. D., Cooper, H., Cordray, D. S., Hartman, H., Hedges, L. V., Light, R. J., Louis, T. A., & Mosteller, F. (1992). *Meta-analysis for explanation: A casebook.* New York: Russell Sage.

Creswell, J. W. (2002). *Educational research: Planning, conducting, and evaluating quantitative and qualitative research.* Upper Saddle River, NJ: Merrill/Prentice Hall.

Derman, E. (2004). *My life as a Quant: Reflections on physics and finance.* New York: John Wiley.

Derry, S. J., Levin, J. R., Osana, H. P., Jones, M. S., & Peterson, M. (2000). Fostering students' statistical and scientific thinking: lessons learned from an innovative college course. *American Educational Research Journal, 37*(3), 747–773.

Dooley, D. (2001). *Social research methods* (4th ed.). Upper Saddle River, NJ: Prentice Hall.

Eliason, S. R. (1993). *Maximum likelihood estimation: Logic and practice.* Thousand Oaks, CA: Sage.

Elliott, M. (1998). School finance and opportunities to learn: Does money well spent enhance students' achievement? *Sociology of Education, 71,* 223–245.

Embretson, S. E., & Reise, S. P. (2000). *Item response theory for psychologists.* New York: John Wiley.

Fitzpatrick, J., & Morris, M. (1999). *Current and emerging ethical challenges in evaluation.* San Francisco: Jossey-Bass.

Fleming, J., & Garcia, N. (1998). Are standardized tests fair to African Americans? *Journal of Higher Education, 69,* 471–495.

Fox, J. (1997). *Applied regression analysis, linear models, and related methods.* Thousand Oaks, CA: Sage.

Gall, J., Gall, M., & Borg, W. (1999). *Applying educational research: A practical guide* (4th ed.). New York: Longman.

Gamoran, A., & Hannigan, E. (2000). Algebra for everyone? Benefits of college-preparatory mathematics for students with diverse abilities in early secondary school. *Educational Evaluation and Policy Analysis, 22,* 241–254.

Gerber, S. B., Finn, J. D., Achilles, C. M., & Boyd-Zaharias, J. (2001). Teacher aides and students' academic achievement. *Educational Evaluation and Policy Analysis, 23,* 123–143.

Gigerenzer, G. (2002). *Calculated risks: How to know when numbers deceive you.* New York: Simon & Schuster.

Glass, G. V., & Hopkins, K. D. (1996). *Statistical methods in education and psychology* (3rd ed.). Boston: Allyn & Bacon.

Glenn, D. (2002, June 21). What the data actually show about welfare reform. *Chronicle of Higher Education,* pp. A14–A16.

Gould, S. J. (1981). *The mismeasure of man.* New York: Norton.

Greenwood, D. J., & Levin, M. (1998). *Introduction to action research: Social research for social change.* Thousand Oaks: Sage.

Gueron, J. M., (1997). Learning about welfare reform: Lessons from state-based evaluations. *New Directions for Evaluation, 76,* 79–94.

Guterman, L. (2002, November 29). Battling for hearts and minds. *Chronicle of Higher Education,* pp. A12–A13.

Haller, E., & Kleine, P. (2001). *Using educational research: A school administrator's guide.* New York: Addison-Wesley/Longman.

Hamilton, L. S. (1998). Gender differences on high school science achievement tests: Do format and content matter? *Educational Evaluation and Policy Analysis, 20,* 179–197.

Harrell, F. E. (2000). *Regression modeling strategies.* New York: Springer.

Harvey, E. (1999). Short-term and long-term effects of early parental employment on children of the National Longitudinal Survey of Youth. *Developmental Psychology, 35*(2), 445–459.

Harwell, M. R., & Gatti, G. G. (2001). Rescaling ordinal data to interval data in educational research. *Review of Educational Research, 71*(1), 105–131.

Heck, R. H. (2004). *Studying educational and social policy: Theoretical concepts and research methods.* Mahwah, NJ: Lawrence Erlbaum.

Henrich, J., Boyd, R., Bowles, S., Camerer, C. Gintis, H., McElreath, R., & Fehr, E. (2001). In search of homo economics: Experiments in 15 small-scale societies. *American Economic Review, 91,* 73–79.

Hinkle, D. E., Wiersma, W., & Jurs, S. G. (1998). *Applied statistics for the behavioral sciences* (4th ed.). Boston: Houghton Mifflin.

Huck, S. W. (2004). *Reading statistics and research* (4th ed.). Boston: Allyn & Bacon.

Hunt, M. (1997). *How science takes stock: The story of meta-analysis.* New York: Russell Sage Foundation.

Ingersoll, R. M. (2001). Teacher turnover and teacher shortages: An organizational analysis. *American Educational Research Journal, 38*(3), 499–534.

Ioannidis, J. P. (2005). Contradicted and initially stronger effects in highly cited clinical research. *Journal of the American Medical Association, 294*(2), 218–228.

Johnson, B. (2001). Toward a new classification of nonexperimental quantitative research. *Educational Researcher, 30*(2), 3–13.

Johnson, R. A., & Wichern, D. W. (2002). *Applied multivariate statistical analysis* (5th ed.). Upper Saddle River, NJ: Prentice Hall.

Kahane, L. (2001). *Regression basics.* Thousand Oaks, CA: Sage.

Kahneman, D., & Tversky, A. (Eds.). (2000). *Choices, values, and frames.* Cambridge: Cambridge University Press.

Kanji, G. K. (1999). *100 statistical tests.* Thousand Oaks, CA: Sage.

Kaplan, D. (2000). *Structural equation modeling: Foundations and extensions.* Thousand Oaks, CA: Sage.

Karen, D. (2002). Changes in access to higher education in the United States. *Sociology of Education, 75,* 191–210.

Keppel, G., & Zedeck, S. (1989). *Data analysis for research designs: Analysis of variance and multiple regression/ correlation approaches.* New York: W. H. Freeman.

Kirk, R. (1996). Practical significance. *Educational and Psychological Measurement, 56,* 746–759.

Klatsky, A. (2003). Drink to your health? *Scientific American, 288*(2), 74–81.

Kline, R. B. (2005). *Principles and practice of structural equation modeling* (2nd ed.). New York: Guilford.

Kraemer, H. C., & Thiemann, S. (1987). *How many subjects? Statistical power analysis in research.* Thousand Oaks, CA: Sage.

Kupermintz, H. (2003). Teacher effects and teacher effectiveness: A validity investigation of the Tennessee value added assessment system. *Educational Evaluation and Policy Analysis, 25*(3), 287–298.

Lee, V., & Loeb, S. (2000). School size in Chicago elementary schools: Effects on teachers' attitudes and students' achievement. *American Educational Research Journal, 37,* 3–31.

Lee, V. E., et al. (2001). The difficulty of identifying rare samples to study: the case of high schools divided into schools within schools. *Educational Evaluation and Policy Analysis, 23*(4), 365–379.

Lewin, K. (1946). Action research and minority problems. *Journal of Social Issues, 2*(4), 34–36.

Liao, T. F. (1994). *Interpreting probability models: Logit, probit, and other generalized linear models.* Thousand Oaks, CA: Sage.

Light, R. J., & Pillemer, D. B. (1984). *Summing up: The science of reviewing research.* Cambridge, MA: Harvard University Press.

Light, R. J., Singer, J. D., & Willett, J. B. (1990). *By design: Planning research on higher education.* Cambridge, MA: Harvard University Press.

Lindbloom, C. E., & Cohen, D. K. (1979). *Useable knowledge: Social science and social problem solving.* New Haven, CT: Yale University Press.

Linn, R. L. (2003a). Accountability: Responsibility and reasonable expectations. *Educational Researcher, 32*(7), 3–13.

Linn, R. L. (2003b). Performance standards: Utility for different uses of assessments. *Educational Policy Analysis Archives, 11*(31). Retrieved from http://epaa.asu.edu/epaa/v11n31.

Linn, R. L., Baker, E. L., & Betebenner, D. W. (2002). Accountability systems: Implications of requirements of the No Child Left Behind Act. *Educational Researcher, 31*(6), 3–16.

Linn, R., & Haug, C. (2002). Stability of school-building accountability scores and gains. *Educational Evaluation and Policy Analysis, 21*(1), 29–36.

Lipsey, M. W. (1997). What can you build with thousands of bricks? Musings on the cumulation of knowledge in program evaluation. In D. Rog & D. Fournier (Eds.), *Progress and future directions in evaluation: Perspectives on theory, practice, and methods* (pp. 7–23). San Francisco: Jossey-Bass.

Lipsey, M. W., & Wilson, D. B. (2001). *Practical meta-analysis.* Thousand Oaks, CA: Sage.

Lissitz, R. (2005). *Value added models in education: Theory and applications.* Maple Grove, MN: Journal of Applied Measurement Press.

Lissitz, R. W., & Huynh, H. (2003). Vertical equating for state assessments: Issues and solutions in determination of adequate yearly progress and school accountability. *Practical Assessment, Research & Evaluation, 8* (10). Retrieved from http://EdResearch.org/pare.

Loehlin, J. C. (2004). *Latent variable models: An introduction to factor, path, and structural equation analysis* (4th ed.). Mahwah, NJ: Lawrence Erlbaum.

Luke, D. A. (2004). *Multilevel modeling.* Thousand Oaks, CA: Sage.

Ma, X., & Willms, J. D. (1999). Dropping out of advanced mathematics: How much do students and schools contribute to the problem? *Educational Evaluation and Policy Analysis, 21,* 365–383.

Matthews, J. (1995). *Quantification and the quest for medical certainty.* Princeton, NJ: Princeton University Press.

Mattingly, D. J., Prislin, R., McKenzie, T. L., Rodriguez, J. L., & Kayzar, B. (2002). Evaluating evaluations: The case of parent involvement programs. *Review of Educational Research, 72*(4), 549–576.

Mayer, R., Heiser, J., & Lonn, S. (2001). Cognitive constraints on multi-media learning: When presenting more material results in less understanding. *Journal of Educational Psychology, 93*(1), 187–198.

McCloskey, D., & Ziliak, S. (1996). The standard error of regressions. *Journal of Economic Literature, 34*(1), 97–114.

McMillan, J. (2004). *Educational research* (4th ed.) Boston: Allyn & Bacon.

Meltzoff, J. (1997). *Critical thinking about research: Psychology and related fields.* Washington, DC: American Psychological Association.

Menard, S. (2002). *Applied logistic regression* (2nd ed.). Thousand Oaks, CA: Sage.

Mohr, L. B. (1995). *Impact analysis for program evaluation.* Thousand Oaks, CA: Sage.

Mueller, C., & Dweck, C. (1998). Praise for intelligence can undermine children's motivation and performance. *Journal of Personality and Social Psychology, 75*(1), 33–52.

Mullen, A. L., Goyette, K. A., & Soares, J. A. (2003). Who goes to graduate school? Social and academic correlates of educational continuation after college. *Sociology of Education, 76,* 143–169.

Myers, J., & Well, A. (2003). *Research design and statistical analysis* (2nd ed.). London: Lawrence Erlbaum.

Namboodiri, K. (1984). *Matrix algebra.* Thousand Oaks, CA: Sage.

Nardi, P. (2003). *Doing survey research.* Boston: Allyn & Bacon.

NCES (National Center for Education Statistics). (2002, June 20). Profile of undergraduates in U.S. postsecondary education institutions: 1999–2000. [NCES number, 2002168]

Newman, F. M., Smith, B., Allensworth, E., & Bryk, A. S. (2001). Instructional program coherence: What it is and why it should guide school improvement policy. *Educational Evaluation and Policy Analysis, 23*(4), 297–321.

Newman, M. (2001). Longitudinal assessment of neurocognitive function after coronary-artery bypass surgery. *New England Journal of Medicine, 344*(6), 395–402.

Newton, R. R., & Rudestam, K. E. (1999). *Your statistical consultant.* Thousand Oaks, CA: Sage.

NICHD (National Institute of Child Health and Human Development). (2002). Early child care and children's development prior to school entry. *American Educational Research Journal, 39*(1), 133–164.

Pampel, F. C. (2000). *Logistic regression: A primer.* Thousand Oaks, CA: Sage.

Parker, R. A., & Bergman, N. G. (2003). Sample size: More than just calculations. *American Statistician, 57*(3), 166–170.

Paxton, P., & Bollen, K. A. (2003). Perceived quality and methodology in graduate department ratings. *Sociology of Education, 76,* 71–88.

Pearl, J. (2000). *Causality: Models, reasoning, and inference.* Cambridge: Cambridge University Press.

Pedhazur, E., & Schmelkin, L. (1991). *Measurement, design, and analysis: An integrated approach.* Hillsdale, NJ: Lawrence Erlbaum.

Pett, M. A., Lackey, N. R., & Sullivan, J. J. (2003). *Making sense of factor analysis.* Thousand Oaks, CA: Sage.

Pong, S., & Pallas, A. (2001). Class size and eighth-grade math achievement in the U.S. and abroad. *Educational Evaluation and Policy Analysis, 23,* 251–273.

Quinones, S., & Kirshstein, R. (1998). *An educator's guide to evaluating the use of technology in schools and classrooms.* U.S. Department of Education. Retreived from www.ed.gov/pubs/EdTechGuide.

Ragin, C. C. (1994). *Constructing social research: The unity and diversity of method.* Thousand Oaks, CA: Sage.

Raudenbush, S. W. (2003, April). Schooling, statistics, and poverty: Can we measure school improvement? Paper presented at the annual meeting of the American Educational Research Association, San Diego, CA.

Raudenbush, S. W., & Bryk, A. S. (2002). *Hierarchical linear models: Applications and data analysis methods* (2nd ed.). Thousand Oaks, CA: Sage.

Roderick, M., & Camburn, E. (1999). Risk and recovery from course failure in the early years of high school. *American Educational Research Journal, 37,* 303–343.

Rog, D. J., & Fournier, D. (Eds.). (1997). *Progress and future directions in evaluation: Perspectives on theory, practice, and methods. New directions for evaluation.* San Francisco: Jossey-Bass.

Rosenthal, R. (1979). The "file-drawer problem" and tolerance of null results. *Psychological Bulletin, 86,* 638–641.

Rosenthal, R. (1991). *Meta-analytic procedures for social research* (rev. ed.). Thousand Oaks, CA: Sage.

Ross, C. E., & Broh, B. A. (2000). The roles of self-esteem and the sense of personal control in the academic achievement process. *Sociology of Education, 73,* 270–284.

Salmon, W. C. (1998). *Causality and explanation.* Oxford: Oxford University Press.

Salsburg, D. (2001). *Lady tasting tea: How statistics revolutionized science in the 20th century.* New York: W. H. Freeman.

Schumacker, R. E., & Lomax, R. G. (1996). *A beginner's guide to structural equation modeling.* Mahwah, NJ: Lawrence Erlbaum.

Seltzer, M., Choi, K., & Thum, Y. M. (2003). Examining relationships between where students start and how rapidly they progress. *Educational Evaluation and Policy Analysis, 25*(3), 263–286.

Sennum, S. (2002). *The relationship between change facilitator styles and school climate as perceived by teachers in Thailand.* Unpublished doctoral dissertation. Illinois State University, Normal, IL.

Seppa, N. (2002). Antibody warfare: Vaccine halts microbes in dialysis patients. *Science News, 161,* 99–100.

Shadish, W. R., Cook, T. D., & Campbell, D. T. (2002). *Experimental and quasi-experimental designs for generalized causal inference.* Boston: Houghton Mifflin.

Shiller, R. J. (2000). *Irrational exuberance.* New York: Broadway Books.

Slavin, R. E. (2002). Evidence-based education policies: Transforming educational practice and research. *Educational Researcher, 31*(7), 15–21.

Smith, B. (2000). Quantity matters: Annual instructional time in an urban school system. *Educational Administration Quarterly, 36*(5), 652–682.

Stern, P. C., & Kaloff, L. (1996). *Evaluating social science research* (2nd ed.). New York: Oxford University Press.

Stutz, B. (2003). Pumphead. *Scientific American, 289*(1), 76–81.

Sui-Chu, E. H., & Willms, J. D. (1996). Effects of parental involvement on eighth-grade achievement. *Sociology of Education, 69,* 126–141.

Tabachnick, B. G., & Fidel, L. S. (2001a). *Using multivariate statistics* (4th ed.). Boston: Allyn & Bacon.

Tabachnick, B. G., & Fidel, L. S. (2001b). *Computer-assisted research design and analysis.* Boston: Allyn & Bacon.

Taleb, N. N. (2001). *Fooled by randomness.* New York: Texere.

Tashakkori, A., & Teddlie, C. (1998). *Mixed methodology.* Thousand Oaks, CA: Sage.

Thompson, B. (2002). What future quantitative social science research could look like: confidence intervals for effect sizes. *Educational Researcher, 31*(3), 25–32.

Thompson, B. (2004). *Exploratory and confirmatory factor analysis: Understanding concepts and applications.* Washington, DC: American Psychological Association.

Thorndike, R. M. (2005). *Measurement and evaluation in psychology and education* (7th ed.). Upper Saddle River, NJ: Merrill/Prentice Hall.

Thurstone, L. L. (1947). *Multiple factor analysis.* Chicago: University of Chicago Press.

Tracey, T. J. G. (2000). Development of interests and competency beliefs: A 1-year longitudinal study of fifth- to eighth-grade students using the ICA-R and structural equation modeling. *Journal of Counseling Psychology, 49*(2), 148–163.

U.S. Congress. (1993). Government Performance and Results Act of 1993. Retrieved June 27, 2003, from http://govinfo.library.unt.edu/npr/library/misc/s20.html.

Vogt, W. P. (1997). *Tolerance and education.* Thousand Oaks, CA: Sage.

Vogt, W. P. (2002a, April). *Isn't this program too complex to evaluate? A case study of evaluation of a multi-method, multi-level, multi-university teacher education grant.* Paper presented at the annual meeting of the American Educational Research Association, New Orleans, LA.

Vogt, W. P. (2002b, April). *What are the grounds for choosing research methods and do multi-method options exacerbate the choice problem?* Paper presented at the annual meeting of the American Educational Research Association, New Orleans, LA.

Vogt, W. P. (2005). *Dictionary of statistics and methodology* (3rd ed.). Thousand Oaks, CA: Sage.

Vogt, W. P., & McKenna, B. (1998, April). *Teachers' tolerance: Their attitudes toward political, social, and moral diversity.* Paper presented at the annual meeting of the American Educational Research Association, San Diego, CA.

Wainer, H., & Brown, L. (2004). Two statistical paradoxes in the interpretation of group differences illustrated with medical school admission and licensing data. *The American Statistician, 58*(2), 117–123.

Warren, J. R., Le Pore, P. C., & Mare, R. D. (2000). Employment during high school: Consequences for students' grades in academic courses. *American Educational Research Journal, 37,* 943–969.

Weisberg, H., Krosnic, A., & Bowen, B. (1996). *An introduction to survey research, polling, and data analysis* (3rd ed.). Thousand Oaks, CA: Sage.

Wong, C. J., Anthony, S., Sigmon, S. C., Mongeon, J. A., Badger, G. J., & Higgins, S. T. (2004). Examining the interrelationships between abstinence and coping self-efficacy in cocaine-dependent outpatients. *Experimental and Clinical Psychopharmacology, 12*(3), 190–199.

Young, S., & Shaw, D. G. (1999). Profiles of effective college and university teachers. *Journal of Higher Education, 70,* 670–686.

Zernike, K. (2001, February 15). Antidrug program says it will adopt a new strategy. *The New York Times,* National Section.

Index